THE MACDONALD ENCYCLOPEDIA OF
FLOWERS
FOR BALCONY AND GARDEN

THE MACDONALD ENCYCLOPEDIA OF
FLOWERS
FOR BALCONY AND GARDEN

MACDONALD & CO
LONDON & SYDNEY

This edition first published in Great
Britain in 1983 by Macdonald & Co
(Publishers) Ltd
London & Sydney

Maxwell House
74 Worship Street, London EC2A 2EN

ISBN 0 356 09148 1

Translated from the Italian
by Sylvia Mulcahy

Printed in Italy by Officine Grafiche
Arnoldo Mondadori Editore, Verona

CONTENTS

PREFACE

The beautiful book I have the pleasure of introducing to you reflects perfectly the great love for flowers I share with the authors of the text, Guido Moggi and Luciano Giugnolini, of the University of Florence, and with the photographer, Giuseppe Mazza, who lives in the Principality and has already so skillfully illustrated books on fish, exotic plants and shells.

I am convinced that this work will prove most useful to all garden lovers, and that it will enable them to recognize the different species and varieties of flowers with ease.

I hope that the clarity of the text and the wonderful photographs that illustrate this book will assist the work of all gardening enthusiasts who read it, and that their knowledge of this fascinating subject will be greatly enriched.

(signed) *Grace de Monaco*

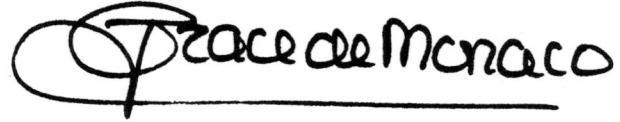

KEY TO SYMBOLS

Plant type

Annual plant

Perennial plant with sub-
terranean rootlike stem
(bulb, rhyzome, tuber,
etc.)

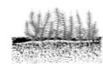

Perennial plant
with more or less
woody base

Water plant

Deciduous shrub

Evergreen shrub

Deciduous tree

Evergreen tree

Deciduous climber

Evergreen climber

Suitability

Plant suitable for cut flowers

Ideal for borders, rock gardens and alpine gardens

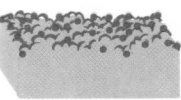

Suitable for flowering hedge

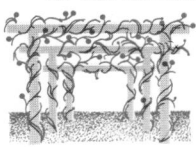

For use on espaliers, arbors, hanging baskets, arches, etc.

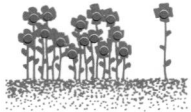

For use in groups or as an isolated plant

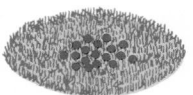

Bedding plants, suitable for floral carpets and patches of color

Maps showing distribution

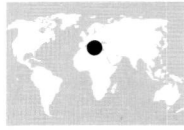

The plant is indigenous. The map indicates its area of natural distribution.

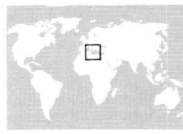

The plant is a cultivated form derived from indigenous plants. The map indicates the country of origin of its probable natural progenitors.

The plant is either a hybrid or a horticultural variety whose origin is clear. There is no sign on the map at all.

A NOTE TO THE READER

Species are listed in alphabetical order according to scientific name. The binomial for each species is in capital letters, followed by an abbreviation for, or the full name of, its originator. Synonyms and the English common name (where it exists) are also included. The following information is also given for each species: a short description; its average height; measurements of the flower (for Composite flowers the measurements of the whole head are given); place of origin; flowering period; cultural requirements and possible problems; propagation methods; hardiness and ease of cultivation.

Flowers——the outward expression of the plant world

The plant world makes an impression on our senses in many ways, but the most obvious is through flowers. Flowers represent that part of the plant world that can be most readily appreciated by everyone, regardless of social status, cultural level, age or environment.

Man's most important contact with plant life occurs mainly in two ways. The first involves his need to survive. This requires constant research into ways in which plants can be utilized as food, as healing agents and so on. Although the first link is with material needs, the second may be defined as spiritual; that is to say, the need to satisfy hopes and dreams of which we are aware only through our senses of sight and smell.

Thus flowers represent the outward material achievement of an aesthetic satisfaction for which man unconsciously yearns. This has manifested itself through the ages in mankind's progressive interest in flowers——an interest that continues unabated. While the botanist can see in the flower the fundamental structure for the reproduction of the finest plants and the poet discovers in it an indefinable source of inspiration, the painter and architect turn to it for the principles of design. In literature, religion and folklore, too, flowers have always been a fundamental well from which inspiration has been drawn.

Attracted by their beauty, therefore, man has credited them with the widest range of attributes. From time immemorial he has sought to retain their natural qualities under cultivation in order to be able to enjoy their beneficial effects, without seasonal interruption. Flowers were cultivated and the first gardens were in bloom as long as 5,000 years ago. Flower gardens were certainly created and enjoyed by the Chinese, and it is believed that chrysanthemums began to be cultivated there almost 4,000 years ago. In Babylon, Persia, Egypt and Greece, gardens were features of the palaces and wealthy homes.

As flowers were increasingly cultivated, gardens became more and more imaginative in their design, and simultaneously with the introduction of flowering plants, the first attempts were made to grow shrubs and trees in the garden as well——not so much for their flowers as for the architectural possibilities they offered in providing solid areas of green in the form of hedges, bowers, etc. Thus the flower garden became associated with a park in which hedges, paths and flower beds were made more interesting by the introduction of statues and fountains to create a harmonious whole. Such gardens were widespread in antiquity, especially in the Far East and Asia Minor.

In search of flowers for the gardens of Europe

The early part of the Middle Ages saw the destruction of many gardens with origins in antiquity. So devastating was the obliteration of what had become a centuries-old tradition that, until the eleventh century, the growing of flowers degenerated into an almost forgotten skill. The reemergence of interest expressed itself at first in the utilitarian garden, which contained plants valuable for food, medicine and other practical purposes.

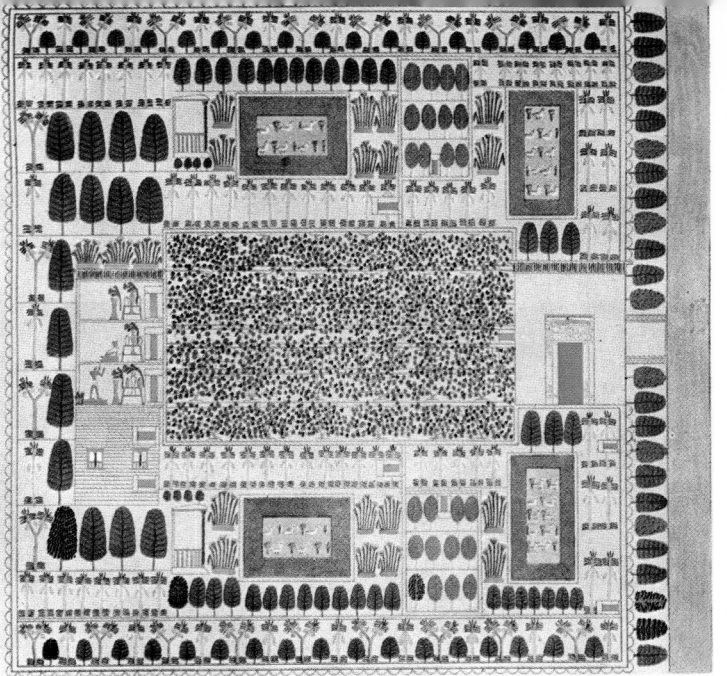

In the sixteenth and seventeenth centuries the flower garden came back into favor——a revival that coincided with new humanistic ideas and the development of those sciences regarded as being in the service of man. The architectural style of the gardens of this period stemmed from this humanist movement. In fact, the Italian garden was a direct result of this philosophy because architecture was regarded as one of the professions serving mankind. Still followed in the gardens of many of Europe's older houses, the principle behind the Italian garden is to treat everything——hedges, shrubs, fountains and flowering plants——as architectural features within the harmonious whole. The flowers, therefore, are used not so much for their beauty as for the contribution their colors and shapes make in creating decorative patterns. To achieve this effect, the plants have to be massed together in blocks of color. The main elements of an Italian garden are the box or yew hedges enclosing flower beds, each of which is planted with a number of different species. These are all of one color and their flowering habits synchronize with a neighboring bed; for example, an entirely yellow bed may contrast with a blue one.

This kind of layout obviously required a wide range of flowers. It was not enough merely to consider their color; the appearance of each plant, its life-span, flowering period, etc., were also important. The fact that many widely differing genera were available was due to those intrepid navigators and explorers who undertook journeys into unknown parts of the world. Many of the most beautiful and interesting flowers that

This print, which is in the British Museum, shows the winter camp established in the early nineteenth century by the Scottish botanist David Douglas for collecting North American plants.

found their way into the gardens of Europe were the result of such travels. By the seventeenth century, the main flowers in European gardens were lilies, tulips, violets, roses and irises, soon to be supplemented by hydrangeas, petunias, pelargoniums and fuchsias, while magnolias, gardenias and begonias appeared a little later.

The great botanical expeditions that were organized to seek out new and rare flowers took place mainly in the eighteenth and nineteenth centuries. Such naturalists as Bartram, Commerson, Banks, Kerr and Douglas undertook journeys to far-off lands in search of rare or unknown plants. They returned with bulbs and seeds as well as living plants, which were introduced into the gardens of Europe. During this time there was an influx of new plants into Europe from Brazil, Mexico, the United States, Australia, Japan and China.

One problem proved particularly difficult to overcome. Plants from temperate climates not too dissimilar from those of Europe or the Mediterranean region became acclimatized rather easily——but tropical plants from places with an equatorial climate were unable to survive without special attention, and even then, they did well only in gardens in warmer, more humid areas. Consequently a new type of building sprang up in the gardens of the great houses——the greenhouse. This meant that tropical plants could be nurtured indoors. Proper heating and humidification enabled orchids, exotic ferns and bromeliads to be grown quite well, even when the temperature outside was chilly.

Chinese painting of 1100 depicting hibiscus flowers.

The introduction of tropical flowers into the gardens of Europe is discussed elsewhere in this book. Suffice to say here that the period from the late eighteenth to the early nineteenth centuries is very important in the history of gardening. Not only was great interest aroused by the sight of plants thriving so far from their natural environment; interest in the protection of the natural vegetation of the countryside was also aroused. If it is true that these biological-scientific expeditions were responsible for the enthusiastic cultivation of exotic flowers, it is equally true that such excursions were responsible for considerably impoverishing the natural heritage of the countries to which the plants were indigenous. As a result, at the beginning of the 1800s, there was some outcry against the transference of exotic plants to cooler countries, the argument being that for every plant successfully brought into a European country alive, thousands had been lost, either during the collecting process or the journey home. According to a calculation made in the early nineteenth century, only 1,400 of the 13,000 different species that were being grown in Britain alone were indigenous to the British Isles. So it is not hard to imagine the amount of work involved in collecting and transporting samples from the tropics to Europe and, at the same time, to consider how many plants must have been lost.

There was, however, a positive aspect of this collecting. The enthusiasm with which plants were tracked down enabled scientists to discover many new species, thus providing opportunity to broaden their knowledge of flowering plants. In *Curtis'*

15

Botanical Magazine, first published in 1787, there began to appear a description of each new plant that was received in England by the Royal Botanic Gardens at Ke√ from the exploratory voyages being undertaken. This magazine, now in its 183rd volume, is still being published for the same purpose.

The intensive activity in the search for new plants is evident from the names given to new genera and species. The names of botanists, gardeners and explorers were perpetuated in many genera now commonly found in the warm or temperate conditions of European gardens. Examples are: J. Tradescant (*Tradescantia*), W. Forsyth (*Forsythia*), A. Buddle (*Buddleia*) and W. Kerr (*Kerria*), all of Britain; L. Fuchs (*Fuchsia*), A. Dahl (*Dahlia*) and C. E. Weigel (*Weigela*) of Germany; P. Magnol (*Magnolia*) and L. B. de Bougainville (*Bougainvillea*) of France; P. Mattioli (*Matthiola*) of Italy; A. Garden (*Gardenia*) of America; and O. Rudbeck (*Rudbeckia*) of Sweden.

Another outcome of this vigorous cultivation of exotic flowers was the opportunity that was opened up for experimentation with the crossing of plants originating from widely separate parts of the world and growing in totally disparate environments. This not only proved to be a major factor in horticultural advancement, as new kinds of flowering plants were produced, but it also laid the foundations for a completely new science. Genetics, although initiated simply as an empirical activity, was to develop into an experimental science of tremendous relevance to all forms of life. In fact, it was as a result of experiments carried out on the hybridization of flowering plants that the basic elements that provide the foundation for all research into inherited characteristics in plants and animals emerged. The laws and theories of heredity in general also trace back to early work in plant hybridization.

The Italian garden——and, in particular, the French garden that derived from it——was originally based on elegant architectural features that, as time passed, became more and more unrelated to nature. So elaborate did these layouts become that a reaction set in against such artificiality. In tune with the eighteenth-century emergence of the spirit of Enlightenment, the so-called English garden came into being. The new schools of thought were encouraging ideas of freedom and a return to nature. The picturesque structure of the English garden, with its more or less "spontaneous" arrangements was a reflection of this philosophy. Straight lines were abolished; trees and shrubs were allowed to grow in their natural shapes; and flowering plants were positioned to give the impression that they grew there of their own accord. Nevertheless, to achieve this freedom within the bounds of a pictorial composition, definite rules had to be followed. These related to the curves of flower beds, the relative sizes of the shrubs and trees used to create different shades of green and, most important, the balance of light and shade used to reproduce the chiaroscuro that had become an important feature in pictorial art. In such gardens, flowers obviously played a rather different role, their purpose being to provide contrasting patches of color—almost as though by chance——against the slightly monotonous expanses of green grass and the dense groups of leafy bushes. In this atmosphere of a "return to nature," interest in exotic plants declined and local flowers came into favor. Even

Cobaea scandens *flower. This plant was introduced into Europe, in Kew Gardens, about 1780 and was described by Cavanilles in 1791 as a new specie* (Curtis' Botanical Magazine, *1805, No. 22).*

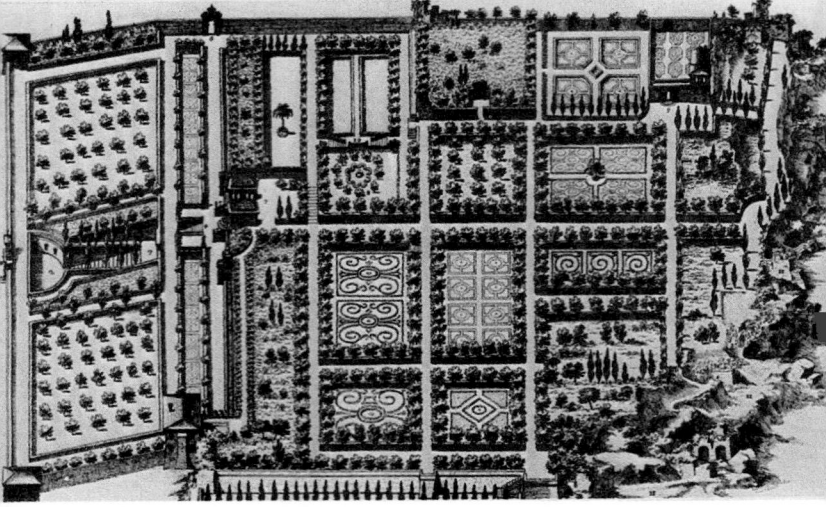

A print showing the Farnese Gardens in Rome (sixteenth century) designed by Giovanni Vignola and realized by Pope Paul III.

wild flowers were encouraged as symbols of the spirit of freedom that permeated the entire concept of the garden.

The idea of the landscaped garden, which originated in England, developed extensively during the nineteenth century while, at the same time, the number of exploratory expeditions in search of new flowering plants was diminishing. The cost of such expeditions had risen tremendously since the first voyages three centuries earlier, and collectors were forced to pay more attention to reducing the loss of botanical material. As a result, while amateur collecting declined rapidly, scientific collecting by professional naturalists increased. This trend has continued right up to the present day and is likely to continue.

The flower gardens of the world

The development of floriculture and the improvements in modern gardening techniques have given great scope to flower growing on every continent, regardless of climate or soil conditions. Whether it be a world-famous botanical garden or a small cottage garden, a plant-laden balcony or rolling lawns punctuated by colorful flower beds, any garden has the magical power of brightening up the gray monotony of an industrial environment or the repetitive regularity of agricultural scenery. Flowering plants are seen to best advantage, however, in "thematic" gardens or at least in gardens where the flowers are treated as an integral part of the overall design.

In the case of the Italian (or formal) garden, as well as in the shrubbery or woodland area—sometimes referred to as the

An example of an alpine rock garden: the Hruska Garden in Gardone Riviera, Brescia (northern Italy).

wilderness——of the English (or informal) garden, the flowers are subsidiary to the design. They are used to emphasize the interplay of shades of green and the shapes of the bushes, which, in turn, contrast with the different forms of the trees.

The most important part in the cultivation of flowering plants is, of course, played by the botanical gardens. Here, flowers, apart from providing beauty, are grown mainly so they can be correctly classified according to their botanical characteristics. They are frequently found growing in their natural surroundings (though, of course, these often have to be simulated).

Of the so-called thematic gardens, three types are discussed here. They are all examples of design in which the flowers stand out, sometimes because there are so many of them, sometimes because of their long blooming period, sometimes because of their exquisite beauty.

Alpine gardens are an example of the first type. These are devoted to those charming little plants that grow at high altitudes, particularly in great mountain chains such as the Alps, the Pyrenees, the Caucasus and the Rockies. Such gardens are interesting not only because they unite plants from the mountains of every continent, but also because of the many different plants and the beauty of their flowers. An alpine garden, therefore, is a wonderful microcosm of color and form.

More uniform in design but equally attractive is the bulb garden, so called because it is devoted to those perennial plants——such as tulips, hyacinths, lilies, and bulbous irises——

Part of the Royal Botanic Gardens at Kew, near London.

that grow from an underground reservoir of nourishment. Holland is the country where these gardens can be seen at their best, but there are also associations of bulb growers in many parts of the world who produce spectacular results.

A third example of a thematic garden is one that concentrates on succulents. These are often seen in American desert regions, Mexico and the Mediterranean countries. Most succulents produce few flowers and, since the flowers seldom bloom for long, they do not have the color impact that a bed of tulips or a rocky outcrop covered in tiny alpine saxifrage has. However, the flowers are very beautiful and often remarkably large. Although they may remain open for only a short time, their sudden display of brilliance is all the more precious.

Every type of garden has its special features. But, whether it be a rose garden, a path lined with azaleas, multicolored flower beds or an avenue of brilliantly flowering trees, each leaves an indelible impression on the observer.

As already mentioned, botanical gardens serve rather a different purpose. Botanical gardens include not only the official botanical gardens but also the parks and gardens in which plants have been properly identified and labeled with their names (both botanical and popular), habitat and, possibly, a brief history. Such places are invaluable both for research and for the layman who wishes to increase his knowledge of plants. They also often exchange plants with similar organizations.

Botanical gardens, which began to develop in Europe in the sixteenth century, soon became established throughout the world, and many countries now have one or more. Probably the best known are the Royal Botanic Gardens at Kew, England. Here is a splendid example of coordination between scientific research and horticultural and floricultural education combined with aesthetic purpose. Kew Gardens, as they are popularly called, not only fill an important——even indispensable——teaching and scientific role; they also provide delightful surroundings, close to London, in which the tourist or local resident can refresh his spirit.

There are many other gardens in Europe, some very old, that deserve to be regarded as botanical gardens even though they may not all be officially classified as such. Among the most famous and beautiful are the Jardin des Plantes in Paris, the Botanischer Garten in Berlin, the small but charming and well-organized Botanic Garden in England's Cambridge University and the Mediterranean Garden of Yalta in the Crimea. Many parks, both private and public, have become botanical gardens over the years without actually being so designated. In northern Italy, for instance, there is the Villa Taranto, on Lake Maggiore, which is well known for its rhododendrons, and the Villa Mortola, near Ventimiglia, renowned for its Mediterranean and subtropical flora; in Austria there is one at Schonbrunn; in France are Les Cedres on the Côte d'Azur.

This section would be incomplete without mentioning some of the oldest botanical gardens in Europe. In these, besides the usual facilities for study and aesthetic appreciation, there is also what might be termed artistic-historical interest. In fact, the gardens' very antiquity makes them more than a center for research and educational relaxation, because they represent a cultural heritage, part of which had blended into the scientific culture of the sixteenth and seventeenth centuries. Some good examples in Italy are the botanical gardens in Padua and Florence, the oldest in the world. In the rest of Europe there are similarly long-established botanical gardens in Leyden in Holland, Montpellier in France and Heidelberg in Germany.

Many of the emergent countries in Africa are still suffering from the effects of their recent troubles, and the establishment of botanical gardens has inevitably had low priority. Only in the last few years, in fact, has the majority of newly independent countries been able to start organizing national botanical gardens. One famous garden, however, is in Kirstenbosch, South Africa. This has a complete collection of all the best-known flowers that grow on the Cape of Good Hope as well as the indigenous plants of South Africa as a whole.

The Canary Isles, too, possess two delightful botanical gardens, the Orotova in Tenerife and the Viera y Clavijo on the island of Grand Canary. These are best known for their native trees, shrubs and plants and for a wide range of succulents.

It is difficult to decide which are the best known of the North American botanical gardens. There are so many of them and they are invariably so well laid out as to defy comparison. However, the most beautiful and most functional of all is probably the Arnold Arboretum in Boston. One of the largest in the world, it is renowned for its collections of magnolias, ornamental prunus, forsythias, rhododendrons and lilacs. The Brooklyn Botanical Gardens in New York, Huntington Botanical Gardens in San Marino, California (known particularly for succulents and camellias), the Strybing Arboretum and Botanic Gardens in San Francisco, Fairchild Tropical Garden in Coconut Grove, Florida, Morton Arboretum just west of Chicago, Missouri Botanical Garden in St. Louis (water lilies), Longwood Gardens in Kennett Square, Pennsylvania, are other fine ones.

In South America, the botanical garden in Rio de Janeiro and the Jardín Botánico Carlos Thays in Buenos Aires are outstanding.

The most impressive botanical gardens in Asia are in Bogor in Indonesia, Peradeniya in Ceylon (Sri Lanka) and the city of Singapore as well as those in Kyoto, Mikko and Sapporo in Japan, Peking in China, and Calcutta in India. The first three are undoubtedly the best examples of tropical gardens. Here can be seen the luxuriant vitality of the tropical plant kingdom and one can feel the full impact of color when the flowers burst into bloom. Tropical water lilies, ferns, palms, bamboos, camellias, India-rubber plants, anthuriums (flamingo flowers, painter's palettes, etc.) and orchids (of which Singapore has a particularly famous collection) are all grown in the open air. There are none of the problems of limited space or acclimatization that have to be contended with in greenhouses.

Before bringing this survey of the world botanical gardens to a close, reference must certainly be made to those in Melbourne and Sydney, Australia, and Christchurch, New Zealand. The first two provide an interesting record of the indigenous plant life of the Australian continent and include eucalyptus, acacia, callistemon (bottle brush), metrosideros and melaleucas as well as a wide variety of plants that are typical of—and often exclusive to—the land down under.

Flowering plants (angiosperms)

When we think of flowering plants, we often forget that the flower is only one part of the plant and that, even though it is of importance to the continuance of the species, it may last only a short time, leaving the parent plant intact. It is true, of course, that many plants do not have flowers at all——ferns and conifers are examples——but it is also true that every flowering plant produces at least one flower no matter how insignificant, in order to reproduce. In the broad spectrum of plant evolution, flowering plants——or angiosperms, the correct botanical name——represent the most advanced level. They are the visible evidence of that long, unceasing process to develop the plant kingdom over the earth's surface.

Since aquatic plants began acquiring the land habit about 400 or 500 million years ago, plants have been undergoing a very gradual modification. Their shape has become increasingly complex as their adaptation to existence on land, in all climates and on all the land masses, has improved. Thus it is possible to trace the development of plants, through ferns and conifers, until the angiosperms——identifiable by the presence of a flower——eventually evolved.

The flower, which is the reproductive organ of an angiosperm, is certainly the most characteristic feature of these plants. But they have other attributes typical of the group, both physically and behaviorally, which enable us to distinguish

23

The structure of flowering plants. Left, diagram of a plant: 1. roots; 2. basal leaves; 3. stalk; 4. leaf; 5. fruit; 6. flower.
Right, diagram of a tree: 1. roots; 2. trunk; 3. crown.

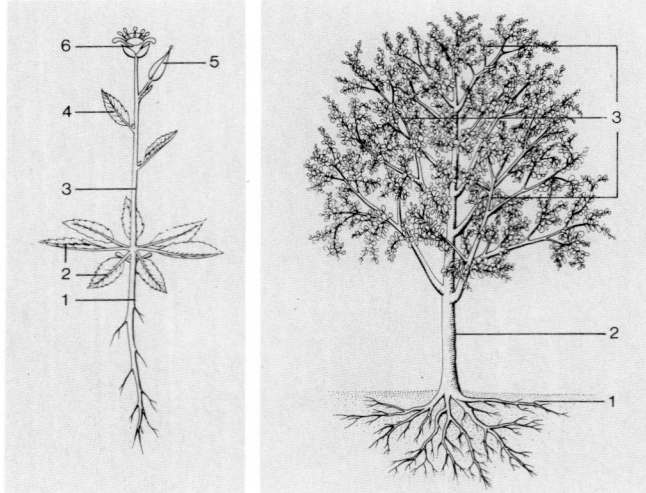

them from, for example, gymnosperms (plants producing their seeds in cones, such as the pines) and filicins (ferns).

A typical feature of angiosperms is their wide variation in size, ranging from some of the largest to the smallest plants in the world. One of the smallest is the common duckweed (diameter ⅛ in./2–3 mm.) while one of the largest is the eucalyptus tree (height 330 ft./100 m.). Their appearance is also extremely varied, depending on their environmental conditions. Some angiosperms that live on the sea bed near the coast have a filamentous, or threadlike, appearance; there are some very tiny ones, too, that grow near the continental glaciers and perpetually snow-covered land. There are giant grasses, such as the bamboo, which can reach heights of 96–132 ft. (30–40 m.) and dwarf trees, such as the Japanese hollies, sometimes less than 12 in (305 mm.) tall.

This variability of habit, which frequently corresponds to variability in the plant's capacity to adapt, has made it possible for angiosperms to exist in almost every kind of environment. Specific growth habits can be related to specific groups of flowering plants: grasses, shrubs, trees, lianas (climbing plants that need supporting), epiphytes (plants that grow on the branches of trees without touching the ground at all, like many orchids), etc. In each of these groups, the basic structure of the angiosperm can be recognized. This consists of a root and a stem from which side branches may grow, and an inside which contains the latent leaves. The flower is nothing more than a modification of a branch and its leaves. This com-

24

position of stem, leaves and root can be identified in all angiosperms even though it may be found in radically modified forms, and at first sight may be hardly apparent.

The root is the supportive organ of the plant, designed to provide it with water and mineral salts. It may be quite simple—i.e., a taproot—or it may be fibrous and branch out in different directions. The way the latter form develops depends in good part on the kind of soil and substratum in which the plant is growing and whether it is growing on land or in water.

The stem is the axial organ and backbone of the angiosperm. In most plants it is more or less upright, stout and capable of supporting the branches, leaves, flowers and fruits that take off from it. But in grasses it is often quite simple, without branches, and as in the case of bulbs, rhyzomes, tubers, etc., it sometimes takes a different form and may be underground. This enables it to remain in good condition for a long time, thus ensuring that the plant gets off to a good start in the spring. During the dormant period it accumulates reserves of nutrients and builds up the leaves and flowers in embryo, ready to emerge as soon as the right conditions pertain.

Branch systems are similar in structure to the stem. While not very developed in grasses, they are an important part of the framework of shrubs and, particularly, trees. They constitute the head, or crown, of the tree, which is its characteristic feature, and it is often possible to recognize a species of tree by the shape of the head. In fact, the types of branch system, the color of the foliage, the direction in which the branches grow, and even the appearance and color of the bark are all contributory factors in identification. The stem——or trunk, as it becomes in trees——and limbs sometimes undergo such a degree of modification as to be almost unrecognizable. This can be seen, for instance, in the fleshy stems of some cacti; in the flattened branches (cladodes), which look like leaves, of the evergreen subshrub *Ruscus aculeatus* (butcher's broom); in the spiny branches of the cotoneasters.

The leaves of a flowering plant are, perhaps, its most characteristic feature as far as its vegetative system is concerned. They are the organs by which the plant carries out photosynthesis and transpiration, whether this be through the great leaves of a palm tree or the tiny umbrellalike leaves of tropaeolums, through cactus spines or the tendrils of many leguminous plants, through the fleshy leaves of mesembryanthemums, the delicate leaves of the linden or the leathery leaves of the magnolia. Leaves vary a great deal in shape, size, lifespan, subdivision into leaflets, thickness, color, etc. They are therefore a very important element in the identification of the various species of angiosperm.

Regardless of the importance of roots, stems and leaves, no angiosperm can complete its natural cycle or be fully reproductive unless flowers are formed. The flower is the final stage in the reproductive cycle of an angiosperm, and its seeds are the natural means by which each species is propagated. In other words, the reproductive cycle of an angiosperm starts with the germination of a seed and the formation of a seedling and ends with the formation of a flower, then a fruit and finally new seeds. As these ripen and leave the parent plant, they all have the potential to start the cycle all over again.

The vegetative period of an angiosperm may last for almost any length of time, depending on the species and environment. When the first flowers begin to form, representing reproductive maturity, this may mean not only the end of the plant's reproductive cycle but also the end of the whole plant. Thus some plants that die after seed dissemination leave the task of reproducing the next generation to their seeds. In annuals, for example, the entire life cycle——germination of the seed, development of the stem(s) and leaves, production of flowers, formation of fruit and seeds, dissemination——may take place within the space of a few months or, in the case of desert plants, a few days. But perennials, although they have an equally rapid reproductive cycle, do not die after dissemination and the parts of the plant beneath the soil become responsible for forming new leaves, flowers and fruit the following year. (Of course, perennials are also reproduced by seeds.)

The reproductive cycle of shrubs and trees is rather different. Many require several years——between ten and twenty or even more——to reach maturity. This accounts for the fact that flowers very often do not appear until a shrub or tree has reached a fair size, after a long vegetative phase.

The actual flowering period of angiosperms varies widely from genus to genus and species to species, according to climatic conditions. Some tropical plants produce flowers spasmodically throughout the whole year in their natural environment; but when transferred to more temperate zones they

Some examples of fruit: 1. achene of the Compositae family; 2. blackberry; 3. jimson weed capsule; 4. legume (edible pod); 5. apple (cross section).

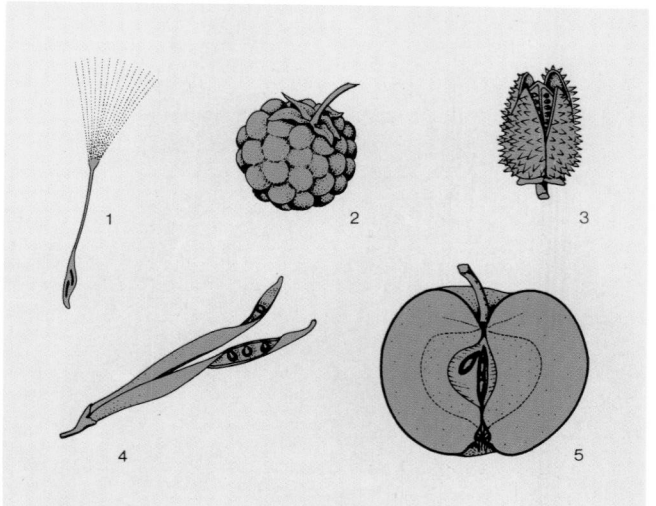

adjust their flowering period to the new climatic conditions and are in bloom for only 15 to 20 days a year. Generally speaking, the flowering period of plants in their natural surroundings rarely corresponds to the time they will remain in bloom in conditions which have been imposed on them—unless the conditions closely resemble those of their place of origin.

Among the plants whose flowers remain open for only a short time are the cacti, irises, tulips and cistus (rock or sun roses). Among long-blooming plants are orchids and azaleas.

Timing of blooming is equally variable. A genus such as prunus, whose 430 species include such ornamental flowering trees and shrubs as almonds, cherries and peaches, tends to put out a great deal of bloom at one time. The effect is beautiful, even spectacular, but it is short-lived. Other plants produce many flowers that individually have an equally brief life; but they bloom intermittently, providing a less dramatic display but lasting much longer. Fuchsia, tagetes, hibiscus and viburnum are among those with extended blooming periods.

When the flowering season ends, plants rely on their seeds to propagate the species. Some trees produce indehiscent fruits that do not split open when ripe; consequently their seeds must be distributed by other means. For example, the fleshy fruit of the flowering currants and roses (which produce hips) and the stone fruits of cherries and peaches are eaten by birds, and these contribute to dissemination by carrying the seeds away from the parent plant. On the other hand, many plants produce dehiscent fruits that burst open on maturity so that the seeds can be scattered by the winds or carried away

Cornus florida (*flowering dogwood*), *var.* Rubra, *in bloom.*

by animals, birds and other agents. For example, the feathery seeds of the oleander can easily be seen in summertime as they drift lightly away from the open fruit on currents of air.

The origin and evolution of the flower

One feature of the scenery that impresses all of us is the beauty of flowers. The wealth of color they provide, together with their variety of shapes and sizes, are a constant wonder. And in the public parks and gardens of cities, flowers dominate the scene, enlivening everything with their vivid hues. Were there flowers in prehistoric landscapes when plant forms first appeared? In fact there were not. Flowering plants——angiosperms——are, from a geological point of view, of relatively recent origin, as they did not become fairly widespread until 150 to 200 million years ago. And when one realizes that the earth is about 4 billion years old, one may regard angiosperms as quite young.

Land masses started to be populated by plants about 500 million years ago. This was at the beginning of the Paleozoic Era, when lichens, mosses, algae and very primitive plants covered the rocks, which had themselves only recently been formed and emerged from the oceans. The first land plants sufficiently developed to bear any resemblance to some of those we know today began to take shape in the Silurian Period——400 million years ago——and continued to develop through the Carboniferous and Permian Periods of 250 to 300

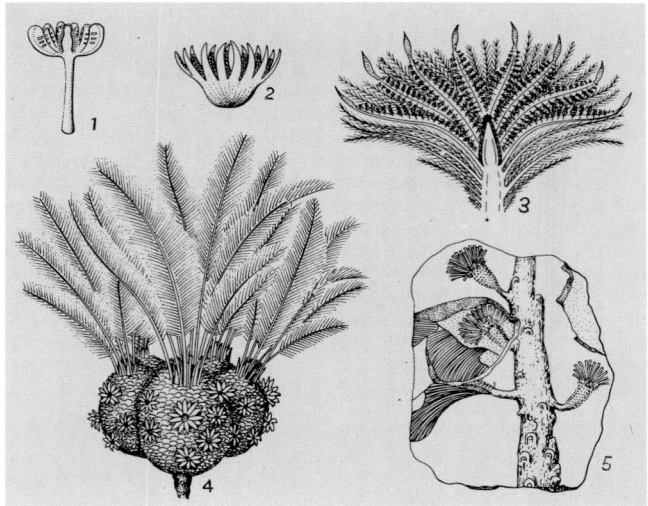

Fossil structures illustrating flowers of 100–300 million years ago: 1. Williamsoniella; *2.* Williamsonia; *3 and 4.* Cycadeoidea; *5.* Vojnowskya.

million years ago. Flowering plants, however, were still unknown. Vegetation consisted of shrubs or large trees with more or less developed leaves, climbing plants, ferns and conifers. This was the period of the great tree ferns, the lepidodendrons and sigillarids, of which there were vast forests in North America and central Europe. By the end of the Palaeozoic Era, however, these had become extinct, leaving only their fossilized tissues, which now exist as underground coal seams.

Plants with flowers did not make their appearance on earth until the Mesozoic Era, although we have no means of knowing which were the first representatives of angiosperms or how they were made. The results of certain palaeontological studies have, in fact, demonstrated that, toward the end of the Mesozoic Era—130 million years ago in the Cretaceous Period—angiosperms were already widely dispersed over almost the entire earth, in a great variety of flower forms. Scientists maintain, however, that the first flowers had already made a timid appearance—albeit in very primitive form—in the early stages of the Mesozoic Era, 225 million years ago.

During this era there were to be found in various areas a number of plant types that were structured similarly to flowers. The forerunners of the angiosperms, they included such things as the glossopteris of the Triassic Period, the caytoniales of the Jurassic Period and the bennettitales of the Cretaceous Period. All had a reproductive apparatus bearing some resemblance to the structure of the modern flower. But, geologically

29

speaking, they had a comparatively short life and died out at the end of the Mesozoic Era to make way for other types.

The first "true" flowering plants became widespread during the Cretaceous Period but did not really develop extensively until the Tertiary Period (30 to 70 million years ago). These have come down to us with only slight modifications in the structure of the flower.

Scientists regard the magnolia and similar plants as the most primitive angiosperms currently in existence. These have, in fact, retained in their flowers the same features that were found in angiosperm fossils over 100 million years old. In their primitive form the flowers consisted of a central axis with all its floral appendages attached spirally (acyclic structure) and continuing upward from the sterile components to the reproductive ones. In the course of evolution the axis shortened until the spiral was almost level with the sterile floral envelope on the outside and the fertile components in the center. We see this structure today in the magnolia flower. In most flowers, however, the floral parts form verticils, or whorls, on the same level around the axis, producing a cyclic structure. In this, two whorls are external and sterile——the perianth——and two or more whorls are internal and fertile——the andoecium (stamens) and the gynoecium (carpels).

The structure of the flower

The essential parts of a flower are its bearing axis——that is, its peduncle, or stalk, supporting at its apex the receptacle, or torus, from which grow the floral components, arranged in whorls. The outer components, forming the involucre, or perianth, are sterile and act as a protective covering; the inner ones——the androecium and gynoecium——are reproductive.

Perianth. The sterile components of the perianth are usually arranged in two whorls that may be the same color, shape and size or quite different. When the two whorls are more or less equal, the perianth is known as the perigonium and its two appendages are called tepals. When they differ from each other, however, the outer whorl——which is usually green——is called the calyx and is formed of sepals while the inner whorl——which is usually brightly colored——is known as the corolla. The components of the corolla are called petals. Each part of the calyx may be quite separate (dialysepalous) or joined together (gamosepalous). The corolla may also consist of individual petals (dialypetalous) or of petals that are joined to each other (gamopetalous or sympetalous). If there is a perigonium, rather than a calyx and corolla, this is also found in two forms, dialytepalous and gamotepalous. The calyx generally acts as a protective covering for the fertile organs and, when flowering is over, may either fall off or continue to enclose the fruit. The corolla, like the perigonium, is usually brightly colored, and where this is so, it seems to aid pollination by attracting pollen-carrying insects. This is confirmed by the fact that in wind-pollinated flowers the corolla is generally very small and insignificant, without any coloration other than green.

Some types of flower have no perianth at all. In these, the protective function is entrusted to other organs such as bracts, and pollination is carried out by the wind. Flowering plants are classified by the basic characteristics of their perianthal struc-

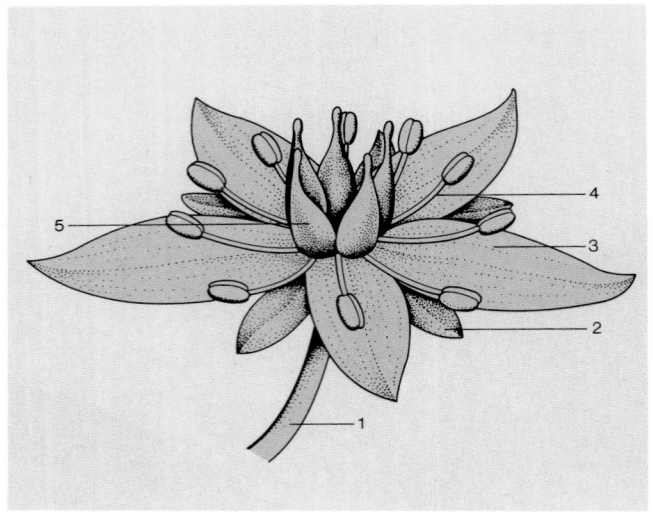

ture, which takes many forms. Such factors as the number of petals or tepals, how they are positioned, the way in which such organs are joined to the axis, and the shape of the corolla or perigonium make it easy to distinguish between a rose and a tulip, a mallow and a saxifrage, an orchid and a lily, and so on. The form variations of the corolla—and of the perigonium—in particular have given rise to a wide range of flower types, all of which have specific names such as campanulate (bell-shaped), rotate, urceolate (pitcher-shaped), tubulate (trumpet- or tube-shaped), papilionaceous (butterfly-like), labiate (lipped), etc. Each of these names is highly descriptive of the various corolla structures and makes identification quite easy.

Many people are first attracted to flowers growing and collecting by the brilliant colors of the corolla or perigonium and the beauty of their structures. But in many plants this signaling function is performed by quite different parts of the flower. For example, in the aconite it is the calyx that becomes colored while the corolla is reduced to a mere appendage. In the bougainvillaea, too, the flower itself is insignificant while the leaves—the bracts—that envelop it are large and brilliantly colored. On the other hand, some flowers are quite tiny but very numerous; they are also colored but their effect *en masse* rather than the individual flowers is attractive.

The reproductive system. The reproductive system—or sporophylls—of the flower consists of the androecium, whose floral parts are the stamens, and the gynoecium, which is formed by the carpels. These, in turn, are the constituent units

Cross sections of flowers illustrating the different positions of the ovary. Top: superior ovary; bottom: left, seminiferous ovary; right, inferior ovary. 1. peduncle; 2. receptacle; 3. calyx; 4. corolla; 5. androecium (stamens); 6. gynoecium (ovary).

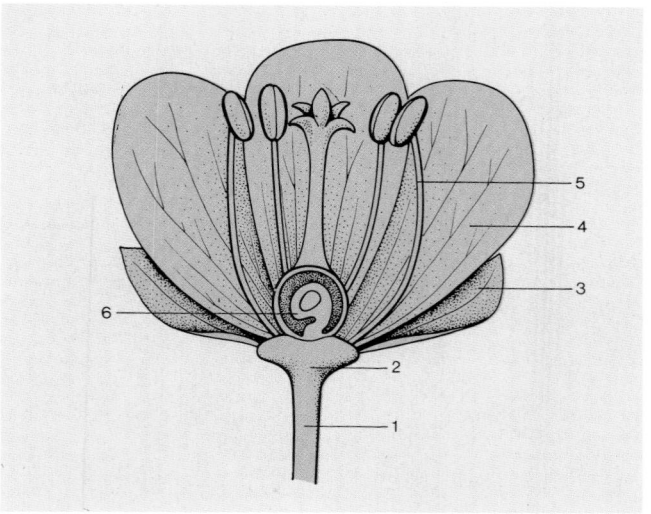

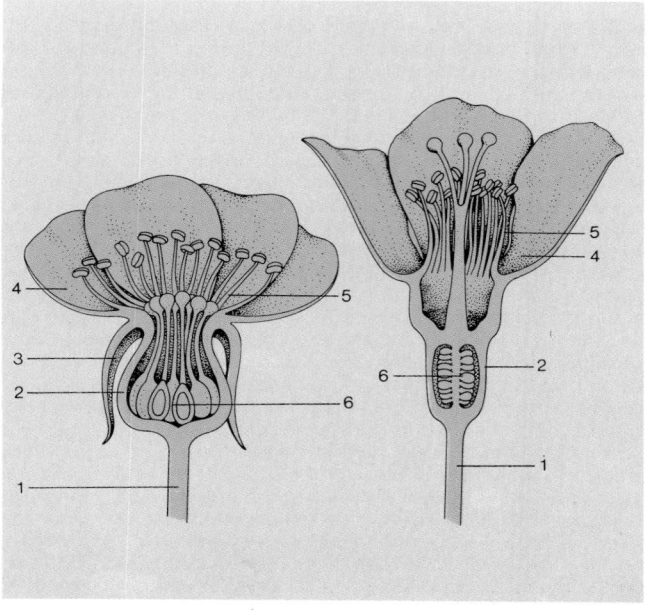

Some examples of corollas: 1. ligulate (Compositae); 2. tubulous (Pentstemon); 3. personate (Scrophulariaceae); 4. campanulate (Campanulaceae); 5. papilionaceous (Leguminosae); 6. rosaceous (Rosaceae).

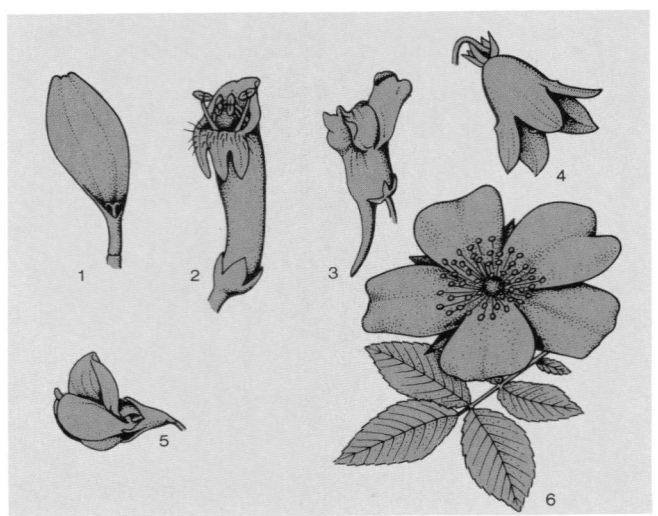

of the ovary. In a sexually complete flower——a hermaphrodite, or bisexual, flower——the androecium and gynoecium are both present and are positioned in such a way that the androecium is either underneath or on the outside and the gynoecium is either on top or on the inside. Flowers that have only an androecium or a gynoecium are called unisexual. Plants with unisexual flowers are categorized according to the distribution of the flowers. For example, in monoecious plants, the unisexual flowers are distributed in different areas of the same plant, those bearing the androecia, or male flowers, being carried on one branch and those with the gynoecia, or female flowers, on another. In dioecious plants, by contrast, the male flowers are borne by one plant and the female flowers by another plant; thus the gardener must deal with individual male and female plants for purposes of propagation. In hermaphrodite (or monoecious) plants, pollination clearly presents no problems since the androecium (stamens) and gynoecium (ovary) are close together. In the case of dioecious plants, however, fertilization may be quite difficult because the stamens and ovary are on separate plants and the intervention of some external agent is required, especially if the plants are some distance apart.

Androecium. The fertile male appendages that produce the male spores——microspores or pollen grains——are called stamens. A typical stamen consists of a supportive axis (the filament) and a fertile part (the anther). The latter is divided into two lobes, each containing two pollen sacs in which the pollen is produced. The number of stamens ranges from three in

Close-up of a poppy flower, clearly showing androecium and gynoecium.

irises to five in campanulas, six in lilies, ten in broom and wisteria. Roses have even more. The stamens' shape and structure may vary considerably from one type of plant to another. Orchids, for instance, have no recognizable stamens. Their pollen, which is not powdery, remains in two, four, six or eight spherical masses called polliniae.

Stamens may be free-standing or joined together. They may also vary in length and color, the filament being white with red anthers, for instance, or blue with white anthers, etc. The filament holds the anther high in order to make it easier for the anther's pollen to be carried away. In some cases there is no filament at all. The anther, however, is almost always present because it is the fertile part (there are a few cases in which there is no anther but these are exceptional). When the moment of maturation arrives, the anther opens to release the pollen, which is then carried away by insects, the wind or other agents, and the process of pollination is set in motion.

The word ''pollen'' refers to the whole powdery mass made up of a great many minute grains that are produced inside the anther (in Latin, *pollen* means fine flour). Pollen grains possess variable features and are enclosed in two casings, the outer one being equipped with all kinds of defensive structures or appendages such as thorns, prickles or crestlike protuberances. These enable the pollen of one plant to be distinguished from that of another. The study of pollen has, in fact, given rise to a relatively new science, palynology, which is a great help in systematic biology, phytography, paleoclimatol-

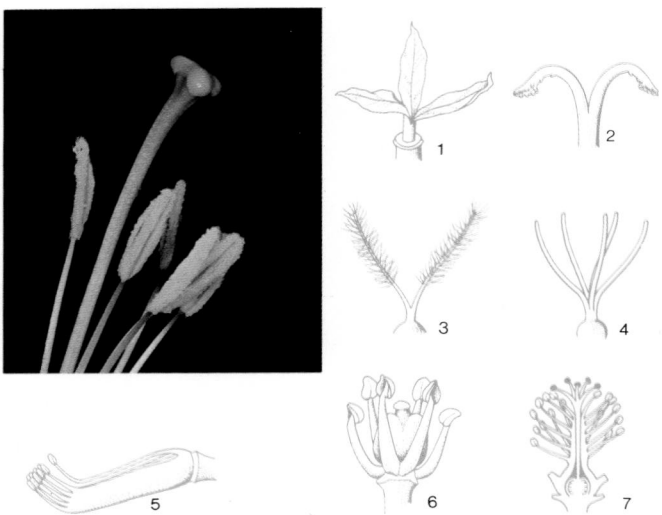

Details of the reproductive organs of flowers: 1, 2, 3, 4, various types of stigmas; 5, 6, 7, examples of stamens. The photograph is of the stamens and stigma of a lily.

ogy and in the applied areas, too. In the study of pollen-induced allergies, therefore, and in increasing our understanding of the properties of honey, an analytical knowledge of pollen has become essential.

Gynoecium. The gynoecium consists of the female reproductive organ, or carpels, which are fused together in many plants to form the ovary, which is the most pronounced part of the gynoecium. Each carpel contains an ovule in which the female gamete, or oosphere, is formed. Projecting from the carpel is a kind of stalk, called a style, on the end of which is the stigma. This varies in size but its purpose is always to trap pollen when it comes near enough. The whole organ, comprising the ovary, style and stigma, comprises the pistil.

The gynoecium may be formed by a single carpel, and is then described as a monocarpic gynoecium such as is found in the papilionaceae and compositae families. On the other hand, the gynoecium may be composed of more than one carpel, in which case these may be free-standing to form the same number of pistils. This is known as an apocarpous gynoecium and is found in such plant families as the magnoliaceae and ranunculaceae. Alternatively the carpels may be fused together to form a single pistil called a synacarpous gynoecium, as in the caryophyllaceae and liliaceae families. As has already been mentioned, the gynoecium is in the apical, or central, part of the flower but its position in relation to the other parts, such as the perianth and androecium, may vary. However, there are three particular positions by which ovaries are distin-

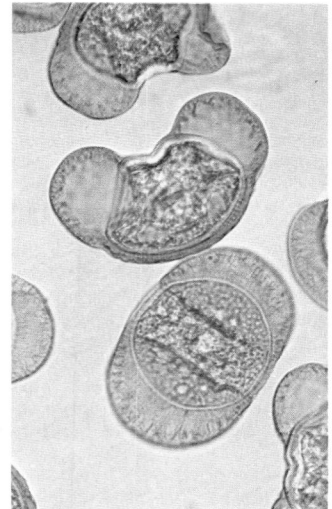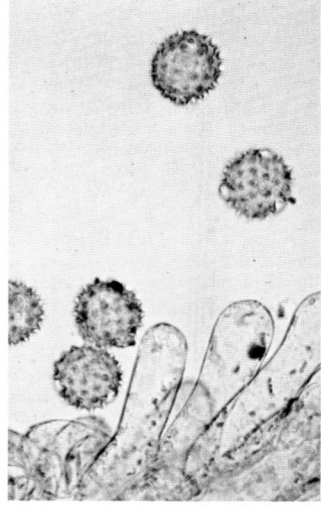

Pollen grains under the microscope. Left, pine pollen; Right, purple clover pollen.

guished——superior, inferior and seminiferous. In the first case, the gynoecium is positioned over the other floral appendages (a hypogynous flower), as in the papilionaceae and liliaceae families. In the second, the gynoecium is positioned below the other parts (an epigynous flower), as in the iridaceae and compositae families. In the third, with its seminiferous gynoecium or perigynous flower, the perianth and androecium are fused together to form a cup that surrounds and partially envelops the ovary, as in the rosaceae family. The ovules——in some cases only one——are inside the ovary, attached by the placentae in an orderly arrangement. This positioning, known as the placentation, varies from one family to another.

The ovary may consist of a single cavity or lobe——a unilocular ovary——as, for example, in the papilionaceae family; or there may be several cavities——a plurilocular ovary——as in the campanulaceae and liliaceae families. When pollination has taken place——and often fertilization, too——the structure of the ovary changes in accordance with certain determinate physiological processes that are involved in the ripening of the fruit. As a result of these processes, the carpels forming the walls of the ovary are transformed and grow to become the wall of the fruit——the pericarp. The ovules develop into seeds. And the whole ovary enlarges to become a fruit. During the transformation of the ovary into a ripening fruit, the other parts of the flower——perianth, androecium, style and stigma——usually shrivel and fall off, since their purpose has been served. This when flowering is said to have finished, because the most important part of the process is represented by the fading of the flower and the fall of the corolla (or perigonium). In a few cases, these organs may remain intact as the fruit ripens, and may even grow, thus participating in the formation of the fruit itself.

Inflorescences

So far we have discussed the flower as a single structure, but in many plants it is found in groups of various sizes and degrees of orderliness. These groupings are known as inflorescences. In plants that produce their flowers singly, flowers are usually borne on a main flower stalk, or peduncle. For example, tulips, cyclamens and pansies have single, terminally positioned blooms even though the plants, when cultivated in groups, may sometimes give the impression of bearing clusters of flowers or inflorescences.

A great many flowers do, of course, grow in collective heads consisting of such tiny, closely packed flowers that they look like a single flower. For instance, all the compositae, such as daisies, dahlias, chrysanthemums and cornflowers, grow in this way. An inflorescence, therefore, is a cluster of flowers arranged in a distinctive way on small stalks, or pedicels, which, while not bearing normal leaves, carry modified leaves called bracts. Every plant family that bears its flowers in an inflorescent structure repeats the essential features of the clusters constantly.

Classification of the various types of inflorescence is based on only a few characteristics, such as the branching of the main stalk, the speed of growth of the secondary stalks, the size to which the flowers grow and the order in which the individual flowers open, whether or not there is a floral peduncle. Inflorescences are usually divided into two main categories. One is the racemose (or indefinite) inflorescence in which the main stem, or raceme, continues to grow, putting out new flowers toward the tips of short pedicels. In this case, the oldest flowers are those farthest from the apex while the youngest are those nearest it, and the inflorescence does not finish growing until a flower has been formed at the summit of the stalk. The other category is the cymose (or definite) inflorescence in which the main inflorescent stem ceases to grow quite early with the opening of a terminal flower, while secondary axes and higher orders continue to branch out to produce new flowers that open successively once the terminal flower has faded. The most important types of racemose inflorescence are the raceme, as in delphiniums, lilies, hyacinths, etc.; the spike, as in veronicas; the umbel, as in the umbelliferae (carrot family) and alliums; the corymb, as in spiraea, ligustrum and some types of saxifraga; and the capitulum, which is present in all the compositae. Similarly, among the cymose inflorescences there are the helicoid, or simple monochasium, as in the iris and gladiolus; the scorpioid, or compound monochasium, as in the myosotis (forget-me-not); the simple dichasium, as in the dianthus and other members of the caryophyllaceae family; and the pleiochasium, or compound dichasium, as in the sambucus (elder). A few inflorescences do not fit into any of these main categories; for example, the cyathium of the euphorbia; the vertillicasters of the labiates; compound inflorescences, as in the achillea, which has a corymb of capitula.

One of the more common and distinctive inflorescences is, in fact, the capitulum. One of the main families in which this is found is the compositae. Many members of this group are cultivated specifically for their flowers, such as the ox-eye daisy, cornflower, chrysanthemum, zinnia, etc. The capitulum is formed from a single enlarged receptacle, expanded into a disc, on which are crowded numerous tiny sessile (i.e. attached by their base without a stalk or pedicel) florets arranged spirally from the outer edge to the center. The whole capitulum is encircled by a whorl of bracts, usually green in color, which constitute the involucre and which, at first glance, resembles the calyx of a single flower. The little flowers that make up the capitulum may be of two types—tubulate (tube-shaped) or ligulate (strap-shaped). Tubulate florets are cylindrical, with a gamopetalous (joined petals) corolla and usually without a calyx, although they may have a calyx that has been transformed into fine hairs called a pappus. Ligulate flowers are also gamopetalous but, at the end of a very short tube, they open up into a broad, tonguelike lamina that varies in length. Depending on the species, tubulate and ligulate flowers may be found in the same capitulum. They have three different combinations of characteristics. In one the tiny flowers that constitute the capitulum are all tubulate and more or less equal; for example, some of the senecio, carduus and cirsium genera. In another, all the flowers are ligulate; for example, taraxacum, scorzonera and hieracium. In the third possibility, the peripheral flowers are ligulate and known as ray flowers, forming a sort of external corona, while those in the center, the disc flowers, are all tubulate and frequently differ from the ray flowers in size and color. Most of the cultivated compositae belong to this group. Seen as a whole, these inflorescences resemble single flowers because the ray flowers can look very much like a corolla while the disc flowers are easily mistaken for the stamens and carpels of a single flower.

Pollination

Pollination involves the transfer of pollen from the anther to the stigma of the gynoecium. This is essential for fertilization to take place, since the male and female gametes develop in organs that are some distance from each other and are unable to make physical contact. The intervention of an intermediary is therefore necessary if a plant is to reproduce.

Pollination may occur from the stamen to the pistil of the same flower, this system being known as autogamy, or direct pollination. More frequently, however, it occurs between the stamens of one flower and the pistils of another flower on either the same plant or a separate plant. This is called heterogamy, or cross-pollination. While heterogamy has to take place in dioecious plants and monoecious plants with unisexual flowers for structural reasons, it is optional in plants with hermaphrodite flowers (although cross-pollination is quite widespread here, too, and might even be said to be the prevalent system). Hermaphrodite plants do, in fact, often have rather unusual structures, or certain phenomena occur in them, that prevent autogamy and consequently make heterogamy inevitable. One such phenomenon, for example, is the dif-

The wide range of colors demonstrated in these cineraria (Senecio cruentus) capitula gives some idea of the variations found in this type of inflorescence.

Some examples of inflorescences: 1. capitulum of a ligulate composite flower (each floret is ligulate); 2. a capitulum of a tubulate composite flower (a) tubulous disc-florets; (b) ligulate ray-florets; 3. umbel; 4. dichasium; 5. spike; 6. raceme.

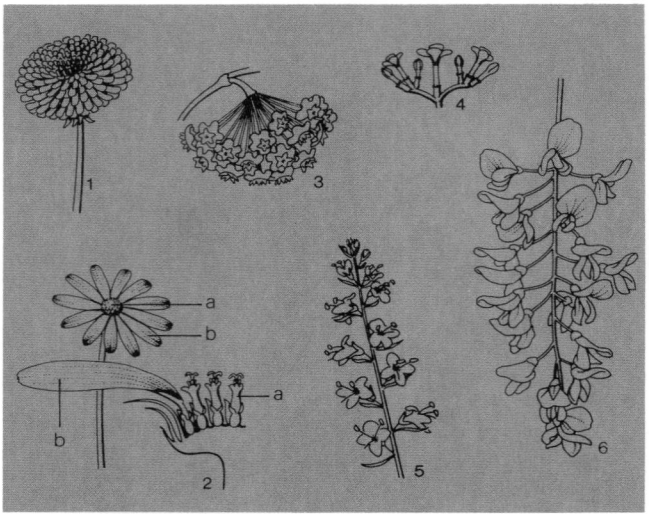

ference in the maturation period of the stamens and the pistils. In such instances, when the anthers have matured and the pollen is released, the stigma of the gynoecium may still not be completely developed and is therefore unable to receive the pollen. Alternatively, it may already have faded. Cross-pollination, which involves the transference of pollen across a space, can only be effected through the intervention of external factors that act as pollen carriers, albeit unwittingly. These are, for the most part, the wind, animals and water. Pollination carried out with the help of these agents is called, respectively, anemophily, zoophily and hydrophily. In anemophilous plants, the pollen is committed to the wind until it lands on an appropriate stigma. Obviously, in this kind of pollination, only a minimal amount of pollen ever reaches a stigma, because its dispersal is entirely haphazard. As a precautionary measure, therefore, plants that rely upon wind pollination produce vast quantities of pollen to increase the likelihood of a successful union. There are several groups of plants that are completely anemophilous, such as the salicaceae (willows), fagaceae (beeches) and graminaceae (grasses).

Zoophily, which requires the intervention of animals, is most frequently found as entomophily—pollination through the medium of insects. Insects are believed to be attracted to some flowers by the bright colors of the perianth. In other flowers, the nectaries at the base of the petals secrete a strong, sweet liquid that appeals to certain pollinating insects: and to make sure that the insects can get it, the corolla or perigonium are

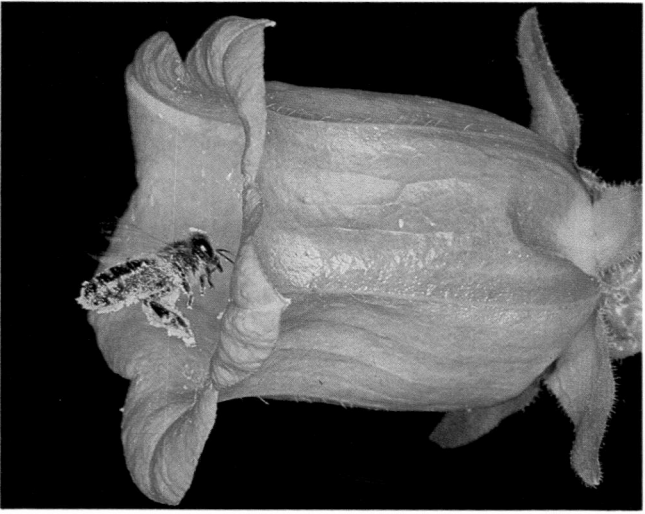

specially constructed to provide ready access. There are also entomphilous plants for which only one species of insect can serve as the pollinator. If this insect does not live in the present environment of such a plant, it must be pollinated by the gardener himself.

Hybridization
Man frequently acts as a pollinating agent when he wants to produce particular varieties and hybrids. When this operation is effected between plants of the same species it is known as intraspecific artificial pollination. If it is performed between different types of plants, it is called interspecific artificial pollination. The result of the latter process is the production of a hybrid—a plant having some of the characteristics of the male flower and some of the female. The technique of artificial hybridization is fairly easy but it is often difficult to get satisfactory results. In fact, to obtain a hybrid plant in a good vegetative and fertile condition it is necessary to follow interspecific pollination with regular fertilization between gametes of different species, thus ensuring the formation of an embryo and of a seed capable of germinating and producing a new plant. If the procedure is successful, a plant is produced with different features from those of its parents. Varieties that are produced artificially in this way, through hybridization under controlled conditions of cultivation, together with those obtained through meticulous methods of artificial selection, are known as cultivars. This word, which has come into being through interna-

tional agreement, is a contraction of the words "cultivated variety" and is abbreviated "cv." If, however, one is referring to hybrids produced from different species—or even, sometimes, from different genera—it is customary to indicate the hybridization with a multiplication sign. For example, *Clematis x violacea* is a deciduous hybrid obtained by crossing C. flammula and C. viticella to give cv. "Rubromarginata." Similarly *Deutzia x rosea* gives cv. "Carminea" or cv. "Campanulata" and *Rosa x odorata* (tea rose) gives cv. "Old Velvet."

Although hybridization techniques are relatively simple, they need to be applied with a certain degree of accuracy. For a successful hybridization, it is essential first to select the plants to be hybridized and to decide from which plant the mother flower will be taken and from which the father. The flower chosen for the maternal role will, after pollination, have to produce fruit whose seeds are of top quality, and the mother must therefore be brought to the peak of vegetative and fertile condition. All the anthers have to be removed from the flower of this plant while the flower is still young to prevent it from pollinating its own stigma. The flower is then enclosed in a gauze or muslin bag that acts as protection against the arrival of pollen from other flowers that may be quite a distance away. When the covered flower is fully developed, artificial pollination can be carried out. After removing pollen with a fine brush from the anthers of the plant selected for the paternal role (in the case of an interspecific hybrid this must, of course, belong to a different species), the human pollinator opens the muslin bag for an instant and brushes the pollen onto the stigma of the mother flower. Then the bag is immediately closed. If pollination has been successful—that is, if fertilization has taken place and the embryo matured—the ovary swells and develops into a fruit while the ovules change into seeds. Now the bag can be removed and complete maturation of the fruit awaited. When it is fully ripe, the seeds are collected for sowing. Each seed should produce a hybrid plant to whose genetic makeup both parent plants have contributed. It may then be given the name of both parents, as described above.

Reproduction
The reproduction of angiosperms does not simply involve fertilization of the female gamete, or oosphere, situated in the ovule, by the male gamete, or antherozoid, contained in pollen, followed by the formation of the embryo inside the seed. A second act of fertilization is also necessary. This occurs parallel to the act already described, between a second male gamete and the so-called secondary female cells (the polar nuclei) situated within the ovule, close to the oosphere. As a result of this second fertilization, there develops a special type of material, called endosperm, which is rich in the nutritive substances that will feed the embryo as it forms. This phenomenon is called double fertilization. It is found exclusively in flowering plants, and represents a fundamental feature in the evolution of plants. It is through this double gametic act that the embryo is assured of a reserve of nourishment that will enable it to develop autonomously when the moment of germination arrives.

Once pollination has taken place, the pollen granule deposited on the stigma of the gynoecium germinates to produce a

pollen tube that grows down inside the style into the ovule. The two male gametes contained in the pollen granule, having passed along the pollen tube, arrive at the ovule, and this is where the second fertilization takes place. The first gamete unites with the oosphere, or egg, to produce a zygote——the first cell of the new embryo; the second gamete fuses with the secondary nucleus to produce one cell——a proendospermatic cell——which will produce the endosperm, or albumen.

As a result of these processes, the ovule undergoes certain changes, gets larger and eventually becomes a seed, while at the same time the ovary grows bigger into a fruit. At this stage, the reproductive cycle is concluded. The plant must now concern itself with the propagation of the new plantlets contained in the seed to ensure, by a process of dissemination, the survival of future generations.

The variability and beauty of flowers

Just what is it about flowers that makes them so beautiful? Undoubtedly, in most cases, it is the color and shape and, to a lesser extent, the fragrance of the corolla or perigonium. For instance, roses, carnations, tulips and azaleas all owe their striking beauty to these structures, and without them the plants would be insignificant——in no way to be compared with, say, a stately conifer or a fragile fern. Yet in some cases it is not the corolla that is the center of the flower's attraction; and it may not even be one of the flower's components. In the eucalyptus and mimosa, for example, the brilliance of the flowers is attrib-

Hybrid passiflora bloom (cv. "Empresse Eugénie": P. quadrangularis x P. caerulea).

utable to the stamens. In the eucalyptus these occur in tufts with white or cream-colored filaments, while in the mimosa they are fluffy balls of brilliant yellow. In the bougainvillaea and poinsettia, the flowers themselves are tiny and unimportant but the bracts that envelop them are brilliantly colored and large.

If flowers have such natural beauty, why do men persist in trying to develop new varieties? Partly, of course, it's because man is a tinkerer. But mainly it's because many people believe they honestly can improve on nature.

Undoubtedly most new varieties and hybrids are developed simply to extend the color range of a given genus or to make it available in new shapes, forms or sizes. But some are developed to improve a flower's fragrance (in the great and continuing effort to create more beautiful and more trouble-free roses, earlier hybridizers unfortunately bred most of the fragrance out of the flowers, so now efforts are being made to breed it back in). Some are developed to improve a flower's resistance to cold; to reduce or increase the plant's overall size; to make the plant resistant to, or immune to, diseases; and so on.

It is true that today most of this development work is being done for commercial purposes——to increase the market for a flower or, more crassly, to woo buyers away from the old, cheaper varieties to new, expensive varieties. But whatever the motive, the result is to expand the number of flowers available to gardeners and thus to increase the beauty and reliability of gardens and also to simplify the gardener's labors.

Which are the most beautiful flowers? Everyone has his own subjective view. No one has ever assembled in one place at one time all the flowers of the world to be judged like girls in a Miss America contest. In one way or another all flowers have beauty and scores have exceptional beauty.

In which natural environments are the most beautiful flowers to be found? Botanists and others who have traveled the world over generally rate the equatorial forests first. Here the vegetation, consisting of a great mixture of plants varying widely in shape and size, is always lush. This is attributable to ideal climatic conditions: high temperatures, frequent and plentiful rains and extremely high humidity. In this complex ecosystem the flowers are among the most exotically beautiful known to man: orchids in thousands of species, verbenas, anthuriums, arum and trumpet lilies, spathiphyllums and countless bromeliads.

A completely different type of ecosystem that produces a wealth of brilliant flowers is, paradoxical though it may seem, the desert. Those arid zones——the North American and Chilean deserts, the Kalahari in south-central Africa, the peripheral strip of the Sahara and Arabian deserts as well as the great deserts of central Australia——may look parched and bare for the greater part of the year, but when the rains come they are transformed into vast carpets of little green plants. The bushes, trees and grassy plants become covered with brightly colored flowers that, although frequently very large, sometimes have only a fleeting flowering period. The American cactus, the South African stapelia, the mesembryanthemums of the Kalahari and the aeonium of the Canary Islands are just a few examples of the spectacular blooms.

A third type of natural environment is in the upper mountain reaches, renowned for their wonderful wild plant life. There are natural shrubberies, pasturelands, plateaus that resemble moorlands and, perhaps the most rewarding of all, the crevices, nooks and corners that abound among the rocks to provide all that is needed by innumerable species of flowering plants. Hidden among the crags and ravines of the terrain or in the shelter of windswept bushes or spread out over the high meadows, plant life cycles are completed and renewed in compatible surroundings. Some of the most glorious mountain flowers are to be found in the Alps, the Rocky Mountains, the Caucasus, the Andes, the Himalayas, the Ruwenzori Mountains in Uganda/Zaire, the Smokies. Many much-loved flowers belong to this mountain flora. Among them are gentians, saxifrages, rhododendrons, campanulas, violets and sempervivums.

Flowers in history, art, tradition and folklore

In art, literature, poetry and music, man has always drawn inspiration from flowers. And he often credits them with religious and magical powers. Mythology tells us, for example, that the carnation originated from the unrequited love of Diana for a shepherd boy. Angered by his lack of response, she removed his eyes and threw them as far as she could. Two beautiful flowers sprang up from the ground where they fell. They were carnations.

A happier legend from Spain tells of the way in which the world was first populated with flowers. Prior to that time the world was beautiful, with soaring mountains, deep-blue waters, lovely trees——but no flowers. The angels who had created this picture assembled on the rainbow to view their work. They were so numerous that the rainbow broke and the millions of pieces that fell to earth turned into flowers in every color.

Most religions abound in references to flowers. In the Bible, where mention is frequently made of food-producing plants, flowers are often cited as well. Flax, poppies and daisies are mentioned in several places in both Testaments. And perhaps the best known of all, the "lilies of the field," are referred to by Saint Matthew in Chapter 6, verses 28–29: "And why take ye thought for raiment? Consider the lilies of the field, how they grow; they toil not, neither do they spin: And yet I say unto you that even Solomon in all his glory was not arrayed like one of these." According to reliable sources, the lilies Jesus had in mind were the *Anemone coronaria* that flourishes in the fields of Israel.

In literature, references to flowers occur time and again. In painting, sculpture and architecture they are reproduced in innumerable ways, while in poetry they are a constant source of inspiration. Who cannot recall the floral background of the paintings of Botticelli and Fra Angelico, or van Gogh's "Sunflowers," or the flowery decorations of the Pompeian frescoes? Or the roses mentioned by Thomas Moore: "Tis the last rose of Summer left blooming alone," or Wordsworth's "The

A collection of several species of flowers demonstrating great variety of form and color.

rainbow comes and goes, and lovely is the rose," or Shakespeare's "What's in a name? That which we call a rose by any other name would smell as sweet" and, of course, Gertrude Stein's "Rose is a rose is a rose is a rose"?

Architecture, too, is inspired by flowers—for example in the distinctive rose windows in so many churches, especially churches of the fourteenth and fifteenth centuries. These were clearly inspired by the repetitive regularity of a flower (the window's name came later). Similarly, flowers as well as fruits and leaves appear over and over again in friezes, medallions and capitals—even in lighting fixtures and ornate lavatories.

In heraldry, flowers recur with remarkable frequency. And because of the important part that noble families played in determining historical events, it is inevitable that flowers, sometimes in stylized form, should be found representing certain periods (such as that of the War of the Roses) or particular nations. For example, the lily, adopted by Louis VII of France as the symbol of his family, soon came to represent the whole of France and remained its emblem until the French Revolution. A rose without thorns is the emblem of England; a thistle, of Scotland; the national flower of Wales is a daffodil.

Appropriately enough, the ornamental cherry is the choice of Japan. In the United States, every state has its state flower.

The floral theme is frequently found in philately and numismatology. As a means of constantly making the general public more aware of flowers, philately is especially effective because flowers are often depicted on stamps on new issues throughout the world. It might even be said that the postal authorities of all modern countries vie with each other to produce the best flowers on their stamps. In recent years there has been a new trend to feature indigenous wild flowers, especially when these are rare and in danger of disappearing altogether, or are of particular national interest.

Flowers are featured prominently in the traditions and folklore of nearly all countries and play a part on family occasions such as births, weddings and funerals. However, the meaning given to specific flowers is not always the same. In many parts of Europe the white chrysanthemum is a sign of mourning while in China it symbolizes happiness and joy.

Flowers also have a prominent role in national and state ceremonies and festivals throughout the world and are the central theme of many of these. Probably the most famous examples are in the United States—the Parade of Roses, followed by the Tournament of Roses, in Pasadena, California and the Cherry Blossom Festival in Washington, D.C. But there are many others, and not all are so frankly commercial, well publicized or even happy. In many coastal communities a wreath of greens and flowers is frequently tossed into the sea to commemorate the local men and ships that have disappeared into the depths. The use of flowers in many ceremonies is often linked to the meaning, sometimes symbolic, attributed to them. The orange blossoms carried by brides on their wedding day represent purity while white lilies signify innocence. Other traits evoked by certain flowers are noble-mindedness, courage, deceitfulness, kindness, and so on.

Flowers are a part of many popular proverbs and sayings. Among the proverbs on different sides of the world are those that refer to some biological feature of flowers or to their brief flowering period, as in the Chinese "The wise bee does not take pollen from a fallen bloom," or in one from Italy that says, "If they are roses, they will bloom." Among sayings that refer simply to the beauty of flowers there is the Korean "In a flower bed, even a stone seems lovely." And some sayings refer to undesirable features: for example, "There's no rose without thorns."

Finally, we are constantly reminded of flowers by the first names of millions of people—primarily women—throughout the world: Jasmine, Rose, Violet, Margaret, Lily, Daphne, Pansy, Cherry, Daisy, etc.

The protection of flowering plants

It is clear that flowers play an important part in man's existence. From this it might be inferred that man would hold the flora around him in respect, delighting in all it has to offer. Unfortunately, the opposite is largely the case. Man has—whether knowingly or not—destroyed the wild flowers to such an extent that their very survival is now threatened. The motives behind such destruction have varied over the years. Sometimes they have been quite reasonable, being unavoidably associated with the necessities of the human environment; but many of the motives have been totally unjustified and wanton. The transformation of forests and natural open spaces into grazing and agricultural land, the flooding of vast areas for the building of dams, urban and industrial development involving complex road systems, etc., are all situations in which plants and flowers are destroyed. It is true that, by and large, such activities can be justified on social grounds despite the frequently haphazard and clumsy way in which they are approached. But the disappearance of many wild flowers is often due to other causes that invariably have no valid justification. A glaring example is uncontrolled resort development along so many of the coasts. Such developments not only disturb the environment for wildlife by increasing traffic on local roads; the incidence of fires goes up as well. Another cause for concern is indiscriminate wild-flower picking and collecting of plants for the garden—plants which, taken from their natural habitat, rarely survive—and the area is deprived of seeds and thus natural propagation is prevented.

Because several species of plants have been irretrievably lost in recent years, botanical authorities have launched a vigorous campaign to safeguard the wild flower. This effort has been welcomed and its principles incorporated into the policies of international organizations such as the International Union for the Protection of Nature, and the World Wildlife Fund. Since 1968, the experts have identified 20,000 species of higher (vascular) plants that are very rare and are in danger of disappearing completely. Of these, 250 species are seriously menaced—in some cases only a very few specimens are known still to be surviving as individual plants in the wild. These include several types of iris (*Iris winogradowii* of the USSR and *Iris lortetii* of Israel), saxifrages (*Saxifraga florulenta* of the western Alps), orchids (*Cypripedium candidum* of North America and *Paphiopedilum druryi* of India) and gladioli (*Gladiolus aureus* of South Africa). In consequence, a documented

list of endangered plants was published in 1978. Called the *Red Data Book,* it contains information on the threats to which the plants are exposed and suggestions about ways to ensure their protection.

Scientists and public administrators in all member communities of the European Economic Community are giving the subject considerable thought, and laws have already been passed in several countries for the protection of wild flowers. In the United States, garden clubs, wild-flower preservation societies, women's clubs and comparable organizations have conducted all-out campaigns to save the wild flowers; as a result most states have passed laws forbidding the picking or digging of a number of species such as the dogwoods in Arkansas and Washington, the trailing arbutus in Massachusetts and other states and the American bittersweet in Connecticut and other states. (Most countries have a *National Plant Conservation Guide* which lists protected plants.)

Local authorities have also, in many cases, provided an efficient public information service in the form of brochures, leaflets and posters. In fact, one of the reasons why plants are inadvertently destroyed is lack of information. There are many ways to collect wild flowers but anyone who pulls a plant up by its roots in order to have both the flowers and leaves causes irreparable damage because reproduction is no longer possible. By cutting—not pulling—the flowers at ground level, less damage is caused, since the underground systems of the plant will, after a while, generate new flowers. But it is much better to

leave flowers growing for everyone to enjoy and where they can propagate themselves naturally. Our interdependence on flowers is undeniable and the complete destruction of even one more species of plant could mean the disappearance from the world of yet another part of our unique genetic inheritance. If everyone were to remember these arguments, there would be some chance of protecting our remaining flora. This would involve the cooperation of every individual in preserving the species that are still in existence rather than depending on laws. It is just as much within our power to encourage and nurture this natural source of beauty as it is to destroy it——and far more to the benefit not only of ourselves but also of the generations to come.

The cultivation of flowers

Since history began, and perhaps before that, man has felt the need to surround himself with gardens——if possible with some areas of green and some of flowers. His feeling for plants has even led him into investing them with an almost sacred significance and sometimes crediting them with supernatural powers. The latter custom is well documented in historical writings and the remains of edifices that can still be seen in many long-established gardens. On a less grandiose scale, there is a hankering in people for the perfume of flowers and for their aesthetic appeal. We may have only a few window boxes or a small balcony or basement area, but a few flowering plants in pots can brighten the dreariest living quarters.

And the flowers are a pleasure that will be shared by all who see them.

Everyone can grow plants. Once one realizes the possibilities that open up from the available vast range of flowering plants, all that is left to do is to make the right choice. There are plants that will grow to an enormous size and there are others that remain tiny. Some demand a great deal of attention and others prefer to be left almost entirely alone. In every case they repay our care with the satisfying sight of germination, healthy development and beautiful blooms.

Gardening—or floriculture—is a skill that cannot be learned in a few minutes or fully described in a few pages. It would be presumptuous to attempt it. What we have tried to do here is to explain some of the basic facts that will help you choose suitable and rewarding plants. The main aspects dealt with are the soil, added nutrients, water, methods of propagation and cultivation, diseases, pests and, finally, some suggestions on how to plan a garden.

The soil

Most plants, with the exception of the epiphytes and aquatic plants, send roots down into the soil, no more than 3–3½ ft. (1 m.). The stratum most explored by roots, therefore, is between 12–30 in. (30–50 cm.) deep. Cultivable soil is that superficial part of the earth's crust able to sustain and provide nourishment to plants. Practically speaking, there are few types of ground that cannot be cultivated; with the aid of modern equipment and technology, even deserts can be made to produce crops. But the main obstacle is usually the cost, which may make the task economically unviable.

The superficial strata of the ground have been perennially exposed to the action of natural agents such as heat, cold and water, as well as to the action of the microorganisms—aerobics and anaerobics—that bring about the gradual disintegration of the parent rock material and the decomposition and transformation of vegetable and animal material. This enables certain soluble mineral substances to be released so they can be absorbed and transformed by plants during the various phases of that perpetual cycle known as the food chain.

Soil that derives from parent rock material is generally divided into three strata: active, inert and subsoil.

The various types of ground are referred to as: arable land, or that which is usually reserved for agricultural cultivation (in this book, it is generally referred to as "good garden soil"); argillaceous (clayey) soil, when it is composed of more than 30 percent clay; alluvial soil, when it has been formed from particles of material transported by glaciers, water or wind or deposited as sediment in old river beds; argillaceous-calcareous soil, when there is a certain amount of lime present; argillaceous-siliceous, when it is made up of 50 percent silica or silicate sand; argillaceous-humic soil, with a reasonable humus content; calcareous soil, with a predominance of lime; cretaceous soil, when, apart from the lime, a certain amount of chalk is also present; sandy soil, when a great deal of sand is present; and woodland mold, when the soil consists mainly of undergrowth detritus, humus and rotted turf.

Aeonium nobile
Aloe polyphylla
Caryota no
Crinum mauritianum
Cypripedium candidum
Daphne arbuscula
Doronicum cataractarum
Echium pininana
Epidendrum mutelianum
Erica chrysocodon
Erica jasminiflora
Gladiolus aureus
Glomeropitcairnia
  erectiflora
Iris lortetii

Iris winogradowii
Johannesteijsmannia
  altifrons
Lilium rhodopaeum
Limonium arborescens
Myosotidium hortensia
Orothamnus zeyheri
Rafflesia arnoldii
Roystonea elata
Saxifraga florulenta
Sobralia xantholeuca
Tibouchina chamaecistus
Trochetia erythroxylon
Xeronema callistemon

Quality, in gardening terms, is denoted as follows: soil is fertile or rich when it is rich in organic and mineral substances favorable to cultivation; poor soil lacks nourishing material; compact or heavy soil is generally argillaceous, calcareous-cretaceous ground that is very cohesive, not friable, and hard to work; light or well-aerated soil has little or no cohesion and contains a certain amount of humus; moist soil is created by the water present in underground strata rising to the surface through capillarity; impermeable soil is so cohesive that water can barely penetrate it and thus lies on the surface.

Prepared soils, composts and substrates

Whether the aim of the gardener is specialized cultivation, or to produce beautiful blooms for cutting, or to have a fine display of mixed flowering plants, various additives almost inevitably must be worked into the soil. It may be necessary to introduce different types of soil, compost or foundation materials, according to the species to be grown. The following are principal additives: Loam is a fairly even mixture of sand, clay and silt——usually with some humus. Topsoil comes from land that has been well maintained and manured many times. Heath mold is the acid peaty soil in which heath and heather have grown and is taken from the surface layer under clumps of heather; it is a reddish color if it contains clay, and is dark——the best kind——if rich in humus. Finally, river or quarried sand.

Leaf mold is dug from the surface of the ground in woods or taken from piles of raked-up leaves. It is rich in humus from the

Lavender (Lavandula officinalis) cultivation.

decayed plant material. The powdery, splintery sawdust from decomposed stumps and tree trunks is also good humus. In either case, the humus is neutral (with a pH of 7) if the leaves or wood come from most broad-leaved deciduous trees. It is somewhat acid if taken from conifers and very acid if taken from oak trees. (This is an important point to remember, because some plants, such as rhododendrons, require an acid soil. Most, however, do best in a more or less neutral soil.)

Compost is obtained from layers of different materials—leaves, grass, kitchen waste, etc.—alternated with shallow layers of damp soil and sprayed or sprinkled with liquid manure or mineral fertilizers. A good dusting with powdered lime neutralizes any excess acidity. From time to time the compost heap should be turned over with a fork and, finally, sieved—although this is a refinement that can be omitted if the thoroughly rotted material is dug well into the ground before planting.

In modern floriculture, sterilized natural and artificial materials are widely used as a sterile foundation in the propagation of plants, to help aerate seed and potting composts by making them lighter, and in several of the hydroponic (soilless) cultures. Expanded vermiculite and perlite, baked clay granules, coarse sand, etc., come within this category.

Feeding the soil—fertilizers and top dressings

All soil that is being intensely cultivated for long periods of time gradually loses its fertility to the point of becoming unproductive. This is sometimes known as "losing heart." To restore the balance of the soil's nutritive content, therefore, it is necessary to introduce appropriate additives. Although a number of chemical elements are essential to ensure that plants develop to their full potential, they do not need to be present in equal amounts. Some are necessary in quite large quantities; others in smaller quantities; and some are required as trace elements only. But all are essential, and the absence of even one may give rise to what is known as a soil deficiency. Those elements required by plants are oxygen, carbon, hydrogen (which are obtained from air and water), nitrogen, phosphorous and potassium (obtained from the soil). Required in smaller quantities are calcium, magnesium, iron and sulfur; and the trace elements are boron, manganese, zinc, copper and molybdenum. (A little sodium, chlorine and silicon are also beneficial.)

Two main kinds of compound are used to feed the soil—organic and inorganic. They are usually used in conjunction with one another—largely because organic fertilizers have certain advantages such as a long period of activity in the soil, slow absorption by the plants, improvement of the physiochemical and bacterial structure of the soil and increased resistance to leaching from heavy rain or prolonged watering. In the inorganic compounds, however, the minerals are highly concentrated and ready for fast assimilation by the roots as soon as contact is made; thus they have an immediate effect on the development of plants. An inorganic fertilizer is therefore frequently used as a quick-acting tonic or "pick-me-up." It also has the advantage that more than one element can be introduced at a time, although prolonged use can ultimately produce negative symptoms in the soil structure. The best way to start is by combining both types of fertilizer, using organic compounds as a basic feed supplemented by inorganic additives when certain elements are particularly lacking.

Stable and farmyard manures head the list of the most widely used organic fertilizers. These are closely followed by poultry manure, fish meal, guano, dried blood, bonemeal, shoddy (wool and cotton waste), hop manure (made from used hops), chopped seaweed, old mushroom-bed compost and dry wood ash. Liquid organic fertilizer also gives excellent results. It is made by immersing half a sackful of animal manure in water for about two weeks. The resulting fluid can then be diluted to about twice the volume, applied directly to the plant roots and watered in thoroughly. There are, of course, many soluble mineral preparations on the market that are adapted to the requirements of particular groups of plants. They are all easy to apply and give good results if the instructions are carefully followed.

The inorganic or mineral fertilizers in most general use are sulphate of ammonia, calcium nitrate, sodium nitrate, potassium nitrate, sulphate of potash (potassium sulphate) and superphosphate. Also used are combinations of minerals such as potassium phosphate, ammonium phosphate, nitrogen-potassium-phosphate, etc. These are called ''balanced fertilizers'' and are identified on the package by three numbers— 5–10–5, 10–6–4, etc. The first represents the concentration of nitrogen; the next, phosphorus; the last, potassium.

Mineral fertilizers should be used only according to the particular requirements of plant types, methods of cultivation, the condition of the soil, the season of the year, and so on. Nitrogen influences a plant's development—growth and foliage. Phosphorous affects its productive features—flowers, fruit and seeds—by acting on the plant in advance of the various stages of development. Potassium helps to strengthen the parts of the plant that are above ground, thus improving its perfume, the color of its flowers and the quality of its fruit and seeds. Calcium, generally applied as ground limestone—separately from fertilizer—affects soil acidity and thus influences growth and helps the plant to assimilate the organic material in the soil. It also stimulates leaf development.

Nitrates should be applied as a top dressing and the surface given a light hoeing. All the other minerals can be dug into the ground to suitable depths.

A system of fertilization that is rapidly gaining favor these days is foliar feeding. This involves spraying the plant with appropriate nutritive solutions that are easily assimilated by the plant through its leaves. The nutritive elements in these solutions must be so pure that they can be taken in by the green parts of the plant and circulated through its vascular tissues to give immediate benefit. These fertilizers, which are marketed extensively, are produced with one or more basic elements or with a combination of macro- and micro-elements. By carefully selecting those that meet the requirements of your plants, you ensure a correctly balanced intake of nourishment.

Foliar fertilizer is especially useful in particular circumstances and is indispensable when urgent first aid or compensatory action is required. For example, it is very helpful after transplanting, because it quickly assists plants in recovering the functions of the root system; during the growing stage,

when there is a lack of some particular nutritive elements or there are signs of general weakness; when plants are recovering from hailstorms, frosts, prolonged droughts or even pruning; and in supplementing the food of pot-bound plants or plants growing in soil lacking the necessary nourishment.

Solutions intended for foliar feeding can be mixed with several types of pest-control sprays, which means that two jobs can be done in a single operation.

Water and watering

Water enables plants to absorb through their roots the soluble part of the mineral elements that are present in the soil. It is also the main constituent of plants, some of which consist of as much as 90 percent water.

Watering in dry weather is therefore one of the most important—and demanding—of all the tasks the gardener has to do. Every plant has certain water and humidity requirements and only after long experience is it possible to judge exactly when to start using the hose and how much water to give. The following basic precepts may prove helpful:

Plants are just as likely to be damaged or even to die from too much watering as from too little.

It is not advisable to let plants dry out until they show signs of thirst by drooping or wilting. Some may revive well but many cannot.

Evergreen plants with large, abundant leaves require more water than flowering plants.

An example of leaves being rotted down to make organic manure (compost).

If the ground is allowed to dry out completely, it may become almost impermeable and much of the water that is applied will run off.

Shrubs and trees with surface root systems should be kept well watered during the summer months.

Bedding plants that have a concentrated period of flowering—cannas, dahlias, petunias, zinnias, etc.—need to be watered generously and frequently.

Recently planted trees and shrubs need not only to be watered at the roots but also sprayed over their trunks or stems and heads to compensate for the sluggish action of the root system while it is recovering from transplanting shock.

During the summer many plants, such as azaleas, rhododendrons, gardenias, camellias and hydrangeas, benefit from having their heads sprayed every evening.

Plants grown in light, sandy, porous soils that do not hold water need frequent but light watering, preferably daily.

In particularly dry regions, where plants have to be watered even in the winter, watering should be done during the warmest hours of the morning. It should also be remembered that it is better to give plants an occasional thorough soaking than frequent small amounts of water. It is advisable to apply water at fairly low pressure or in a fine spray so you don't beat down the plants or compact or erode the soil. Rainwater is prefera-

Feeding the soil with manure or fertilizer is very important to the growth of flowers. This photograph shows a field of dandelions (Taraxacum officinale).

ble to tap water and should be collected and used whenever possible. If the water is extremely cold, it should, ideally, be allowed to stand in the sun in buckets until it reaches the temperature of the atmosphere. The alternative is to apply it in a fine spray and never straight on the plants. Some plants do not like hard water, so this should, if possible, be passed through a water softener before it is applied to such plants. In desert areas of the southwestern part of the United States, where both the water and soil are extremely saline, water must be applied in the spring in exceptionally large amounts to wash the insoluble salts in the soil deep into the ground, more or less out of reach of the roots. Thereafter, whenever more water is applied, it must be poured on heavily to prevent a new buildup of salts in the soil.

Plant propagation

In nature, most plants propagate themselves by means of seeds. This is known as gamic reproduction.

Earlier in this book the biological processes that lead to the formation of fruit and seeds, as well as the different methods of natural seed dispersal, were discussed. In floriculture, propagation through seeds is, of course, the most widely used propagation method and starts with the gathering of the seeds as soon as the fruit is ripe. It does not follow, however, that reproduction through seed is always the most satisfactory method, because the plants thus produced may not "come true" (because of hybridization, they may revert to their origi-

61

nal form and color). If plants are not being grown under strictly controlled conditions, this danger is always present; and this, in turn, means that no guarantee can be given that the strain will remain pure in the next generation (i.e., that the complete genetic makeup of the parent plant will be reproduced exactly). In cases like this——and whenever propagation through seed presents difficulties——it is advisable to adopt agamic reproduction through cuttings, stem layering or air layering. Each of these systems ensures that the new plants will have exactly the same biological characteristics as the parent plant.

Gamic reproduction: collection and selection of seeds
Reproduction by seed involves a series of processes, from the gathering of the seeds from the parent plants and carrying through to their sowing, thinning out, transplanting, etc.

The production and collection of seeds for sowing is a very exacting process involving meticulous application of certain principles in order to ensure the success of the end product. Professional seed growers employ a considerable amount of land for experiment as well as actual production. But this is only one side of their work, a great deal of which is done in specially equipped laboratories in which complex operations of selection, hybridization, control and research are constantly being carried out. The motivation behind all this activity is to obtain new varieties or strains, to avoid the setting in of various types of degenerative processes and to improve the overall quality. In their selection of seeds, plant breeders and seed merchants have to observe specific regulations on methods of production, standards of purity and germination.

The amateur who would like to save seed for his own use must acquire some knowledge of the subject. Many species—especially cultivated ones—are subject to an inevitable process of natural degeneration. It is essential, therefore, to select a plant or plants that display the best qualities of growth and healthiness, flowering, leaf and fruit production, early or late cropping, etc., in the expectation that these characteristics will be passed on to their descendants. To achieve this, selection may be made either *en masse* or individually. The flowers on those plants chosen as seed-bearers can be isolated by placing small bags of paper or fine gauze over them to prevent pollination from other plants. Several generations must be produced from the selected seed, each one being treated as described, before a pure strain that will remain true to type through successive generations is achieved.

The seed must be gathered just at the right moment of ripeness. This can be assessed from such visible signs as coloration and a tendency of the fruit to open or become detached from the plant. The seeds of dehiscent fruit, which tend to burst spontaneously from their pod or capsule, should be collected slightly before they reach this stage. They are then cleaned by threshing, screening and winnowing. The seeds of soft, fleshy fruit, however, are removed by gentle pulping followed by washing. After this they can be left to dry in the shade, protected from birds.

Essential features of good seeds. It is of prime importance to ensure that the seed will germinate and produce a new plant. The period during which seeds remain viable varies from spe-

Watering the flowers with a simple, reasonably priced automatic sprinkler—a boon in the garden.

Marigold seeds. Reproduction by seed is the most commonly used propagation method in floriculture.

cies to species. Some have a life of many years; others may remain germinable for only a few months or even days. Germinative qualities can be assessed by sowing small sample quantities of seed in special containers known as germinators; if they put out rootlets, and plantules begin to emerge within the proper time, the seed can be regarded as germinable.

Seeds to be stored in their dormant state should be kept in a dry, shady, well-ventilated place where the temperature remains cool and where neither insects nor rodents can reach them. Seeds that are inclined to be oily should be packed between layers of fresh moss and sown as soon as possible, because they quickly lose their germinability.

Hard-coated seeds or those that are slow or poor germinators can be stratified. This means layering them in pots or boxes in a mixture of damp peat and sand. The containers can then be left in a sheltered position outdoors. Cover them with wire netting to protect them against birds or rodents.

The outer husk of very hard seeds should, if possible, be slightly nicked before sowing. Alternatively, they are softened in lukewarm water for at least 24 hours.

Vernalization. Vernalization is a modern technique that influences the germinative rhythm of seeds, permitting their seasonal behavior to be controlled. For example, quite remarkable results are obtained by keeping seeds in a refrigerator—usually in glass containers in a mixture of peat and sand—at low temperatures for certain lengths of time.

Seed sowing

There are various ways in which seed can be sown, depending upon local conditions and plant requirements. The simplest method is to sow directly in the open ground, where the plants are intended to bloom. The site must be reasonably sheltered from excessive sun and wind; water must be available in case of a dry spell; the seedlings must have room to grow.

In preparing the ground, some additives will probably be necessary. For instance, peat and sand assist drainage and give breathing room to the roots in heavy soil, while well-rotted manure, vegetable compost or similar materials can be dug in to provide nourishment as the plants develop. Once the bed is prepared, sowing can be carried out. Most hardy annuals and tap-rooted plants that do not like being transplanted can be sown in the spring in this way for summer flowering.

The less sturdy half-hardy annuals that require more protection can be sown in shallow, well-drained containers. These may include pots of clay, plastic or compressed peat; seed boxes of wood or plastic; or special seed pans.

A well-prepared seed container is shown above in cross section. The best type of seed compost consists of a mixture of light materials. This varies slightly with the species of plants to be grown but the basic ingredients are peat, bark, well-rotted and sieved manure and garden compost, coarse sand and dried, shredded sphagnum moss.

Several types of seed compost are on the market. Some are

soilless. The John Innes mixture is made by mixing together 2 parts sterilized loam, 1 part granulated peat, 1 part coarse sand plus 1½ ounces (43 grams) superphosphate and ¾ ounce (21 grams) ground limestone to each bushel (36 liters).

Depth of sowing. This varies with the species. A useful guideline is to cover the seed with its own depth of soil or slightly more. Very tiny seeds such as begonia, nicotiana and petunia can either be left uncovered or given just a light sprinkling of seed compost or sieved dried sphagnum moss. The surface is then pressed lightly all over with a flat piece of wood to firm the seeds into the soil.

When to sow. There is no fixed time for sowing seeds, as many factors such as position in the garden, weather, etc., have to be taken into account. Generally speaking, though, the sowing period lasts from the middle of spring until summer for perennials and biennials that flower the next year——such as cyclamen, cineraria, pansy, myosotis (forget-me-not), bellis (daisies). Spring–summer flowering annuals such as salvia, aster, marigold and zinnia can be sown at the end of the winter or early spring indoors in the same year.

Plants that are to spend all their life in a greenhouse can be sown throughout the year as their seed ripens.

Precautions to be taken during the sowing season. When seeds are not sown directly in the ground, the containers in which they are placed should generally be put under cover in either a coldframe or a greenhouse. There are three essential factors for good germination: humidity, shade and controlled warmth. In most cases, temperatures should not fall below 54–65° F. (12–18° C.) and not rise above 68–72° F. (20–22° C.). Great care should also be given to watering and to maintaining the level of humidity. Protect the containers from too much direct sunlight until the seedlings are established.

Attacks by cryptogams (parasitic fungi) such as *Phytophthora parasitica* and *Pythium debaryanum,* which often bring about damping-off (stem rot), can be easily avoided in two ways: (1) Dust the seeds before planting with a seed disinfectant such as captan. (2) Sow the seeds in a sterile medium such as vermiculite, sand or peat. Or you can sterilize ordinary soil by baking it in a 180° oven for two hours; but this is practical only for small quantities of soil.

Transplanting and pricking out
When seeds have been sown close together, the seedlings should remain in their original containers only long enough to establish growth. When they are strong enough to be handled——usually when the seed leaves have expanded fully and the second pair of leaves is showing——they should be transplanted into prepared containers. The new soil should be richer in nutrients than the seed compost. Remove the seedlings in clumps with a wooden spatula or garden label. The seedlings are then laid on a flat surface to let the soil fall away from their roots and permit easy separation. Replant each seedling by first making a hole with a dibble or pencil just deep enough to ensure that the roots touch the bottom. Leave about 1½–2 in. (3.5–5.00 cm.) between holes. Firm in by pressing

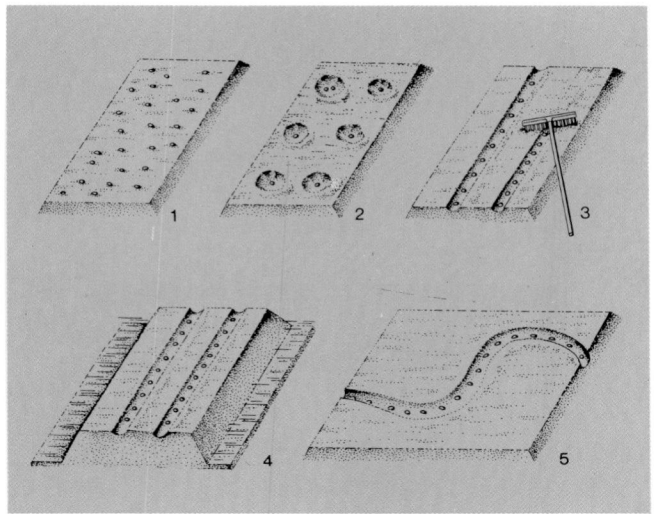

gently around each plantlet. Finally, spray lightly with tepid water or a seed-starting mixture containing plant nutrients.

Agamic reproduction

To reproduce plants that are difficult or impossible to raise from seed, there are several methods of vegetative propagation: stem and shoot cuttings, air (or aerial) layering, shoot layering, division, budding and grafting.

Cuttings. The most widely used method is to make cuttings from small pieces of stem, young nonflowering side shoots or other parts of the plant on which there are one or two nodes (leaf buds). The illustration on opposite page shows the common types of cuttings. Half-ripe stem cuttings are pieces of one-year-old stem, fairly firm at the base, with a growing tip and a few leaves. They can be taken from biennial or perennial plants such as geraniums, fuchsias and hydrangeas and should be placed in a sheltered position while rooting. Soft-wood cuttings are young shoots taken from new growth and are less mature than half-ripe cuttings. Herbaceous cuttings are immature shoots or pieces of herbaceous plants such as carnations, phlox and begonias that have reached a certain stage of growth. They are quite delicate and should be rooted in pots or boxes in a coldframe or greenhouse. Leaf cuttings are made from the mature leaves and stalks of plants that have latent buds, invisible on the surface, in their veins. The leaf-stalks will root at their bases even though the leaves are cut into pieces. This applies to such plants as saintpaulia (African

Systematic preparation of a seed tray: 1. top layer (a minimal amount of sieved soil or seed compost); 2. seeds; 3. sandy soil or seed compost; 4. layer of organic material; 5. drainage material; 6. drainage holes; 7. crocks.

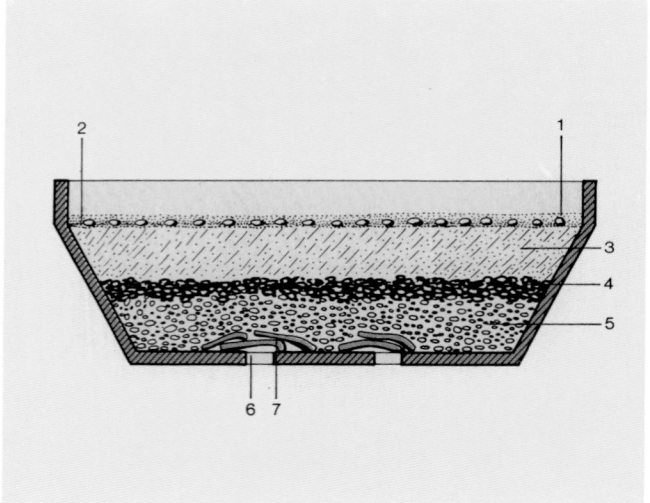

violet), peperomia and rex begonia, which can be rooted by placing or planting the cut leaf-stalk and stem on suitable material (equal parts of peat and sand) with a small stone resting on the leaf to maintain contact with the compost. Root cuttings can be taken from several types of plant that produce buds on their root system or that throw up suckers (in the latter case, grafted plants should be avoided since only the understock will be reproduced). Pieces of root about 1½–2½ in. (3–6 cm.) in length can be placed in pots containing peat, sand and loam to root in a warm greenhouse. This system is suitable for peony, Anemone japonica (Japanese Anemone), etc.

In general, the length of cuttings can vary, according to plant species, from about ½ in. (1 cm.) with only one bud, to 20–24 in. (50–60 cm.) with anything from two to eight buds.

Successful rooting depends largely on cuttings being taken from healthy, vigorous plants at the right time—which varies according to species and climatic conditions. Usually, softwood cuttings can be taken in the spring and early summer; semi-hardwood cuttings at the end of the summer to autumn; herbaceous and leaf cuttings in the spring or any time more or less provided the right conditions are available. Cuttings are usually rooted first in sand or a similar inert substance such as vermiculite and the materials already mentioned for hydroponic cultures, since no food is necessary during the root-forming stage. Alternatively, a light compost may be used containing about 70–75 percent sand. As soon as the cuttings have made good roots, they should be transplanted into a

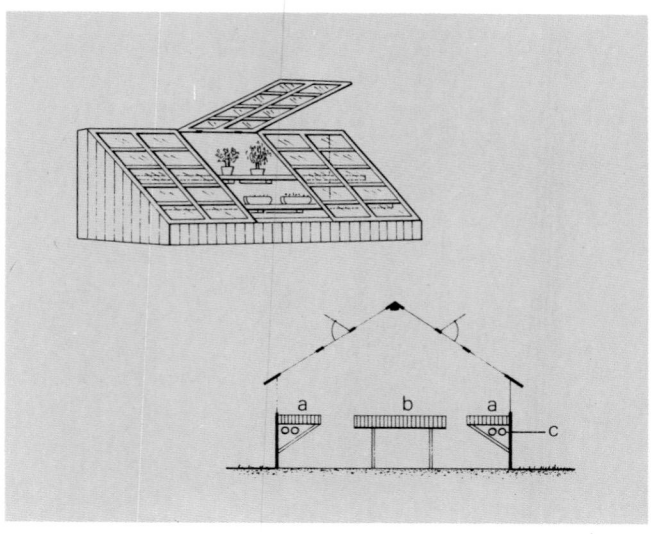

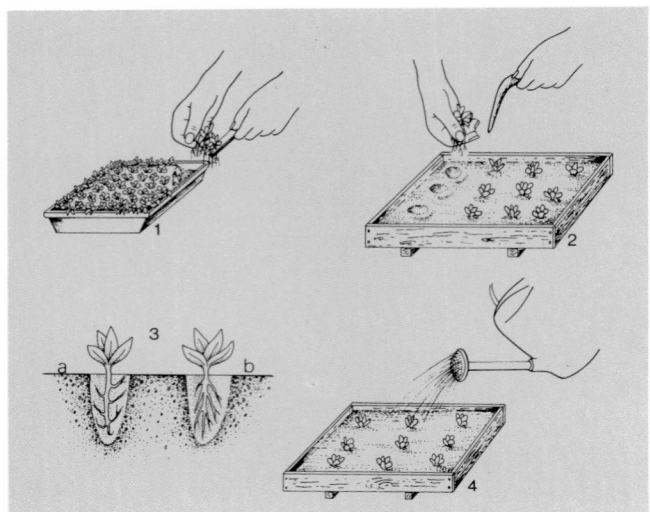

light, nourishing soil and placed in a well-ventilated, well-lighted position where the humidity and watering can be controlled. It is sometimes helpful to mulch with grass cuttings to encourage new growth. The use of one of the hormone rooting compounds—in some of which a fungicide is incorporated to discourage basal rotting—can increase the success rate considerably. Conditions to be avoided are: cuttings placed too close together; insufficient light, which will "draw" the new shoot and make it long, spindly and pallid; poor drainage and ventilation, which will cause rotting; unsuitable siting.

Air layering. This system is widely used to induce the stem or a one- to two-year-old branch of an established shrub or tree to produce roots. The main advantage is that quite sizable plants that retain all the characteristics of the parent plant can be obtained in a relatively short time (two to three months). Air layering is usually carried out in the spring or early summer, following the method shown in the illustrations.

Shoot layering. With this system, known also as simple layering, ordinary layering or stem layering, one or more low-growing, flexible lateral branches are brought down to ground level, fastened with wooden pegs in previously made holes about 3 in. (8 cm.) deep, and packed firmly with soil. Nicking the underside of the branch at the burial point helps to hasten root formation. In most cases, roots and shoots emerge after about a year. Then, if the section that has been buried and rooted is severed from the main shoot, it can be transplanted into its permanent position.

Types of cuttings: 1. hardwood; 2. semi-hardwood; 3. softwood; 4–5. leaf; 6. root.

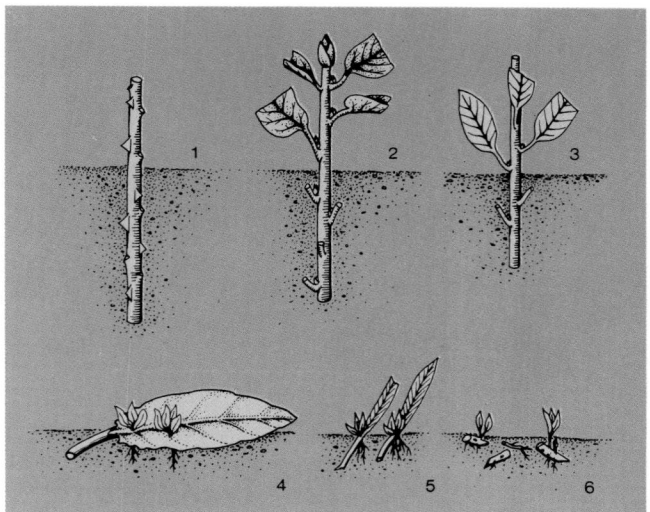

Suckers, which are thrown off by many species of plants, can also be treated as naturally layered shoots, but only when they come from ungrafted or unbudded stick.

Division.   In this method of propagation, which is very commonly used with garden perennials, the roots of the parent plant are dug up and divided during the dormant period (usually late fall, late winter or early spring) and the small plants are set into the garden again. The way in which a plant is divided depends on the structure of its roots. Some plants, such as chrysanthemums, put out roots in many directions, and these are simply cut off and replanted. Plants that form a clump of fibrous roots are pulled apart with the fingers. Plants forming a dense mat of large, intertwining fleshy roots may have to be chopped apart with a spade or forcibly pulled apart with two spading forks placed back to back.

In all cases, the new plant sections should contain the buds or shoots that will develop into new stems.

Budding and grafting.   These are complicated methods that require a knowledge of basic principles plus considerable experience. Both systems involve uniting one or more individual buds—or a shoot with several buds—with another type of plant (rootstock). Various ways of introducing the scion (the shoot or bud) into the rootstock plant, are shown on the opposite page. These methods are adopted for a number of reasons, the most usual being to fix a variety; to replace one variety with another, to grow a plant that is prone to certain root diseases on the rootstock of one that is immune.

Various types of cuttings (of hoyas, fuchsias, geraniums and salvias) placed in a plunge bed in a frame to root.

Potting

The typical flowerpot is made of red clay. It tapers up from its base to a height slightly greater than the diameter of its top edge. One or more holes in the base allow surplus water to escape. Several other materials are also used, such as concrete and wood, to make containers in a variety of shapes and sizes. The most popular material today is plastic. Whatever the material, any pot must be in proportion to the plant it is to hold and, if it is to be on display, it must have eye appeal.

If the pot selected for a plant has been used before, it must be thoroughly cleaned inside and out. This is done with a stiff brush to remove any encrustation. Then, to be absolutely certain no disease will be transmitted to the new occupant, scrub the pot with soap and water containing a little chlorine bleach. The next step is to ensure good drainage by placing a layer of clean shards (broken pieces of pot) or gravel in the bottom. This is followed by a layer of fibrous material, the depth of which will depend on how long the plant is to remain in the pot. This layer may consist of such material as bark, leaf mold, heath mold, well-rotted manure, etc., with a handful of potting compost pressed on top. The roots of the plant are then spread as evenly as possible over this base. (If the roots are well compacted into their original potting medium, they can be left undisturbed.) The pot is now filled with soil that is lightly firmed around the roots. The collar of the plant should not be embedded deeply and, in most cases, should be left on a level

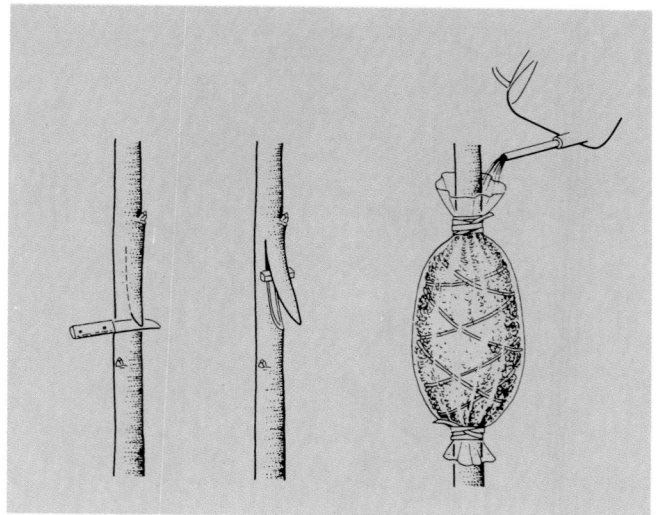

with the surface of the soil. To facilitate watering, do not bring the soil right up to the rim; it should be about ½ to 1 in. below the rim. The final stage in potting is to water the plant well—if possible with air-temperature rainwater.

Several potting-on operations may be necessary, according to the life cycle of the species, to keep pace with growth and ensure sufficient root space. The process should be gradual, however, replacing each pot by another only an inch or so larger each time. It is better to make several changes of pot rather than to let a plant be overpotted in a pot that is too large for it. If a plant is to remain in a pot, once a certain size has been reached, it may no longer be possible to use a larger pot, for obvious reasons. In this case, it is advisable to remove the plant periodically and renew the drainage material and as much of the potting compost as possible. It may also be necessary to reduce the root system slightly by trimming back the root ends with a sharp knife.

Transplanting into the open ground

The best times of year for planting out are in the early spring or (second best) early autumn. However, a few plants—especially those of tropical origin such as palms and citrus fruits—respond better to summer planting.

The hole dug for any plant should be proportionate to its size. For small plants (for example, *Potentilla fruticosa* and *Hypericum moserianum*) it should generally be about 12 × 12 × 12 in. (30 × 30 × 30 cm.); for small shrubs such as *Cotoneaster horizontalis*, *Rosmarinus repens*, about 20 × 20 × 20

73

Top, various types of propagation by division: 1. dividing a clump; 2. dividing rhizomes; 3. dividing tubers; detaching offset bulbils.
Bottom, various methods of budding and grafting: 1, 2, 3. budding; 4. crown grafting; 5. saddle grafting; 6. approach grafting.

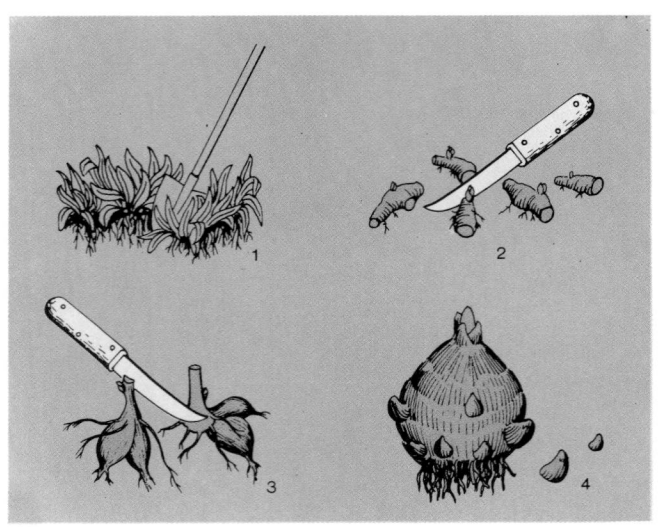

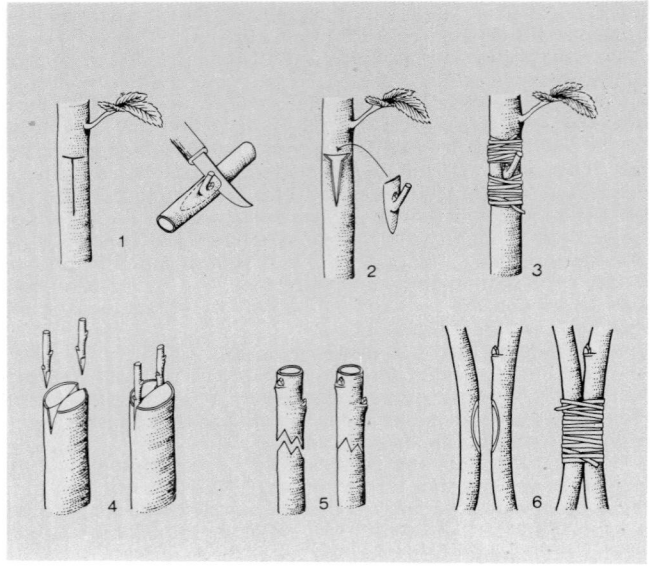

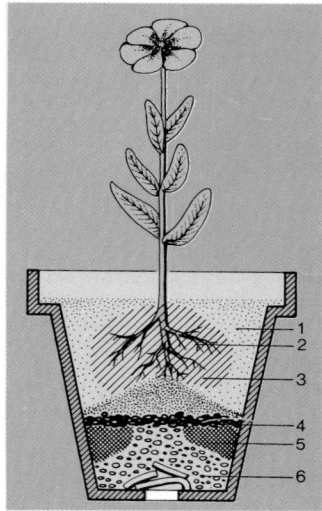

Systematic preparation of a flowerpot: 1. potting compost; 2. roots; 3. possible ball of soil on roots; 4. organic material (manure); 5. rotted leaves; 6. inert material (gravel, vermiculite, perlite, etc.). Right, succulent plants just after potting.

1
2
3
4
5
6

in. (50 × 50 × 50 cm.); for small trees or medium-size bushes (*Prunus malus*, deutzia, weigela) about 28 × 28 × 28 in. (70 × 70 × 70 cm.); and at least 40 × 40 × 40 in. (1 cubic meter) for trees (pines, *Magnolia grandiflora*). It is often helpful to dig the hole some time before it is required in order to aerate the soil. If the ground tends to hold water, some form of drainage material such as gravel or sand should be spread into the bottom of the hole.

To prepare a hole for a plant, a layer of good topsoil mixed with well-rotted organic compost should first be spread over the bottom, then followed by a layer of topsoil over which the roots can be spread. The root system can be cut back by about one-third, or if there is a taproot or a straggly growth of roots, a reduction of about one-quarter can be made. If the roots are encased in a soil ball, great care must be taken that this does not break away.

No plant should ever be planted deeper than it previously grew. When it's in position, firm the soil around the roots. Then form a collar of soil on the ground all the way around the hole to create a saucer to hold water. This can be removed once the plant is well established.

When supports such as canes, stakes or posts are required, it is a good idea to set them into position while the hole is still open to avoid subsequent root damage. When tying the young shrub or tree to its support, use strips of cloth or run string or wire through short lengths of hose bent around the plant stem in order to keep the tie from cutting through the bark.

Pruning

Pruning covers all operations related to the cutting back and removal of parts of a plant. But there is no doubt that a great many plants are more beautiful if left to grow naturally.

Pruning is done for a number of reasons and is often essential. It may have to be done merely to get rid of dead, misshapen or diseased wood. Alternatively, a branch may have become potentially dangerous. A plant——whether tree, shrub, or bush——may be required to grow in a particular shape or within a restricted space. A balance may have to be maintained between root absorption and top growth in a confined growing area. Pruning also improves and controls the production of flowers and fruit by advancing or retarding, within certain limits, their natural seasons; it encourages root and growth recovery after transplanting, and new growth in old or tired plants or where a disease, although cured, has debilitated a plant.

Autumn or end-of-winter pruning is carried out on woody branches during the dormant period, before the sap begins to rise. Quite heavy, even drastic, pruning can take place during this period. Light pruning, however, can be done in the spring and summer on new growth in certain cases.

The average gardener generally uses the following pruning methods:

Shoot-thinning: Crowded or deformed shoots are removed to open up the center of the plant in order to allow light and air to reach the remaining branches.

Cutting back: Branch lengths are reduced to encourage new growth nearer the trunk or central stems.

Spur-pruning: The season's growth is cut back to one, two or three buds, according to the species (espalier-trained roses, crape myrtle, etc.) to encourage compact, strong new growth from each main shoot.

Pollarding: This should be carried out only on extremely strong-growing trees. The main branches are taken back quite close to the fork——or even back to the trunk——of the tree to create a bushy head that requires pruning every year or so. When done for the first time (as in all instances when considerable wounds are inflicted on the limbs) brush the cuts over with an appropriate disinfectant such as iron or copper sulfate, and then cover them with paint or tar.

Topiary: This is the art of shaping hedges and bushes into geometric or even more imaginative shapes by careful and frequent clipping of new growth. While not all shrubs lend themselves to topiary work, the following are suitable examples: *Buxus sempervirens,* (box), *Euonymus japonicus* (Japanese spindle tree), *Crataegus pyracantha* (ornamental thorn), *Laurus nobilis* (sweet bay), *Prunus laurocerasus* (cherry or common laurel).

Side-shoot and sucker removal: Remove suckers and unwanted shoots springing up from the roots and collar of the plant especially if the plant was grafted onto a rootstock.

With herbaceous plants, control growth by:

Disbudding: Removing the secondary lateral shoots or the leaf buds from which such shoots will develop so the sap will concentrate in the main shoots. An equally important purpose

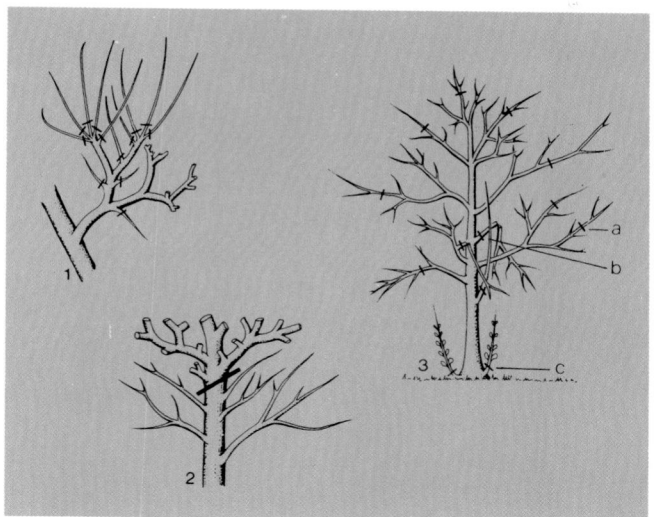

is to encourage the plant to develop into a more shapely plant.

Stopping: Removing the growing point on each shoot to encourage the side shoots to grow or to restrain too vigorous growth.

Pinching: Nipping off all but the terminal buds on each stem in order to force the development of a few flowers of maximum size. In some cases, gardeners who are entering exhibitions pinch out all buds except one or two.

Leaf removal: Taking off superfluous leaves in order to expose previously over-leaved flowers or fruit to the light and air, thus to encourage stronger plant growth.

Growing plants on terraces, decks and balconies

When you grow ornamental plants on terraces, decks and balconies, the containers you use are almost as important as the plants. These may be purchased from commercial sources or specially built on the site. There are many types and sizes on the market, and in a wide variety of materials. Look for porosity, light weight and ease of handling. If a container is to be set on a balcony ledge or windowsill, it should have a wide, flat base to ensure its stability. In some cases, you should also fasten it to the floor or a nearby wall.

Permanent containers for plants range upward from about 6 in. (15 cm.) in depth and 8 in. (20 cm.) in width. Rectangular and square containers can be placed close together to form a single group that makes the best use of the available space. Very effective screens or windbreaks can be constructed ad-

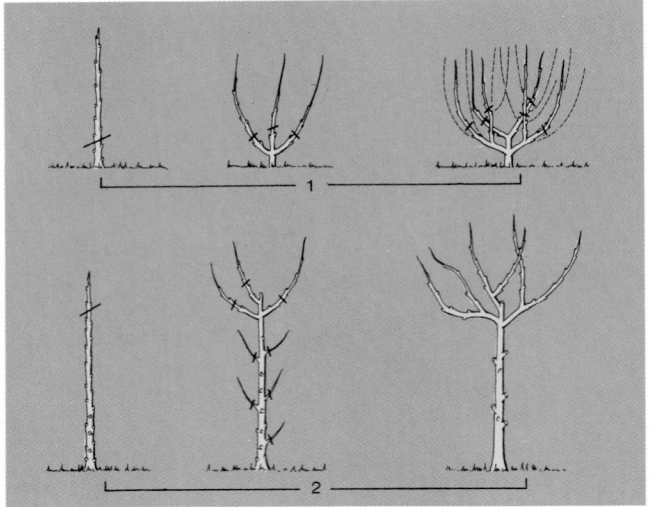

Initial pruning to form a bush or a tree; 1. the formation of a low-growing bush; 2. the formation of a tree. Diagonal lines show where cuts are made.

jacent to the containers out of wires, netting or trellis. These look beautiful when flowering plants are trained against them.

Large balconies and roof gardens can be transformed into true hanging gardens. Ideally, these structures should be built specifically for the purpose so that the containers can be made to fit exactly into the available space—which may even be large enough to encompass real flower beds. Once the supporting floor has been suitably reinforced, the flower-bed containers, made of copper, galvanized steel or aluminum sheets or laminated plastic or strong, flexible plastic, can be positioned. While the beds are under construction, some form of channeling should be incorporated and provision made for running water and drains. Automatic watering devices will keep the soil at the correct level of dampness at all times. The best system is a so-called drip system made up of very small plastic tubes laid on the soil surface or underneath. Control the system manually or with an automatic timer.

Hanging baskets and pots of flowering plants are especially decorative on terraces and balconies, but require more care than plants in ordinary containers because they must be watered more frequently—even once or twice a day. This is especially true of baskets, which are made of open-mesh wire lined with sphagnum moss and then filled almost to the top with good potting soil. Maintaining the water supply for container-grown plants is probably the worst problem you will run into when growing flowers in this way. But there are two others that must not be overlooked.

One, you must make sure that the plants are not too large for their containers. Many terraces and balconies are rather exposed, and heavy rains and high winds can create havoc by upsetting the containers and even ripping the plants from their anchorage in the shallow soil. This applies particularly to small trees and shrubs. These require heavy, deep containers, and perhaps even being tied to posts or walls.

Two, you must consider the soil. Since there is so little of it, it must be very rich. A good basic soil (for all except calciphobous plants that hate lime) is made up of one-third good topsoil, one-third humus mixed with coarse leaf mold or bark, and one-third well-rotted manure with another slow-acting organic fertilizer added. During the growing season the plants also require periodic feeding with organic and mineral fertilizers as well as frequent applications of foliar fertilizers.

Terrace, deck, balcony and roof gardens are generally most successful when there is a good mixture of low-growing flowering and foliage plants with a few tall ones; for example, hosta with gladiolus, forget-me-nots with tulips, French marigolds with zinnia, and so on. Nor must green plants be overlooked, since they make a fine backdrop to the annual color display and keep the scene alive during the winter. The following fill this role particularly well: *Pinus mugo, Chamaecyparis obtusa* "Nana Gracilis," *Chamaecyparis* "Ellwoodii," *Juniperus chinensis* "Pfitzeriana," *Juniperus communis repanda, Juniperus squamata* "Meyeri," *Picea pungens* "Glauca Globosa," *Picea glauca* "Albertiana Conica," *Taxus baccata, Thuja orientalis* "Pyramidalis Aurea," *Thuja orientalis* "Compacta Nana Aurea," *Mahonia, Prunus Laurocerasus* "Otto Luyken," *Ilex aquifolium* "Argentea Variegata," *Elaeagnus pungens* "variegata aurea." Use some ferns, too: *Phyllitis scolopendrium* (hart's tongue), *Polystichum setiferum* (soft shield fern).

Another thematic variation is to make a water garden out of one or more of the plant containers. This can look extremely beautiful during the summer and, in temperate climates, throughout the year. Some aquatic plants that look decorative together are *Cyperus papyrus* (Egyptian paper rush), *Cyperus alternifolius* (umbrella grass) and *Cyperus gracilis, Thalia dealbata, Typha, Iris kaempferi, Sagittaria sagittifolia* (common arrowhead), *Pontederia cordata* (pickerel weed), *Eichhornia crassipes* (floating water hyacinth) and *Nymphaea* (water lily).

Diseases and pests

Plants, like all living things, are subject to disease. In practice, a disease is regarded as anything that disturbs the physiological and morphological balance of a plant by changing its functions in some way. Because of the scope and complexity of the subject this chapter is restricted to listing the causes of diseases. It also briefly indicates the commonest pathogenic agents and the remedies that can be applied.

—Diseases attributable to poor climatic conditions such as too much or too little heat. Provide shade, spray with tepid rainwater, mulch, cover with straw, provide temporary shelter such as cloches and coldframes.

—Diseases attributable to the lack of certain physicochemical substances in the soil; nutritional deficiencies and imbal-

An example of a terrace winter garden. *1*. Codiaeum; *2*. Dieffenbachia; *3*. Pilea repens; *4*. Cyathea arborea; *5*. Asparagus sprengeri; *6*. Hedera; *7*. Cyrtomium falcatum; *8*. Gynura sarmentosa.

ance; badly aerated or waterlogged soil that has negative effects on its microflora, compactness and permeability; deficiencies or insolubility of the mineral elements. Such conditions can cause stunted growth, chlorosis, albinism, etc. Correction is effected by addition to the soil of the appropriate organic/mineral fertilizers.

—Constitutional diseases caused by defects in the vegetal organs brought about by a latent predisposition in the seeds or in those parts of the plant that have been used in propagation. Chlorosis, albinism, etc., may result. Great care should be taken to propagate only from healthy stock.

—Traumatic diseases produced by external agents such as high winds, hailstones, exceptionally heavy snow, and pruning injuries. When possible, the damaged area should be removed completely, and followed by preventive-curative spraying with anti-cryptogamic copper-based disinfectant solutions (Bordeaux mixture, oxychloride of copper) and iron sulfate.

—Virus diseases contracted from little-known ultramicroscopic microorganisms. The best treatment is to select all propagatory plants with great care and to take all preventive measures possible. Infected plants must be destroyed.

—Diseases caused by external organic agents in the form of parasitic animals. The main culprits are the phytophagous (plant-eating) insects belonging to the following orders: (1) *Lepidopterae:* butterflies (larvae and caterpillars), leaf miners, goat moths, silkworms, cutworms, pyralid caterpillars, etc. Infestations by insects such as these can be treated only with

An example of effective placing of plants of different shades of green on a large balcony: 1. Dizygotheca elegantissima; 2. Tetrastigma voinerianum; 3. Scindapsus aureus; 4. Ficus elastica; 5. Hibiscus rosa-sinensis; 6. Codiaeum; 7. Aphelandra squarrosa.

insecticides based on systemic phosphoric esters, carbamates, mastic grease bands and moth-repellant substances. (2) *Coleopterae: Cerambycidae* (longicorn or long-horned beetles), *Curculionidae* (weevils), *Elateridae* (click beetles), etc. In these cases, treatment with phosphor-organic and carbamate insecticides is necessary. (3) *Hemipterae: Aphides* (aphis [aphid], green and black plant lice), *Tingidae* (lacebugs), *Psilidae* (*Psila rosae* = carrot fly, *Psila nigricornis* = chrysanthemum stool miner), *Coccoidea* (mealybugs and scale insects), *Aleurodidae* or *Aleyrodidae* (whiteflies), *Cicadidae* (cicadas), *Cimicidae* (bedbugs), etc. For these the best insecticides are those with a plant base such as pyrethrum or nicotine, although chemically based insecticides containing a mixture of white oils combined with phosphor-organics or carbamates and phosphor-organics can also be used. (4) *Hymenopterae: Tenthredinidae* (sawflies), *Vespidae* (wasps), *Formicoidea* or *Formicidae* (ants), etc. Combat with insecticides based on DDT or phosphorous such as malathion. (5) *Orthopterae: Forficula auriculariae* (earwigs), *Gryllotalpidae* (molecrickets), *Acridoidea* (short-horned grasshoppers and locusts). Treat with phosphor-organic and carbamate insecticides.

Other parasitic animals are: mites——*Tetranychus urticae* (two-spotted spider mite) and *Tetranychus telarius* (linnalus, the common red spider mite)——controlled with insecticide based on acaricides, chloro-organics——and eelworms (foliar and root nematodes [*Anguillae* or *Nematodae*]), which are mi-

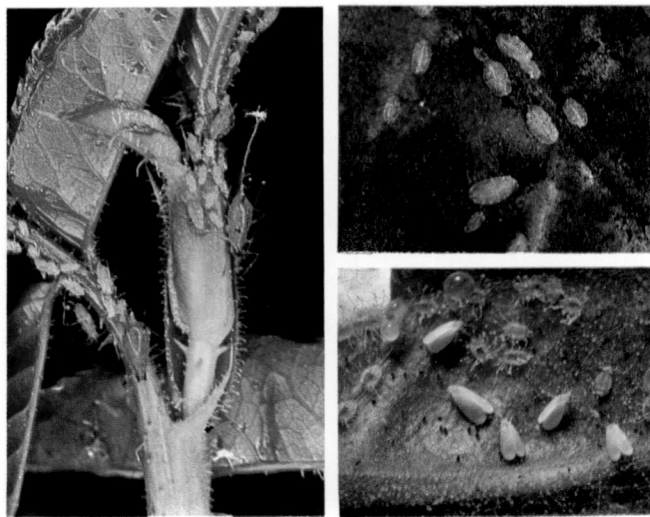

Some types of insect pests: left, aphids (greenfly) on roses; top right, scale insects; bottom right, whiteflies (snowflies).

croscopic worms living in the roots of many herbaceous and woody plants, where they cause distortion and swelling. Treatment consists of insecticides based on nematicide, holoidrous-carbide, phosphor-organic materials or thyadiazine.

Some natural ways to combat insect pests

In some instances, a particular type of insect pest can be got rid of only by growing another type of plant that is not receptive to it. A system of rotational cultivation under which host plants are alternated with immune ones can also be used.

Insects are living organisms and can be victims of other parasites—predatory insects, endoparasites, hyperparasites, etc.—whose natural habit helps to restrain or even prevent the spread of the destructive species. Entomological research is looking for and developing ways to exploit this natural form of control. It certainly seems to offer a solution both effective and economically viable while at the same time ecologically acceptable because it presents no pollution problems.

Cryptogamic diseases (moss, fungi, etc.)

Cryptogamic diseases are caused by the action of vegetal parasites, usually of microscopic proportions, belonging to the thallophytes (cryptogams)—especially to the myxomycetes, bacteria and fungi (phycomycetes, ascomycetes, basidiomycetes and imperfect fungi) division. These microorganisms penetrate the natural apertures (stomata) of a plant or enter through damaged cells; thus their microscopic filaments (hy-

phae and mycelia) infiltrate the tissues of the plant with devastating results. A number of microscopic fungi (mycetofungi) belong to this group; their cycle develops in two phases—as saprophytes (molds) on the soil and as parasites on plants. The best known and commonest cryptogamic diseases are:
Oidium or powdery mildew: This is a whitish powdery formation that first appears on the upper side of leaves and then spreads, in a damp atmosphere, to the underside, making the leaves curl and arresting growth. These spores can also affect flowers. Oidium is caused by various species of the genus *Oidium* and by *Sphaeroteca pannosa*. It thrives in humidity and attacks many familiar garden plants such as the zinnia, dahlia, rose and euonymus. Preventive/curative measures can be taken by spraying with copper-based fungicides such as Bordeaux mixture or oxychloride of copper. Alternatively, a lime-sulfur spray can be used or a dusting of powdered flowers of sulfur given. Nitrophenol is also effective.
Rust: Reddish-brown or black marks caused by *Uromyces caryophillinus, Puccinia pruni, Puccinia* species, etc., appear on leaves and stems. Carnations, roses and geraniums are all susceptible. The plants should be treated with a fungicide containing copper, sulfur, dithiocarbamate or phthalate products as soon as an attack is noticed.
Black spot: Infected leaves become speckled with black spots that may develop into holes as the affected tissue is killed. Black spot is caused by *venturia, fusicladium, diplocarpon*, etc., attacking roses, *Prunus*, greenhouse plants, bul-

Euonymus leaves infected with oidium.

bous plants. Treatment: preventive/curative spraying with copper-dithiocarbamate or phthalate-based fungicides.

Scab and growths on green parts and roots: When plant tissues react to the action of a pathogenic agent, the cells develop abnormal growths to form rough corklike excrescences that may become quite large. Such formations are very persistent and are caused by *Pseudomonas savastanoi, Agrobacterium tumefaciens,* etc. Among the susceptible plants are hydrangeas, *Prunus* and olive trees. Treatment: removal and burning of infected parts or complete destruction of badly affected plants. (All tools used in the treatment must be disinfected.) Spray plants with a strong concentration of fungicide after pruning——Bordeaux mixture, iron sulfate, etc.

Gray mold on flowers and fruit: Caused by *Botrytis cinerea,* which does look like a gray mold. Treat with fungicides containing phthalics or having an oxazolidine base.

Downy mildew: This includes various diseases induced by fungi (*peronospora,* phytophthora *infestans, plasmopara*) with the characteristic of developing inside the green organs of the host plant, especially in the leaves. Mildew can be seen in the white patches on the underside of leaves, which shrivel and dry up. In tuberous-rooted or rhizomed plants, downy mildew also causes the tubers and rhizomes to rot. It is a very common problem and chrysanthemums, roses, solanums, etc., are especially vulnerable. Treatment: preventive/curative fungicides based on copper and phthalic products.

Bulb rot: A softening of the tissues caused by spores of the

Rust is a common cryptogamic disease of which this is an example.

fungi *fusarium* and *Botrytis cinerea* (gray mold). It attacks tulips (then it is called ''Tulip fire''), narcissi, gladioli, etc. Treatment: phthalic fungicides.

Dry rot in bulbs and tubers: The tissues rot and the tubers and bulbs dry up. The rot is caused by the fungi *Corticium solani* (Rhizoctonia) and *fusarium*. All affected tubers and bulbs must be destroyed but preventive treatment with liquid or powder anticryptogamics or fungicides is worth trying. Do not replant in the same place.

Regulations on the use of pesticides

As has been shown, there are many ways of combating the diseases and pests that attack plants. Among the commonest remedies are the antiparasitic substances and pesticides that either destroy the parasites or prevent the attack altogether.

The production and sale of insecticides and fungicides containing substances that are toxic to all warm-blooded creatures, including ourselves, are subject to strict legal control in nearly every country in the world. Approved insecticides, miticides and fungicides sold to the public are divided into four categories, according to toxicity. Those in the first category are the most toxic and the container must be clearly marked ''Poison.'' Those in the second category, although highly toxic, are distinguished by the Cross of St. Andrew and the word ''Harmful'' or ''Dangerous.'' In order to buy any of the materials in the first two categories, a special license must be obtained from agricultural authorities. Any antiparasitic materials

Top photograph: damage caused on a leaf by Peronospora or downy mildew; bottom photograph: spraying with pesticides in a nursery garden.

in the third category must be marked "Handle with care" and represent only a small risk to adults. The risks involved with the fourth category are so minor as to be discounted. All products belonging to the last two categories are freely available.

During the preparation and application of all these mixtures, the instructions, always printed on the label, must be adhered to scrupulously. Keep all such products locked up in a dry place, well out of the reach of children and domestic animals. Any leftover material should be burned, but on no account should aerosol cans ever be put on a fire; these should be buried where they cannot be dug up again by either people or animals.

In spraying or dusting toxic materials on plants, it is advisable to wear a nose-and-mouth mask, a protective eye shield or glasses, rubber gloves and waterproof overalls, and to do the work in early morning or late afternoon on very still, windless days. Do not smoke or eat while carrying out any of these treatments. When the task is finished, every container and piece of equipment used should be thoroughly washed or cleaned. If you feel at all unwell during the operation, stop immediately and, if the symptoms persist, contact a doctor as soon as possible. Details as to the appropriate antidote to any toxic chemical on the market should be found on the container.

Planning a garden

Flowers can be grown anywhere around your property as long as they make a contribution to the overall scene. Generally, however, flowering shrubs and trees are grown in shrubbery borders. (Trees may also be set off by themselves.) Smaller flowering perennials and annuals are usually grown in flower beds (some people prefer to call these flower borders). But they are also sometimes planted in with shrubs.

Laying out all the various flower beds and borders—and perhaps small clumps, too—on a property is not easy to do successfully; you may wish to consult a landscape architect or a knowledgeable gardener. If, however, you do this yourself, you should be guided by these four very general rules:

1. There must be some reason for the display; it must make a contribution to the scene. Too often, it doesn't.

2. The shape of the bed or border should relate to its location; otherwise it may look strange (even though masses of flowers cover many sins in bed and border arrangement).

3. The length of the bed is immaterial. But the depth—front to back—must be such that you can work in the bed and pick flowers without trampling the plants. If you can get at a bed from only one side, the bed should not be more than 4 feet deep; 3 feet is actually better. On the other hand a bed that can be worked from both front and back can be 6 feet deep.

4. Strange as it may seem, many gardeners maintain that a border of perennials, annuals and/or bulbs should not be placed where you have direct view of them from the house in winter. The reason for this is that the border is not at all pretty at this time of year, when the plants are cut to the ground. Even a shrubbery border can be ugly unless it contains evergreens or deciduous shrubs with interesting structures, persistent fruit or attractive bark. This rule, of course, applies only to gardens

A garden in bloom with geraniums, petunias and strelitzias.

in cold climates, not to those in warm climates, where plants grow and often bloom in the winter.

Actually laying out a bed or border is quite easy. The best way to start is to draw a sketch that is as accurate as possible. Then, if the bed is to be of geometrical shape—rectangular, square, round, etc.—stake it out carefully and stretch strings between the stakes. An undulating or free-form bed is laid out by laying a flexible hose on the ground.

Arranging the plants is more difficult. The lowest usually go in the front of the bed; then come the intermediates, and finally at the back of the bed the tall species. Annuals, perennials and bulbs are generally arranged in clumps of three, five or seven plants of the same variety. These can be intermingled with a few large single plants used as accents; and frequently there are one or two ribbonlike drifts of a single variety.

Shrubs and trees, though larger, are arranged in much the same way, although in single species. A few clumps, however, may be used. In most cases these are very small plants such as the heaths and heathers. The ground between may be left bare or planted to a groundcover or mulched.

Spacing the plants is important. Beginning gardeners have a tendency to cram plants close together. But most plants grow faster than we think, and unless you have given each specimen elbow room, you soon wind up with an unsightly jumble. Try to determine before planting the garden how much each plant spreads. You can get this information from the nursery where you buy shrubs and trees. The growth habits of annuals

A close-up photograph of the orange blossom (Citrus aurantium *var.* Myrtifolia), *an especially decorative flower.*

and perennials vary greatly. As a very rough rule of thumb, however, allow 6 to 8 inches between flowers no more than 6 inches tall; 8 to 10 inches between flowers 6 to 12 inches tall; 12 to 15 inches between flowers over 12 inches tall; and 2 to 3 feet between giant flowers such as tithonia and cosmos.

Most beds and borders are edged simply by cutting a little trench around them with a sharp spade. Unfortunately, this must usually be recut at least once a year, because it tends to fill with grass clippings, soil, twigs, etc., and becomes indistinct. A permanent edging is therefore a work saver besides, for the most part, more attractive. The metal edgings that are widely sold, however, are of no value because they quickly crumple as you walk and mow over them. A brick edging is far better. To keep the bricks from tilting or sliding, stand them on end in a trench with the tops flush with the surrounding lawn. Ideally (although this means you must buy more bricks) the wide edges should be perpendicular to the bed. This results in an edging approximately 3½ inches wide—plenty wide enough to support the wheels on one side of your lawn mower so you can mow the grass beside the edging rather than clipping it by hand. Redwood, cedar or cypress 4 × 4-inch timbers can also be used, but must be held in place with stakes.

Raised beds are being used with increasing frequency today. They are just like ordinary beds except that they are raised from about 6 inches to 30 inches above the surrounding ground. They have a number of advantages:

An example of a flourishing corner with fuchsia at the top, Colocasia antiquorum *in the center and impatiens around the edge*

Azaleas in bloom in Villa Taranto, on Lake Maggiore, a famous Italian garden.

——They protect the plants from the people who are walking through the garden and from children playing.

——They tend to keep tree roots and grass from invading the beds.

——They provide flat, erosion-free growing space on sloping land.

——They raise plants above the water table so they won't be drowned in very wet weather.

——They take the backache out of planting and cultivating plants by bringing the soil level up closer to your hands. You can even sit on the edge of the bed while working.

——They may make a flat garden more interesting by giving it elevation.

——They give greater importance to the very small plants which tend to become ''lost'' among larger plants.

——They can be used——just like a low hedge——to separate one garden area from another.

——If built in front of a high, blank wall or fence, they make the wall or fence look lower and less forbidding.

To build a raised bed you simply construct a sturdy wall around it. This can be made of 2-inch-thick planks, bricks, stone, concrete blocks, poured concrete, etc. Make sure that the wall extends well below ground so it will not heave in cold weather. After the wall is in place, fill the bed with good soil. The surface of the soil must be at least 1 inch below the top of the wall so the soil cannot wash out.

ENTRIES

1   ABUTILON MEGAPOTAMICUM Auguste de Saint Hilaire and Charles Naudin

Syn.: *A. vexillarium* Edouard Morren. Common name: Abutilon

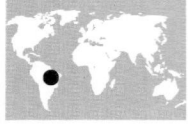

Family   Malvaceae.

Description   Shrub with slender branches, often pendulous. Bright-green lanceolate-sagittate leaves, alternate, with irregularly toothed margins. Flowers are axillary, borne singly and pendent with interesting pentagonal shape of Chinese lanterns; red calyx with yellow petals with blackish-brown anthers protruding. Not long-lived.

Height of plant   3–5 ft. (1–1.50 m.).

Size of flower   1½–2¾ in. (4–7 cm.).

Place of origin   Brazil.

Flowering time   Spring–summer.

Cultivation   Sunny, sheltered position. Will grow outdoors in a temperate climate, otherwise treat as a pot plant in a cool greenhouse and put outside during the summer. Not frost-resistant. Prefers good, rich topsoil or a good depth of well-drained, noncalcareous soil. Requires frequent watering. Prune by cutting back lateral shoots and shortening main stems. Pests: aphids and red spider mites.

Propagation   By seed and by softwood or semi-hardwood cuttings in the spring–summer.

Qualities   Half-hardy. Very easy to grow.

2   ACACIA LINEARIS John Sims

Syn.: *A. longissima* Hermann Wendland. Common name: Wattle

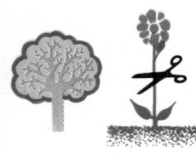

Family   Mimosaceae

Description   Arborescent stem with a mass of rather untidy, erect branches which bend over with the weight of the flowers and foliage. Evergreen, with long, lanceolate leaves (phyllodes), obtuse at the end and coriaceous, with clearly marked veins. Numerous flowers borne in globulose capitula on axillary spikes. One of the most vigorous of the acacias, its prolific blooming makes it a great favorite for outdoor cultivation in temperate zones and warm coastal areas.

Height of plant   10–26 ft. (3–8 m.).

Size of flower   ¼–⅜ in. (0.5–0.8 cm.) each capitulum.

Place of origin   New South Wales, Australia.

Flowering time   Spring.

Cultivation   Full sun. Temperate climate. Very little resistance to cold. Prefers uncultivated, siliceous-argillaceous, open-textured ground but adapts to almost all types of fertile garden soil. Periodic feeding with organic and mineral fertilizers helps to promote growth. Requires regular watering. Light pruning to thin out dense growth may be desirable. Pests: often subject to scale insects.

Propagation   By seed in the spring, in pans or flowerpots. The young plants need to be potted-on at least twice before final planting out.

Qualities   Not hardy. Easy to grow.

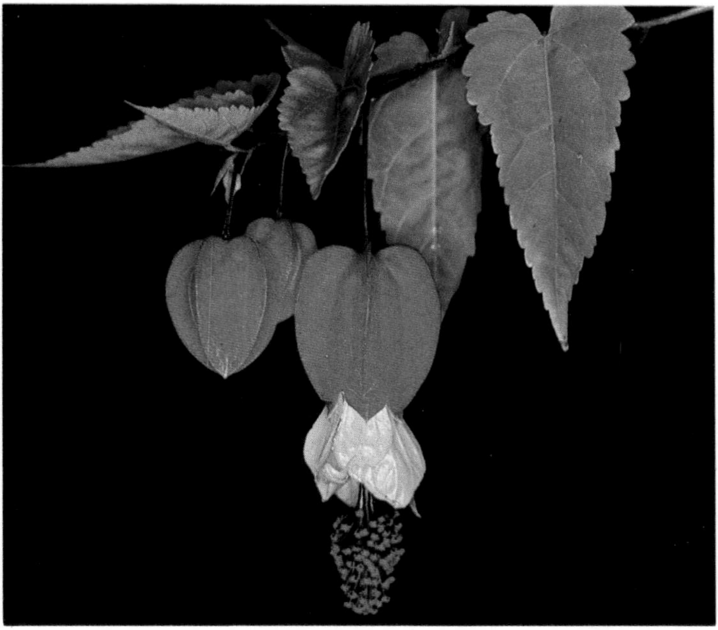

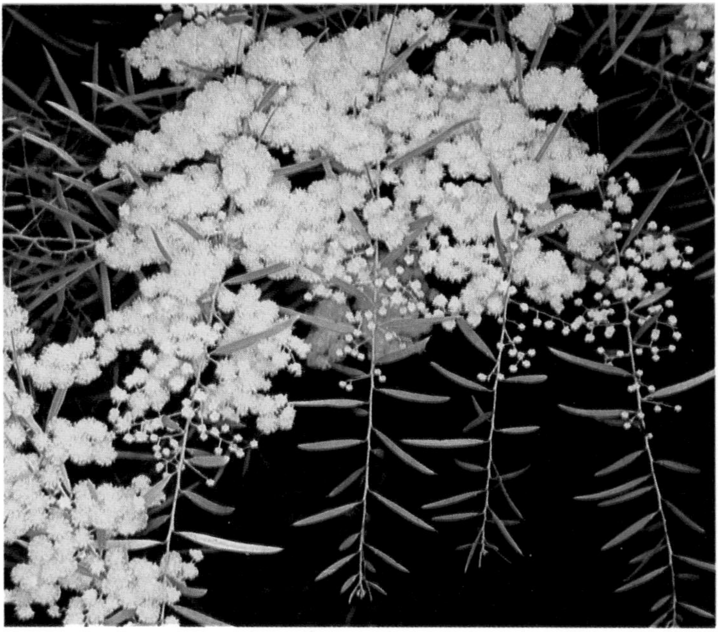

3 **ACACIA DEALBATA** Heinrich Friedrich Link
Syn.: *A. decurrens* Karl Ludwig Willdenow, var.
dealbata F. Muller. Common name: Mimosa

Family Mimosaceae.
Description Evergreen tree widely grown in temperate areas and, when climate is warm enough, near the sea. Compound, bipinnate leaves 2⅜–4¾ in. (6–12 cm.), formed by about 20 lobes which, in turn, are composed of about 50 silvery gray-green leaflets. Frequent yellow flowers borne in globular capitula on axillary and terminal panicles 3¼–4 in. (8–10 cm.) long. In some countries there is considerable demand for sprays of mimosa for its symbolic significance during the annual celebration of International Women's Day.
Height of plant 16–30 ft. (5–9 m.).
Size of flower ¼–⅜ in. (0.6–1 cm.) each capitulum.
Place of origin Tasmania, Australia.
Flowering time End of winter–spring.
Cultivation Full sun. Temperate climate, in positions sheltered from frost and wind. Rich, deep soil, fairly damp, with a subacid reaction, permeable and with a tendency to be calcareous. Resistant to dry conditions. Benefits from regular watering and periodic applications of organic and mineral fertilizers. No pruning necessary. Pests: subject to scale insects. Special problem: frost.
Propagation By seed, previously well soaked, under glass, in the spring. Grafting on hardy acacias such as *A. retinoides* or *A. nerifolia*.
Qualities Not hardy. Easy to grow.

Opposite above: a complete Acacia dealbata, *or mimosa tree, whose flowers have been chosen as a symbol of the emancipation of women in some parts of the world. Bottom: A close-up of the same plant. The globose capitula of the mimosa flowers can clearly be seen.*

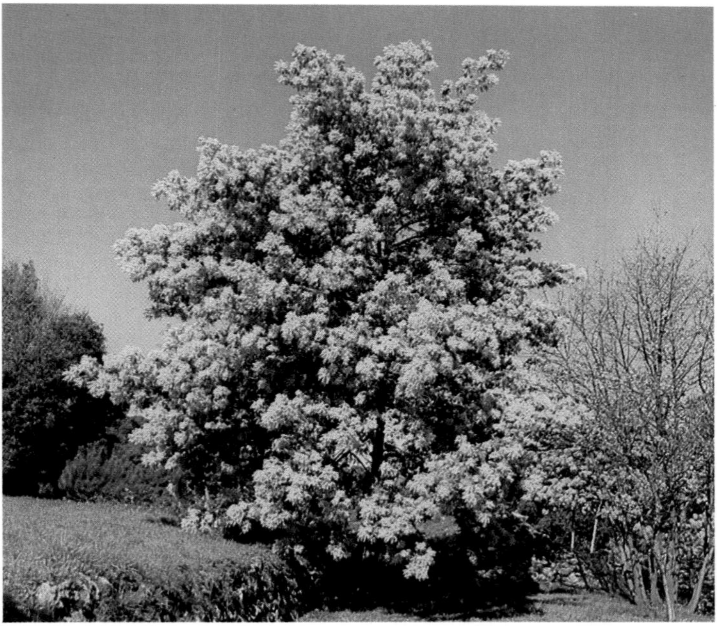

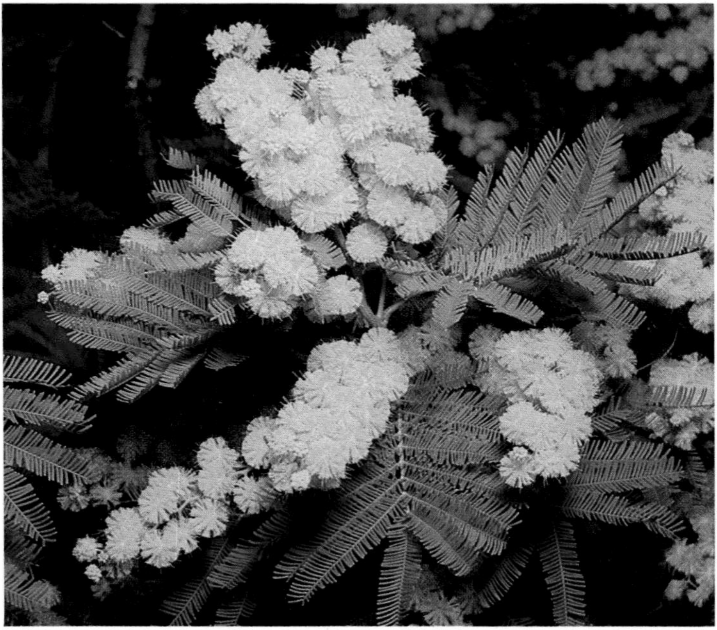

4 ACACIA LONGIFOLIA (Henry C. Andrews) Karl Ludwig Willdenow

Syns.: *A. obtusifolia* Allan Cunningham; *A. intertenta* von Siebold and Zuccarini

Family   Mimosaceae.
Description   Small tree widely grown in temperate areas; like the other acacias, it has an arborescent-bushlike habit with considerable irregular branching that bends under the weight of foliage. Alternate light-green leaves (phyllodes), oblong-lanceolate, obtuse and coriaceous. Very decorative, prolific blooming. It is one of the hardiest of the acacias.
Height of plant   10–20 ft. (3–6 m.).
Size of flower   ¼ in. (0.5 cm.).
Place of origin   Australia.
Flowering time   Spring.
Cultivation   Full sun. Temperate climate. Likes deep, open-textured, silaceous soil. Also does well in ground tending to be clayey-sandy, open-textured and well drained. Benefits from periodic applications of organic and mineral fertilizers. Very fast growing and very resistant to drought but responds to regular watering. Can be pruned if necessary. Pests: mealybugs.
Propagation   By seed in the spring in pans in a coldframe, transplanted into pots and then potted-on before finally being planted out.
Qualities   Not hardy. Easy to grow.

5 ACACIA PODALIRIAEFOLIA Allan Cunningham

Syn.: *A. motteana* Hortorum. Common name: Acacia

Family   Mimosaceae.
Description   Shrubby or arborescent evergreen plant that branches freely and has a wide spread. An extremely decorative plant because of its foliage and free-flowering habit. Small oval leaves (phyllodes), obovate or triangular-obovate; they are sessile, silkily-pubescent and ash-gray-green in color. The flowers are prolific, like little round feathers, borne on simple racemes and slightly scented.
Height of plant   13–20 ft. (4–6 m.).
Size of flower   About ⅜ in. (1 cm.).
Place of origin   New South Wales, Australia.
Flowering time   Winter.
Cultivation   Full sun and sheltered position. Temperate climate. Can withstand one or two light frosts without coming to much harm. Calcareous, calcium-rich soil with plenty of organic matter; or of a moist clayey-sandy nature. Responds to seasonal applications of organic and mineral fertilizers as well as generous watering. Light pruning after flowering. Pests: Scale insects.
Propagation   By seed, in autumn or spring, in pots placed in the shade. By grafting onto *A. longifolia*.
Qualities   Hardy in a temperate climate. Easy to grow.

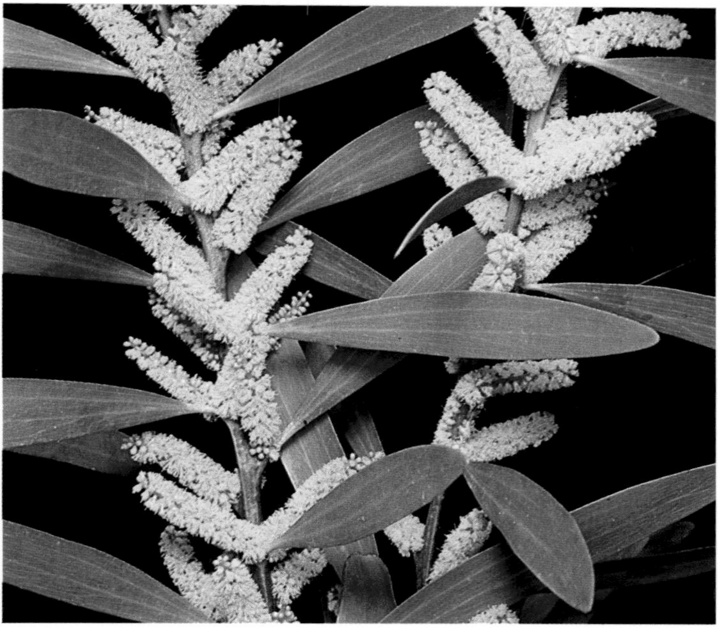

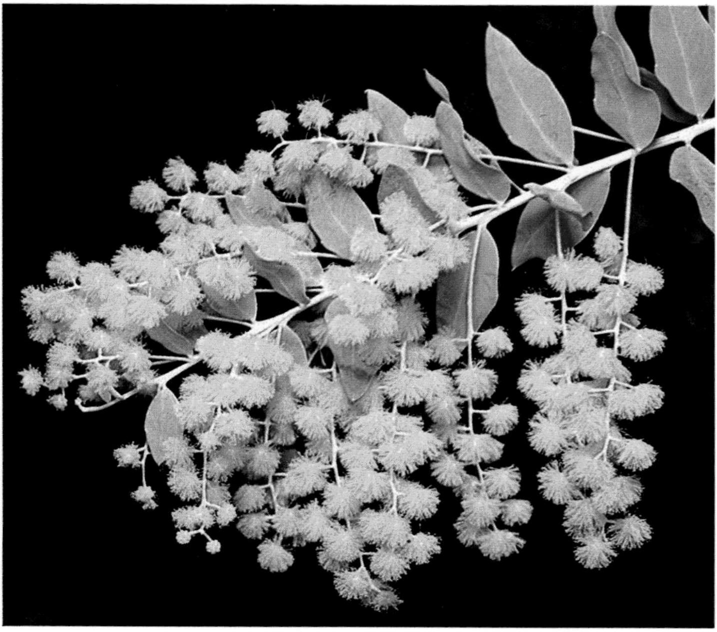

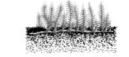

6   ACANTHUS MOLLIS Carolus Linnaeus
Common name: Bear's breeches

Family   Acanthaceae.
Description   Deciduous perennial plant with large fasciculate roots. Its decorative glossy mid-green leaves are oblong with sinuate-pinnatifid margins, toothed, with deeply indented lobes; borne on short pedicels, they are about 13–20 in. (35–50 cm.) long. Numerous flowers are carried on spikes about 27–36 in. (70–90 cm.) long; each flower is set in the axil of a broad bract whose inferior part is sinuate-dentate and rather bristly while the superior is purple and entire. The tubulate corolla is pinkish-white with reddish venation; it widens at the end into a large single trilobate lip.

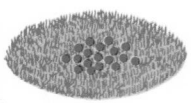

Height of plant   24–40 in. (0.60–1 m.).
Size of flower   ¾–1⅛ in. (2–3 cm.).
Place of origin   Mediterranean area of Europe.
Flowering time   Spring–early summer.
Cultivation   Shady, cool position. Temperate climate. Frost-resistant. Deep soil, rich in humus and fairly compact, moist and permeable. Does not require special care but will not flower in poor soil.

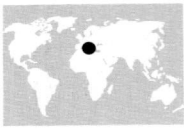

Propagation   By seed, in the spring, in pots, and subsequent transplanting. Clump division is easier.
Qualities   Ground cover under trees. Hardy. Easy to grow.

---

7   AESCHYNANTHUS SPECIOSUS   Joseph Dalton Hooker
Syn.: *Trichosporum splendens* Otto Kuntze

Family   Gesneriaceae.
Description   Decorative perennial plant for a temperate-hot climate; grown more as an indoor or greenhouse plant than outdoors. Bushy habit with slender cylindrical branches that grow from the base and trail or climb. The thick leaves are arranged in twos or threes in opposite groups; obovate-lanceolate, with crenate-dentate margins and averse tips. Flowers borne singly or in dense racemes at the ends of the branches.
Height of plant   15–32 in. (40–80 cm.).
Size of flower   2–2⅜ in. (5–6 cm.).
Place of origin   Indonesia.
Flowering time   Spring–summer; sporadically in other seasons.

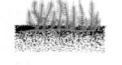

Cultivation   Shady position. Temperate-hot and humid climate. Dislikes low temperatures. For potting up as an indoor plant, use a mixture of equal parts heather litter, leaf mold, peat and well-rotted organic manure with a little sand. Water regularly. Pruning limited to controlling the shoots. Pests and diseases: various insects and rot.

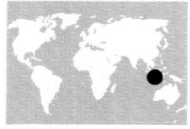

Propagation   By cuttings, in a warm greenhouse, in autumn or spring.
Qualities   Suitable for balcony, terrace and indoors. Not hardy. Requires considerable care.

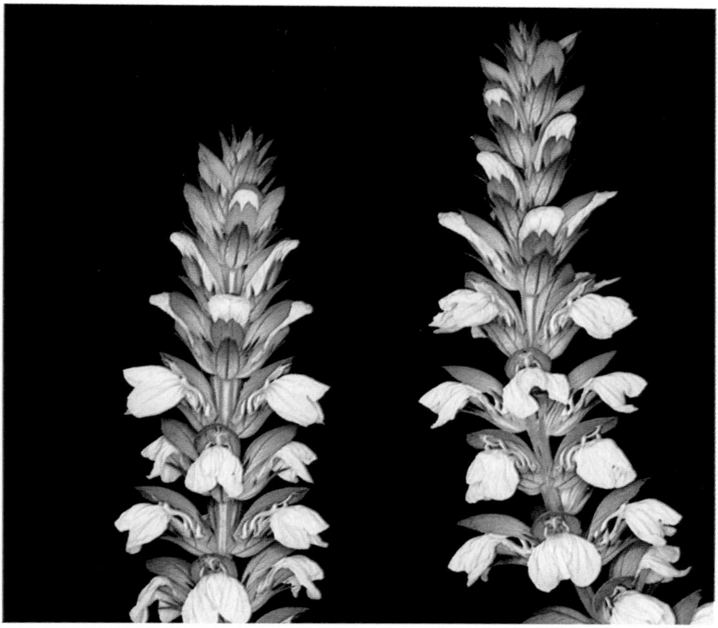

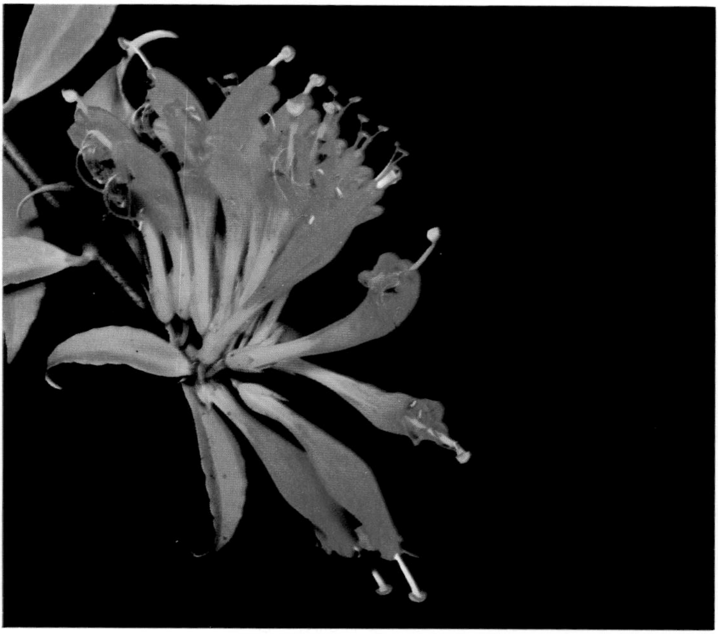

8 AESCULUS PARVIFLORA Thomas Walter
Syn.: *A. macrostachya* François André Michaux.
Common name: Dwarf horse chestnut.

Family Hippocastanaceae.
Description One of the less vigorous species of horse chestnut, it is especially suitable for small gardens. An upright, compact shrub with a broad spread, it often becomes rather bushy due to the number of suckers that may grow from the base. Leaves are alternate, digitate, with five to seven elliptic or oblong-ovate leaflets, crenulate-dentate and pubescent. White flowers with long pale-pink stamens, in erect racemes. Prolific and decorative when in bloom.
Height of plant 10–13 ft. (3–4 m.).
Size of flower 1½–2 in. (4–5 cm.).
Place of origin Alabama, South Carolina.
Flowering time Summer.
Cultivation Shady position. Temperate climate, well able to withstand the cold. Flourishes in all types of soil, with a preference for forest litter if it is well aerated and damp. No particular care necessary and requires watering only in very dry periods. It should not be pruned but allowed to grow naturally. Remove suckers, however. Special problem: the leaves are susceptible to sunscald.
Propagation By seed, in a nursery bed in the autumn, or by stratifying the seeds and then sowing in the spring. It can also be grafted onto the common horse chestnut.
Qualities Hardy and easy to grow.

---

9 AETHIONEMA GRANDIFLORUM Edmond
Boissier and Hohen.
Common name: Persian stonecress.

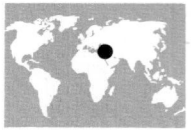

Family Cruciferae.
Description A dwarf subshrub, suffruticose, with a spreading habit. Its small leaves are dense, alternate and lanceolate-oblong. Flowers profusely in spicate racemes, giving the plant the appearance of a dark-pink cushion.
Height of plant 8–12 in. (20–30 cm.).
Size of flower $3/16$–$5/16$ in. (0.5–0.8 cm.).
Place of origin Middle East; Caucasus.
Flowering time Spring–summer.
Cultivation Sunny position. Temperate climate. Fairly frost-resistant. Hillside or mountainous sites. Damp, rich, humic soil. Requires some feeding with liquid fertilizers, and regular watering. Trim lightly after flowering to remove dead growth. Trouble-free.
Propagation By seed in the autumn, providing shelter during the winter; or in the spring. By division in autumn or spring.
Qualities Hardy. Easy to grow.

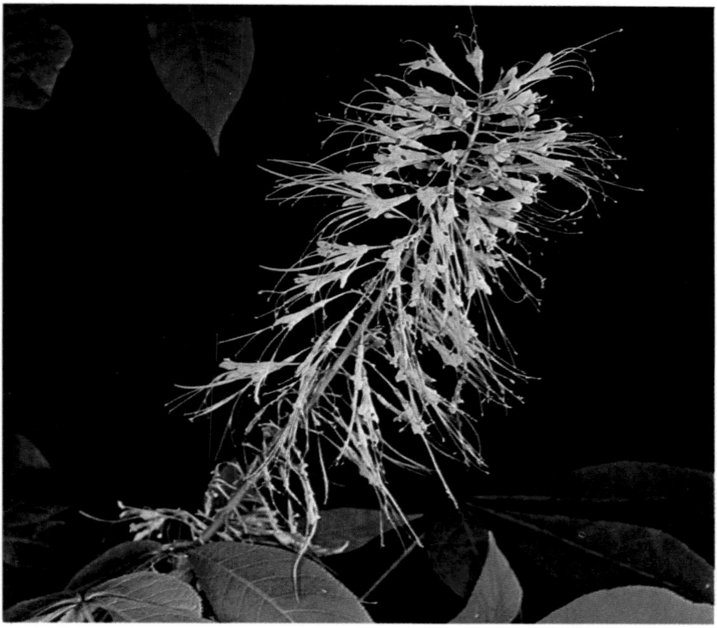

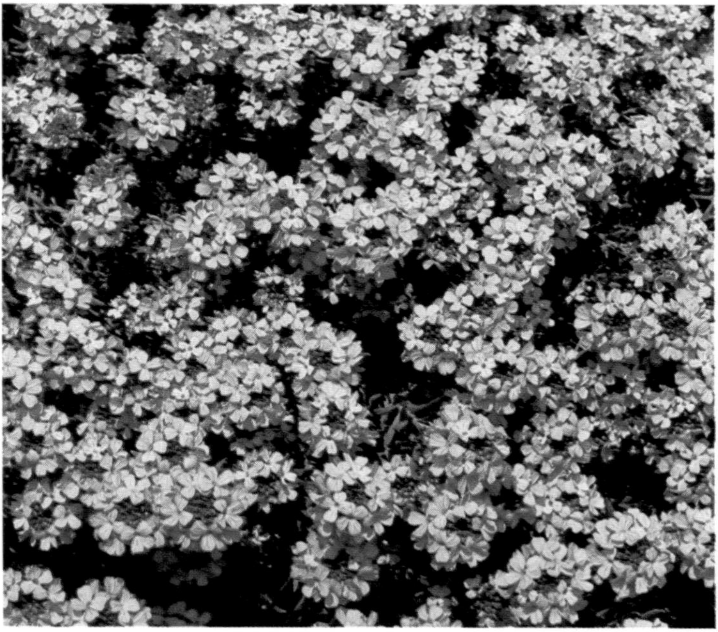

10 AGAPANTHUS AFRICANUS Georg Franz Hoffmann

Syn.: *A. umbellatus* C. L. L'Heritier. Common name: African lily

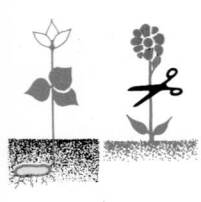

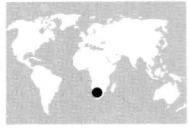

Family Liliaceae.

Description Herbaceous perennial forming a clump. Its bright green, liguliform leaves are canaliculate and sheathed at the base, 10–20 in. (25–50 cm.) long, coriaceous and outcurving. The scape is almost tuberous, with fleshy roots. Flowers are produced in dense, rounded umbels at the end of each upright floral scape, with long peduncles. Color varies from white to azure and purplish-blue, according to variety. No perfume. Grown commercially for cutting.

Height of plant 2–4 ft. (0.60–1.20 m.).

Size of flower 1½–2½ in. (4–6 cm.) long.

Place of origin South Africa.

Flowering time Spring–summer.

Cultivation From full sun to slight shade. Temperate climate; can withstand some light frost, especially if well mulched. Prefers deep, moist soil, tending to be heavy and clayey. Requires plenty of well-rotted manure and frequent watering. In colder area best grown in large pots or tubs. Does not like to have its deep roots disturbed. Pests and diseases: ground insects and root rot.

Propagation Spring sowing in pots under glass. Because it is slow-growing, pot it on at least twice before finally planting out. Or by division of the clump.

Qualities Fairly hardy. Easy to grow.

11 AGERATUM HOUSTONIANUM Phillip Miller

Syn.: *A. mexicanum* John Sims

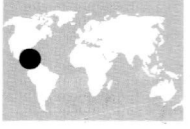

Family Compositae.

Description Half-hardy annual, this bedding plant forms a low bush that is popular for its long flowering period. Triangular-ovate, obtuse, pubescent leaves with crenulate-dentate margins. Numerous flowers carried on tiny capitula, tubulous and featherlike, joined in compact terminal corymbs; fairly deep lavender-blue. There are many horticultural varieties, all quite compact, in various shades.

Height of plant 8–24 in. (20–60 cm.).

Size of flower $^3/_{16}$–$^5/_{16}$ in. (0.5–0.8 cm.).

Place of origin Central America.

Flowering time Spring, summer and autumn, until the first frosts.

Cultivation From full sun to half shade. No particular soil requirements but does especially well in open-textured garden soil rich in organic material and well drained. Requires regular and plentiful watering. Pests and diseases: aphids; root rot, oidium and various cryptogams in damp conditions.

Propagation By seed, in pans or boxes, under glass at the end of the winter or early in spring; they will first need to be pricked off and then planted out when the seedlings are about 2–3 in. (5–8 cm.) high.

Qualities Suitable for growing in pots, window boxes and on balconies. Easy to grow.

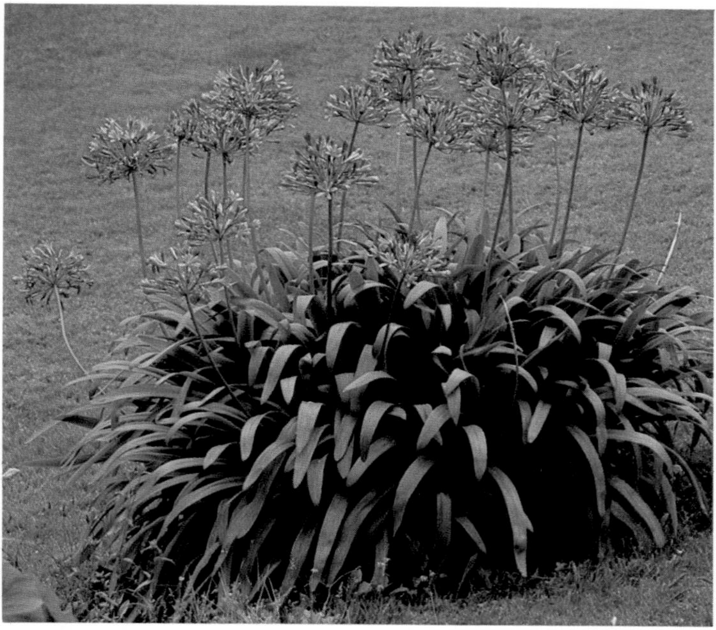

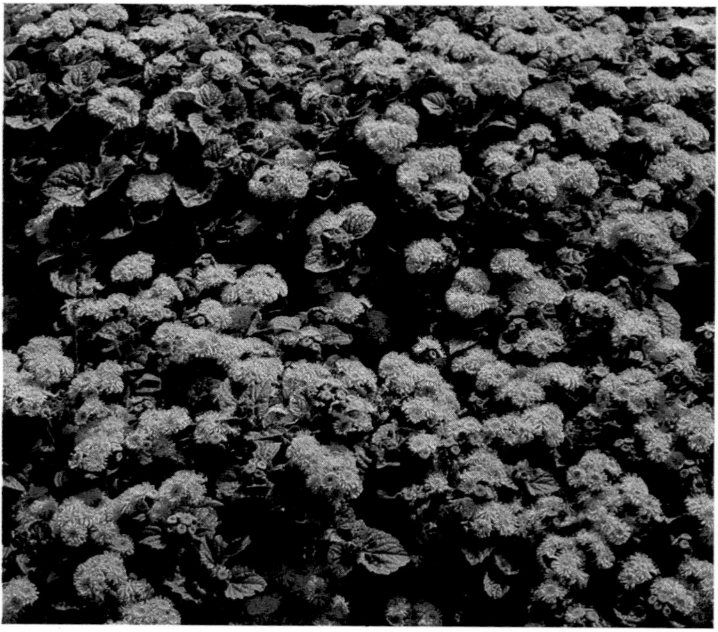

12 AJUGA REPTANS Carolus Linnaeus
Common name: Bugle

Family Labiatae.
Description A charming little herbaceous plant; excellent ground cover but can get out of hand. Basal leaves are oblong-spatulate and glabrous with smaller, sinuate-dentate caulines. Floral stem is quadrangular in cross section. Sky-blue axillary flowers are carried on a composite spike, each with a pilose calyx with five teeth, bilabiate tubulous corolla with large four-lobed lower labium. There is also a variety with deep reddish leaves.
Height of plant 6–8 in. (15–20 cm.).
Size of flower $^3/_8$–$^5/_8$ in. (1–1.5 cm.).

Place of origin Europe.
Flowering time Spring–summer.
Cultivation Shady position. Temperate climate but can withstand the cold well. Prefers damp, humic—even heavy—soil. Spreads quickly but requires regular watering. No special cultural care usually necessary.
Propagation By rooting stolons, preferably in spring or autumn.
Qualities Useful in wildernesses and on poor land. Hardy, very easy to grow.

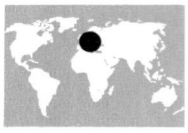

---

13 AKEBIA QUINATA (M. Houttuyn) Joseph Decaisne

Family Lardizabalaceae.
Description Climbing deciduous woody plant, ornamental both for its foliage and flowers. Quick-growing, its stem twines around any support, throwing out numerous slender offshoots. It deserves to be used more widely than it is, as it adapts quickly to all kinds of surroundings. Leaves are alternate, digitate and composed of five ovate-oblong leaflets. It produces a large number of strange little yellowish-violet flowers joined into small racemes.
Height of plant 15–25 ft. (5–8 m.).
Size of flower 1⅛ in. (3 cm.).
Place of origin China; Japan.
Flowering time Spring–summer.
Cultivation From full sun to deep shade. Temperate climate. Frost-resistant. Can adapt to any garden soil, even if poor and coarse, provided it is moist. Requires periodic feeding with organic/mineral fertilizers. Watering not usually necessary except in very dry conditions. Winter pruning to thin out and tidy up. Needs to be supported. Trouble-free.
Propagation By layering, or by softwood or semi-hardwood cuttings, in spring or autumn. Sometimes by seed.
Qualities Suitable for patios, terraces and large balconies as a climber. Hardy. Easy to grow.

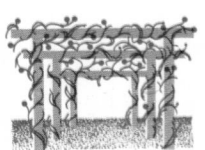

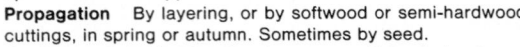

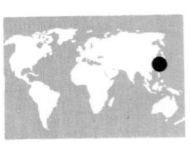

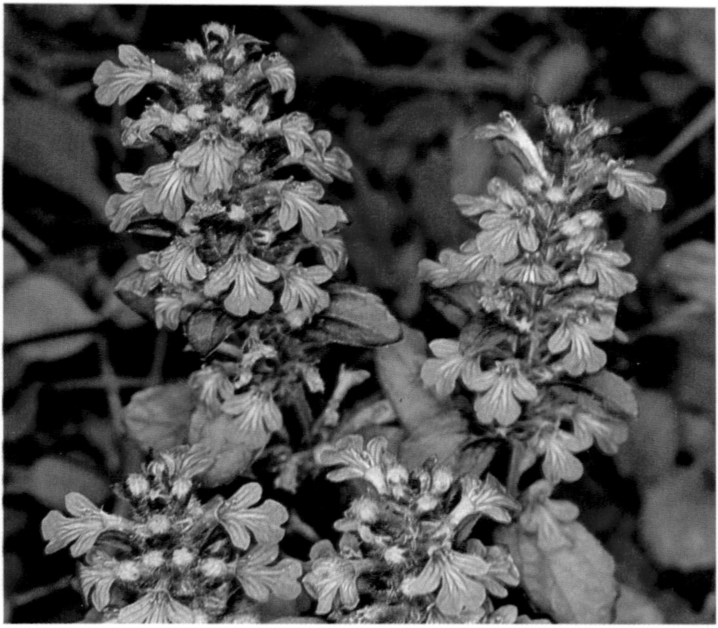

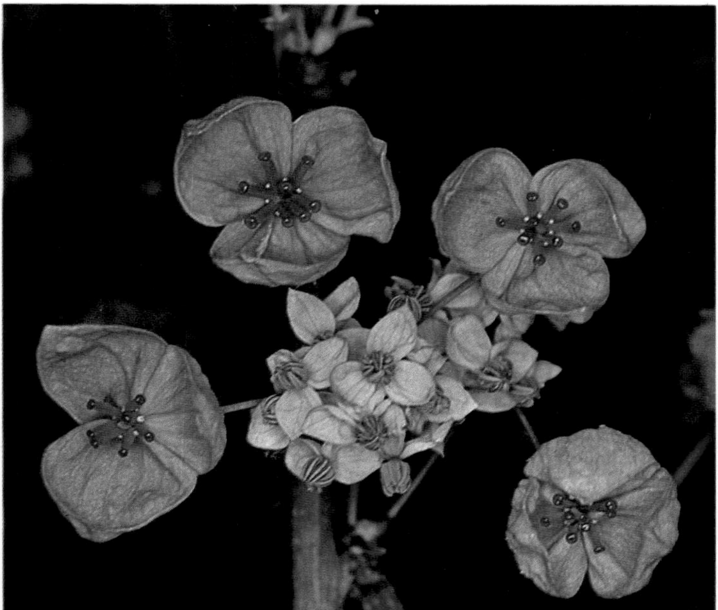

14 ALCEA ROSEA Carolus Linnaeus
Syns.: *Althaea rosea* (Linnaeus) Antonio Jose Cavanilles; *A. chinensis.* Common name: Hollyhock

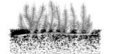

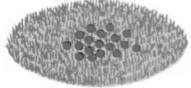

Family Malvaceae.
Description Hardy annual, biennial or perennial depending upon the variety and method of growth; generally a biennial. Stems are erect, semi-woody and covered with quite stiff hairs. Large, rounded, cordate leaves, five to seven lobes and crinkly margins, smaller toward top of stem. Flowers borne singly or in pairs along the spikes. Also single- and double-flowering forms. The corolla has five fused petals. The yellow stamens joined in a central column. Colors: white and yellow to violet, purple and crimson.
Height of plant 6½–11½ ft. (2–3.5 m.).
Size of flower 2¾–4¾ in. (7–12 cm.).
Place of origin Uncertain but probably Asia Minor or China.
Flowering time End of spring–summer.
Cultivation Full sun, temperate climate. Tolerates light frost. Prefers fairly clayey soil, rich in organic material and even sewage sludge. Resistant to dry conditions; likes moderate watering. In too rich and humid soils it may develop a cryptogamic rust peculiar to this plant family (*Puccinia malvacearum*). As winter sets in, cut stems to ground level and cover with mulch.
Propagation By seed, at the end of winter, in pots or pans in a sheltered position. Transplant seedlings with three to four leaves to their permanent site. To ensure plants of the same species, take root cuttings or divide clumps.
Qualities Hardy. Easy to grow.

15 ALLIUM NEAPOLITANUM D. Cyrillo
Syn.: *A. album Santi*

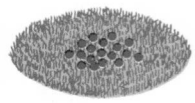

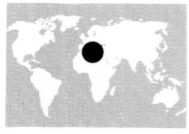

Family Liliaceae.
Description Perennial deciduous bulbous plant. Very prolific small, whitish globose bulb. The shiny green leaves are basal, linear, slightly caniculate, obtuse-acute and spreading. As many as 30 flowers borne in terminal umbels on upright triangular scapes. White perigonium with six oblong stellate tepals. The flowers are very conspicuous, especially in grass. Its only drawback is that the whole plant smells of garlic.
Height of plant 10–12 in. (25–30 cm.).
Size of flower ¾ in. (2 cm.).
Place of origin Mediterranean areas.
Flowering time Spring.
Cultivation Semishaded position, even under trees. Temperate climate with limited resistance to heavy frosts. Suited to all types of soil enriched with humus or forest litter. Naturalizes well in grassy areas, banks and on poor land. Requires no special attention. Trouble-free.
Propagation Easily propagated from bulblets during the resting period.
Qualities Hardy. Easy to grow.

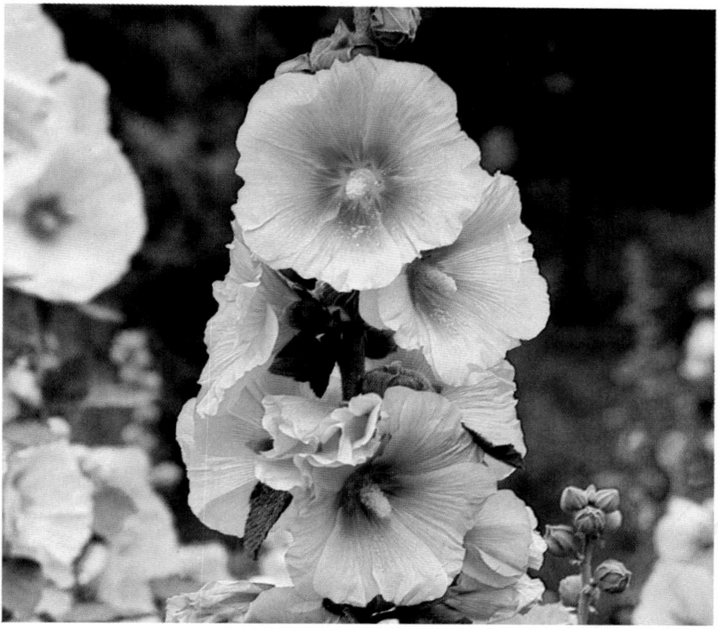

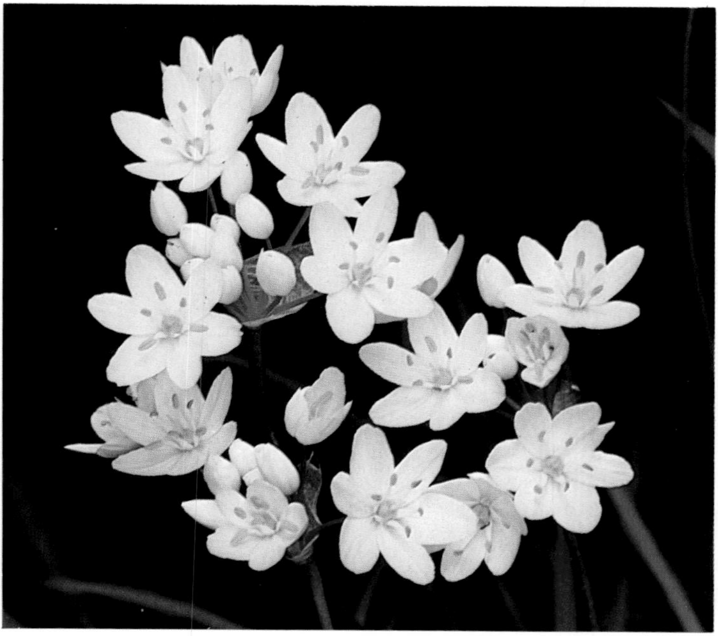

16 ALOE ARBORESCENS Phillip Miller
Common name: Tree aloe

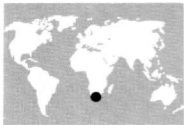

Family Liliaceae.
Description Treelike upright cylindrical stem, branching out in bushy formation. The sessile leaves are persistent, long, succulent, triangular-acuminate with prickly edges, springing from the stem in terminal rosettes. Numerous flowers are borne in spiky racemes on long terminal peduncles. Frequently seen among the succulents grown in warm coastal or temperate inland areas.
Height of plant 40–60 in. (1–1.50 m.).
Size of flower 1⅛–1½ in. (3–4 cm.).
Place of origin Cape of Good Hope, South Africa.
Flowering time Spring–summer.
Cultivation Full sun. Temperate-warm climate; cannot withstand low temperatures or shade. Undemanding——suited to all kinds of soil, even when dry, stony or rocky, but prefers clayey-sandy soils. Excellent resistance to dryness, requires little watering. No cutting back required except for removal of dead parts, which should be cut from the base. Pests: sometimes attacked by mealybugs, scale insects and aphids.
Propagation Reproduction is from basal shoots and leaf cuttings, in spring–summer, in a coldframe.
Qualities Half-hardy unless in a warm climate. Easy to grow.

17 ALOE x PRINCIPIS (Adrian Hardy Haworth) Stearn
Syn.: *A. salmdyckiana* Joseph August Schultes.
Common name: Aloe.

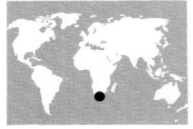

Family Liliaceae.
Description This ornamental shrub is a beautiful succulent that can be grown in a temperate climate near the sea. The upright cylindrical stem is branched with persistent leaves, attached in large subterminal rosettes, long, pointed and triangular with prickly edges. Decorative flowers are carried in large, dense cylindrical racemes on branching steles, like candelabra. Cylindrical perigonium with six linear tube-shaped tepals, fairly close together.
Height of plant 3½–11½ ft. (1–3.50 m.).
Size of flower ¾–1⅜ in. (2–3.5 cm.).
Place of origin South Africa.
Flowering time Spring–summer.
Cultivation Full sun. Not frost-resistant. Sheltered positions shaded by walls or rocks. Adapts to any soil, even if poor and stony. Prefers humus-rich, clayey-sandy soil, dry conditions. Cut back only to remove dead parts. Pests and diseases: scale insects and root rot.
Propagation By sowing in the spring under glass in boxes or pots. After potting up, plantlets require potting on once or twice before finally planting out. Also by leaf cuttings and side shoots cut from the base of the mother plant.
Qualities Hardy in a warm climate. Easy to grow.

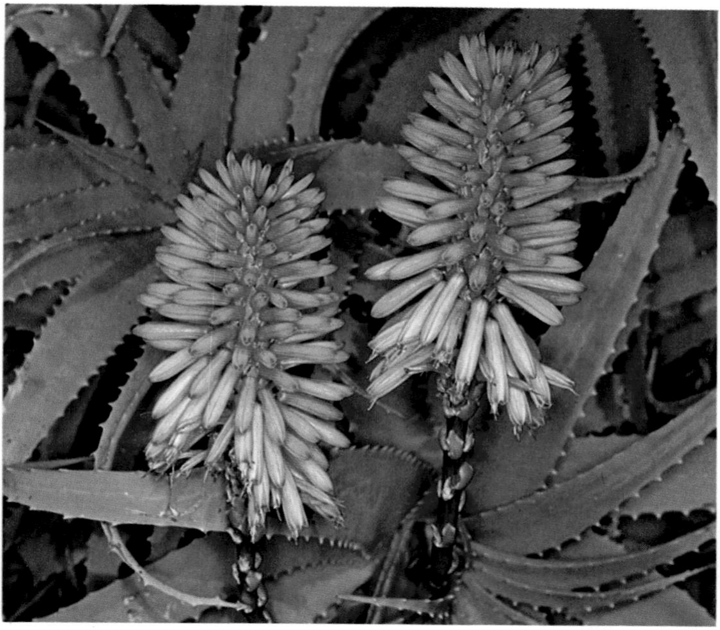

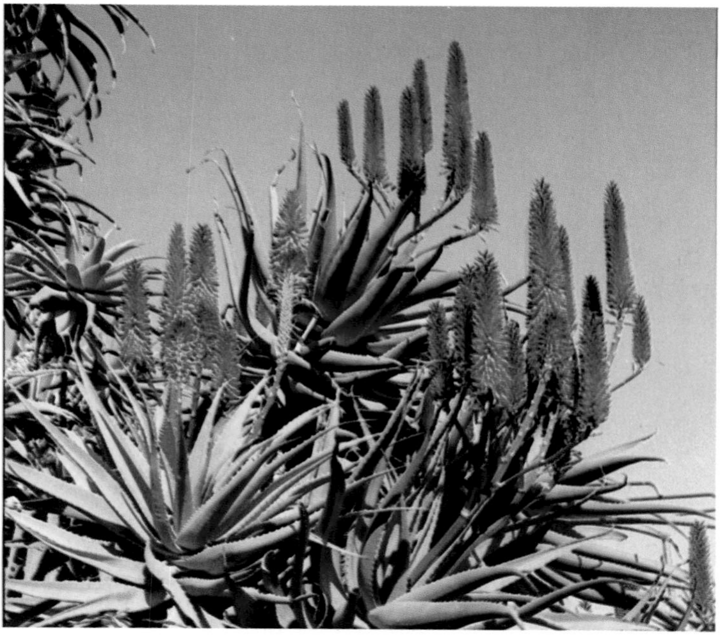

18 ALSTROEMERIA VERSICOLOR Hipolito Ruiz Lopez and Jose Pavon
Syns.: *A. sulphurea* Hortorum; *A. tigrina* Hortorum.
Common name: Peruvian lily

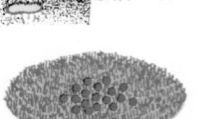

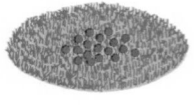

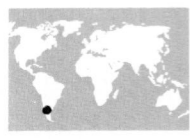

Family Amaryllidaceae.

Description Very floriferous herbaceous plant with fleshy tuberous roots that grow quickly to produce numerous plants. Its slender stems terminate in an umbrella-shaped cluster of alternately arranged leaves; these are winglike, oval-lanceolate and rather undulate, and carried on elongated pedicels, with an oblong, loose-fitting sessile sheath. The upright floral stems bear sturdy floral peduncles in groups of two or three, with a whorl of leaves crowning the point at which they are joined into four or five umbels. Perigonium has six open tepals which form the calyx; the color varies, sometimes even on the same flower. There are several horticultural cultivars.

Height of plant 20–28 in. (50–70 cm.).

Size of flower 1½–2 in. (4–5 cm.).

Place of origin Chile.

Flowering time Spring–summer.

Cultivation A light, sheltered position. Temperate, frost-free climate. Open-textured, fertile and well-drained soil. Apply organic manure and some slow-release minerals when the ground is prepared. Water often. Pests and diseases: insects (slugs, swift moth caterpillars); fungus diseases.

Propagation By division in the spring. Sometimes by seed in a coldframe or cool greenhouse.

Qualities Half-hardy. Very easy to grow.

---

19 ALYSSUM SAXATILE Carolus Linnaeus cv. ''sulphureum''
Syn.: *Aurina saxatilis* (Linnaeus) Augustin Nicaise Desvaux. Common name: Basket of gold.

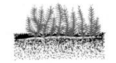

Family Cruciferae.

Description A shrubby perennial sometimes grown as a biennial. Alternate oblong-lanceolate, tomentose, gray-green leaves. Numerous sulphur-yellow flowers branching out in terminal panicles. This plant is subject to visible morphological mutations according to the soil and climatic conditions. There are several cultivars.

Height of plant 8–12 in. (20–30 cm.).

Size of flower 1½–3 in. (0.4–0.8 cm.) each panicle.

Place of origin Central and Southern Europe; Asia Minor.

Flowering time Spring.

Cultivation Full sun and sheltered; temperate climate. Flourishes in almost any soil but prefers a calcareous-clayey composition, fairly compact, well drained and dry. Organic manure should be dug in before planting and one or two liquid feeds given during the growing period. Water only during periods of drought. Cut well back after flowering. Pests and diseases: caterpillars, slugs and snails; root rot and oidium.

Propagation By seed in the spring, in boxes or pots, in a sheltered position. Use good garden soil mixed with sand.

Qualities Can be grown in pots, window boxes, cracks in walls and between paving stones. Hardy. Easy to grow.

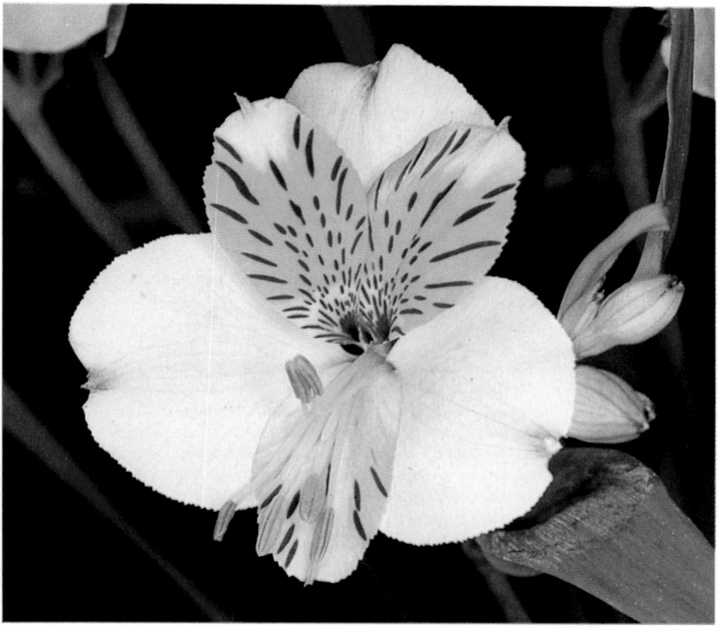

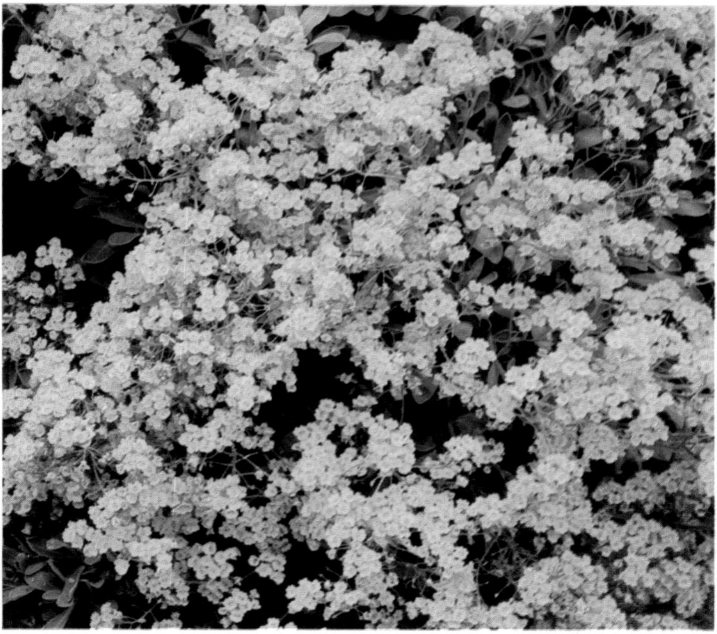

20   AMARANTHUS CAUDATUS Carolus Linneaus.
Common name: Love-lies-bleeding.

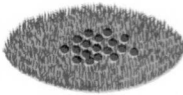

Family   Amaranthaceae.
Description   Half-hardy annual with an upright reddish stem. Its alternate leaves are oval and obtuse, varying in size from 2 to 6 in. (5–15 cm.) in length, on a petiole the same length as the blade. The tiny rich crimson flowers are arranged close together on a group of compact spikes or on large flexible panicles, rather like cats' tails.
Height of plant   20–40 in. (0.50–1 m.).
Size of flower   Length of the floral racemes 6–14 in. (15–35 cm.).
Place of origin   The tropics, possibly Central and South America.
Flowering time   Summer–autumn.
Cultivation   Full sun to half-shade. Good garden soil of average consistency but slightly sandy and humus-rich. Apply well-rotted manure when preparing the ground. Benefits from liquid nitrogenous feeding during growth. Requires plentiful watering. Pests and diseases: aphids, caterpillars and sometimes fungus diseases.
Propagation   By seed, at the end of winter, in a warm place; transplant seedlings when ready. Alternatively, seeds can be sown directly in flower bed and subsequently thinned out.
Qualities   Suitable for pots, decorative tubs, etc. Hardy. Easy to grow.

21   AMARYLLIS BELLADONNA Carolus Linnaeus
Common name: Belladonna lily.

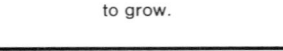

Family   Amaryllidaceae.
Description   Deciduous bulbous plant. The large bulb, which is pyriform, elongated and tunicate, is slow to develop new bulbs. The four to eight upright leaves curve back slightly; they are linear, obtuse, glabrous and caniculate. The floral scape is erect, bearing six to ten slightly pendulous fragrant flowers that spring from an umbel. A beautiful plant to include in the summer display. Warning: This plant is poisonous.
Height of plant   20–28 in. (50–70 cm.).
Size of flower   4 in. (10 cm.).
Place of origin   South Africa.
Flowering time   Midsummer.
Cultivation   A light or semishaded position. Temperate climate. Can withstand the frost well, even in the north, if protected by a good mulch. Prefers open-textured soils that are sandy, rich and well fertilized. Dislikes waterlogged ground. Requires periodic feeding and plentiful watering. It has a resting period after blooming. Trouble-free.
Propagation   By bulblets, removed during the resting period.
Qualities   Hardy. Easy to grow.

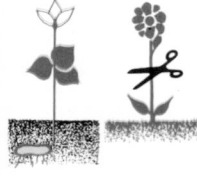
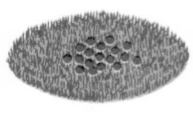
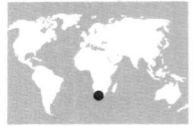

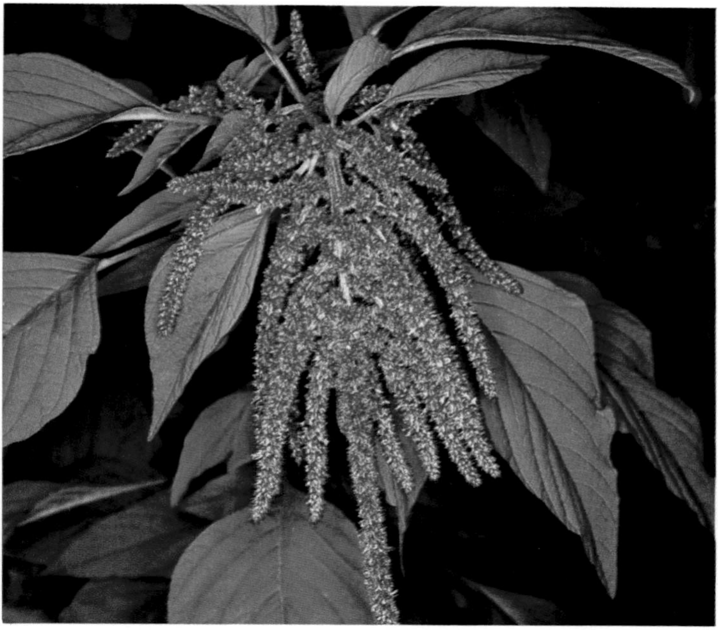

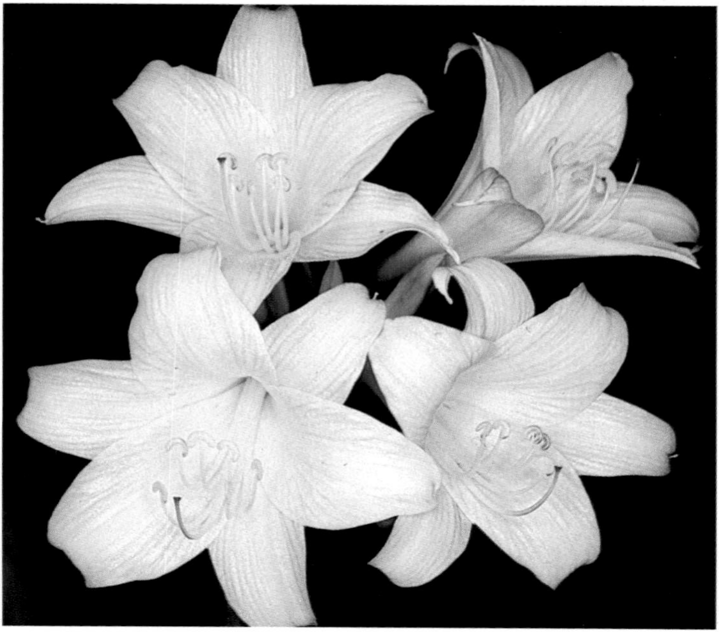

22 ANEMONE CORONARIA Carolus Linnaeus
Common names: Windflower; poppy anemone; lily of the field

Family Ranunculaceae.

Description Herbaceous tuberous plant enjoyed particularly for its reliable habit of blooming in time to herald the spring. The rhizome, which is nearly always branched, puts down roots from all sides. Each leaf has seven pubescent leaflets carried on a long petiole. Flowers are borne terminally on a stalk that has three or four bracts a little below the calyx; these may be single, semidouble or double according to the cultivar, of which there are many. Colors range from white to shades of red, blue and purple. The stamens are a strikingly dark blackish-blue.

Height of plant 4¾–10 in. (12–25 cm.).

Size of flower 1⅛–2 in. (3–5 cm.).

Place of origin Uncertain, but probably from the East and naturalized in the eastern Mediterranean regions.

Flowering time Spring.

Cultivation Shady position. Temperate climate. Prefers damp, humus-rich situations or clayey-siliceous soils. Dislikes organic manures. Requires regular watering. Goes into a rest period after blooming. The rhizomes can be lifted and kept by storing them in layers in sand or dry peat. Pests and diseases: flea beetles, caterpillars, cutworms, aphids and slugs; also subject to certain viruses and fungus diseases.

Propagation By seed, in pans or boxes, in the spring in a coldframe or cool greenhouse. Seedlings will require pricking out and be ready to plant out in nursery beds by early autumn. They flower in their second year. Use a rich loam or potting compost, not too light, mixed with sand. Propagation can also be achieved by dividing the rhizomes in October or in spring.

Qualities Suitable for pots and containers on the terrace, patio or balcony. Hardy. Easy to grow.

Opposite above: Anemone coronaria cv. ''De Caen.'' Bottom: an ornamental variety of Anemone, cv. ''St. Brigid.''

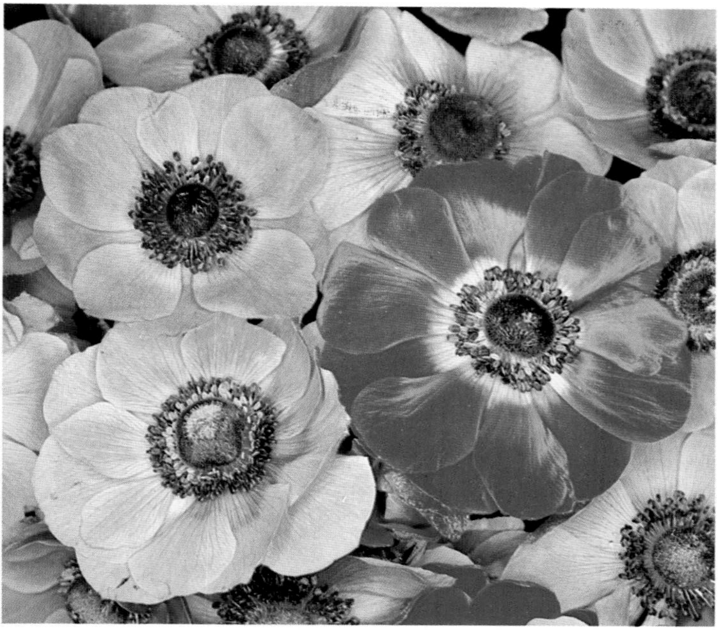

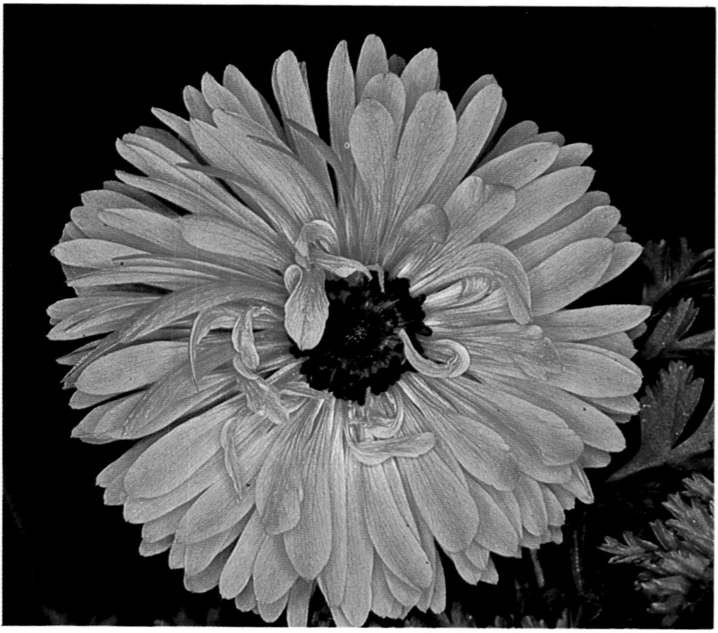

23 ANTIRRHINUM MAJUS Carolus Linnaeus
Common name: Snapdragon

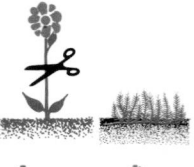

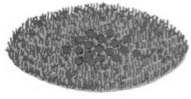
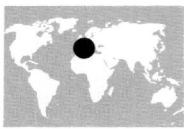

Family   Scrophulariaceae.
Description   A bushy perennial usually grown in numerous cultivated varieties as an annual. The lower leaves are opposite and spatulate while the upper are alternate, lanceolate-oblong and pubescent. The fragrant flowers, arranged in pyramidal spikes, have a distended tubulous corolla whose vertical upper lip is bilobate and the lower one trilobate, the medial lobe adhering to the upper lip to close the throat. This accounts for the name "Snapdragon," because the two lips can be manually squeezed open and allowed to snap shut.
Height of plant   6–38 in. (15–95 cm.).
Size of flower   1½–2 in. (4–5 cm.).
Place of origin   Southern Europe; North Africa.
Flowering time   Spring, summer, autumn.
Cultivation   Full sun. Temperate climate. Any type of calcium-rich soil, even if it is stony, provided it is not too clayey or too acid. Plant even grows in cracks in old walls and paving stones. Appreciates some liquid fertilizer during growth and regular watering. In warm areas, cut stalks to ground after blooming stops; plants will come up again in the spring. Pests and diseases: aphids; rust and oidium.
Propagation   By seed in late winter in pans; prick off before planting out.
Qualities   Hardy. Easy to grow.

---

24 AQUILEGIA VULGARIS Carolus Linnaeus
Common name: European columbine

Family   Ranunculaceae.
Description   Herbaceous perennial with upright floral stem, branched, bearing a few leaves. The main leaves spring from the roots; they are biternate in form with cuneate segments with crenate interspaces and rounded lobes. The free-flowering blooms are quite distinctive, borne in broad panicles; they have five ovate-oblong colored sepals and five spoon-shaped petals of the same or a different color, each one equipped with a long spur that may be straight or curved. There are many subspecies and cultivars with double or semidouble flowers in various colors.
Height of plant   20–36 in. (50–90 cm.).
Size of flower   1½–2⅜ in. (4–6 cm.).
Place of origin   Europe.
Flowering time   Spring–summer.
Cultivation   A light or semishaded position. Temperate-cool climate. Grows well in a light, sandy soil of the rich woodland type, even if clayey, provided it is damp but permeable. Dislikes dry conditions. Stems and dry leaves should be cut back in the autumn. Not long-lived. Pests: the scale insect *Nematus aquilegiae*, and the columbine leaf miner *Phytomyza aquilegiae*.
Propagation   Spring sowing in pans in light compost. Prick out before transplanting. Flowers the following year. Self-sows freely.
Qualities   Hardy. Easy to grow.

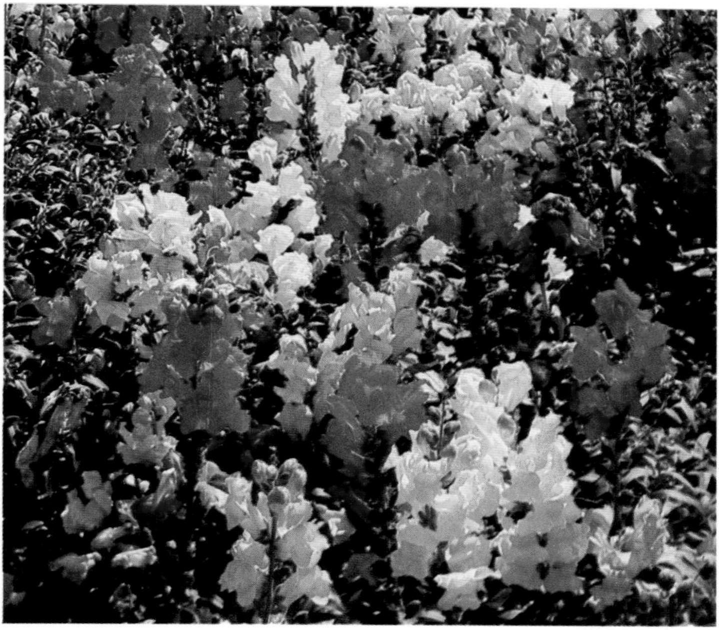

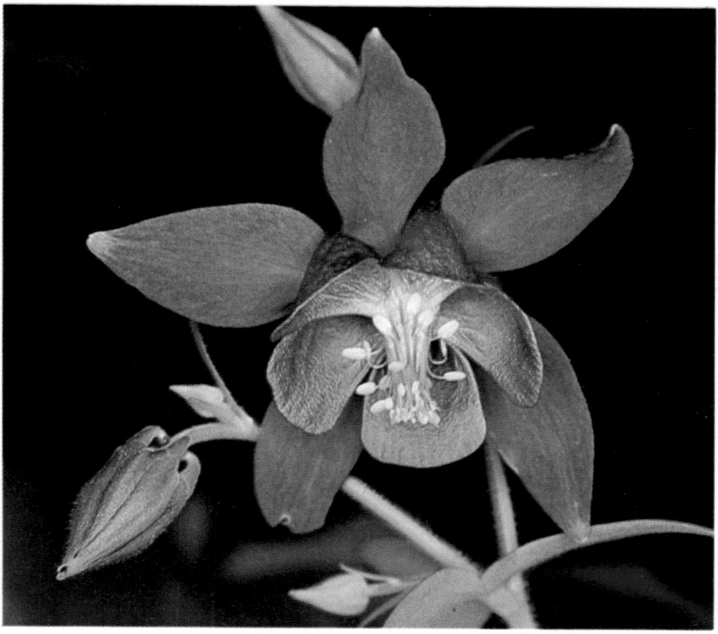

25 ARCTOTIS x HYBRIDA Hortorum
Common name: African daisy

Family Compositae.
Description Perennial generally treated as an annual. It is grown like the gazania for its interesting flower but is more delicate and shorter-lived. There are several cultivars, differing both in the color of the flower and shape of the leaves. Tomentose stems branch out from the upright base. The linear leaves are roughly dentate-laciniate in form, pilose and whitish on both sides. The flowers grow singly in simple capitula, the colors ranging from red to yellow, often with different shades on the same head.
Height of plant 15–24 in. (40–60 cm.).
Size of flower 2–2¾ in. (5–7 cm.).
Place of origin A cultivated hybrid, its progenitors came from South Africa.
Flowering time Summer.
Cultivation Full sun or open, sunny positions. Temperate climate. Dislikes very cold weather and wet conditions. Prefers rich, damp soil of average consistency. Responds well to organic feeding and regular watering. Bushy growth can be encouraged by pinching out the growing points of the young plants.
Propagation By seed. Start seeds under glass in pans or sow directly in the garden after last frost.
Qualities Hardy. Easy to grow.

26 ARUNCUS DIOICUS (Thomas Walter) Merritt Lyndon Fernald
Syns.: *A. sylvestris* Vincinz Franz Kosteletzky; *Spiraea aruncus* Carolus Linnaeus. Common name: Goat's beard.

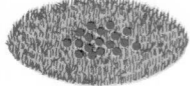

Family Rosaceae.
Description This bushy perennial is often very useful in improving shadowy corners in shrubberies because of its plumes of flowers. Its fairly large leaves, which are carried on long petioles, are bi- or tri-pinnate with double-serrated ovate-acute leaflets. The tiny whitish flowers are clustered in dense spicate racemes to form plumelike terminal panicles.
Height of plant 40–60 in. (1–1.50 m.).
Size of flower 10–20 in. (25–50 cm.) each panicle.
Place of origin Central Europe.
Flowering time Summer.
Cultivation Partial shade. Fairly frost-resistant. Prefers moist or very moist noncalcareous humus-rich soils or the natural leaf mold of a shrubbery. Requires organic feeding in the spring and generous watering, because it loses leaves and flowers in dry conditions. Cut all stems back to ground level in the autumn. This plant does not flower well in poor, dry soil.
Propagation By division of the clump in autumn.
Qualities Grows well by a pool, stream or marshy ground. Hardy. Easy to grow.

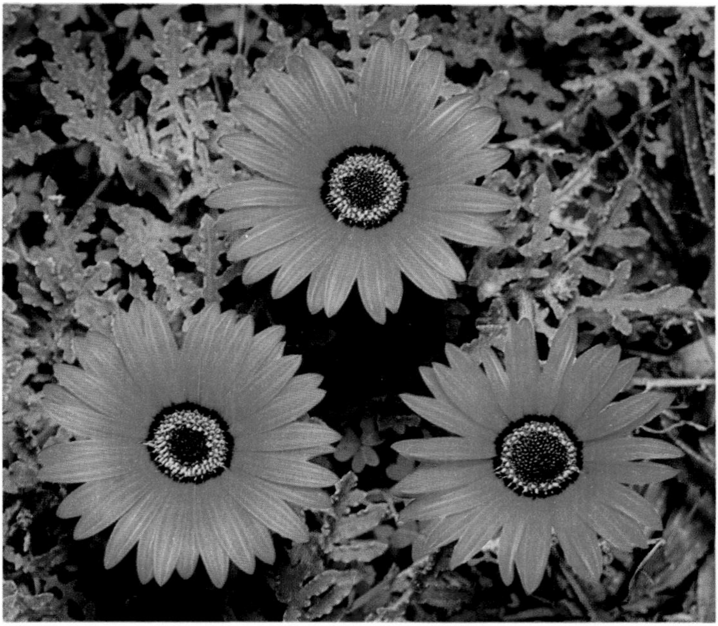

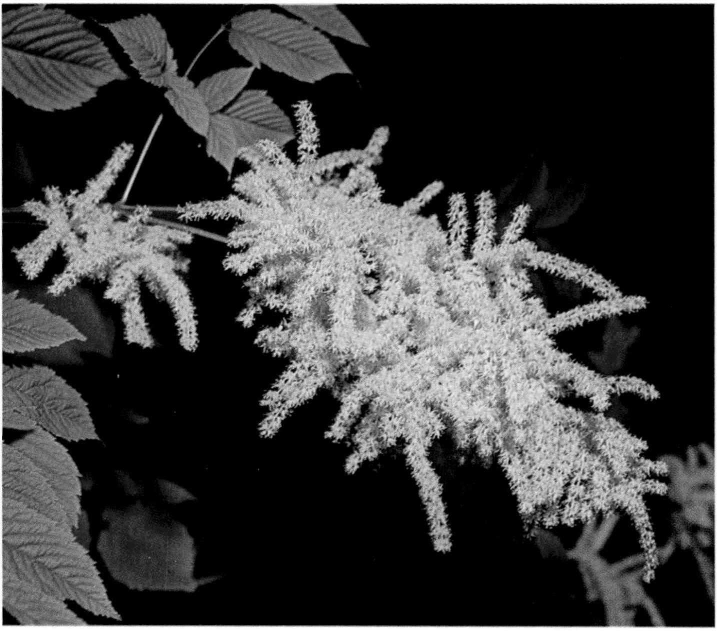

27 ASTER AMELLUS Carolus Linnaeus
Common name: Italian aster

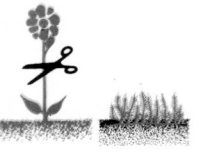

Family Compositae.
Description Bushy perennial with slender, pubescent, up-right stems which branch out toward the top. The dark-green leaves are alternate, ovate-lanceolate and dentate. Flowers are borne in daisylike capitula, the linear ray flowers being blue or violet with a golden-yellow central disc. The flowers are often joined together in loose corymbs. The plant, of which there are several cultivars, is very popular because of its free-flowering habit.
Height of plant 16–24 in. (40–60 cm.).
Size of flower 1¾–2½ in. (4.5–6 cm.).
Place of origin Southern Europe, Western Asia.
Flowering time Late summer–early autumn.

Cultivation A very sunny position—full sun if possible. Temperate climate but can withstand the cold well. Any deep, fertile, open-textured soil, rich in organic material, moist but permeable. Requires feeding with organic manure and minerals such as phosphates, nitrogen and potash. Water plentifully. Light cutting back of top growth encourages sprouting. Pests and diseases: aphids, rusts and oidium.
Propagation Sow in boxes under glass in the spring and prick out. Also by clump division in the spring or autumn.
Qualities Hardy. Easy to grow.

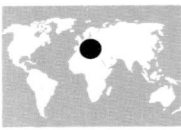

---

28 AUBRIETA DELTOIDEA Augustin Pyramus De Candolle
Common name: Purple rock-cress.

Family Cruciferae.
Description A dainty little perennial that spreads into a large cushionlike formation—whether on level ground, in a rockery or tumbling down a wall—covered with a mass of brilliant flowers. Its prostrate-ascending stems are well branched. The small leaves are persistent, alternate, pubescent and spatulate in shape, joined into rosettes. The flowers grow in small racemes and are so numerous that they hide the leaves. The four-petal corolla is cruciate. The colors range, depending on the cultivar, from violet, mauve, pink and white to wine-red.
Height of plant 4–6 in. (10–15 cm.).
Size of flower ⅜ in. (1 cm.).
Place of origin Southern Europe; Asia minor.
Flowering time Spring.

Cultivation Full sun to partial shade. Temperate climate. Fairly frost-resistant. Prefers a moist, permeable soil or rich, clayey-sandy loam. Does not require watering and needs no particular attention.
Propagation By division in spring or autumn; by cuttings in spring; by seed sown in pans in spring and put into a cold-frame.
Qualities Hardy. Easy to grow.

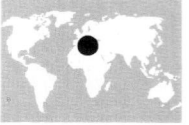

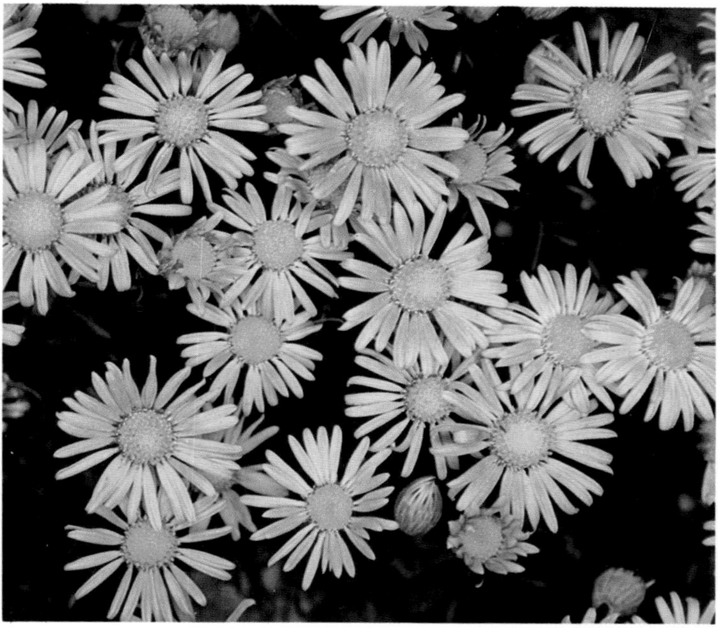

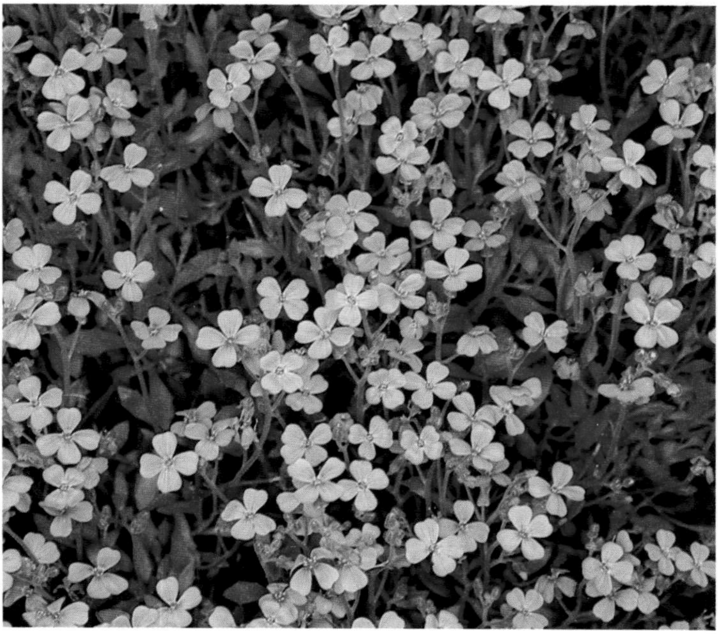

29 BAUHINIA GRANDIFLORA Antoine Laurent Jussieu
Common name: Orchid tree

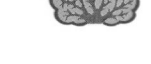

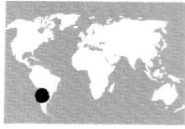

Family   Caesalpiniaceae.
Description   A semi-evergreen tree that likes a warm-temperate climate, this will grow outdoors in the gardens of warm coastal areas or where the winters are mild and rarely reach 32° F. (0° C.). It has a treelike stem with strong, slightly drooping branches; its head is shaped like an umbrella. The leaves, set alternately, are unusually oval-subcordate, almost coriaceous and divided into two distinct lobes. The large flowers are axillary, sometimes growing in clusters, strongly reminiscent of a flight of butterflies. Other good species are *B. blakeana* (red tones), *B. forficata* (creamy white), *B. variegata* (lavender, white or pink).
Height of plant   13–17 ft. (4–5 m.).
Size of flower   2–3 in. (5–8 cm.).
Flowering time   Summer.

Cultivation   Sunny but very sheltered position. Climate temperate. Grows in almost any kind of well-drained, rich, moist soil, even if slightly clayey. Appreciates occasional organic/mineral feeding. Requires a lot of watering. Cutting back after flowering encourages new growth.
Propagation   By spring or autumn sowing in small pots in a warm greenhouse. Will be ready for planting in the flowering position in the second or third year.
Qualities   Half-hardy. Very easy to grow.

---

30 BEGONIA SEMPERFLORENS Heinrich Friedrich Link and Friedrich Otto
Common name: Wax begonia

Family   Begoniaceae.
Description   Bushy annual bedding plant with articulate-nodose succulent stems. Its fragile leaves are set alternately; they are ovate-oblong or subcordate, bright green with metallic shading and carried on long petioles. The stems and petioles are a brownish-red. The flowers are simple, plentiful and joined together in the top axillaries to spread out and bloom in ascending order. There are many cultivars in various colors.
Height of plant   4–16 in. (10–40 cm.).
Size of flower   ½–¾ in. (1.5–2 cm.).
Place of origin   Originally from Brazil but now widespread.
Flowering time   Spring–summer.

Cultivation   A light position, out of direct sunlight. Temperate climate. Soilless compost—or forest litter, if available—mixed with peat, sand and well-sieved and seasoned organic manure. Requires regular and plentiful watering and a periodic liquid feed during growth. Pests and diseases: Insects; various types of rot, oidium and various cryptogams.

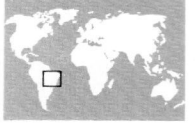

Propagation   By seed in pans at the end of the winter under glass. Prick out as soon as two or three leaves appear and pot on into boxes or flowerpots. When plant begins to look straggly, cut back on a level with new growth to encourage sprouting. Take cuttings from the adult plant.
Qualities   Very hardy. Easy to grow.

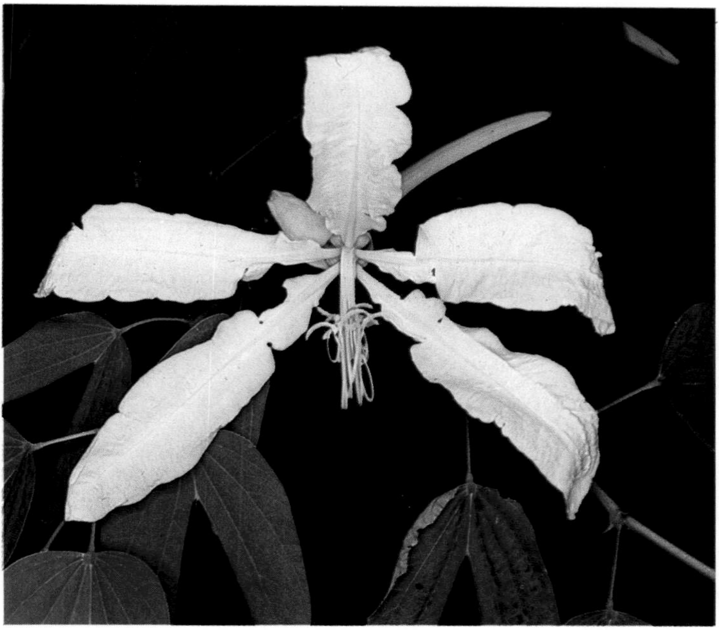

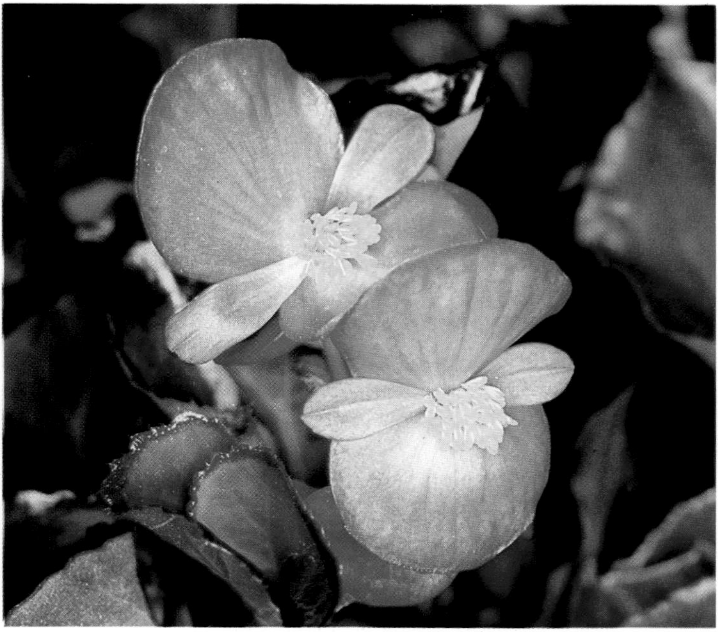

31 BEGONIA x TUBERHYBRIDA A. Voss
Syn.: *B. tuberosa* Hortorum

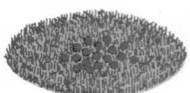

Family Begoniaceae.

Description A herbaceous perennial with a flattened succulent tuber and fibrous capillary roots. Its bushy, reddish-green stem is fleshy and articulate-nodose. The rather thick leaves are irregularly alternate and oblique cordate with lobed dentate rugose margins; they are medium green with metallic highlights. The single and double flowers are generally produced in groups of three on upright stems and resemble small camellias. Long flowering period. Colors: pink, salmon, white and yellow.

Height of plant 8–16 in. (20–40 cm.).

Size of flower 2½–6 in. (6–15 cm.).

Place of origin Cultivated hybrid.

Flowering time Summer.

Cultivation A moist position in partial shade. Thrives in foggy areas. Well-drained, rich, light soil or a mixture of equal parts well-rotted leaf mold and peat, sand and dry, well-seasoned manure with a little dried blood. Likes an occasional liquid feed and plenty of watering. After blooming, allow it to die back and overwinter tubers in dry peat indoors. Diseases: root rot, leaf spot, cucumber mosaic, tomato spotted wilt, oidium.

Propagation By fully developed commercially grown tubers. By seed, although this is a laborious process. By stem cuttings from basal shoots thrown up by tubers put to germinate at the end of the winter in a heated greenhouse.

Qualities Very easy to grow. Half-hardy.

32 BELLIS PERENNIS Carolus Linnaeus, cv. flore pleno
Common name: English daisy

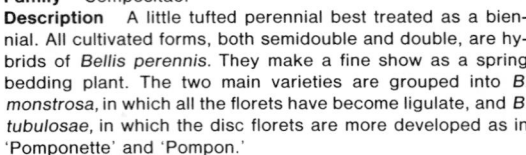

Family Compositae.

Description A little tufted perennial best treated as a biennial. All cultivated forms, both semidouble and double, are hybrids of *Bellis perennis*. They make a fine show as a spring bedding plant. The two main varieties are grouped into *B. monstrosa,* in which all the florets have become ligulate, and *B. tubulosae,* in which the disc florets are more developed as in 'Pomponette' and 'Pompon.'

Height of plant 4–6 in. (10–15 cm.).

Size of flower 1⅛–4 in. (3–10 cm.).

Place of origin Parent species originated in Europe.

Flowering time Spring–summer.

Cultivation A light or partially shaded position. Temperate climate. Withstands the cold quite well. Prefers soils that are rich in organic materials and moderately calcareous or sandy-clayey. Responds well to liquid feeding in the early stages of growth and frequent watering. Pests and diseases: aphids, oidium and rust.

Propagation Sow seed outdoors in the spring. Plants can be treated as annuals if seed is sown under glass in late winter. The large, sterile flowered varieties of *B. monstrosa* can be increased by clump division after flowering, the small plants being brought on in a sheltered coldframe.

Qualities Hardy. Easy to grow.

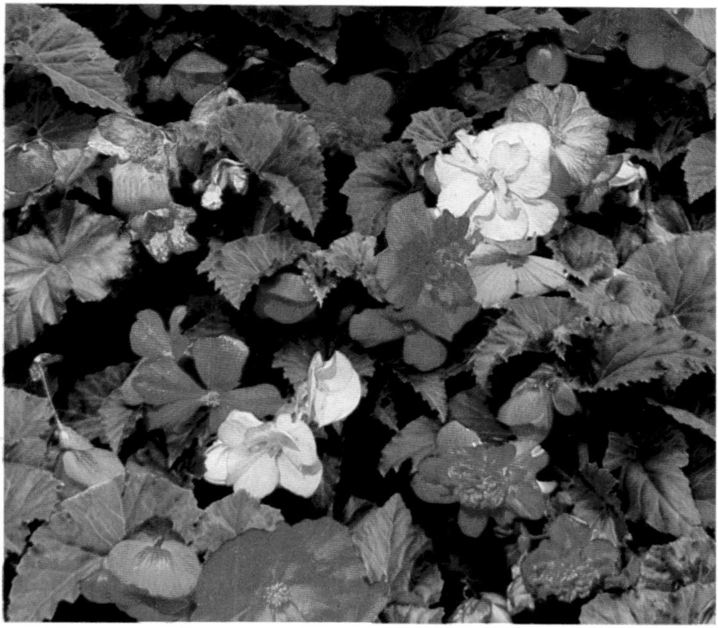

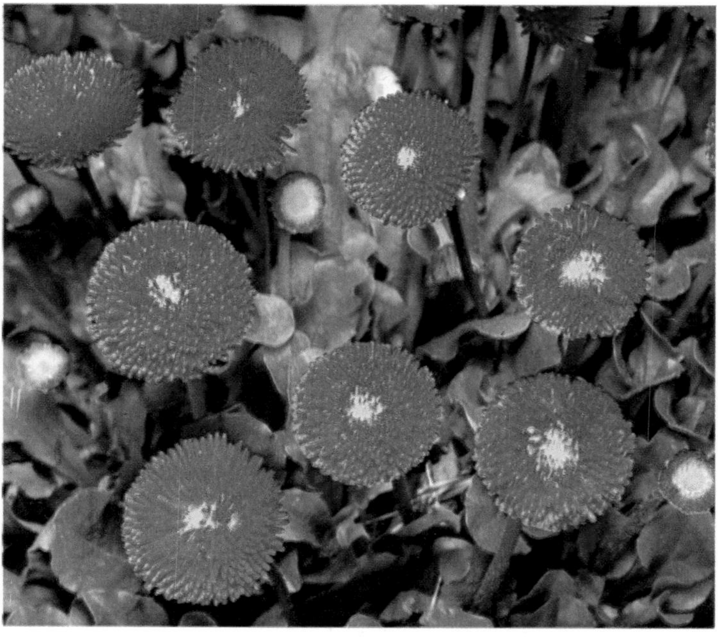

33 BELLIS PERENNIS Carolus Linnaeus cv. fl. simpl.
Common name: Single English daisy

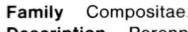

Family Compositae.
Description Perennial in its natural form but grown as an annual in its various cultivated species for its floriferousness. Grows in low tufts in a tight rosette of oblong-spatulate, crenulate leaves. The flowers are borne in single capitula with a large yellow disc surrounded by a dense crown of ligulate florets. Several selected colors are available: white, pink, red and striped.
Height of plant 3–6 in. (8–15 cm.).
Size of flower ¾–2 in. (2–5 cm.).
Place of origin Parent species originated in Europe.
Flowering time Spring–summer.
Cultivation A light or partially shaded position. Temperate climate. Withstands the cold quite well. Suited to all types of soil but prefers clayey-humus, moist ground that has been prepared with well-seasoned manure. Appreciates occasional liquid feeding and frequent watering.
Propagation Sow in late winter in pans under glass and prick out.
Qualities Hardy. Easy to grow.

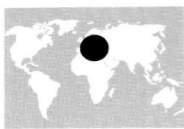

---

34 BERBERIS DARWINII William Jackson Hooker
Common name: Barberry

Family Berberidaceae.
Description Evergreen shrub of bushy habit which branches up prolifically from the base. The leaves grow in axillary clusters; they are alternate, sessile, oblong or cuneate-dentate, coriaceous, with prickly margins and about ⅜–1 in. (1–2.5 cm.) long. Orange flowers are abundantly borne on long peduncles and arranged in pendulous racemes of 15–20 flowers. The little blue-black berries have a turquoisy bloom. There are dwarf and a semi-prostrate and spreading variety as well.
Height of plant 5–10 ft. (1.50–3 m.).
Size of flower ⅜–½ in. (1–1.3 cm.).
Place of origin Chile and Patagonia (Argentina).
Flowering time Spring and sporadically in the autumn.

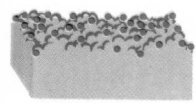

Cultivation A light or partially shaded position. Frost-resistant. Undemanding, it prefers an acid soil but also grows in moist, moderately calcareous or humus-rich ground. Watering necessary only in very dry periods. Appreciates periodic organic feeding. Pruning limited to thinning and trimming. Very disease-resistant.
Propagation By seed sown in the spring after stratification, although very slow. Alternatively, lateral-shoot, semi-hardwood or hardwood cuttings, treated with hormone powder, taken in autumn or spring and brought on in a coldframe.
Qualities Hardy. Easy to grow.

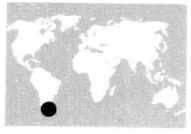

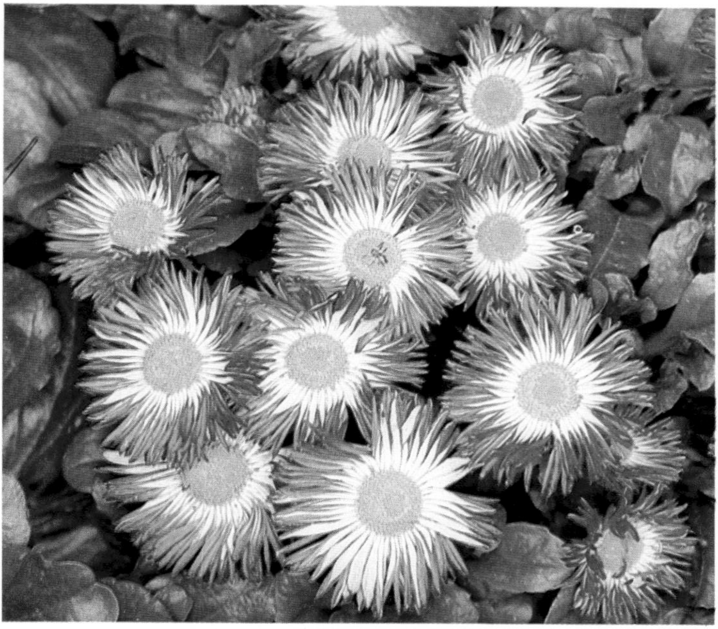

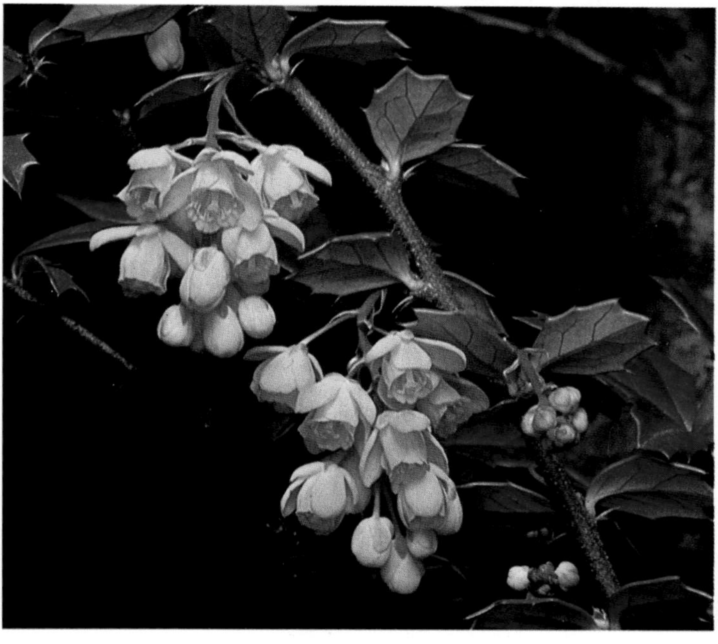

35 BERGENIA CRASSIFOLIA (Carolus Linnaeus) K. Fritsch
Syn.: *Megasea*

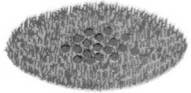
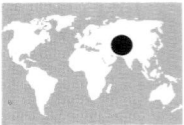

Family Saxifragaceae.
Description Thick-stemmed perennial, strongly branching, of prostrate-ascending habit. Its large persistent leaves are ovate-rounded, gibbous and quite thick. The flowers are numerous and arranged in axillary cymes. Very hardy, this is a rewarding plant in the spring because of its floriferousness. The varieties include several shades of pink.
Height of plant 6–12 in. (15–30 cm.).
Size of flower ¾–1 in. (2–2.5 cm.).
Place of origin Nepal and Siberia (Central Asia).
Flowering time Spring.
Cultivation Sun or shade. Frost-resistant. Will grow in almost any soil, preferring well-drained garden soil with humus, but also does well in stony ground and rockeries. Light organic feeding produces luxuriant growth. It can withstand dry conditions very well but appreciates some watering in the summer. No cutting back required except for the removal of dead flowers and leaves. Replant in a new position about every three or four years.
Propagation By clump division or rhizome cuttings in the spring.

36 BIGNONIA CAPREOLATA Carolus Linnaeus
Syn.: *Tecoma crucigera* (Linnaeus) Bureau, *Doxantha capreolata* Miers Common names: Crossvine, trumpet flower.

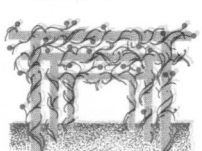

Family Bignoniaceae.
Description A vigorous climbing evergreen plant of compact habit with long, slender branches. Its compound, ovate-lanceolate leaves are binate and arranged opposite each other; they are coriaceous, pale green and equipped with tendrils. The flowers, which have very showy red or yellow-orange corollas, are clustered into axillary cymes. The fruits are like long, pendulous siliquae.
Height of plant 33–50 ft. (10–15 m.).
Size of flower 2–2¾ in. (5–7 cm.).
Place of origin Southeastern United States.
Flowering time Summer.
Cultivation A sunny position. Cannot withstand heavy frosts. Climbs by means of tendrils and requires supporting. Will grow in any soil but prefers rich clay. Requires feeding with manure and plenty of watering in the summer. Prune in the autumn or winter to prevent the plant from getting straggly; all dead material and weak growth should be cut away. Spray frequently with insecticides; bignonia attracts aphids and other insects.
Propagation By cuttings, layering and air layering in the spring or summer. Or by spring seed sowing under glass.
Qualities Half-hardy. Easy to grow.

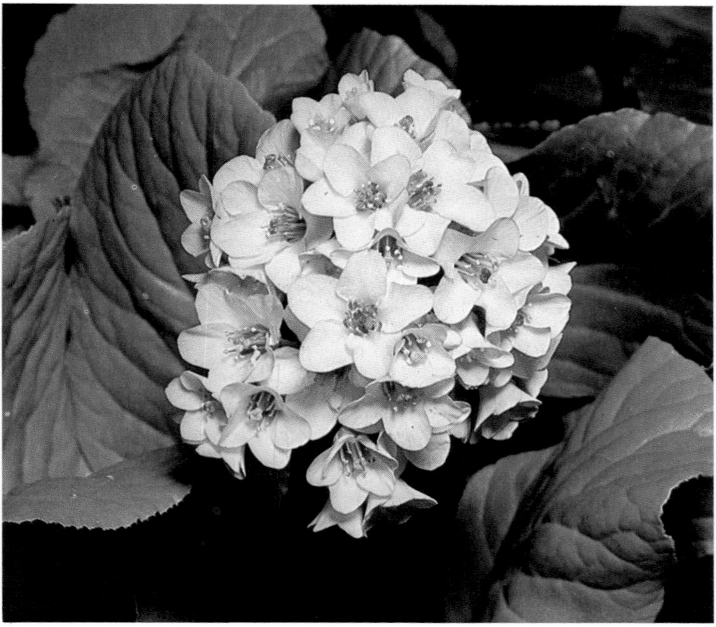

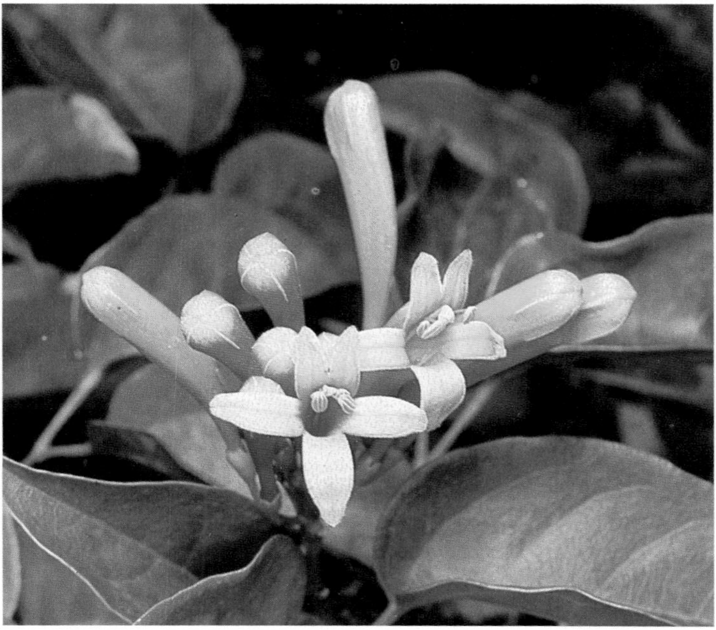

37 BIGNONIA UNGUIS-CATI Carolus Linnaeus
Syn.: *B. Tweediana* John Lindley

Family Bignoniaceae.
Description Although a member of the beautiful bignonia genus, this is less hardy than the others and thrives only in temperate climates. A vigorous climber, it puts out numerous slender branches that either hang down or entwine themselves around supports. Leaves are small and fused into groups of ovate-acute leaflets, truncated at the base. Axillary flowers are borne singly or in pairs. Its dehiscent fruits are like cylindrical siliquae, about 12 in. (30 cm.) long and ⅜–¾ in. (1–2 cm.) broad.
Height of plant 39–65 ft. (12–20 m.).
Size of flower 2–2¾ in. (5–7 cm.).
Place of origin Argentina and Brazil.
Flowering time Summer.
Cultivation An open, sunny position. Not frost-resistant. Likes a soil that is fairly compact, clayey-sandy, rich in organic material, moist but well-drained. Periodic organic/mineral feeding. Can withstand a certain amount of dryness but appreciates regular watering. Trimming back and quite severe thinning encourages more flowers.
Propagation By hardwood or semi-hardwood cuttings in summer. Or by layering or air layering.
Qualities Easy to grow.

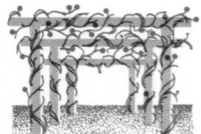

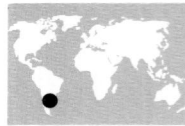

38 BILDERDYKIA AUBERTII (Louis Henry) Moldenke
Syn.: *Polygonum aubertii* Henry. Common name: Silver lace vine

Family Polygonaceae.
Description A quick-growing and prolific climbing plant. Its dainty habit and exceptional floriferousness give the impression of a cloud of white florets enveloping the whole plant. It has slender, twining stems and branches out in all directions. Its alternate leaves are spear-shaped/cordate or lanceolate and sinuate-undulate. The innumerable white or greenish-white flowers are arranged in long axillary or terminal panicles. This plant is often confused with *P. baldschuanicum* (Russian vine), which can be distinguished by its pinkish-white flowers.
Height of plant 33–50 ft. (10–15 m.).
Size of flower 2 in. (5 cm.).
Place of origin Turkestan, Western China and Tibet.
Flowering time Summer–autumn.
Cultivation Sunny or partially shaded position. Can withstand the cold very well. Flourishes in nearly all types of soil provided it is moist and rich. Requires a lot of watering. It loses most of its leaves and flowers under dry conditions. Cut back in the autumn. Trouble-free.
Propagation By layering or by semi-hardwood cuttings in the summer or autumn. Sometimes by seed in the spring in a cold-frame.
Qualities Hardy. Easy to grow.

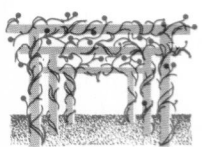

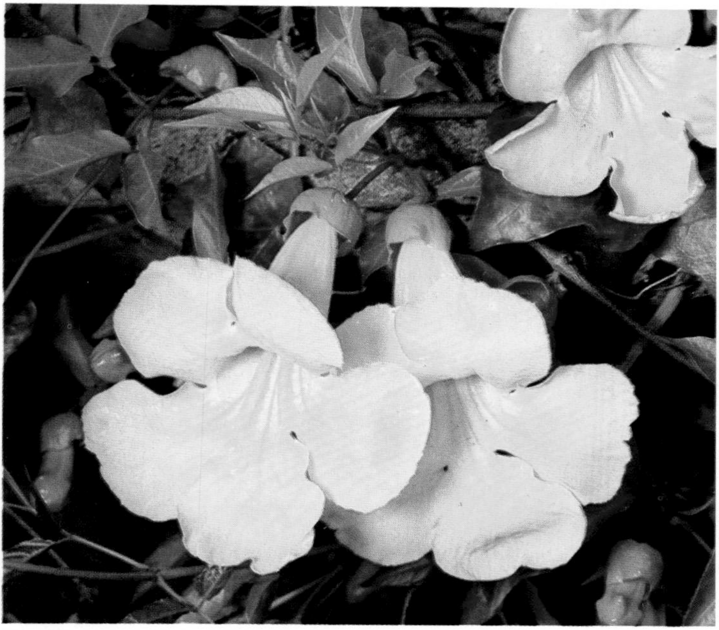

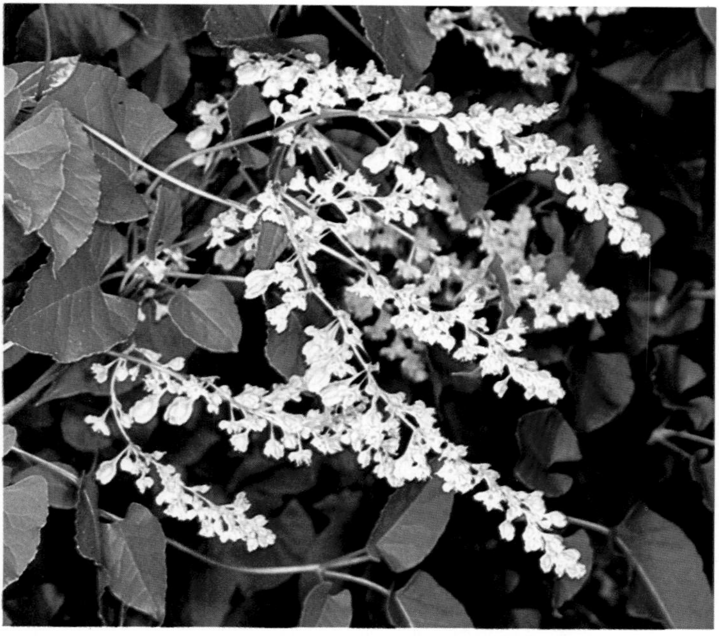

39 BLETILLA HYACINTHYNA Heinrich Gustav Reichenbach
Syns.: *B. striata, Bletia hyacinthyna*

Family Orchidaceae.
Description A tufted plant with numerous flattened, rounded pseudobulbs growing just beneath the surface. The cartilagenous leaves are fasciculate-lanceolate and averse, leaving the venation in relief. Five to ten flowers are borne on upright stems, accompanied by small bracts at the base of a short peduncle. This most attractive terrestrial orchid is both hardy and exotic; it can be grown outdoors in temperate areas. There is also a white-flowered variety.
Height of plant 12–16 in. (30–40 cm.).
Size of flower 1½–2 in. (4–5 cm.).
Place of origin China and Japan.
Flowering time Summer.
Cultivation Partial shade. Temperate climate and can withstand frost if well mulched with leaves or straw. Prefers a humus-rich leaf-mold type of soil or ordinary garden soil with peat and heath mold added. It can be grown in pots and containers on a terrace, deck, etc., but needs regular watering. Before it takes its winter rest, all stems and leaves should be cut down to ground level.
Propagation By clump division in autumn or spring.
Qualities Half-hardy. Easy to grow.

40 BOUGAINVILLEA x BUTTIANA Hortorum

Family Nyctaginaceae.
Description Several varieties of bougainvillea are available that offer a wide choice of flower size and color. Many are very lovely and give a fine show. Even the leaves are now often larger than on the original species. These hybrids have been produced by crossing various species and it is now almost impossible for them to revert to the parent plants—however, they are frequently less vigorous and hardy than *B. glabra* and *B. spectabilis*. They make good pot plants.
Height of plant 6½–16 ft. (2–5 m.).
Size of flower 1⅛–2 in. (3–5 cm.).
Place of origin A cultivated hybrid of *B. globosa* (originating from Brazil).
Flowering time Summer.
Cultivation Full sun. Warm temperate climate. Sheltered position, even in a warm coastal zone. Cannot withstand the cold. In northern areas this plant must be treated as a pot plant and kept in a heated greenhouse, to be put outdoors during the summer. Clayey-sandy soil or good garden soil, adding plenty of leaf mold. Periodic feeding with organic/mineral fertilizers, and regular watering. Prune to shorten main and lateral growths and remove any weak or dead material.
Propagation Semi-hardwood or hardwood cuttings in summer to bring on in a greenhouse. Air layering in spring or summer.
Qualities Half-hardy unless in a warm climate. Very easy.

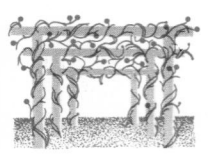

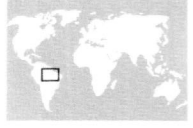

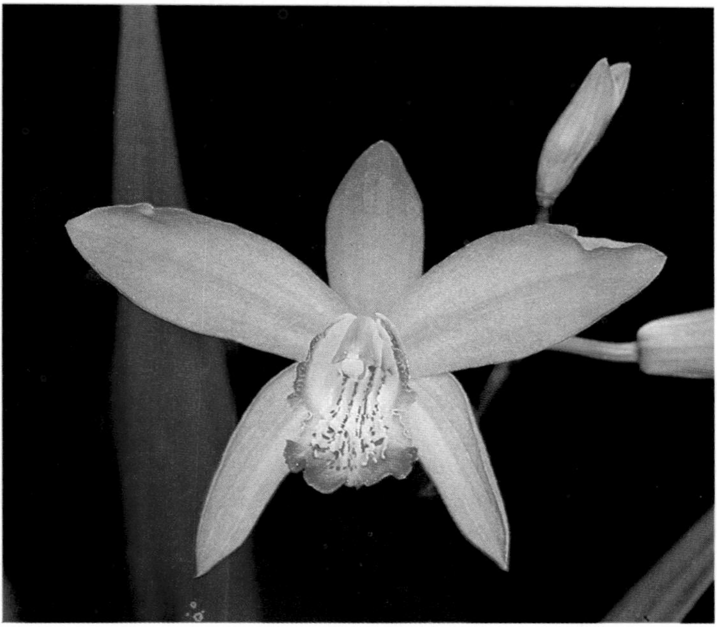

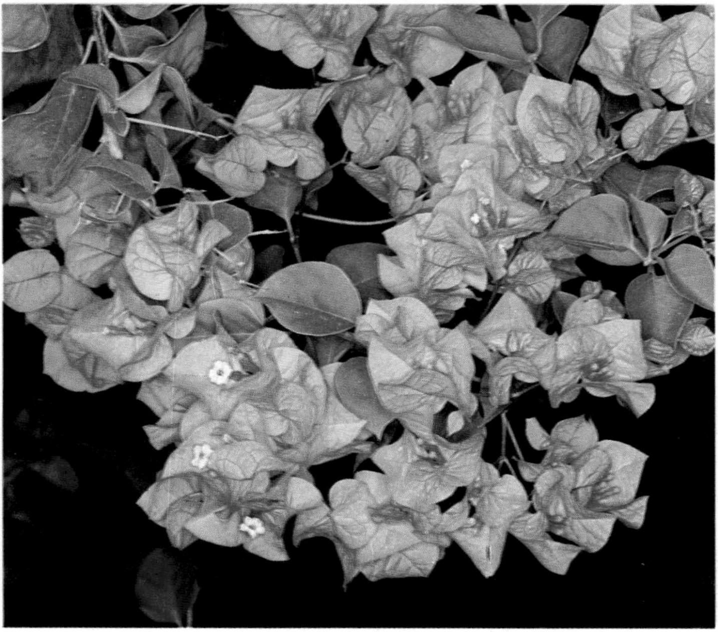

41 BOUGAINVILLEA GLABRA Jacques Denys Choisy, *var. sanderiana* Hortorum

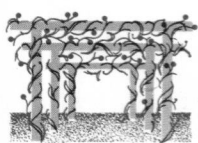

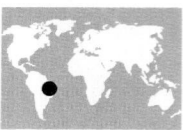

Family Nyctaginaceae.

Description Grown as a flowering climber in areas that enjoy a temperate to hot climate, this is a spectacular sight with its wealth of brilliant purple bracts, which contrast strikingly with the medium-green foliage. It ramifies strongly into spined branches. Leaves are small, ovate-acute and alternate. The little pale-yellow, tubulous flowers are arranged in threes within an involucre of three broad ovate-acute bracts that are often mistaken for flowers.

Height of plant 13–23 ft. (4–7 m.).

Size of flower 1⅛–1⅜ in. (3–3.5 cm.) each group of bracts.

Place of origin Brazil.

Flowering time Summer.

Cultivation Full sun. Temperate to hot climate in sheltered areas, against a wall; does well even if near the sea. Cannot withstand the cold and should be protected from it with plastic screens or covers. Can be grown as a pot plant in a warm greenhouse. Prefers a clayey-sandy soil enriched with manure. Requires occasional feeding with minerals but watering is not always necessary. Prune to shorten and contain the exuberant growth. Generally trouble-free.

Propagation By hardwood or semi-hardwood cuttings in the summer. Also by air layering.

Qualities Half-hardy. Easy to grow.

Opposite: a fine example of Bougainvillea glabra *var.* Sanderiana; *a close-up of the plant in which its small tubulous flowers, emerging between the brightly colored purple bracts, can clearly be seen.*

42 BUDDLEIA DAVIDII A. Franchet

Syn.: *B. variabilis* W. Botting Hemsley; Buddleja.
Common name: Butterfly bush.

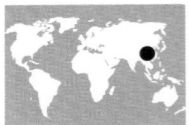

Family Loganiaceae.
Description A deciduous shrub, widely grown for its long, profuse flower spikes. From its base it throws up sturdy growths that are at first upright, then decumbent. Its leaves are entire—although crenulate-serrated—lanceolate and opposite; they are green on top and a cottony-white underneath. The flowers are borne in panicles that are dense, conical and terminal, composed of numerous clusters of agglomerate flowers. There are more than 15 cultivars of different colors.
Height of plant 6–16 ft. (2–5 m.).
Size of flower $3/8$–$9/16$ in. (1–1.5 cm.), each panicle 12–24 in. (30–60 cm.) long.
Place of origin China.
Flowering time Summer.
Cultivation Full sun to partial shade. Withstands the cold well, especially if protected by a good mulch in the autumn. Flourishes in almost any type of soil, even if calcareous, provided it is rich and moist. If growth is slow, enrich soil with manure and minerals. Requires regular watering. Prune hard in the autumn. Pests and diseases: aphids and viruses.
Propagation By semi-hardwood and hardwood cuttings taken in spring or autumn.
Qualities Hardy. Easy to grow.

---

43 BUDDLEIA MADAGASCARIENSIS Jean Baptiste Lamarck

Common name: Yellow buddleia

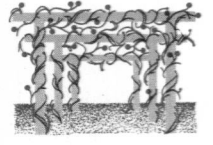

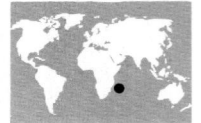

Family Loganiaceae.
Description This species is a very rewarding climbing plant. It is often to be seen clambering over the walls and on the sloping banks of gardens in warm coastal areas. Its long sarmentose ramifications require support. It is deciduous, with very large, rugose leaves. Its very striking inflorescences are composed of a great many tubulous ray florets, each with four yellow-orange petals arranged on long, stiff spikes.
Height of plant 6–20 ft. (2–6 m.).
Size of flower $1/8$–$3/8$ in. (0.5–1 cm.).
Place of origin Madagascar.
Flowering time Spring.
Cultivation Full sun or partial shade. Warm-temperate climate in a sheltered position. Cannot withstand the cold. Where these requirements cannot be met, this makes a good greenhouse plant. It prefers good garden soil that is well-aerated, rich and moist. Requires organic/mineral feeding and plenty of water in the summer. Prune hard in autumn or winter.
Propagation By taking semi-hardwood and hardwood cuttings in the summer. Alternatively, by air layering.
Qualities Suitable for growing in large flowerpots or containers. Very easy to grow.

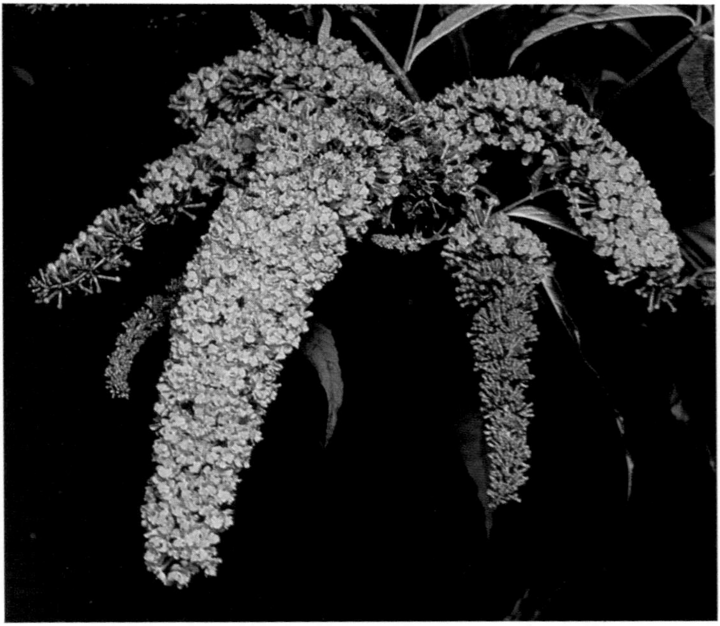

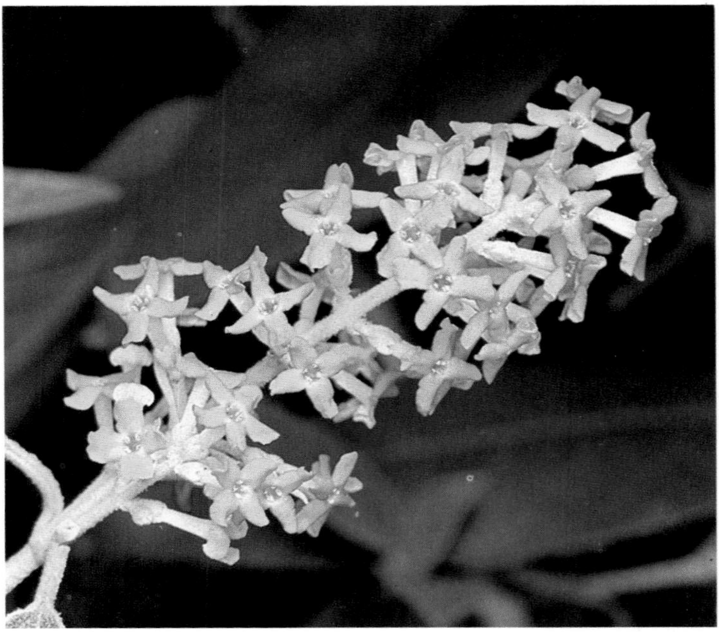

44 CAESALPINA GILLIESII Nathanael Wallich
Syn.: *Poinciana gilliesii* William Jackson Hooker. Common name: Bird of paradise.

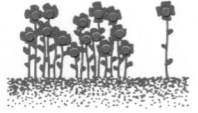

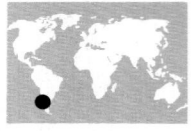

Family Caesalpiniaceae.
Description A small tree, attractive for its tiny foliage and its prolonged period of flowering. Its ramifications are sparse and loose-growing with bright-green leaves that are alternate and bipinnate-compound. Its flowers are large and numerous, clustered into terminal pyramidal racemes and opening in an orderly way from the bottom upward. The corolla has five unequal petals and numerous fiery-red stamens joined into a delightful little plume that gives an elegance to the inflorescence.
Height of plant 6½–13 ft. (2–4 m.).
Size of flower 2⅜–4 in. (6–10 cm.).
Place of origin Argentina and Chile.
Flowering time Summer.
Cultivation Full sun. Warm-temperate climate. Sheltered but open position, even in coastal areas. Not frost-resistant, although can withstand temperatures of 28–27° F. (−2/−3° C.) if well mulched. Likes a well-aerated, damp, fertile, even sandy, soil. Appreciates occasional organic/mineral feeding; the area around its base should be lightly worked. Requires plenty of watering. The branches should be pruned hard in the autumn or late winter to encourage the plant to flower more freely.
Propagation By late-winter seed sowing in pans or, better still, pots placed in a greenhouse or heated frame. Pot on twice before planting out in the open.
Qualities Easy to grow.

45 CALCEOLARIA HERBEO-HYBRIDA A. Voss
Syn.: *C. herbacea* Hortorum. Common name: Calceolaria

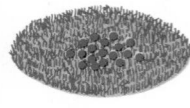

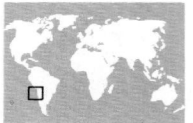

Family Scrophulariaceae.
Description A herbaceous annual, its basal leaves are arranged in a rosette; they are oval-rugose, crenulate, tomentose and tender. The floral stems are upright and the vesicular, highly decorative flowers are of particular interest for their strange inflated bag shape; they are joined together in terminal clusters. Color and size vary according to the different cultivars. The plant can be grown in a heated greenhouse.
Height of plant 10–18 in. (25–45 cm.).
Size of flower 1–1½ in. (2.5–4 cm.).
Place of origin A cultivated hybrid produced by crossing the numerous species of calceolaria, which originally came from Central and South America.
Flowering time End of spring.
Cultivation A light position but not in direct sunlight. Temperate climate. It is usually grown in a greenhouse and planted in the open when flowering has almost begun. Likes a loose-textured, porous mold enriched with equal parts leaf mold, peat, heath mold and sand, as well as an occasional feed with an organic/mineral fertilizer. Liquid feeding can be combined with watering but must be scrupulously controlled. Pests and diseases: aphids, root rot and fungus diseases.
Propagation By sowing in pans in early summer in a greenhouse and potting on at least twice.
Qualities Very delicate. Requires great care to grow.

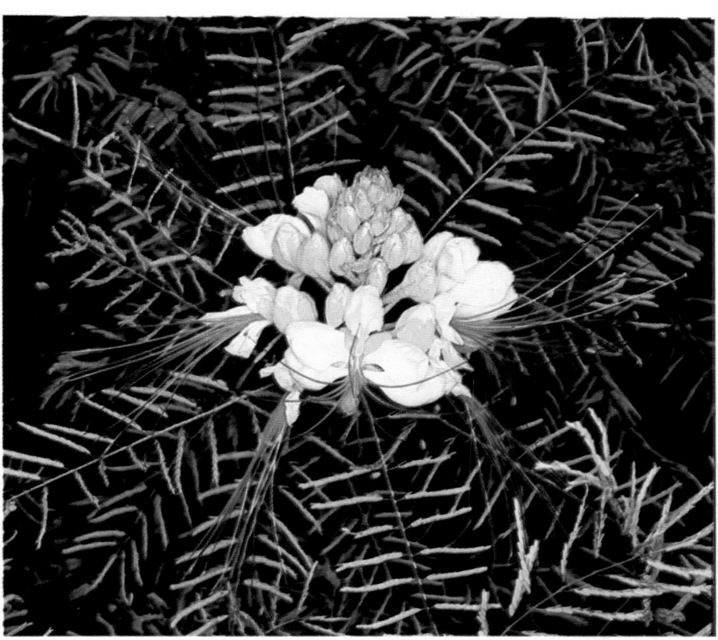

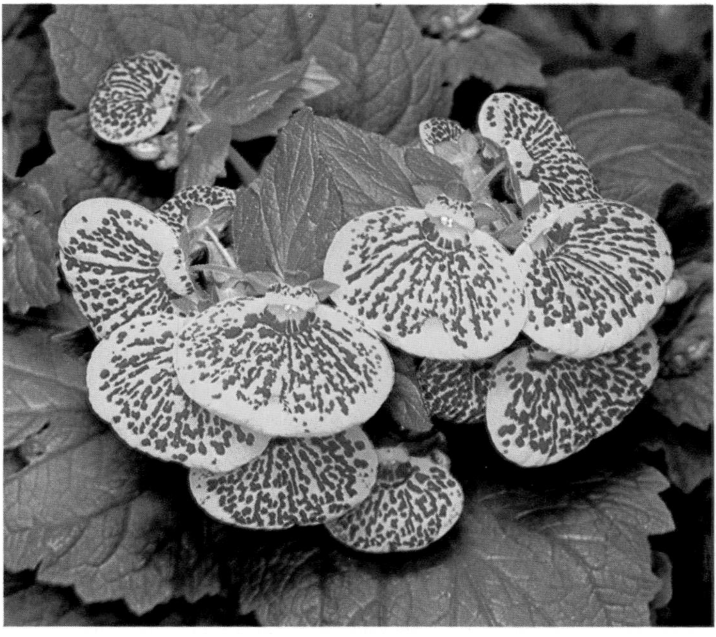

46 CALENDULA OFFICINALIS Carolus Linnaeus, cv. "Hortensis"
Common name: Pot marigold

Family Compositae.

Description A bushy annual with numerous ramifications from the base. Its light-green leaves are alternate, sessile and oblong-spatulate. The whole plant is glandulous-pubescent and gives off a pungent aroma. Its orange flowers, which are formed in large capitula, are terminal and prolific. The species has single flowers but the many cultivars that have been developed have semidouble and double flowers in various shades. Its floriferousness, combined with long flowering time, are useful attributes when flowers are scarce.

Height of plant 8–16 in. (20–40 cm.).

Size of flower 1⅛–2 in. (3–5 cm.).

Place of origin Originally from southern Europe, its many cultivated varieties are now widespread.

Flowering time Spring, summer or autumn, depending on the climate and time of sowing.

Cultivation Sunny position. Can withstand fairly cold weather but not heavy frosts. Grows in almost any type of soil. Benefits from organic and liquid feeding as well as plenty of watering. Pests and diseases: aphids and root rot; also prone to oidium and rusts in damp conditions.

Propagation By seed sown in pans under glass or directly in the garden after frost is over.

Qualities Suitable for pots, terraces, balconies. Hardy. Easy to grow.

47 CALLISTEMON SPECIOSUS Augustin Pyramus DeCandolle
Syn.: *Metrosideros speciosus* John Sims. Common name: Bottle brush

Family Myrtaceae.

Description An attractive evergreen shrub that can be regarded as hardy in temperate regions. Slow-growing but very effective with its strange flowers. Its branches are sparse and upright with alternate, linear-lanceolate leaves. Abundant flowers are borne on cylindrical spikes with distinctively long stamens arranged like a brush. The globose, woody fruits remain tightly adherent to the branches for several years. Often grown in gardens in warm, coastal areas.

Height of plant 10–13 ft. (3–4 m.).

Size of flower 1–1⅛ in. (2.5–3 cm.).

Place of origin Southwestern Australia.

Flowering time Spring–summer.

Cultivation As sunny a position as possible and sheltered. Warm-temperate climate. Not very resistant to frost. Well-aerated soil, whether acid or calcareous, and not too rich. It can be grown in pots in heath mold mixed with shredded bark or forest litter. Feed like azaleas and water regularly. This plant may suddenly die because of an imbalance of absorption.

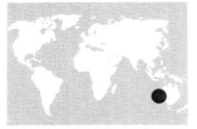

Propagation By springtime sowing in pans in a cool greenhouse; prick out and pot up. By semi-hardwood cuttings taken in late spring, planted in sand and brought on in a cool greenhouse.

Qualities Half-hardy. Very easy to grow.

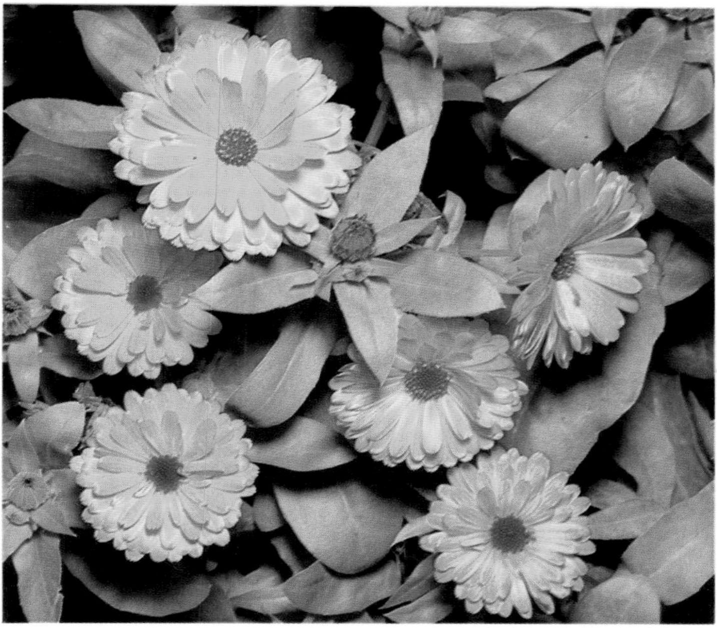

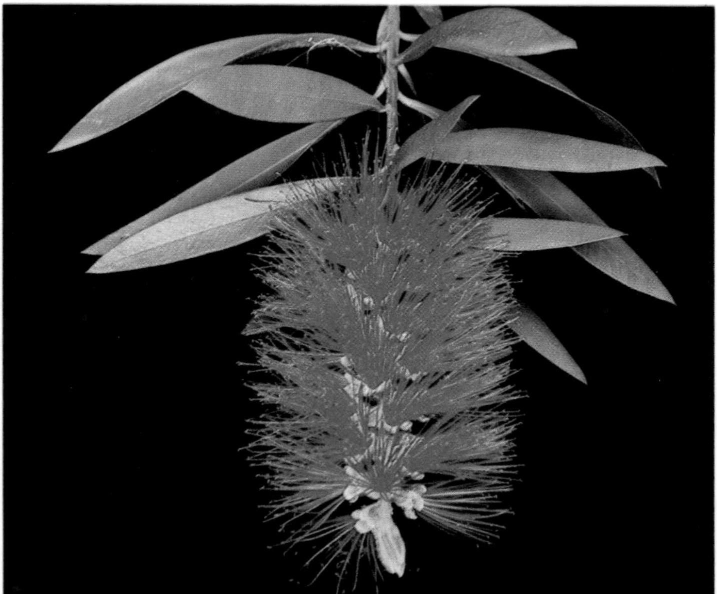

48 CALLISTEPHUS CHINENSIS Christian Gottfried Nees von Esenbeck
Syns.: *Aster sinensis* Carolus Linnaeus, *Callistephus hortensis* Alexandre Henri Gabriel Cassini.
Common name: China aster

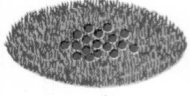

Family Compositae.
Description An annual that is widely grown for its lovely, brightly colored summer flowers. The species produces long upright ramifications bearing large terminal inflorescences in capitulum form. Its alternate leaves vary in shape and size, the lower ones being spatulate, rhomboidal and carried on petioles, the upper ones smaller, sessile and oblong. A great many varieties derive from the species. These include plants of various heights bearing single, semidouble and double flowers.
Height of plant 6–31 in. (15–80 cm.).
Size of flower 1½–4 in. (4–10 cm.).
Place of origin China and Japan.
Flowering time Spring–summer.
Cultivation These flowers need at least 14 hours of daylight to grow well. Temperate climate. Well-prepared garden soil with the addition of potassium phosphate. Watering should be well distributed. Excessive nitrogenous feeding makes the plants vulnerable to various diseases such as root rot, oidium and rusts, as well as parasitic animals.
Propagation Late winter or spring sowing under glass for summer flowers. Also directly in the garden after frost.

49 CALTHA PALUSTRIS Carolus Linnaeus
Common names: Marsh marigold, cowslip

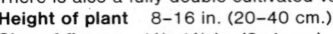

Family Ranunculaceae.
Description A perennial, this plant enjoys marshy, damp conditions. It is useful in shallow water and places where water seeps through. Floriferous stems are borne on divaricate ramifications, often stoloniferous. Its crenulate-dentate leaves are cordate or reniform. The abundant flowers are borne singly. There is also a fully double cultivated variety.
Height of plant 8–16 in. (20–40 cm.).
Size of flower 1⅛–1½ in. (3–4 cm.).
Place of origin Europe, in wet places in mountainous areas.
Flowering time Spring–summer.
Cultivation Shady position. Cool temperate climate; it withstands the cold well and likes constant moisture, even in mountainous terrain. It prefers a clayey, siliceous woodland soil, preferably humus-rich; can also grow in calcareous ground. It thrives at pool edges and by slow-running streams where the water is semi-static. In the winter it loses its leaves. Does not require any special care.
Propagation By clump division or by seed in the spring.
Qualities Hardy. Easy to grow.

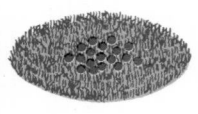
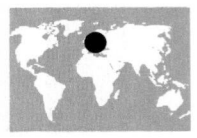

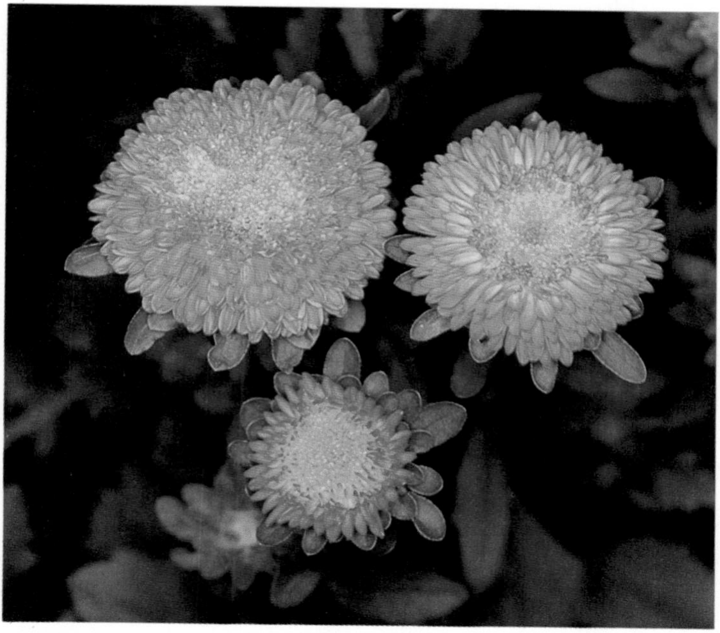

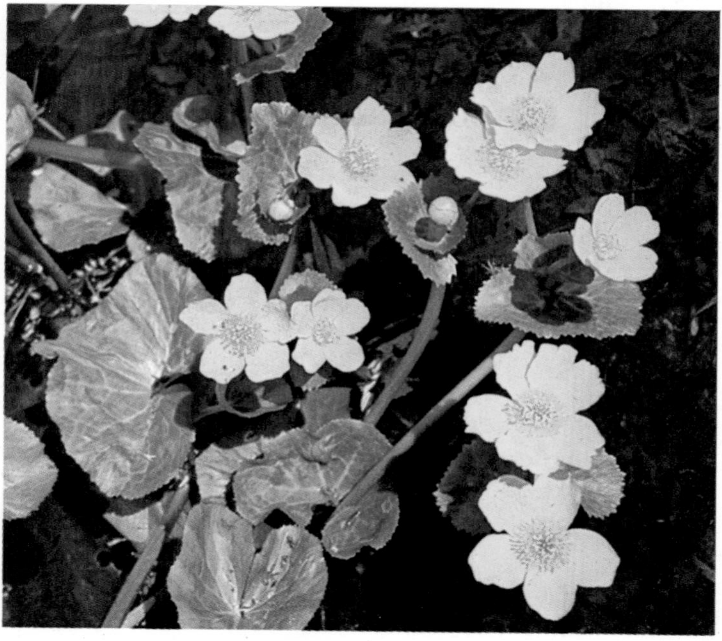

50 CAMELLIA JAPONICA Carolus Linnaeus cv. ''Flore Pleno''
Common name: Common camellia

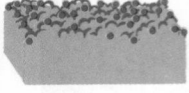

Family Theaceae.
Description An arborescent evergreen shrub or tree, of fairly compact habit and conical-pyramidal in shape. Its leaves are alternate, oval and crenulate-denticulate. The cultivated forms and varieties differ from *C. japonica* in the form of the flower—which is double—in size, and in the wide range of colors. Plants are very floriferous. The petals may be arranged in a tight rosette, fimbriated in the center or as an open rosette. A great many cultivars are available commercially. They are slower-growing than the species and those that have been produced by grafting do not usually grow very large.
Height of plant 6½–16½ ft. (2–5 m.).
Size of flower 2⅜–4¾ in. (6–12 cm.).
Place of origin Cultivated hybrid. Parent stock from Japan and Korea.
Flowering time Late winter, early spring.

Cultivation Slightly shaded, sheltered position. Temperate climate. Can withstand the cold well. Dislikes calcareous soil although this can be amended with the introduction of leaf mold, peat and heath mold in equal parts. Shredded lupines also make a good organic manure. If any yellowing of the leaves occurs, give an occasional application of chelated iron. Keep well watered with lime-free water. Pruning limited to light trimming of branches that are weak or too vigorous. Pests and diseases: subject to aphids and particularly to scale insects; excessive cold may damage the flower buds.
Propagation By semi-hardwood cuttings in the summer and by leaf cuttings, treated with hormone powder and put to root in a greenhouse. Also by air layering and grafting on to *C. japonica*.
Qualities Also suitable for containers on terraces, balconies. Hardy. Easy to grow.

Opposite: two cultivated double-flowered varieties of Camellia japonica; *top, the cv. ''Martin Cachet.''*

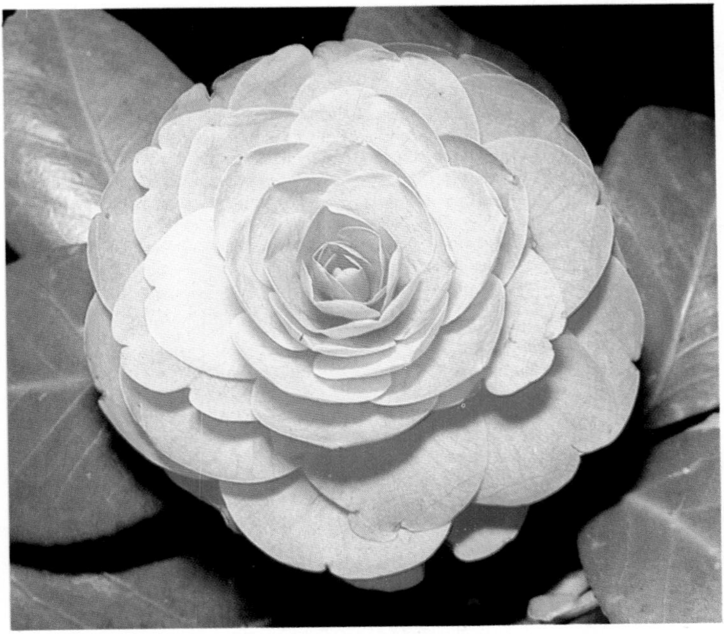

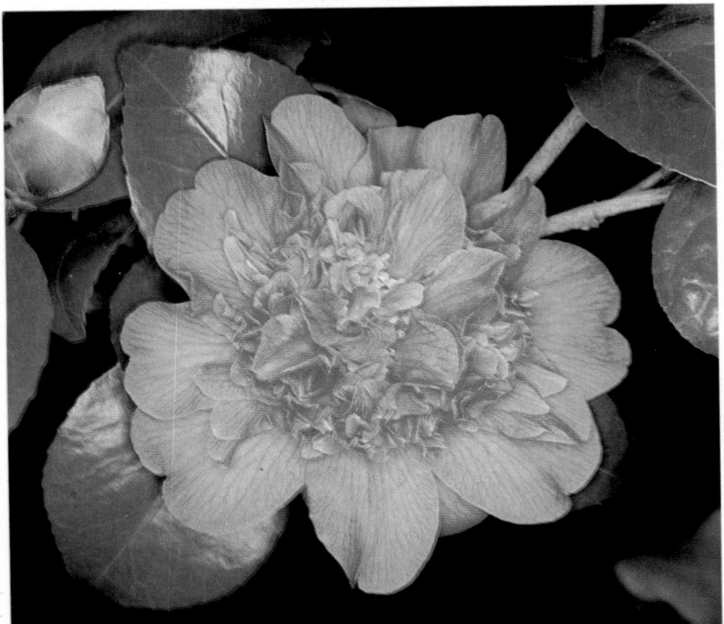

51 CAMELLIA JAPONICA Carolus Linnaeus cv. "Adolphe Audusson"

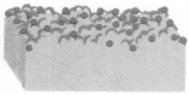

Family Theaceae.
Description One of the loveliest of evergreen shrubs, both for its flowers and foliage, this is of erect habit and conical-pyramidal in shape. Its numerous woody branches bear alternate, oval leaves with crenulate-denticulate margins. They are coriaceous in texture, a deep glossy green on top and pale underneath. The very decorative axillary and terminal flowers are carried individually or in groups of two or three. Crimson, violet or white according to the cultivar.
Height of plant 10–20 ft. (3–6 m.).
Size of flower 2–3⅛ in. (5–8 cm.).
Place of origin China and Japan.
Flowering time Late winter, early spring.
Cultivation Partial shade. Temperate climate but able to withstand temperatures down to 14° F. (−10° C.). Noncalcareous soil. Prefers rich soil, even a little clayey; if necessary, amend with equal parts heath mold or peat, shredded bark and a little sand. Slow-release fertilizer. Keep well watered with lime-free water and spray the leaves during the summer. Remove dead flowers and prune out dead or weak growth. Pests and diseases: scale insects and mealybugs, chlorosis.
Propagation By seed—a very slow process. By semi-hardwood cuttings taken in the summer. By air layering and grafting.
Qualities Suitable for pots or small tubs on balconies, terraces. Relatively easy to grow.

52 CAMPANULA CARPATICA Nicolous Joseph Jacquin
Common name: Carpathian bellflower

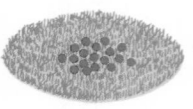

Family Campanulaceae.
Description A dainty, clump-forming perennial, especially attractive for its compact, dwarf habit and floriferousness. Its campanulate open flowers are carried terminally on numerous slender, erect stems. The leaves are cordate or oval-acute and dentate. This is one of the larger-flowered campanulas among the dwarf types. It is available in a number of cultivated varieties.
Height of plant 10–12 in. (25–30 cm.).
Size of flower 1 in. (2.5 cm.).
Place of origin Carpathian Mountains of eastern Europe.
Flowering time Late spring–summer.
Cultivation Shade-loving. Temperate climate, reasonably frostproof. Moist, well-drained position in any fertile soil that is neither very compact nor too calcareous. Requires plenty of watering. Does not like to be disturbed. Trouble-free.
Propagation By clump division in autumn or spring. By spring seed sowing in a coldframe, although the color may be different from that of the mother plant.
Qualities Hardy. Easy to grow.

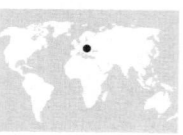

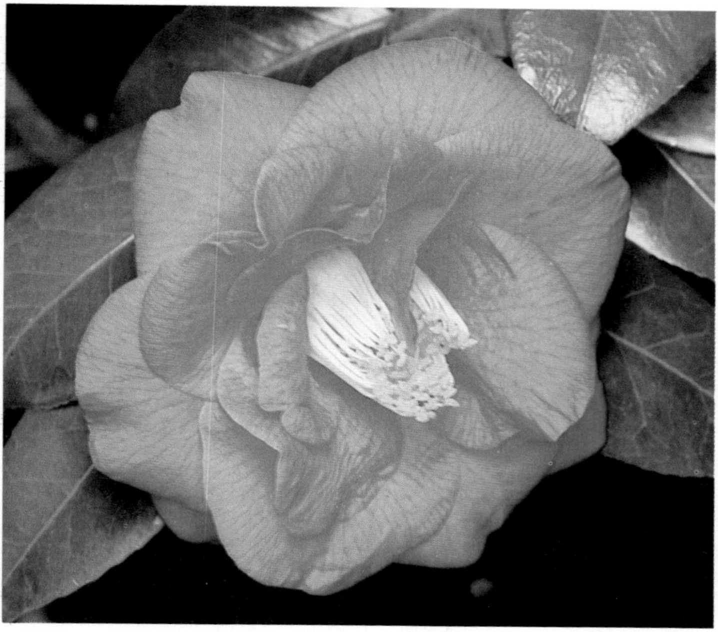

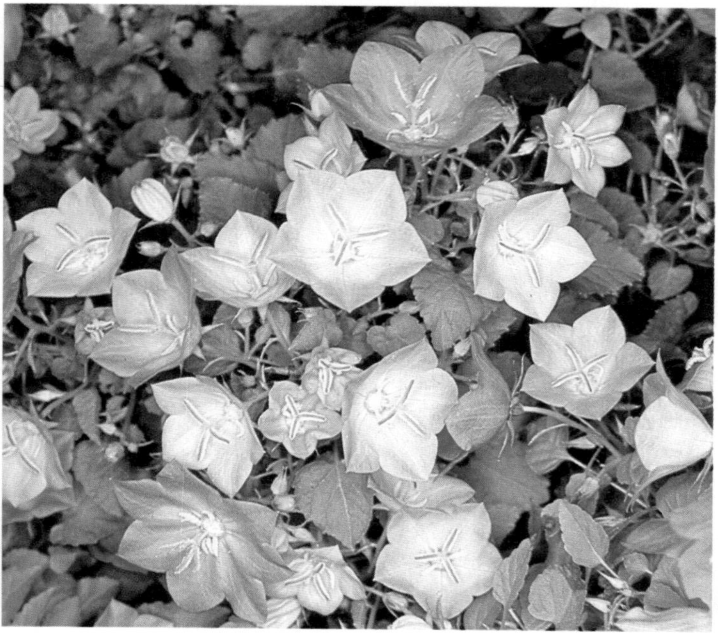

53 CAMPANULA MEDIUM Carolus Linnaeus
Syn.: *C. grandiflora* Jean Baptiste Lamarck. Common name: Canterbury bells

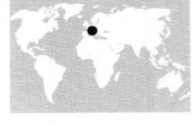

Family Campanulaceae.
Description A perennial that is often regarded as a biennial because it is not long-lived. Its erect stems branch out in pyramid form. Basal leaves are arranged in rosettes, the rest being alternate, oblong-lanceolate, sometimes small and sessile, hispid and rough-textured. The flowers are borne decoratively in large terminal racemes. There are some cultivated varieties with a more open double calyx in different colors (*C. medium*. cv. "Calycanthema").
Height of plant 12–18 in. (30–45 cm.).
Size of flower 1⅛–2 in. (3–5 cm.).
Place of origin Central Europe.
Flowering time Spring–summer.
Cultivation Full sun to partial shade. Temperate climate. Can withstand light frosts especially if protected by a good mulch. Prefers good humus-rich, calcareous soil; also well-aerated but moist conditions. Feed with manure and some liquid fertilizer. Requires regular and plentiful watering. Pests: likely to attract aphids and red spider mites.
Propagation By summer seed sowing in pans placed in a cool, shady place. Transplant in late autumn or, even better, the following spring.
Qualities Hardy. Easy to grow.

---

54 CAMPANULA PORTENSCHLAGIANA
Johann Jacob Roemer
Syn.: *C. muralis* Portenschlag-Mebermeyer. Common name: Dalmatian bellflower.

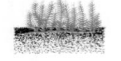

Family Campanulaceae.
Description A perennial with procumbent or climbing stems with numerous little cordate, rotundate-dentate leaves; it forms attractive cushions of small, lavender-blue flowers with a goblet-shaped corolla.
Height of plant 2–5 in. (6–12 cm.).
Size of flower ⅜–¾ in. (1–2 cm.).
Place of origin Dalmatia.
Flowering time Spring–summer.
Cultivation Shady position. Temperate climate, fairly frost-resistant. Rich, moist soil, quite well aerated and moderately calcareous. Also flourishes in cracks in dry walls, stone steps and rockeries. Requires no special attention but likes regular watering. Pests and diseases: slugs, snails and froghoppers; root rot.
Propagation By spring sowing in pots in a coldframe or directly in its flowering position. By clump division in late winter or autumn.
Qualities Hardy. Easy to grow.

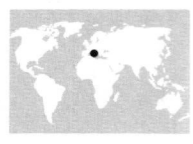

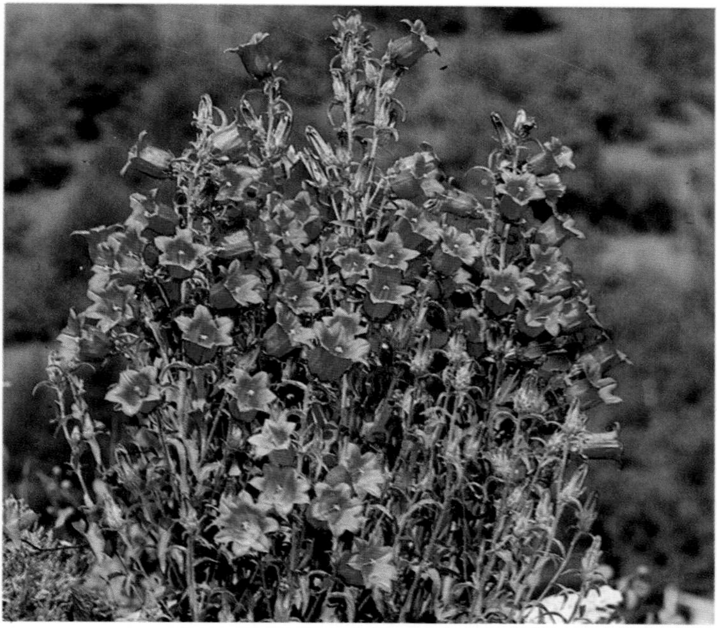

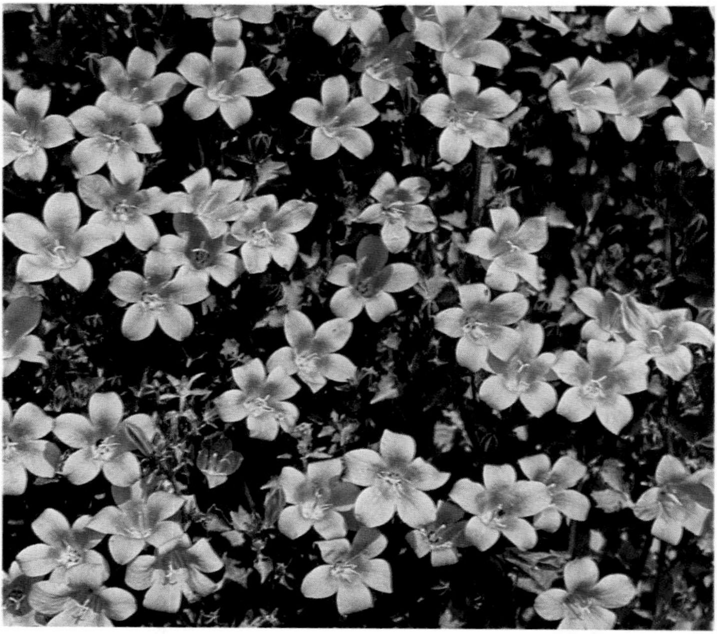

55 CAMPSIS RADICANS Berthold Seemann

Syns.: *Bignonia radicans* Carolus Linnaeus, *Tecoma radicans* Antoine Laurent Jussieu. Common names: Trumpet creeper, trumpet vine.

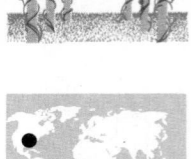

Family Bignoniaceae.
Description One of the most beautiful flowering deciduous climbers, this has woody stems and vigorous, spreading branches. Its leaves are imparipinnate with nine to eleven elliptical, ovate-oblong leaflets with dentate-acuminate margins. The orange flowers, with a campanulate calyx and funnel-shaped corolla, are borne in terminal racemes of three to twelve. The main stem produces a number of adventitious, self-clinging aerial rootlets.
Height of plant 33–36 ft. (10–11 m.).
Size of flower 1½–2¾ in. (4–7 cm.).
Place of origin Eastern United States.
Flowering time Summer.
Cultivation Sunny, sheltered position. Temperate climate. Is damaged by heavy frosts. Moist, compact soil, moderately fertile but well drained. Needs strong support. Some organic/mineral fertilizers required and some loosening of the surface. Regular watering. Hard pruning necessary during the resting period. This plant attracts ants. Pests: aphids.
Propagation By cuttings or air layers that take easily in the spring. By spring seed sowing in boxes or, even better, in pots in a greenhouse or coldframe.
Qualities Hardy. Easy to grow.

56 CANARINA CANARIENSIS Augustin Pyramus DeCandolle

Syn.: *C. campanula* Carolus Linnaeus

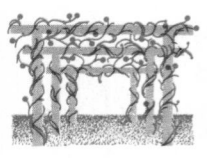
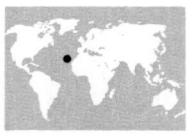

Family Campanulaceae.
Description Perennial rhizomatose plant with several erect herbaceous-carnose stems that have an almost sarmentose-climbing appearance. Its light green leaves are opposite or verticillate. This plant is especially interesting for its strange habit and for the beauty of its numerous flowers, which are showy, campanulate, pendulous and carried singly. It rests for about three months during the summer.
Height of plant 4–8 ft. (1.20–2.50 cm.).
Size of flower 1½–2 in. (4–5 cm.).
Place of origin Canary Islands.
Flowering time Late winter–spring.
Cultivation Partial shade, well protected from rough weather as it is a delicate plant. Temperate climate. Cannot withstand frost. Can be grown as a pot plant in a cool greenhouse. It likes a light, rich, permeable compost. Needs support. Remove stems when they have dried out. Pests and diseases: aphids, earth-borne insects, fungus diseases.
Propagation By late summer seed sowing in a greenhouse. By clump division.
Qualities Suitable as a pot plant if supported. Delicate. Quite easy to grow.

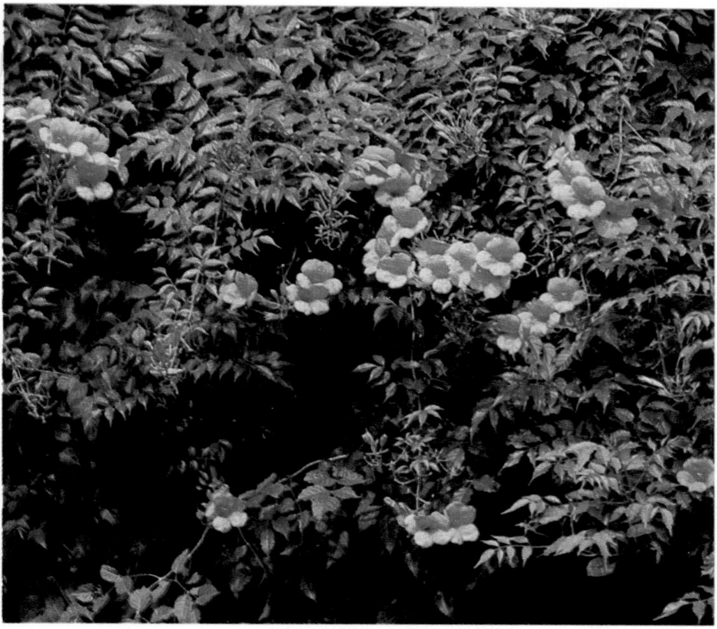

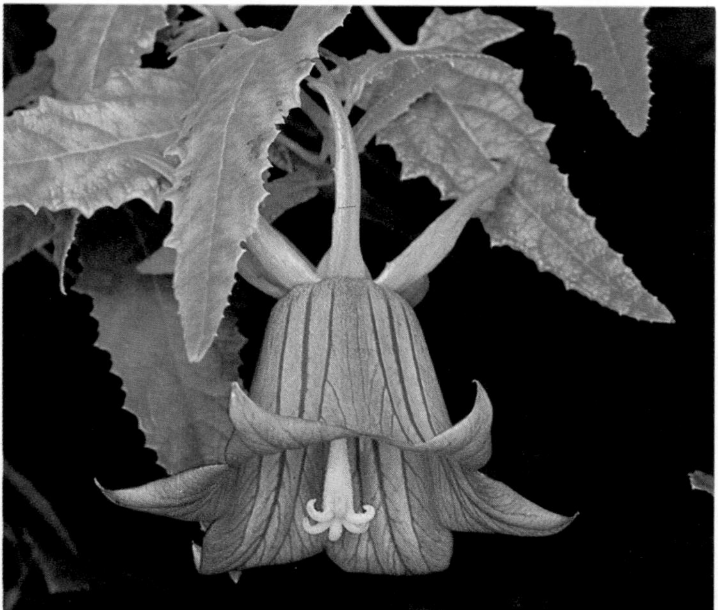

57 CANNA x GENERALIS L. H. Bailey
Syns.: C. x indica Carolus Linnaeus, C. x hybrida

Family Cannaceae.
Description *Canna indica* comprises a large number of cultivated species that are all hybrids obtained by crossing *C. indica* with *C. flaccida*, *C. coccinea* and *C. glauca*. They are among the loveliest of decorative plants, for both flowers and foliage. Canna leaves are large, alternate and oblong-acute or ovate-lanceolate. The very showy flowers are borne in terminal racemes and consist of colored sepals and petaloid stamens. There are many cultivars with flowers in a variety of colors and green or brown/purple leaves.
Height of plant 4–5 ft. (1.20–1.60 m.).
Size of flower 3–4¾ in. (8–12 cm.).
Place of origin Cultivated from tropical parentage (South America, Indonesia).
Flowering time Summer–autumn.
Cultivation Full sun. Temperate climate. Grows in almost any kind of soil provided it is rich and moist. It is a plant that requires a lot of feeding with organic manure, and generous watering. In the autumn, cut dead leaves and stems back to just above ground level and mulch well to protect from frost; alternatively, the rhizomes can be lifted and stored in layers of moist peat in a frost-free place. Trouble-free.
Propagation By allowing the rhizomes to sprout in the spring and dividing them.
Qualities Also suitable for growing in containers on terraces, balconies. Hardy. Easy to grow.

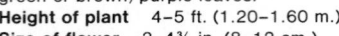

58 CANTUA BUXIFOLIA Jean Baptiste Lamarck
Common name: Magic flower of the Incas

Family Polemoniaceae.
Description A little-known evergreen shrub originating from the upper reaches of the cordillera of the Andes. A bushy plant, it is densely branched, with small, alternate, lanceolate-elliptical leaves. Floriferous, each flower has a long tubulous corolla and either grows singly or in racemes hanging from the ends of the branches. At one time, Cantua flowers were used to adorn young girls in the religious ceremonies of the South American Indian Aymara tribe.
Height of plant 5–8 ft. (1.50–2.50 m.).
Size of flower 2⅜–2¾ in. (6–7 cm.).
Place of origin Peru, Bolivia and Chile.
Flowering time Summer.
Cultivation An open, sunny position. Temperate climate. Not frost-resistant. Moist garden soil, rich or fairly clayey, with ample humus and well-drained. If grown in a pot, it requires a good, clayey woodland mold enriched with well-matured horse manure, peat and a little sand. Overall watering. Pruning restricted mainly to shortening all growths slightly after flowering. Pests and diseases: aphids; root rot and fungus diseases in conditions that are too damp.
Propagation By cuttings taken in the spring and brought on in a greenhouse in boxes of sandy compost. Also by seed, but this is hard to find.
Qualities Half-hardy. Very easy to grow.

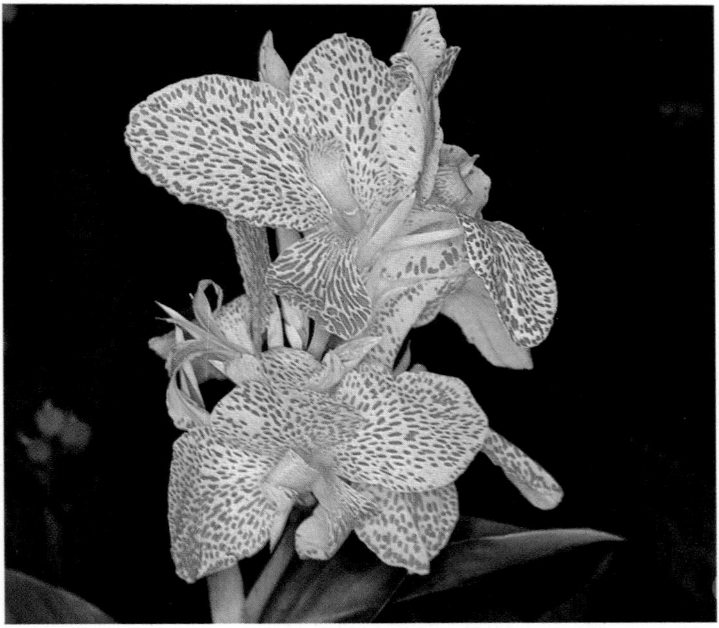

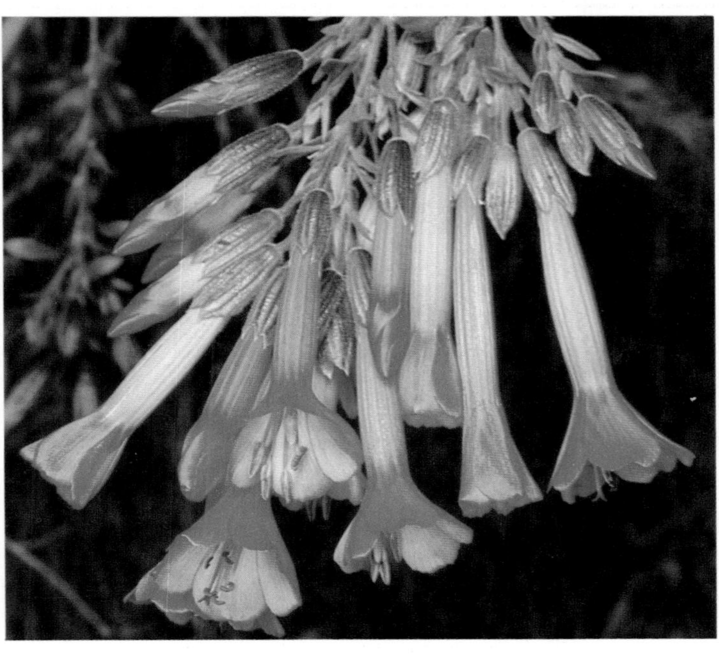

59 CARPOBROTUS ACINACIFORMIS (Carolus Linnaeus), L. Bolus.
Syn.: *Mesembryanthemum acinaciforme* Linnaeus.
Common name: Mesembryanthemum

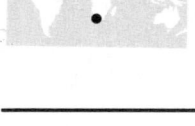

Family   Aizoaceae.
Description   A suffrutescent plant that grows wild but is also cultivated for its decorativeness. Its creeping, branched stems carry sessile, succulent leaves; these are opposite, decussate and triangular in cross section. It is floriferous, the axillary flowers being borne singly. They have a daisylike appearance with a great many bright pink linear petals and yellow stamens. An excellent plant for dry, stony or rocky sites by the sea.
Height of plant   8–12 in. (20–30 cm.).
Size of flower   2¾–3⅛ in. (7–8 cm.).
Place of origin   South Africa.
Flowering time   Spring–summer.
Cultivation   Full sun but sheltered position. Dislikes frost but can withstand a temperature down to 28° F. (−2° C.) for a short time. Grows in any kind of soil, preferably well drained and stony or sandy. Withstands salt air very well. Does not require watering or any particular attention. Pruning restricted to removal of dry material. Diseases: rather prone to root rot and other fungus diseases caused by damp conditions.
Propagation   By autumn or spring sowing in a sandy-based compost in pans in a coldframe or greenhouse. Also by cuttings taken in spring or early summer and brought on in a sheltered coldframe.
Qualities   Hardy. Easy to grow.

60 CASSIA MARILANDICA Carolus Linnaeus
Common name: Wild senna, American senna.

Family   Caesalpiniaceae.
Description   A good ornamental shrubby perennial for a garden in a temperate climate. Bushy in habit, it has an erect, semi-arborescent stem with numerous long, upright branches. Its leaves are alternate, paripinnate and composed of six to eight pairs of oblong-lanceolate leaflets. The numerous flowers are borne in axillary racemes made up of five petals shaped unevenly and arched like a spoon, with yellow-orange or reddish anthers. The plant is often grown for its attractive floral display in mild coastal districts.
Height of plant   6½–13 ft. (2–4 m.).
Size of flower   ¾–1⅛ in. (2–3 cm.).
Place of origin   North America.
Flowering time   Summer.
Cultivation   Sunny, sheltered position. Temperate climate. Not frost-resistant. Grows in any soil but prefers it to be fairly compact, even clayey, provided it is rich. Appreciates plenty of feeding. Can withstand dry conditions quite well. Quite hard pruning, both by cutting back and thinning out, improves flowering the following year.
Propagation   By seed or cutting in the spring, brought on in a sheltered coldframe.
Qualities   Easy to grow.

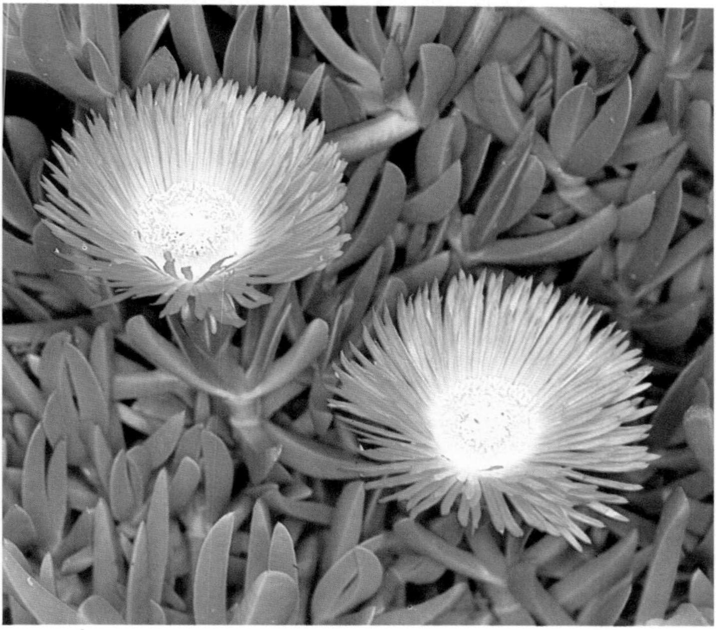

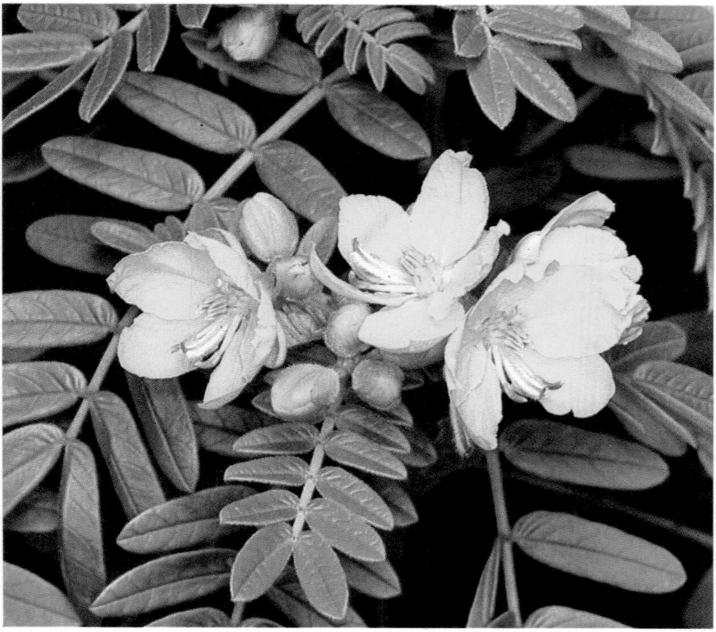

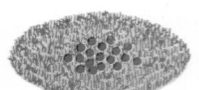

61   CATHARANTHUS ROSEUS (Carolus Linnaeus) George Don
Syns.: *Lochnera rosea* Heinrich Gottlieb Ludwig Reichenboch, *Vinca rosea* Linnaeus. Common name: Madagascar periwinkle

Family   Apocynaceae.
Description   Perennial grown as an annual with very attractive flowers. Upright stem, producing latex when cut. Its leaves are opposite, elliptical-lanceolate, glossy and glabrous. The flowers are either axillary or borne terminally and singly. Fairly tall cultivars can be found with white, deep pink, plum-purple and bicolored flowers.
Height of plant   12–16 in. (30–40 cm.).
Size of flower   1⅛–1½ in. (3–4 cm.).
Place of origin   Madagascar.
Flowering time   Summer.
Cultivation   A sunny position with little shade. Warm to temperate climate. It likes a moist, well-aerated soil, rich in leaf mold or humus. Requires a little liquid feeding in the early stages of growth and plenty of watering. Does not like heavy rain. Usually trouble-free.
Propagation   By spring sowing in a coldframe; transplant seedlings into a nursery bed and then into flowering position.
Qualities   Half-hardy. Easy to grow.

---

62   CEANOTHUS x DELILIANUS Eduard Spach
Syns.: *C. arnoldii* Hortorum, *C. intermedius* Hortorum. Common name: Wild lilac

Family   Rhamnaceae.
Description   A very ornamental deciduous shrub but not always easy to grow. Its ramifications are upright with opposite, oblong leaves with serrated margins and venation in relief on the underside. The numerous flowers are tiny, clustered into dense terminal and axillary panicles toward the ends of the branches. There are known to be more than 15 cultivars.
Height of plant   40–60 in. (1–1.50 m.).
Size of flower   6–8 in. (15–20 cm.) each panicle.
Place of origin   Cultivated from North American parentage (*C. americanus* Linnaeus, *C. còeruleus* Mariano Lagasca)
Flowering time   Summer.
Cultivation   Sunny or slightly shady position. Temperate climate. Not frost-resistant. Bring under cover in a hard winter. Prefers well-aerated or sandy soil, humus-rich or amended with mixed heath mold or peat and sand. Periodic organic/mineral feeds. Regular and plentiful watering. Light pruning in the autumn or late winter encourages new flowering. Diseases: susceptible to chlorosis and stunted growth.
Propagation   By hardwood cuttings taken in the autumn and brought on in a sheltered position. By softwood cuttings taken in the spring and brought on in a coldframe. By air layering and sometimes by grafting onto the roots of *C. americanus*.
Qualities   Half-hardy. Very easy to grow.

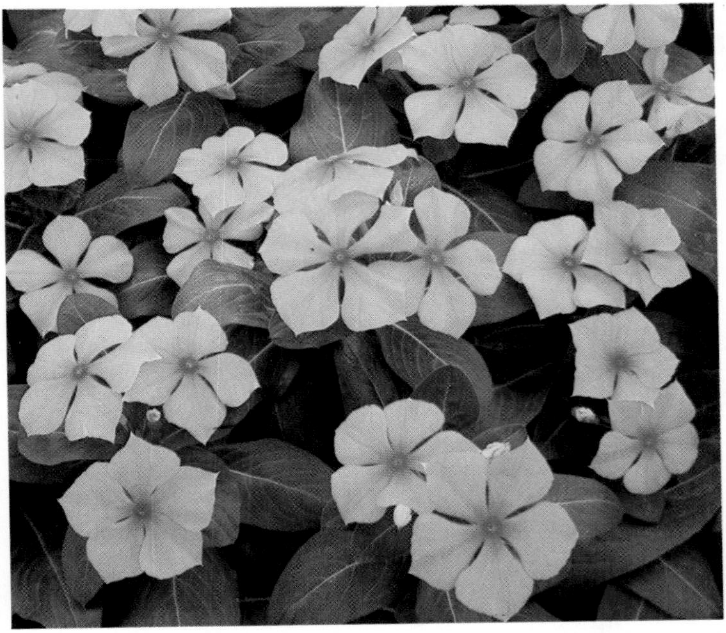

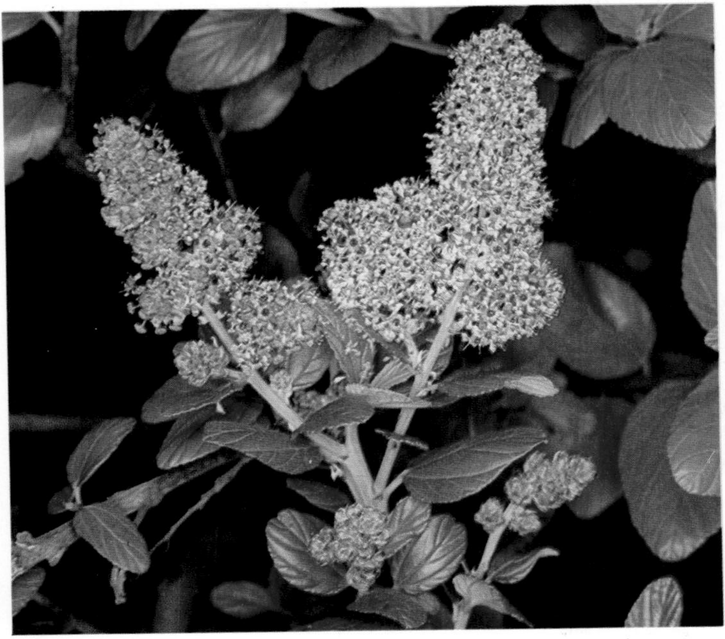

63 CELOSIA ARGENTEA Carolus Linnaeus var. *cristata* (Linnaeus) Otto Kuntze
Common name: Cockscomb

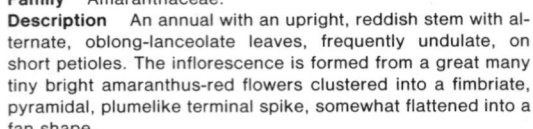

Family Amaranthaceae.
Description An annual with an upright, reddish stem with alternate, oblong-lanceolate leaves, frequently undulate, on short petioles. The inflorescence is formed from a great many tiny bright amaranthus-red flowers clustered into a fimbriate, pyramidal, plumelike terminal spike, somewhat flattened into a fan shape.
Height of plant 13–26 in. (35–65 cm.).
Size of flower 2–8 in. (5–20 cm.) the whole inflorescence.
Place of origin Uncertain but probably the tropics.
Flowering time Summer–autumn.

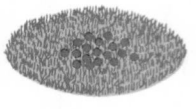

Cultivation Full sun or light shade. Temperate climate. Grows in any type of soil, whether well aerated, sandy or fairly heavy, provided it is organically well manured and moist. Appreciates a little liquid feeding during growth. Requires generous watering. Pests and diseases: attracts various insects; black spot and oidium.

Propagation By late winter sowing under glass. Prick off seedlings and grow at moderate temperature. May be sown directly in the garden in the spring after frost is over.
Qualities Also suitable for containers on balconies, terraces. Hardy. Easy to grow.

64 CELOSIA ARGENTEA Carolus Linnaeus cv. "Plumosa"
Syn.: *C. pyramidalis*

Family Amaranthaceae.
Description An upright herbaceous plant with ramifications from the base. Its leaves are alternate, lanceolate-acuminate and carried on long petioles. Inflorescence: terminal compound panicles growing close together bearing tiny flowers with no corolla but with a calyx accompanied by two or three bracts in various mother-of-pearl colors (yellow, gold or shades of red).
Height of plant 6–32 in. (15–80 cm.).
Size of flower 4–8 in. (10–20 cm.).
Place of origin Uncertain but probably the tropics.
Flowering time Summer–autumn.

Cultivation Full sun or very light position. Temperate climate. Good garden soil, fertile and moist; can even be moderately heavy provided it is rich. Pests and diseases: attracts caterpillars and aphids; subject to black spot and oidium in a damp climate.

Propagation By spring sowing in boxes under glass with subsequent pricking off and growing on. Alternatively, by sowing directly in flowering positions and then thinning out. Self-seeds freely.
Qualities Also suitable for containers on balconies, terraces. Hardy. Easy to grow.

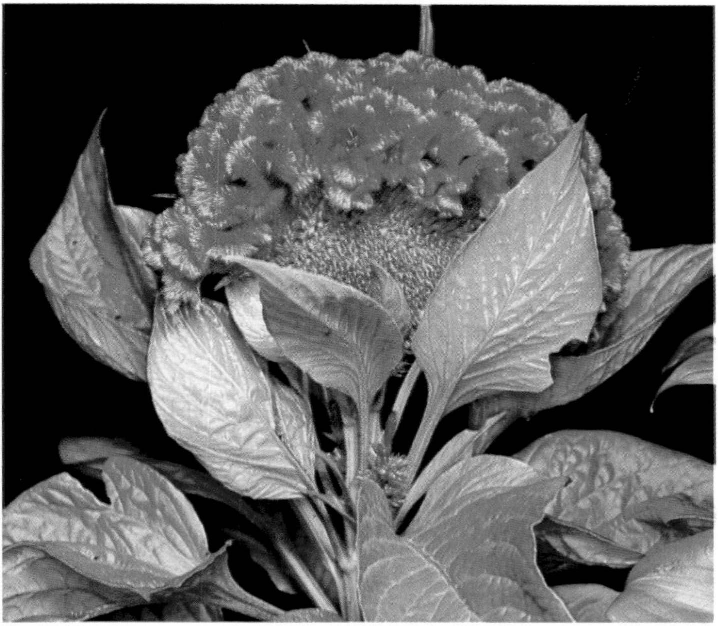

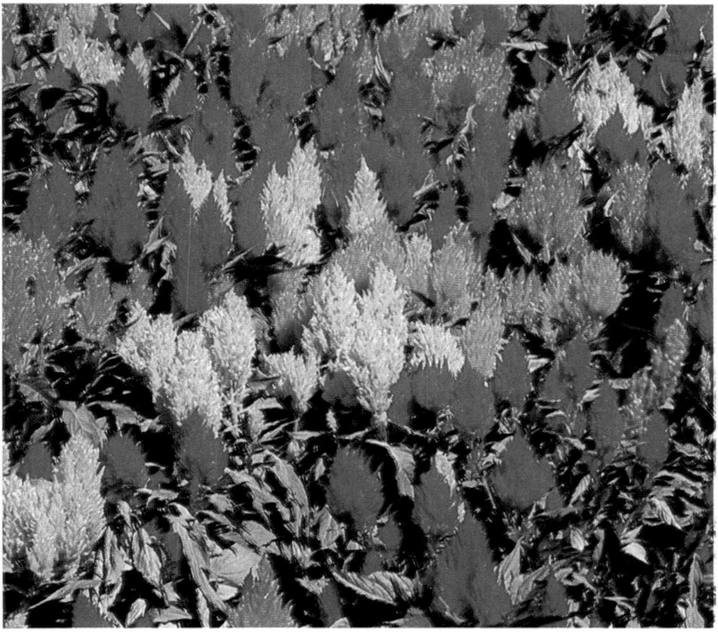

65 CENTAUREA CYANUS Carolus Linnaeus

Common names: Cornflower, bachelor's button, ragged robin, blue bottle.

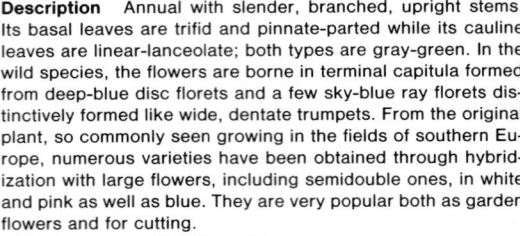
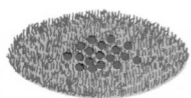
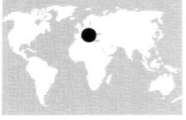

Family Compositae.

Description Annual with slender, branched, upright stems. Its basal leaves are trifid and pinnate-parted while its cauline leaves are linear-lanceolate; both types are gray-green. In the wild species, the flowers are borne in terminal capitula formed from deep-blue disc florets and a few sky-blue ray florets distinctively formed like wide, dentate trumpets. From the original plant, so commonly seen growing in the fields of southern Europe, numerous varieties have been obtained through hybridization with large flowers, including semidouble ones, in white and pink as well as blue. They are very popular both as garden flowers and for cutting.

Height of plant 20–28 in. (50–70 cm.).
Size of flower 1⅛–1½ in. (3–4 cm.).
Place of origin Southern Europe.
Flowering time Spring–summer.
Cultivation Sunny position. Temperate climate. Well-aerated, rich, moist soil, tending to be light. Compact, clayey and wet ground should be avoided. Does not like being transplanted. Likes regular watering. Pests and diseases: insects; chlorosis in unsuitable soil.
Propagation By spring sowing under glass or directly in the garden.
Qualities Hardy. Easy to grow.

66 CENTAUREA DEALBATA Karl Ludwig Willdenow

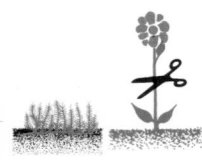
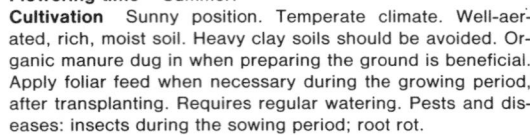

Family Compositae.

Description A sturdy perennial with erect, branched stems. Its lower leaves are pinnatisect, in acute segments and borne on petioles; its upper ones surrounding the capitula are sessile and either pinnatisect or entire. All the leaves are green on top and silver-gray underneath. The capitula consist of light- and deep-pink flowers; the ray florets spread out widely, deeply laciniated into numerous linear lobes.

Height of plant 16–32 in. (40–80 cm.).
Size of flower 2–2¾ in. (5–7 cm.).
Place of origin Asia Minor and Iran.
Flowering time Summer.
Cultivation Sunny position. Temperate climate. Well-aerated, rich, moist soil. Heavy clay soils should be avoided. Organic manure dug in when preparing the ground is beneficial. Apply foliar feed when necessary during the growing period, after transplanting. Requires regular watering. Pests and diseases: insects during the sowing period; root rot.
Propagation By spring sowing in a humus-rich, sandy-based compost. Divide plants every three to four years to maintain vigor.
Qualities Half-hardy. Very easy to grow.

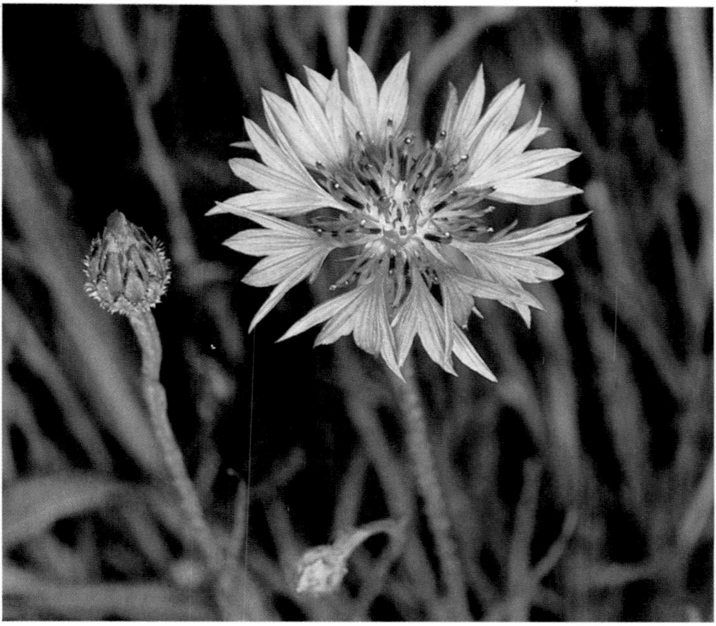

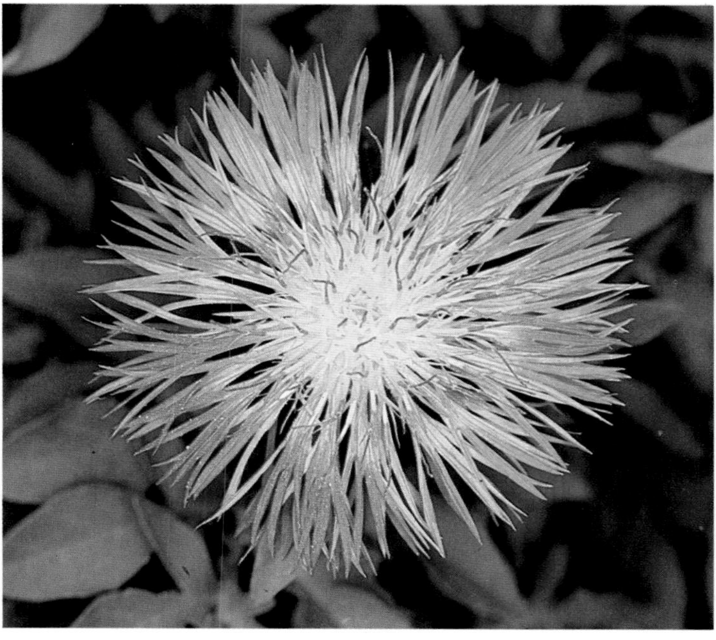

67 CENTRANTHUS RUBER Augustin Pyramus DeCandolle

Syns.: *Valeriana rubra* Carolus Linnaeus, *Kentranthus ruber* (alternative spelling preferred by some botanists). Common name: Red valerian

Family Valerianaceae.

Description A bushy perennial with numerous light, glaucous, hollow stems, slightly branched. Its oval leaves are opposite, ovate-lanceolate, acute and acuminate; the basal leaves are petiolate and the rest are sessile. The numerous little deep-pink flowers are tubulous and borne in terminal corymbiform cymes. There are also several cultivars in red and white. A useful plant because of its ability to grow in the most unlikely rocky places.

Height of plant 20–35 in. (50–90 cm.).
Size of flower ⅛ in. (0.5 cm.).
Place of origin Southern Europe.
Flowering time Summer-autumn.

Cultivation Full sun. Temperate climate. Not frost-resistant. Grows in poor ground, preferably in cracks in old walls, limestone quarries, rocky ground and calcareous soil. Does not transplant well. Does not require watering. Cut stems to the ground in winter. Dislikes dampness and frost.

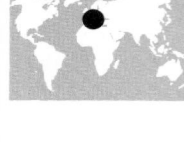

Propagation By sowing directly in flowering sites shortly after seeds have ripened. Alternatively, by sowing in peat pots so plants can be set into the garden without being disturbed.
Qualities Hardy. Easy to grow.

---

68 CERASTIUM TOMENTOSUM Carolus Linnaeus

Common name: Snow-in-summer

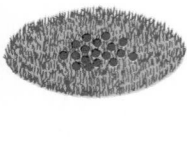

Family Caryophyllaceae.

Description Cottony white perennial with radicant, prostrate-ascendent stems. Its numerous leaves are opposite alternate, oblong-lanceolate or linear and tomentose-argentate. Its numerous small white flowers have a corolla with five open bifid petals like a bell, arranged in cymes. An attractive little plant, widely used in borders because of its adaptability.

Height of plant 8–12 in. (20–30 cm.).
Size of flower ⅜–⅝ in. (1–1.5 cm.).
Place of origin Southern and eastern Europe.
Flowering time Spring–summer.

Cultivation Sunny and partially shaded positions. Temperate climate. Tolerates poor soil and usually requires no special care. Prefers moist sites but can also tolerate dryness. Likes regular watering. Sometimes tends to become invasive. Usually trouble-free.

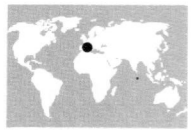

Propagation Nearly always by clump division in spring or autumn. Also by spring sowing in flowering site.
Qualities Hardy. Easy to grow.

69 CERATOSTIGMA PLUMBAGINOIDES
Alexander von Bunge.
Syn.: *Plumbago larpentae* John Lindley. Common name: Leadwort

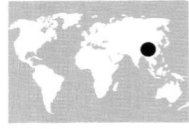

Family Plumbaginaceae.
Description A good ground-cover subshrub, its delightful appearance, long flowering period and hardiness have made it a great favorite. Its slender, branched, violet-colored stems are creeping in habit at first and then stand erect. The leaves are alternate, spatulate-acuminate and often crenulate-curved. The long, tubulous flowers are sessile and open into five rotate lobes; they are carried in terminal and axillary cymes.
Height of plant 8–12 in. (20–30 cm.).
Size of flower 1–1½ in. (2.5–4 cm.).
Place of origin China.
Flowering time Summer–autumn.
Cultivation Full sun to partial shade. Temperate climate. Withstands frost well. Likes poor, stony areas, especially cracks in old walls and between paving stones. Prefers soil that tends to be heavy. Does not require any special care. Slow to settle down, it usually takes about two or three years to make a uniform carpet. Likes regular watering. Cut back to ground level in the autumn.
Propagation By clump division or by pieces of rhizome in the autumn or, even better, late winter.
Qualities Hardy. Easy to grow.

70 CERCIS SILIQUASTRUM Carolus Linnaeus
Common name: Judas tree

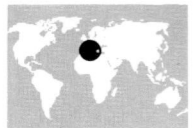

Family Caesalpiniaceae.
Description A small deciduous tree, well branched, the trunk and branches covered with blackish bark. Leaves are alternate, rotundate-reniform; dark green on top and glaucous underneath, borne on a petiole half their length. The numerous flowers appear before the leaves and are carried in clusters on the trunk and branches. The flowers have a papilionaceous corolla and are a deep rose or purplish-pink. There is also a white-flowered variety.
Height of plant 11–20 ft. (3.50–6 m.).
Size of flower ¾ in. (2 cm.).
Place of origin Southern Europe and Asia Minor.
Flowering time Spring.
Cultivation Full sun and a little shade. Temperate climate but can withstand frost well. It grows in almost any kind of soil but prefers rich, moist, clayey ground. Does not require any attention normally. This tree should be left to grow naturally but it will tolerate light pruning during the winter.
Propagation By autumn or spring sowing in a sheltered seedbed. By root shoots.
Qualities Hardy. Easy to grow.

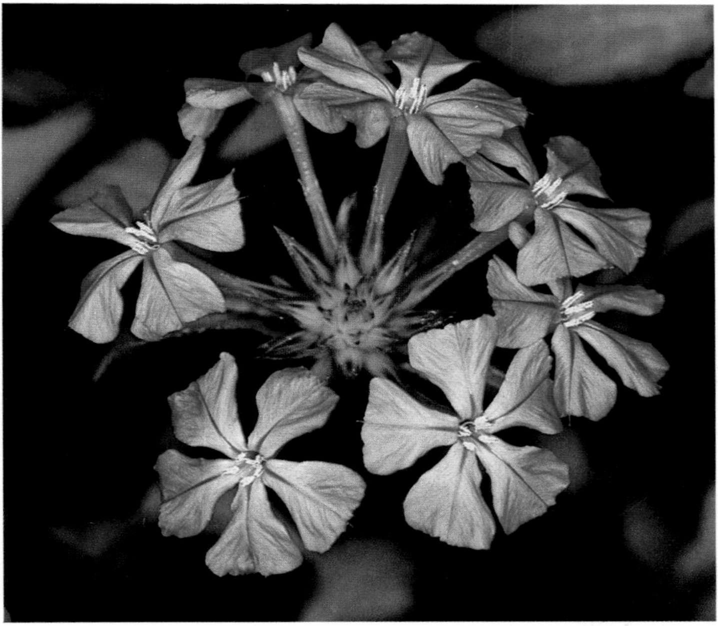

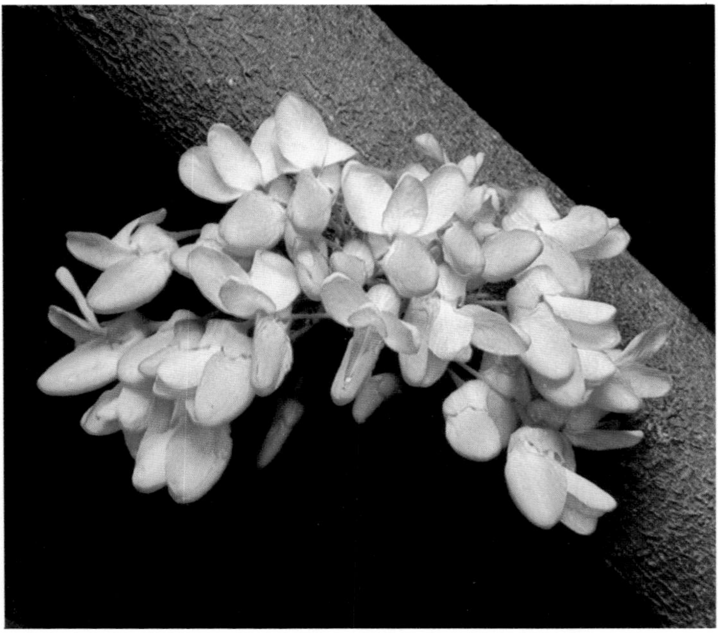

71 CESTRUM ELEGANS Diedrich Franz Leonhard von Schlectendahl
Syn.: *C. purpureum* Standley

Family Solanaceae.
Description A deciduous, shrubby-bushy plant with long pubescent ramifications arching a little at the end; its leaves are alternate, ovate-lanceolate, scabrid and pubescent on the underside. They exude an unpleasant smell when touched. The numerous flowers have a long, tubulous, wine-red corolla; they are long-lasting and grow in corymbiform clusters borne in compound cymes. The fruit consists of pea-sized berries.
Height of plant 6½–10 ft. (2–3 m.).
Size of flower ¾–1⅛ in. (2–3 cm.).
Place of origin Mexico.
Flowering time Winter–spring.
Cultivation Partial shade. Very sheltered position. Temperate climate. Not frost-resistant. Prefers a rich, loamy, well-aerated soil with organic manuring augmented by light mineral feeding. Requires plenty of water in the summer. Prune to control growth in February or March. Pests: insects.
Propagation By herbaceous or half-ripened cuttings in spring or summer. Sometimes by seed shortly after seed has been collected.
Qualities Half-hardy. Very easy to grow.

---

72 CHAENOMELES JAPONICA (Carl Peter Thunberg) Eduard Spach
Syns.: *Cydonia maulei* Thomas Moore, *Pyrus japonica* Thunberg. Common name: Japanese quince

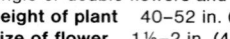

Family Rosaceae.
Description A popular deciduous shrub, confused with the similar *C. speciosa* from which it differs by not flowering until nearly finished leafing and by bearing rounder fruit. A bushy, spreading habit and short, spiny secondary branches. Its leaves are alternate, ovate-oblong, with serrated margins. The numerous flowers grow either singly or in racemes of two to four. The fruits have a bitter-dry taste. There are varieties with single or double flowers and different colors.
Height of plant 40–52 in. (1–1.30 m.).
Size of flower 1½–2 in. (4–5 cm.).
Place of origin Japan.
Flowering time Spring.
Cultivation Full sun to partial shade. Temperate climate. It can withstand cold. Suitable for fairly heavy soils, even calcareous or clayey. Give a little organic manure occasionally. Prune after flowering to encourage new growth, and remove dead growth or weak growth. Moderate watering. It is subject to chlorosis.
Propagation By division, layering and air layering in the spring or summer. By herbaceous and half-ripened cuttings in the spring. By seed, but new plants may not come true to type.
Qualities Hardy. Easy to grow.

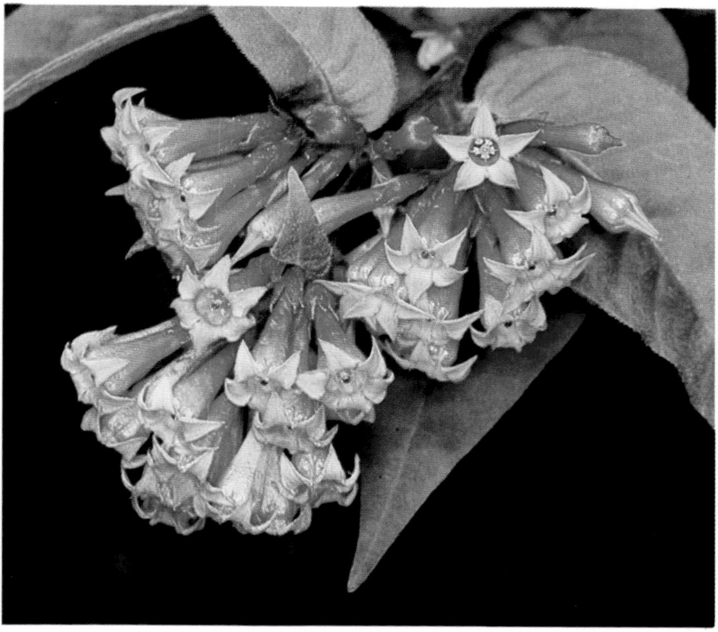

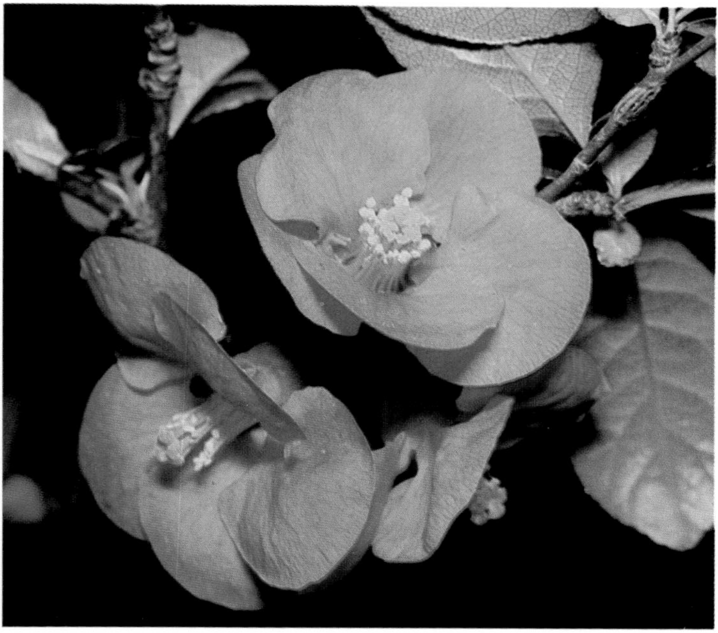

73 CHEIRANTHUS CHEIRI Carolus Linnaeus
Common name: Wallflower

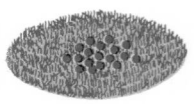

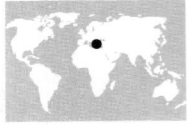

Family Cruciferae.
Description A perennial, usually grown as an annual or biennial, this plant is popular for its showy floriferousness, adaptability and hardiness. It is subshrubby with sturdy, upright ramifications. Its leaves are sparse, linear-lanceolate, and they undulate on a short petiole. It produces numerous flowers in a spike at the end of each branch. It often reacts against cultivation and reverts to the species. There are many cultivars with colors including cream, yellow, orange, coppery-red and purple.
Height of plant 15–24 in. (40–60 cm.).
Size of flower ¾ in. (2 cm.).
Place of origin Originally from the Aegean Islands but naturalized in southern Europe.
Flowering time Spring–summer.
Cultivation Sunny position. Temperate climate. Prefers permeable calcareous soil, not too rich. Thrives in cracks in walls and on rubble containing old plaster, etc. Appreciates moderate watering. Pests and diseases: aphids, caterpillars and cabbage root fly maggots; root tumors, rots and fungus diseases.
Propagation By seed in late summer in the shelter of an open frame, in spring in pans in a coldframe or directly in the flowering site. Or by self-seeding.
Qualities Hardy. Easy to grow.

74 CHOISYA TERNATA Carl Sigismund Kunth
Common name: Mexican orange

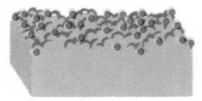

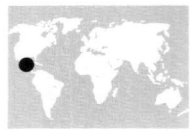

Family Rutaceae.
Description A charming, fairly small, bushy, slow-growing evergreen shrub. It has sturdy green ramifications. Its trifoliate leaves are sparse and opposite, ovate-elliptic and carried on a long petiole. The numerous fragrant flowers have five white petals arranged in terminal clusters.
Height of plant 40–60 in. (1–1.50 m.).
Size of flower ¾–1 ⅛ in. (2–3 cm.).
Place of origin Mexico.
Flowering time Late winter.
Cultivation Cool, slightly shady position. Temperate climate. Damaged by heavy frosts. Compact, rich, moist soil with clayey-humus content. Manure and minerals help to stimulate growth. Requires regular watering. No need to prune, apart from slight shortening and thinning out of weak growth, especially while the plant is growing. Pests: sometimes attracts scale insects and red spider mites.
Propagation By half-ripened cuttings taken in the spring or summer and rooted in boxes in a sand-based compost in a coldframe.
Qualities Hardy. Easy to grow.

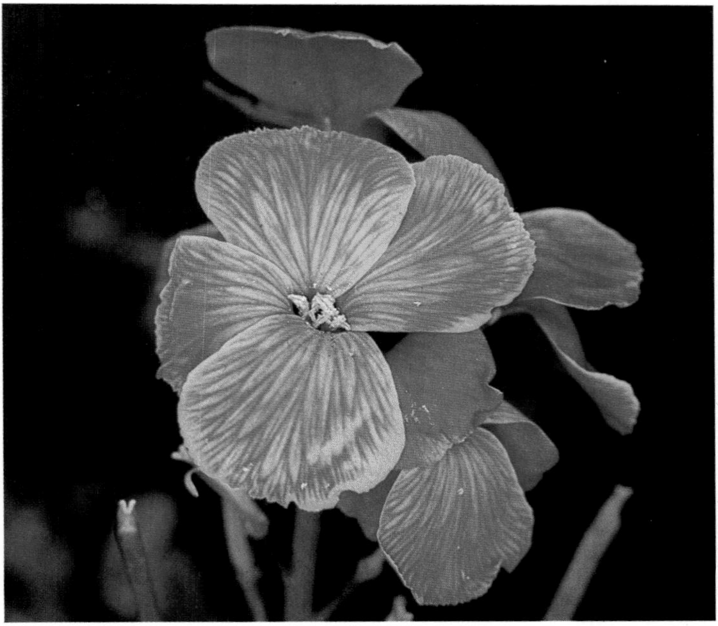

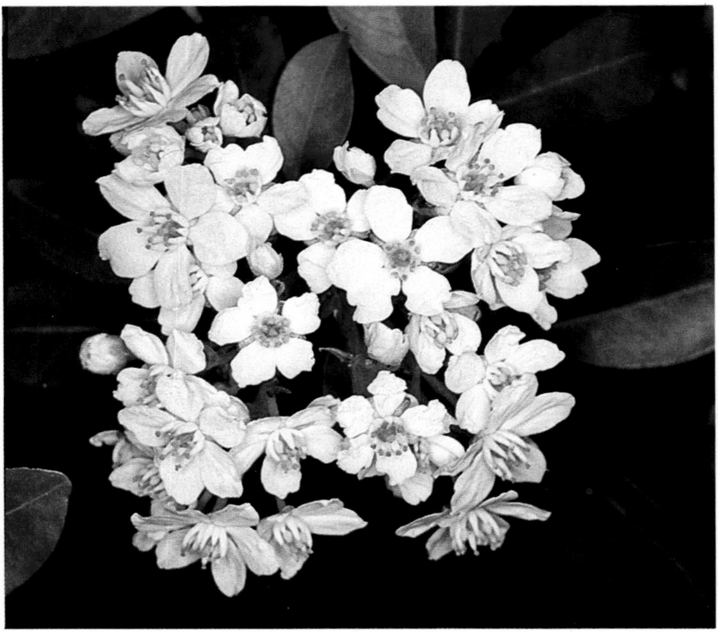

75 CHRYSANTHEMUM COCCINEUM Karl Ludwig Willdenow

Syns.: *Pyrethrum roseum* Friedrich August Marschall von Bieberstein, *Chrysanthemum roseum* M. F. Adams. Common names: Painted daisy, pyrethrum

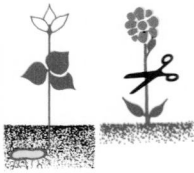
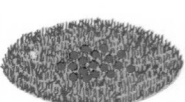
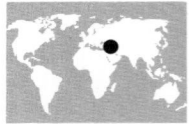

Family Compositae.
Description A popular garden perennial, this bears numerous upright, rigid floral stems, slightly branched. Its basal leaves are bipinnatisect and laciniate. The cauline leaves are alternate, small and sparse. The attractive flowers are like large daisies and may be single or double, depending on the variety. Colors include white, pink, light red and scarlet.
Height of plant 27–32 in. (70–80 cm.).
Size of flower 2–3 in. (5–8 cm.).
Place of origin Iran and the Caucasus.
Flowering time Early summer.
Cultivation Sunny position. Temperate climate. Dislikes the cold and prefers a position that is open yet sheltered. Protect with a good mulch for the winter. Prefers soil that is clayey, rich in humus and organic material, moist and well manured. Appreciates liquid feeding during the growing period, and generous watering. The clumps should be divided every three years. Pests and diseases: aphids and fungus diseases.
Propagation By spring seed sowing or clump division in early fall.
Qualities Hardy. Easy to grow.

76 CHRYSANTHEMUM FRUTESCENS Carolus Linnaeus

Syns.: *Anthemis frutescens* Hortorum, *Pyrethrum frutescens* Karl Ludwig Willdenow. Common names: Marguerite, Paris daisy

Family Compositae.
Description An evergreen suffruticose subshrub, rather short-lived. Its leaves are pinnate-lobate or pinnate-parted. Its single white flowers are in capitula and have the classic daisy form with a large yellow disc, borne on long peduncles in terminal racemes. The plant is well known and extensively grown as a bedding plant and for cutting in warm regions.
Height of plant 40–48 in. (1–1.20 m.).
Size of flower 1–1½ in. (2.5–4 cm.).
Place of origin Canary Islands.
Flowering time Spring–summer and sporadically in winter.
Cultivation Full sun to partial shade. Temperate climate. Frost-tender; should be put in a sheltered position during the winter as it cannot withstand a temperature below freezing. Prefers a humus-rich, clayey soil. Occasional organic/mineral feeding. Likes plenty of watering. Dead-head as flowers fade. Pests and diseases: aphids, fungus diseases and root rot.
Propagation By nonflowering side shoots in the spring or semiherbaceous cuttings in the summer. Pinch out the tops to encourage side shoots.
Qualities Suitable for containers on balconies, terraces. Hardy. Easy to grow.

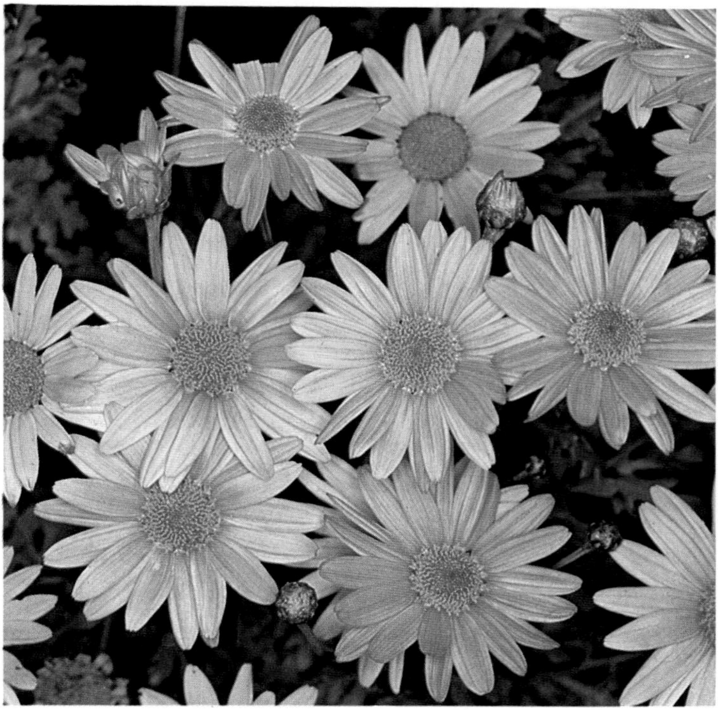

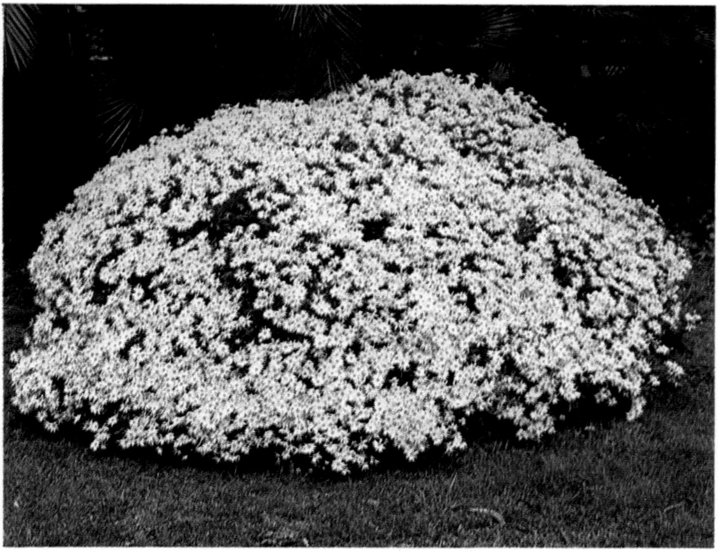

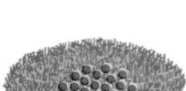

77 CHRYSANTHEMUM x INDICUM Carolus Linnaeus

Syns.: *C. sinense* Joseph Sabine, C. x Hortorum.
Common name: Chrysanthemum

Family   Compositae.

Description   The wild native species is almost unknown today. It originated in China and is responsible for countless varieties and cultivated forms that have succeeded one another in gardens, nurseries and greenhouses. As long ago as 500 B.C. the chrysanthemum was already being widely grown in China, about a thousand years before it was to become the national flower of Japan. It is now one of the most cultivated flowers throughout every continent. Only in Italy is there prejudice against it because it is associated there with funerals.

The Chinese and Japanese remain the best growers of this plant. By applying the knowledge of chrysanthemum growing they have gained over the centuries, they can produce hundreds of blooms, each more than 4 in. (10 cm.) in diameter, on single plants, appearing like huge bouquets.

The chrysanthemum is also grown commercially as a cut flower. There are a great many varieties suitable for growing as pot plants for indoors or greenhouse, in the open ground, in rockeries and on terrace or deck. Depending on the variety and with the necessary cutting back, the plants can even be trained to different shapes.

Chrysanthemums are classified according to the shape of the flower, but unfortunately these classifications vary considerably from country to country. The following main categories define the shape and petal arrangement: incurved or spherical, reflexed, intermediate, sub-globose or pompon, semipompon, single, anemone-centered, spray and cascade (Korean). In other, more complex, classifications are: decorative, spoon, thread-petaled or spider, Fuji and quill.

The plant is suffruticose and if left to itself is of a bushy, well-branched habit. Its light-green leaves are alternate and either pinnate-lobate or incised-lobate, dentate, slightly tomentose on the underside with an alate, stipellate petiole. Stems and leaves emit a rather pungent aromatic smell when touched. The numerous flowers are in capitula arranged in terminal corymbs.

Height of plant   6 in.–4 ft. (0.15–1.20 m.).

Size of flower   1½–10–12 in. (25–30 cm.), depending on the cultivar.

Place of origin   China and Japan.

Flowering time   Autumn–winter.

Cultivation   An open, sunny position. Cool, temperate climate. They are "short-day" plants; that is, photosensitive (light-sensitive) and produce flower buds only as the days become shorter and the nights considerably longer. Commercial chrysanthemum growers produce blooms all year by artificially controlling the light and temperature in special greenhouses.

Opposite: some cultivars of Chrysanthemum x indicum—*top, an incurved form; center, cv. "Ritz," single-flowered daisy type; bottom, semidouble flower.*

More cultivars of Chrysanthemum x indicum—*top, thread-petaled; center, cv. "Lancier"; bottom, typical form of the spoon-shaped flower.*

When chrysanthemums are grown in the open ground, they should be planted in a sheltered, south-facing bed. The soil—preferably clayey—should be humus-rich and thoroughly prepared with plenty of well-rotted manure dug in and a slow-release compound mineral fertilizer. When the young plants are ready to be planted out, they should be planted complete with their soil ball or peat pot—so that the roots need not be disturbed. Occasional liquid feeds greatly encourage good growth, since the plants are greedy for nitrogen. If they are to be grown to produce single exhibition blooms or sprays, pinching out or regular disbudding has to be carried out.

If necessary, the young plants should be tied to a support which should be put in the ground during planting and be at least as long as the ultimate height of the plant. If plants are to be grown in pots, it is wise to put only one in each pot, the size of which may range from 7–8–10 inches (18–20–25 cm.) in diameter, depending on the number of flowers to be allowed to grow on the plant. Prior to this final potting-on, there will be two changes of pots.

To obtain one to twelve flowers of 4–6 in. (10–15 cm.) in diameter, it is necessary to pinch out four to six pairs of leaves by removing the growing tip when the plant has produced about ten pairs of leaves (in May). Following this operation, lateral shoots appear in the leaf axils; it is these that produce the flowers, and it is now necessary to select the sturdiest, equal in length, in the number you require, and remove the rest. All subsequent lateral shoots, apart from those chosen to flower, must be removed. At the same time, a number of tiny floral buds begin to appear on the selected stems, of which only the main, central ones can be allowed to remain. This is known as "disbudding." Some growers prefer to remove the main bud as soon as it appears, leaving the one immediately below it to develop, because the main bud is frequently prone to distortion due to an accumulation of sap. Everyone has his own beliefs. There are certain specialized methods of cultivation that enable blooming to be retarded or accelerated, but space prevents a description here.

Pests and diseases Chrysanthemums require vigilant attention to protect them from attack as they attract such harmful insects as aphids, leaf miners, capsid bugs, caterpillars, earwigs, snails, red spider mites, eelworms and cutworms. They are also subject to viruses, root rot and various fungus diseases such as oidium, gray mold, powdery mildew, rust and petal blight.

Propagation By cuttings made from the shoots that spring from the roots, when they have put out four or five leaves; these can be rooted in sand in a coldframe or cool greenhouse in late winter. Subsequently they should be transplanted and potted on according to the type of cultivation required. Suckers can also be rooted in the spring. Air layering is another possibility. With mature perennial plants, clump division can also be carried out. Usually sowing is only resorted to in late winter or early spring, when new varieties are being sought. This can be done in pans or boxes, in light, sandy compost, in a heated greenhouse or frame.

Qualities Half-hardy. Demanding to grow but rewarding.

78 CISTUS ALBIDUS Carolus Linnaeus
Common name: Rock rose

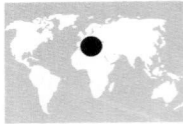

Family Cistaceae.
Description A well-branched upright evergreen shrub of bushy habit. Its dull whitish-gray leaves are tomentose, sessile, ovate-elliptical and reticulate. Its short-lived pink or mauve flowers are similar to those of a wild rose with central yellow stamens. They are borne in terminal groups of three to five. There is also a white variety.
Height of plant 20–60 in. (0.50–1.50 m.).
Size of flower 2–2½ in. (5–6 cm.).
Place of origin Mediterranean region.
Cultivation Full sun. Temperate climate. Can withstand light frosts. Prefers rocky, calcareous, poor soil. It likes an open position and does not need watering or any particular attention. Pruning is limited to removal of dead wood and any straggly growth. Does not like excessive moisture, which may cause root rot.
Propagation By spring sowing in pots in a coldframe; but it is better to sow directly into flowering sites, since plants do not like being transplanted.
Qualities Hardy. Easy to grow.

---

79 CISTUS LADANIFERUS Carolus Linnaeus
Common name: Rock rose

Family Cistaceae.
Description One of the loveliest of this genus, both for its foliage and the beauty of its abundant flowers. Open, upright branches spring from the base. The vegetal growth is sticky and resinous, with an aromatic fragrance. The leaves are almost sessile, linear-lanceolate and of a whitish cottony texture on the lower surface. Flowers are carried singly or in groups of three to eight on long peduncles at the end of short branches. The large corolla consists of white petals, each with a dark red blotch toward its base.
Height of plant 5–6½ ft. (1.50–2 m.).
Size of flower 2–2¾ in. (5–7 cm.).
Place of origin Western Mediterranean region.
Flowering time Spring–early summer.
Cultivation Full sun to partial shade. Temperate climate. Frost-tender. Although the plant grows in poor soil, it prefers siliceous soils low in calcium but with ample humus. Does not like to be transplanted, and watering can often have deleterious effects. The best results are obtained by sowing seed directly in the garden. Usually requires no particular attention. Prune only to remove dead material and straggly growth.
Propagation By autumn or spring sowing in the garden or in peat pots that can be planted without disturbing the young plants when they are set out.
Qualities Hardy. Easy to grow.

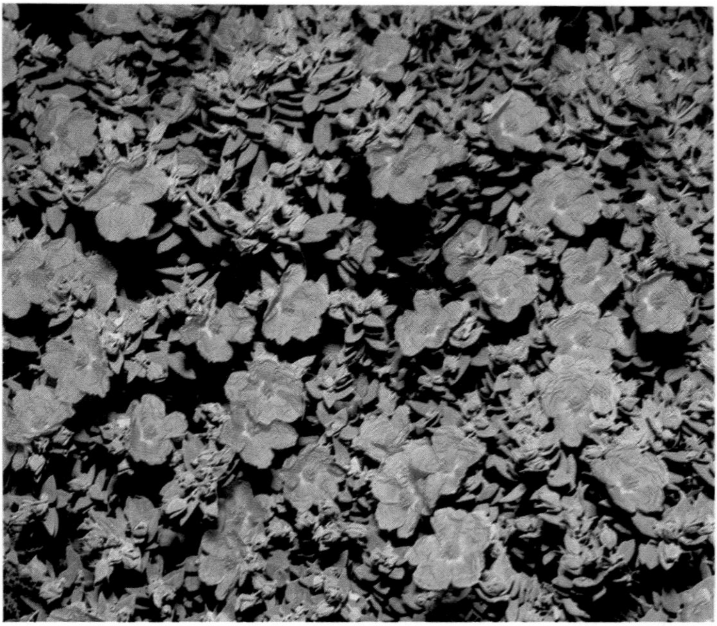

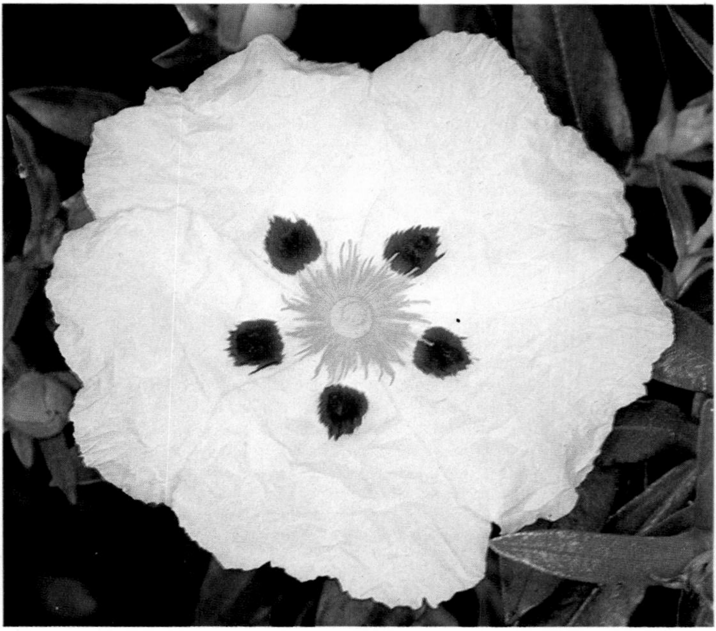

80 CLARKIA ELEGANS David Douglas
Syn.: *C. unguiculata*

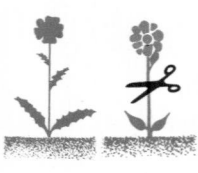

Family Onagraceae.
Description This annual plant branches up from its base with fragile, slender stems. Its alternate leaves are ovate-lanceolate, glabrous and tender. Its numerous single or double flowers are distributed in long, lax spikes, depending on the variety. The tubulous corolla opens out into four or five divaricate lobes. The color range includes red, pink, white and salmon.
Height of plant 20–43 in. (50–110 cm.).
Size of flower ¾–1⅛ in. (2–3 cm.).
Place of origin Western South and North America—especially California.
Flowering time Early summer.

Cultivation Sun to partial shade. Temperate climate. Fertile, slightly acid soil. Excessive moisture and too much feeding can harm the plant, causing the stems to collapse. High temperatures shorten its flowering period. Pests and diseases: often attacked by harmful insects and fungus diseases.
Propagation By sowing seed in the garden when soil is warm. Plants do not like to be transplanted.
Qualities Very hardy. Quite easy to grow.

---

81 CLEMATIS x JACKMANII Thomas Moore

Family Ranunculaceae.
Description A slender deciduous vine with nodular stems with long fragile ramifications. The leaves are opposite, trifoliate or ternate, with cartilagenous ovate-acute leaflets. The solitary axillary flowers are a very striking shade of deep violet-blue. This species probably originates from a cross between *C. hendersonii* and *C. lanuginosa* effected in the Jackman plant-breeding nursery in Great Britain.
Height of plant 10–16½ ft. (3–5 m.).
Size of flower 4–4¾ in. (10–12 cm.).
Place of origin Hybrid of horticultural origin.
Flowering time Summer.

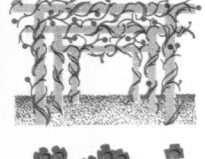

Cultivation Shady, moist situation. Temperate climate with fair resistance to cold. Prefers humus-rich, woodland-type soil, not too compact; enrich occasionally with leaf mold, well-rotted manure and sand. Also periodic applications of liquid fertilizers or minerals. Plenty of watering. Prune in late winter to stimulate new growth. Diseases: root rot and fungus diseases.

Propagation By layering and air layering. By cuttings of half-ripened wood rooted in a coldframe. By seed, but this is a very slow process and the resulting plants may not be true to type.
Qualities Suitable for growing in containers on a terrace or deck. Half-hardy. Very easy to grow.

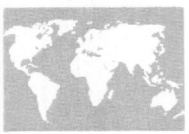

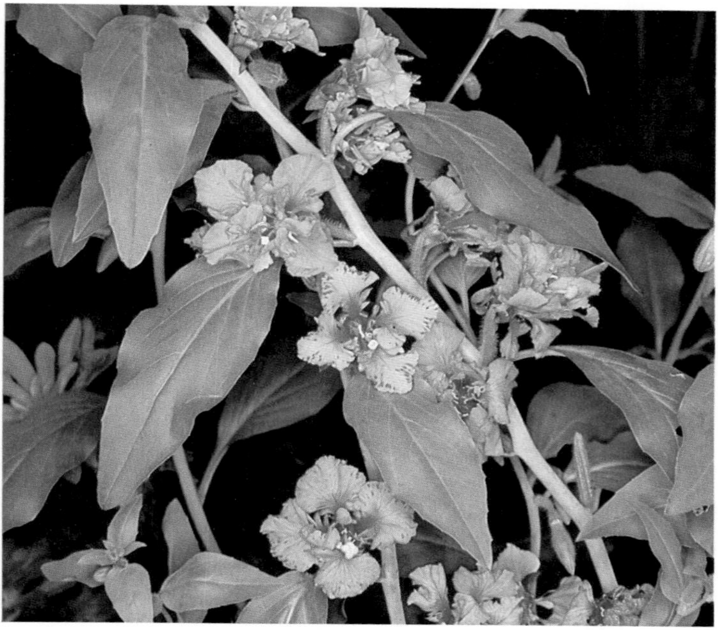

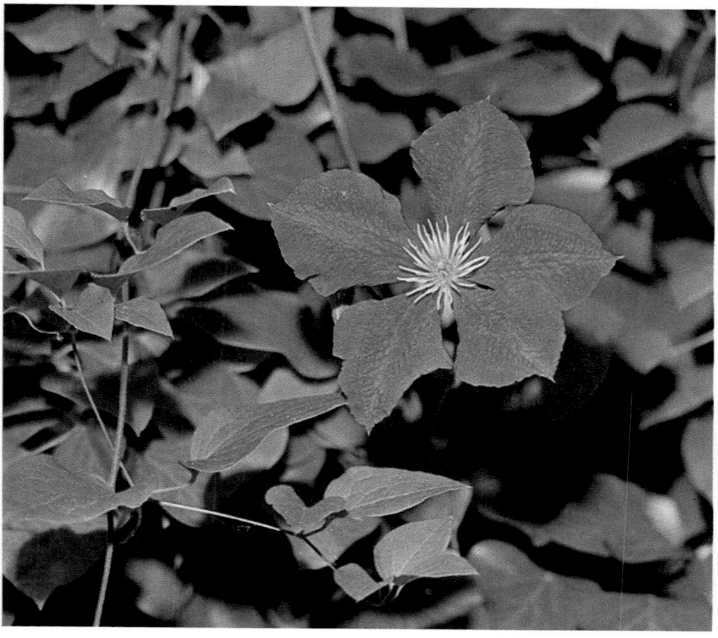

82 CLEMATIS MONTANA Francis Buchanan

Family Ranunculaceae.
Description A vigorous deciduous climbing perennial with numerous slender nodular and fragile stems. Its leaves are opposite, binate or ternate, ovate-acute and dentate. The numerous single white flowers are fragrant, delicately tinged with pink, and make a fine display, almost covering the plant. One of the best climbers.
Height of plant 10–26 ft. (3–8 m.).
Size of flower 2–2⅜ in. (5–6 cm.).
Place of origin Himalayas.
Flowering time Spring–early summer.

Cultivation Full sun to partial shade in a sheltered position. Temperate climate. Woodland-type or organically rich soil, well manured, moist but well drained. Plenty of watering during the summer. Minimum of pruning, since the plant flowers on old wood. Usually trouble-free.
Propagation Mainly by air or stem layering. By grafting on *C. vitalba*. By stem cuttings of half-ripened wood taken in the summer and rooted under glass.
Qualities Hardy. Quite easy to grow.

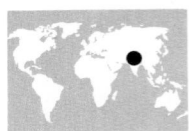

---

83 CLEOME SPINOSA Nicolaus Joseph Jacquin

Syn.: *C. pungens* Karl Ludwig Willdenow. Common name: Spider flower

Family Capparidaceae.
Description A simple annual with a single upright sturdy stem. Its deep-green leaves, borne on long petioles with a thorn at the base of each, consist of five lanceolate or ovate-acute leaflets. The flower heads have a strange but striking appearance, with very long, protruding stamens that are reminiscent of a cat's whiskers. Arranged in long terminal racemes, the flowers continue opening over a long period, starting from the bottom. Several colors are available among the cultivars: white, pink, pinkish-purple and others.
Height of plant 3–4 ft. (0.90–1.20 m.).
Size of flower ¾–1⅜ in. (2–3.5 cm.).
Place of origin South America.
Flowering time Summer.

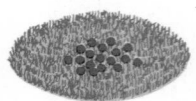

Cultivation Sunny to partial shade. Temperate climate, sheltered position. Frost-tender. Suited to any soil tending to be calcareous, deep, rich, moist and even sandy; liquid feeding during early growth. Plenty of watering. Pests and diseases: aphids; rots and chlorosis.
Propagation By sowing in the garden after last frost. Self-seeds freely.

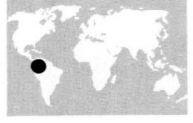

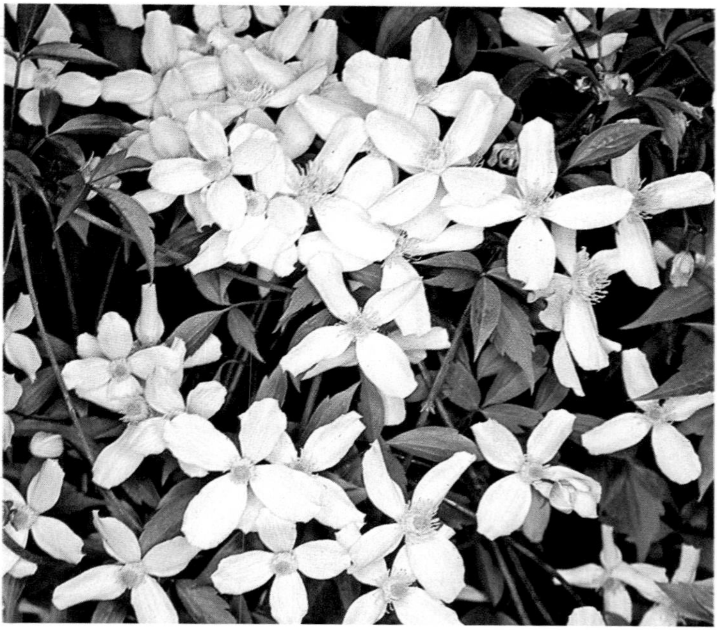

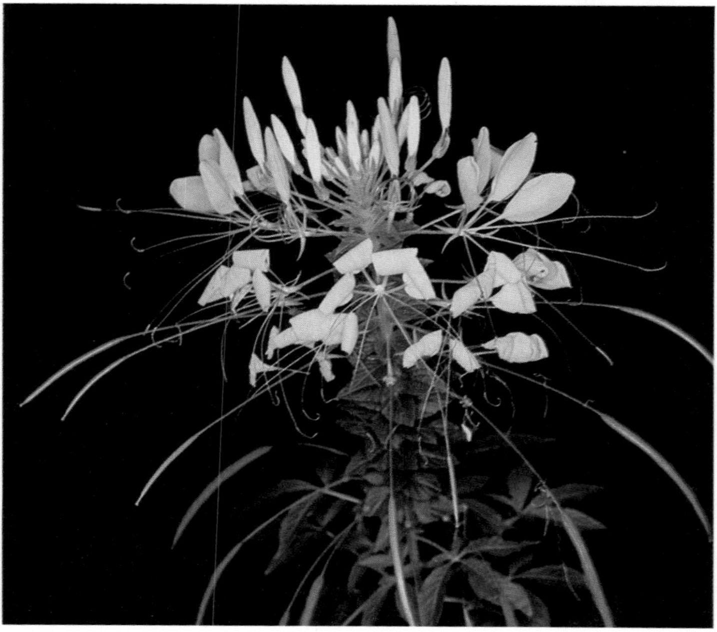

84 CLERODENDRON BUNGEI Ernst Gottlieb Steudel

Syn.: *C. foetidum* Alexander von Bunge. Common name: Glory bower

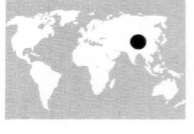

Family Verbenaceae
Description A bushy shrub, as decorative for its foliage as for the abundance and unusual quality of its carmine-pink inflorescences. It throws up vigorous suckers, which make the plant very thick. Its leaves are opposite, ovate-subcordate, acute and pubescent, giving off an unpleasant odor when touched. The numerous fragrant flowers are arranged in compact corymbiform cymes.
Height of plant 5–7 ft. (1.50–2 m.).
Size of flower ¾–1 in. (2–2.5 cm.).
Place of origin China.
Flowering time Summer.
Cultivation Full sun to partial shade. Temperate climate. Frost damage likely but new growth springs from the base. In cold areas the stems should be protected with a good mulch. Prefers well-aerated, moist, sandy soil and benefits from generous organic manuring. Plenty of watering. Very little pruning required. Well-established plants can be kept to an acceptable size by pollarding.
Propagation By division, detaching the rooted suckers. By cuttings of half-ripened wood in the spring for rooting under glass. By seed.
Qualities Hardy. Easy to grow.

85 CLERODENDRON TRICHOTOMUM Carl Peter Thunberg

Syns.: *C. serotinum* Elie Abel Carriere, *Volkameria japonica* Hortorum. Common name: Harlequin glory bower

Family Verbenaceae.
Description A charming bushy plant or small decorative tree of open habit with branches that are quadrangular in cross section toward the cyme. Its leaves are opposite, ovate-acuminate, sub-cordate and dentate, exuding an unpleasant odor when touched. Numerous delicately scented flowers are arranged in fan-shaped, branched cymes. After flowering, the red calyces remain on the plant, each bearing a light metallic-blue berry, thus prolonging the plant's decorative value.
Height of plant 6½–10 ft. (2–3 m.).
Size of flower 1⅛ in. (3 cm.).
Place of origin Japan and eastern China.
Flowering time Summer–autumn.
Cultivation In partial shade. Temperate climate. Good resistance to frost (18° to 14° F./−8° to −10° C.). It likes well-aerated, deep, rich, moist soil. Benefits from occasional applications of organic/mineral fertilizers. Requires watering in the summer. Pruning: shorten branches by one-third during the winter. If necessary, prune hard.
Propagation By cuttings taken in the spring for rooting under glass, in a sheltered nursery bed outdoors or in a greenhouse. By spring seed sowing under glass.

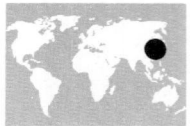

Qualities Hardy. Easy to grow.

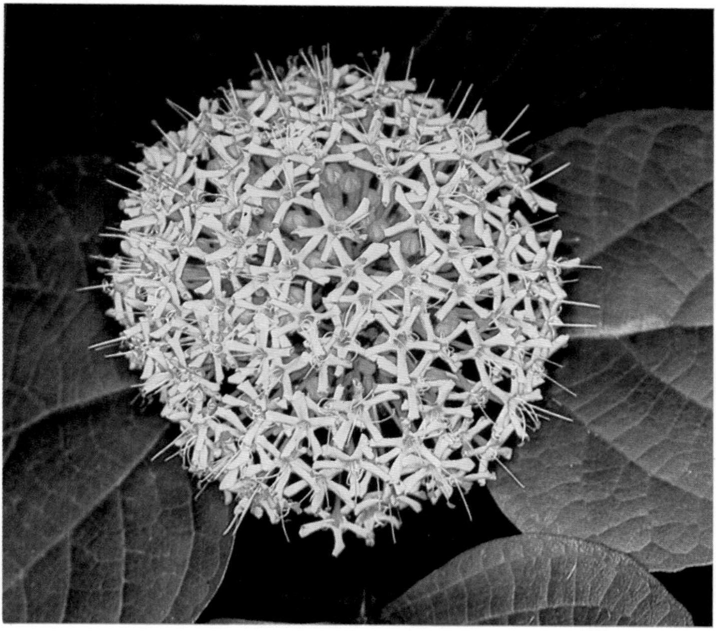

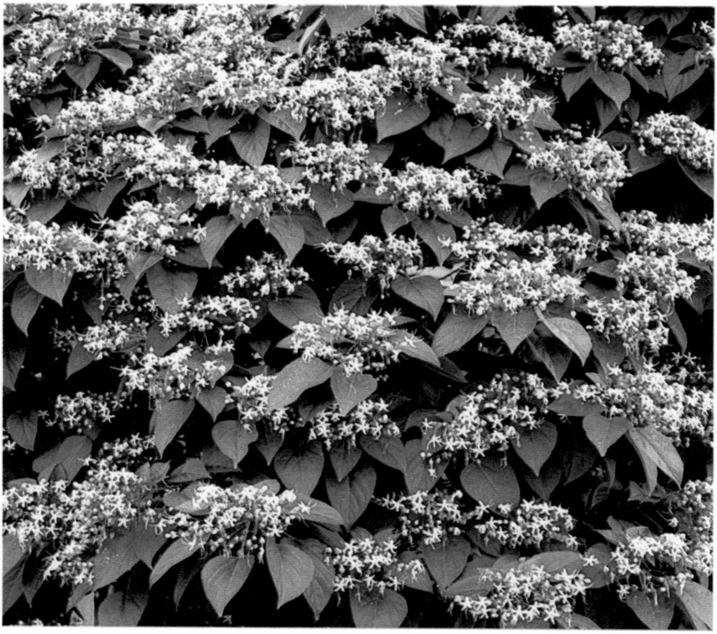

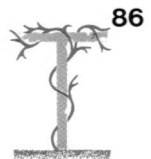

86 CLIANTHUS PUNICEUS Banks and Daniel Solander
Syn.: *Donia punicea* George Don. Common name: Parrot's beak

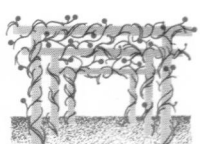

Family Papilionaceae.
Description An attractive shrub for temperate regions, with strange, showy inflorescences and delicate foliage. It is of climbing habit and well-branched. Its alternate leaves are imparipinnate with ten to twelve pairs of leaflets. Its flowers are borne in pendulous axillary clusters, each having a long, acuminate falciform carina and averse vexillum.

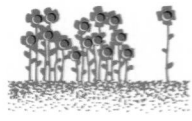

Height of plant 40–60 in. (1–1.50 m.).
Size of flower 1⅛–2 in. (3–5 cm.).
Place of origin New Zealand.
Flowering time Spring or winter, according to the climate of the continent it is grown in.

Cultivation Sunny position. Cannot withstand the cold. Warm, sheltered coastal areas suit it well. To grow this plant outdoors in northern areas, plant it out for the summer months and then pot it up to overwinter in a cool greenhouse. Rich, lime-free loam, somewhat compact; add organic/mineral fertilizers when planting. Regular watering. Cut back lightly after flowering. Pests: scale insects and greenhouse red spider mites.
Propagation By spring sowing in pots under glass. By long heel cuttings of lateral shoots in the spring or summer.
Qualities Half-hardy. Very easy to grow.

87 CLIVIA MINIATA Eduard von Regal
Syn.: *Imantophyllum miniatum* William Jackson Hooker. Common name: Kaffir lily

Family Amaryllidaceae.
Description A herbaceous plant with a short rhizome and large, carnose, fasciculate roots. Its symmetrical leaves are arcuate, liguliform, consistent and distichous with sheathed leaf bases. Its numerous flowers are in groups of six to fifteen, borne terminally on a succulent stalk and consisting of an infundibuliform perigonium deeply divided into six spatulate lobes. This plant can live outdoors in warm-temperate climates but is generally grown as an indoor plant to brighten a rather dark corner.

Height of plant 20–24 in. (50–60 cm.).
Size of flower 2⅜–4 in. (6–10 cm.).
Place of origin South Africa.
Flowering time Late winter–spring.

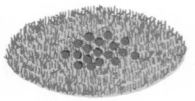

Cultivation A shady position. Frost-tender. But rarely planted in the garden except in the tropics. Elsewhere treated as a pot plant. It prefers good topsoil amended with equal parts peat and leaf mold plus some well-rotted manure and sand. Frequent watering. Repot every three or four years. Pests and diseases: ground insects and mealybugs; various rots.

Propagation By clump division in the autumn or after flowering. By seed, which must be fresh; this is slow to produce new plants.
Qualities Hardy only in its natural environment. Easy to grow.

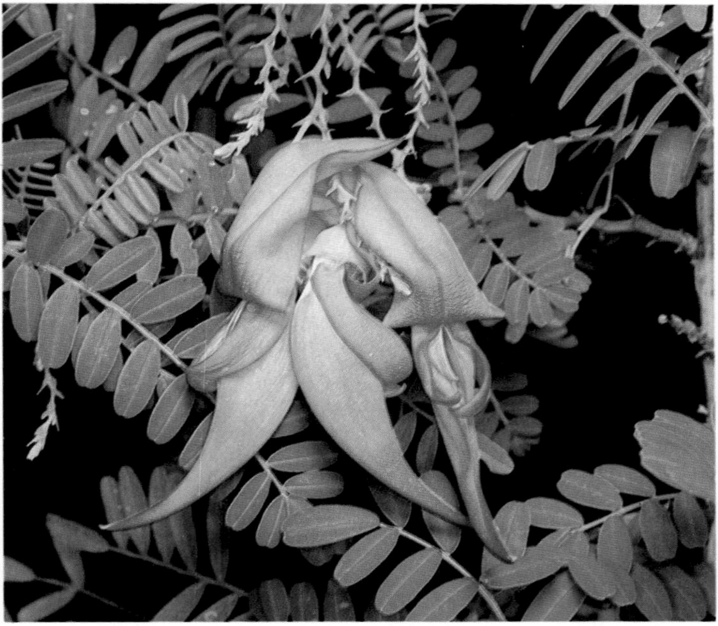

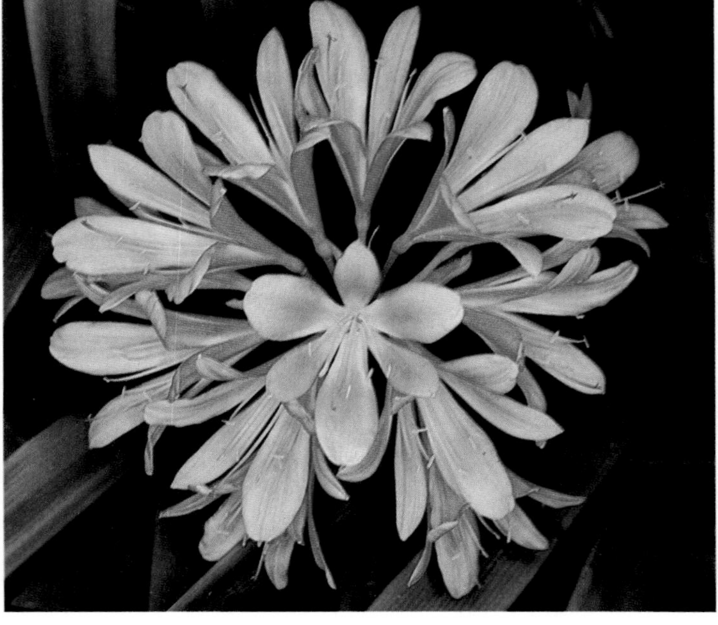

88 COBAEA SCANDENS Antonio Jose Cavanilles
Common name: Cup and saucer vine

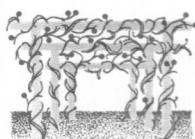

Family Polemoniaceae.
Description Perennial climbing plant with an unusual inflorescence in the shape of a bell. Often grown as an annual because of its aversion to the cold. Its vigorous climbing stems grow rapidly, with alternate, sessile, rugose, paripinnate leaves, which end in a long cirrus; they consist of four to eight oval acute leaflets. The flowers, borne on long peduncles, have a very showy calyx with open lobes and a campanulate corolla. The similarity to a Chinese handleless teacup and saucer accounts for the name "cup and saucer vine." There is also a rare white variety.
Height of plant 20–33 ft. (6–10 m.).
Size of flower 2⅜–3⅛ in. (6–8 cm.).
Place of origin Mexico.
Flowering time Summer–autumn.
Cultivation Full sun, partial shade. Temperate climate. In sheltered, warm inland and coastal areas it will live in the open for several years. A greedy plant, it requires good, well-aerated garden soil that has been well manured. Occasional liquid feeds. Plenty of watering. Prune to control growth in early spring. Pests: aphids, red spider mites and gnawing insects.
Propagation By late winter sowing in individual pots under glass. Use a sandy, medium-light compost.
Qualities Half-hardy. Very easy to grow.

---

89 COLEUS BLUMEI George Bentham cv. hybrid
Common name: Painted nettle

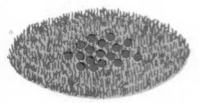

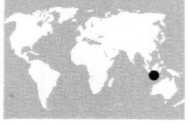

Family Labiatae.
Description A perennial although usually treated as an annual, this is extensively grown for the colors of its foliage, which is spectacular (the flowers are insignificant). It has a herbaceous, succulent, quadrangular stem with open ascendent ramifications. Its large opposite leaves are ovate-acuminate and dentate-sinuate on the margin; their green edges are accompanied by a brilliant range of colors including cream, yellow, red and purplish-red. The tiny white or azure flowers are bilabiate.
Height of plant 15–32 in. (40–80 cm.).
Size of flower ⅛ in. (0.5 cm.).
Place of origin Java.
Flowering time Summer.
Cultivation Full sun or very light shade. Temperate climate. Frost-tender. Grows in any well-aerated, moist, sandy soil that is either naturally rich or well manured. Frequent and plentiful watering. Pinch out growing tops to encourage side shoots and prevent legginess. Remove inflorescences as soon as they appear in order not to weaken the plant. May be damaged by wind and heavy rain. Pests and diseases: aphids; various rots.
Propagation By late winter seed sowing in pans under glass. By cuttings taken in summer or fall and rooted in a warm place.
Qualities Easy to grow and propagate.

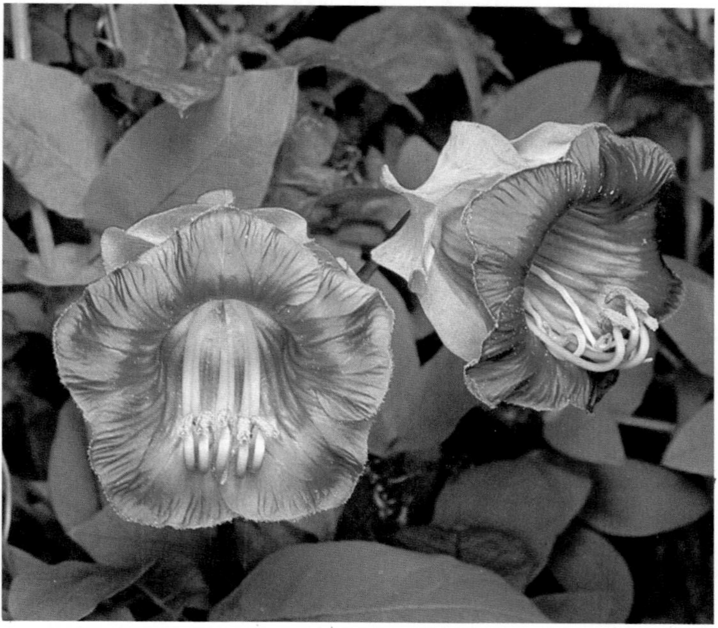

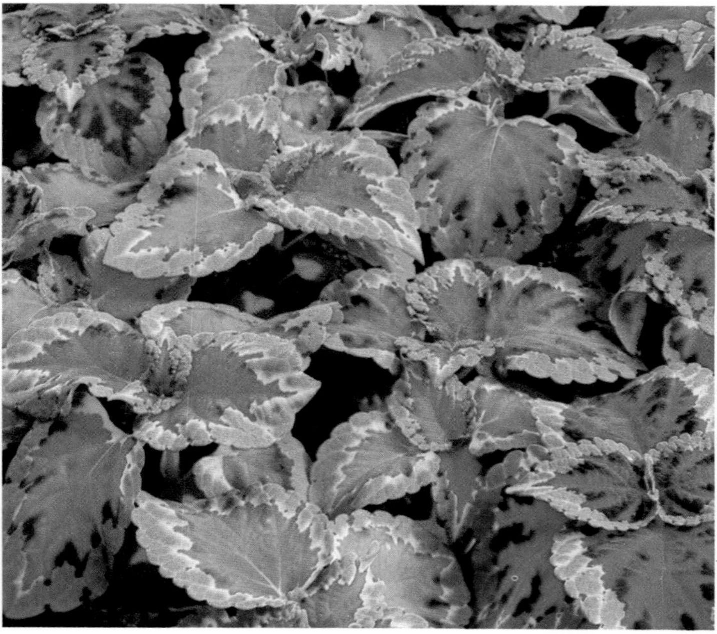

90 CONVALLARIA MAJALIS Carolus Linnaeus
Common name: Lily of the valley

Family Liliaceae.
Description This deciduous herbaceous plant grows from a small, branched, underground rhizome. Its glaucous green leaves are ovate-lanceolate and surround the pure white, sweetly scented flowers, which are borne in racemes of six to twelve on a slender scape. Fruit: quite large, pealike orange berries.
Height of plant 6–8 in. (15–20 cm.).
Size of flower ⅛ in. (0.5 cm.).
Place of origin Temperate zones of Europe.
Flowering time Spring.

Cultivation Shady position. Temperate climate. Prefers well-aerated fertile soil, rich in calcium and organic material, moist but well drained. The crowns should be lifted and divided every four or five years to avoid overcrowding. As the growing period begins, feed with a complete mineral fertilizer. If necessary, water regularly until flowering has started, then less frequently as the plants enter their resting period.
Propagation By rhizomes in the spring.
Qualities Also suitable for containers. Hardy. Easy to grow.

91 CONVOLVULUS MAURITANICUS Edmond Boissier
Common name: Ground morning glory

Family Convolvulaceae.
Description A small evergreen, perennial, decumbent or procumbent (prostrate) climber, this makes a most decorative addition to a rockery or an old wall. Its slender stem carries alternate, oval-obtuse, pubescent leaves on a short panicle. The flaring, bell-shaped flowers are abundant and appear over a long period.
Height of plant 40–60 in. (1–1.50 cm.).
Size of flower 1⅛–1½ in. (3–4 cm.).
Place of origin North Africa.
Flowering time Spring–autumn.

Cultivation Full sun. Temperate climate. Frost-tender. Prefers a stony site and thrives among rocks and crevices. Grows in any moderately heavy soil. Likes regular watering but can withstand dry conditions. No particular attention needed. The best results come from sowing directly in flowering positions.
Propagation By sowing or taking cuttings in spring or autumn.
Qualities Hardy. Easy to grow.

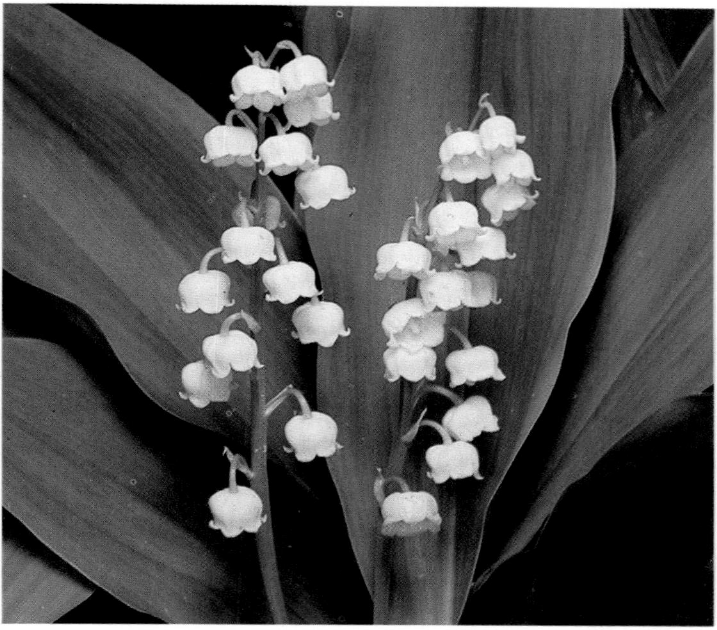

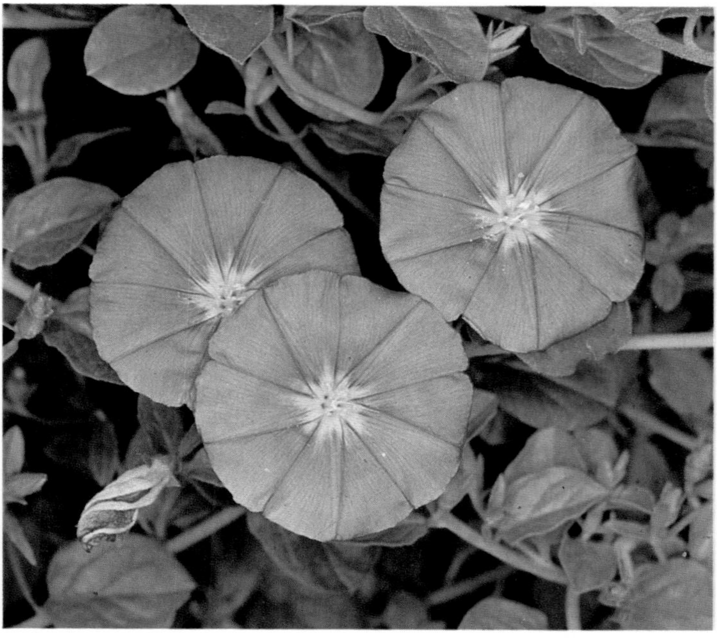

92 CONVOLVULUS TRICOLOR Carolus Linnaeus
Syn.: *C. minor*. Common name: Dwarf morning glory.

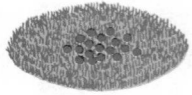
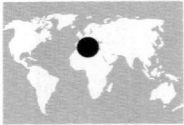

Family Compositae.
Description A herbaceous, climbing or prostrate annual with well-branched stems. It has alternate oblong leaves with ciliate edges and venation beneath. Its solitary flowers are axillary and carried on long peduncles; they have a large infundibuliform corolla in three bands of color—dark blue on the outside, white on the median plane and, in the throat, sulphur yellow. The flowers open in the morning and close in the evening.
Height of plant 15–20 in. (40–50 cm.).
Size of flower 1⅛–1½ in. (3–4 cm.).
Place of origin Southern Europe and North Africa.
Flowering time Summer.
Cultivation Full sun. Temperate climate. Cannot withstand very low temperatures. Prefers calcium-rich soil but can adapt to any good, fertile soil. Averse to overmoist conditions. Organic manure should be dug into the ground before sowing or planting out and occasional applications of liquid fertilizers given during the growing period. The plants need small supports if required to climb, but nothing if they are to hang down.
Propagation By spring sowing into flowering site or in peat pots under glass. Does not like to be transplanted
Qualities Hardy. Easy to grow.

93 COREOPSIS LANCEOLATA Carolus Linnaeus
Common name: Tickseed

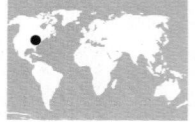
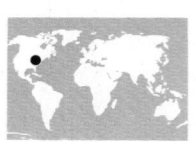

Family Compositae.
Description A bushy perennial that is remarkable for its abundant and free-flowering qualities. It naturalizes well. Its slender upward-branching stems carry opposite leaves which are either entire or pinnatisect at the base, while the rest are oblong-lanceolate. The showy, decorative, golden-yellow flowers are borne in capitula, like small single sunflowers, with a little disc. The ray florets have a ligule-dentate margin.
Height of plant 24–40 in. (0.60–1, m.).
Size of flower 1½–2 in. (4–5 cm.).
Place of origin Eastern United States.
Flowering time Spring–early summer.
Cultivation Sunny to partial shade. Temperate climate. Fairly frost-resistant especially if well mulched. Prefers well-aerated, sandy soil with some humus; but the soil should not be too good, as the plant produces more leaves than flowers in fertile ground. Regular but restrained watering. Dead flowers should be cut off at stem base. Does not like to be disturbed. Short-lived.
Propagation By spring sowing in pans in a coldframe. By clump division in the spring or autumn. Also self-seeding.
Qualities Hardy. Easy to grow.

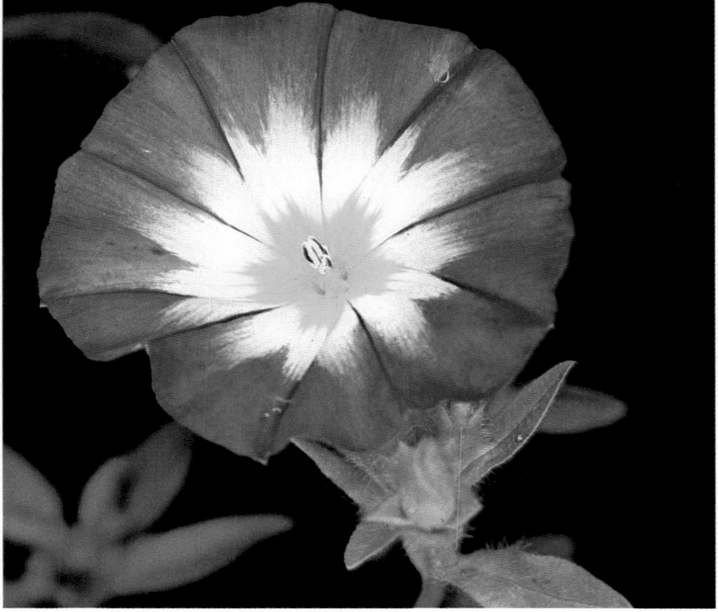

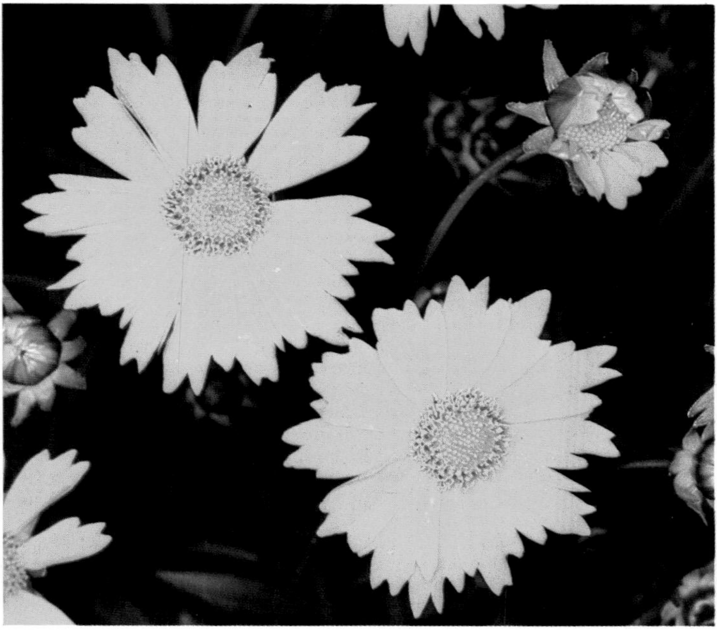

94 COREOPSIS TINCTORIA Thomas Nuttall cv. ''Atropurpurea''
Syn.: *C. bicolor* Augustin Pyramus DeCandolle

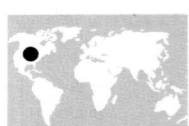

Family   Compositae.

Description   A herbaceous, upright, bushy annual of great charm due to its floriferousness. Its pubescent leaves are parted into three to five ovate-oblong lobes. The species has yellow outer flowers with a dark, brownish center but there are numerous other single and double varieties in colors ranging from yellow to chestnut-brown. The flowers are arranged in open capitula borne terminally on long, slender peduncles.

Height of plant   24–40 in. (0.60–1 m.).

Size of flower   2 in. (5 cm.).

Place of origin   Central United States.

Flowering time   Late spring–summer.

Cultivation   Full sun or partial shade, sheltered from the wind. Temperate climate. Well-aerated, sandy soil, even slightly argillaceous, but not too rich because then the plants tend to topple over. Frequent watering. Remove dead flowers at once. Trouble-free.

Propagation   By sowing in late winter in boxes in a warm greenhouse. Prick off once before planting out. Or by spring sowing directly in the flowering site in well-aerated ground.

Qualities   Hardy. Easy to grow.

95 CORNUS FLORIDA Carolus Linnaeus cv. ''Rubra''
Common name: Flowering dogwood

Family   Cornaceae.

Description   A deciduous shrub or small tree with a wide spread. Its dark-green leaves are opposite, oval-acuminate and undulate, turning a gorgeous red in autumn. Its insignificant greenish-yellow flowers are arranged in the center of four large white or rose-pink spatulate oblong bracts that look like a flower. Showy coral-red berries in the autumn.

Height of plant   10–16 ft. (3–5 m.) but up to 39 ft. (12 m.) in its habitat.

Size of flower   2–4 in. (5–10 cm.) with bracts.

Place of origin   Eastern United States.

Flowering time   Spring.

Cultivation   Sunny to partially shaded position. Temperate climate. Dislikes excessive heat. Grows in any soil or humus-rich, moist woodland mold. Requires regular watering and an occasional complete feed. These plants look more natural if left unpruned. Insects and diseases: borers; chlorosis in unsuitable soils.

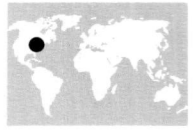

Propagation   By spring seed sowing in pots in a coldframe, but this is a very slow method. By layering of lateral shoots. Or by cuttings in the spring or summer.

Qualities   Hardy. Easy to grow.

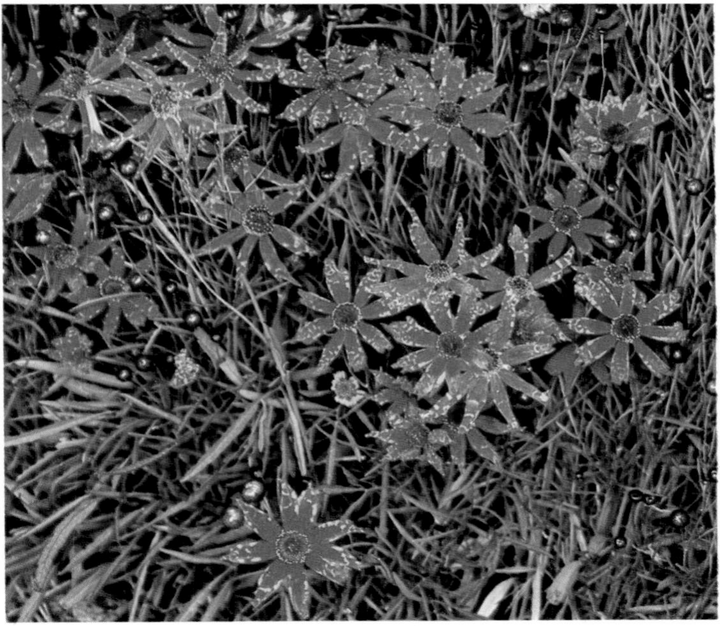

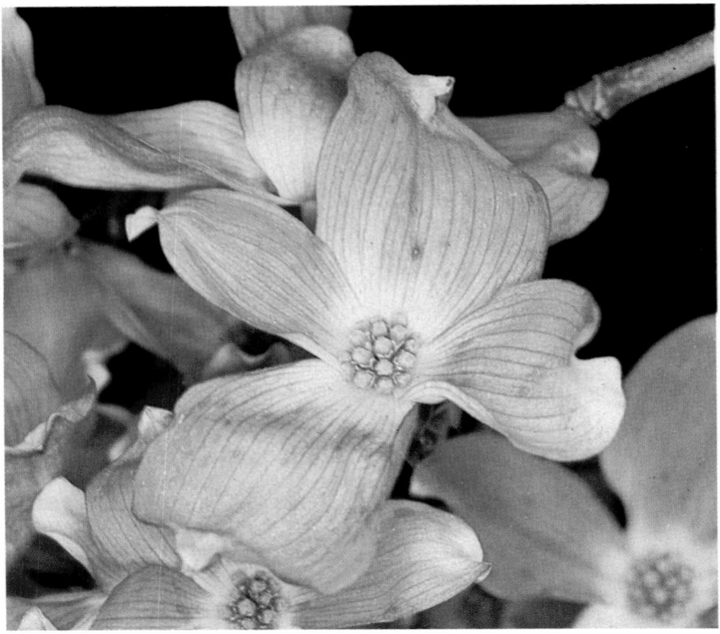

96 CORONILLA GLAUCA Carolus Linnaeus

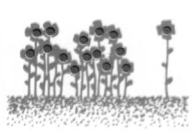

Family Papilionaceae.
Description A delightful shrub that requires a temperate climate and grows particularly well in California. It is well branched with alternate, imparipinnate leaves composed of five to seven leaflets. It has numerous flowers arranged in an open umbel and borne on a slender peduncle; they are only noticeably scented when exposed to the sun.
Height of plant 5–10 ft. (1.50–3 m.).
Size of flower ¼–½ in. (0.7–1.5 cm.).
Place of origin Mediterranean area.
Flowering time Spring–summer.

Cultivation Full sun or slight shade. Temperate climate. Dislikes the cold and is subject to frost damage. Prefers sandy-clayey soil. An undemanding plant, it self-sows easily. A moderate feeding can be given occasionally if really necessary. Watering should be restricted to a bare minimum. Pruning consists of cutting off the dead growth and shortening the stems in the autumn–winter period. Trouble-free.
Propagation By spring sowing in pots (peat, if possible) so that the plants can be planted out later complete with soil ball. The seeds should be brought on in a coldframe. Where the climate is warm enough, seeds can be sown directly in the garden and thinned out later if required.
Qualities Hardy. Easy to grow.

---

97 CORTADERIA SELLOANA (Joseph August Schultes and son) Paul Ascherson and Graebner
Syns.: *C. argentea* O. Stapf, *Gynerium argenteum* Christian Gottfried Nees von Esenbeck. Common name: Pampas grass

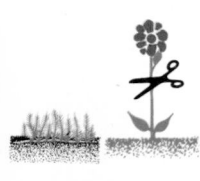

Family Gramineae.
Description A sturdy, vigorous grass forming a large, impenetrable mass. Its evergreen leaves are liguliform, sheathed at the base, with sharp edges. Its floral culms terminate in a dense setaceous plumelike panicle consisting of short silvery-white spikes with gramineous flowers that, in themselves, are insignificant. It is often grown by itself to display its beautiful plumes.

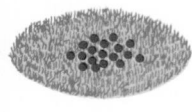

Height of plant 5–10 ft. (1.50–3 m.).
Size of flower 12–16 in. (30–40 cm.) each panicle.
Place of origin Brazil, Paraguay and Argentina.
Flowering time Late summer.

Cultivation Some, but preferably full sun. Temperate climate. Sensitive to frost and excessive moisture in the winter. Grows in almost any ground, but prefers a well-aerated, sandy soil. Requires no special attention except an occasional trim to remove dead or straggly growth, including the dry floral stems. Diseases: root rot.
Propagation By clump division in autumn or spring. Sometimes by seed in pans of sandy compost under glass.
Qualities Hardy. Easy to grow.

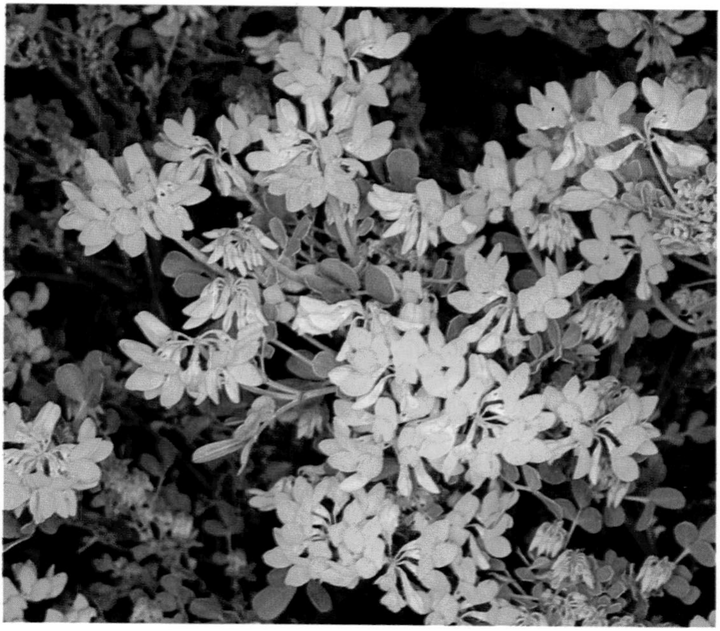

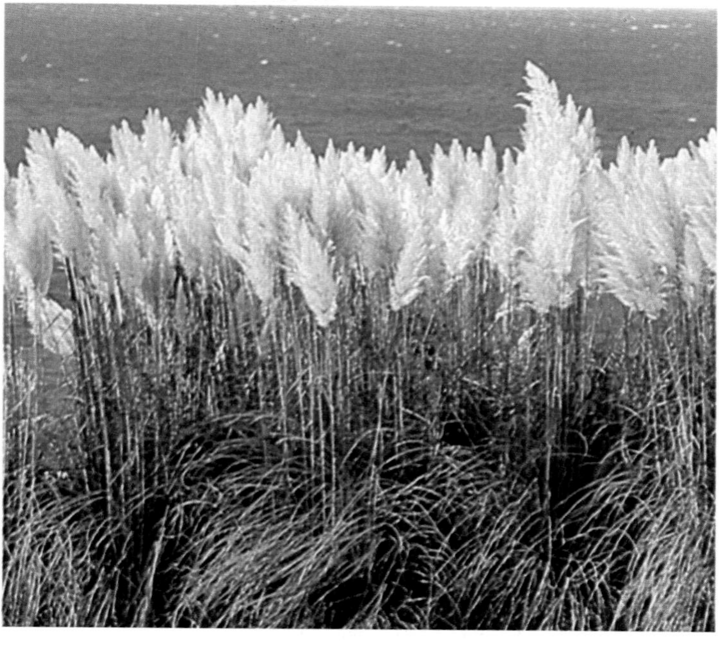

98 COSMOS SULPHUREUS Antonio Jose Cavanilles cv. "Diablo"
Syn.: Cosmea. Common name: Yellow cosmos

Family Compositae.
Description An annual with slender upright stems and delicate, polypinnatisect leaves. Its numerous terminal flowers are in a single capitulum with a large central disc, the colors ranging from shades of yellow to orange and red. "Diablo" is more compact than the others and has bright-red ray florets.
Height of plant 31–40 in. (0.80–1 m.).
Size of flower 3⅛–4¾ in. (8–12 cm.).
Place of origin Central America.
Flowering time Summer–early autumn.

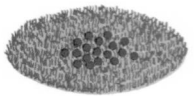

Cultivation Full sun to partial shade, sheltered from the wind. Temperate climate. Good, well-aerated, fertile soil. Requires plenty of watering and light organic/mineral feeding. It needs a little support from sticks, since it can get straggly. Usually trouble-free.
Propagation By spring sowing in pans of light, sandy soil under glass. Alternatively, by sowing directly in the garden, thinning out seedlings if too crowded.
Qualities Hardy. Easy to grow.

---

99 COTONEASTER HORIZONTALIS Joseph Decaisne
Common name: Rockspray cotoneaster

Family Rosaceae.
Description A popular semi-evergreen shrub, often found in rockeries. Its prostrate habit, attractive little flowers, reddish leaves in the autumn and red fruits that stay on the branches for most of the winter give this plant year-round appeal. The numerous stiff branches are arranged in a sort of fan shape, almost horizontally, with semipersistent, coriaceous, ovate-acute leaves. The small, hawthorn-like flowers are purplish-red with pink edges. Fruit is coral-red and bacciform.
Height of plant 40–60 in. (1–1.50 m.).
Size of flower ⅛–¾ in. (0.5–2 cm.).
Place of origin Western China.
Flowering time Spring.

Cultivation Full sun to partial shade. Cool-temperate climate. Frost-resistant. Give ample room to spread. Grows in almost any position, if not too shaded or damp, and in any humus-rich soil with a calcarious tendency, provided it is well drained. Benefits from a yearly application of well-rotted manure. Requires watering during dry periods. Pruning limited to tidying up straggly branches and cutting out weak or dead growth.
Propagation By cuttings of half-ripened shoots taken in the summer and put to root in sand in a coldframe; alternatively, of ripened shoots in the autumn. By air layering in the spring or summer. By seed, but this is a very slow method.
Qualities Hardy. Easy to grow.

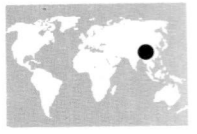

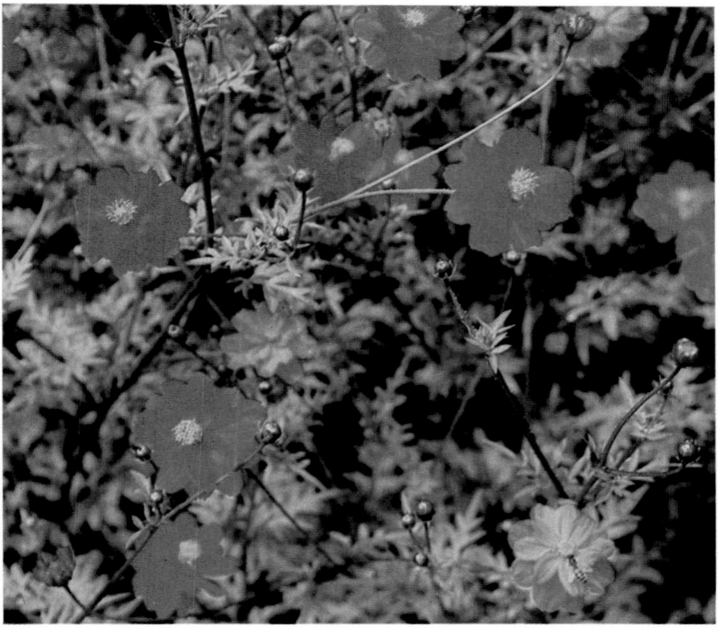

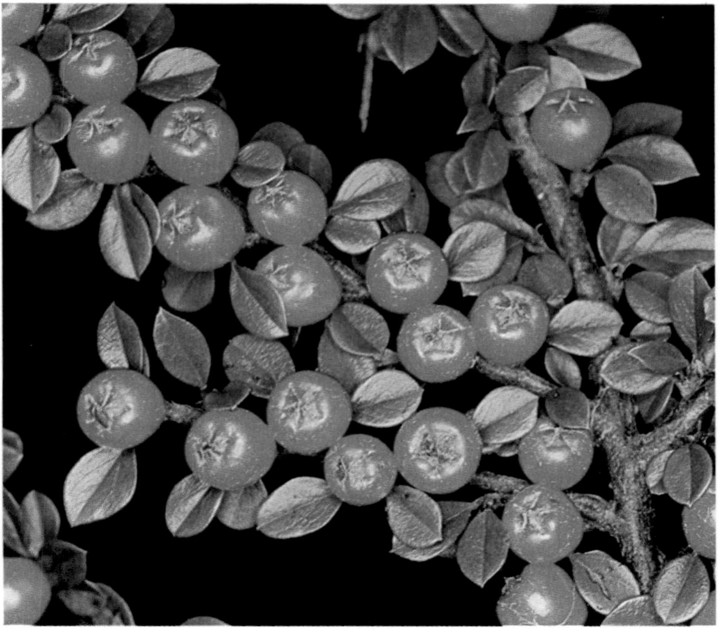

100 CRASSULA FALCATA Hermann Wendland
Syn.: *Rochea falcata* Augustin Pyramus DeCandolle

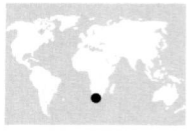

Family Crassulaceae.
Description A particularly charming succulent with an almost unbranched, upright stem. Its velvety leaves are persistent, distichous, opposite and succulent; they are also oblong, obtuse, slightly falciform and lightly fused to the base. Numerous little flowers are arranged in dense, open corymbiform cymes. The showy florescence is quite long-lasting.
Height of plant 20–32 in. (50–80 cm.) but in its own habitat 40–60 in. (1–1.50 m.).
Size of flower ⅛ in. (0.5 cm.); each cyme 2¾–4 in. (7–10 cm.).
Place of origin South Africa.
Flowering time Late summer.
Cultivation Full sun. Temperate climate. Frost-tender. Grown as an indoor or warm-climate rock-garden plant. Prefers a humus-rich, sandy soil mixed with a little peat. Water regularly in summer but less often in winter. In northern regions, keep it in a warm atmosphere or heated greenhouse. Diseases: root rot, rust and dry patches on the leaves.
Propagation By cuttings or seed in pans of light, very sandy compost in autumn or spring; bring on in a warm greenhouse, later pricking off and transplanting to small pots.
Qualities A good plant for terraces, balconies. Half-hardy. Easy to grow.

101 CROCUS SPECIES

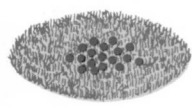

Family Iridaceae.
Description The Dutch are undoubtedly the leading authority on the production of hybrid crocus bulbs. Ornamental Dutch crocuses derive mainly from patient work carried out in crossing *C. vernus*, *C. flavus*, *C. sativus*, *C. susianus* and *C. versicolor*. They have a fairly small, piriform bulb with reticulate fibrous tunics and white nervature. One or two flowers spring direct from the corm through the crown of leaves.
Height of plant 3⅛–4¾ in. (8–12 cm.).
Size of flower 2–2¾ in. (5–7 cm.).
Place of origin Cultivated hybrid.
Flowering time Late winter–spring.
Cultivation A light or semishaded position. Temperate climate. Can withstand frost well, especially if protected by a light mulch. The plant grows in almost any type of ground but prefers good, fertile, moist, sandy garden soil mixed with leaf mold and a little well-rotted manure. There is usually no need to water crocuses. The bulbs can be left in the ground for two or three years before they are taken up and moved. Usually trouble-free.
Propagation By removing the small bulb offsets during the resting period and planting where they are to grow. Corms are freely available commercially.
Qualities Suitable for balconies, terraces. Hardy. Easy to grow.

102 CUPHEA IGNEA Augustin Pyramus DeCandolle
Syn.: *C. platycentra* Charles Lemaire. Common name: Cigar plant

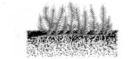
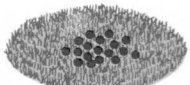

Family   Lythraceae.

Description   Suffrutescent, evergreen perennial subshrub often grown as an annual. It has numerous little reddish stems and a shrubby habit. Its shiny green leaves are alternate or opposite and ovate-lanceolate. The attractive, abundant flowers remain in bloom throughout the year if brought under cover during the coldest months; if left outdoors, they bloom from spring to winter. The tubulous flowers are borne singly in the terminal leaf axils.

Height of plant   8–20 in. (20–50 cm.).

Size of flower   ¾–1⅛ in. (2–3 cm.).

Place of origin   Mexico.

Flowering time   Best through summer and fall.

Cultivation   Partial shade. Temperate climate. Cannot withstand the cold. Woodland type, fairly heavy, humus-rich soil enriched with farmyard manure. Regular watering. Usually trouble-free. In colder climates, overwinter indoors.

Propagation   By cuttings taken in the spring or autumn and rooted under glass. By spring sowing in pans of light sandy compost.

Qualities   Half-hardy. Very easy to grow.

---

103 CYCLAMEN REPANDUM John Sibthorp and James Edward Smith
Syn.: *C. vernale* O. Schwarz

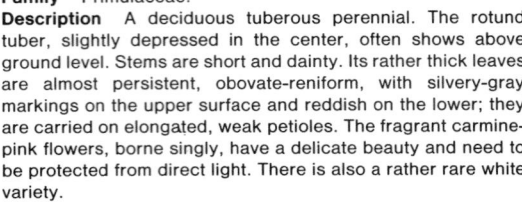

Family   Primulaceae.

Description   A deciduous tuberous perennial. The rotund tuber, slightly depressed in the center, often shows above ground level. Stems are short and dainty. Its rather thick leaves are almost persistent, obovate-reniform, with silvery-gray markings on the upper surface and reddish on the lower; they are carried on elongated, weak petioles. The fragrant carmine-pink flowers, borne singly, have a delicate beauty and need to be protected from direct light. There is also a rather rare white variety.

Height of plant   3⅛–4¾ in. (8–12 cm.).

Size of flower   ¾–1⅛ in. (2–3 cm.).

Place of origin   Eastern Mediterranean area.

Flowering time   Spring.

Cultivation   In full or partial shade. Cool-temperate climate. Fairly frost-resistant if well mulched. The plant likes soil that is rich in lime and humus; if necessary, add plenty of leaf mold to keep the ground moist. Regular watering, but not during the resting period. Does not like to be disturbed and should be left to naturalize. Pests: mice, tarsonemid mites, aphids and thrips.

Propagation   By summer sowing in pans under glass. The young plants have to be potted up and then repotted more than once before planting out into flowering site.

Qualities   Hardy. Very easy to grow.

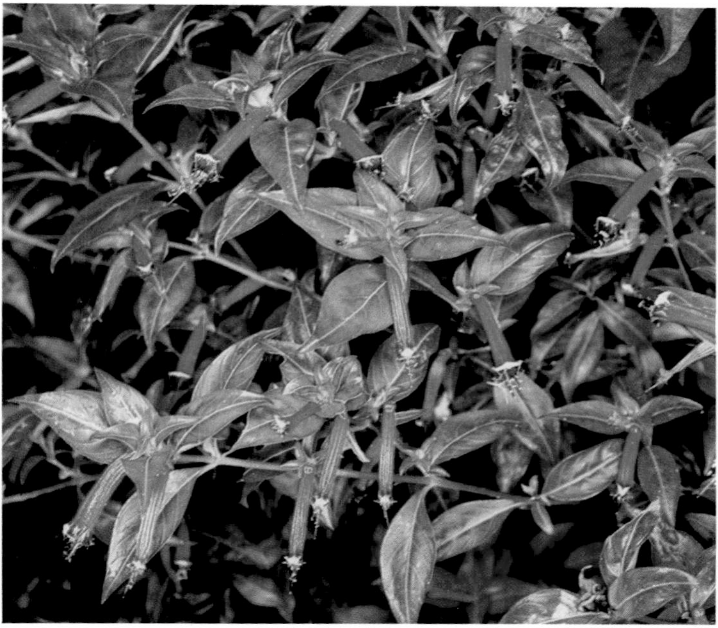

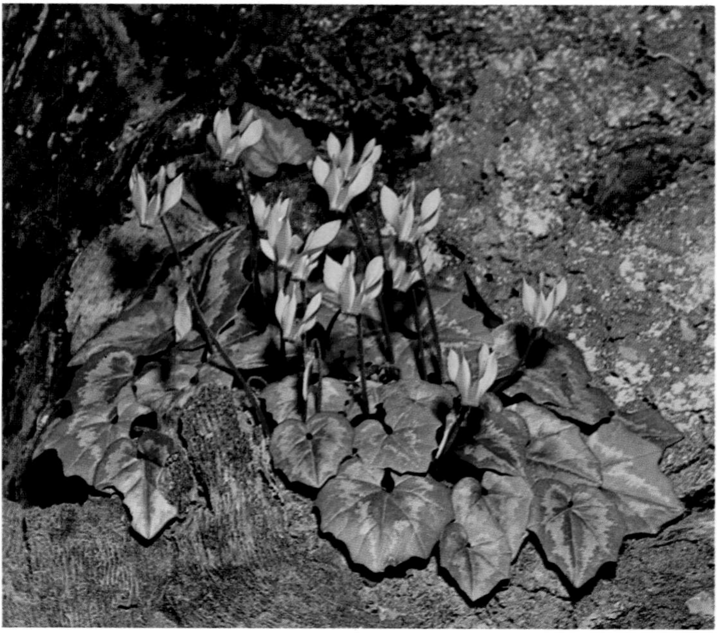

104 CYCLAMEN PERSICUM Phillip Miller
Syn.: *C. latifolium* John Sibthorp and James Edward Smith

Family Primulaceae.
Description Tuberous deciduous perennial. Its globose, depressed tuber puts out numerous roots. Cultivated varieties regarded as biennials. The radical leaves are rotundate-cordate, crenulate-denticulate, with marbled upper surface and plain lower one. Fragrant flowers borne singly on carnose stems. The winter-flowering indoor plant today is very different from the original species, due to the many hybridizations. A wide range of horticultural cultivars. A greenhouse pot plant.
Height of plant 8–10 in. (20–25 cm.).
Size of flower 1⅛–2⅜ in. (3–6 cm.).

Place of origin Eastern Mediterranean area and Asia Minor.
Flowering time Winter–spring.
Cultivation Shady but light position. Temperate climate. Compost of heath mold, fibrous humus and sand in equal parts, dried, powdered stable manure and a handful of dried blood. Water thoroughly from the base, on no account allowing the tuber or flower stems to get wet. Apply liquid fertilizer regularly until end of flowering period. Pests and diseases: eelworms (nematodes) and red spider mites; fungus diseases.

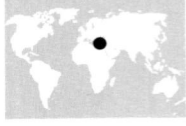

Propagation By midsummer sowing in boxes in a coldframe. Pot up, then pot on at least twice. Flowers the following year.
Qualities A delicate plant. Rather demanding to grow.

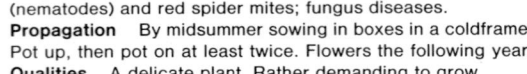

105 DAHLIA IMPERIALIS Roezl.
Common name: Tree dahlia

Family Compositae.
Description A tuberous deciduous perennial, this is the largest of all dahlias. Its nodose, hollow stems are frequently over 16½ ft. (5 m.) tall with opposite, bipinnate or tripinnate leaves. Its flowers are grouped in capitula with a yellow disc and white rays shot with pink. The numerous capitula are semipendulous and arranged in large terminal panicles.
Height of plant 8–18 ft. (2.50–5.50 m.).
Size of flower 4–6 in. (10–15 cm.).
Place of origin Uncertain but probably Mexico.
Flowering time Autumn.

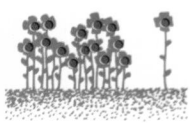

Cultivation Full sun. Deep, moist soil, even fairly heavy, provided it is rich or well manured. Plenty of watering. A position sheltered from the wind with some means of support for the long stems. Can also be grown in large pots, but this will restrict its size somewhat. After flowering, the plant enters a resting period and the peduncles can be cut back to within about 4 in. (10 cm.) of the ground. In cold areas, lift the tubers and store them, stratified in dry peat, in a frost-free place.

Propagation By clump division, each piece to include a portion of the collar bearing shoots. By herbaceous cuttings taken from the new shoots thrown up by the tubers after they have been stratified in damp sand in a heated greenhouse at the end of winter.
Qualities Fairly hardy. Easy to grow.

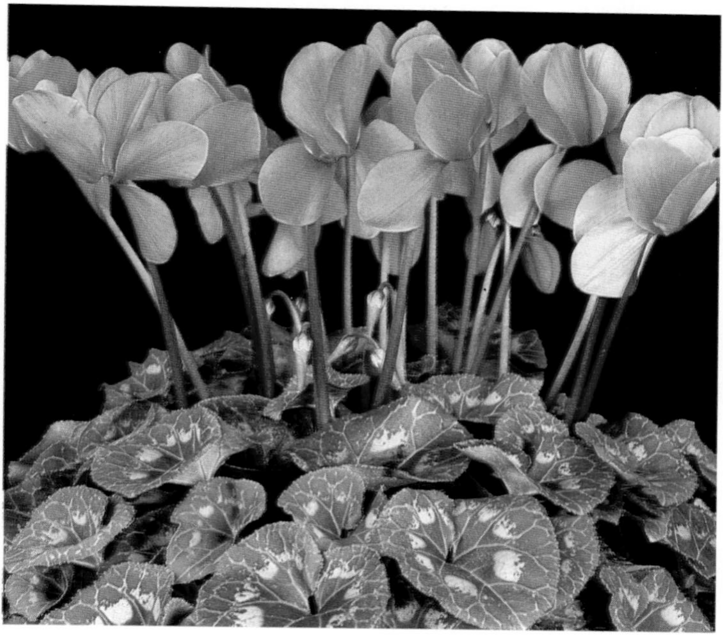

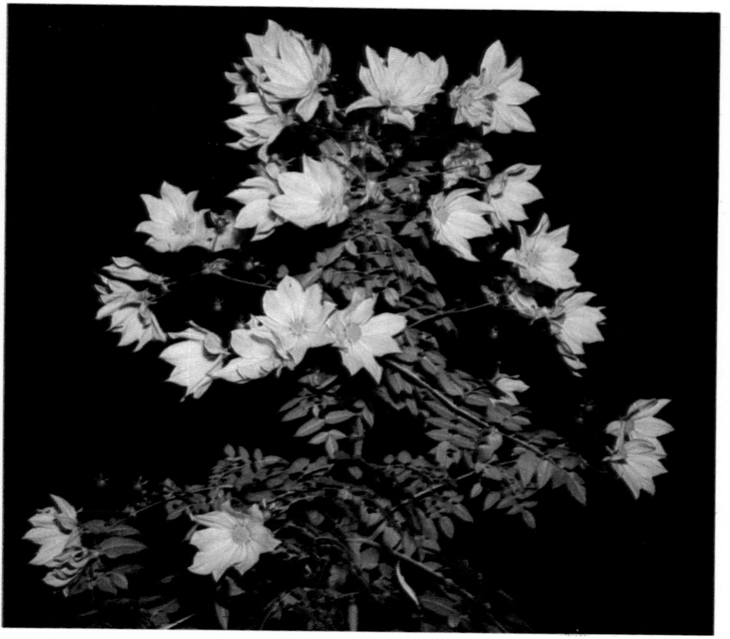

106 DAHLIA VARIABILIS Rene Louiche Desfontaines cv.

Family Compositae.

Description A herbaceous plant with large, fasciculate-tuberous, carnose, oblong roots terminating in a long, cylindrical-conical root. Its upright stems are nodose, hollow, herbaceous and fragile, with opposite ramifications. Leaves are opposite, pinnatisect or deeply dentate, with five to seven ovate-acute, dentate lobes. Flowers are in very variable medium-sized or large capitula; some have disc and unequal ray florets; other variations in single-flowered and anemone-flowered types.

Dahlias grown nowadays are mostly hybrid forms deriving from three Mexican species, commonly known as *Dahlia variabilis*. Continuous cultivation and breeding from first half of nineteenth century on have resulted in numerous hybrids, and we have lost sight of the original species. Consequently, dahlias are now divided into groups according to the form of their capitula and their flowers. Best-known are: those whose disc is in strong contrast to the ray, which often has only a few ligulate florets (single-flowered dahlia and collerette dahlia—recognizable by the little collar of florets inside the ray); those with a double or semidouble globular capitulum with large, ligulate

Cultivar of Dahlia variabilis: *below, cactus; opposite above, single-flowered dwarf; opposite below, decorative.*

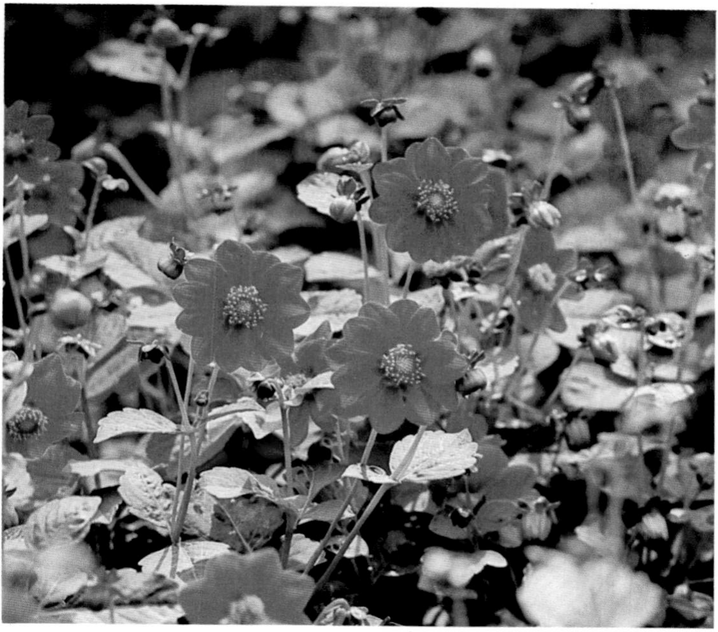

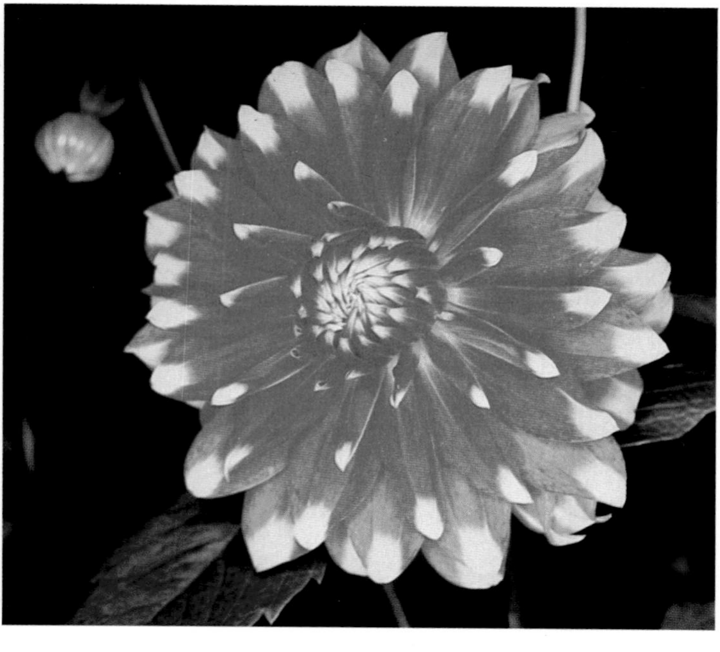

florets either oval, oblong or spoon-shaped (decorative, pom-pon and ball dahlias); and those with a globular capitulum and numerous ray florets either linear, cylindrical or acuminate (cactus or semi-cactus dahlia).

Height of plant   28–60 in. (0.7–1.5 m.); dwarf varieties—12–20 in. (0.30–0.50 m.).

Size of flower   2–10 in. (5–25 cm.), according to the variety.

Place of origin   Cultivated hybrids from Mexican species.

Flowering time   Summer–autumn.

Cultivation   Full sun or partial shade. Temperate climate. Prefers deep, rich, moist soil, even clayey or slightly cal-careous, well manured before planting. Plenty of watering with some liquid feeding initially. Pinch out to encourage side shoots. Cut stems of dead flowers back to two or three nodes from the base. In autumn, lift plants and overwinter them in boxes of dry peat in a frost-free place. Pests and diseases: gnawing insects and aphids; root rot and, in dampness, oidium and rust.

Propagation   By division of the tuberous clump, each part re-taining a portion of the collar bearing buds. By cuttings ob-tained by removing the shoots that grow from the tuberous clumps after they have been stratified in damp sand in a heated greenhouse at the end of winter, require potting up and proba-bly potting on before planting out. The single, fertile varieties can be reproduced from seed by sowing in pans in late winter under glass, but they may not come true to type.

Qualities   Very hardy. Quite easy to grow.

Opposite: Dahlia variabilis *cv. ''Pompon.''*

---

107   **DATURA SANGUINEA** Hipolito Ruiz Lopez and Jose Pavon

Family   Solanaceae.

Description   An evergreen shrub. Its branches are not very woody; they are fragile and very medullate. Its leaves are in groups of five or six, ovate-lanceolate, velutinous on both sur-faces and 6–10 in. (15–25 cm.) long by 2¾–6 in. (7–15 cm.) wide. The orange-red flowers, longitudinally veined in yellow, have an elongated trumpet-shaped corolla and are pendulous and unscented. The plant can be grown outdoors only in a tem-perate climate; otherwise it should be treated as a warm greenhouse pot plant to be put out in the open during the sum-mer.

Height of plant   6½–13 ft. (2–4 m.).

Size of flower   6–8 in. (15–20 cm.).

Place of origin   Peru.

Flowering time   Late summer–autumn.

Cultivation   A light, sheltered position, since the plant cannot withstand a temperature below freezing point. It prefers a fairly clayey soil, rich in organic material. Requires plenty of water-ing in the summer. After flowering, it can be pruned fairly hard to encourage new flowering growth. Diseases: root rot, chlorosis and stunted growth (rickets) in unsuitable ground.

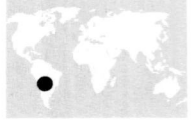

Propagation   By cuttings rooted in a warm greenhouse in late spring–summer; these take a long time to become established. By air layering in the spring.

Qualities   Half-hardy. Easy to grow.

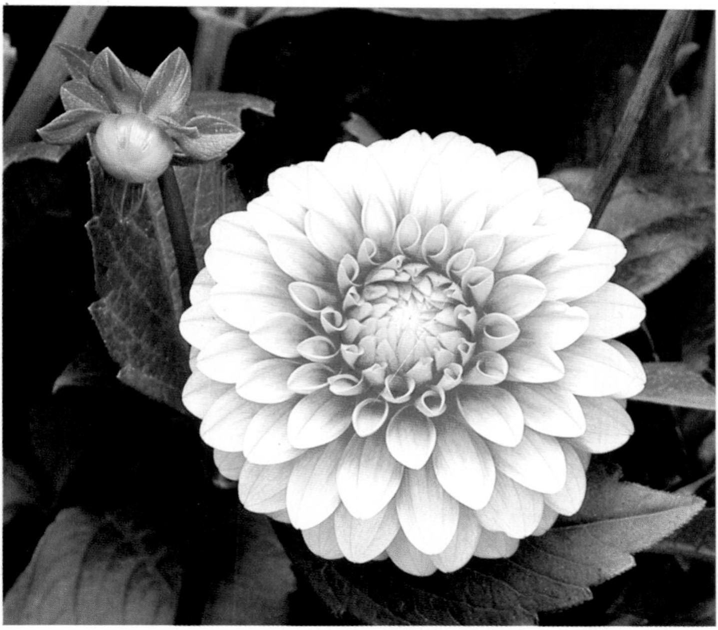

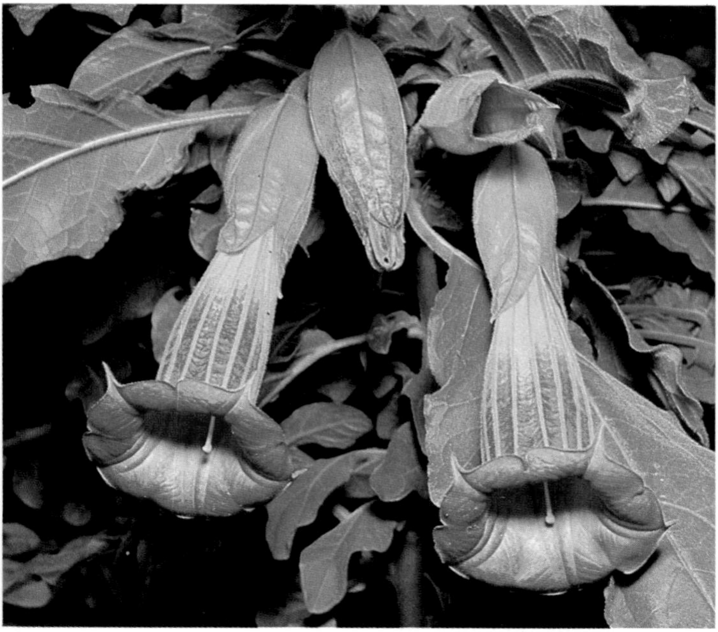

108 DELPHINIUM ELATUM Carolus Linnaeus cv. hybrid.

Syn.: *D. x cultorum* Hortorum. Common name: Candle larkspur

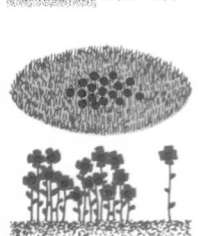

Family Ranunculaceae.
Description A herbaceous perennial, but short-lived and often grown as a biennial, it has particularly lovely flowers. Its upright stem is pubescent and has few branches. Its leaves are alternate, the lower ones being petiolate while the upper are sessile; they are palmate-parted and irregularly laciniate. The spurred flowers are borne in terminal racemes in the form of a large, dense panicle that may be as long as 20 in. (50 cm.). There are numerous single, semidouble and double cultivars, in various colors and sizes. Warning: this plant is poisonous.
Height of plant 20–80 in. (0.50–2 m.).
Size of flower 1½–3⅛ in. (4–8 cm.).
Place of origin Central and eastern Europe.
Flowering time Summer.
Cultivation A light to partially shaded position. Temperate climate. Prefers a deep, rich, acid soil; cannot tolerate lime. When necessary amend with leaf mold and peat. Plentiful watering during the summer. Cut the stems down to ground level in the autumn. Every three or four years divide the crowns and replant in different sites to strengthen growth. Diseases: root rot, chlorosis and viruses.
Propagation By clump division in spring. By root cuttings with buds from the collar taken in the same season. By summer sowing, putting the seed boxes in a coldframe.
Qualities Half-hardy. Fairly demanding to grow.

109 DEUTZIA x LEMOINEI Hortorum

Family Saxifragaceae.
Description A deciduous shrub with upright stems and fragile, abundant ramifications. Its leaves are opposite and ovate-lanceolate with a crenulate-dentate margin. Its numerous white flowers are carried in a great many erect thyrsiform panicles. The plant makes an unparalleled floral display in the spring. It is a cultivated hybrid of *Deutzia gracilis x D. parviflora*.
Height of plant 60–80 in. (1.50–2 m.).
Size of flower ½–1 in. (1.5–2.5 cm.).
Place of origin A cultivated hybrid, the parent plants originated in China and Japan.

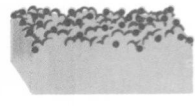

Flowering time Spring.
Cultivation A light to partially shaded position. Temperate climate. Although able to grow in any type of soil, it prefers moist, fairly clayey, humus-rich ground. Benefits from periodic feeding with organic/mineral fertilizers. Limited watering during dry spells. Cut out dead wood and overlong branches after flowering.

Propagation By division, by means of the radical suckers. By semi-hardwood cuttings at the end of summer. By air layering.
Qualities Also suitable for growing in large containers on terraces and balconies. Hardy. Easy to grow.

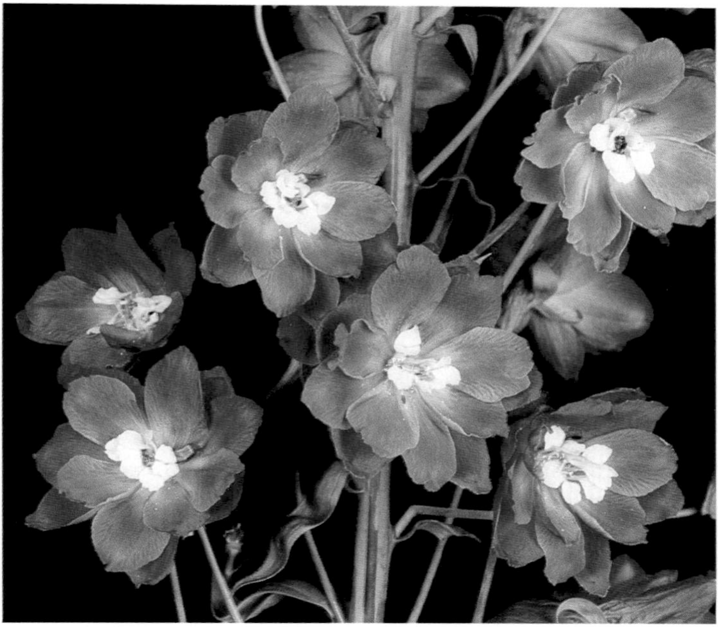

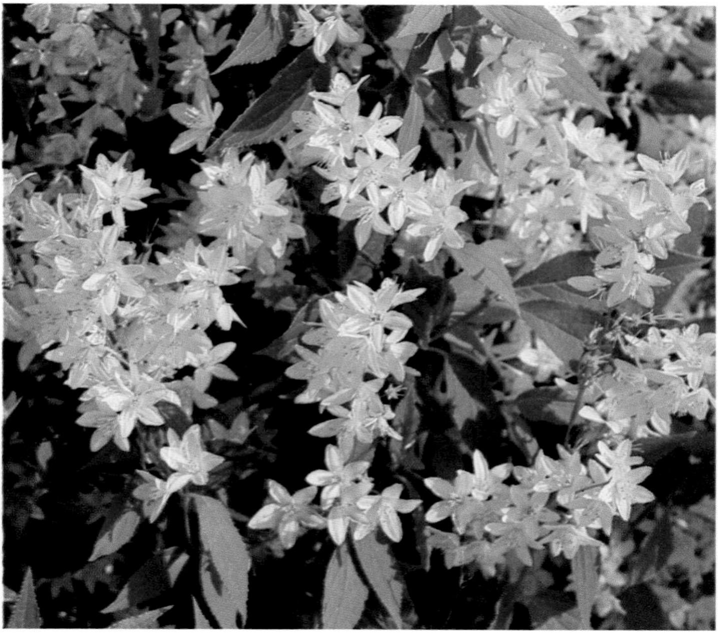

110 **DEUTZIA PULCHRA** M. L. Vidal

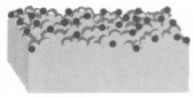

Family Saxifragaceae.
Description A charming, bushy plant that makes a particularly fine show in the spring. Its ramifications are upright, tending to open outward. Its leaves are opposite, cuneate at their base, ovate-lanceolate, acute and rough. Its numerous flowers are borne in pendulous panicles. There are also varieties in purplish-red, pink and white.
Height of plant 5 ft.–8 ft. 4 in. (1.50–2.50 m.).
Size of flower ⅜–½ in. (1–1.5 cm.).
Place of origin China.
Flowering time Spring.
Cultivation A partially shaded to half-shaded position. Temperate climate. Withstands the cold well. Will grow in any fairly compact, moist, humus-rich soil. Benefits from periodic applications of mineral fertilizer and manure. Plentiful watering during the summer. Remove all old flowering stems from the base. Usually trouble-free.
Propagation By basal suckers or air layering in the spring or summer. By semi-hardwood cuttings rooted in a coldframe.
Qualities Hardy. Easy to grow.

---

111 **DIANTHUS BARBATUS** Carolus Linnaeus
Common name: Sweet William

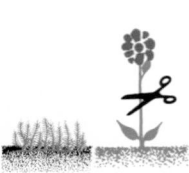

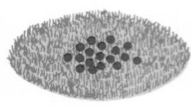

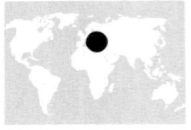

Family Caryophyllaceae.
Description A bushy little plant with sturdy, articulate-nodose, erect, green stems. Its shiny green leaves are opposite and oblong-lanceolate, the basal ones arranged in rosette form. Its little flowers are numerous and carried in dense, broad, terminal, umbelliform inflorescences. Their colors range through pink, red, violet, white. Although a perennial, the plant is nearly always grown as a biennial. There are numerous cultivars.
Height of plant 8–20 in. (20–50 cm.).
Size of flower ¾ in. (2 cm.).
Place of origin Eastern Europe, including Russia.
Flowering time Spring–summer.
Cultivation A sunny position. Temperate climate. Calcareous or clayey soil mixed with good woodland mold and well-rotted organic manure plus a little sand. Regular watering and a few liquid feeds during the early growth period. The young plants are usually planted out in the autumn with some protection such as straw or peat mulch against the winter cold. Subject to attack from various insects and fungus diseases.
Propagation By spring seed sowing in pans in a frame; prick off and plant out in the autumn.
Qualities Hardy. Easy to grow.

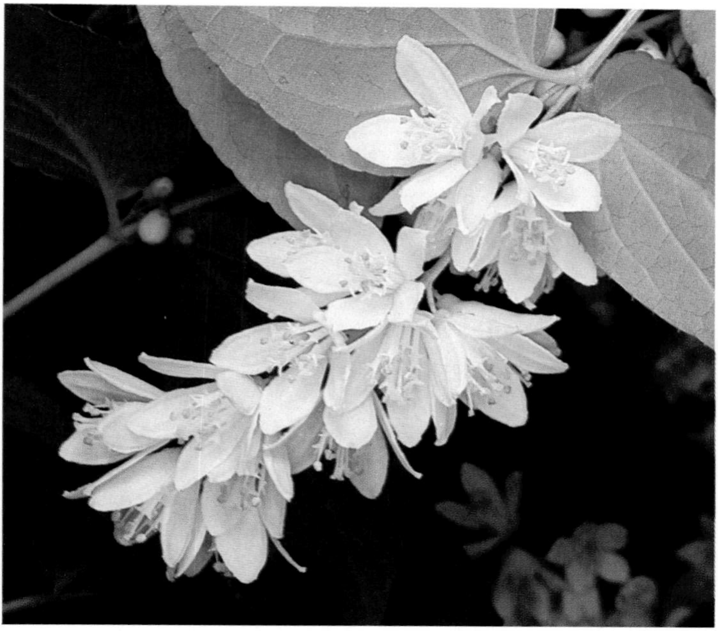

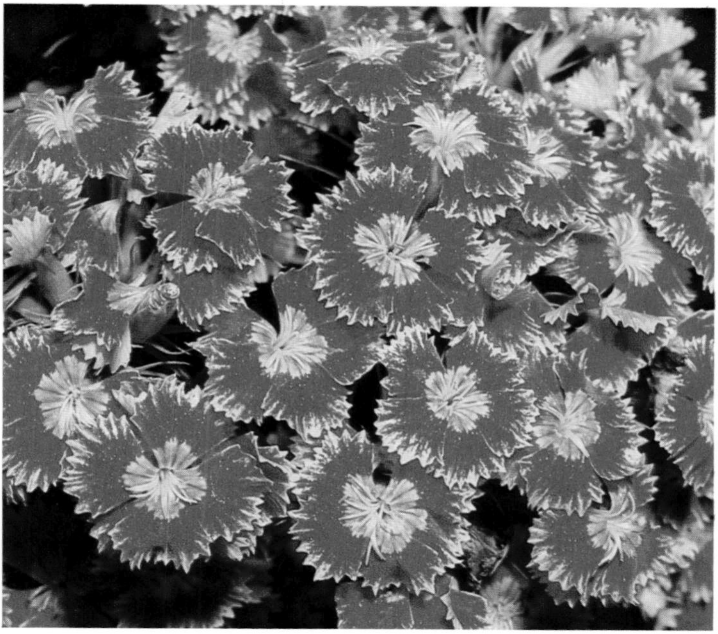

112 DIANTHUS CARYOPHYLLUS Carolus Linnaeus cv. "Florepleno" Hortorum
Common names: Carnation, clove pink

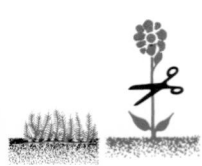
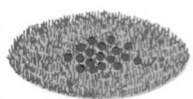
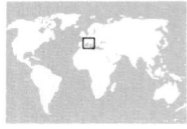

Family Caryophyllaceae.
Description This border perennial has a suffrutescent stem with short, open, erect ramifications elongated into articulate-nodose floriferous stems. Its leaves are sessile, linear-acuminate, consistent and rigid. The flowers are often sweetly scented and borne singly; they may be semidouble or double. Having been crossed innumerable times, the numerous carnation cultivars that we know today have been obtained from the original species; many are particularly suited to forced greenhouse cultivation.
Height of plant 20–40 in. (0.50–1 m.).
Size of flower 1–2 in. (2.5–5 cm.).
Place of origin Horticultural hybrid from parents originating in the western Mediterranean area.
Flowering time Spring.
Cultivation A sunny position. Temperate climate. Has a preference for good, clayey garden soil mixed with well-rotted leaf mold, well-seasoned farmyard manure and a little sand. Liquid feeding during the growing period. Regular overall watering. Pests and diseases: insects such as eelworms; fungus diseases and viruses.
Propagation By cuttings in autumn or spring and rooted under glass. By seed, in spring in a coldframe or cool greenhouse; seedlings should be pricked off and then potted up.
Qualities Half-hardy. Rather demanding to grow.

113 DIANTHUS DELTOIDES Carolus Linnaeus
Common name: Maiden pink

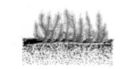

Family Caryophyllaceae.
Description A graceful, tufted perennial of prostrate habit with numerous slender, upright, diffuse stems. Its tiny dark-green leaves are linear and opposite. Its abundant flowers are carried terminally in small, compact inflorescences or are borne singly; they have a long, tubulous calyx and a distinctive dialypetalous corolla, their colors ranging from white to pink and dark red.
Height of plant 6–12 in. (15–30 cm.).
Size of flower ⅜–¾ in. (1–2 cm.).
Place of origin Europe.
Flowering time Spring–summer.
Cultivation Full sun. Temperate climate. Prefers well-aerated, sandy, very dry soil, even if not particularly fertile. Limited watering during very dry periods. No special care required. Old flowering stems should be cut off.
Propagation By spring sowing in a coldframe; seedlings should be pricked off into small pots and the young plants planted out into flower beds in the autumn.
Qualities Hardy. Suitable for balconies, terraces. Easy to grow.

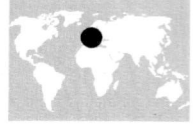

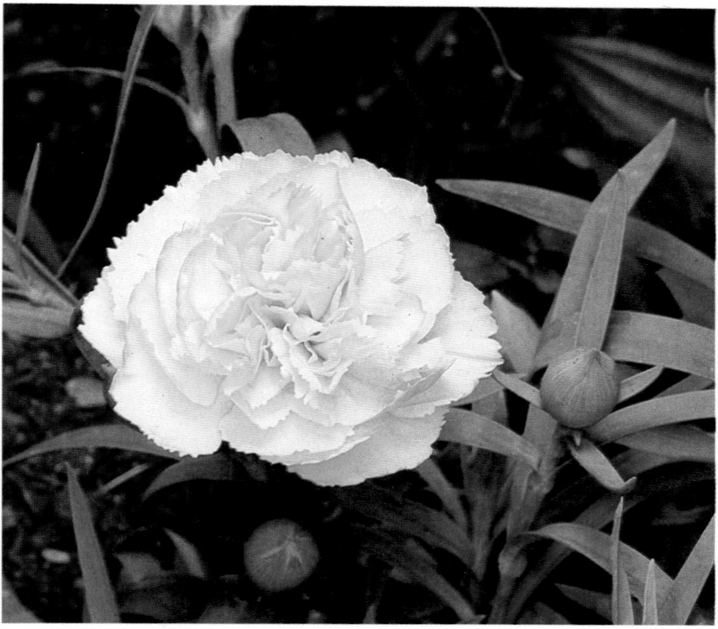

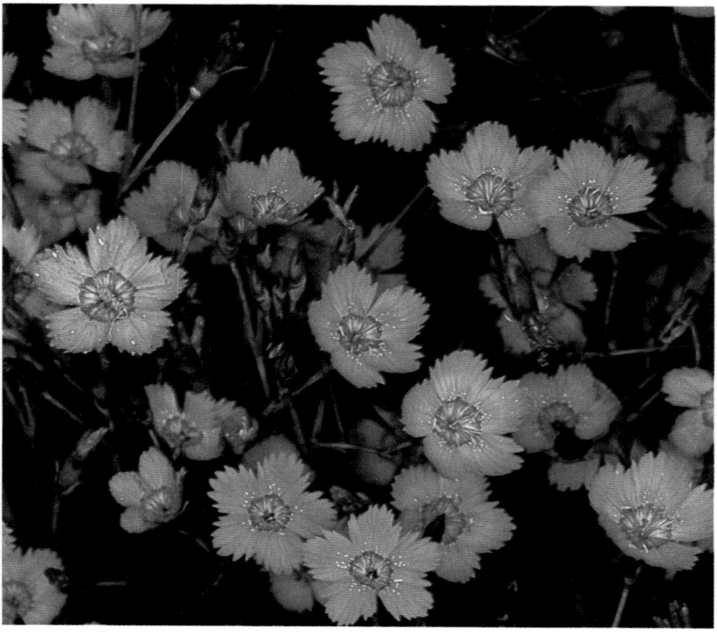

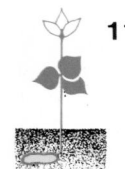

114 DICENTRA SPECTABILIS (Carolus Linnaeus) Charles Lemaire

Syn.: *Dielytra spectabilis* George Don. Common name: Bleeding heart

Family Fumariaceae.
Description A bushy herbaceous plant with numerous reddish-glaucous green stems. Its alternate leaves are pluriternate in cordate trilobate segments. The numerous pendulous flowers are borne in delightful lax arcuate racemes and are distinguished for their rose-pink calyx and white corolla. The plant flowers freely and for a long time.
Height of plant 16–32 in. (40–80 cm.).
Size of flower 1⅛–1⅜ in. (3–3.5 cm.).
Place of origin Manchuria and Korea.
Flowering time Spring–early summer.
Cultivation A position that is fairly shaded but in an open, protected site. Cool-temperate climate. May be damaged by heavy frosts. Prefers a light, porous soil that is either naturally rich or enriched with plenty of leaf mold and peat. Likes to be kept well watered. Pests and diseases: aphids; root rot.
Propagation Divide roots in early spring; take root cuttings in early summer; or sow seeds in midsummer in pans.
Qualities Easy to grow. Suitable to wild as well as formal gardens and rock gardens.

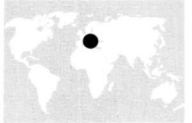

115 DICTAMNUS ALBUS Carolus Linnaeus

Syn.: *D. fraxinella* Christian Hendrick Persoon
Common names: Gas plant, dittany

Family Rutaceae.
Description A bushy perennial with simple upright stems. Not cultivated extensively but worth growing for the delightful balsamic perfume of its flowers. Its alternate leaves are compound and imparipinnate with oval-lanceolate leaflets. The numerous flowers are pink or white, borne in pubescent terminal racemes. The stems exude a volatile gas that can be lighted with a match.
Height of plant 20–36 in. (50–90 cm.).
Size of flower 1⅛–1½ in. (3–4 cm.).
Place of origin Southern and eastern Europe.
Flowering time Summer.
Cultivation Full sun. Temperate climate. Fairly resistant to the cold. Prefers rich, fertile, calcareous soil enriched with well-rotted manure. The stems should be cut back to the base in the autumn and the crown protected from the cold with a good mulch. Regular, moderate watering. Does not like being transplanted.
Propagation Best grown from seed sown directly in the garden in the spring and early summer. Or start seed in peat pots that can be put in the ground without disturbing the roots.
Qualities Hardy. Very easy to grow.

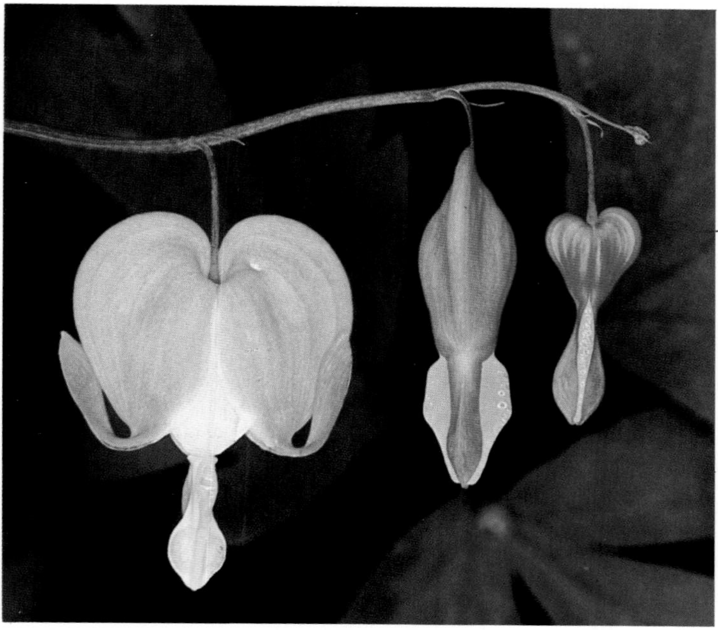

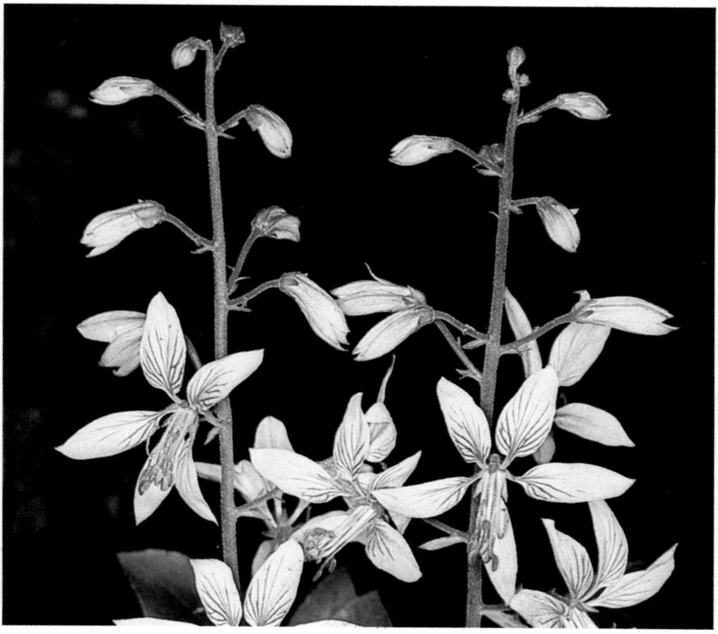

116 DIGITALIS LUTEA Carolus Linnaeus
Common name: Straw foxglove

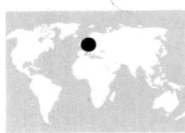

Family Scrophulariaceae.
Description A herbaceous perennial with an unbranched upright stem. Basal leaves are ovate-lanceolate with a very short petiole, while the stem leaves tend to become smaller toward the top; all the leaves are dark green. The inflorescence consists of a raceme bearing numerous greenish-yellow flowers on one side only; they are tubulous-campanulate with a down-turned corolla. The leaves contain alkaloids.
Height of plant 16–32 in. (40–80 cm.).
Size of flower 1–1⅜ in. (2.5–3.5 cm.).
Place of origin Western Europe.
Flowering time Summer.
Cultivation A shaded position. Temperate climate. Can withstand the cold fairly well. Prefers rich, sandy-siliceous, very dry soil. Water only if conditions become extremely dry. No particular care required. The old flowering stems should be cut down to the ground.
Propagation By seed in peat pots that can be sunk into the soil, since the plant does not like being transplanted. It is better to sow directly in the flowering site in the spring.
Qualities Hardy. Very easy to grow.

117 DIGITALIS PURPUREA Carolus Linnaeus
Common name: Common foxglove

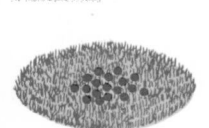

Family Scrophulariaceae.
Description A beautiful herbaceous flowering plant with a sturdy, upright stem, grown as a biennial. (Although a perennial, its life-span is only two to three years.) Its large basal leaves are oblong-lanceolate, averse, rugose and tomentose; on the stem they are alternate and small. The numerous large flowers are pendulous and tubulous-campanulate, borne in spicate racemes. This plant contains alkaloids. There are several cultivated varieties, some of the best being *D. maculata-superba*, *D. gloxiniaeflora* and the double *D. p. monstruosa*.
Height of plant 2–4 ft. (0.60–1.20 m.).
Size of flower 1½–2 in. (4–5 cm.).
Place of origin Western Europe.
Flowering time Spring–summer.
Cultivation Partial shade. Temperate climate. It likes a light, humus-rich, moist, permeable soil; it is a calcifuge plant. Regular watering. Cut all old flowering stems down to the collar. Diseases: chlorosis and root rot.
Propagation By spring sowing in a coldframe and planting out in the autumn. Seed can also be sown in the garden and the seedlings subsequently thinned out.
Qualities Hardy. Easy to grow.

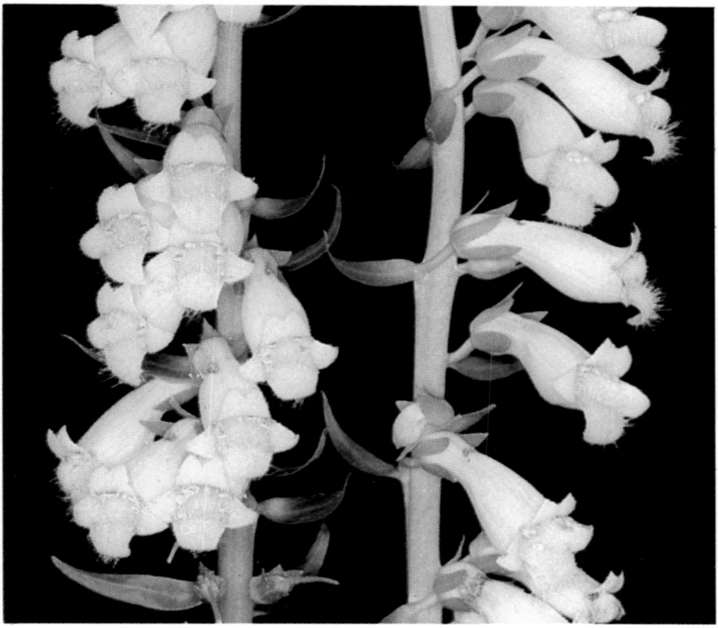

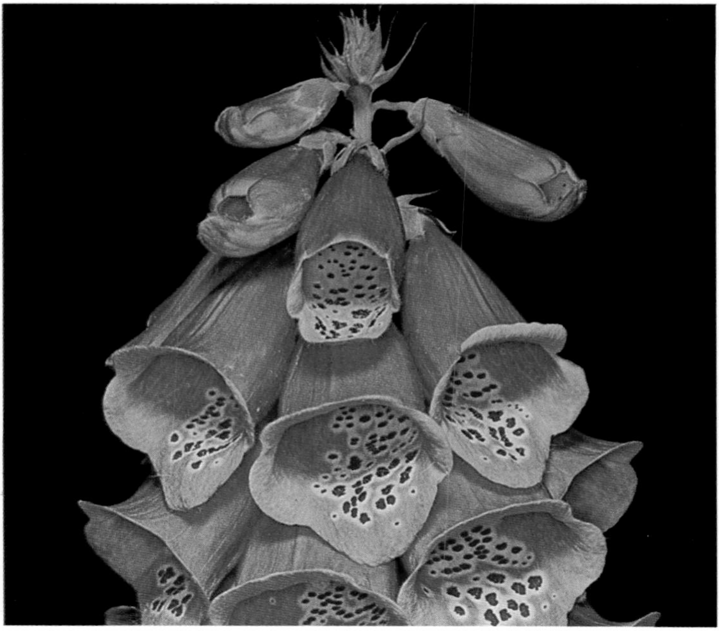

118 DIMORPHOTHECA BARBERIAE Adrian Hardy Haworth

Syns.: *D. lilacina* Eduard von Regel, *Osteospermum barberiae* (Haworth) Norlindh. Common name: Cape marigold

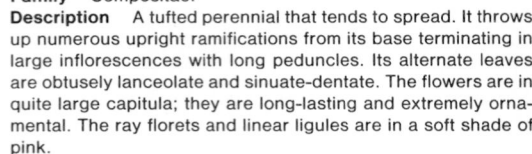

Family Compositae.

Description A tufted perennial that tends to spread. It throws up numerous upright ramifications from its base terminating in large inflorescences with long peduncles. Its alternate leaves are obtusely lanceolate and sinuate-dentate. The flowers are in quite large capitula; they are long-lasting and extremely ornamental. The ray florets and linear ligules are in a soft shade of pink.

Height of plant 12–16 in. (30–40 cm.).
Size of flower 2¾–3⅛ in. (7–8 cm.).
Place of origin South Africa.
Flowering time Summer.

Cultivation Very sunny position. Temperate climate. Cannot withstand cold. Grows in any soil that is well aerated, sandy and rich or enriched with organic manure. Requires frequent watering. All old flowering stems should be cut off at the base. Does not like being transplanted. Pests and diseases: aphids; stunted growth (rickets).

Propagation By spring sowing at the flowering site, with just a light covering of sand; germination is difficult.

Qualities Half-hardy. Quite demanding to grow.

119 DISTICTIS BUCCINATORIA (Augustin Pyramus DeCandolle)

Syns.: *Phaedranthus buccinatorius* (DeCandolle) Miers, *Bignonia buccinatoria* Mairet and DeCandolle

Family Bignoniaceae.

Description An evergreen climber with tendrils, its habit is to creep as high as possible. It is semitropical but grows well in sheltered positions in a warm coastal area. Its compound leaves are bifoliate—formed of two ovate-oblong leaflets, acuminate or obtuse, glabrous and coriaceous, with a petiole and branched filiform tendrils. The flowers are borne in pendulous terminal racemes with a tomentose peduncle and a campanulate tubulous corolla with four rose-pink or red lobes and a tube with a yellow base.

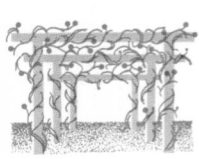

Height of plant 5–10 ft. (1.50–3 m.).
Size of flower 3⅛–5½ in. (8–14 cm.).
Place of origin Mexico.
Flowering time Summer.

Cultivation A very light position, sheltered from the wind but exposed to the sun. Warm-temperate climate. Frost-tender. Grows even in moderately calcareous soil if rich and moist. Needs frequent watering in summer. Insect-prone. Can be grown as a pot plant in a heated greenhouse.

Propagation By layering or air layering in the spring–summer. By half-ripened and hardwood cuttings taken in the summer and rooted in a greenhouse.

Qualities Half-hardy. Very easy to grow.

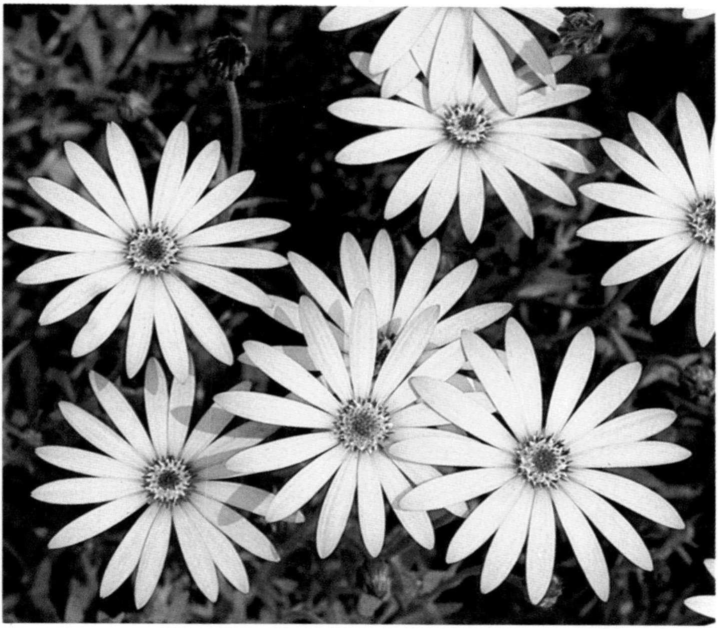

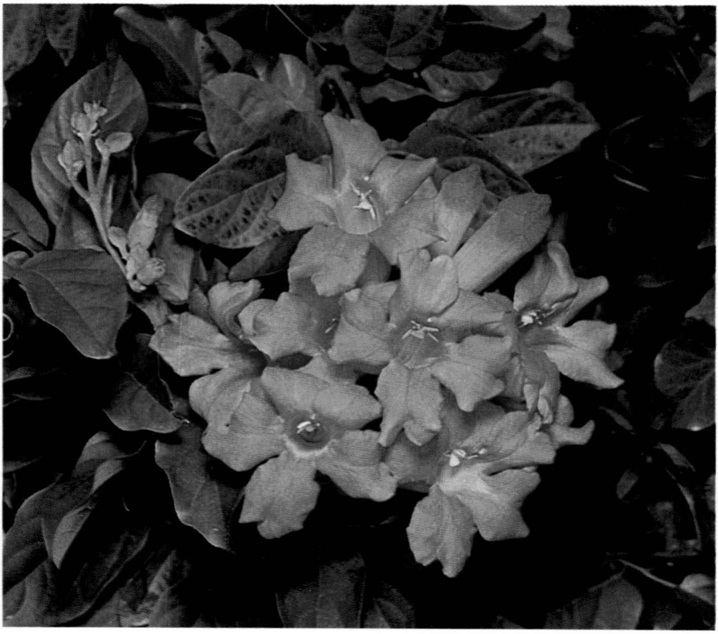

120 DORONICUM GRANDIFLORUM Jean Baptiste Lamarck
Common name: Leopard's bane

Family Compositae.
Description A shrubby perennial with numerous tightly packed upright stems growing from the rhizome. Its floriferous display of large yellow daisylike flowers contrasts strongly with the bright green of the foliage, making this a very decorative plant. The lower leaves are petiolate and ovate-rotundate with a crenulate-dentate margin; the upper ones are cordate and sessile. Flowers are borne in large capitula with a dark disc and numerous lighter ray florets.
Height of plant 12–16 in. (30–40 cm.).
Size of flower 1½–2⅜ in. (4–6 cm.).
Place of origin Central and southern Europe.
Flowering time Spring.
Cultivation A sunny to partially shaded position. Temperate climate. Fairly frost-resistant. Grows in almost any kind of soil provided it is rich, deep and moist. If left in the same place, the plant soon becomes exhausted; it should therefore be moved every two or three years. Frequent watering in the summer. The stems should be cut back in the autumn and the crown well mulched to protect from winter frosts.
Propagation By clump division in the spring or autumn. By spring sowing in pans under glass; seedlings will subsequently require pricking off.
Qualities Hardy. Easy to grow.

121 ECHINOPS RITRO Carolus Linnaeus
Common name: Globe thistle

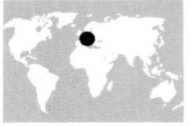

Family Compositae.
Description A perennial with erect stems branched upward, argentate-cottony. Its alternate leaves are lobate-pinnatifid and dentate-spinose; cottony underneath. Its flowers are borne in globular, metallic-blue terminal capitula and are very decorative. This plant is a little untidy but makes a useful contribution in enlivening difficult parts of a garden.
Height of plant 40–51 in. (1–1.30 m.).
Size of flower 2–2⅜ in. (5–6 cm.) each capitulum.
Place of origin Southeastern Europe.
Flowering time Summer–autumn.
Cultivation A sunny to partially shaded position. Temperate climate. Grows in almost any type of soil, even alkaline, if it is well aerated, sandy and moderately fertile. Occasional watering in very dry weather. The plant can be left to naturalize. The old flowering stems should be cut back to the ground in the autumn. Usually trouble-free.
Propagation By spring sowing in pans in a coldframe. It can also be sown directly in the flowering site. Alternatively, it can be divided in the spring.
Qualities Hardy. Easy to grow.

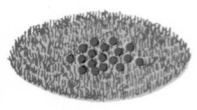
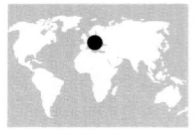

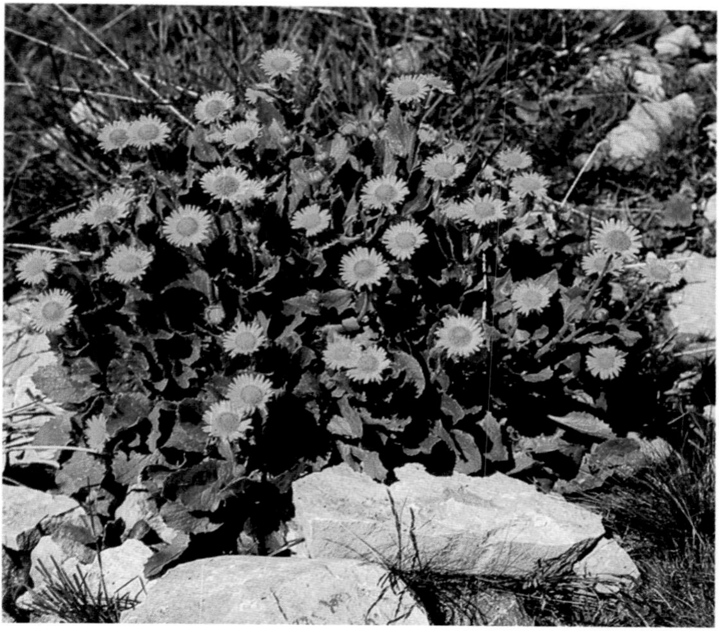

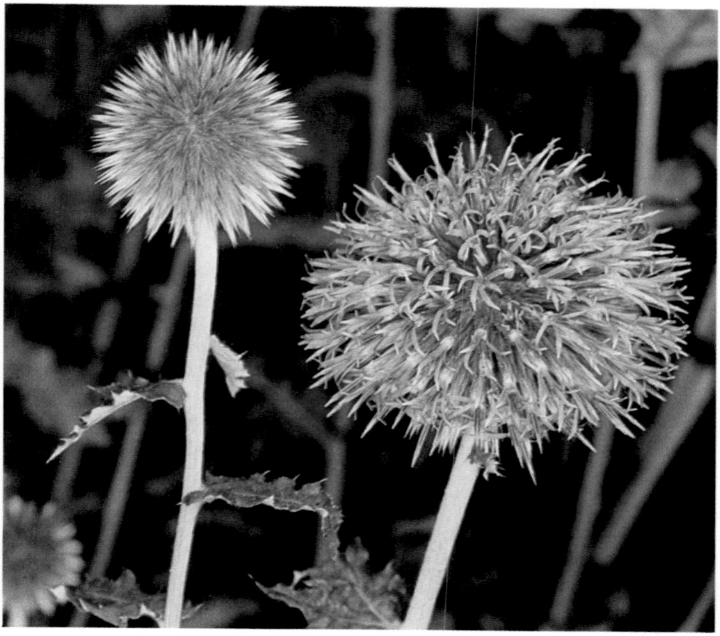

122 ECHIUM FASTUOSUM William Aiton
Common name: Pride of Madeira

Family Boraginaceae.
Description An evergreen shrubby perennial with an untidy habit. Its grayish-green leaves are lanceolate or linear-lanceolate and tomentose-hirsute. Its numerous flowers are small, tubulous-campanulate and borne on dense terminal racemes; they are particularly attractive because of their azure color.
Height of plant 60–80 in. (1.50–2 m.).
Size of flower ⅜–½ in. (1–1.5 cm.).
Place of origin Canary Islands.
Flowering time Summer.
Cultivation A sunny position, well sheltered from the cold. Temperate climate. Cannot withstand heavy frosts. Well-drained, calcareous soil. The plant benefits from an occasional light hoeing and an application of organic/mineral fertilizers. No pruning is necessary. If water is badly distributed or inadequate, it may well do damage. Diseases: stunted growth (rickets) and chlorosis in unsuitable ground.
Propagation By spring sowing and cuttings taken from the best plants. The young plants need to be potted on at least twice. When planting out, the soil ball must remain intact, because the plant suffers in transplanting.
Qualities Hardy in its own environment. Not always easy to grow.

---

123 EICHORNIA CRASSIPES (Karl Friedrich Philipp von Martius) Solms-Laubach
Syns.: *E. speciosa* Karl Sigismund Kunth, *Pontederia crassipes* von Martius. Common name: Water hyacinth

Family Pontederiaceae.
Description A floating, rhizomatose, aquatic plant that puts out quantities of stolons which spread to form large clumps. Its cordate leaves are in open rosettes with a vesicular petiole, dilated at the center, which ensures that the plant will float, and a big bract at the base. The delicate, short-lived flowers are borne on a spike, like a hyacinth. The plant is very floriferous. In tropical areas it is regarded as a troublesome weed.
Height of plant 6–8 in. (15–20 cm.).
Size of flower 1½–2 in. (4–5 cm.).
Place of origin Tropical America.
Flowering time Summer.
Cultivation Full sun. Temperate climate. Frost-tender. Will grow in shallow artificial ponds in almost static water with the long roots just touching the mud at bottom. Can also be planted in large earthenware pots in muddy soil with plenty of well-seasoned organic manure; the pots can then be immersed to just below surface of the water. Thus the plants can be transferred indoors to a greenhouse in winter.
Propagation Plant basal shoots in pots and immerse in a container of water in a warm greenhouse; they will be ready for transferring to their flowering site within 15 to 20 days.
Qualities A pond plant. Easy to grow.

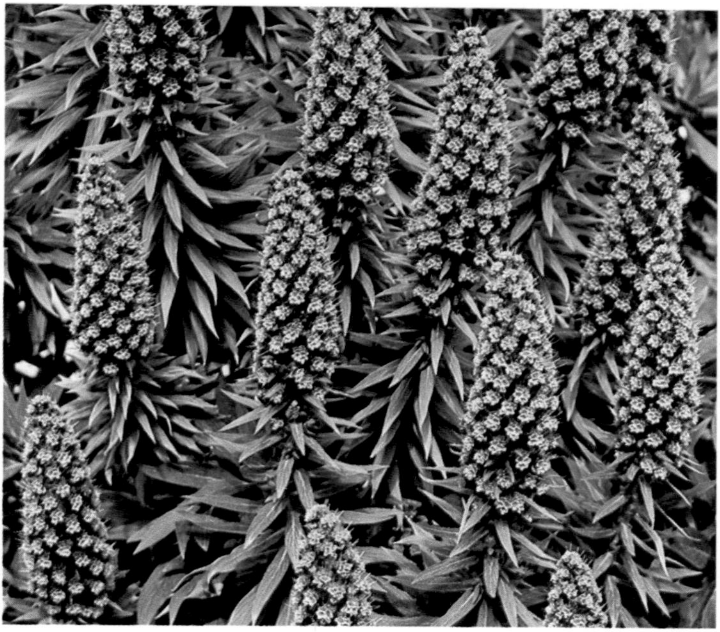

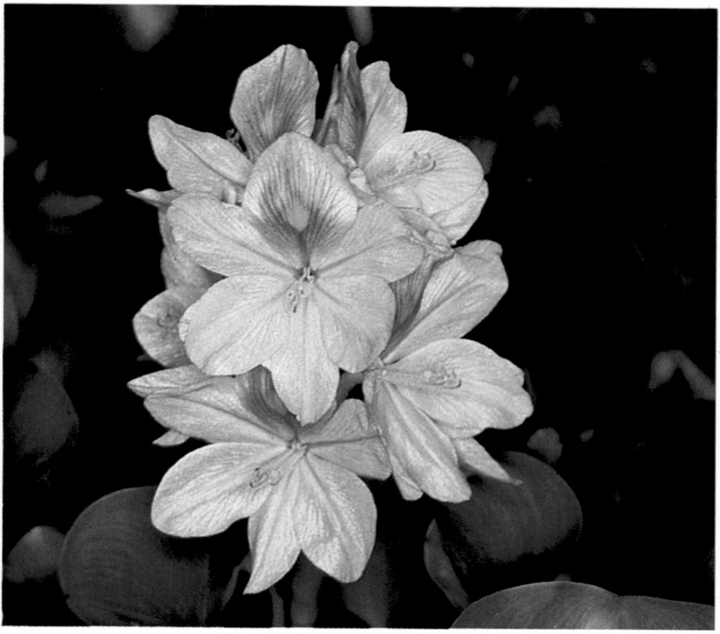

124 ENKIANTHUS CAMPANULATUS (Friedrich Anton Wilhelm Miguel) George Nicholson
Syn.: *Andromeda campanulata* Miguel

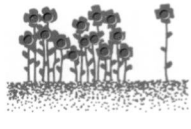

Family   Ericaceae.

Description   A deciduous shrub with numerous wide-spreading branches arranged almost geometrically and covered with an attractive reddish bark. The leaves, grouped in fascicles, are spatulate-elliptical or acuminate-dentate and slightly pilose-setose on both surfaces. The pendulous campanulate flowers appear on the season's new growth, grouped in terminal racemes of ten to fifteen flowers. There is also a white-flowering variety, *E. albiflorus,* and a red one, *E. rubicundus.*

Height of plant   40–120 in. (1–3 m.).

Size of flower   ⅜ in. (1 cm.).

Place of origin   Japan.

Flowering time   Spring.

Cultivation   A shady but light position. Temperate climate. This calcifuge plant likes moist, well-aerated, acid soil; if necessary, the soil can be amended with heath mold, shredded bark, peat or leaf mold in equal parts. Frequent watering over the whole root system. No pruning necessary. Slow-release organic fertilizers. This is a slow-growing plant. Diseases: chlorosis and stunted growth in unsuitable soils.

Propagation   By spring cuttings of two-year-old wood, treated with root-stimulating hormones and rooted.

Qualities   Half-hardy. Very easy to grow.

125 EPIPHYLLUM x ACKERMANNII Hortorum
Syn.: *Phyllocactus x hybridus Hortorum*

Family   *Cactaceae.*

Description   A succulent plant deriving from *P. ackermannii* and *P. phyllanthoides.* All the epiphyllums are very interesting plants and worth getting to know. They have flattened, upright, angular stems, fairly well branched and succulent, with sinuate-crenulate margins and equipped with whitish hairs. The bright-red flowers are very beautiful and, in other cultivars, range from pure white to pink and salmon-pink. The flowers emerge from the edges of the flat stems and the purplish-violet fruits are globose.

Height of plant   24–36 in. (60–90 cm.).

Size of flower   3⅛–4 in. (8–10 cm.).

Place of origin   A cultivated hybrid; habitat of parent stock, Mexico.

Flowering time   Summer.

Cultivation   Full sun. Temperate climate. Cannot withstand frost but, if put in a dry place, survives at temperatures just above freezing point. It prefers good, well-drained, clayey-sandy soil mixed with leaf mold and sand. Watering should be regular but restrained and minimal in the winter. Diseases: various types of rot.

Propagation   By cuttings taken from the preceding year's stems before they have started to grow. By seed in a warm greenhouse——a process that requires a great deal of care.

Qualities   Half-hardy. Very easy to grow.

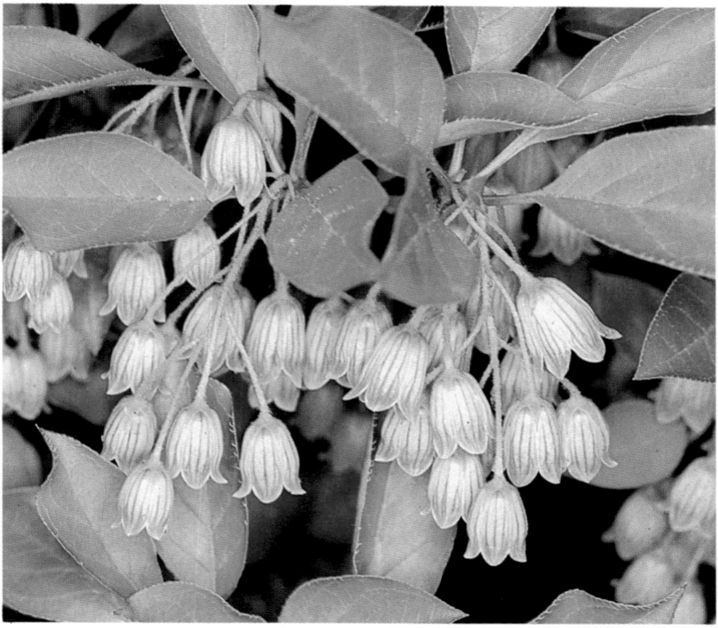

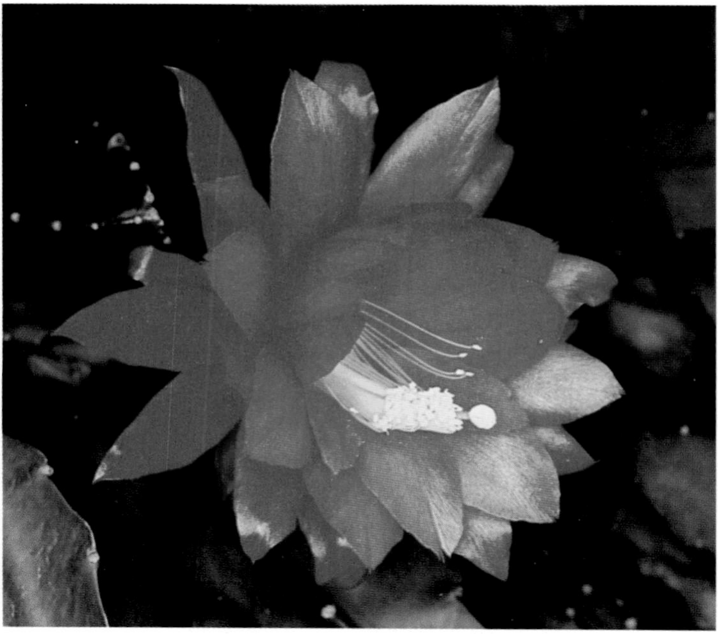

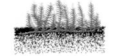

126 ERICA HERBACEA Carolus Linnaeus
Syn.: *E. carnea* Linnaeus. Common name: Spring heath

Family Ericaceae.
Description A thickly branched evergreen suffrutescent subshrub of prostrate-erect habit. Its numerous leaves are glabrous, linear-acute, between ¼ and ½ in. (only a few millimeters) long and grouped in fours. The flowers start to form a year prior to blooming. They create a tightly packed, cylindrical, spicate raceme about 2–2¾ in. (5–7 cm.) long. Their bright-pink corollas are tubulous-urceolate, from which emerge the brownish-red anthers.

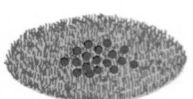

Height of plant 12–24 in. (30–60 cm.).
Size of flower ⅛–⅜ in. (0.5–0.8 cm.).
Place of origin Central Europe.
Flowering time Late winter–early spring.
Cultivation A fairly sunny position. Cool-temperate climate. Frost-resistant. An acid soil, preferably siliceous and peaty. Excessively dry conditions are harmful to the plant and manure should also be avoided. Generous watering, when necessary, all around, as well as over the plants themselves. Pruning usually unnecessary. Often not long-lived.

Propagation By semi-hardwood cuttings taken in the summer and put to root in a light compost (equal parts of peat, heath mold and sand) in a coldframe.
Qualities Hardy in its natural environment. Rather demanding to grow.

---

127 ERICA x WILMOREI Knowles and F. Westcott
cv. Roi Eduard''

Family Ericaceae.
Description One of the most beautiful of the cultivated hybrid ericas, generally grown by specialist amateurs. It is suffruticose, bushy and well branched with ascendent-erect stems. Its green leaves are linear, grouped in threes and ¼–⅜ in. (5–7 mm.) long. Its flowers have a tubulous corolla, slightly incurving, pink suffused with white at the apex, and borne in dense terminal foliose racemes.

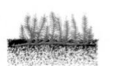

Height of plant 10–16 in. (25–40 cm.).
Size of flower ¾–1 in. (1.8–2.5 cm.).
Place of origin A hybrid of cultivated origin.
Flowering time Late winter–early spring.

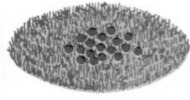

Cultivation A sunny, open position. Cool-temperate climate. Frost-tender. Lime-free soil—the ground should be acid or slightly alkaline, with plenty of fibrous peat and a little sand added. No manure should ever be applied. Chopped, dried seaweed can be given, if feeding is necessary. Water all around the plants with frequent spraying in hot weather. Can also be grown as a pot plant, often with greater success than in open ground. Pruning: this type of plant is usually left to grow naturally.

Propagation By cuttings taken from the cymes of the branches and rooted in a greenhouse in a porous compost of peat and sand in pots protected with transparent plastic.
Qualities Half-hardy. Rather demanding to grow.

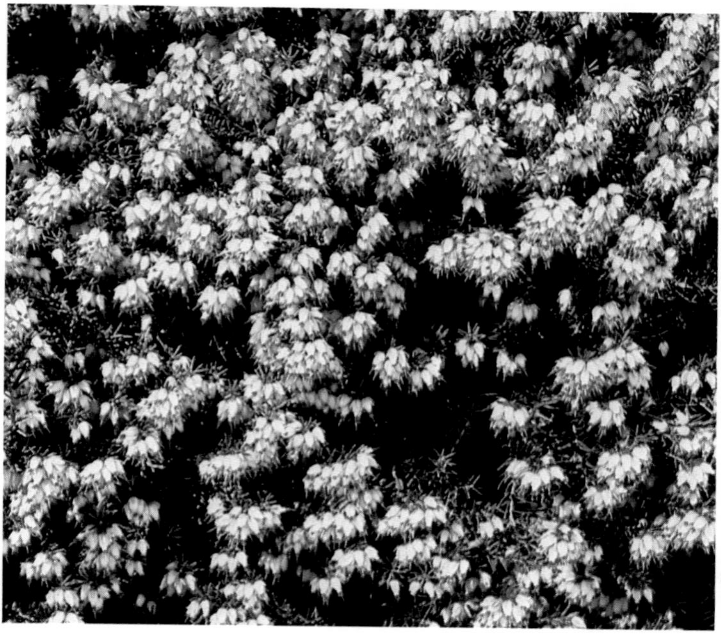
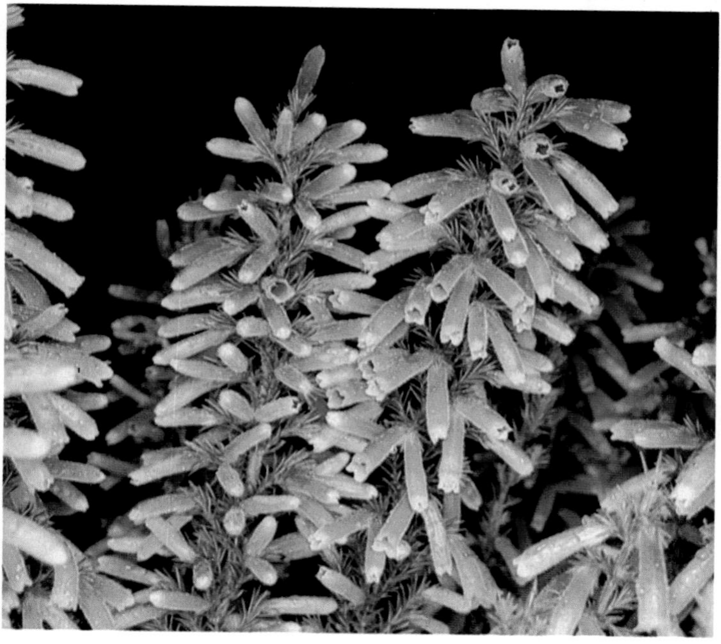

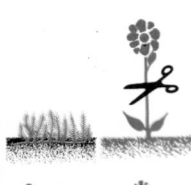

128 ERYNGIUM ALPINUM Carolus Linnaeus
Common name: Alpine sea-holly

Family Umbelliferae.
Description A perennial grown mainly for the unusual appearance created by its stems, leaves, and especially by the metallic azure bracts surrounding the flowers like fins or dusty cobwebs. The stems are erect with oval, sub-cordate, dentate-spinose basal leaves. The upper leaves are pinnate-parted with dentate-spinose laciniae. Flowers are borne in oblong capitula, surrounded by a corona of deep sky-blue, spinate, pinnate-parted leaflets that are often mistaken for floral petals.
Height of plant 12–28 in. (30–70 cm.).
Size of flower 2⅜–4 in. (6–10 cm.) each capitulum.
Place of origin Southern Europe.
Flowering time Summer.
Cultivation Full sun or very sunny. Temperate climate. Can withstand the cold well. Prefers a dry, stony position or calcareous soil with a little humus. Requires no particular care. This plant is usually left unpruned as the flowers dry out and remain decorative for a long time. Trouble-free.
Propagation By spring sowing in small pots or directly in the garden.
Qualities Hardy. Easy to grow.

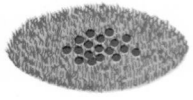

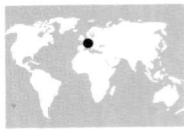

129 ERYTHRINA CRISTA-GALLI Carolus Linnaeus
Syn.: *E. laurifolia* Jacquemont. Common name: Cockspur coral tree

Family Papilionaceae.
Description A small tree with a thick, woody rootstock. Its green, upright ramifications are sturdy and equipped with large thorns. To survive the cold, the current year's branches often do not lignify. The leaves are alternate, trifoliate with oblong-elliptical leaflets, coriaceous with a long petiole. The flowers are papilionaceous with a large arcuate vesicle borne in long terminal racemes on the branches.
Height of plant 5–8 ft. (1.50–2.50 m.) (13–16 ft. in its natural environment).
Size of flower 1½–2 in. (4–5 cm.).
Place of origin Brazil.
Flowering time Summer.
Cultivation Full sun. Warm-temperate climate, sheltered position. In northern areas it must be well protected from the cold or put in a cool greenhouse. Grows in almost any kind of soil but prefers it to be well aerated, fertile and moist. Regular watering. All stems can be cut to the base for the winter; new growth will start vigorously in the spring.
Propagation By spring sowing, placing one seed in a pot, in a coldframe or warm greenhouse. Young plants have to be potted on at least twice before planting out in the garden.
Qualities Half-hardy except in its own climate. Easy to grow.

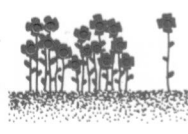

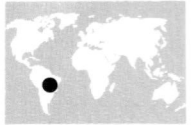

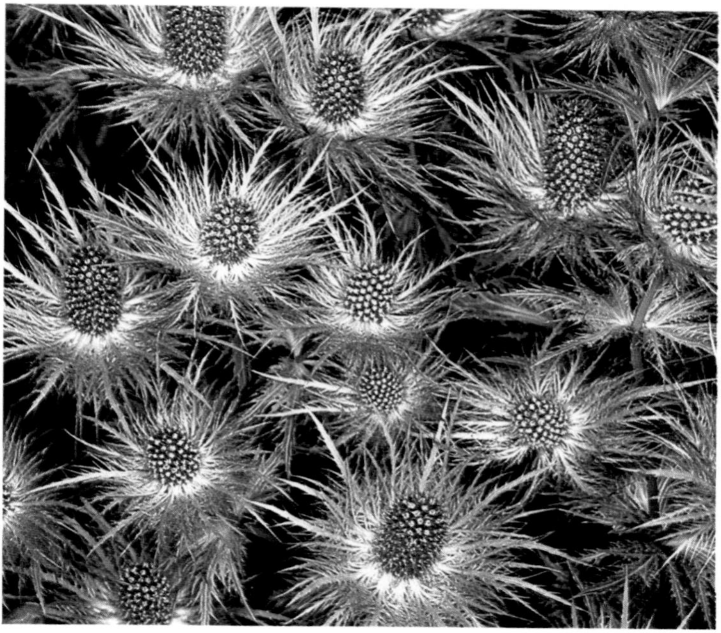

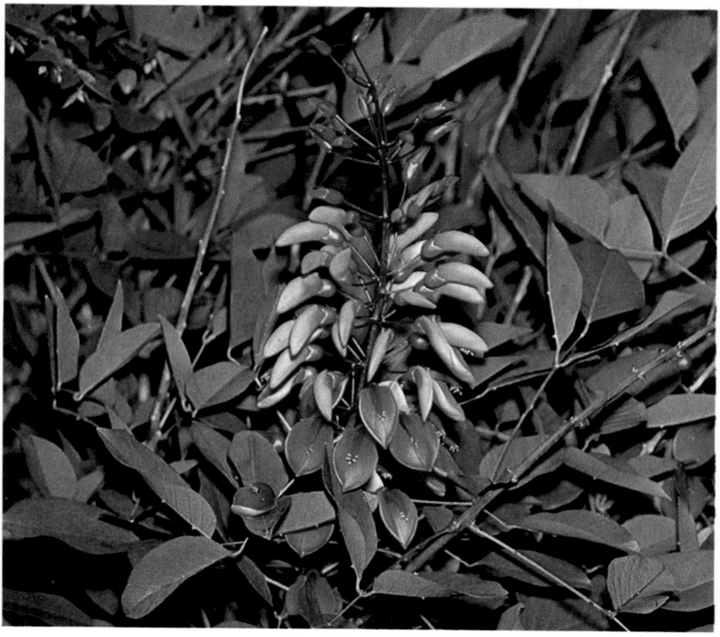

130 ESCALLONIA MACRANTHA William Jackson Hooker and George Arnold Walker Arnott

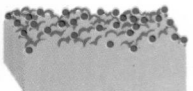

Family Escalloniaceae.
Description A delightful evergreen shrub, this also makes a good flowering hedge. Its woody rootstock sends up dense ramifications from the base. These slender branches carry alternate, rather coriaceous, ovate-elliptical or obovate leaves. The delicately scented flowers are tubulous-campanulate and borne in small pendulous clusters over a long flowering period. There are three cultivars: "Alba," "Rosea" and "Duplicato-serrata."
Height of plant 5–13 ft. (1.50–4 m.).
Size of flower ½–¾ in. (1.5–2 cm.).
Place of origin Chile.
Flowering time Summer.

Cultivation Sunny or partially shaded position. Cool-temperate climate. Prone to damage from heavy frosts. Grows in any type of damp, well-drained soil, even if it is clayey. Resistant to coastal weather conditions. Pruning necessary only if the plant is grown as a hedge. Usually trouble-free.
Propagation By semi-hardwood cuttings taken in the summer and rooted in a frame. Also by air layering.
Qualities Hardy. Easy to grow.

---

131 ESCHSCHOLTZIA CALIFORNICA Adalbert von Chamisso
Common name: California poppy

Family Papaveraceae.
Description A perennial grown as an annual, this throws up numerous erect ramifications from the base. Its gray-green leaves are alternate, pinnatisect and minutely divided into linear laciniae. Its numerous flowers are borne terminally on slender peduncles and formed of four large petals and many stamens. It makes a very colorful display. There are numerous cultivars in various colors; some are double-flowered.
Height of plant 12–18 in. (30–45 cm.).
Size of flower 2–2¾ in. (5–7 cm.).
Place of origin California and Oregon.
Flowering time Late spring–summer.

Cultivation Sunny position. Warm-temperate climate. Prefers well-drained, calcareous-sandy soil. Moderate all-around watering. Does not like to be transplanted. Pests and diseases: aphids; root rot.
Propagation By spring sowing, preferably in the garden.
Qualities Very hardy. Easy to grow.

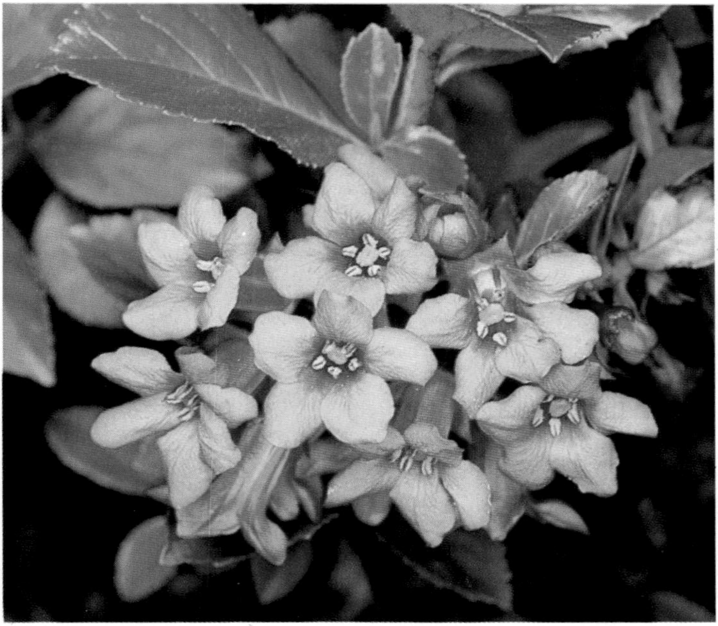

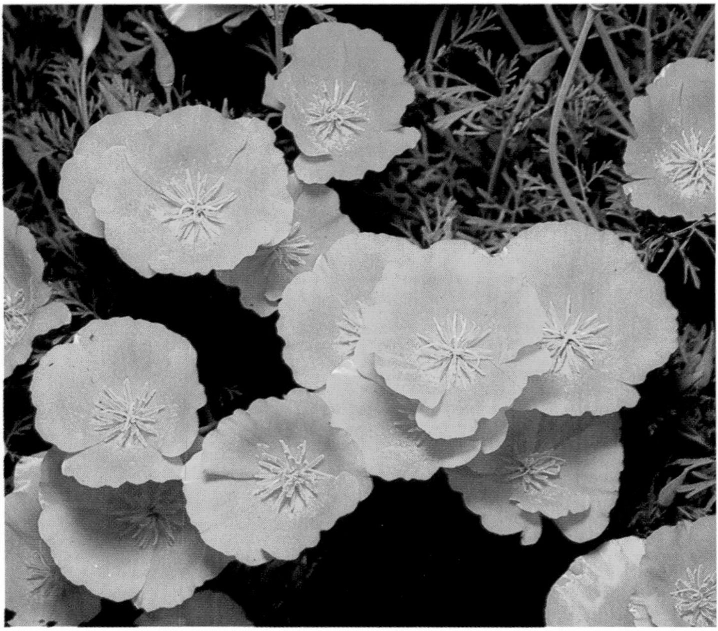

132 EUCALYPTUS FICIFOLIA Ferdinand von Mueller
Common name: Red-flowering gum

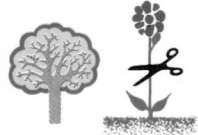

Family Myrtaceae.
Description A vigorous tree that can be regarded as one of the best ornamental eucalyptuses growing in temperate regions. It can be cultivated successfully in sheltered positions in warm coastal areas. It has an upright trunk with numerous slender, pendulous and flexuous ramifications with a blackish, cracked and peeling (deciduous) bark. Its vertical leaves are alternate and lanceolate. Its flowers are distinctive because of their long red stamens—the corolla falls prematurely—borne in umbelliform cymes of six or seven flowers at the base of the young branches.
Height of plant 1C–50 ft. (5–15 m.).
Size of flower ¾ in. (2 cm.).
Place of origin Southwestern Australia.
Flowering time Late winter–early spring.
Cultivation Full sun. Temperate climate. Frost-tender. Sheltered position. Prefers moist, fertile, clayey-sandy soil. The only pruning that may be necessary is to cut back wayward branches and dead or adventitious growth.
Propagation By spring sowing in boxes in a frame or greenhouse. Transplant into pots and pot on one or more times before finally planting out.
Qualities Half-hardy except in its own climate. Easy to grow.

133 EUPHORBIA MARGINATA Frederick T. Pursh
Syn.: *E. variegata* John Sims. Common name: Snow-on-the-mountain

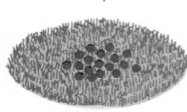

Family Euphorbiaceae.
Description A particularly ornamental annual. Its variegated white leaves are grouped in terminal clusters. This gives the effect of a sensational display of flowers that lasts the whole life cycle of the plant. It is erect, with divaricate ramifications, and is at its best in the summer. Its alternate leaves are oval and oblong-acute, the lower ones being green and the upper ones white variegated with green. The flowers, grouped in small, distinctive florescences, are insignificant.
Height of plant 16–32 in. (40–80 cm.).
Size of flower ⅛–⅜ in. (0.5–1 cm.).
Place of origin North America.
Flowering time Spring–summer.
Cultivation Full sun. Temperate climate, sheltered from the wind. Grows in any kind of soil but prefers moist, clayey-sandy soil even if poor. Fairly frequent watering. Usually trouble-free.
Propagation By spring sowing directly into flowering site, because it transplants badly.
Qualities Hardy. Easy to grow.

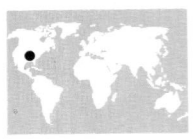

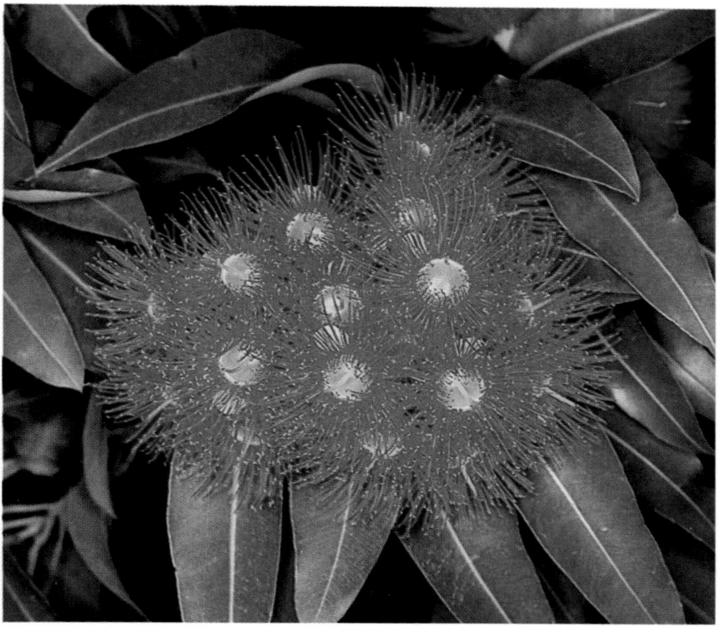

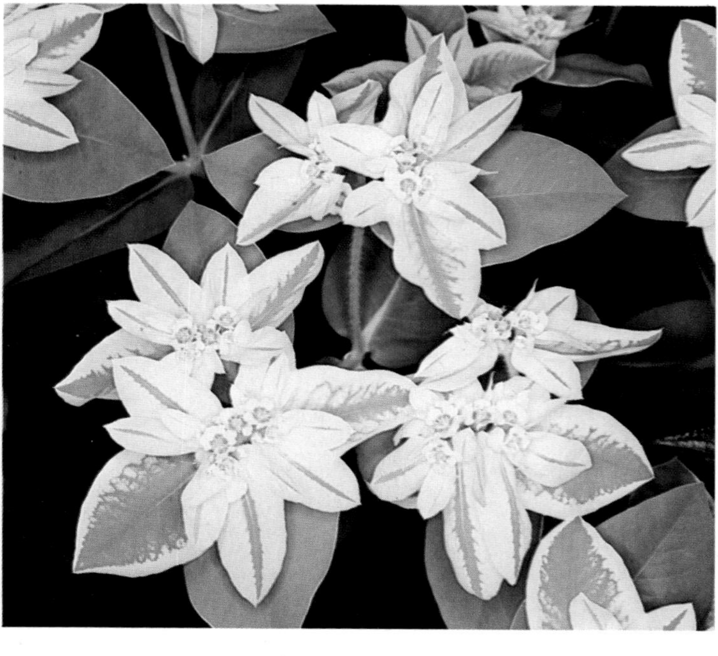

134 EUPHORBIA PULCHERRIMA Karl Ludwig Willdenow

Syn.: *Poinsettia pulcherrima* R. C. Graham. Common name: Poinsettia

Family Euphorbiaceae.

Description A plant of the warm-temperate climes, this is widely grown indoors and out, particularly for Christmas. In its natural state it has a shrubby habit with a few cylindrical, tubulous ramifications; if damaged, it oozes latex. Its alternate leaves have seven lobes. The insignificant flowers are surrounded by large, bright-red, unequal foliaceous bracts, sometimes lanceolate-dentate, often mistaken for the flower petals.

Height of plant 2–10 ft. (0.60–3 m.).

Size of flower 6–10 in. (15–25 cm.), including the bracts.

Place of origin Mexico.

Flowering time Winter.

Cultivation Full sun. Warm-temperate climate. Cannot withstand the cold. Very sheltered position or grown as a greenhouse plant. Well-aerated, clayey-sandy soil, rich in organic material, and with a little peat. Periodic applications of liquid mineral fertilizer. Water and spray freely during growing period but reduce after flowering, finally ceasing altogether for about 40–50 days. The soil can then be changed and the cycle of cultivation starts again. Prune back to two or three buds. Diseases: chlorosis, fungus diseases and viruses.

Propagation By hardwood cuttings taken during the resting period and put to root in sandy compost in a greenhouse.

Qualities Half-hardy. Quite demanding to grow.

---

135 EXOCHORDA RACEMOSA Alfred Rehder

Syns.: *E. grandiflora* John Lindley, *Spiraea grandiflora* William Jackson Hooker. Common name: Pearlbush

Family Rosaceae.

Description A deciduous shrub, this is one of the few to flower at the end of winter. It has numerous open, flexuous, slightly averse ramifications. Its alternate leaves are close together, elliptical or oblong-lanceolate, with a short petiole. Its numerous pure white flowers, opening from pearllike buds, have five petals and are carried in terminal racemes. There are two varieties and one cultivar: *E. dentata*, *E. prostrata* and cv. "The Bride."

Height of plant 10–11½ ft. (3–3.5 m.).

Size of flower 1⅛–1½ in. (3–4 cm.).

Place of origin China.

Flowering time Early spring.

Cultivation Full sun to partial shade. Temperate climate. Can withstand the cold well. Grows in any clayey-sandy, fertile, moist soil. A periodic application of well-rotted farmyard manure incorporated with some mineral fertilizer ensures good flowers. An occasional thinning out may sometimes be necessary but regular pruning is not needed. Generally trouble-free.

Propagation By softwood cuttings in the spring. By air layering in the spring or summer. Sometimes by seed in the spring.

Qualities Hardy. Easy to grow.

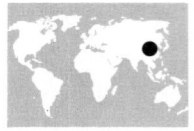

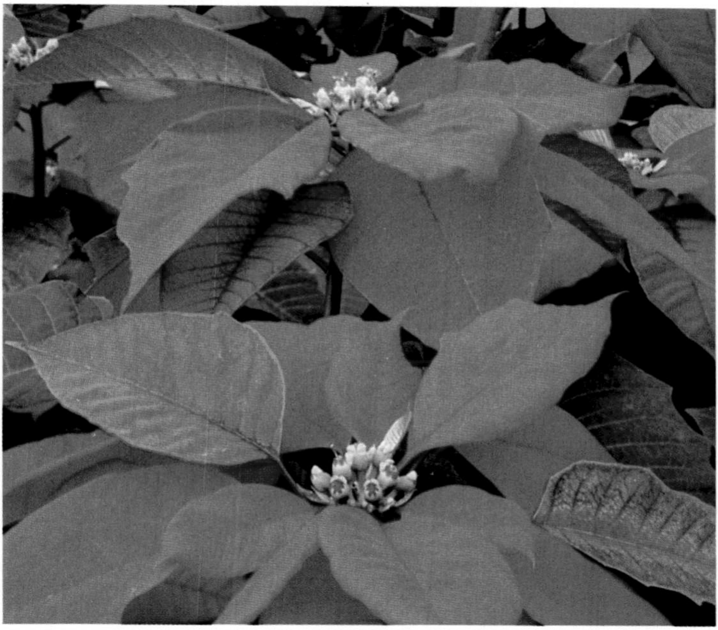

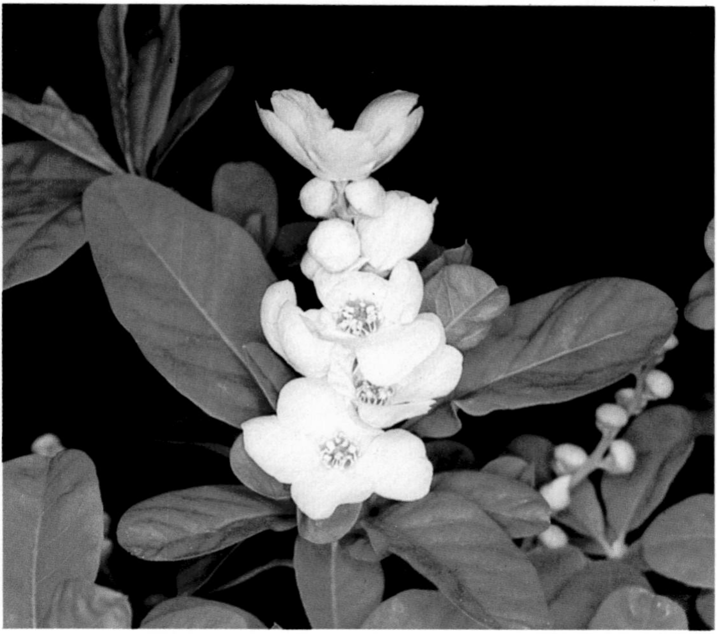

136 FELICIA AMELLOIDES A. Voss.

Syns.: *Agathaea coelestis* Alexandre Henri Gabriel Cassini, *Aster rotundifolius* Carl Peter Thunberg.
Common name: Blue marguerite

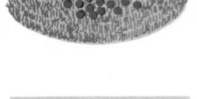
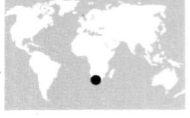

Family Compositae.
Description A quick-growing, suffruticose, bushy, semiprostrate plant. Its persistent leaves are alternate and ovate-rotundate. Its flowers are in numerous capitula borne singly on long stalks. Each capitulum has a yellow disc and deep sky-blue linear ray florets.
Height of plant 16–20 in. (40–50 cm.).
Size of flower ¾–1⅜ in. (2–3.5 cm.).
Place of origin South Africa.
Flowering time Almost throughout the year but mainly in the spring and summer.
Cultivation Full sun. Temperate climate. Shelter from frost, although it can withstand a few light frosts. Grows in almost any well-aerated, fertile, humus-rich soil, even if a little argillaceous. Frequent watering. The whole plant should be lightly trimmed in autumn–winter. Needs protection during the cold season. Trouble-free.
Propagation By spring sowing under glass. By cuttings taken from the tips of the branches in the spring.
Qualities Suitable for balconies, terraces. Half-hardy. Easy to grow.

137 FELICIA FRUTICOSA (Carolus Linnaeus) George Nicholson

Syn.: *Aster fruticosus* Linnaeus

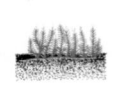
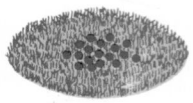

Family Compositae.
Description A bushy suffruticose perennial with a mass of slightly prostrate ramifications. Its tiny leaves are alternate and linear-acute, crowded onto rather short ramifications. Its flowers are borne in isolated terminal capitula, a great many on each plant, with long peduncles. The flowering period is long and flowering is extremely abundant.
Height of plant 16–28 in. (40–70 cm.).
Size of flower 1⅜ in. (3.5 cm.).
Place of origin South Africa.
Flowering time Spring–summer.
Cultivation An open, light position. Temperate climate. Frost-tender. Prefers well-aerated, rich, moist soil with a calcareous or argillaceous basis. It also grows well in the sandy soil of coastal areas. Benefits from organic manure and plentiful watering. When it has finished flowering—or in autumn—it is desirable to trim the whole plant to ensure an even display of flowers the following year.
Propagation By clump division in autumn. By cuttings taken in summer–autumn and rooted in a coldframe.
Qualities Suitable for balconies, terraces. Half-hardy. Easy to grow.

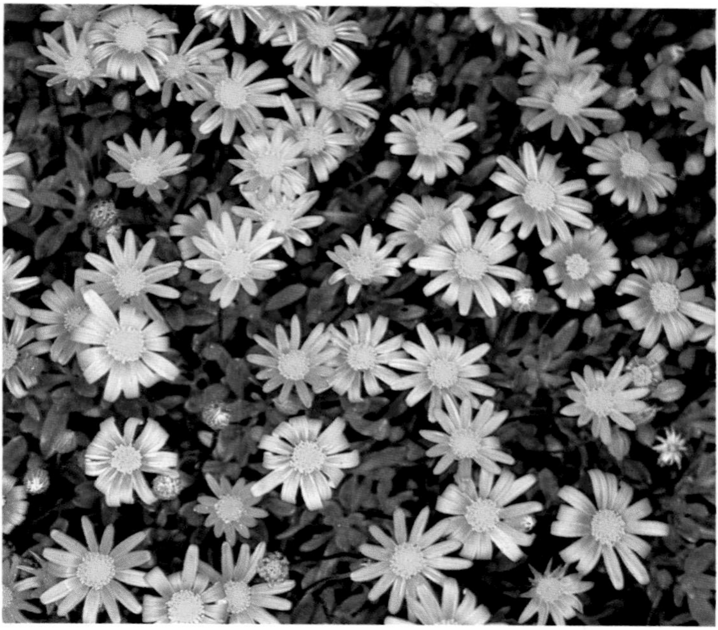

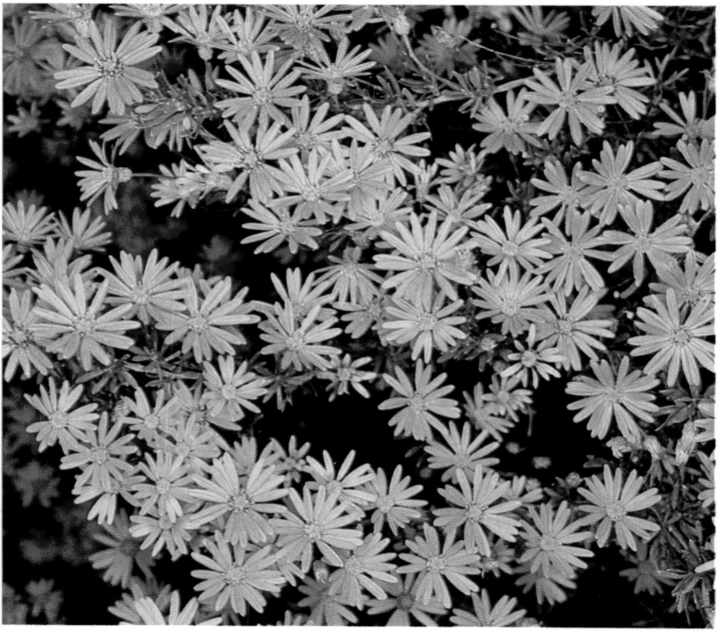

138 FORSYTHIA x INTERMEDIA Hermann Zabel

Family Oleaceae.
Description A shrubby-bushy plant with long, flexuous branches which are often quadrangular in cross section at the end. Its deciduous leaves are opposite, ovate-oblong and serrated. Its bright-yellow flowers are either borne singly or in groups of two or three along almost the entire length of the branches. Floriferous and very decorative. This forsythia is a hybrid derived by crossing *F. suspensa* with *F. viridissima*. It differs from *F. suspensa* in having more erect ramifications and a later flowering period. There are some attractive cultivars of this hybrid such as ''Spring glory,'' ''Arnold Gran'' and ''Beatrix Farrand.''
Height of plant 6–10 ft. (2–3 m.).
Size of flower ¾–1⅛ in. (2–3 cm.).
Place of origin A hybrid of cultivated origin; habitat of parents: China and Japan.
Flowering time Early spring.
Cultivation Full sun to partial shade. Temperate climate but plant can withstand the frost very well. Grows in any type of soil, even heavy. Plentiful watering. Periodic applications of organic/mineral fertilizers. Prune after flowering, removing the old wood and shortening the newer growth.
Propagation By semi-hardwood cuttings in summer and autumn. By clump division. By layering.
Qualities Hardy. Easy to grow.

139 FREESIA x KEWENSIS Hortorum
Syn.: *F. refracta* Friedrich Wilhelm Klatt. cv.

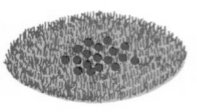

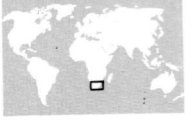

Family Iridaceae.
Description A proliferous bulbous plant, obovate-truncate at the base and covered with a fibrous tunic. Its long leaves are distichous, ensiform, narrow and overlapping. Its fragrant flowers are borne on short, upturning peduncles with an infundibuliform-campanulate perigonium of six unequal lobes, in groups of five to ten and carried on short racemes on a slender but rigid stem that is slightly arched like the neck of a swan. There are about 20 cultivars of various sizes and colors.
Height of plant 8–18 in. (20–45 cm.).
Size of flower 2–2¾ in. (5–7 cm.).
Place of origin A hybrid derived from parents originating from South Africa.
Flowering time Spring.
Cultivation A sunny position. Temperate climate. Frost-tender. Prefers good, rather light garden soil mixed with leaf mold and sand. Add a little organic manure. Plentiful watering prior to flowering; then taper off and discontinue as bulbs go into resting period.
Propagation By bulblets removed during the resting period. By seed, but this takes two or three years before plants come into flower.
Qualities Half-hardy. Easy to grow.

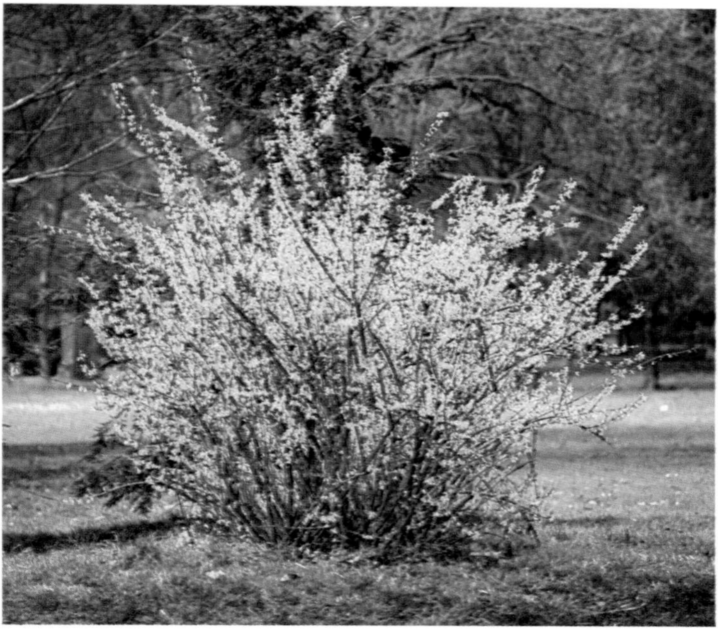

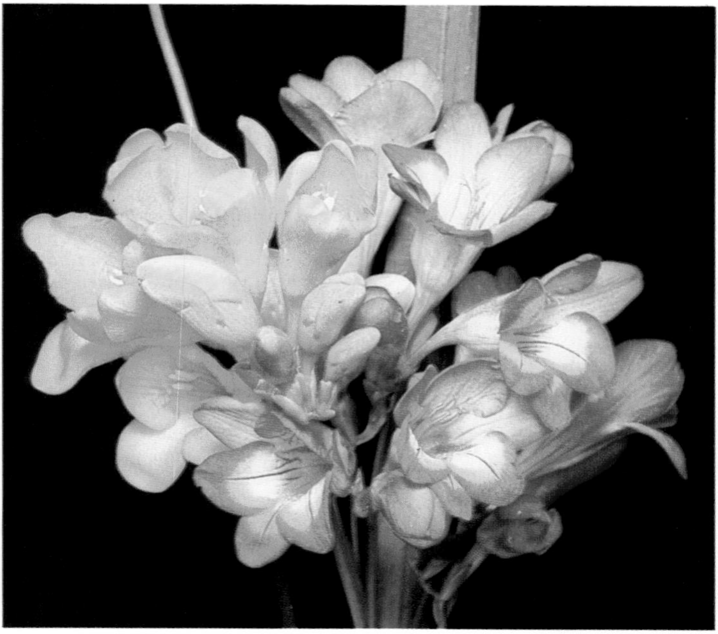

140 FRITILLARIA IMPERIALIS Carolus Linnaeus
Common name: Crown imperial

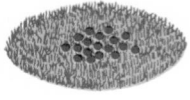

Family Liliaceae.
Description Produced from a large scaly bulb, this vigorous and decorative plant has numerous sessile leaves, broadening at the base, verticillate and arranged halfway up the stem, or lower. It bears a strange inflorescence formed of numerous campanulate, pendulous flowers in a corona at the top of a long, upright stem, surmounted by a tuft of leaves. It has an unpleasant odor. Its color may be orange, yellow or red, depending on the variety.
Height of plant 31–47 in. (0.80–1.20 m.).
Size of flower 2–3⅛ in. (5–8 cm.).
Place of origin Western Asia.
Flowering time Spring–early summer.
Cultivation Slight to half-shade. Temperate climate. Frost-tender. Grows in any fertile, well-drained, moist garden soil provided it is not too compact. If necessary, the ground can be amended with peat and sand. The bulb should be planted at a depth of 8 in. (20 cm.). Feed with bonemeal. Regular watering. After flowering, cut the stems down. The plant likes to be left undisturbed but deteriorates after a few years, even so.
Propagation Flowering bulbs are usually imported. Bulblets can be removed during the resting period and replanted. Plants sown from seed take four or five years before coming into flower.
Qualities Half-hardy. Rather demanding to grow.

141 FRITILLARIA MELEAGRIS Carolus Linnaeus
Common names: Snake's-head fritillary, guinea flower, checkered lily

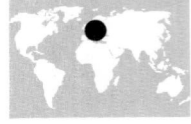

Family Liliaceae.
Description A bulbous plant with a deciduous, depressed, tunicate bulb. Its sparse leaves are linear-caniculate. This plant is not widely grown although it is attractive for its curious pendulous, campanulate, violet-colored flowers with their rusty-purple markings suggesting snakeskin. It can be found growing wild, with unmarked flowers, in yellow, white and purple; these have an unpleasant smell.
Height of plant 12–16 in. (30–40 cm.).
Size of flower 1½–2⅜ in. (4–6 cm.).
Place of origin Central Europe.
Flowering time Spring.
Cultivation Shade. Cool-temperate climate. Frost-resistant. Fertile, moist garden soil, even if compact. If necessary, ground can be amended with a little peat and sand. Regular watering. Rests in the summer. Not a long-lived plant; it is exhausted after two or three years.
Propagation By seed, but very slow. By bulblets removed during the resting period.
Qualities Very hardy. Easy to grow.

142 FUCHSIA CORYMBIFLORA Hipolito Ruiz Lopez and Jose Pavon

Family Onagraceae.
Description A shrubby plant with almost-persistent leaves and reddish, pubescent, fragile ramifications. Its leaves are opposite, often verticillate in threes, oblong-lanceolate, pubescent and a greenish bronze with reddish venation. It has numerous flowers, each with a long, tubulous calyx and divaricate lobes; the corolla is the same length as the calyx. The flowers are borne in pendulous terminal corymbs. There are several cultivars of this species whose colors vary slightly in brightness, and with reddish leaves.
Height of plant 3–8 ft. (1–2.50 m.).
Size of flower 2¾–4 in. (7–10 cm.).
Place of origin Peru and Ecuador.
Flowering time Summer–autumn.
Cultivation Shade. Temperate climate. Frost-tender. Must be kept under cover during the winter. Moist, fertile, clayey-sandy soil. If pot-grown, a mixture of 2 parts leaf mold, 1 part heath mold, 1 part well-rotted manure, 1 part sand and a sprinkling of bonemeal. Periodic liquid feeds. Plentiful watering. Prune lightly during resting period. Subject to attack by insects.
Propagation By half-ripened and semi-hardwood cuttings in spring and summer, rooted in a coldframe.
Qualities Half-hardy. Easy to grow.

143 FUCHSIA x sp. cv. "Marin Glow"
Syn.: *F. macrostemma* Hipolito Ruiz Lopez and Jose Pavon, hybrid.

Family Onagraceae.
Description The many types of fuchsia being grown in our gardens are mostly hybrids derived from crossings between the original species *Fuchsia magellanica* and *F. fulgens*. They are deciduous shrubs with numerous slender, fragile branches, forming fairly compact bushes. The tender leaves are opposite or verticillate in threes, oval-acute and crenulate-serrated. The flowers are pendulous and either borne singly or in small terminal clusters; they may be single, semidouble or double. Fruit: blackish-red berries like morello cherries.
Height of plant 40–60 in. (1–1.50 m.).
Size of flower 1½–2 in. (4–5 cm.).
Place of origin The countries of origin of its likely parents are Mexico (*F. fulgens*); Chile and Argentina (*F. magellanica*).
Flowering time Summer.
Cultivation A light but shaded position. Temperate climate. Not able to withstand the cold well. An acid soil, rich in organic material. A good mixture for pot culture is: 2 parts clay, 1 part leaf mold, 1 part well-rotted manure, 1 part sand and a little bonemeal. Plentiful watering. Occasionally a little liquid fertilizer. A trim or light pruning in the winter. Subject to aphids, fungus diseases and root rot.
Propagation By half-ripened and semi-hardwood cuttings in the spring and summer, rooted in a coldframe. Or by seed.
Qualities Half-hardy. Easy to grow.

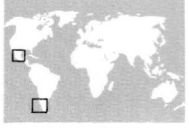

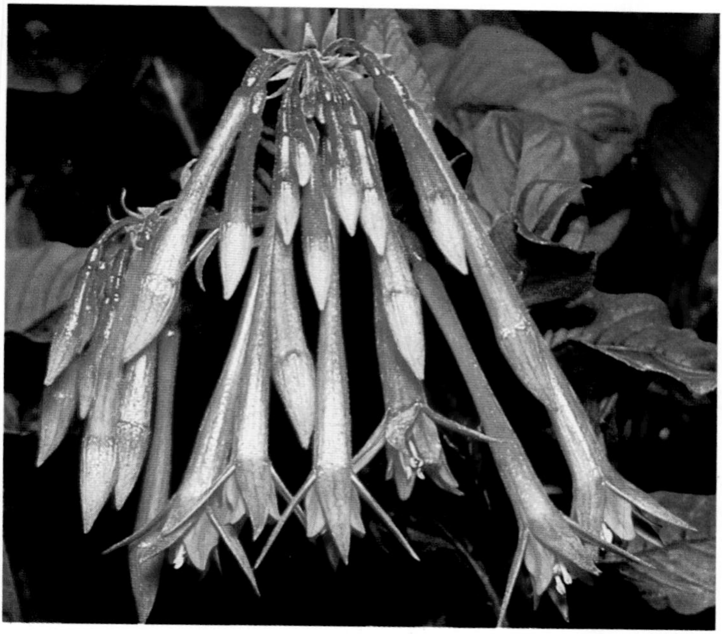

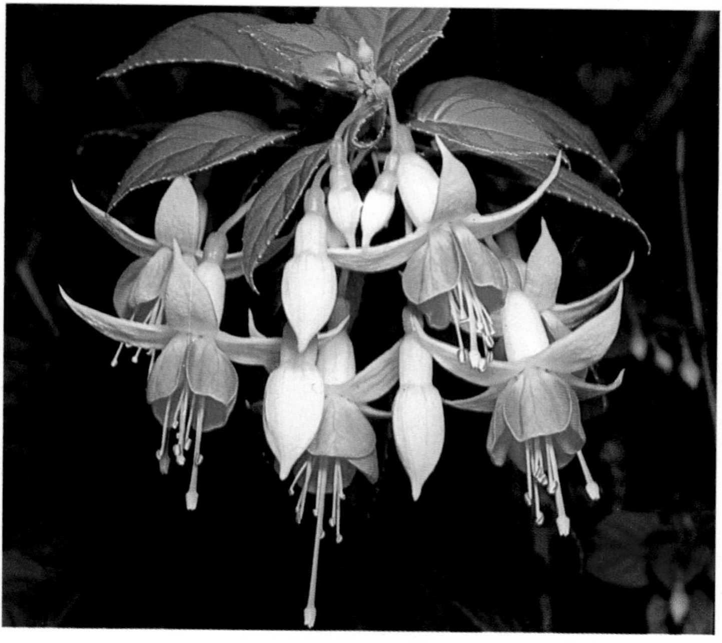

144 GAILLARDIA ARISTATA Frederick T. Pursh
Syns.: *G. lanceolata* André Michaux, *G. grandiflora*.
Common name: Blanketflower

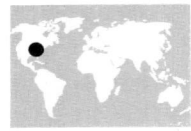

Family   Compositae.
Description   A perennial, tufted, herbaceous flowering plant. Its upright, branched stems are a little divaricate. Its dark-green, alternate leaves are oblong-lanceolate or lobed and rough. The purplish-orange flowers are in numerous capitula on branched peduncles. It has a prolonged flowering period and is very decorative.
Height of plant   15–24 in. (40–60 cm.).
Size of flower   2–4 in. (5–10 cm.).
Place of origin   North America.
Flowering time   Late spring–summer.
Cultivation   Full sun or very sunny position. Temperate climate. Can withstand a few light frosts, especially if well mulched. Prefers well-aerated, moist, sandy soil. Fertilizers should be applied cautiously, since the plant tends to collapse if overfed. Plentiful watering. The stems should be cut down in the autumn. Fairly trouble-free, although insects and rot may cause problems.
Propagation   By spring sowing in boxes in a greenhouse or coldframe; seedlings will have to be pricked off before planting out.
Qualities   Hardy. Easy to grow.

---

145 GARDENIA JASMINOIDES John Ellis cv. flore pleno
Syn.: *G. florida* Carolus Linnaeus. Common name: Cape jasmine

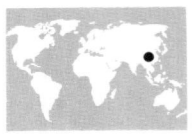

Family   Rubiaceae.
Description   Evergreen shrub widely grown for delicate beauty of its many flowers and heady fragrance. Generally regarded as a delicate pot or greenhouse plant although it can be grown successfully in open ground in warm areas. Has a shrubby, robust rootstock that branches up from the base. Its numerous leaves are opposite, oblong-lanceolate, acute and almost coriaceous.
Height of plant   40–80 in. (1–2 m.).
Size of flower   2–3⅛ in. (5–8 cm.).
Place of origin   China.
Flowering time   Spring–summer.
Cultivation   Partial shade. Temperate climate. Overwinter in cool greenhouse. Prefers woodland-type soil with shredded bark, heath mold and peat with a little sand. Slow-release organic fertilizers: bonemeal, etc. It is a calcifuge but requires plenty of lime-free water overall and light spraying of leaves on summer evenings. Remove dead growth. Subject to chlorosis, eelworms, scale insects and root canker.
Propagation   By semi-hardwood cuttings taken in the summer and rooted in sand and shredded bark or peat in equal parts under glass at about 77° F. (25° C.). Or by air layering.
Qualities   Half-hardy. Very easy to grow.

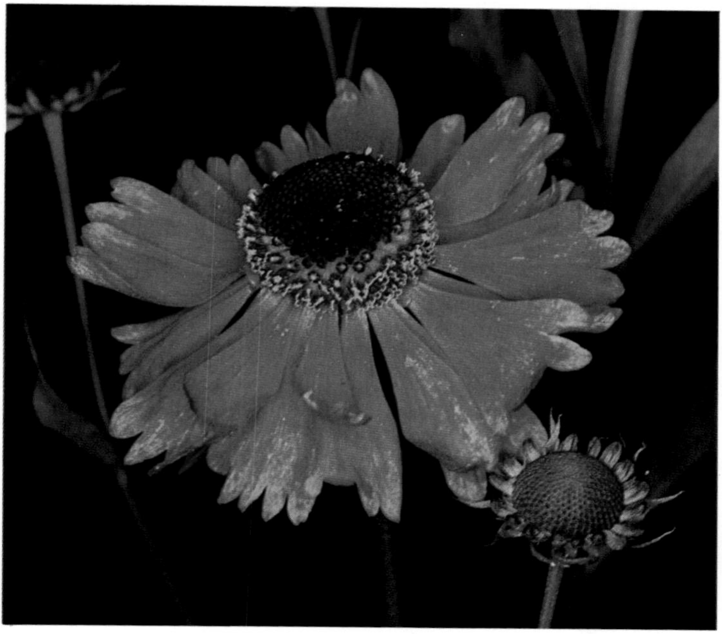

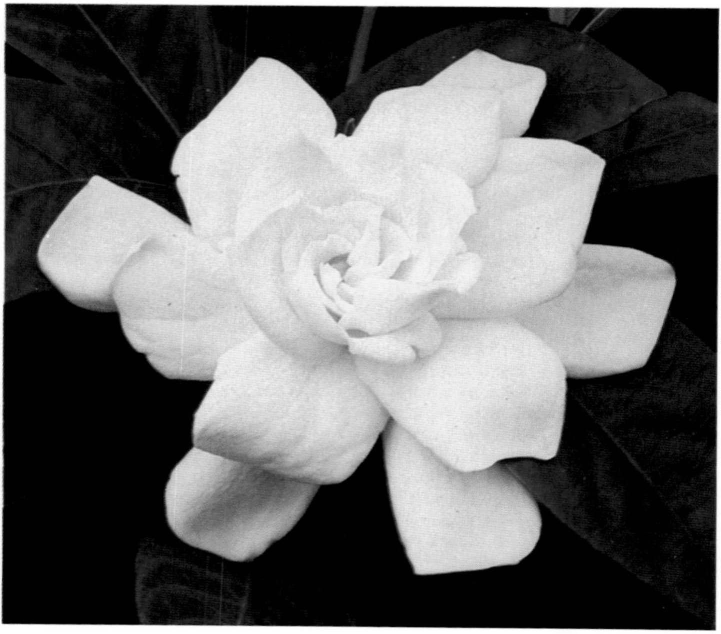

146 GAZANIA NIVEA C. F. Lessing

Family Compositae.
Description A bushy, herbaceous perennial often grown as an annual or biennial, depending on the climate. Its whitish-gray leaves are sessile, lanceolate-spatulate and tomentose. Its flowers are carried in solitary axillary capitula ranging in color from golden-yellow to chestnut-brown and red, with a darker disc.
Height of plant 8–14 in. (20–35 cm.).
Size of flower 2¾–3⅛ in. (7–8 cm.).
Place of origin South Africa.
Flowering time Spring–summer.
Cultivation Full sun or partial shade. Temperate climate. Dislikes frost and winter dampness. Prefers well-aerated, sandy soil that is humus-rich or well manured with organic material and phosphate fertilizers. Can withstand dry conditions well. Regular watering. At end of flowering season, remove old stems and leaves and protect plant for the winter by mulching well. Pests and diseases: aphids; various rots.
Propagation By clump division in spring or autumn. By early spring seed sowing under glass.
Qualities Suitable for balconies, terraces. Half-hardy. Easy to grow.

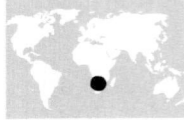

147 GENTIANA ACAULIS Carolus Linnaeus
Syn.: *G. kochiana* Perrier and Songeon. Common name: Stemless gentian

Family Gentianaceae.
Description A beautiful little perennial with magnificent dark-blue flowers, best grown in an alpine garden where its natural surroundings can be reproduced. It is often difficult to obtain good results when trying to raise it in any other conditions. It has short stems, each bearing one flower. Its lower leaves form a basal rosette while the rest are opposite, ovate-lanceolate and sessile. Flowers are campanulate and very large in relation to the size of the plant.
Height of plant 2⅜–4 in. (6–10 cm.).
Size of flower 2–2¾ in. (5–7 cm.).
Place of origin The mountains of central and southern Europe.
Flowering time Spring–summer.
Cultivation A shady, sheltered position. Cool-temperate climate. Frost-resistant. Likes a woodland-type soil, siliceous-argillaceous and moist; quite at home among rocks. Overall watering that keeps the soil constantly damp without becoming waterlogged. The plant likes to be left undisturbed.
Propagation By late-summer sowing in woodland mold enriched with humus.
Qualities Hardy. Rather demanding to grow.

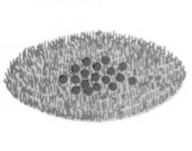

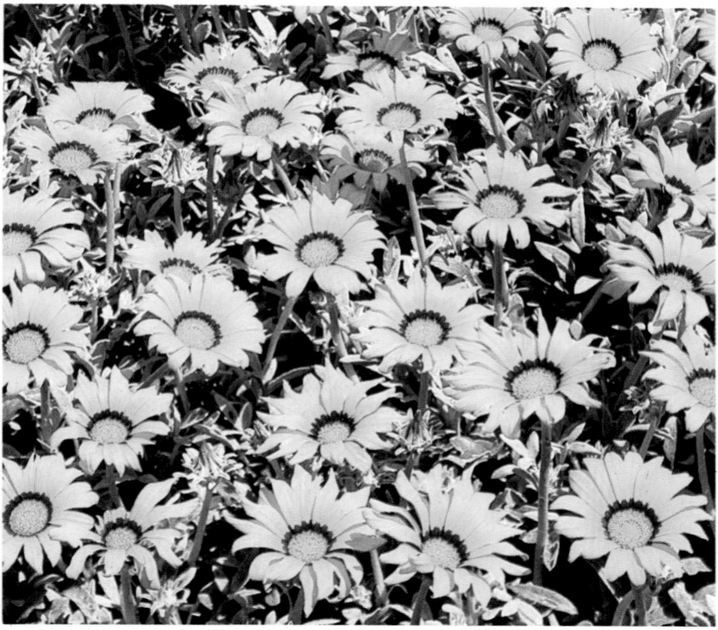

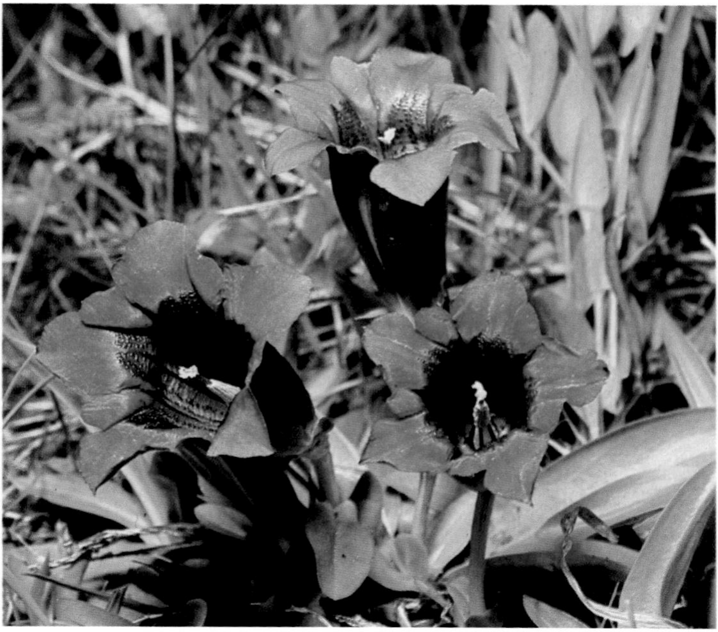

148 GERANIUM PALMATUM Antonio Jose Cavanilles
Syn.: *G. anemonaefolium* C. L. L'Héritier de Brutelle

Family Geraniaceae.
Description A bushy, suffruticose perennial. Its leaves are palmate-compound, each with a very long petiole (up to 12 in./30 cm.) and a lamina formed of five pinnatifid leaflets with laciniate-parted lobes. Its terminal flowers are in lax inflorescences, with a rose-pink flared corolla and protruding stamens. This distinctive, uncommon plant is, unfortunately, not long-lived.
Height of plant 12–20 in. (30–50 cm.).
Size of flower ¾–1⅛ in. (2–3 cm.).
Place of origin Canary Islands.
Flowering time Spring–summer.

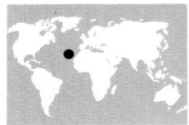

Cultivation A light, open position. Temperate climate. It cannot withstand much cold. Grows in almost any kind of garden soil, if it is rather compact, fertile and moist. Regular but limited watering. New growth can be encouraged by removing all dead inflorescences. Pests and diseases: insects; root rot as well as rust and oidium in damp conditions.
Propagation By spring sowing in pans under glass followed by pricking off and potting up before planting out.
Qualities Half-hardy. Easy to grow.

149 GERBERA JAMESONII William Jackson Hooker
Common names: Barberton daisy, Transvaal daisy

Family Compositae.
Description An acaulose, slightly tufted perennial with upright, pinnatifid, irregularly lobed leaves with strong venation and a sturdy petiole. Its flowers are in very lovely capitula, like ox-eye daisies, on robust stems with numerous linear ligules grouped together. The colors range from orange to red, white and yellow, according to the cultivar. There are semidouble and double-flowered varieties. They lend themselves to greenhouse forcing.
Height of plant 20–24 in. (50–60 cm.).
Size of flower 2–2¾ in. (5–7 cm.).
Place of origin South Africa.
Flowering time Spring–summer.
Cultivation Sunny to partial shade. Dry warm-temperate climate. Dislikes frost and needs to be sheltered but in an open position. Prefers a fertile, sandy soil but not calcareous, as the plant will then become chlorotic. Benefits from solid and liquid organic feeding and overall watering. During the winter it should be protected. Pests and diseases: aphids and tarsonemid mites; chlorosis, viruses, fungus diseases and stunted growth (rickets).
Propagation By seed, but this is not easy; seeds are viable for only about three months. By division in summer or autumn; protect young plants in a warm greenhouse.
Qualities Half-hardy. Quite demanding to grow.

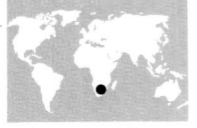

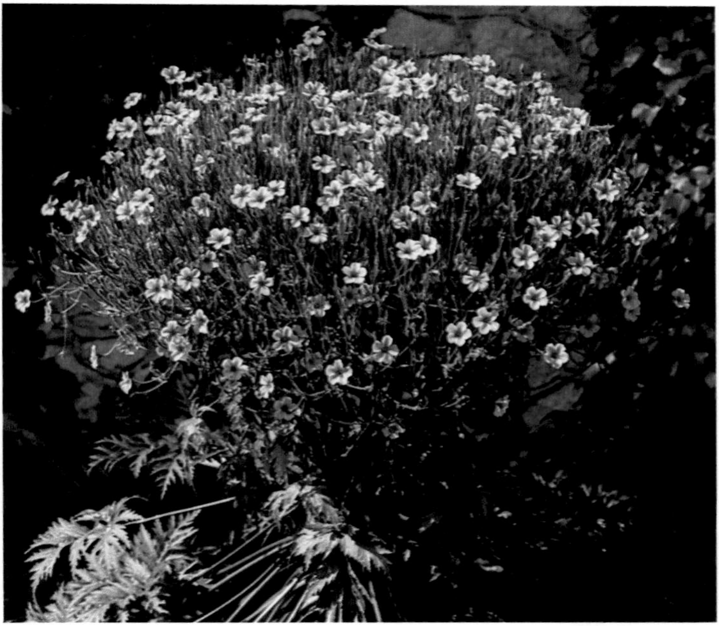

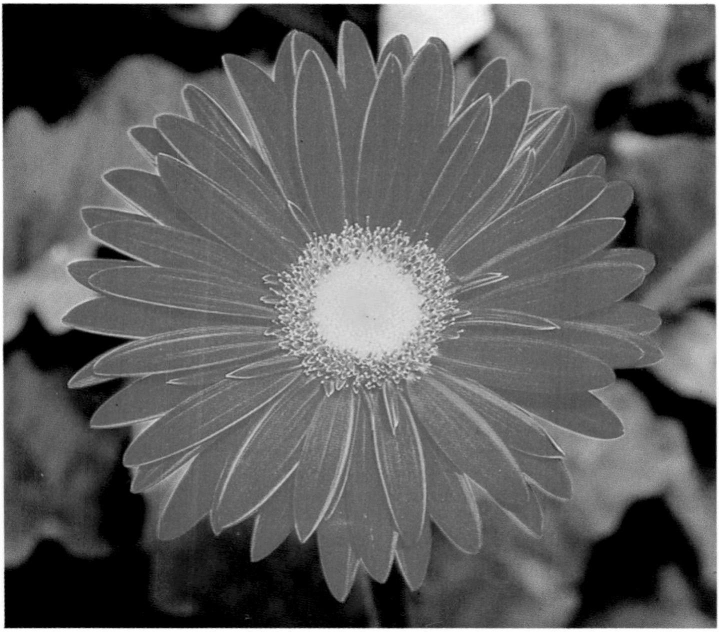

150 GLADIOLUS x GANDAVENSIS Hortorum, hybrid.

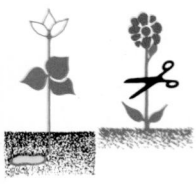

Family Iridaceae.
Description A very showy bulbous plant, extensively grown for its highly decorative flowers. It has an upright, rigid stem. Its linear, ensiform leaves, which cling closely to the stem, are long and acuminate. Its large flowers are carried in a dense, spicate inflorescence which is often unilateral. The corolla is zygomorphic with six unequal, spatulate tepals in a subcampanulate form. There are numerous horticultural varieties of the large-flowered hybrids in a wide variety of colors.
Height of plant 24–60 in. (0.60–1.50 m.).
Size of flower 4–8 in. (10–20 cm.).
Place of origin A hybrid of horticultural origin.
Flowering time Summer.

Cultivation Full sun. Temperate climate. Growing period limited to the summer months; or the corms can be forced in a greenhouse. Will grow in almost any soil that is slightly acid, well aerated, rich and moist. The soil can be enriched with a little organic material and mineral fertilizers (sulfate of ammonia and ammonium nitrate) but if too much nourishment is given, the vegetation may become deformed. Plenty of watering. The corms should be lifted in the fall, allowed to dry out and overwintered in a frost-free place.
Propagation By cormels in the spring; put them outdoors in a sheltered nursery bed. By seed, to obtain new varieties.
Qualities Hardy. Easy to grow.

151 GLADIOLUS SEGETUM John Bellenden Ker
Syn.: *G. italicum* Phillip Miller

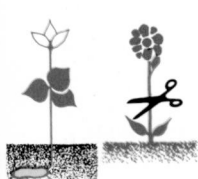

Family Iridaceae.
Description A bulbous perennial. A rather depressed corm with fibrous tunics. The green leaves are distichous, ensiform, narrow, erect and acuminate. The numerous flowers are borne in lax unilateral spikes with a zygomorphic perigonium of six slightly unequal tepals. Not widely grown but lends itself well to naturalization in a wild area or poor ground.
Height of plant 20–28 in. (50–70 cm.).
Size of flower 1⅛–1½ in. (3–4 cm.).
Place of origin Southern Europe.
Flowering time Spring.
Cultivation A sunny or very slightly shaded position. Temperate climate, but frost-resistant. Grows in any type of soil, preferably clayey, compact and humus-rich. Does not require any particular care. Watering should be done only with great restraint, if at all. After flowering, it should be cut back to ground level as it goes into its resting period. It tends to become invasive.
Propagation By cormels removed during the resting stage. By seed. Also by self-sowing.
Qualities Hardy. Easy to grow.

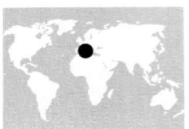

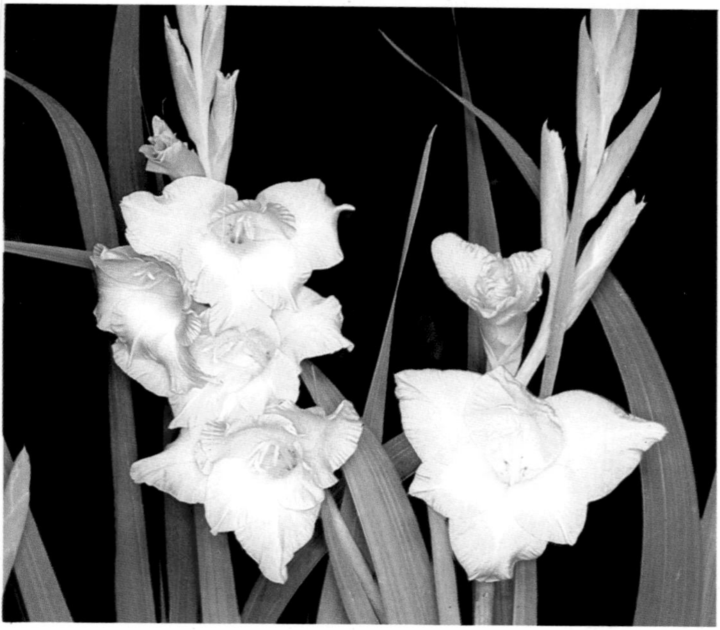

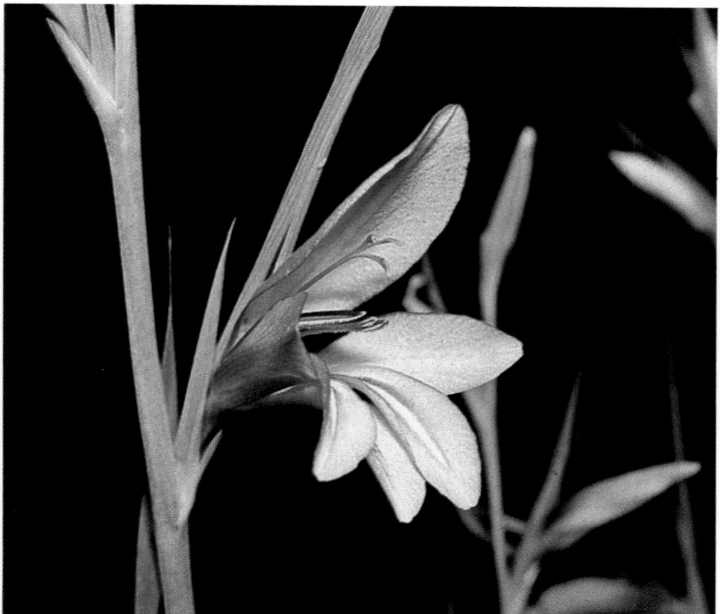

152 **GLADIOLUS TRISTIS** Carolus Linnaeus

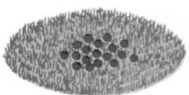

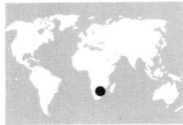

Family Iridaceae.
Description A bulbous perennial, this gladiolus has dark-green, slender, cylindrical-conical leaves about 18–24 inches (45–60 cm.) long. Three, four or five flowers are arranged on terminal spikes on a stem with two or three leaves toward the base; they consist of six acuminate, lanceolate-spatulate, unequal tepals. Colors range from ivory to sulfur yellow with red streaks on the reverse. It is one of the few species with scented flowers.
Height of plant 18–24 in. (45–60 cm.).
Size of flower 2–3⅛ in. (5–8 cm.).
Place of origin South Africa.
Flowering time Spring.
Cultivation Full sun. This is one of the species most resistant to cold. It likes a fertile, fairly compact, neutral or slightly acid, permeable type of garden soil. Too much nitrogen encourages too much leaf growth and tends to distort the stems. Regular watering during the active period of the plant; after flowering, it goes into a resting period and watering is harmful. Pests and diseases: aphids; fungus diseases.
Propagation By the cormels that proliferate at the base of the corms; these can be removed during the resting stage.
Qualities Hardy. Suitable for balconies, terraces. Easy to grow.

---

153 **GLOBULARIA CORDIFOLIA** Carolus Linnaeus

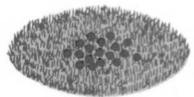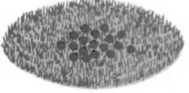

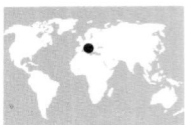

Family Globulariaceae.
Description A small perennial with slender, branched, creeping stems. Its bright-green leaves are semideciduous and obovate-spatulate. Its numerous azure flowers are very attractive; they are grouped in globose capitula to form clusters of many flowers, each growing singly at the apex of a short peduncle. It has a long flowering period.
Height of plant 3⅛–4 in. (8–10 cm.).
Size of flower ⅝–⅞ in. (1.5–2 cm.).
Place of origin Mountains of southern Europe.
Flowering time Spring. Sporadically in autumn.
Cultivation Sun or partial shade. Suited to any type of soil that tends to be heavy, even calcareous. Undemanding; usually requires no particular care. Regular watering. A little liquid fertilizer, if necessary. Trim lightly with scissors to increase the carpeting effect. Generally trouble-free.
Propagation By division in spring or autumn.
Qualities Hardy. Easy to grow.

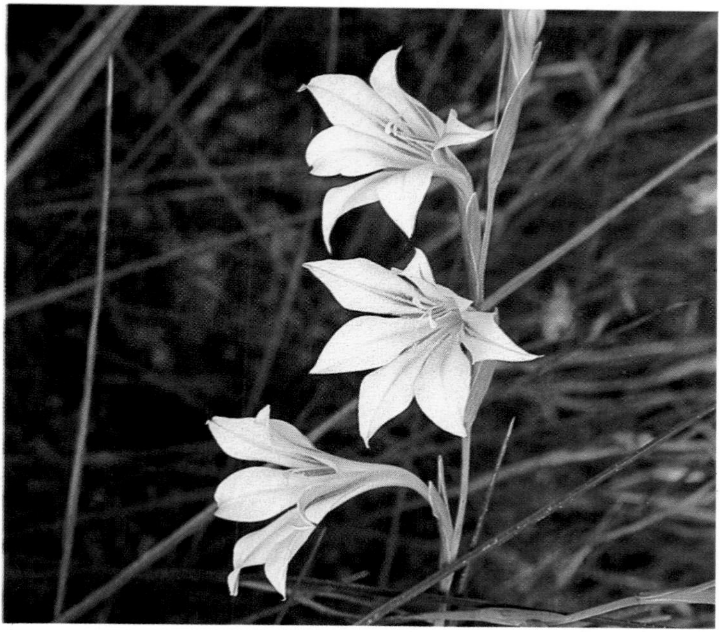

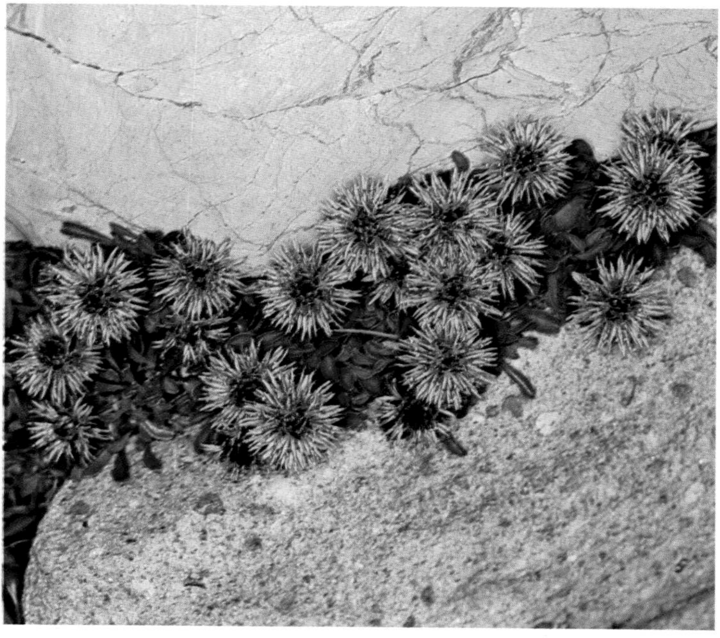

154 GODETIA GRANDIFLORA John Lindley cv.

Syns.: *G. whitneyi* Hortorum, *Oenothera whitneyi* Asa Gray, *G. amoena whitneyi.* Common name: Satinflower

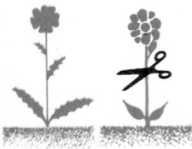

Family   Onagraceae.
Description   A bushy annual with an upright, ligneous stem and low, erect ramifications spreading outward. Its alternate leaves are oblong-lanceolate with a short pedicel. The axillary flowers are grouped in foliose racemes with a corolla of four or five unequal petals that are predominantly pink with broad basal markings. There are many horticultural cultivars. It is now difficult to find the pure species since nearly all are hybrid forms derived from *G. grandiflora* and *G. amoena.*
Height of plant   12–20 in. (30–50 cm.).
Size of flower   2–4 in. (5–10 cm.).
Place of origin   Western North America.
Flowering time   Late spring–summer.
Cultivation   A sunny to slightly shaded position. Prefers cool to warm areas. Well-aerated, rich soil mixed with leaf mold. Some well-rotted manure should be worked into the ground when preparing the bed and liquid fertilizers applied during growth. Plenty of watering. Pests and diseases: harmful insects; foot, stem and root rot.
Propagation   By spring sowing—preferably directly in the garden because the plant does not transplant well.
Qualities   Half-hardy. Easy to grow.

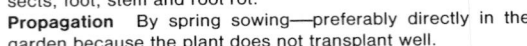

155 GREVILLEA ROSMARINIFOLIA Allan Cunningham

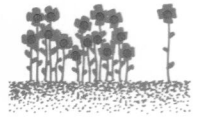

Family   Proteaceae
Description   When this evergreen shrub is grown outside its natural habitat it becomes somewhat inhibited. It is to be seen in gardens in warm coastal areas, such as the French Riviera, where it can develop treelike proportions. It has numerous ramifications and a fairly wide spread. Its alternate leaves, which grow close together, are sessile and linear-acute. The flowers are very strange, grouped in dense racemes toward the top of the branches.
Height of plant   5–10 ft. (1.50–3 m.).
Size of flower   ¾ in. (2 cm.).
Place of origin   Australia.
Flowering time   Spring.
Cultivation   Full sun or partial shade, and sheltered. Warm-temperate climate. Soil moist, tending to be clayey-sandy and humus-rich or amended with peat or leaf mold. Work well-rotted organic material into soil when preparing the ground for planting. Can withstand dry conditions fairly well. Usually not pruned.
Propagation   By spring sowing in a greenhouse or coldframe. Needs to be repotted at least twice before planting out.
Qualities   Half-hardy. Very easy to grow.

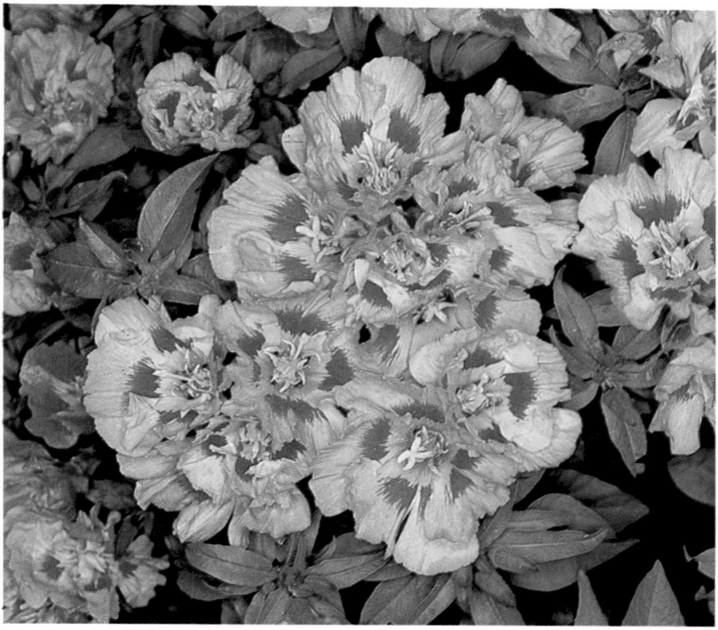

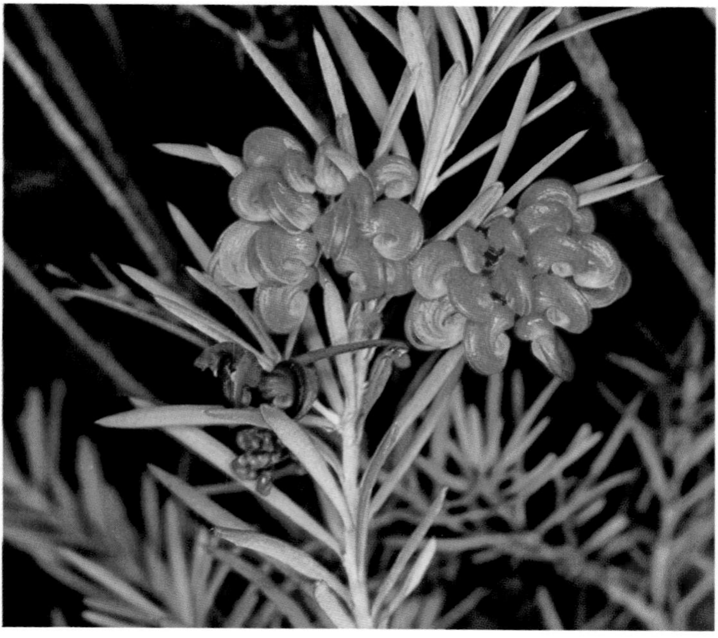

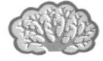

156 HEBE TRAVERSII (Joseph Dalton Hooker) Cockayne and H.H.B. Allan
Syn.: *Veronica brachysiphon* Hortorum

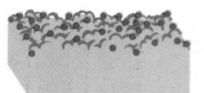

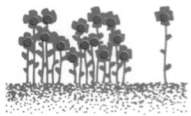

Family Scrophulariaceae.
Description A plant often known by the old name of *Veronica*, since the genus *Hebe* has only recently been introduced. The arborescent species, with ligneous stems, are now attributed to this new genus; the herbaceous species are attributed to the *Veronica* genus. An evergreen shrub with numerous erect ramifications, it has a compact habit. Its opposite leaves are sessile, elliptical-oblong or oblong-oval. The flowers are tiny, pinkish-white or reddish-purple, and borne in short axillary racemes.

Height of plant 40–80 in. (1–2 m.).
Size of flower ¾–1⅛ in. (2–3 cm.) the whole raceme.
Place of origin New Zealand.
Flowering time Summer–autumn.
Cultivation Full sun. Temperate climate. Frost-tender. Prefers ordinary, well-aerated, moist garden soil, even a little calcareous. A seasonal application of organic/mineral nutritive materials. Regular watering. Prune after flowering; the shrub can be pruned into quite a nice shape. It is subject to fungus diseases in a damp climate.
Propagation By cuttings in the spring under glass. By air layering in spring–summer. Sometimes by seed.
Qualities Half-hardy. Easy to grow.

157 HEDYCHIUM GARDNERIANUM William Roscoe
Common name: Ginger lily

Family Zingiberaceae.
Description A little-known plant that is attractive both for its flowers and its foliage. Its habit is rather similar to that of *Canna indica*. It has a short, articulate rhizome with sparse roots and sturdy green stems. Its alternate leaves are oval-lanceolate with a sheathing pedicel. Its numerous fragrant flowers, carried in a cylindrical-pyramidal terminal spike, are irregular and unusual. They have a very long, protruding stamen and filiform style.

Height of plant 2 ft. 6 in.–4 ft. (0.80–1.20 m.).
Size of flower 2–2¾ in. (5–7 cm.).
Place of origin India.
Flowering time Summer.
Cultivation Sunny to partial shade. Warm-temperate climate. Frost-tender. Although greedy for rich soil, this plant adapts itself to any well-aerated, sandy and damp ground. Plenty of watering. Can also be grown as a pot plant. The old flowering stems can be cut back to the base in the autumn. Pests: insects.

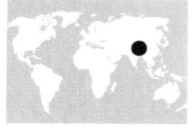

Propagation By division of the rhizomes in spring or autumn. By spring sowing in a cool greenhouse.
Qualities Half-hardy. Easy to grow.

158 HELIANTHEMUM NUMMULARIUM (Carolus Linnaeus) Phillip Miller

Syns.: *H. chamaecistus* Miller, *H. vulgare* Joseph Gaertner. Common name: Sun rose

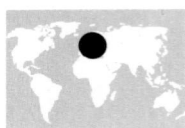

Family Cistaceae.

Description A subshrubby, suffruticose evergreen plant with wide-spreading, ascendent branches. Its small, opposite leaves are lanceolate and ovate, revolute at the margin and a greenish-gray on the reverse. The flowers are borne singly or in modest racemes with a corolla of five petals and numerous stamens in paintbrush formation. Although the most common color is yellow, among the cultivated varieties the flowers may be pink and white as well.

Height of plant 12–24 in. (30–60 cm.).

Size of flower ¾–1⅛ in. (2–3 cm.).

Place of origin Europe.

Flowering time Spring–summer.

Cultivation Full sun. Temperate climate. Can withstand a few frosts. Prefers a dry, sheltered site with calcareous or sandy soil. Does not require watering. Should be cut back hard after flowering or in the autumn. Requires no particular care.

Propagation By sowing in pots and putting in a coldframe in early spring. Sometimes by semi-hardwood cuttings taken in the summer, under glass.

Qualities Hardy. Easy to grow.

159 HELIANTHUS ANNUUS Carolus Linnaeus cv. "Globosus" Hortorum

Syn.: *H. annuus* Linnaeus cv. "Flore Pleno." Common name: Sunflower

Family Compositae.

Description An annual with one upright, sturdy, pithy and hispid stem with few branches. Its bright-green, alternate leaves are oval-acute, somewhat cordate at the base, and dentate. The flowers are borne in large, sometimes tilted, capitula. Basically golden-yellow, the various horticultural cultivars can be found in a range of tones. It flowers abundantly and for a long time.

Height of plant 2½–12 ft. (0.80–3.6 m.).

Size of flower 3⅛–8 in. (8–20 cm.).

Place of origin Minnesota to the West Coast.

Flowering time Summer–mid-autumn.

Cultivation Full sun. Temperate climate. Prefers a flat, fairly low-lying area with deep, moist, rich soil and adapts to any type of ground with these qualities. Plenty of organic manure and minerals should be worked into the soil at planting time and the plants kept well watered throughout their life. Tall varieties may require staking. Diseases: subject to oidium and various rusts in a wet climate.

Propagation By spring sowing in the garden where plants are to grow.

Qualities Hardy. Easy to grow.

160 HELIOTROPIUM ARBORESCENS Carolus Linnaeus

Syn.: *H. peruvianum* Linnaeus. Common name: Heliotrope

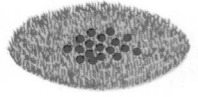

Family Boraginaceae.

Description A suffruticose, evergreen shrub, this is ramified from its ligneous base and has an open habit. Its alternate leaves are ovate-oblong and rugose-pubescent. Its numerous small flowers are borne in compact corymbiform cymes; the tubulous-campanulate, flaring corolla has five lobes. With their delicious vanilla fragrance and light-blue or mauve-blue color, the flowers have great charm.

Height of plant 2½–6½ ft. (0.80–2 m.).

Size of flower about ⅛ in. (0.5 cm.).

Place of origin Peru.

Flowering time More or less throughout the year.

Cultivation A bright, very sheltered position. Warm-temperate climate. Frost-tender. A moist, rich, fairly compact soil. Benefits from applications of well-rotted organic material and regular watering. Prune lightly after the main flowering. Pests and diseases: insects; various rots in overdamp sites.

Propagation By cuttings taken in autumn or spring and rooted in a frame or greenhouse. By spring sowing, but this method is seldom used.

Qualities Half-hardy. Easy to grow.

---

161 HELLEBORUS NIGER Carolus Linnaeus

Common name: Christmas rose

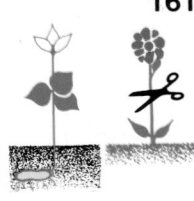

Family Ranunculaceae.

Description A bushy, herbaceous, evergreen perennial with a creeping rhizomatose stem with sparse roots. Its coriaceous leaves are pedate-parted with dentate edges at the top and an erect petiole. Its flowers are single, rather like large anemones, retroflexed at the end of the peduncle, with five white petaloid sepals sometimes tinged with pink.

Height of plant 8–14 in. (20–35 cm.).

Size of flower 2–2¾ in. (5–7 cm.).

Place of origin Southern Europe.

Flowering time Winter.

Cultivation A shady position, also shrubberies and woodlands. Temperate climate. Withstands the cold well. Chalk-rich, even clayey, soil, with humus. An occasional dressing of manure. Likes to be left undisturbed. Regular watering beneficial but it can survive well in dry conditions. Remove dead flowers and any dead or yellowing growth in the autumn. Usually trouble-free.

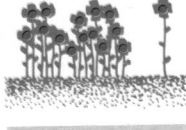

Propagation By clump division in autumn or spring. By seed, but this is a very slow method.

Qualities Hardy. Easy to grow.

79 ▬ 0217

020

0217

FREE GIFT

Tiger Token

Tiger Tokens and Esso Collection gifts are only available at participating Esso Service Stations.

You are entitled to one Tiger Token every time you spend £6 on Esso Petrol or Diesel.

All Tiger Tokens can be redeemed for any Esso Collection gift.

For full details and terms and conditions of the Esso Collection see colour leaflet obtainable from participating Esso Service Stations.

(Esso)

The Esso Collection

79 ▬ 0217

Redemption value 0.001p

06885

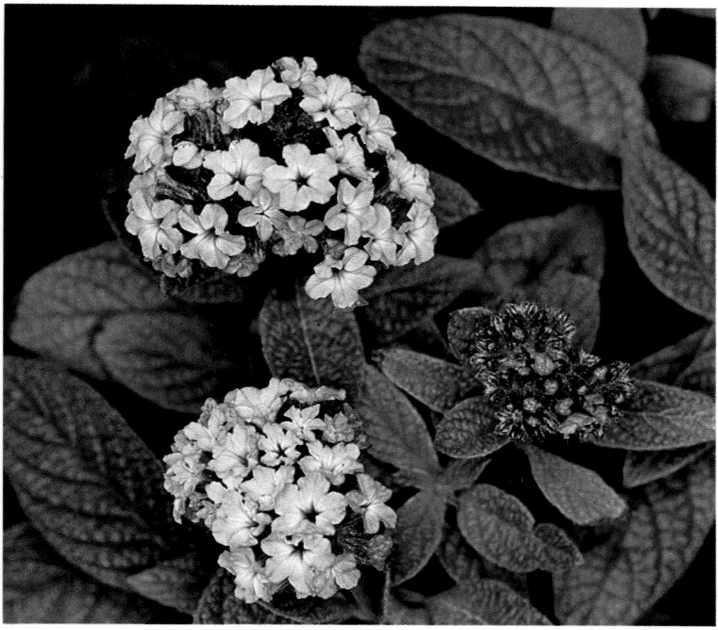

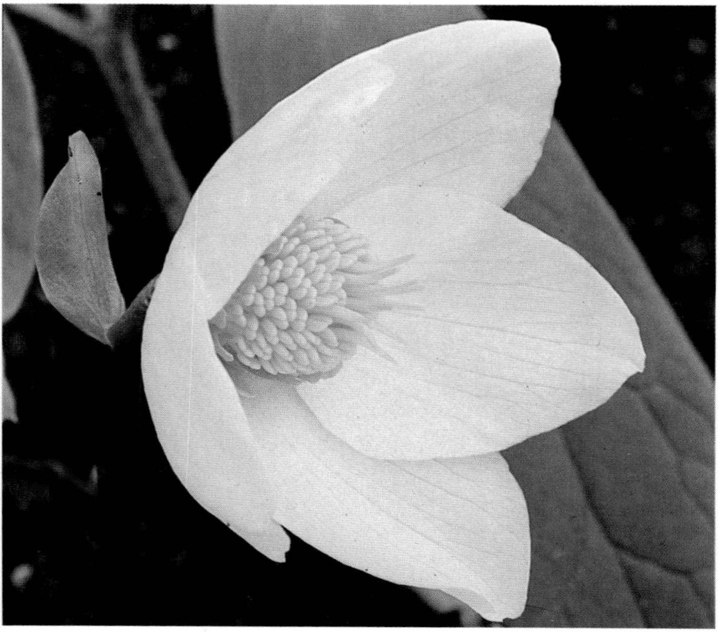

162 HELLEBORUS ORIENTALIS Jean Baptiste
Lamarck cv. "Fr. Irene Heinemann"
Common name: Lenten rose

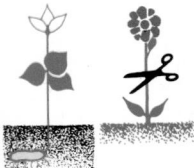

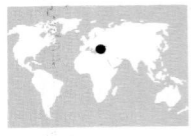

Family Ranunculaceae.
Description A rhizomatose-cespitose herbaceous plant. It is a very variable species from which a number of horticultural hybrids of various colors derive; they are all welcome, however, as they bloom during the period of transition between winter and spring. Its coriaceous leaves are pedate-parted with oblong, dentate segments borne on a sturdy, upright petiole. Its erect floral scapes are equipped with dentate, ovate-lanceolate foliar bracts. Its large flowers are softly shaded with carmine-pink marked with small dark blotches and lines on the inside.
Height of plant 8–14 in. (20–35 cm.).
Size of flower 2–2¾ in. (5–7 cm.).
Place of origin Greece and Asia Minor.
Flowering time Late winter–early spring.
Cultivation Shady position. Temperate climate. Withstands the cold well. Calcareous or clayey-sandy soil with moist humus. Periodic dressing of manure. Does not like to be disturbed. Regular watering. Dry growth should be removed during resting period.
Propagation By clump division, after flowering, in the spring.
Qualities Hardy. Easy to grow. Suitable for containers on terraces, balconies.

---

163 HEMEROCALLIS FULVA Carolus Linnaeus
Common name: Tawny daylily

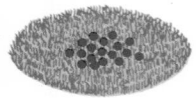

Family Liliaceae.
Description Cespitose-rhizomatose herbaceous perennial with large, carnose roots. Its leaves are distichous, linear, acuminate. Its flowers are infundibuliform and retroflexed; color is orange with yellowish striations.
Height of plant 27–32 in. (70–80 cm.).
Size of flower 4–6 in. (10–15 cm.).
Place of origin China, Japan and eastern Siberia.
Flowering time Late spring–summer.
Cultivation Bright to partially shaded position. Temperate climate. Deep, moist, fertile, even clayey, soil. A light organic/mineral spring dressing, worked into the surface. Stems should be cut down after flowering. Plenty of water during the spring–summer flowering season. Usually trouble-free.
Propagation By clump division in the spring or autumn.
Qualities Hardy. Suitable for terraces, balconies. Easy to grow.

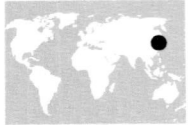

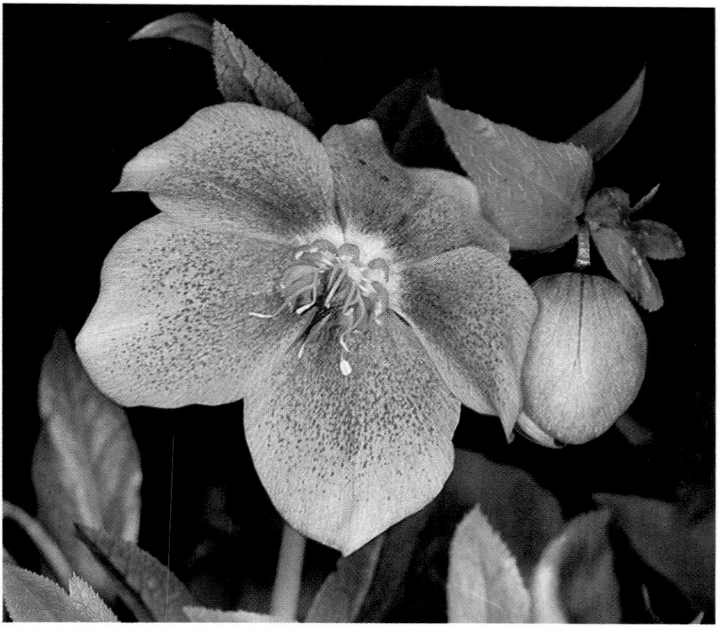

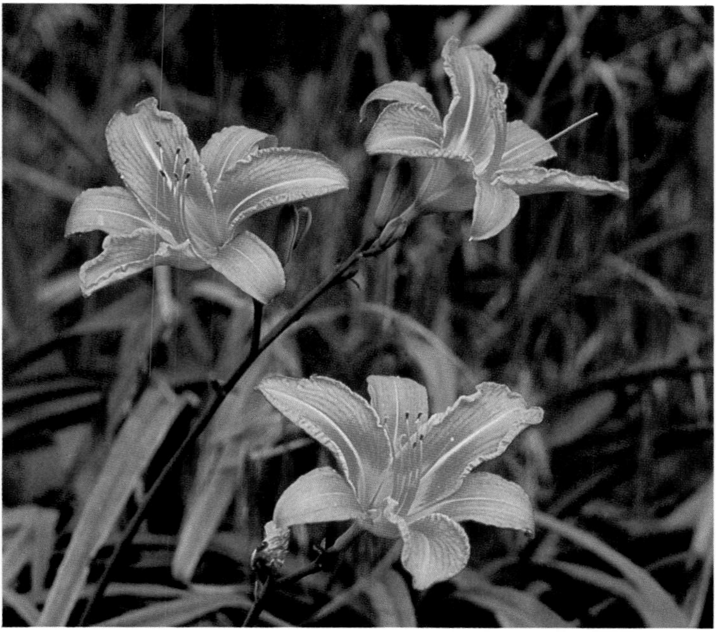

164 HEPATICA NOBILIS Phillip Miller

Syns.: *H. triloba* D. Chaix, *Anemone hepatica* Carolus Linnaeus, *H. trifolia*

Family Ranunculaceae.
Description A herbaceous perennial, rhizomatose with fasciculate leaves; it contains glucosides that are poisonous to man and to animals. Its basal leaves are trilobate and sub-cordate at the base with long petioles; they are dark green on the upper surface and liver-colored on the lower. Its numerous flowers, borne singly on erect scapes, are slightly pilose; they have six to nine deep-blue petals that vary in intensity according to the nature of the soil and the site.

Height of plant 4–4¾ in. (10–12 cm.).
Size of flower ½–1 in. (1.5–2.5 cm.).
Place of origin Europe, Asia.
Flowering time Late winter–early spring.
Cultivation Partial shade; shrubberies and woodlands. Cool-temperate areas. Reasonably frost-resistant. Light soil with humus content, rich in leaf litter, well drained, even a little calcareous. Regular watering. Usually requires no particular care.

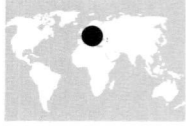

Propagation By clump division in the fall brought on in pots containing peaty leaf mold; slow-growing. Transplant in the spring.
Qualities Hardy. Easy to grow.

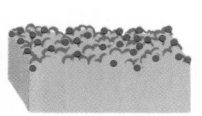

165 HIBISCUS SYRIACUS Carolus Linnaeus

Syn.: *Althaea frutex* Hortorum. Common name: Rose of Sharon

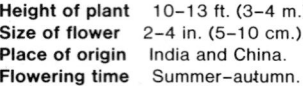

Family Malvaceae.
Description An ornamental deciduous shrub, its stem is arborescent with numerous open, pubescent ramifications. Its alternate leaves are rhombo-ovoid, more or less trilobate and sometimes ovate-lanceolate or dentate-lobate. Its abundant flowers are borne singly in the upper foliar axils and terminally. There are over 40 delightful single, semidouble and double-flowering horticultural cultivars of various colors.

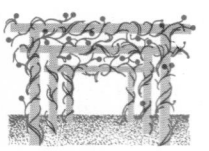

Height of plant 10–13 ft. (3–4 m.).
Size of flower 2–4 in. (5–10 cm.).
Place of origin India and China.
Flowering time Summer–autumn.
Cultivation Full sun or partial shade. Temperate climate. Can withstand frost well. Prefers clayey-siliceous, humus-rich soil or soil that has been well prepared with organic manure. Frequent and plentiful watering to avoid bud drop. Reacts well to pruning and can be shaped into a hedge by trimming. If grown as a small bush, it should be pruned hard to two or three buds in autumn to encourage floriferousness. Usually trouble-free.

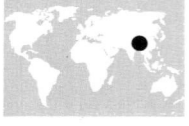

Propagation By cuttings taken in autumn, rooted in a nursery bed and protected during the winter with straw mats or a good mulch; alternatively, in a frost-free coldframe. By spring sowing and subsequent transplanting into boxes before planting out.
Qualities Hardy. Easy to grow.

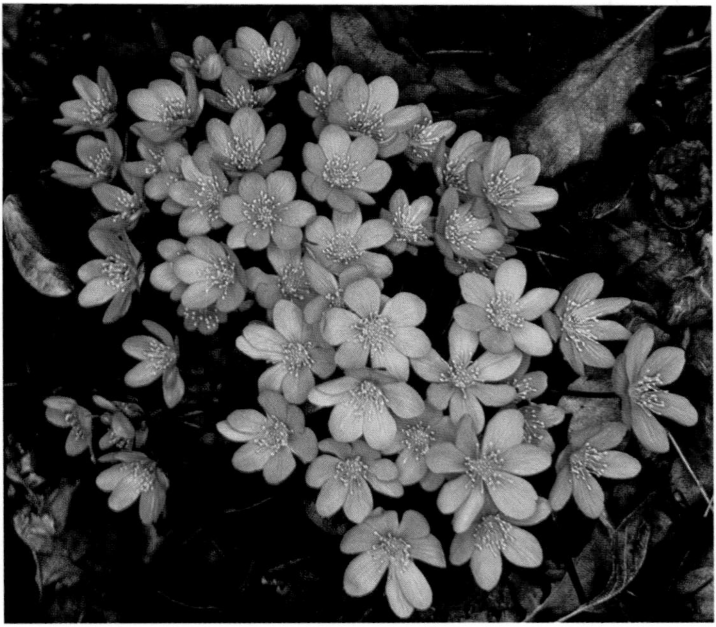

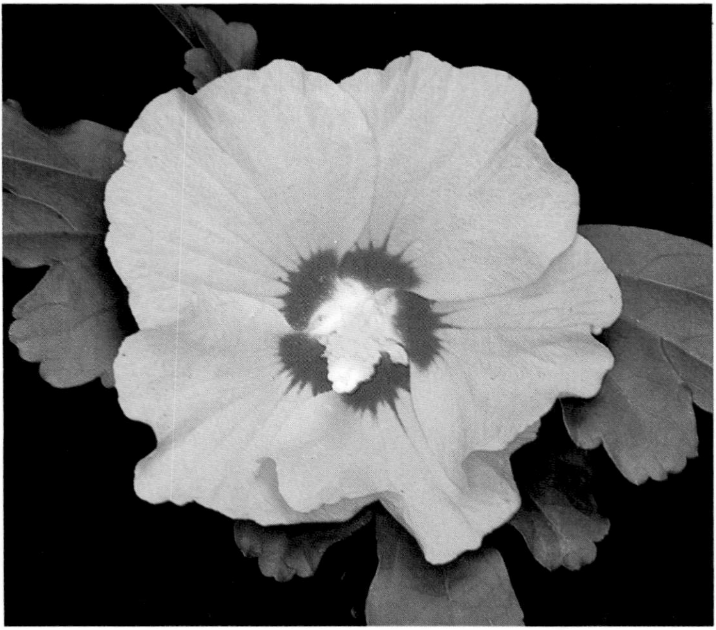

166 HIBISCUS ROSA-SINENSIS
Carolus Linnaeus
Common name: Chinese hibiscus

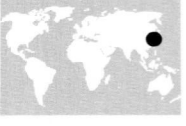

Family Malvaceae.
Description An evergreen shrub, ramified from the base, this has an open, expansive habit. Its bright, dark-green leaves are alternate, persistent, ovate or ovate-lanceolate, sometimes lobate, acute or acuminate, with a dentate-serrated margin. Its large flowers are borne in the upper foliar axils with a widely flaring, gamopetalous, infundibuliform corolla with five sub-rotund lobes from which protrude the very showy stamens and style fused into a single column terminating in yellow anthers and five red styles. The color of the species is a glowing red or bright scarlet-red but there are numerous single, semidouble and double-flowered varieties in shades of pink, orange and yellow. The succession of flowers is excellent and long-lasting.
Height of plant 6–16 ft. (2–5 m.).
Size of flower 3⅛–8 in. (8–20 cm.).
Place of origin China and Japan.
Flowering time Summer; all year in tropical areas.
Cultivation Full sun or partial shade. Warm-temperate climate. Cannot withstand the cold. It is often grown as a pot plant in a heated greenhouse during the autumn and winter and transferred into open ground for the summer. It prefers clayey-siliceous, rich soil. Requires plenty of manure and frequent watering. Pinching out of the growing tips and removal of weak or straggly growth encourages floriferousness. Can also be pruned quite hard in the autumn. Pests: aphids and mealybugs.
Propagation By cuttings taken in the spring and summer and rooted in a coldframe or greenhouse. Also by air layering.
Qualities Hardy only in its natural climate. Very easy to grow.

Opposite: two cultivated varieties of Hibiscus rosa-sinensis—*top, cv. with the typical red flowers; below, cv. "Moonlight," with yellow flowers.*

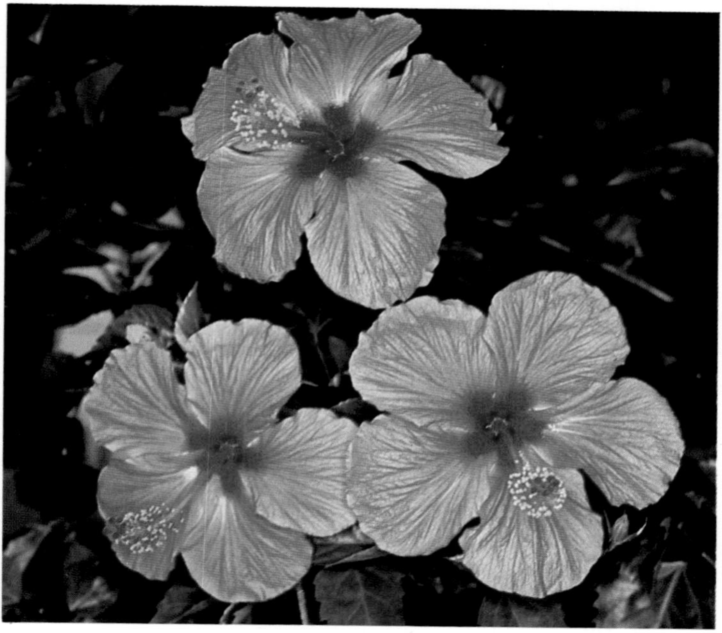

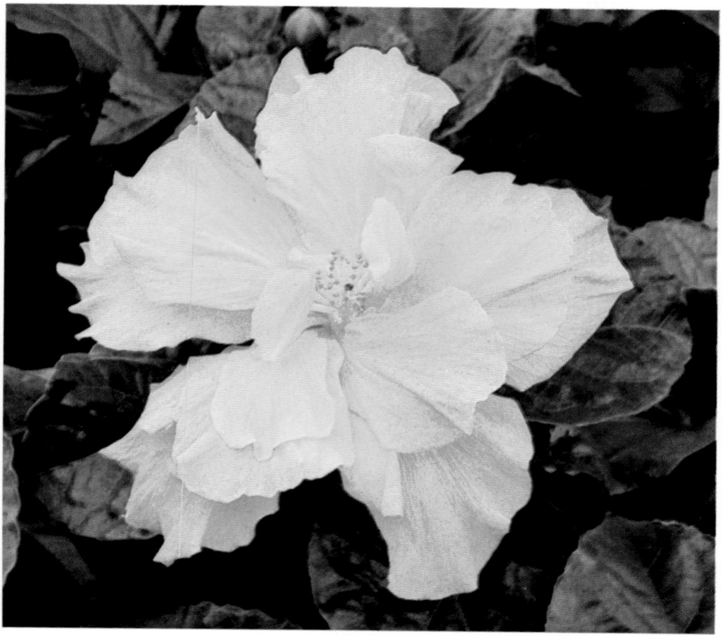

167 HIPPEASTRUM x HYBRIDUM Hortorum
Syn.: *H. hortorum* cv. Common name: Amaryllis

Family Amaryllidaceae.
Description A bulbous perennial growing from a large, piriform, tunicate, chestnut-brown bulb. It has two to six erect, distichous, linear, retroflexed leaves. Its flowers are borne on an upright, robust, fistulose scape in a terminal umbel, and the flaring perigonium has six unequal tepals. Colors vary according to variety, ranging from white to red, rose-pink and striate.
Height of plant 20–36 in. (50–90 cm.).
Size of flower 3⅛–4¾ in. (8–12 cm.).
Place of origin A horticultural hybrid of Peruvian parentage.
Flowering time Spring.
Cultivation A bright, sheltered position. Temperate climate. Frost-tender. Much grown as a pot plant in a warm greenhouse or indoors. Growth may be restarted from the autumn onward, using good garden soil with the addition of leaf mold, peat and sand previously generously composted with well-rotted organic garden material. Moderate overall watering. When flowering has finished, until the leaves turn yellow, apply small applications of liquid manure and water to help the bulb regain its strength.
Propagation New Dutch bulbs are usually obtained. Bulblets can also be used; these should be removed from the parent during the seasonal resting period and planted in boxes or, better still, in individual pots. Seed can also be used, but this is a very slow method.
Qualities Half-hardy to tender. Very easy to grow.

168 HYACINTHOIDES HISPANICA (Phillip Miller)
W. Rothmaler
Syns.: *Scilla hispanica* Miller, *Endymion campanulatus* H. M. Willkolm, *Endymion hispanicus* (Miller) P. Chouard, *Scilla campanulata*. Common name: Spanish bluebell

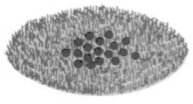
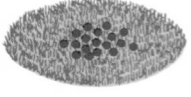

Family Liliaceae.
Description A very prolific perennial with a whitish, oval-rotund, often claviform, bulb. Its leaves are linear-acute, channeled and carnosect. Five or six campanulate flowers are borne in a raceme on each erect scape with short pedicels accompanied by small filiform bracts. The campanulate corollas are pale azure. There are also white and pink varieties.
Height of plant 10–12 in. (25–30 cm.).
Size of flower ⅜–½ in. (1–1.5 cm.).
Place of origin Originally from the Iberian peninsula, it has become naturalized throughout southern Europe.
Flowering time Spring.
Cultivation Partial to full shade. Temperate climate. Withstands the cold well. Grows in any type of soil but prefers it to be rich and well aerated. Needs no watering or particular care. Usually trouble-free. It lends itself well to naturalizing.
Propagation By bulblets removed from the parent bulbs in the summer during their resting period. By spring sowing, but it will be at least three years before flowers are produced.
Qualities Hardy. Easy to grow.

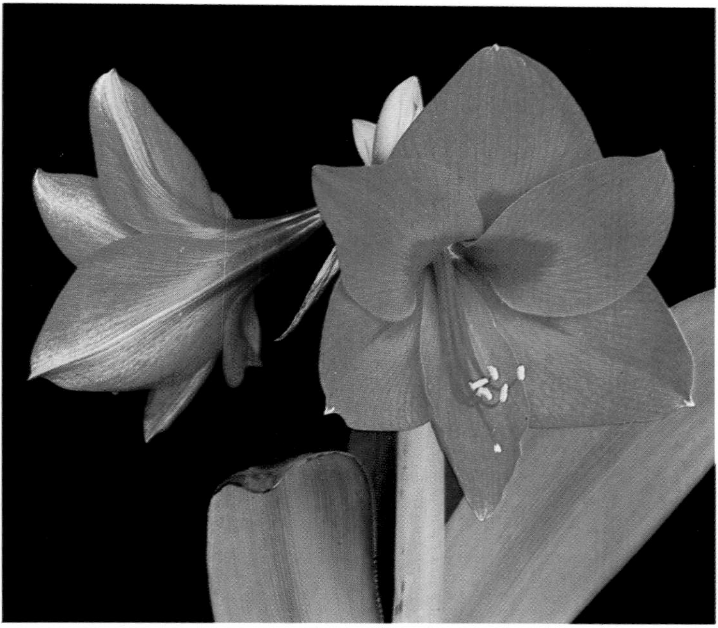

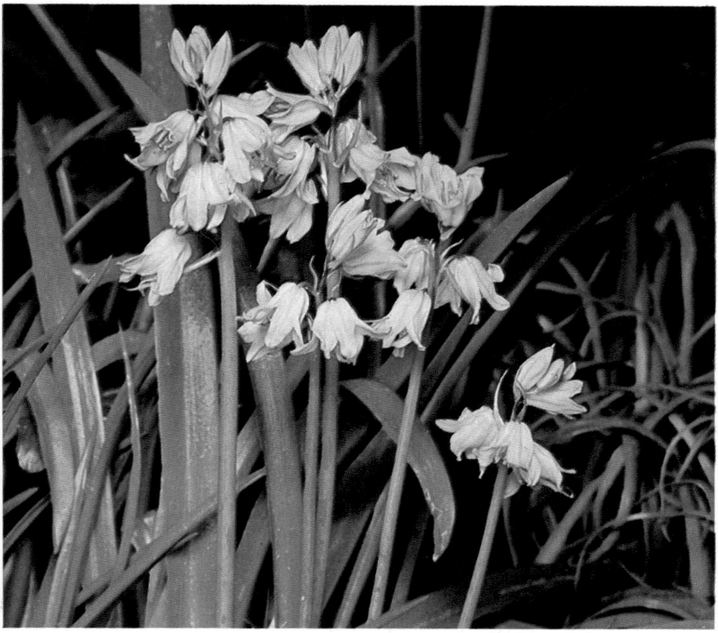

169 HYACINTHOIDES ITALICA
(Carolus Linnaeus) W. Rothmaler
Syns.: *Scilla italica* Linnaeus, *Endymion italicus* (Linnaeus) P. Chouard. Common name: Italian bluebell

Family Liliaceae.
Description A proliferous plant with an oval bulb. Its leaves are linear-channeled, acute and carnosect. Its floral, erect scape terminates in a compact, conic raceme with numerous lavender-blue flowers like a small hyacinth; each perigonium has six divaricate, lanceolate tepals.
Height of plant 6–8 in. (15–20 cm.).
Size of flower ¼–⅜ in. (0.7–1 cm.).
Place of origin Southern France and northwestern Italy.
Flowering time Spring.
Cultivation A shady position. Temperate climate. Can withstand the cold well. Grows in any kind of ground but prefers a slightly clayey, woodland type of soil. Requires no particular care. Suitable for naturalizing. Does not need to be watered. Usually trouble-free.

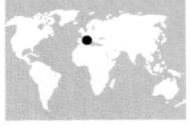

Propagation By bulblets removed from the parent bulbs during their resting period. By spring sowing, but it will be at least three years before flowers are produced.
Qualities Hardy. Easy to grow.

170 HYACINTHUS ORIENTALIS
Carolus Linnaeus cv.
Common name: Hyacinth

Family Liliaceae.
Description A deciduous, bulbous perennial with a large, piriform, tunicate bulb. Its leaves are rather thick and canaliculate; there are usually six or seven of them. Its numerous, very fragrant flowers, each having a tubulous perigonium with six retrocurved lobes, are borne in an almost cylindrical, tight raceme on a thick, upright, carnose scape. Colors include white, pink, deep purple-blue and dark blue, among the many horticultural cultivars. It is a plant that lends itself to forcing and to hydroponic culture.
Height of plant 6–12 in. (15–30 cm.).
Size of flower ¾–1 in. (2–2.5 cm.).
Place of origin Asia Minor.
Flowering time Early spring.
Cultivation A sunny position. Temperate climate. Can withstand a few frosts if well mulched. Prefers a loose, moist, peaty-sandy soil. Water only as required. After flowering, water should be withheld and the plants will go into a resting period; the old flowering stems should be removed and, when the leaves have died off, the bulbs can be lifted and stored in boxes in a well-ventilated, frost-free place.

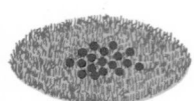

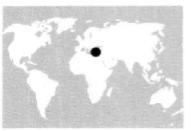

Propagation New Dutch bulbs are generally obtained for autumn planting. By bulblets, but this is a tiresome method.
Qualities Suitable for terraces, etc. Hardy. Easy to grow.

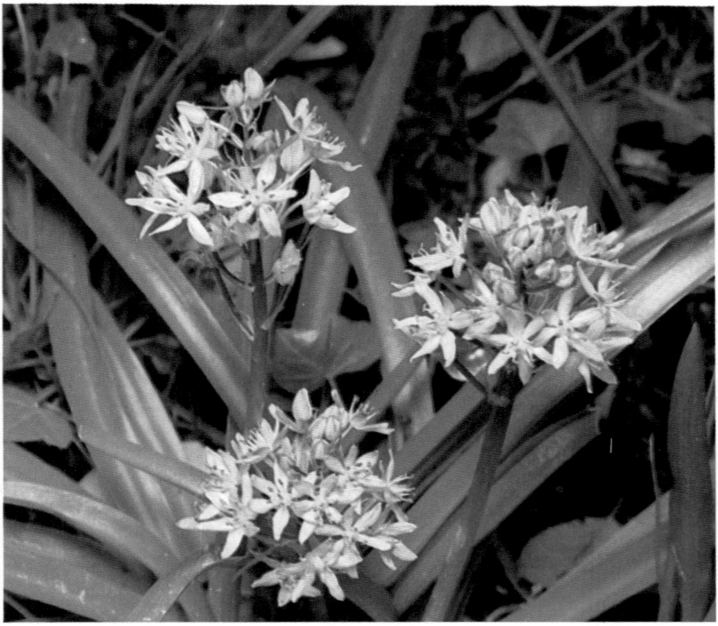

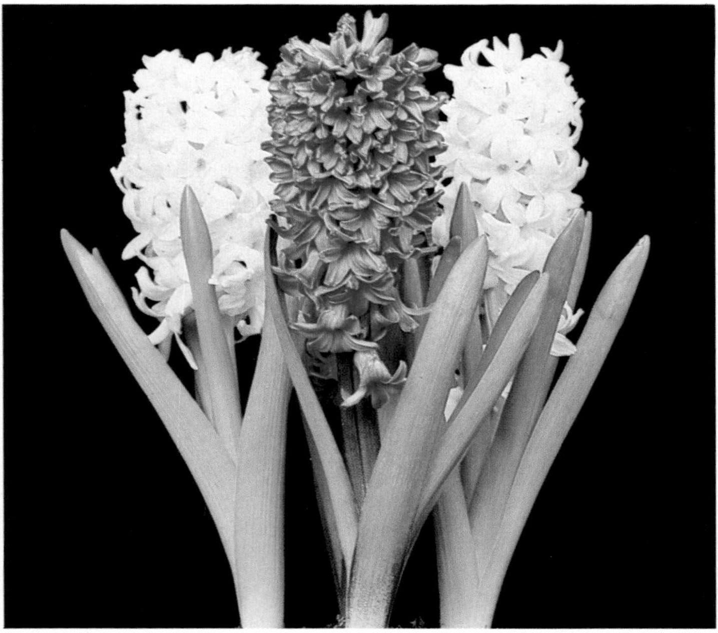

171 HYDRANGEA MACROPHYLLA Augustin
Pyramus DeCandolle
Syns.: *H. hortensis* James Edward Smith, *H. hortensia* Philipp Franz von Siebold, *H. opuloides* Karl Koch. Common name: Common hydrangea

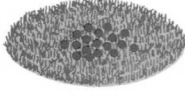

Family Saxifragaceae.

Description A very well-known plant, frequently grown under one or other of the above names, which, as far as floriculturists are concerned, mean the same plant. It is a bushy deciduous shrub that ramifies from the base and has an expansive habit. Its rather thick, opposite leaves are oval-elliptical, serrated and glabrous. The florets may either be fertile——very small, with five short stellulate petals——or sterile, in which case they have three to five (usually four) brightly colored sepals. All the flowers are borne in globose or depressed terminal corymbs.

There are many cultivars differing in color, shape and type of flower. The numerous varieties are generally divided into two groups: "Hortensia," with globose corymbs 6–8 in. (15–20 cm.) across, composed almost entirely of sterile florets; and "Lacecaps," with depressed corymbs 4–6 in. (10–15 cm.) in diameter, with fertile florets in the center and sterile ones around the outside.

Height of plant 2–12 ft. (0.60–3.50 m.).

Size of flower Fertile fiorets: ⅛–³/₁₆ in. (0.3–0.5 cm.); sterile florets: ¾–2 in. (2–5 cm.).

Place of origin China and Japan.

Flowering time Summer–early autumn.

Cultivation Shady but bright position. Cool-temperate climate. Reasonably frost-resistant. The plant dislikes a lime-saturated soil, preferring the loose, rich, moist soil of heaths and woodlands. In preparing ground or potting compost to receive hydrangea plants, the following mixture is recommended: equal parts of heath mold or shredded bark, well-broken-down leaf mold, fibrous peat and very well-seasoned manure with the addition of a little sand and a handful of dried blood. Requires plentiful overall watering alternated with feeds of liquid fertilizer prior to flowering. When the flowers have dried out, the floral stems can be cut back to one or two buds and weak branches removed. Generally the resting period is a good time to shorten the stems of the plants——but leave the new season's floral branches intact. Pests and diseases: aphids; fungus diseases, root rot and viruses.

Propagation By herbaceous or semi-hardwood cuttings, preferably taken in the summer–autumn and protected in a frame or cool greenhouse.

Qualities Suitable for balconies, terraces. Hardy. Easy to grow.

Opposite: two examples of Hydrangea macrophylla——
above, this belongs to the hortensia group; below, this belongs to the lacecap group.

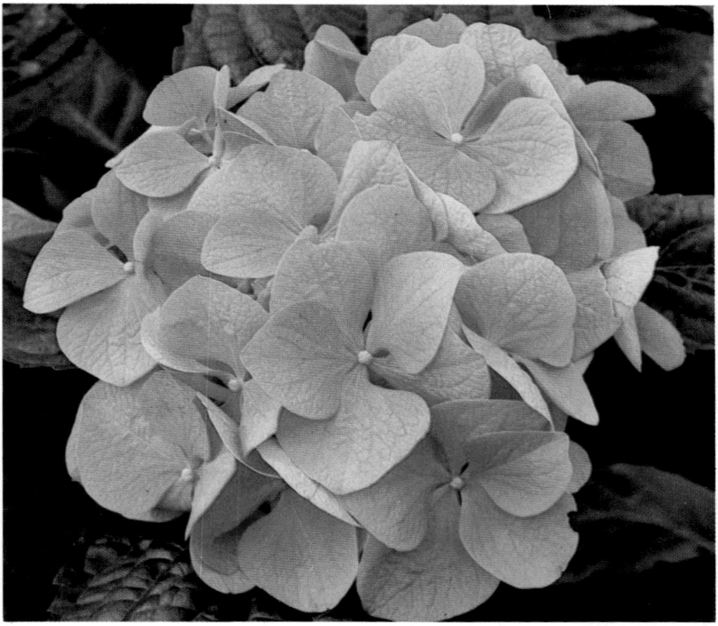

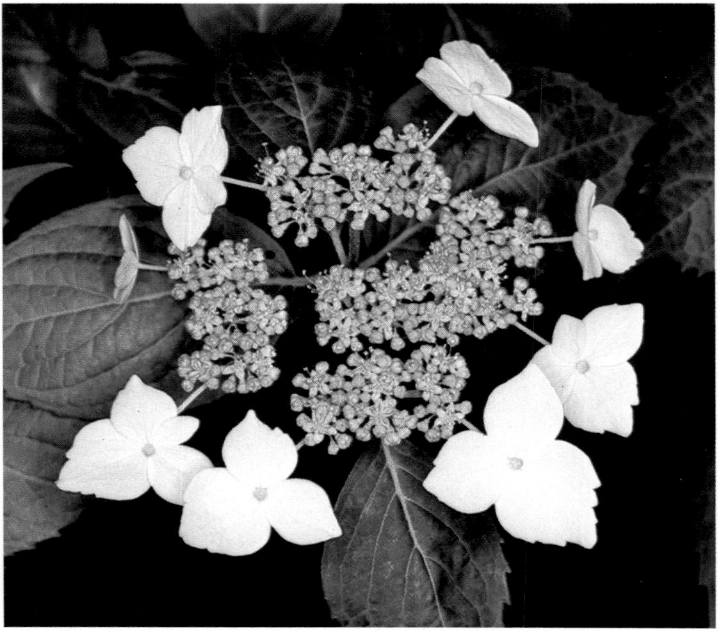

172 HYDRANGEA QUERCIFOLIA William Bartram
Common name: Oak-leaf hydrangea

Family Saxifragaceae.
Description This is one of the least grown of the hydrangea species although it is quite decorative both for its flowers and its deciduous foliage. It is particularly suited to shady positions. A shrub with diffuse, though few, branches, its opposite leaves have three to five lobes—sometimes seven—that are dentate, nervate-rugose, with a green upper surface and a white, cottony lower one. Its widely spaced florets, mostly fertile, are borne in creamy-white corymbiform terminal panicles with a few large, sterile florets around the edge.
Height of plant 40–80 in. (1–2 m.).
Size of flower ¾–1½ in. (2–4 cm.).
Place of origin Southeast United States.
Flowering time Summer.
Cultivation A shady position. Cool-temperate climate. Cannot withstand intense cold. An acid or slightly calcareous soil, especially woodland mold or ordinary rich, moist garden soil amended with well-broken-down leaf mold, peat and sand. Requires a considerable amount of watering. Pruning is limited to removing the old flowering branches because it likes to be left in its natural state. It is subject to chlorosis, which can be treated with iron chelate.
Propagation By herbaceous and semi-herbaceous cuttings taken in the spring–summer and rooted in a coldframe. Also by air layering.
Qualities Hardy. Easy to grow.

---

173 HYPERICUM CALYCINUM Carolus Linnaeus
Common names: Creeping St.-John's-wort, Aaron's beard

Family Hypericaceae.
Description A low-growing, suffruticose, spreading, rhizomatose shrub with stems that creep at first and then throw out erect, lateral branches. Its opposite leaves are persistent, distichous, ovate-elliptical and coriaceous. Its large, singly borne flowers are terminal, with numerous filiform stamens that form a big golden-yellow boss in the center of the corolla.
Height of plant 10–18 in. (25–45 cm.).
Size of flower 2⅜–4 in. (6–10 cm.).
Place of origin Balkan peninsula and Asia Minor.
Flowering time Summer.
Cultivation Grows equally well in full sun or deep shade. Temperate climate. Good resistance to frost. Can adapt to almost any type of soil, even if poor and stony. It often tends to become invasive. Requires no particular care but should be cut down to the ground in autumn to give new, compact spring growth. Usually trouble-free.
Propagation By clump division in autumn. By cuttings taken in summer and put to root in a coldframe. Sometimes by springtime sowing in a nursery bed or, better still, in pots in a coldframe.
Qualities Hardy. Easy to grow.

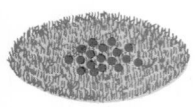

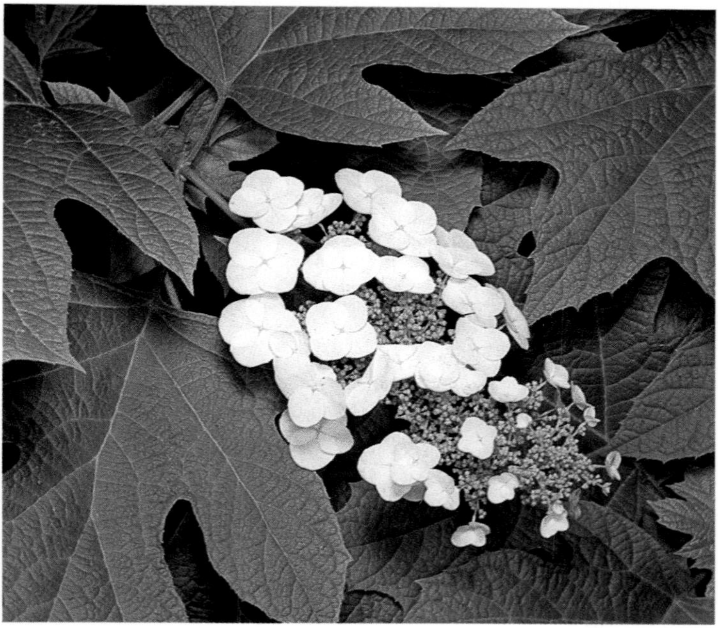

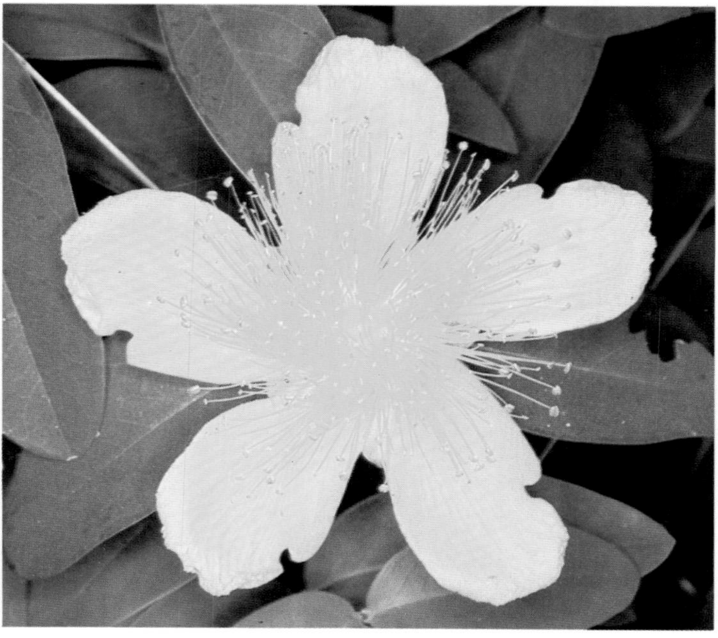

174 HYPERICUM HOOKERIANUM Robert Wight and George Arnold Walker Arnott
Common name: St.-John's-wort

Family Hypericaceae.

Description A small, very decorative plant with a prolonged and abundant flowering period. It has a globose habit and numerous reddish ramifications. Its almost sessile leaves are persistent and ovate-oblong. Its numerous flowers, which are yellow with orange anthers, are borne in terminal clusters of five to seven. There are several cultivated varieties, some of the more notable being var. *leschenaultii*, cv. ''Rogersii,'' cv. ''Rowellane.''

Height of plant 40–60 in. (1–1.50 m.).
Size of flower 1½–2 in. (4–5 cm.).
Place of origin Central Asia.
Flowering time Summer.
Cultivation Full sun to semi-shade. Cool-temperate climate especially in hilly or mountainous areas. Reasonable resistance to frost. Grows in any soil that is fairly compact or clayey-sandy and moderately rich. Limited watering. Light pruning in autumn to remove dead and straggly growth. Trouble-free.

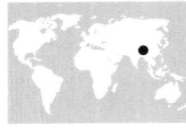

Propagation By seeds and cuttings in spring brought on in a coldframe.
Qualities Hardy. Easy to grow.

175 IBERIS SAXATILIS Carolus Linnaeus
Common name: Perennial candytuft

Family Cruciferae.

Description A semi-herbaceous, low-growing shrubby perennial, ramified from the base and of a cushiony habit. Its leaves are quite thick, entire and linear-lanceolate. It has numerous white or rose-pink flowers with two large petals and two opposite, smaller ones. These are borne in dense umbelliferous corymbs, which are typical of Cruciferae florets.

Height of plant 4–6 in. (10–15 cm.).
Size of flower ⅛–⅜ in. (0.5–0.8 cm.).
Place of origin Southern Europe.
Flowering time Spring–summer.

Cultivation Full sun. Temperate climate. Cannot withstand intense cold. Likes an arid, stony or rocky site but can adapt to any siliceous, calcareous or argillaceous (clayey) soil. Does not require feeding. Limited watering. Usually needs no particular care.

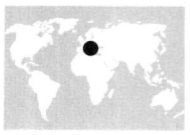

Propagation By spring sowing in pans under glass; will require pricking off before planting out. By cyme cuttings taken in the autumn or spring and put to root under glass.
Qualities Suitable for balconies, window boxes, etc. Hardy. Easy to grow.

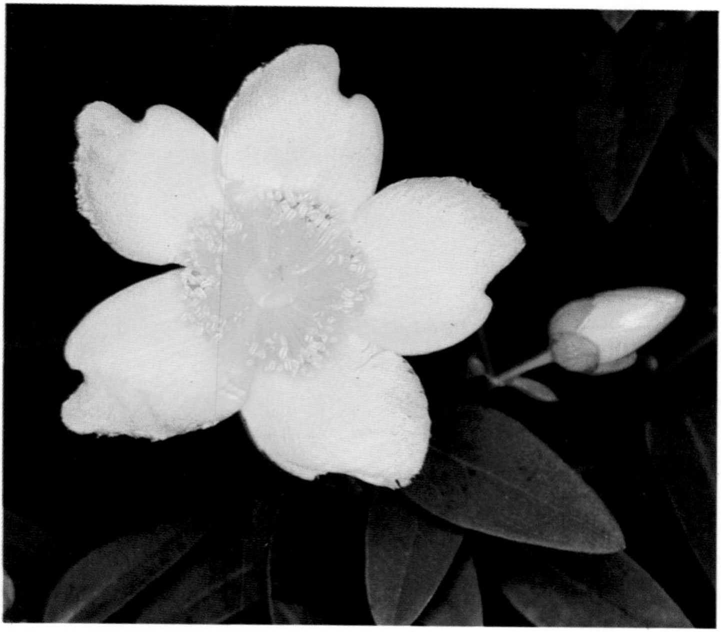

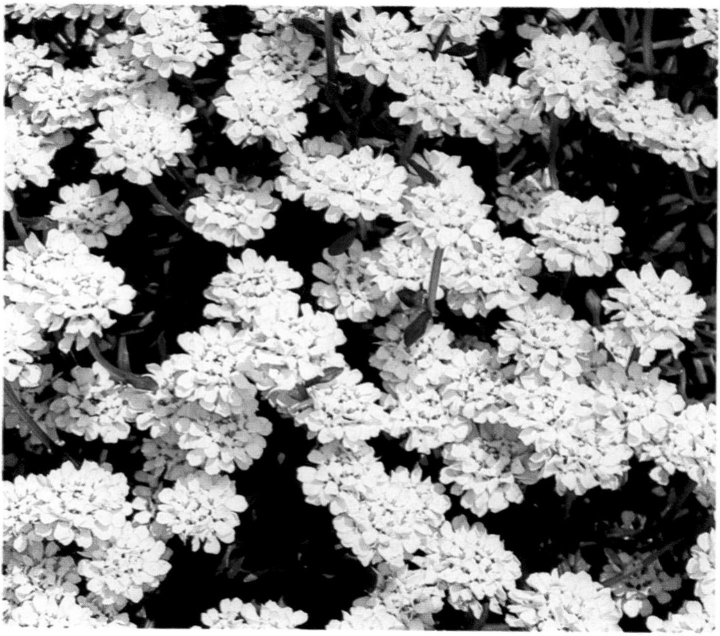

176 IBERIS UMBELLATA Carolus Linnaeus
Syn.: *I. corymbosa* Konrad Moench. Common name: Annual candytuft

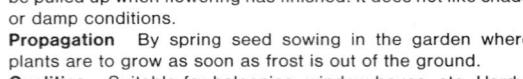

Family Cruciferae.
Description An erect, herbaceous plant that ramifies, particularly at the top. Its leaves are alternate, the lower ones being lanceolate and slightly dentate while the upper ones are linear-lanceolate. Its abundant flowers are borne in umbelliferous corymbs. The colors of the various horticultural cultivars range from white to lilac and a mauvish rose-pink.
Height of plant 10–20 in. (25–50 cm.).
Size of flower ⅛–½ in. (0.5–1.5 cm.).
Place of origin Southern Europe.
Flowering time Spring–summer.
Cultivation A sunny position. Temperate climate. Cannot withstand heavy frosts. Will grow in almost any type of soil but prefers it to be calcareous or siliceous, moist and moderately fertile. Regular, but not excessive, watering. The plants should be pulled up when flowering has finished. It does not like shade or damp conditions.
Propagation By spring seed sowing in the garden where plants are to grow as soon as frost is out of the ground.
Qualities Suitable for balconies, window boxes, etc. Hardy. Easy to grow.

177 IMPATIENS BALFOURII
William Jackson Hooker
Common name: Patience

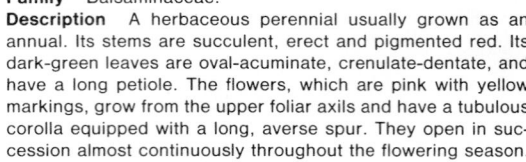

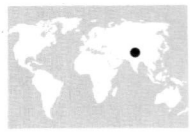

Family Balsaminaceae.
Description A herbaceous perennial usually grown as an annual. Its stems are succulent, erect and pigmented red. Its dark-green leaves are oval-acuminate, crenulate-dentate, and have a long petiole. The flowers, which are pink with yellow markings, grow from the upper foliar axils and have a tubulous corolla equipped with a long, averse spur. They open in succession almost continuously throughout the flowering season.
Height of plant 31–36 in. (80–90 cm.).
Size of flower 1–1⅛ in. (2.5–3 cm.).
Place of origin Western Himalayas.
Flowering time Summer–autumn.
Cultivation A moderately shaded position. Temperate climate. It is a greedy plant and needs well-aerated, humus-rich soil that has been enriched with well-matured manure. It also likes both root and foliar feeding and plenty of watering. Pests and diseases: aphids; various rots, oidium and rust.
Propagation By spring sowing in pans under glass with subsequent pricking off and transplanting. By cuttings taken in spring or autumn, pinching out the tops to encourage branching.
Qualities Easy to grow.

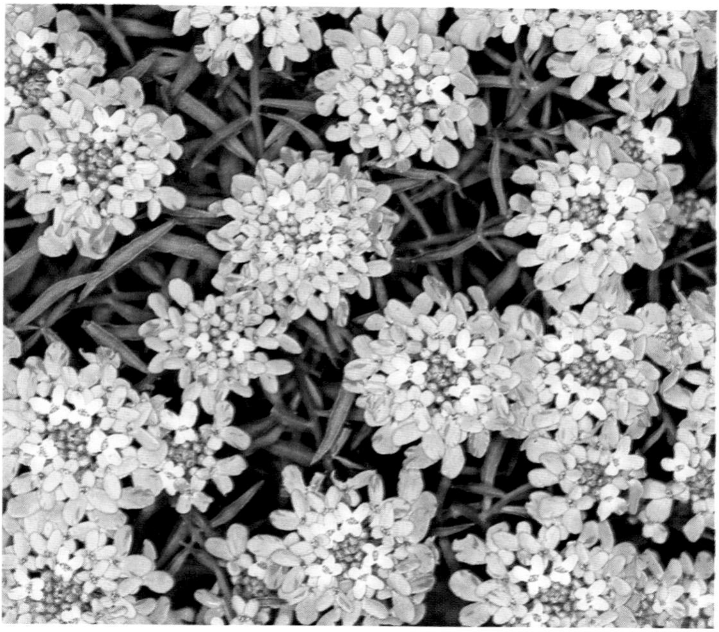

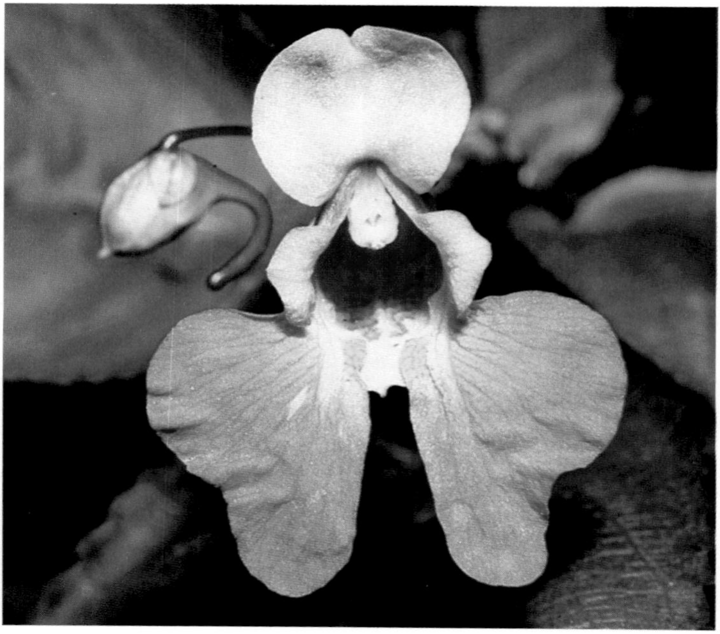

178 IMPATIENS BALSAMINA Carolus Linnaeus
Common name: Balsam

Family Balsaminaceae.
Description A herbaceous annual with a yellowish-green, transparent, erect, succulent, aqueous stem, ramified from the base. Its lower leaves are opposite and its upper ones alternate, lanceolate-dentate. Its abundant axillary-borne flowers are single, semidouble or double according to the various horticultural cultivars. The colors include white, purple and carmine.
Height of plant 8–30 in. (20–75 cm.).
Size of flower 1⅛–1½ in. (3–4 cm.).
Place of origin India, China and Malaysia.
Flowering time Summer–autumn.
Cultivation A bright to partially shaded position. Will grow in almost any type of soil but prefers argillaceous-sandy ground that is rich in organic material. Frequent and plentiful watering. Liquid feeding during the early stages of development to encourage growth. Pests and diseases: aphids; root rot.
Propagation By spring sowing in pans under glass, or directly into flowering site.
Qualities Very hardy. Easy to grow.

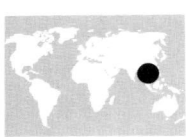

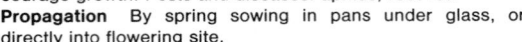

179 IMPATIENS WALLERIANA Joseph Dalton Hooker
Syn.: *I. sultanii* Hooker. Common name: Busy Lizzie

Family Balsaminaceae.
Description A charming herbaceous plant—a perennial usually grown as an annual—with a prolonged flowering period. It is often known as *I. sultanii* although frequently regarded as a species in itself because of its less vigorous growth. In recent years a large number of hybrid varieties have been created, with the consequent division into dwarf, medium and tall. Its erect stems are succulent with a vitreous transparency. Its leaves are alternate, ovate-lanceolate and very slightly dentate. Its flowers are borne singly in the foliar axils.
Height of plant 12–24 in. (30–60 cm.).
Size of flower 1⅛–2 in. (3–5 cm.).
Place of origin Tropical East Africa.
Flowering time Summer–autumn.
Cultivation Moderately sunny places. Temperate climate. Cannot withstand the cold. Likes argillaceous soil enriched with good leaf mold, well-matured farmyard manure and sand. Responds well to liquid feeding during early growth. Plentiful watering. An occasional trim encourages ramification. Pests and diseases: aphids and red spider mites; oidium.
Propagation By spring sowing under glass. By cuttings taken in autumn or spring and placed in a cool greenhouse.
Qualities Good for balconies, etc. Hardy. Easy to grow.

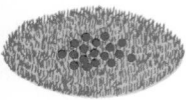

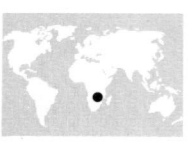

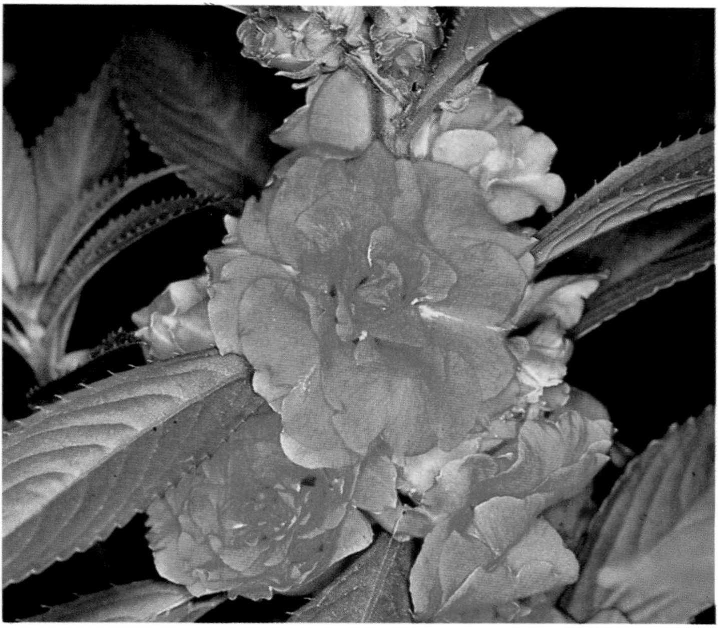
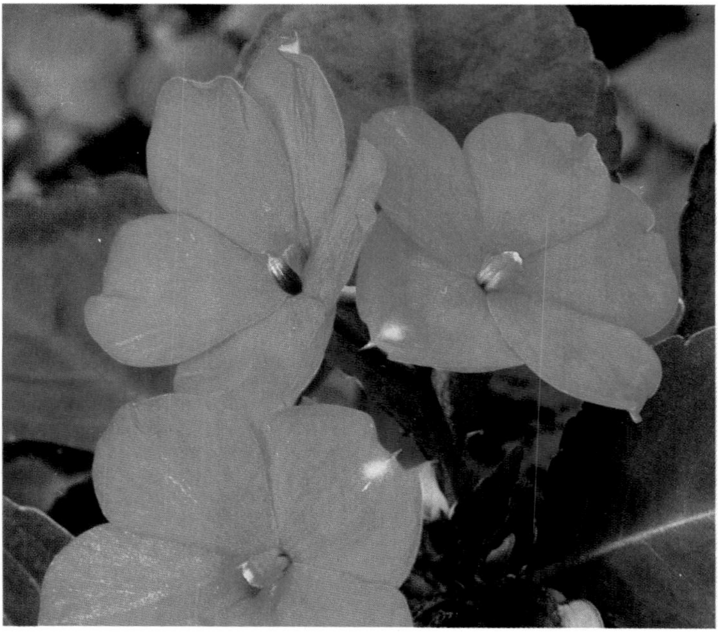

180 IOCHROMA COCCINEA
Michael Joseph Scheidweiler

Family Solanaceae.
Description A very decorative evergreen shrub that can be grown outdoors only in our warmest climates. It has long, fragile, slightly arching ramifications, pubescent at the tip. Its alternate leaves are ovate-lanceolate and pubescent. Its long, pedunculate flowers are tubulous and borne close together in pendulous umbelliferous inflorescences. It produces a fine display and has a long flowering period.
Height of plant 6½–10 ft. (2–3 m.).
Size of flower 2–2¾ in. (5–7 cm.).
Place of origin Mexico.
Flowering time Summer–autumn.
Cultivation A light or moderately shady position. Warm-temperate climate; cannot withstand the cold and is thus often grown as a pot plant in a cool greenhouse. It prefers good, slightly argillaceous garden soil mixed with well-rotted leaf mold and farmyard manure as well as a little sand. Regular watering and periodic liquid feeds. The branches can be cut back to three to five buds after flowering.
Propagation By herbaceous and semi-hardwood cuttings taken in the spring–summer and rooted in a frame or greenhouse.
Qualities Half-hardy to tender. Very easy to grow.

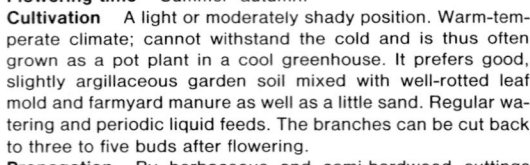

181 IPHEION UNIFLORUM (R. A. Graham)
Constantino Samuel Rafinesque-Schmaitz
Syns.: *Triteleia uniflora* John Lindley, *Brodiaea uniflora, Milla uniflora.* Common name: Spring star flower

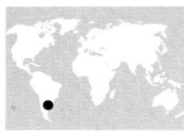

Family Liliaceae.
Description A bulbous, deciduous perennial, this has small oblong bulbs that smell of garlic and glaucous-green linear-acute leaves. Its bluish-white flowers, borne singly, consist of a conical tube opening out to a limb of six divaricate tepals. When massed together the little plants provide a most striking carpet effect during their flowering period.
Height of plant 4–5 in. (10–15 cm.).
Size of flower ¾–1 in. (2–2.5 cm.).
Place of origin Argentina and Uruguay.
Flowering time Spring.
Cultivation Full sun to partial shade. Temperate climate but can withstand frost. Grows in almost any type of well-aerated, even sandy, soil provided it is humus-rich and moist. The plant rests during the summer. It will often naturalize if conditions are right. Does not require watering or any particular care.
Propagation By bulblets removed from the parent bulb during its resting period.
Qualities Hardy. Easy to grow.

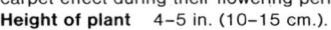

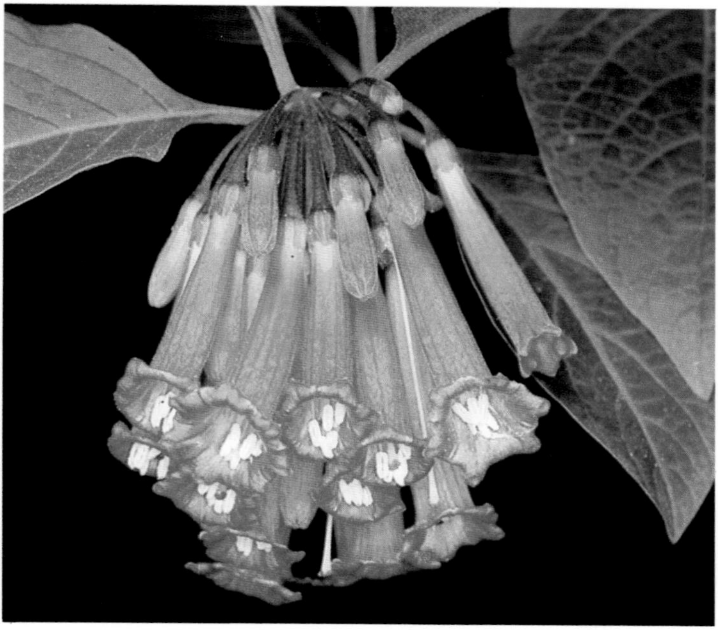

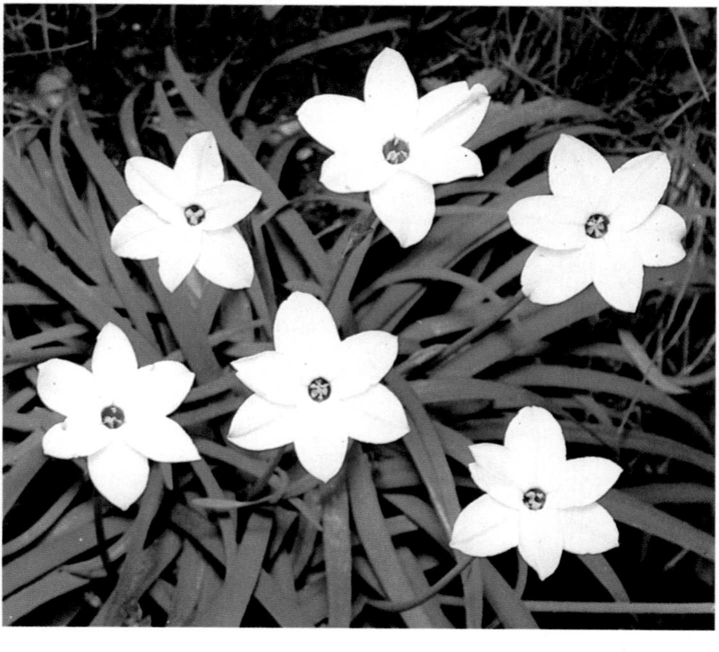

182 IPOMOEA TRICOLOR Antonio Jose Cavanilles

Syns.: *I. rubro-caerulea* Joseph Dalton Hooker, *I. violacea, Pharbitis tricolor.* Common name: Morning glory

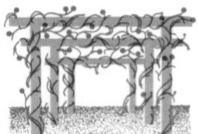

Family Convolvulaceae.
Description Widely grown as an annual, this is a very fast-growing climber. Its slender, twining stems have numerous ramifications. Its alternate leaves are almost persistent, cordate, acuminate and lobate, the lobes being sub-rotund. It grows outdoors in temperate regions, becoming almost woody. It has numerous trumpet-shaped flowers, usually violet or sky-blue with red streaks.
Height of plant 10–20 ft. (3–6 m.).
Size of flower 2⅜–4 in. (6–10 cm.).
Place of origin Mexico.
Flowering time Late spring–summer.
Cultivation A very light or sunny position. Temperate climate. Cannot withstand the cold well. Suited to almost any type of well-aerated, rich, moist soil. Can survive fairly well in dry conditions but likes regular watering. Needs supporting. Usually trouble-free.
Propagation By spring sowing in pots in a coldframe or directly into flowering positions.
Qualities Suitable for balconies, terraces. Hardy. Easy to grow.

183 IRIS JAPONICA Carolus Linnaeus

Syns.: *I. fimbriata* Etienne Pierre Ventenat, *I. chinensis* William Curtis. Common names: Crested iris, orchid iris

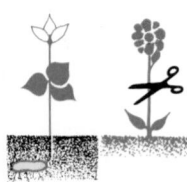

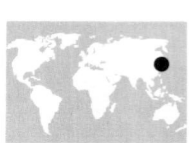

Family Iridaceae.
Description A rhizomatose perennial with a prostrate-ascendent, nodose-ramose stem that creeps on the surface; from this modified stem, other rhizomes grow laterally. These are at first as slender as stolons but soon develop into thick, bushy growth. The leaves are distichous, ensiform and lineate-flexuous. The numerous lavender-colored flowers are borne in loosely arranged, open cymes. Each depressed perigonium has delicately fimbriate laciniae, with markings and a central fringe or crest of golden-yellow.
Height of plant 14–22 in. (35–55 cm.).
Size of flower 2–2¾ in. (5–7 cm.).
Place of origin Japan and China.
Flowering time Spring.
Cultivation A light position but out of direct sunlight. Temperate climate. Does not like heavy frosts. Prefers light, well-aerated, moist soil, rich in organic material or woodland mold. Appreciates being watered during a dry period. Remove dry leaves and floral stems in autumn.
Propagation By rhizome division in autumn; the pieces should not be planted very deeply.
Qualities Hardy. Easy to grow.

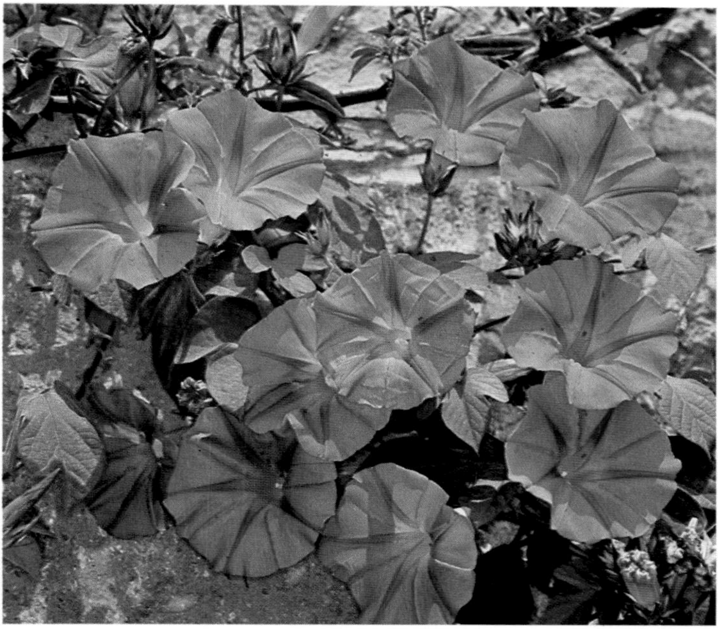

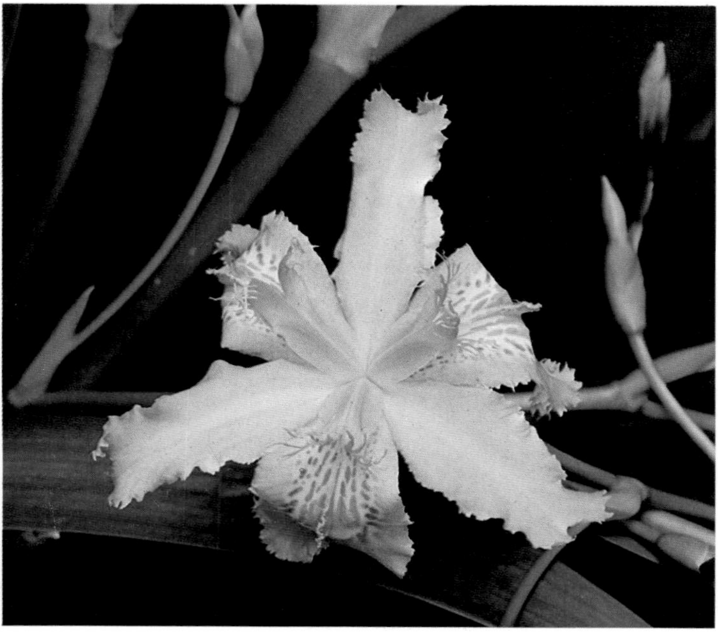

184 IRIS GERMANICA Carolus Linnaeus

Syn.: *I. florentina* (blue-white form). Common name: German iris

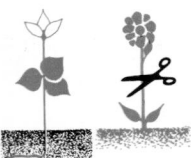

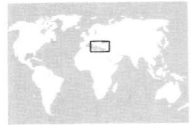

Family Iridaceae.

Description A herbaceous perennial with a large, creeping, ramified rhizome; an aerial shoot that is both foliar and floral forms at the end of each ramification. The light-green upright leaves are distichous, ensiform, equitant and covered with a glaucous pruina. Three to six large flowers are borne on an erect scape, sometimes ramified at the end in a slightly scented inflorescence in the form of a helicoid monochasium.

The perigonium has six tepals, three of which are upturning to converge at the apex toward the center; the others are retro-flexed with a strip of yellow hairs along the central vein, hence the generic term "bearded" for this category of iris. In the species the perigonium is deep purple but the colors of the numerous cultivated hybrids include azure, violet, yellow, white, rose-pink, variegated.

Height of plant 2–3 ft. (60–90 cm.).

Size of flower 4–6 in. (10–15 cm.).

Place of origin A cultivated hybrid whose parents probably originated in the eastern Mediterranean region.

Flowering time Spring–early summer.

Cultivation A sunny position. Temperate climate. Can withstand the cold fairly well. Grows in almost any type of soil but prefers rich, argillaceous-calcareous ground that does not become waterlogged. Does not usually need watering. New plants can be put in at the end of the flowering season, during the summer, keeping the rhizomes near the surface.

Manure should be applied cautiously, since too much causes distortion of the growth and the plants may go limp. If nourishment seems to be necessary, an application of bonemeal will suffice. Cut the floral scapes down to the base immediately after flowering and remove dry leaves in autumn. Pests and diseases: various insects; leaf spot, rhizome rot, rust.

Propagation By rhizome division in the summer, after the flowering period.

Qualities Suitable for terraces, balconies. Hardy. Easy to grow.

Opposite: above, typical flowers of the Iris germanica. *Below, some cultivated varieties; center, cv. "Belle Meade" (Wills, 1952) and cv. "Gudrun" (W. R. Dyches, 1929); bottom, cv. "Rajah Brooke" (L. Worton, 1944) and cv. "Bravado" (1959).*

185   IRIS LUTESCENS Carolus Linnaeus
Syn.: *I. chamaeiris* Carlo Guiseppe Bertero

Family   Iridaceae.
Description   A herbaceous rhizomatose perennial, its rhizome is medium size, creeping and ramified. Its glaucous-green leaves are persistent, distichous, ensiform and short or, quite often, the same height as the flowers, which are quite large in relation to the size of the plant. On each plant there may be one, two or three dark-purple to sky-blue flowers with yellowish striations on the inside. This is an attractive species from which many hybrid species derive from crossings with *I. germanica*.

Height of plant   6–8 in. (15–20 cm.).
Size of flower   2–4 in. (5–10 cm.).
Place of origin   Southwestern Europe.
Flowering time   Spring.
Cultivation   A sunny position. Temperate climate. Withstands frost well. Grows in almost any type of soil, preferably rich, argillaceous-calcareous ground that does not become waterlogged. Usually requires no watering or manuring; too much nourishment tends to make the plants go flabby. If they seem to need feeding, an application of bonemeal will suffice. Rhizomes should always be planted shallowly in the summer after flowering. Dry growth can be removed, but no other type of cutting back is necessary.

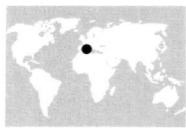

Propagation   Rhizome division, after flowering, in summer.
Qualities   Good for balconies, etc. Hardy. Easy to grow.

---

186   IRIS UNGUICULARIS Jean Louis Marie Poiret
Syns.: *I. stylosa* René Louiche Desfontaines, *I. graminea* Hortorum. Common name: Algerian iris

Family   Iridaceae.
Description   A cespitose-rhizomatose perennial with slender, ramified rhizomes. Its long, narrow leaves are slim, persistent, sheathed and retroflexed. Its numerous fragrant flowers, borne singly, have six azure-lilac tepals with yellow venation and markings inside. There are also white and rose-pink varieties. This plant is particularly well suited to awkward sites and even poor soil.

Height of plant   16–24 in. (40–60 cm.).
Size of flower   2⅜–3⅛ in. (6–8 cm.).
Place of origin   The Mediterranean region of Africa.
Flowering time   Winter–spring.
Cultivation   Full sun and even shade. Temperate climate. Can withstand a few frosts quite well. Sheltered, dry position. Calcareous, argillaceous soil, even if compact and poor. Does not require watering. Likes to be left undisturbed. Occasional thinning out may be necessary if the clumps become too crowded or invasive. Can develop rhizome rot.

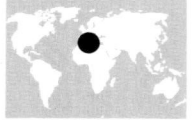

Propagation   By division of the rhizome clumps in late summer, planted shallowly.
Qualities   Hardy. Easy to grow.

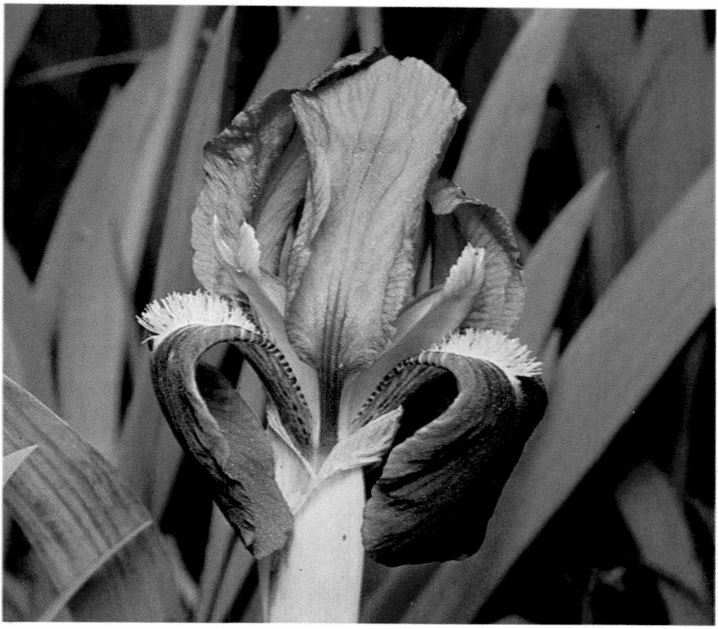

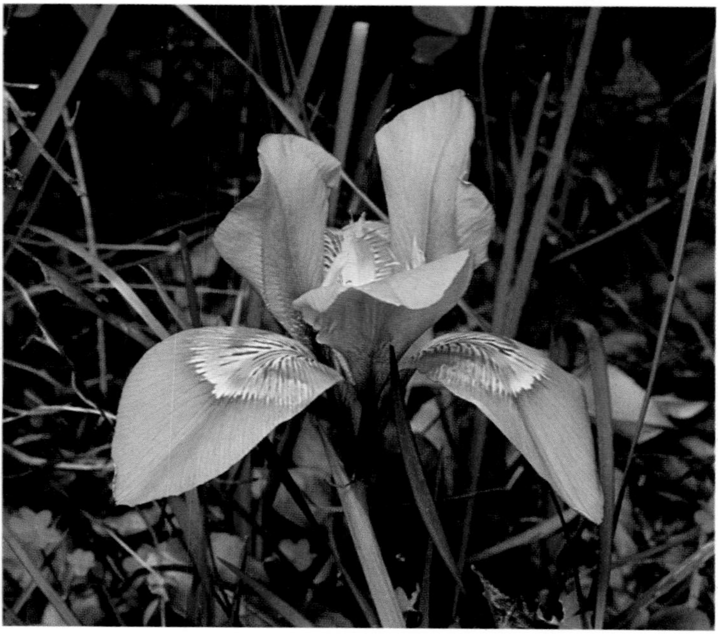

187 IRIS XIPHIUM Carolus Linnaeus
Syn.: *I. hispanica* Hortorum. Common name: Spanish Iris

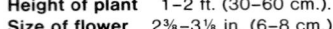

Family Iridaceae.
Description A bulbous perennial with a small oblong-acute, slightly tunicate bulb. Its long leaves are linear-canaliculate and erect or retrocurved. Its one or two flowers are borne on upright peduncles. There are many horticultural varieties, mainly grown for cutting, in white, yellow, purple and azure.
Height of plant 1–2 ft. (30–60 cm.).
Size of flower 2⅜–3⅛ in. (6–8 cm.).
Place of origin Western Mediterranean region.
Flowering time Spring.
Cultivation A sunny position. Temperate climate. Cannot withstand much frost. Well-dug, open, sandy soil, even tending to be calcareous, with plenty of manure worked into the ground before planting. Requires plenty of watering. After flowering and when the leaves have died back, the bulbs should be lifted and left to ripen in a sheltered place.
Propagation By bulblets, but this method is not very common. By bulbs from Holland, ready to flower. Sometimes by seed, although this is a very long process.
Qualities Suitable for terraces, balconies. Hardy. Easy to grow.

188 IXIA MACULATA Carolus Linnaeus
Common name: Corn lily

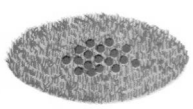

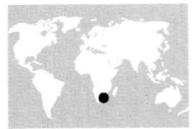

Family Iridaceae.
Description A deciduous perennial that is grown, like freesia, for its very pretty flowers. The little bulbs are depressed, with fibrous tunics. The erect leaves are ensiform and obtuse or rotundate at the end. The flowers are borne on a flexuous peduncle with one or two determinate ramifications of three to seven flowers. The pale-yellow or orange perigonium is divided into six oblong tepals. There are several horticultural varieties.
Height of plant 12–20 in. (30–50 cm.).
Size of flower 1⅛–2 in. (3–5 cm.).
Place of origin South Africa.
Flowering time Spring.
Cultivation Full sun or partial shade in a sheltered position. Temperate climate. Cannot withstand the cold. Prefers well-aerated, rich soil. Can be grown in a pot using a mixture of good, argillaceous-sandy garden soil, woodland mold, peat and a little sieved manure. Regular watering until flowering is over, when the plant can be left to dry off. When the leaves wither, the bulbs can be lifted and stored in a dry, frostproof place until ready for replanting. Pests and diseases: aphids; rust and leaf spot.
Propagation By bulblets removed from the parent bulb during its resting period.
Qualities Half-hardy. Easy to grow.

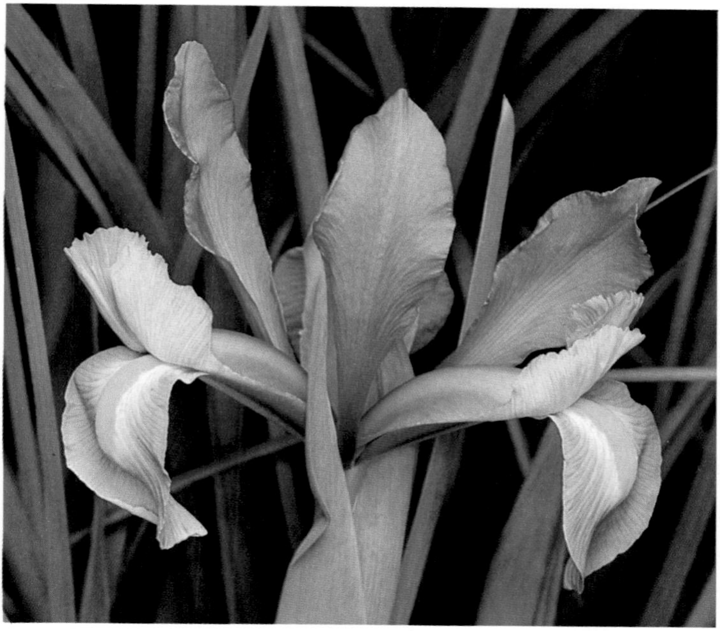

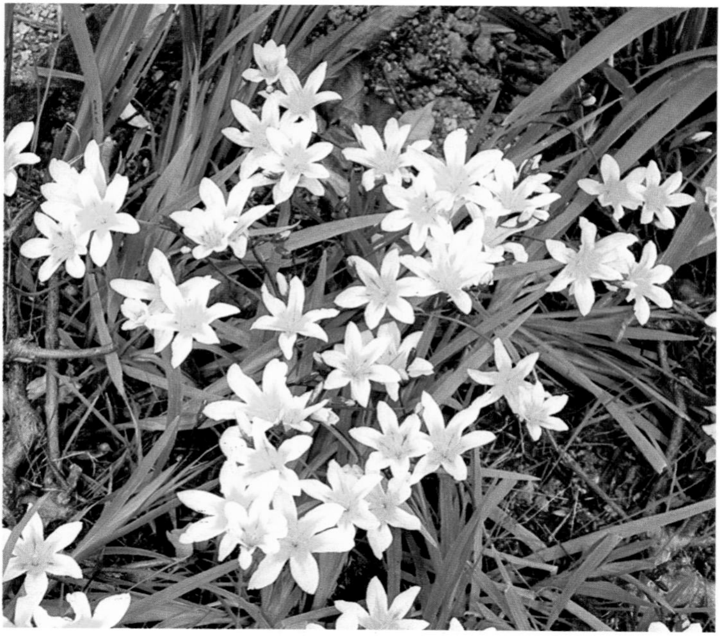

189   JACARANDA MIMOSIFOLIA David Don
Syn.: *J. ovalifolia* Robert Brown

Family   Bignoniaceae.
Description   A large deciduous tree especially appreciated for its wood, which is used in the making of fine furniture. It is also very decorative, with tiny but thickly growing leaves and beautiful clusters of turquoise flowers—in the warm temperate regions where it thrives. Its leaves are opposite, bipinnate-compound, made up of numerous pinnae with ten to fifteen pairs of oblong-rhomboidal leaflets. Its numerous pendulous flowers are borne in alternate clusters.
Height of plant   33–82 ft. (10–25 m.).
Size of flower   1½–2⅜ in. (4–6 cm.).
Place of origin   Northern Argentina.
Flowering time   Spring–summer.
Cultivation   Full sun. Warm-temperate climate. Well-aerated or moderately heavy, deep, fertile, moist soil. Requires organic/mineral feeding and watering for some time after planting, after which it can be left to grow naturally. It tolerates a little pruning from time to time.
Propagation   By spring sowing in pots in a coldframe or cool greenhouse.
Qualities   Hardy only in its own climate. Easy to grow.

---

190   JACOBINIA SUBERECTA Edward André
Syn.: *Dicliptera suberecta* (André) Bremek

Family   Acanthaceae.
Description   A delightful floriferous, suffrutescent subshrub. The rather thick leaves, which are opposite, obovate-acuminate and almost persistent, form dense clumps of green shaded with the argentate sheen of their velutinous surface. Its numerous tubulous flowers are borne in terminal cymes with showy, foliaceous, oblong bracts. The tubulous corolla is brick-red.
Height of plant   20–40 in. (0.50–1 m.).
Size of flower   2–3⅛ in. (5–8 cm.).
Place of origin   Uruguay.
Flowering time   Summer–autumn.
Cultivation   A slightly shaded position. Temperate climate. Frost-tender. Prefers good, well-aerated, rich, sandy, moderately calcareous soil. Requires periodic applications of solid and liquid manure. Makes a good pot plant. Frequent and generous watering. A light trim after flowering gives the plant a tidier appearance. In cool areas, overwinter in a heated greenhouse. Pests and diseases: various insects and fungus diseases.
Propagation   By cuttings of long shoots taken in spring or summer and rooted in a coldframe or cool greenhouse at a temperature of 64–70° F. (18–21° C.).
Qualities   Half-hardy to tender. Easy to grow.

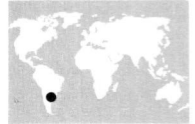

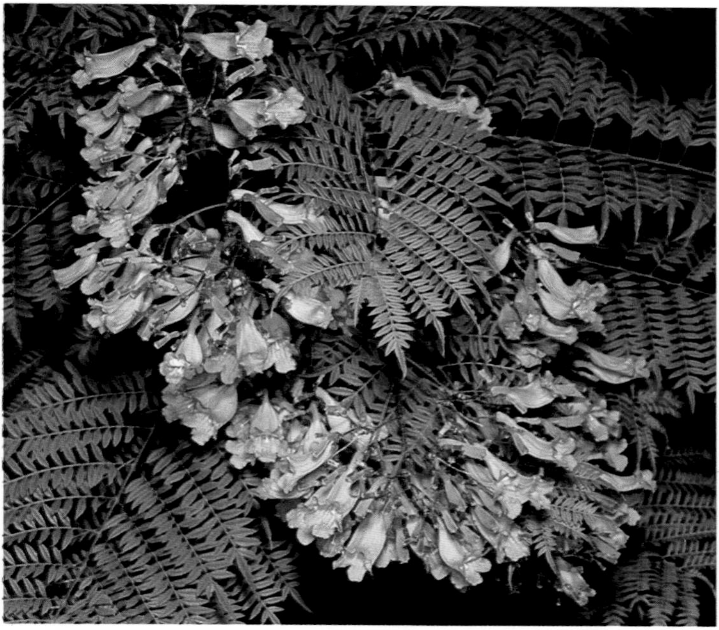

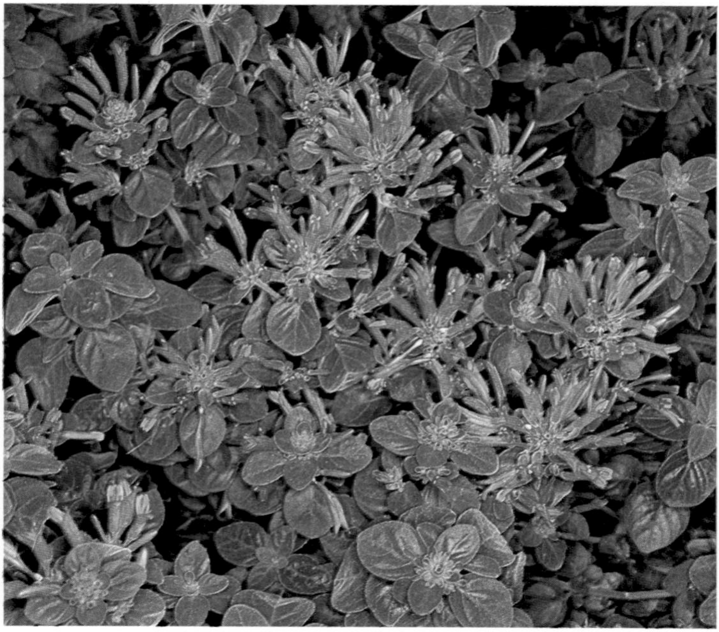

191 JASMINUM AZORICUM Carolus Linnaeus
Syns.: *J. trifoliatum* Konrad Moench, *J. suaveolens* Richard Anthony Salisbury. Common name: Azores jasmine

Family   Oleaceae.
Description   A shrubby-sarmentose evergreen that may, in fact, lose most of its leaves in some climates. It has vigorous stems and slender ramifications. Its opposite leaves are composed of three ovate-acute, consistent leaflets. Its numerous stellate white flowers are borne in axillary cymes and have a sweet, heady perfume. This plant is sometimes confused with the South American *J. fluminense*.
Height of plant   10–16½ ft. (3–5 m.).
Size of flower   ¾ in. (2 cm.).
Place of origin   Azores and Madeira.
Flowering time   Summer; almost throughout the year in temperate regions.
Cultivation   A light position, even in full sun. Temperate climate. Heavy frosts can inflict great damage; it either dies right back to the base or may be killed outright. Suitable for a moist but well-aerated or slightly compact soil that is humus-rich. Regular watering. Periodic applications of organic/mineral fertilizers. Hard pruning encourages the new growth on which flowers are borne. Pests: subject to scale insects.
Propagation   By semi-hardwood and hardwood cuttings taken in the spring–summer. By layering and air layering.
Qualities   Hardy only in its own environment. Easy to grow.

192 JASMINUM NUDIFLORUM John Lindley
Common name: Winter jasmine

Family   Oleaceae.
Description   A shrubby, sarmentose, decumbent perennial with mainly deciduous leaves. Its stems and branches are quadrangular in cross section. Its opposite leaves are trifoliate and ovate-oblong. The numerous flowers are infundibuliform, axillary and unscented, with an open calyx and tubulous, flaring corolla. The flowers open before the leaves appear.
Height of plant   10–16½ ft. (3–5 m.).
Size of flower   ¾–1 in. (2–2.5 cm.).
Place of origin   China.
Flowering time   Late winter–spring.
Cultivation   Full sun to partial shade. Temperate climate but can withstand the cold well. Suitable for almost any type of soil that is rich and moderately compact. An undemanding plant, it requires no particular care. Pruning mainly limited to removal of dead or straggly growth. Generally unaffected by pests or diseases.
Propagation   By cuttings taken in the spring–summer. By layering, which often occurs naturally.
Qualities   Also suitable for terraces. Hardy. Easy to grow.

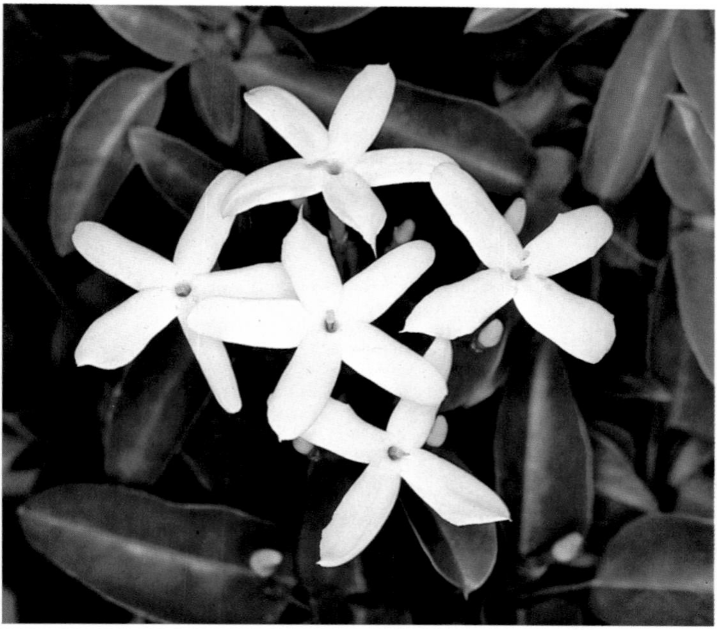

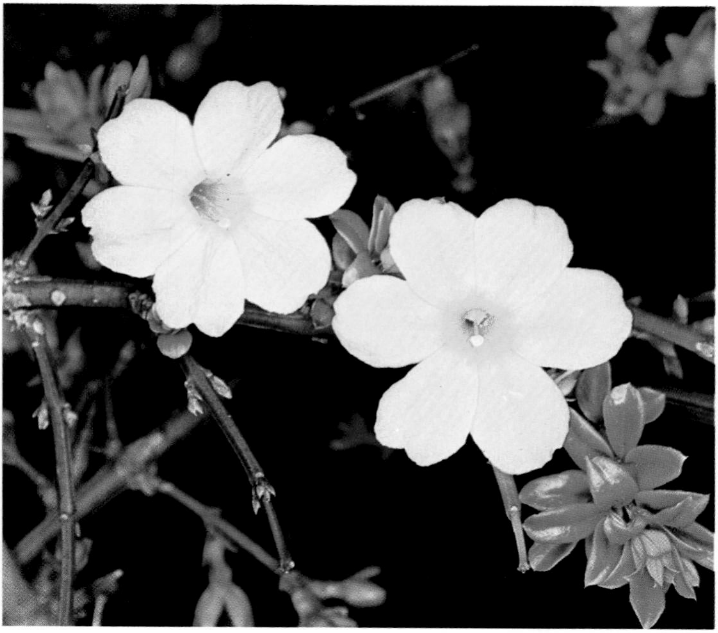

193   JASMINUM POLYANTHUM A. Franchet

Family   Oleaceae.
Description   A shrubby, sarmentose evergreen with numerous slender, twining, climbing stems. Its numerous opposite leaves are imparipinnate with five to seven pointed, ovate-lanceolate leaves. Its abundant floriferousness is striking. The flowers are stellate and delicately scented; rose-pink when in bud but white when fully open.
Height of plant   13–20 ft. (4–6 m.).
Size of flower   ¾–1 in. (2–2.5 cm.).
Place of origin   China.
Flowering time   Summer.
Cultivation   A very light, open position. Temperate climate. Suffers irreparably from frost damage. Suitable for any type of well-aerated, nutritious, humus-rich soil. Regular watering. Occasional applications of organic/mineral fertilizers. Hard-prune in autumn. Generally trouble-free.
Propagation   By semi-hardwood and hardwood cuttings taken in spring or summer and rooted under glass. Or by layering or air layering.
Qualities   Half-hardy. Very easy to grow.

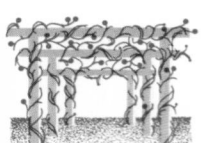

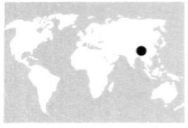

---

194   JASMINUM PRIMULINUM W. Bolting Hemsley
Syn.: *J. mesneyi* Hance. Common name: Primrose jasmine

Family   Oleaceae.
Description   A bushy, semi-pendulous, evergreen shrub with numerous ramifications that are quadrangular at the end. Its opposite leaves are made up of trifoliate dark-green oblong-lanceolate leaflets. Its numerous flowers are borne singly from the foliar axils along the branches; the corolla is yellow and darker in the center.
Height of plant   10–18 ft. (3–4.50 m.).
Size of flower   1⅛–1½ in. (3–4 cm.).
Place of origin   China.
Flowering time   Spring until early summer.
Cultivation   Full sun or as much sun as possible. Temperate climate. Can withstand a few moderate frosts very well. It likes good, deep, moist, humus-rich garden soil. A periodic top dressing of manure and mineral fertilizer ensures continued luxuriant growth and flowers. A certain amount of watering required during very dry spells. Flowered shoots can be cut back and weak or dead wood removed. Usually trouble-free.
Propagation   By cuttings taken in the spring–summer; they root easily. Also by layering.
Qualities   Hardy. Easy to grow.

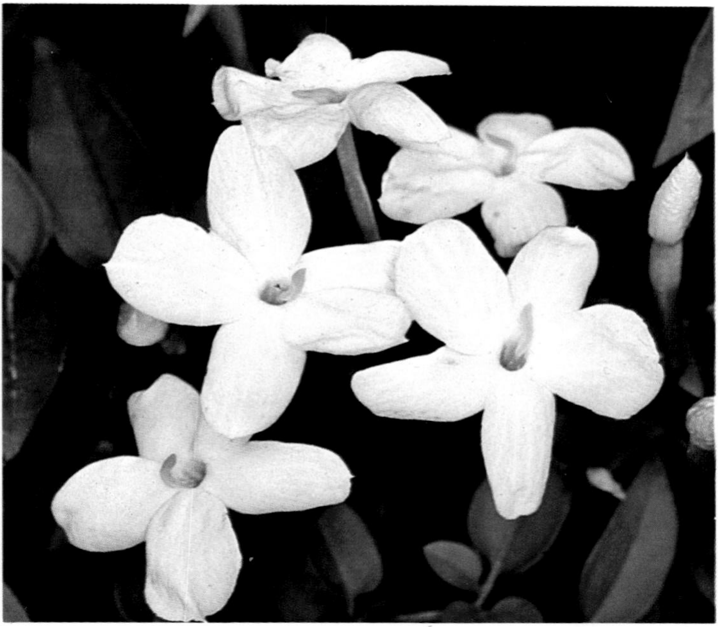
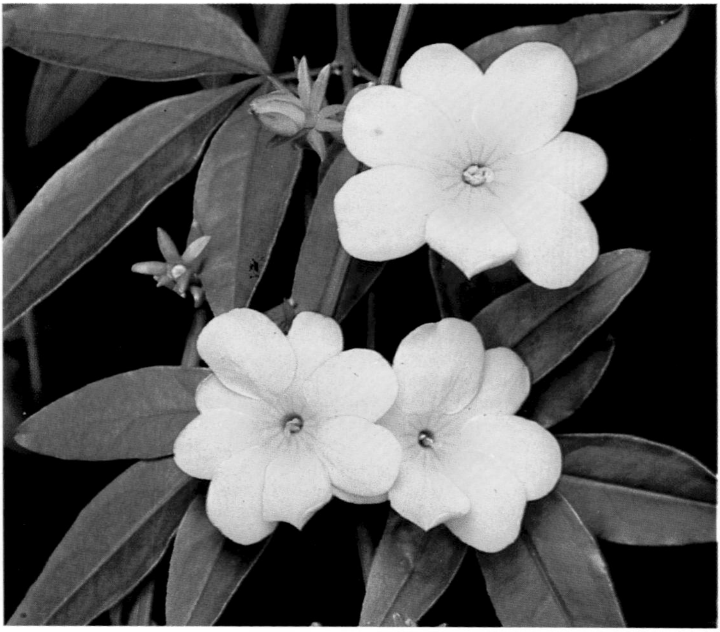

195 KERRIA JAPONICA
Augustin Pyramus De Candolle
Syn.: *Corchorus japonicus* Carl Peter Thunberg

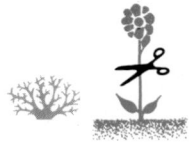

Family Rosaceae.
Description A vigorous, bushy, deciduous shrub with glossy green branches that are recurved or almost sarmentose. Its alternate leaves are ovate-acuminate and doubly serrated. The golden-yellow flowers are not scented but make a fine show, since they are borne singly all along the ends of the previous season's shoots. There are several varieties, the best known being the single-flowered and the cultivar "Pleniflora."
Height of plant 5–10 ft. (1.50–3 m.).
Size of flower 1⅛–1½ in. (3–4 cm.).
Place of origin China and Japan.

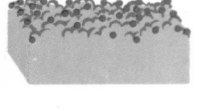

Flowering time Spring
Cultivation A sunny to partially shaded position. Can withstand the frost very well; frost may damage the branch ends but will not kill the plant. Grows in any kind of soil, even if poor. Responds well to a periodic dressing of manure and comprehensive mineral fertilizer in late winter. Does not usually need watering except in very dry spells. Flowered shoots should be cut back to new growths and weak or dead growth removed in the autumn. Usually trouble-free.

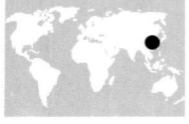

Propagation By hardwood or semi-hardwood cuttings in spring–summer, rooted in a coldframe. By air layering, layering or clump division when shrubs produce adventitious growths.
Qualities Also suitable for growing in containers on terraces. Hardy. Easy to grow.

196 KNIPHOFIA UVARIA (Carolus Linnaeus)
W. Oken
Syns.: *K. aloides* Konrad Moench, *Tritoma uvaria* John Bellenden Ker and Gawl. Common names: Torch lily, red-hot poker

Family Liliaceae.
Description A herbaceous, cespitose perennial. Its long, deep-green leaves are linear-acuminate and caniculate-carinate with a denticulate margin. Its numerous tubulous, pendulous flowers are borne in a large, dense, spicate raceme at the top of a strong cylindrical floral scape; their orange-yellow coloring, tinged with green, makes this a most effective and unusual flower.
Height of plant 24–40 in. (0.60–1 m.).
Size of flower 1⅛ in. (3 cm.).
Place of origin South Africa.

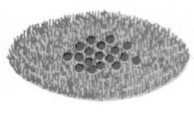

Flowering time Summer.
Cultivation Full sun to partial shade. Temperate climate. Likes a sheltered position, since it cannot withstand heavy frosts. Prefers well-aerated, deep, moist, sandy, even siliceous, soil. Plenty of water in the summer. Faded flower spikes should be cut back to the base. About every four or five years accumulated growth can be thinned out if the plant is becoming ungainly. The leaves can be tied together to protect the crown during the winter, or a good mulch provided.

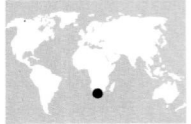

Propagation By clump division in spring.
Qualities Hardy only in its own environment. Easy to grow.

197 KOLKWITZIA AMABILIS Paul Graebner
Common name: Beauty bush

Family Caprifoliaceae.
Description A large deciduous shrub with a compact habit. Its slightly contorted, pink-tinged branches spring from the base. Its opposite leaves are ovate-acute, villose and rugose with the venation in relief. Numerous pinkish-white flowers are borne in compound corymbs at the ends of short lateral twigs. There is also a cultivar "Rosea" with darker pink flowers.
Height of plant 6½–10 ft. (2–3 m.).
Size of flower ½ in. (1.5 cm.).
Place of origin Southwestern China.
Flowering time Late spring–summer.

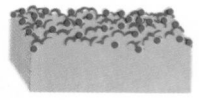

Cultivation Full sun to partial shade. Cool-temperate climate. Grows in any type of soil but prefers rather compact, moist ground with a humus content. Prune in the autumn to remove flowered branches and old wood. Does not need any particular attention. Watering limited to any very dry spells in summer.
Propagation By semi-hardwood cuttings taken in spring–summer and rooted in a coldframe. Sometimes by seed in spring in a greenhouse.
Qualities Hardy. Easy to grow.

---

198 LABURNUM ALPINUM
Heinrich Rudolph August Grisebach
Syn.: *Cystisus alpinus* Phillip Miller. Common names: Golden-chain tree, Scotch laburnum

Family Papilionaceae.
Description A small deciduous tree with trilobate leaves consisting of dark-green ovate-elliptical leaflets on long petioles. It has an elegant habit and its floriferousness is striking. The inflorescences are in pendulous racemes that are longer and more lax than in other species, reaching lengths of 10–16 in. (25–40 cm.). The golden-yellow corollas are papilionaceous. The plant, the seeds in particular, are poisonous.
Height of plant 16–20 ft. (5–6 m.).
Size of flower ¾–1 in. (2–2.5 cm.).
Place of origin Southern Europe.
Flowering time Spring–summer.

Cultivation A north-facing position, preferably in partial shade. Cool-temperate climate. Frost-resistant. Suited to any type of soil, especially that which is siliceous-argillaceous and humus-rich. No pruning or feeding is necessary except at planting time. Watering limited to exceptionally dry spells. Can be grown as a bush or small tree.
Propagation By seed in the fall in a nursery bed.
Qualities Hardy. Easy to grow.

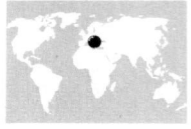

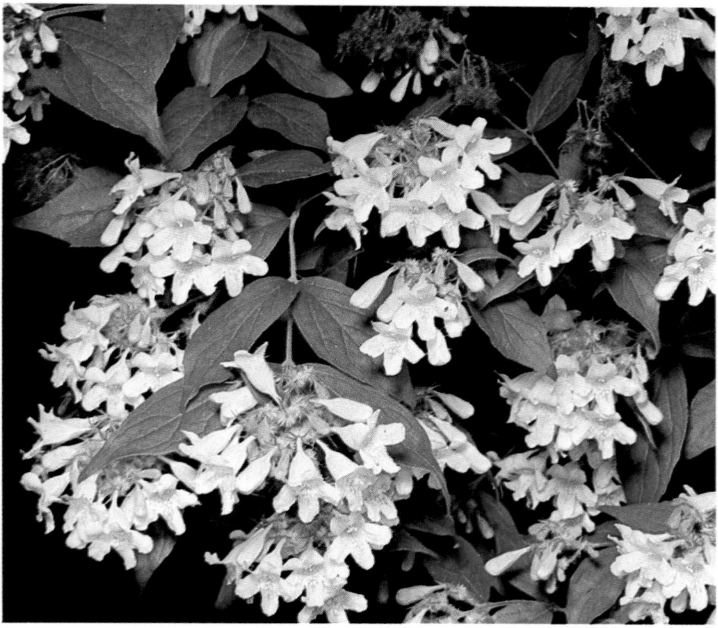

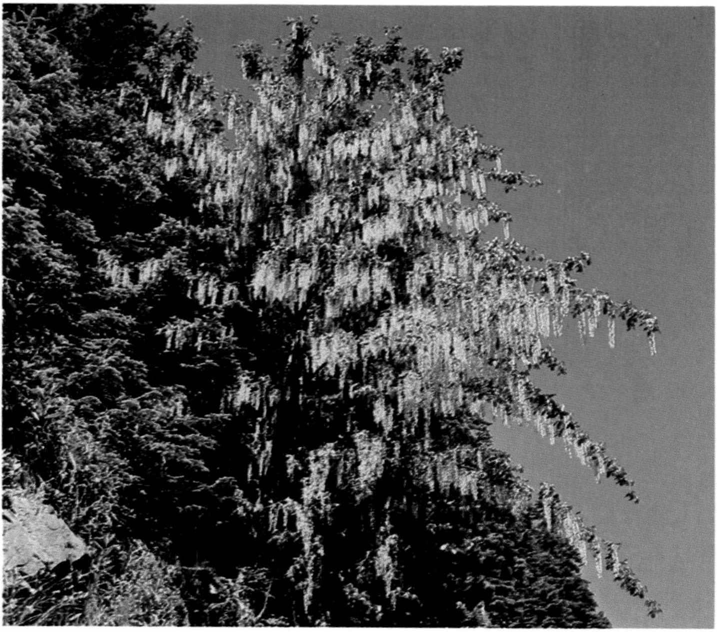

199 LAGERSTROEMIA INDICA Carolus Linnaeus

Syns.: *L. chinensis* Jean Baptiste Lamarck, *L. elegans* Nathanael Wallich. Common name: Crape myrtle

Family Lythraceae.
Description A well-known deciduous shrub or tree that is widely grown because of its long flowering period. It has a sturdy, treelike stem with open, twisted ramifications and peeling bark. It is very slow-growing. The leaves are sub-opposite, ovate-rotundate and almost coriaceous. Its numerous flowers are borne in very showy terminal pyramidal panicles; each purplish-red corolla has five petals. There are several varieties: "Alba," "Elegans," "Rubra" and "Violacea" in white, pink and violet.
Height of plant 13–26 ft. (4–8 m.).
Size of flower 1⅛–1⅜ in. (3–3.5 cm.).
Place of origin China, Japan, Indochina, northern Australia.
Flowering time Summer.

Cultivation Full sun or a very bright position. Temperate climate but can withstand a few degrees below freezing point. Suited to any type of soil but prefers it argillaceous-sandy, fertile and moist. Periodic applications of organic/mineral fertilizers. Regular watering. Requires hard pruning, usually to two or three buds, in the autumn–winter, removing any weak or superfluous branches and adventitious growth.
Propagation By hardwood cuttings taken in the autumn and rooted in a nursery bed.
Qualities Hardy. Easy to grow.

200 LAMPRANTHUS EMARGINATUS (Carolus Linnaeus) N. E. Brown

Syns.: *L. violaceus* (Augustin Pyramus DeCandolle) Schwantes, *Mesembryanthemum violaceum* De Candolle. Common name: Mesembryanthemum

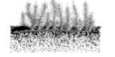

Family Aizoaceae.
Description A succulent, herbaceous-suffruticose plant with compressed, erect, brownish stems on whose apices are borne the numerous solitary flowers. These have a corolla with a yellowish center and a great many pinkish-violet petals. The thick, acuminate leaves are either angular or compressed.
Height of plant 10–12 in. (25–30 cm.).
Size of flower 1–1⅜ in. (2.5–3.5 cm.).
Place of origin Cape of Good Hope.
Flowering time Spring.

Cultivation Full sun in dry ground. Warm-temperate climate. Cannot withstand the cold. Especially suitable for coastal areas in dry, stony ground, since it is well able to live in arid conditions; water should be applied only in exceptionally dry conditions. If grown in beds, the soil can be opened up with humus or peat and a little sand; a little well-rotted organic material can be applied and moderate amounts of water given. Remove dead growth in the autumn. Usually trouble-free.
Propagation By cuttings taken in spring. Sometimes, too, by seed in pans in a coldframe, but the process is a demanding one.
Qualities Hardy in a temperate climate. Easy to grow.

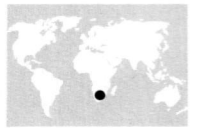

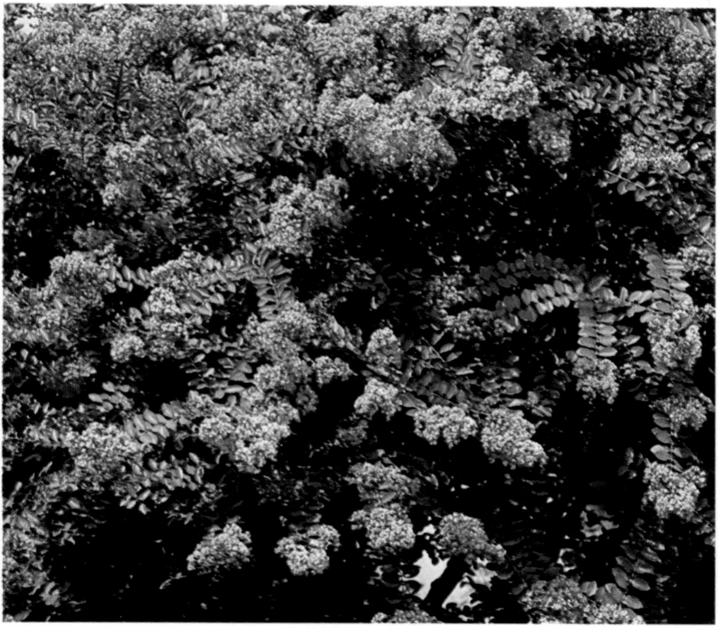

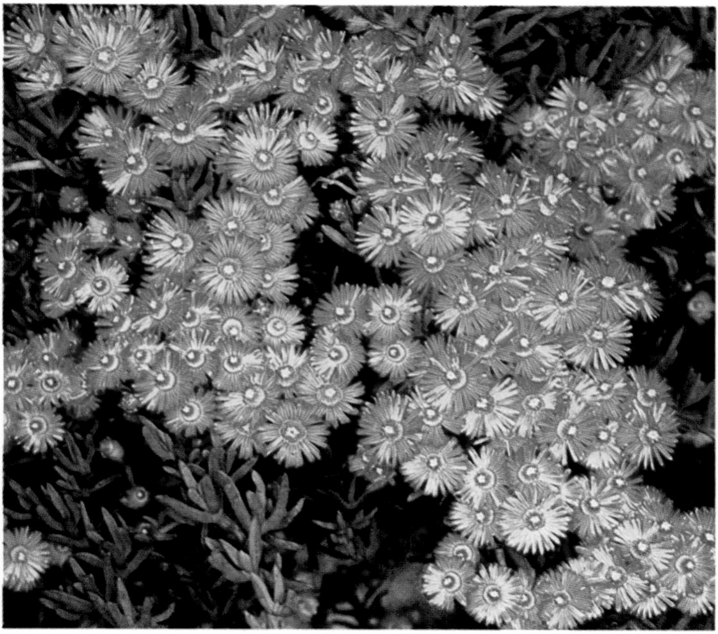

201 LAMPRANTHUS ROSEUS
(Karl Ludwig Willdenow) Schwantes
Syns.: *L. multiradiatus* (Nicolaus Joseph Jacquin)
N. E. Brown, *Mesembryanthemum roseum* Will-
denow. Common name: Mesembryanthemum

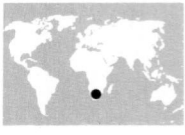

Family Aizoaceae.
Description A herbaceous-suffruticose perennial, its stems
are prostrate with numerous creeping ramifications that carpet
the ground. Its glaucous leaves are opposite, persistent, succulent, linear and acuminate, sometimes trigonal. The flowers
are terminal, solitary but close together, with a large, bright-
yellow button consisting of the stamens and a great many deep
pink petals. The whole effect is that of cushions of showy flowers.
Height of plant 8–12 in. (20–30 cm.).
Size of flower ¾–1⅛ in. (1.8–3 cm.).
Place of origin South Africa.
Flowering time Late spring–summer.
Cultivation Full sun. Warm-temperate climate. Cannot withstand the cold. A sheltered position; dry, sandy ground, even
among rocks and stony screes near the sea. No particular care
required. Water should be given only during exceptionally dry
spells. Dead growth can be removed in the winter.
Propagation By cuttings taken in the spring, rooted in a
sandy compost, under glass, and subsequently transplanted
into pots before planting out. Sometimes grown from seed in
pans in a greenhouse, but this is a rather laborious method.
Qualities Hardy in its own environment. Easy to grow.

202 LANTANA CAMARA Carolus Linnaeus
Syn.: *L. hybrida* Hortorum

Family Verbenaceae.
Description A deciduous shrub especially popular in temperate zones for its long flowering period and multicolored capitula. In tropical areas it often becomes invasive. It has a shrubby
habit. Its opposite leaves are ovate-acute, hispid and rugose;
they emit a rather acrid smell. The numerous small flowers are
borne in umbelliferous cymes of various tones in the same
color group. Its fruit is a dark metallic blue, rather like a blackberry. There is a wide range of horticultural varieties differing
in habit and color that are suitable for flower beds and pots.
Height of plant 40–80 in. (1–2 m.).
Size of flower ⅛–⅜ in. (0.5–1 cm.).
Place of origin Tropical America.
Flowering time Summer–autumn.
Cultivation Full sun to partial shade. Warm-temperate climate. Frost-tender. The plants can be lifted from the garden in
autumn and transferred to a frost-free greenhouse, frame or
pots. Prefers moderately compact or well-aerated soil that is
fertile and very well organically fed. Requires plentiful watering
during the summer but not in winter. Shorten main shoots and
remove weak or dead growth. Generally trouble-free.
Propagation By hardwood or semi-hardwood cuttings taken
in spring or summer and rooted under glass.
Qualities Tender to half-hardy. Suitable for terraces, balconies. Easy to grow.

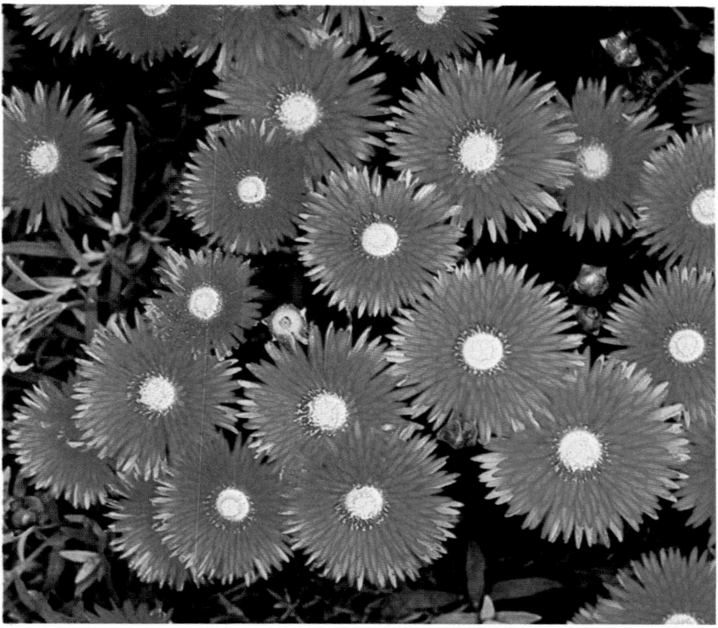

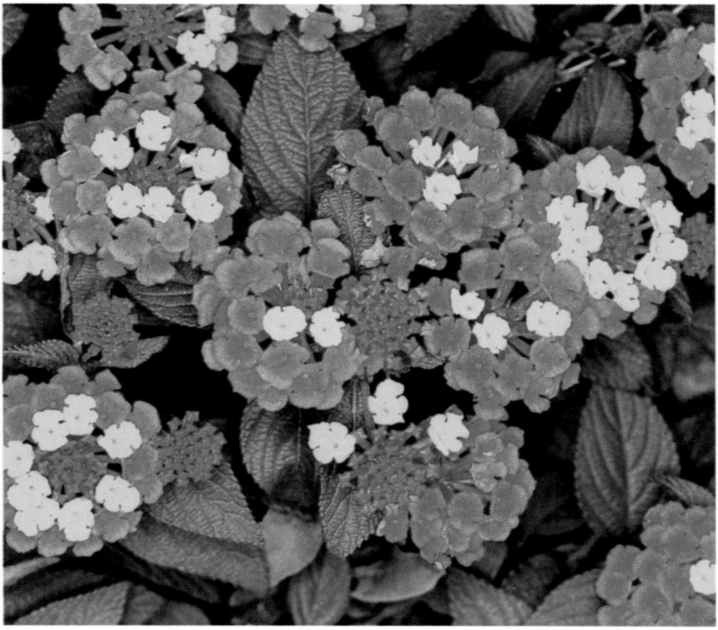

203 **LANTANA MONTEVIDENSIS** (Kurt Sprengel) Briquet
Syn.: *L. sellowiana* Heinrich Friedrich Link and Friedrich Otto

Family Verbenaceae.
Description An evergreen flowering shrub. In warm to hot parts of the world, where the plant is highly regarded for its hardiness and delightful floriferousness, it grows happily outdoors. It has a bushy habit with long, slender tetragonous ramifications. Its opposite leaves are distant, ovate-acute, crenulate-dentate and pubescent. Its numerous flowers emerge from the foliar axils in umbelliferous clusters and continue blooming for a long time.

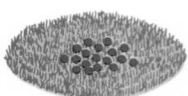

Height of plant 3-5 ft. (1-1.50 m.).
Size of flower ⅛-⅜ in. (0.5-0.8 cm.).
Place of origin Uruguay.
Flowering time Summer–autumn.

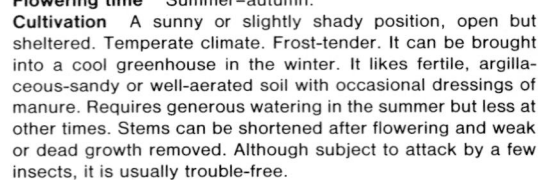

Cultivation A sunny or slightly shady position, open but sheltered. Temperate climate. Frost-tender. It can be brought into a cool greenhouse in the winter. It likes fertile, argillaceous-sandy or well-aerated soil with occasional dressings of manure. Requires generous watering in the summer but less at other times. Stems can be shortened after flowering and weak or dead growth removed. Although subject to attack by a few insects, it is usually trouble-free.
Propagation By cuttings taken in the spring or summer and rooted under glass.
Qualities Hardy. Suitable for terraces, patios. Easy to grow.

204 **LATHYRUS ODORATUS** Carolus Linnaeus
Common name: Sweet pea

Family Papilionaceae.
Description At one time the sweet pea was to be found in most gardens but it is now a little out of fashion. However, it is still well worth growing because of its undoubted beauty. It is a herbaceous climbing annual with very slender ramifications, and most varieties need to be supported with bushy sticks, canes or netting. Its alternate leaves are pinnate-compound, consisting of a pair of leaflets, the petiole ending in a ramose tendril. Some cultivars produce a second crop of flowers.

Height of plant 5-6½ ft. (1.50-2 m.).
Size of flower ¾-1½ in. (2-4 cm.).
Place of origin Southern Europe.
Flowering time Spring.

Cultivation Full sun to partial shade. Temperate climate. It likes fertile, well-aerated, moist garden soil that has been enriched with organic and phosphatic-potassic minerals. Requires plentiful watering during the flowering period. If flowers are not picked, constant dead-heading encourages continued flowering. Pests and diseases: slugs on young plants, aphids, thrips and birds; fungus diseases.

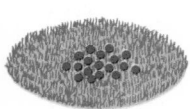

Propagation By spring sowing directly in the flowering site as soon as the soil is workable.
Qualities Hardy annual. Also suitable for terraces, decks. Easy to grow.

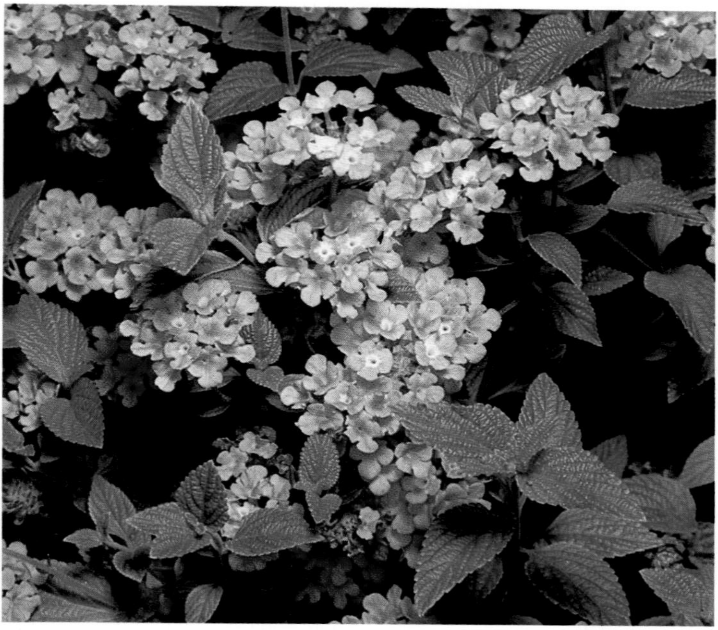

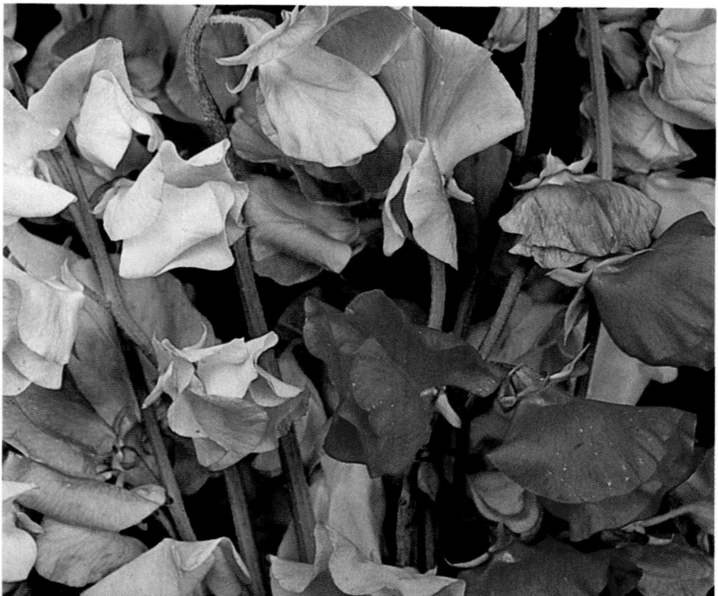

205 **LAVANDULA ANGUSTIFOLIA** Phillip Miller
Syns.: *L. officinalis* D. Chaix, *L. spica*. Common name: English lavender

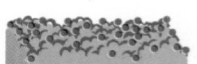

Family Labiatae.

Description A suffruticose semi-evergreen shrub with numerous erect, pubescent, tetragonous ramifications. Its opposite, sessile gray leaves are linear-acute. The whole plant, including the flowers, is very fragrant. Its tiny flowers are carried in groups of six to ten in inflorescences borne on spikes. These are distilled to extract their essential oils for soaps and perfumes.

Height of plant 19–32 in. (50–80 cm.).

Size of flower' 2–4 in. (5–10 cm.) each spike.

Place of origin Mediterranean regions.

Flowering time Summer.

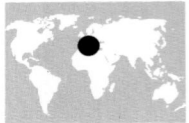

Cultivation Full sun. Temperate climate. Fairly good resistance to frost. Will grow in almost any type of soil, even if poor. Tolerates lime and the salty atmosphere of coastal areas. Does not usually need watering. Periodic dressings of organic/mineral fertilizers. After flowering, it is advisable to cut off all the dead stalks. This plant is not long-lived.

Propagation By spring or summer cuttings, put to root in a sheltered spot outdoors in a nursery bed. Also by layering.

Qualities Hardy. Suitable for terraces, balconies. Easy to grow.

206 **LAVANDULA DENTATA** Carolus Linnaeus
Syn.: *L. delphinensis* Hortorum. Common name: French lavender

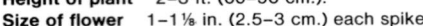

Family Labiatae.

Description A bushy-shrubby or suffruticose plant, it is evergreen with numerous erect ramifications. Its opposite, silvery-gray leaves are tomentose with a dentate-rotundate margin. Its numerous flowers are grouped in terminal spikes, smaller than those of English lavender; they are a fairly deep shade of violet but the depth of color depends on the nature of the ground and position. The whole plant exudes a strong aromatic fragrance.

Height of plant 2–3 ft. (60–90 cm.).

Size of flower 1–1⅛ in. (2.5–3 cm.) each spike.

Place of origin Western Mediterranean region.

Flowering time Spring, summer, autumn.

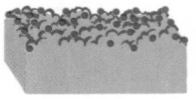

Cultivation Full sun. Temperate climate. May be damaged by hard frosts. Stony, even poor, soil, preferably siliceous and damp but not wet. Generally requires neither watering nor feeding. When flowering has finished—or in the autumn—it is advisable to cut the heads off to avoid exhausting the plant by allowing it to make seed.

Propagation By cuttings taken in spring or late summer and put to root in a sheltered nursery bed.

Qualities Hardy. Easy to grow.

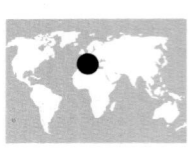

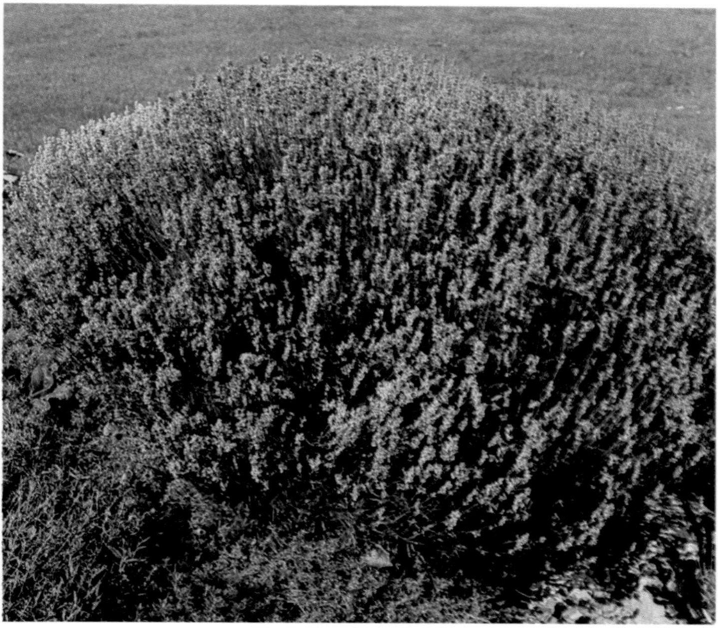

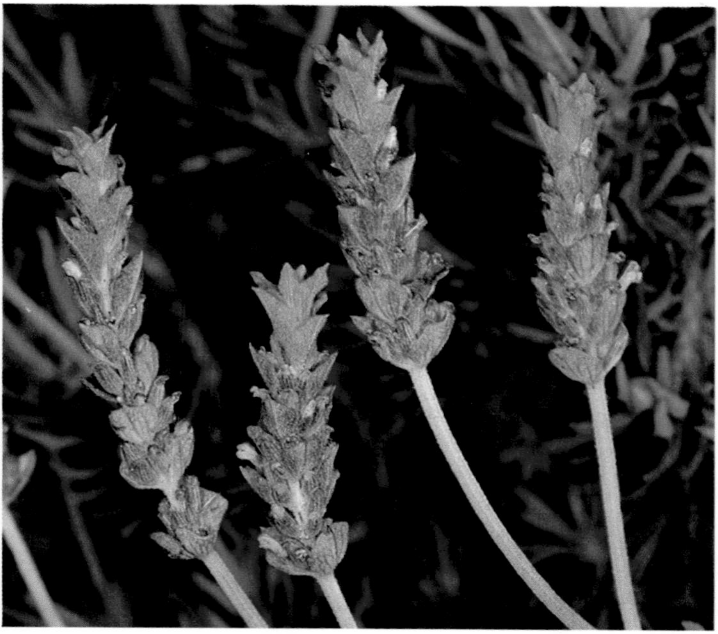

207 LAVATERA TRIMESTRIS Carolus Linnaeus
Syn.: *L. rosea* Friedrich Casmir Medikus. Common name: Mallow

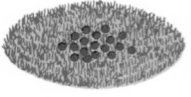

Family Malvaceae.
Description A very vigorous herbaceous annual with an upright, suffrutescent stem. Its alternate leaves are palmate, rotundate-reniform and crenulate-dentate, the inferior ones being quinquelobate and the superior trilobate. The solitary, flared, infundibuliform flowers are most decorative. There are many horticultural varieties among which are the white-flowered cultivar "Alba" and the deep rose-pink "Splendens."
Height of plant 31–40 in. (0.80–1 m.).
Size of flower 3–4 in. (8–10 cm.).
Place of origin Mediterranean regions.
Flowering time Summer–early autumn.
Cultivation Full or almost full sun. Temperate climate. Can adapt to any type of good garden soil that is moist and rich but not too heavy. Regular watering. This plant can be allowed to naturalize. Diseases: sometimes prone to rust and leaf spot.
Propagation By seed sown in spring in the garden where plants are to grow.
Qualities Hardy. Easy to grow.

208 LEUCOJUM AESTIVUM Carolus Linnaeus
Common name: Summer snowflake

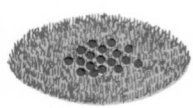

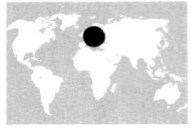

Family Amaryllidaceae.
Description A small, bulbous plant with charming little flowers similar to snowdrops (*Galanthus*). It has proliferous piriform bulbs and four to six fairly thick, linear-obtuse, erect leaves. Its compressed floral scape usually bears two campanulate flowers on long peduncles, with a distinctive green marking at the tip of each tepal.
Height of plant 12–20 in. (30–50 cm.).
Size of flower ¾ in. (2 cm.).
Place of origin Europe, in damp places.
Flowering time Spring–early summer.
Cultivation Shade. Temperate climate. Can withstand the cold well. Any type of soil, preferably moisture-retentive with a good argillaceous-humus content. Watering is not always necessary. Suitable for naturalizing. Does not require any particular attention. Trouble-free.
Propagation By bulblets removed from the parent in the fall. By spring sowing, but it takes about three years for plants to flower.
Qualities Hardy. Easy to grow.

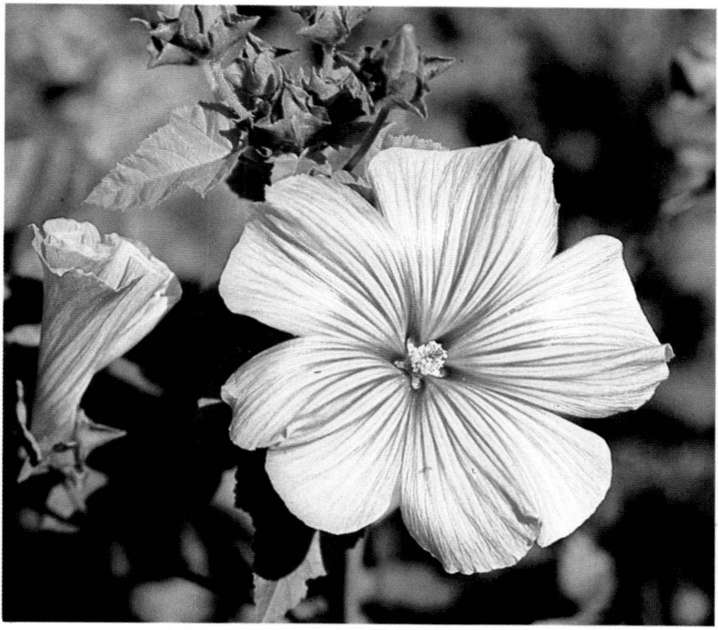

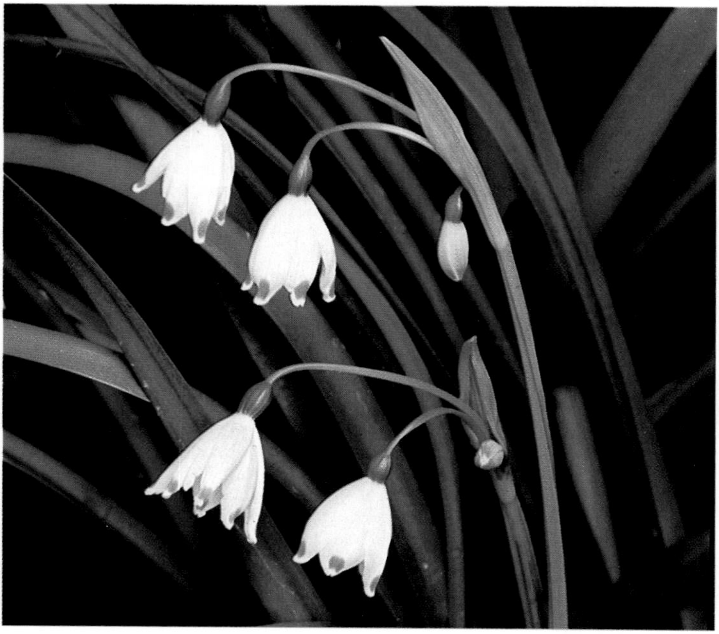

209 LILIUM BULBIFERUM Carolus Linnaeus
Common name: Bulbil lily

Family Liliaceae.
Description A bulbous plant with a compressed, scaly, piriform bulb. At the foliar axils of its rigid, upright stems are produced small, black bulbils. Its cauline leaves are alternate and linear or lanceolate. There are usually one to five flowers to a stem but there may be as many as seven or eight; they are upright and of a tangerine-orange color with darker markings against a blaze of yellow on each petal.
Height of plant 31–40 in. (0.80–1 m.).
Size of flower 2¾–4 in. (7–10 cm.).
Place of origin Central Europe.
Flowering time Summer.
Cultivation A sunny position, but the bulb and roots in the shade. Temperate climate. Light, rich soil that is moist, well prepared prior to planting, with plenty of well-rotted organic material. Regular watering. After flowering, stems should be cut down to ground level. Pests: snails, slugs, the larvae of the lily beetle and cockchafer, aphids, millipedes and other insects that are drawn to its appetizing flowers and leaves.
Propagation By bulbils in late summer.
Qualities Hardy. Easy to grow.

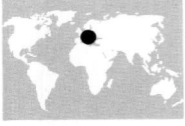

210 LILIUM CANDIDUM Carolus Linnaeus
Common name: Madonna lily

Family Liliaceae.
Description A plant with a large, scaly, compressed-piriform bulb. Its glabrous leaves are sessile, cauline, oblong-lanceolate and ondulate. Its open-campanulate flowers are carried on erect, rigid stems, grouped in varying numbers in thyrsiform racemes. They are white with showy yellow anthers.
Height of plant 2–4 ft. (0.60–1.20 m.).
Size of flower 3⅛–4¾ in. (8–12 cm.).
Place of origin Balkan peninsula, Asia Minor.
Flowering time Summer.
Cultivation A light position but not in too much direct sunlight. Temperate climate. Likes a fairly heavy, well-drained, lime-rich soil. Moderate watering. After flowering, stems should be cut down to ground level. Pests and diseases: slugs, snails, caterpillars, the larvae of the lily beetle and cockchafer, aphids, millipedes and other insects can ruin its leaves and flower; botrytis.
Propagation By the numerous offset bulblets that are found all around the main bulb.
Qualities Hardy. Easy to grow.

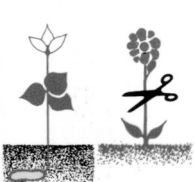

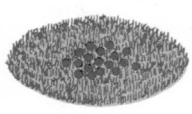

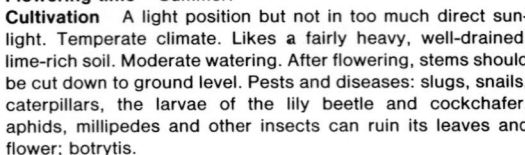

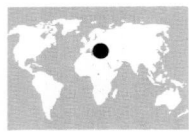

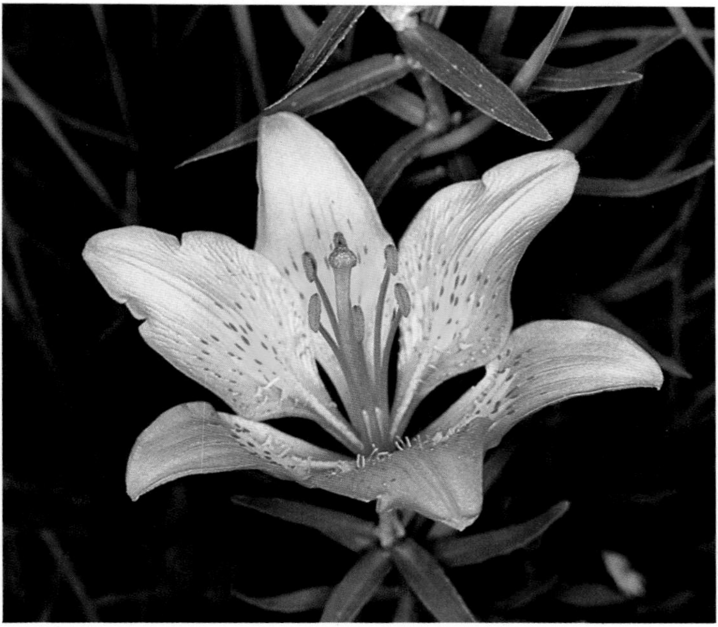

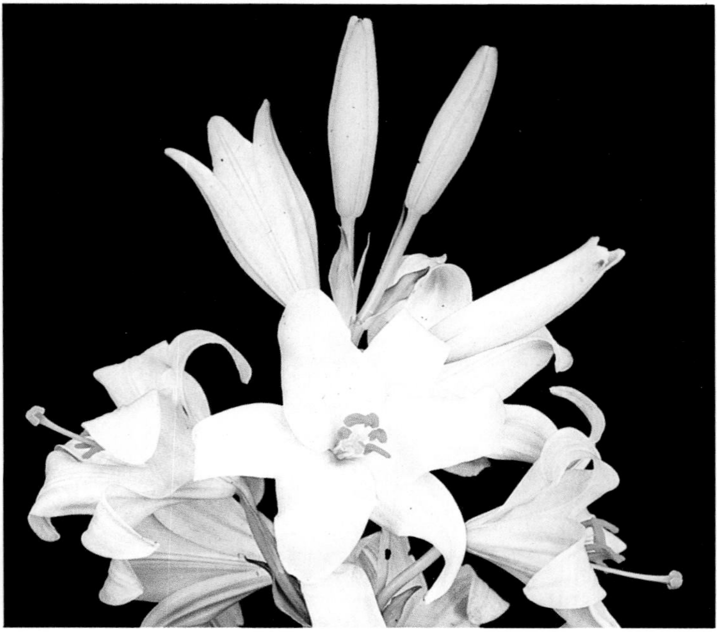

211 LILIUM MARTAGON Carolus Linnaeus
Common names: Martagon lily, Turk's-cap lily

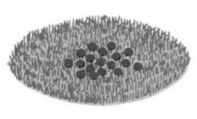

Family Liliaceae.
Description A plant with a compressed piriform bulb. Its cauline leaves are ovate-lanceolate or lanceolate-spathulate, the lower three being verticillate and the upper ones alternate. The greenish, rigid, floriferous stems carry numerous open campanulate flowers, each with six waxlike, pendulous, retro-curved tepals. The flowers, which have a rather unpleasant smell, are in shades of orange-pink to purple-red with dark markings.
Height of plant 40–60 in. (1–1.50 m.).
Size of flower 4–4¾ in. (10–12 cm.).
Place of origin Europe, Siberia, Turkestan, Mongolia.
Flowering time Summer.

Cultivation Full sun or slight shade. Cool-temperate climate. Can withstand the cold up to an altitude of 6,000–6,500 feet above sea level. It likes humus-rich, moist, permeable, even calcareous, soil. Frequent watering. Suitable for naturalizing. Pests and diseases: gnawing insects; stunted growth (rickets) and chlorosis in unsuitable ground.
Propagation By bulblets in late summer; it will be between two and three years before flowers are produced.
Qualities Very hardy. Easy to grow.

212 LILIUM REGALE Ernest H. Wilson
Common name: Regal lily

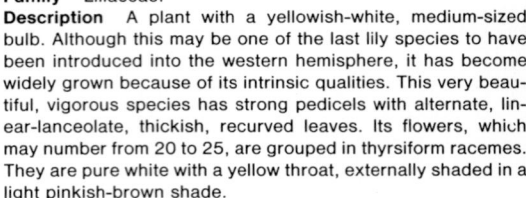

Family Liliaceae.
Description A plant with a yellowish-white, medium-sized bulb. Although this may be one of the last lily species to have been introduced into the western hemisphere, it has become widely grown because of its intrinsic qualities. This very beautiful, vigorous species has strong pedicels with alternate, linear-lanceolate, thickish, recurved leaves. Its flowers, which may number from 20 to 25, are grouped in thyrsiform racemes. They are pure white with a yellow throat, externally shaded in a light pinkish-brown shade.
Height of plant 5–6½ ft. (1.50–2 m.).
Size of flower 4⅜–5⅛ in. (11–13 cm.).
Place of origin Western China.
Flowering time Early summer.

Cultivation A very light position. Temperate climate. Frost-tender. If in an exposed position, the bulbs should be protected from frost with a good mulch or, better still, lifted. It likes a light, moist, well-drained, rich soil with a low lime content, enriched with peat or woodland mold. Regular watering. Manure should be dug into the site well before planting. The flowered stems can be cut down to ground level. Pests: gnawing insects.
Propagation By bulblets in autumn. By autumn or spring seed sowing in a coldframe—but it will be at least two years before the plants are ready to flower.
Qualities Half-hardy. Easy to grow.

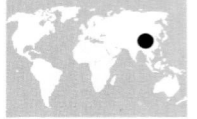

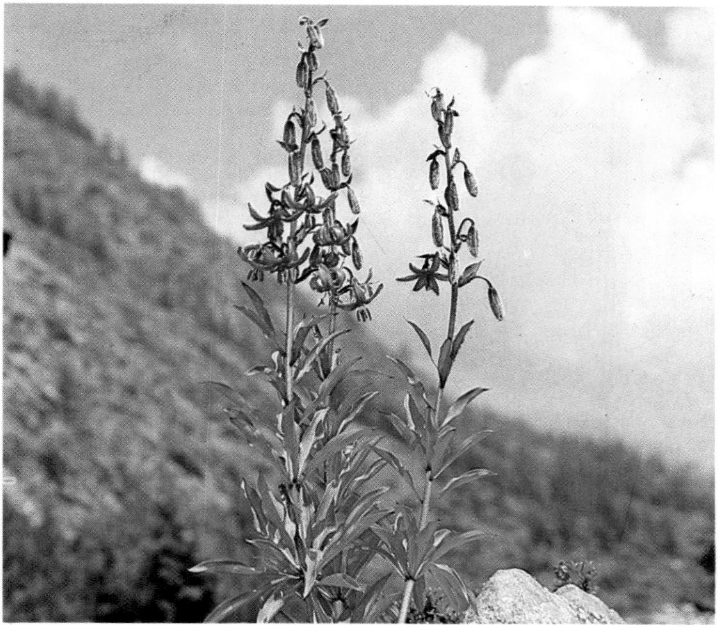

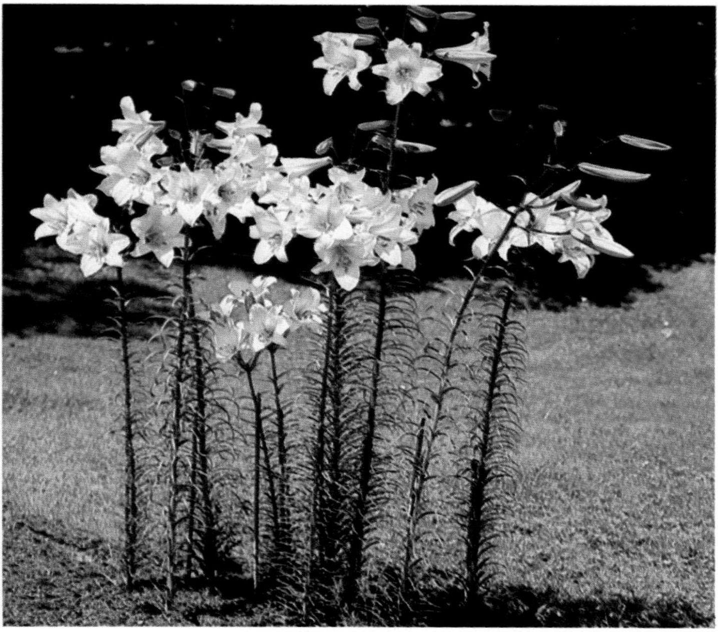

213 LILIUM SPECIOSUM C. P. Thunberg

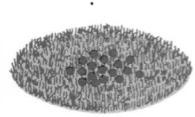

Family Liliaceae.
Description A bulbous plant with a large bulb and an erect, cylindrical, brown stem. Its numerous dark-green leaves are alternate and linear-lanceolate. The white to pink -red flowers are numerous, sometimes exceeding ten to a stem, borne in thyrsiform terminal racemes; each one consists of six strongly recurved tepals and six prominently protruding stamens. The flowers have a delicate vanilla-like fragrance. There are many varieties and cultivars.
Height of plant 40–71 in. (1–1.80 m.).
Size of flower 4–6 in. (10–15 cm.).
Place of origin Japan.
Flowering time Summer.

Cultivation A sunny or partially shaded position. Temperate climate. The bulb can withstand frost fairly well, especially if well mulched. It likes moist, light soil that is rich in organic material and humus but is not argillaceous or sandy. Water can be given freely until the flowering period is ended, then withdrawn during the resting period. After flowering, stems should be cut down. Pests: gnawing insects.
Propagation Usually by bulbils, removed from the parent bulb during the resting period; they take about three years to come into flower. Also by seed, but this method is tedious.
Qualities Fairly hardy. Very easy to grow.

---

214 LOBELIA ERINUS Carolus Linnaeus
Common name: Lobelia

Family Campanulaceae.
Description A herbaceous annual with very slender creeping or trailing stems branching up from the base. Its alternate leaves are in various shapes, the lower ones being obovate or elliptical and crenulate-dentate while the upper ones are almost linear. Its small flowers are produced in great numbers alternately on the stems, looking rather like light-blue or dark-blue butterflies. There are several horticultural varieties in other colors including light azure and purple. The plants die off about two months after flowering.
Height of plant 2–10 in. (5–25 cm.).
Size of flower $^3/_{16}$ in. (0.50 cm.).
Place of origin South Africa.
Flowering time Summer.

Cultivation A light or slightly shady position. Temperate climate. Suitable for any type of fertile, humus-rich, well-aerated garden soil that has been amended with some peat and sand. Frequent watering, preferably light spraying. Pests and diseases: insects sometimes cause trouble but the main problems are damping-off, stem rot and root rot, if conditions are too damp.
Propagation By seed sown in spring under glass.
Qualities Half-hardy annual. Easy to grow.

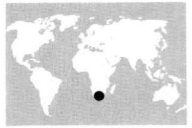

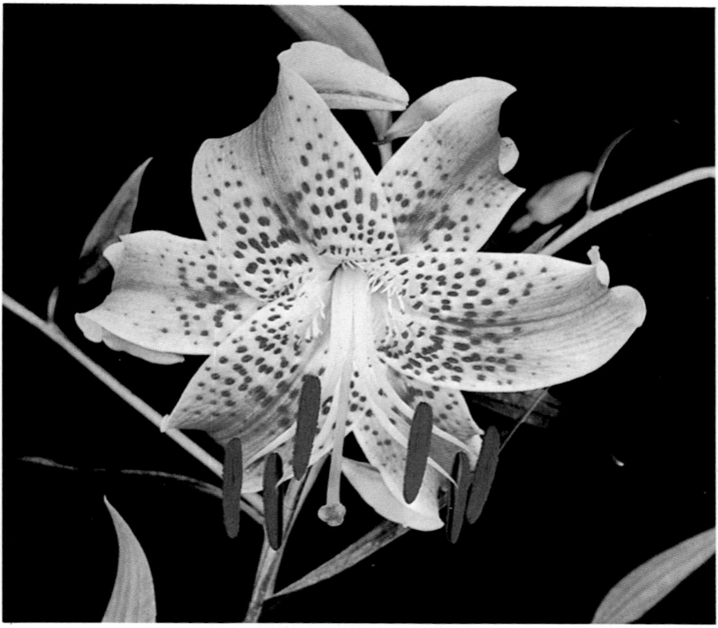

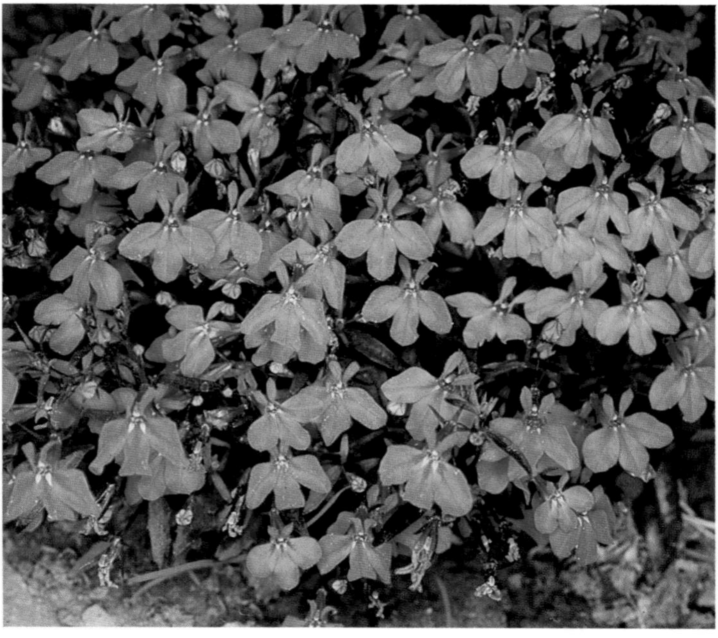

215 **LOBULARIA MARITIMA** (Carolus Linnaeus) Augustin Nicaise Desvaux cv. "Violet Queen"
Syns.: *Alyssum maritimum* (Linnaeus) Jean Baptiste Lamarck, *A. odoratum* Hortorum. Common name: Sweet alyssum

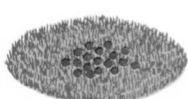

Family   Ranunculaceae.
Description   A perennial herbaceous plant with a semi-creeping habit, but it is grown as an annual. Its numerous small alternate leaves are oblong-lanceolate and ¾–1½ in. (2–4 cm.) long. Its flowers are of the Cruciferae type, with petals in the form of a cross, borne in umbelliferous clusters to form a cushion of white or bluish-violet.
Height of plant   4–8 in. (10–20 cm.).
Size of flower $^3/_{16}$–¼ in. (3–5 mm.).
Place of origin   A cultivated hybrid derived from plants native to the Mediterranean regions.
Flowering time   Spring–early summer.
Cultivation   Full sun or partial shade. Temperate climate. Cannot withstand heavy frosts. Thrives in dry, lime-rich soil, even if not very fertile; it likes crevices in old walls and between paving stones and cobblestones. Does not require watering. Remove flower heads with scissors after each flowering to encourage almost continuous blooming.
Propagation   By spring sowing in boxes or pots; also directly in the flowering site.
Qualities   Hardy annual. Easy to grow.

216 **LONICERA x BROWNII** (Eduard von Regel) Elie Abel Carrière
Syn.: *L. sempervirens* Carolus Linnaeus x *L. hirsuta* Amos Eaton. Common name: Scarlet trumpet honeysuckle

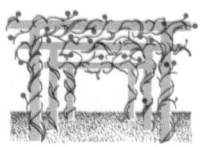

Family   Caprifoliaceae.
Description   One of the loveliest of the cultivated hybrid honeysuckles, it was obtained by the horticulturalist F. E. Brown, in England just before 1850. It is a fairly vigorous evergreen or semi-evergreen climbing shrub with slender, voluble stems and opposite, connate leaves that are amplexicaul at the ends of the stems. Its numerous flowers are borne in umbelliferous verticillasters. There are five cultivars of this hybrid.
Height of plant   16–20 ft. (5–6 m.).
Size of flower   2–2¾ in. (5–7 cm.).
Place of origin   A horticultural hybrid derived from crossing *L. sempervirens* of Japan with *L. hirsuta* of North America.
Flowering time   Spring–early summer.
Cultivation   A bright to partially shaded position. Temperate climate. Grows in any type of soil provided it is moist and humus-rich. Benefits from seasonal applications of general organic/mineral fertilizers. Plentiful watering in summer. Prune only flowered, weak and dead growth. Bear in mind that it flowers on the previous year's wood. Pests: aphids.
Propagation   By cuttings, layering or air layering in the spring or summer.
Qualities   Hardy. Easy to grow.

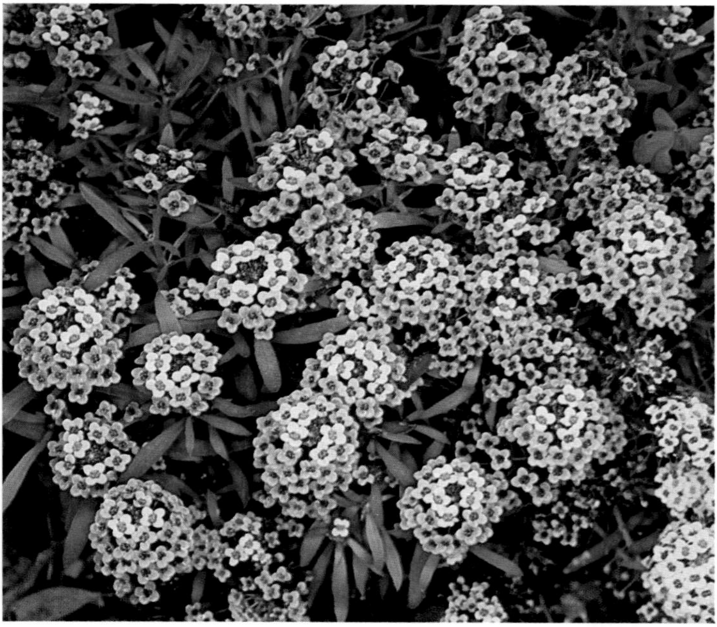

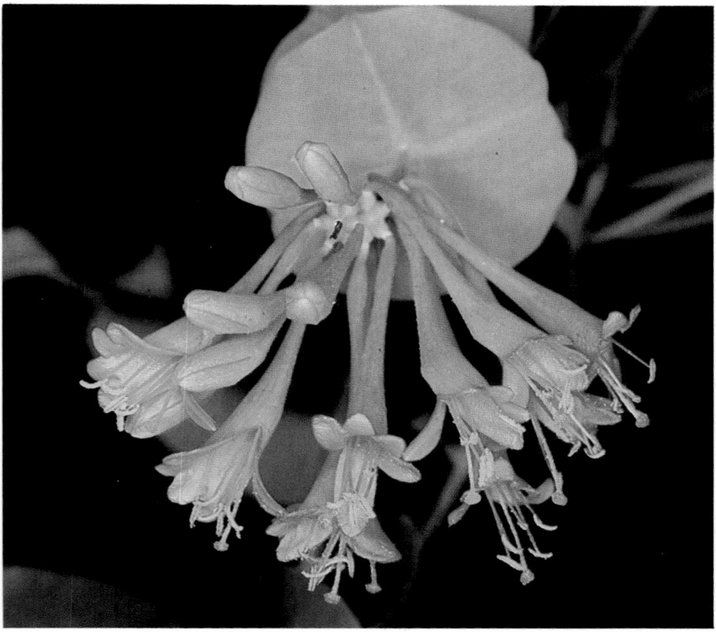

217 LONICERA CAPRIFOLIUM Carolus Linnaeus
Common name: Sweet honeysuckle

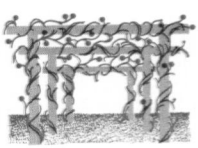

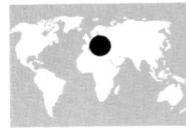

Family Caprifoliaceae.
Description A climbing shrub with a voluble (twining) stem; requires supporting. Its opposite, ovate-elliptical, coriaceous leaves are dark green on the upper surface and glaucous on the lower; almost amplexicaul in the cymes. Its numerous creamy-white fragrant flowers are tubulous, bilabiate and borne in axillary verticels or terminal umbels.
Height of plant 10–13 ft. (3–4 m.).
Size of flower 1½–2 in. (4–5 cm.).
Place of origin Europe.
Flowering time Late spring–summer.
Cultivation A partially shaded position. Temperate climate. Frost-resistant. Suited to any type of moist soil, even if only moderately fertile. Dry conditions impede flowering. Regular watering. Fairly hard annual pruning encourages plant to make new growth. Benefits from periodic applications of organic/mineral fertilizers. Usually trouble-free.
Propagation By cuttings, layering or air layering in the spring or summer. By spring sowing in pots.
Qualities Hardy. Suitable for terraces. Easy to grow.

218 LUPINUS POLYPHYLLUS John Lindley
Common name: Lupine

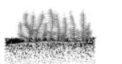

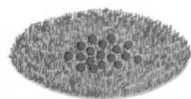

Family Papilionaceae.
Description A herbaceous, cespitose perennial with erect stems and showy, decorative flowers. Its alternate leaves are digitate and articulate, composed of nine to fifteen lanceolate-acute leaflets. Its flowers are borne in upright, conical-spicate racemes about 16 inches (40 cm.) long; the corolla is papilionaceous in a variety of colors, the most usual being violet-blue, lavender, carmine-marked yellow. The Russell hybrids are descended from this species.
Height of plant 24–36 in. (60–90 cm.).
Size of flower ¾–1 in. (2–2.5 cm.).
Place of origin Western North America.
Flowering time Spring–summer.
Cultivation A sunny position. Temperate climate: prefers cool summers. Likes slightly acid, sandy, siliceous soil, if necessary amended with peat. Totally averse to lime. Regular watering. After flowering, stalks should be cut down to the base. Benefits from periodic applications of superphosphate; nitrogen should not be given, since the plants are nitrogen fixers, absorbing nitrogen from the air and imparting it to the soil.
Propagation By spring sowing in pots or directly in the garden.
Qualities Hardy. Easy to grow.

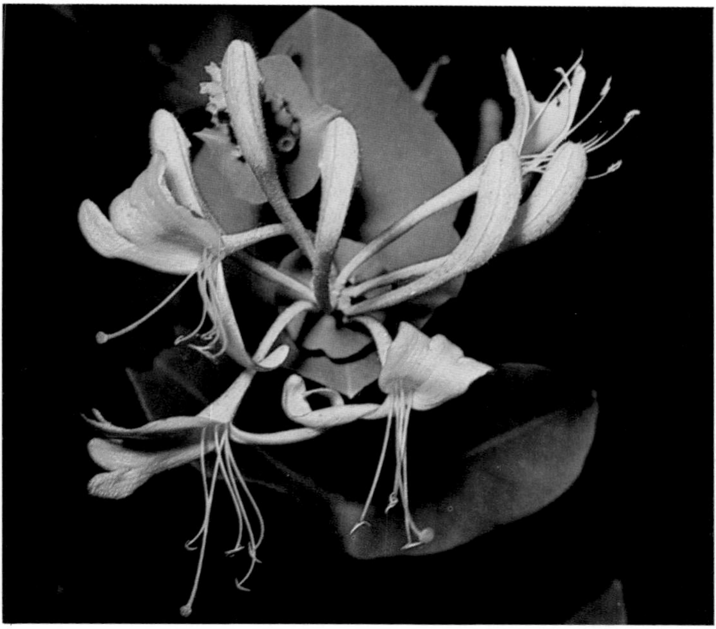

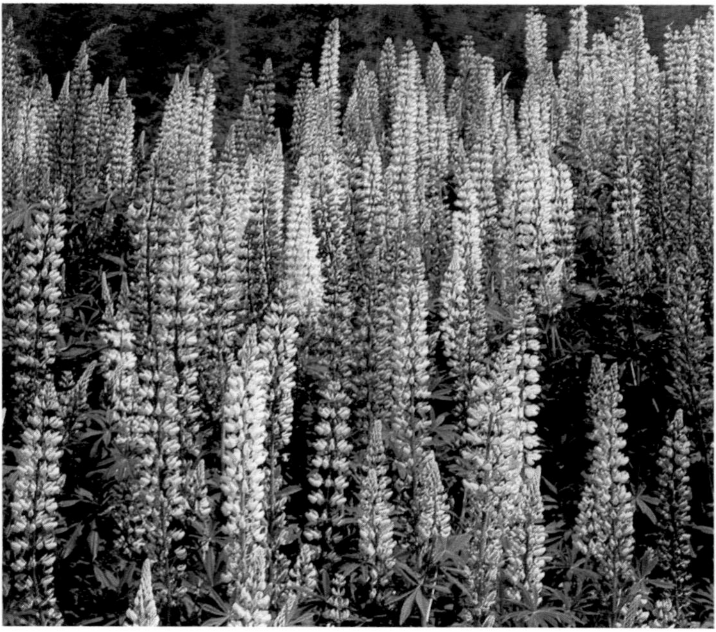

219 MAGNOLIA GRANDIFLORA Carolus Linnaeus
Common name: Bull-bay

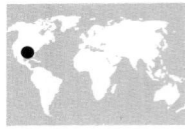

Family Magnoliaceae.
Description One of the most beautiful evergreen flowering trees, esteemed both for its foliage and its blooms, which are exceptionally large. It has strong ramifications that spring from the base to form a large, oval crown. Its oblong leaves are obtusely acute, undulate and coriaceous. Its solitary flowers are terminal and heavily perfumed.
Height of plant 15–25 ft. (4.5–7.6 m.); to 100 ft. in its habitat.
Size of flower 7–7⅞ in. (18–20 cm.).
Place of origin Southeastern United States.
Flowering time Summer.
Cultivation A sunny, isolated position. Warm-temperate climate. Prone to frost damage. It prefers deep, very fertile, humus-rich soil with an acid reaction, and moist without being waterlogged; if necessary, the ground can be amended with plenty of peat. Usually left in its natural shape but tolerates pruning to shape very well. Diseases: prone to various forms of chlorosis, often due to mineral deficiencies in the soil.
Propagation By layering or cuttings in spring or summer. Also by spring sowing, the seed having been stratified, but this is a lengthy process.
Qualities Hardy. Easy to grow.

220 MAGNOLIA HYPOLEUCA Philipp Franz von Siebold and Joseph Gerhard Zuccarini
Syn.: *M. obovata* Carl Peter Thunberg. Common name: Whiteleaf Japanese magnolia

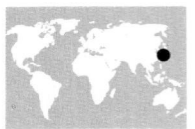

Family Magnoliaceae.
Description A deciduous flowering tree. Its trunk has numerous flexuous ramifications that bear rather fat buds with foliaceous, cottony stipules. Its leaves are alternate, obovate and subsessile. Its numerous flowers, produced terminally on the branches, consist of a number of petals, usually white; stamens have red filaments and yellow or white anthers. There are various cultivars with flowers tinged with another color. It comes into bloom at the same time as the leaves are developing.
Height of plant 6½–13 ft. (2–4 m.); to 100 ft. in its habitat.
Size of flower 3–4¾ in. (8–12 cm.).
Place of origin China and Japan.
Flowering time Early spring.
Cultivation A sunny to partially shaded position. Cool-temperate climate. Withstands the cold well. Prefers siliceous, rich, moist soil or even slightly argillaceous. Periodic applications of organic/mineral fertilizers. It should not be pruned but left to grow naturally. Requires watering in dry periods.
Propagation By layering in spring or summer. Sometimes grown from seed, but this is a lengthy process.
Qualities Hardy. Easy to grow.

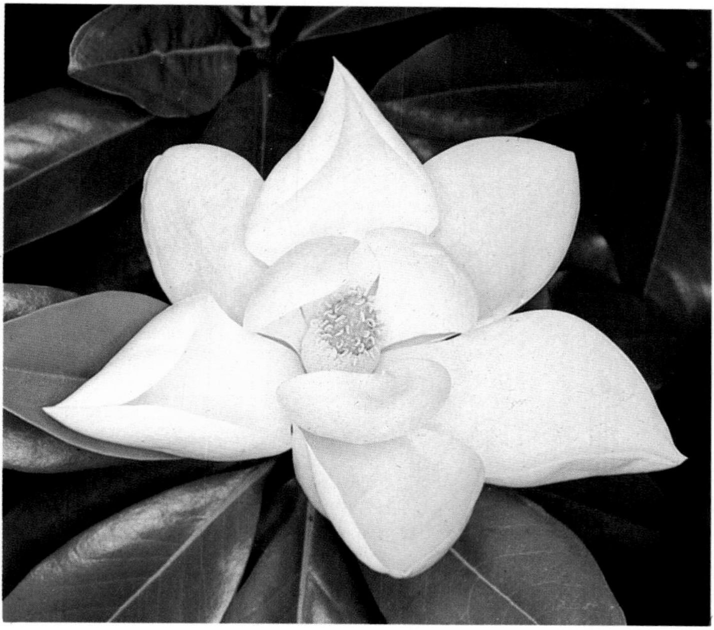

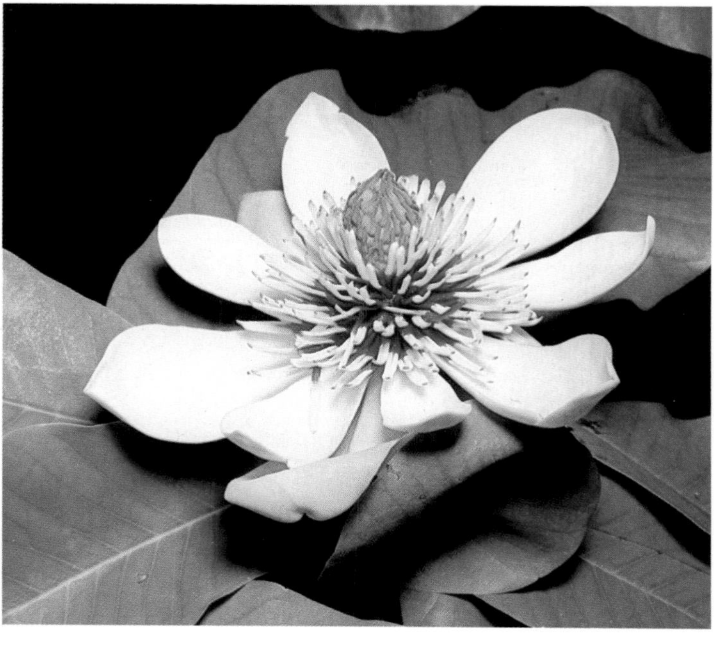

221 MAGNOLIA x SOULANGIANA Soulange Bodin
Common name: Saucer magnolia

Family Magnoliaceae.
Description A deciduous shrub or tree, this is one of the most delightful of the magnolias because of its abundance of flowers in early spring. These are fully open before the plant is in leaf. It has a shrubby, treelike stem with numerous ramifications. Its large, alternate leaves are obovate and obtusely acute, with a short, sturdy petiole. Its flowers are sizable, with erect petals that almost converge; they have very little scent.
Height of plant 13–26 ft. (4–8 m.).
Size of flower 4–4¾ in. (10–12 cm.).
Place of origin A horticultural hybrid derived from *M. liliiflora* (*M. obovata* Hort.) x *M. denudata*, originating from China.
Flowering time Early spring.
Cultivation A sunny or partially shaded position. Cool-temperate climate. Can withstand the cold well. Prefers deep, moist, siliceous soil, rich in organic material or amended with plenty of peat. Periodic applications of general organic/mineral fertilizers. Plentiful watering during the summer. It is particularly beautiful when left in its natural shape but can tolerate considerable pruning.
Propagation By layering or grafting during the spring or summer.
Qualities Hardy. Easy to grow.

222 MAGNOLIA STELLATA (Siebold and Zuccarini) Karl Joseph Maximowicz
Syn.: *M. halleana* S. B. Parsons. Common name: Star magnolia

Family Magnoliaceae.
Description A deciduous shrub or small tree. Very ramified from the base, it has a bushy, compact habit. The bark and leaves exude an aromatic scent. Its alternate leaves are oblong-acute or acuminate. Its isolated, abundant white flowers are stellate and fragrant, with linear-spatulate petals and short stamens. There is also a pink variety and another with more petals.
Height of plant 8–20 ft. (2.50–36.1 m.).
Size of flower 4–6 in. (10–15 cm.).
Place of origin Japan.
Flowering time Early spring.
Cultivation Full sun or slight shade. Temperate climate. Frost-resistant. Prefers deep, rich, lime-free soil enriched with peat and organic manure. Regular watering during the summer. Seasonal applications of general organic/mineral fertilizers. If any signs of chlorosis appear, treat with iron chelates. Usually left unpruned in its natural shape.
Propagation By layering or air layering. Also by cuttings put to root in a greenhouse.
Qualities Hardy. Easy to grow.

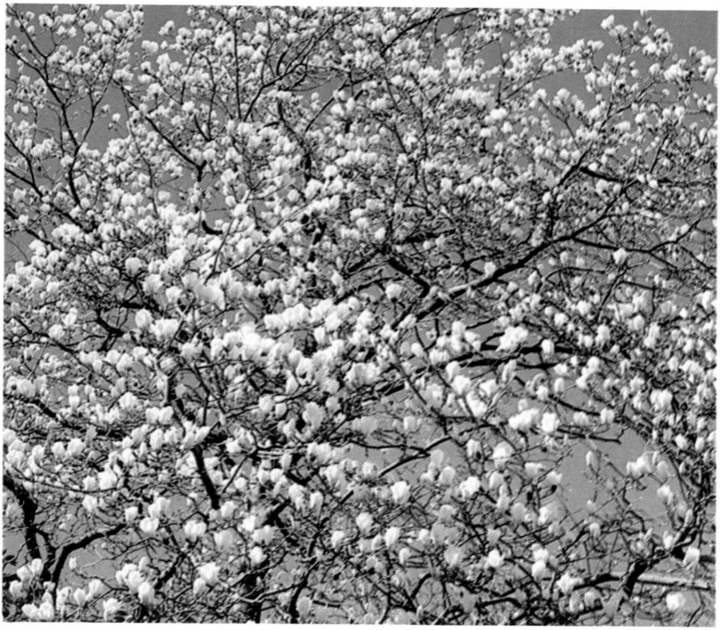

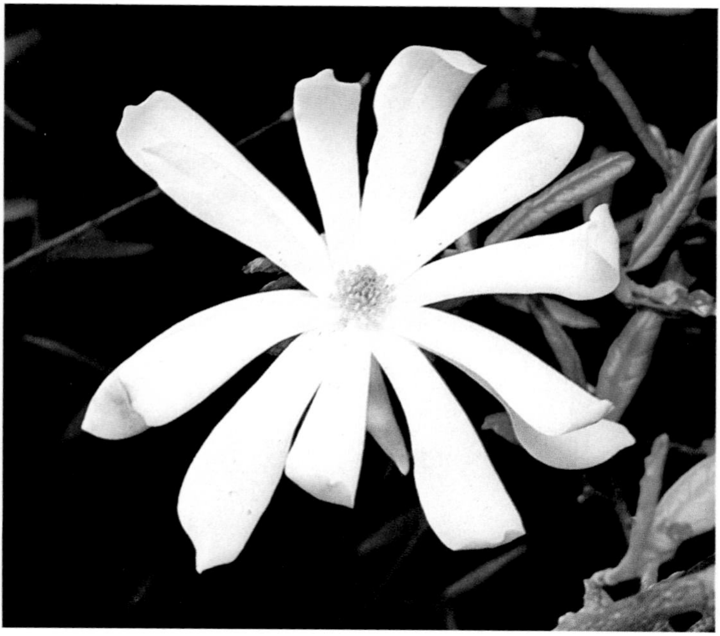

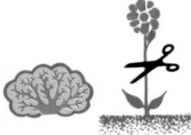

223 MAHONIA AQUIFOLIUM (Frederick T. Pursh) Thomas Nuttall
Syn.: *Berberis aquifolium* Pursh. Common name: Oregon grape

Family Berberidaceae.
Description An evergreen shrub that is decorative for its foliage, flowers and fruit. It is bushy, but not very ramose. Its alternate leaves are imparipinnate, with sessile, ovate-oblong, dentate-spinose, consistent leaflets that turn coppery-red in the winter. Its small yellow flowers are borne in dense racemes at the ends of the branches and in the foliar axils. The blue-black berries are covered with pruina. A slow-growing plant.
Height of plant 40–60 in. (1–1.50 m.).
Size of flower ⅜ in. (1 cm.).
Place of origin Northern California to British Columbia.
Flowering time Early spring.

Cultivation A sunny or, better still, shady position. Cool-temperate climate. Frost-resistant. Undemanding, suited to any type of soil, preferably argillaceous, moderately compact, moist and with a humus content. Regular watering and a periodic application of organic/mineral fertilizers. Little pruning required as the plant grows naturally into an attractive shape.
Propagation By layering or removing and planting underground stems in the spring. Also by spring sowing, but growth is very slow.
Qualities Hardy. Suitable for balconies, terraces. Easy to grow.

224 MALCOLMIA (or MALCOMIA) MARITIMA (Carolus Linnaeus) Robert Brown
Syn.: *Cheiranthus maritimus*. Common name: Virginia stock

Family Cruciferae.
Description A very floriferous and charming annual, it is tap-rooted and has a semi-herbaceous, prostrate-ascendent, purplish-green stem, only slightly ramified. Its alternate leaves are oblong-lanceolate and its numerous flowers bloom in graduated order in short racemes at the end of the branches. Several improved cultivars are on the market in colors that include red, lilac, rose-pink and white.
Height of plant 8–10 in. (20–25 cm.).
Size of flower ⅜–⅝ in. (1–1.5 cm.).
Place of origin Mediterranean regions.
Flowering time Late spring–summer.

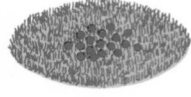

Cultivation In full sun or a very bright position. Temperate climate. Well-aerated, rich, moist soil, even argillaceous-sandy. Plenty of well-rotted manure dug in while the ground is being prepared. Frequent watering. Plants should be removed after flowering. Pests and diseases: aphids; subject to various rots as seedlings.
Propagation By spring sowing directly in flowering site. Subsequent sowings can be made into the summer. Self-sown.
Qualities Hardy annual. Easy to grow.

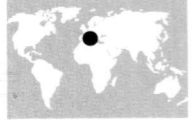

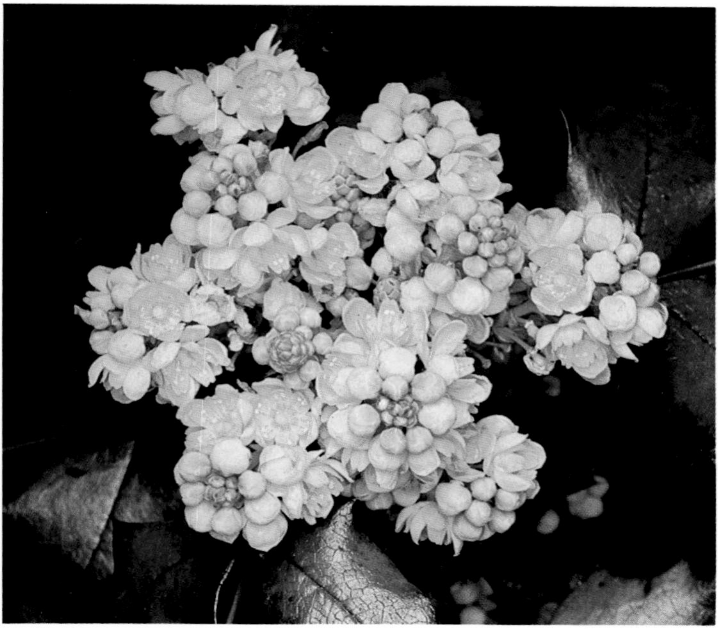

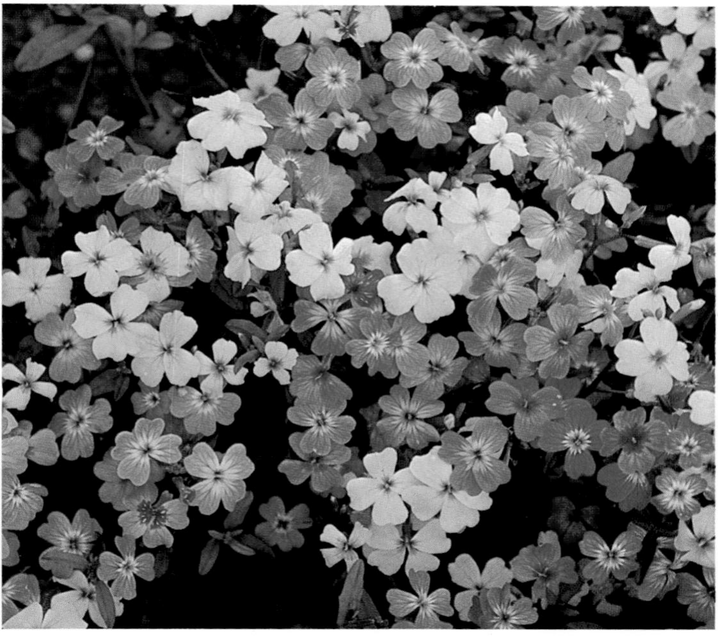

225 MALUS x PURPUREA (Barbier) Alfred Rehder
cv. "Lemoinei"
Common name: Lemoine crabapple

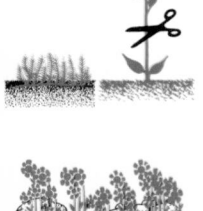

Family Rosaceae.
Description A beautiful tree, ornamental for both the color of its foliage and the numerous ruby-red flowers. It has slightly pendulous ramifications with serrate-crenate, petiolate leaves of a purplish-red color on unfurling. The flowers are borne in clusters of five to seven. Ovoid fruits of a dark blood-red, the size of cherries.
Height of plant 16–23 ft. (5–7 m.).
Size of flower 1⅛ in. (3 cm.).
Place of origin A horticultural hybrid derived from crossings of *M. pumila* cv. "Niedzwetkiana" with *M. floribunda* cv. x "Atrosanguinea." Its progenitors originated in Japan and Siberia.
Flowering time Spring.
Cultivation Full sun to partial shade. Cool-temperate climate. Frost-resistant. A slightly acid, well-aerated, moist, rich soil with a low lime content. Periodic applications of general organic/mineral fertilizers. Requires watering during dry spells. Although a beautiful plant when allowed to grow naturally, a little pruning may be necessary to contain branch lengths and remove weak or dead growth. Pests and diseases: various insects; leaf spot.
Propagation Nearly always by cleft grafting in the spring.
Qualities Hardy. Easy to grow.

---

226 MATTHIOLA INCANA (Carolus Linnaeus) Robert Brown
Syns.: *M. annua, M. graeca.* Common name: Stock

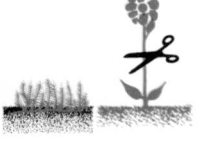

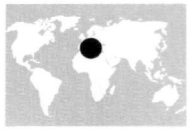

Family Cruciferae.
Description A bushy, short-lived perennial, generally grown as an annual, semi-woody at the base. It produces several irregular, upward-growing branches. Its leaves are entire, lanceolate-obtuse with an ondulate-sinuate margin. Its numerous, very sweetly scented flowers are borne in panicles, ramified at the top of the stalk. Colors include white, pink, red, violet and cream.
Height of plant 19–37 in. (50–95 cm.).
Size of flower 1⅜–1¾ in. (3.5–4.5 cm.).
Place of origin Mediterranean regions.
Flowering time Spring.
Cultivation Full sun. Temperate climate. Cannot withstand heavy frosts. Calcareous, even stony, soil. Prepare ground with superphosphate and apply liquid fertilizer while growing. Requires well-controlled watering during flowering period. Pests and diseases: aphids and aleurodidae (whiteflies); club root, stem rot and various fungus diseases.
Propagation By early spring sowing under glass; move outdoors after last frost.
Qualities Hardy. Fairly easy to grow.

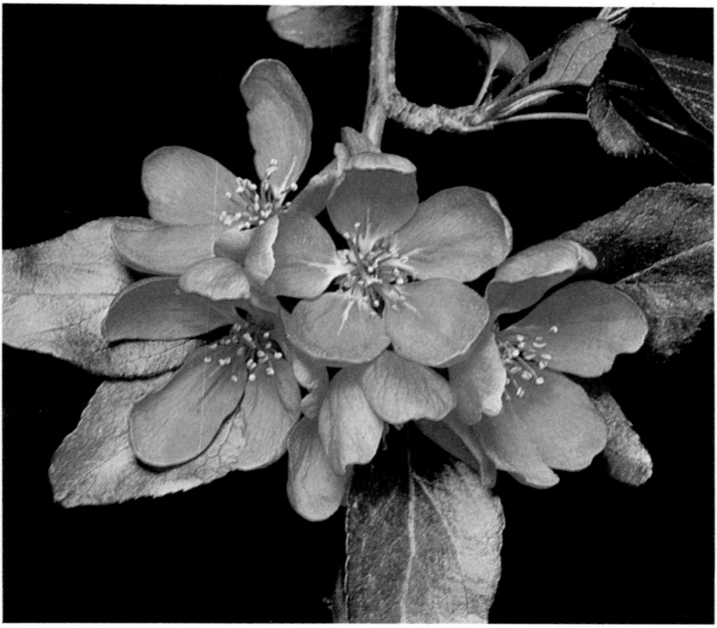

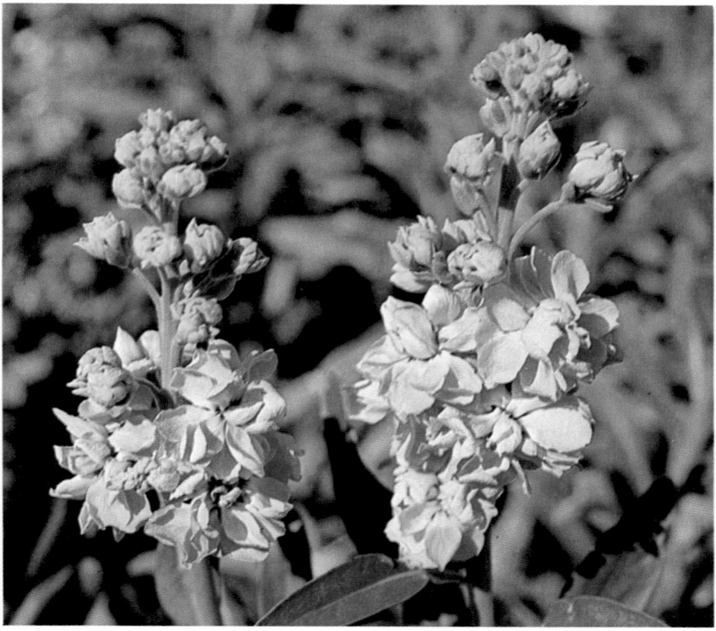

227 MIMULUS LUTEUS Carolus Linnaeus
Syns.: *M. guttatus* Augustin Pyramus DeCandolle, *M. puntatus* Miers. Common name: Monkey flower

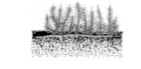

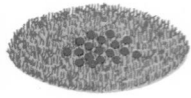

Family Scrophulariaceae.
Description A bushy herbaceous perennial with tetragonous stems. Its bright-green, opposite leaves are ovate sub-cordate and dentate. Its numerous flowers are borne in panicles, their tubulous-campanulate corollas opening out like butterflies. They are yellow heavily marked with reddish-brown.
Height of plant 12–16 in. (30–40 cm.).
Size of flower ¾–1⅜ in. (2–3.5 cm.).
Place of origin Chile.
Flowering time Spring–summer.
Cultivation A bright, slightly shaded position. Temperate climate. Frost-tender. Very damp ground, even an inch or two under water, rich in decomposed organic material; alternatively, frequent watering.
Propagation By spring sowing. By clump division and even by herbaceous cuttings taken from the tops of the branches and put to root in pans with a mixture of sand and peat in a greenhouse.
Qualities Very hardy. Very easy to grow.

---

228 MIRABILIS JALAPA Carolus Linnaeus
Common names: Marvel of Peru, four o'clock

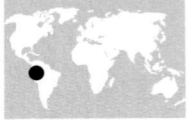

Family Nyctaginaceae.
Description A tuberous perennial, widely grown as an annual. Its adaptability often causes it to be planted in dreary locations where it tends to be overlooked. It grows in a dense bush with strong herbaceous, articulate-nodose stems with divaricate internodes. Its opposite leaves are ovate-acute and sub-cordate. The numerous fragrant flowers are borne in umbelliferous cymes. These open in late afternoon on sunny days; are open all day on cloudy days. There are several cultivars with white, yellow, violet and variegated flowers.
Height of plant 15–35 in. (40–90 cm.).
Size of flower 1½–2 in. (4–5 cm.).
Place of origin Tropical South America.
Flowering time Summer–autumn.
Cultivation A very bright to partially shaded position. Plant even grows under other plants. Temperate climate. It does well in a coastal area. Not very demanding, it thrives in any well-aerated soil even if only moderately fertile. Benefits from a periodic dressing of manure. While liking plenty of water, it can survive dry periods well. The branches should be cut down after flowering, leaving the tubers in the ground; but in cold areas, these should be stored in a frost-free place.
Propagation By spring sowing in pots in a coldframe or directly in the flowering site. Also from stored tubers.
Qualities Suitable for terraces, etc. Hardy. Easy to grow.

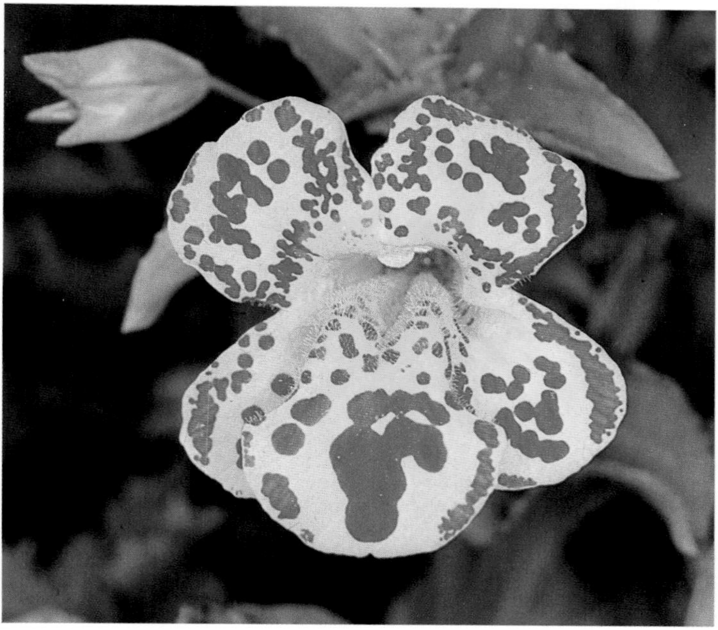

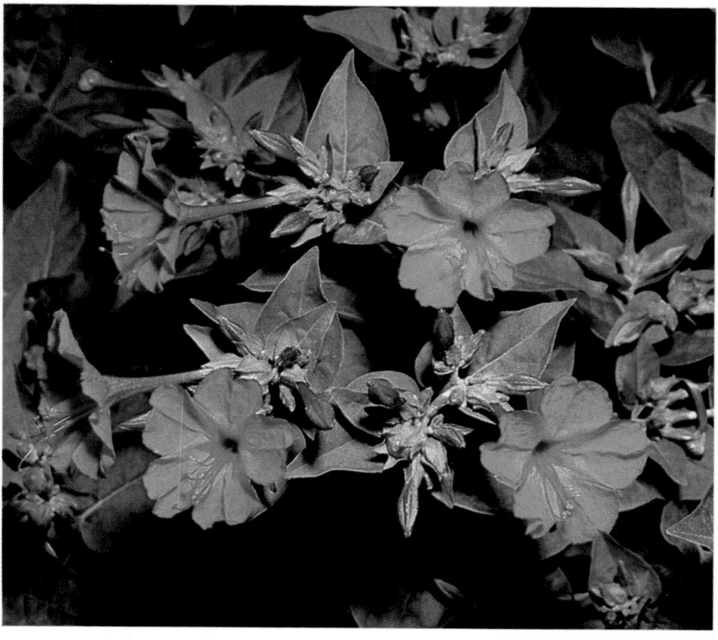

229 MONARDA FISTULOSA Carolus Linnaeus

Syn.: *M. mollis* Linnaeus. Common names: Wild bergamot, horsemint

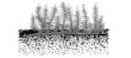

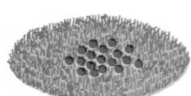

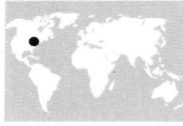

Family Labiatae.

Description An easy plant to grow because of its reliability and abundant floriferousness. Its upright stems are quadrangular, tomentose and not very ramose. Its opposite, oval leaves are oblong, sub-cordate, sinuate-dentate and exude an aromatic scent when touched. The numerous flowers are borne in compact terminal verticels that resemble capitula; their rose-pink corolla is labiate and pubescent. The flowering period is quite long. There are several cultivated varieties.

Height of plant 19–32 in. (50–80 cm.).

Size of flower 1⅜–1½ in. (3.5–4 cm.).

Place of origin Eastern United States.

Flowering time Summer.

Cultivation Partial to full shade. Temperate climate. Can withstand a few frosts, especially if well mulched. Rich, argillaceous-sandy soil enriched with organic material if necessary. Plentiful watering. All flowered stems should be cut off. Usually trouble-free.

Propagation By spring division or by sowing in a nursery bed.

Qualities Hardy. Easy to grow.

230 MUSCARI ARMENIACUM Max Leichtlin

Common name: Grape hyacinth

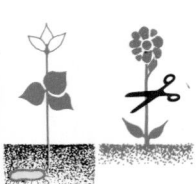

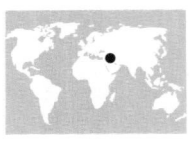

Family Liliaceae.

Description A small bulbous plant from which a number of cultivated hybrids have been developed. It forms dense clumps with numerous bright-blue, white-rimmed inflorescences, and spreads rapidly. The bulb is quite small, whitish, squamous and proliferous. Its three to six fairly thick, alternate leaves are linear and caniculate. Its flowers are slightly scented and borne in dense, cylindrical-conical racemes; the pendent perigonium is urceolate.

Height of plant 4–6 in. (10–15 cm.).

Size of flower ⅛–⅜ in. (0.5–1 cm.).

Place of origin Asia Minor.

Flowering time Spring.

Cultivation A sunny to partially shaded position. Temperate climate. Frost-resistant. Suited to any type of soil, preferably moderately compact, moist and humus-rich. Usually needs no particular attention. Can be allowed to naturalize. It is a good idea to divide the clumps every three or four years.

Propagation By division, removing the bulblets from the parent bulbs during the resting period.

Qualities Hardy. Suitable for balconies, terraces. Easy to grow.

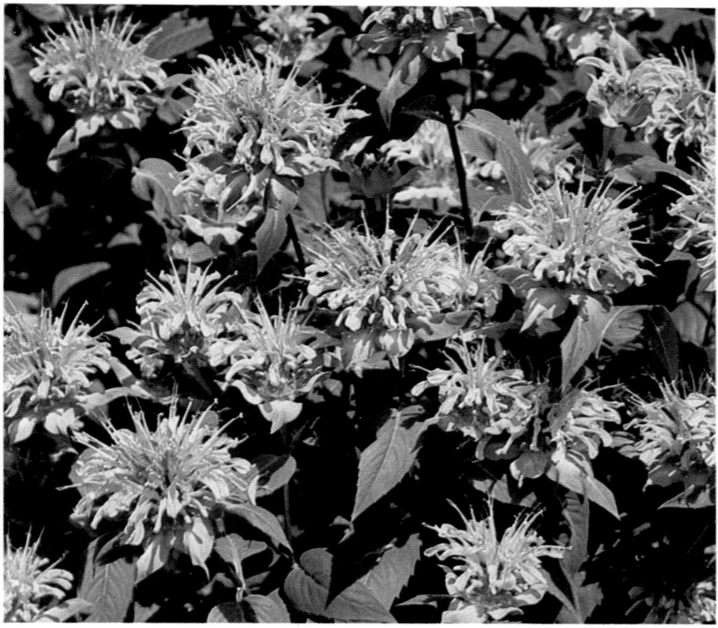

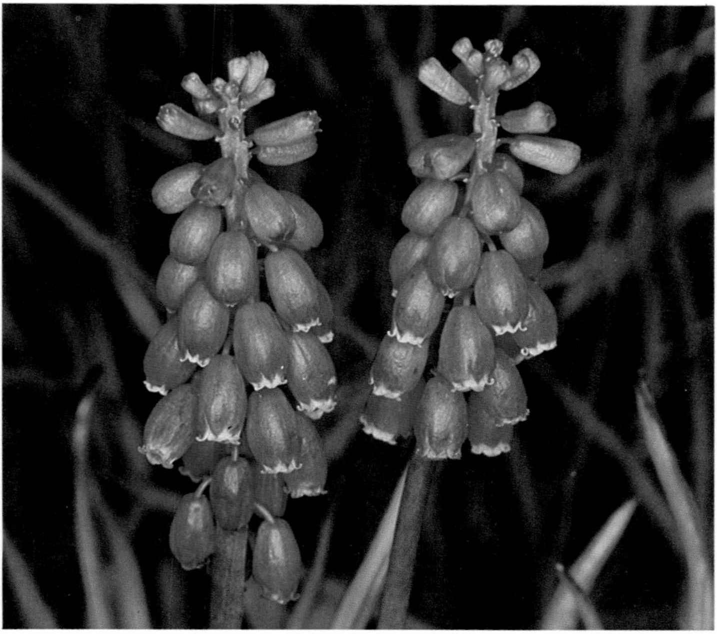

231 MYOSOTIS ALPESTRIS F. W. Schmidt cv.
Syns.: *M. rupicola, M. sylvatica alpestris*. Common name: Forget-me-not

Family Boraginaceae.
Description A small, bushy, herbaceous perennial, often grown as an annual. Its erect stems are well branched, producing alternate, oblong-lanceolate, obtuse and, in part, acute leaves. Leaves and stems are hirsute. The numerous little flowers are borne in scorpioid inflorescences. They are usually azure in color but occasionally white or rose-pink.
Height of plant 4–6 in. (10–15 cm.).
Size of flower ⅛–⅜ in. (0.5–0.8 cm.).
Place of origin Europe.
Flowering time Spring–summer.

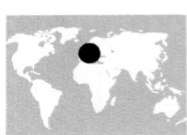

Cultivation A moderately shady, sheltered position. Cool-temperate climate. Fairly frost-resistant. Grows in any type of light, fertile, moist, humus-rich soil. Requires frequent watering. Pull plants up after flowering. Pests and diseases: aphids; oidium.
Propagation By late-summer sowing, pricking off in the autumn and planting out in the spring. Alternatively, by spring sowing in pans under glass, or where the plants are to grow. Self-sows freely.
Qualities Suitable for balconies, terraces. Hardy. Easy to grow.

---

232 MYRTUS COMMUNIS Carolus Linnaeus
Common name: Myrtle

Family Myrtaceae.
Description A compact evergreen shrub. Its small, opposite leaves are oval-acute, obtuse-lanceolate, coriaceous and aromatic; an essence is sometimes distilled from them and they are included in a thirteenth-century recipe for "Hungary Water." The flowers, although small, are numerous and in some countries traditionally regarded as bringers of good luck to newly married couples. In the autumn the branches are thickly covered with very decorative purplish-black ovoid fruits. The "Leucocarpa" variety produces ivory-white fruit. There are also varieties with variegated leaves and double flowers.
Height of plant 3½–10 ft. (1–3 m.).
Size of flower ⅜–¾ in. (1–2 cm.).
Place of origin Mediterranean region.
Flowering time Summer.

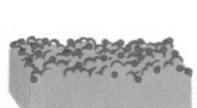

Cultivation In full sun or a sunny, sheltered position. Temperate climate. Can withstand one or two light frosts. Open, fertile ground, even under large trees or near the sea. Does not usually require watering. Tolerant of pruning and can even be trained as a hedge. Usually trouble-free.
Propagation By spring seed sowing. By cuttings taken in the summer and rooted in a sheltered place.
Qualities Hardy. Easy to grow.

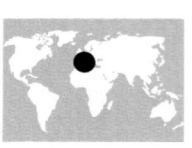

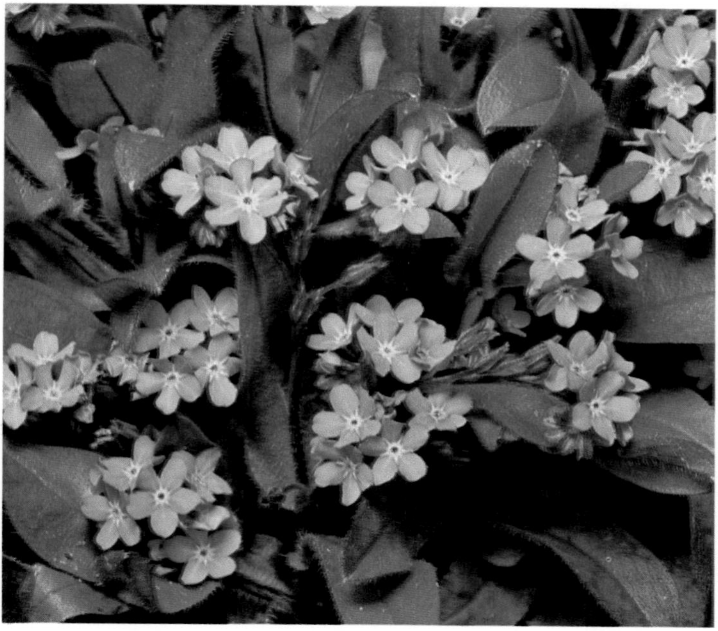

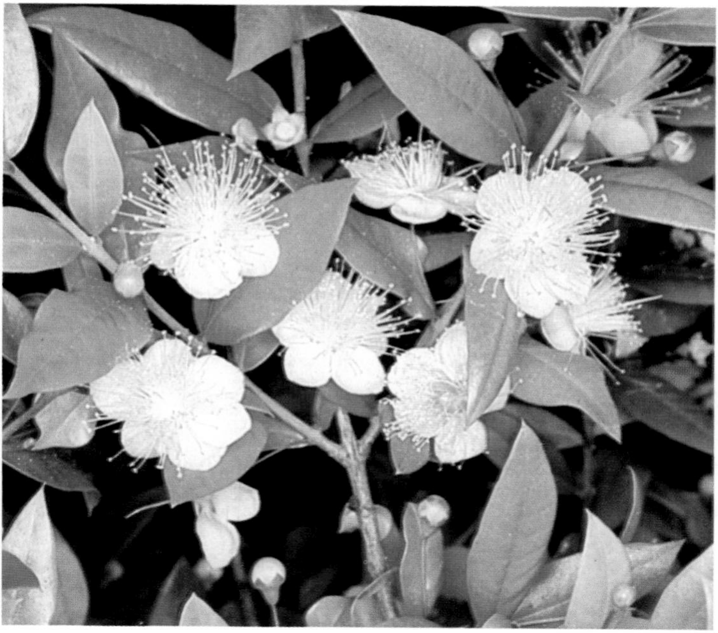

233 NANDINA DOMESTICA Carl Peter Thunberg
Common name: Heavenly bamboo

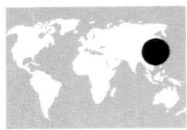

Family Berberidaceae.
Description An elegant, medium-sized evergreen shrub, particularly ornamental in winter when its foliage takes on a metallic, reddish-brown appearance. It also has dainty white flowers and very attractive red berries. Its compound, bi- or tripinnate leaves have ternate, lanceolate leaflets. The numerous flowers are borne in terminal panicles 6–10 inches (15–25 cm.) long. There is also a cultivar, ''Alba,'' with white fruits.
Height of plant 5–6½ ft. (1.50–2 m.).
Size of flower ¼–⅜ in. (0.6–1 cm.).
Place of origin India, China, Japan.
Flowering time Summer.
Cultivation A shady, cool position. Temperate climate. Likely to be damaged by heavy frosts. Prefers well-aerated, humus-rich soil or soil that has been amended with peat and farmyard manure. Periodic light applications of organic/mineral fertilizers. Regular watering during the summer. Should not be pruned. Usually trouble-free.
Propagation By division, cuttings or seed in spring–summer.
Qualities Suitable for terraces. Hardy. Easy to grow.

---

234 NARCISSUS PSEUDONARCISSUS Carolus Linnaeus
Common names: Daffodil, trumpet narcissus

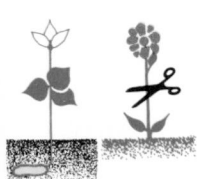

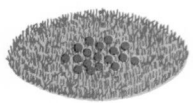

Family Amaryllidaceae.
Description A deciduous bulbous perennial. The bulb is piriform, enveloped in pale tunics. The light-green, upright leaves are linear-obtuse and quite thick. The solitary flowers are very showy with an open, rotate perigonium and a central trumpet-shaped corona. There are many cultivars in colors ranging from white to yellow and orange with a corona and perigonium of the same or contrasting color.
Height of plant 8–14 in. (20–35 cm.).
Size of flower 2–2¾ in. (5–7 cm.).
Place of origin Western Europe; growing wild throughout the whole of Europe.
Flowering time Early spring.
Cultivation A slightly shady position. Temperate climate. Frost-resistant. Any type of soil, with a preference for moderately compact, moist, humus-rich ground. The bulbs do not need to be planted very deep as they tend to work their own way down. The clumps of bulbs generally require splitting up every four or five years. Usually trouble-free.
Propagation By bulblets removed from parent bulbs during the resting period and planted out in October.
Qualities Hardy. Easy to grow.

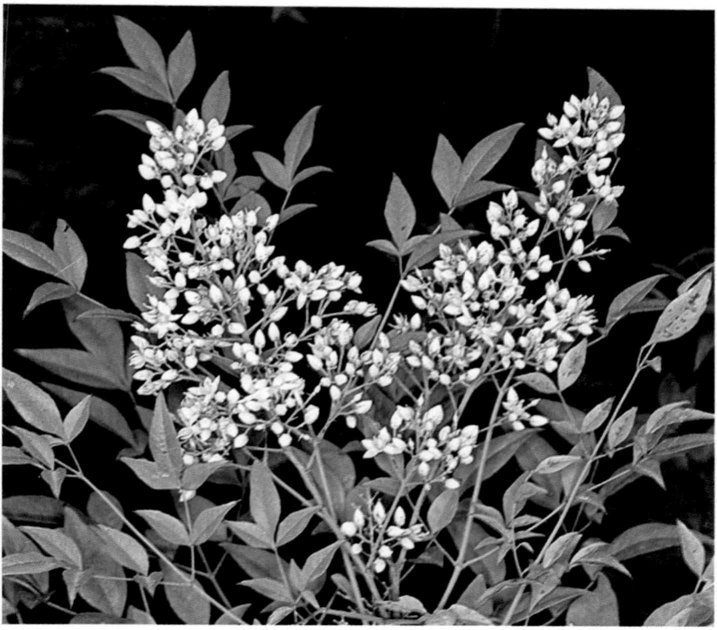

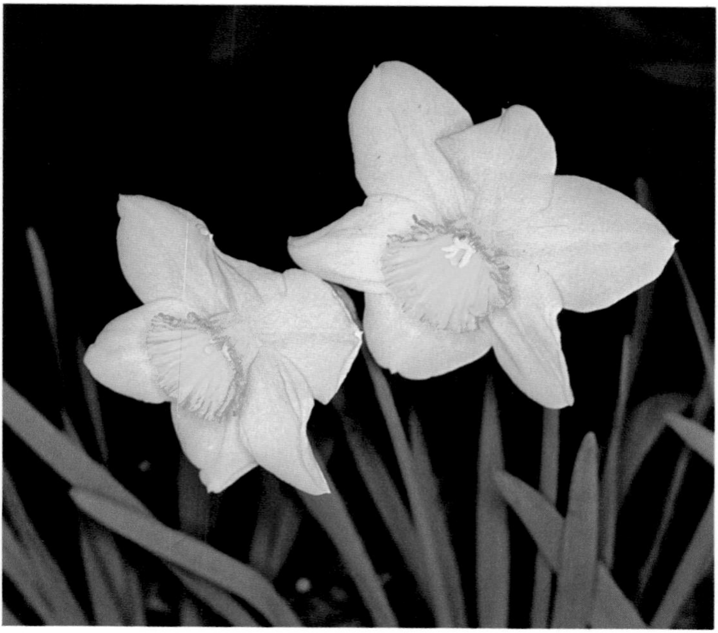

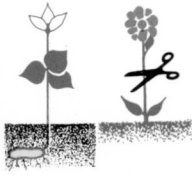

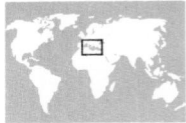

235 NARCISSUS TAZETTA Carolus Linnaeus x **poeticus** Linnaeus cv.
Common names: Polyanthus or poet's narcissus

Family Amaryllidaceae.

Description A bulbous perennial derived from crossing *N. tazetta* with *N. poeticus*. From this, a great many horticultural hybrids have been produced, with varieties in which the color of the perigonium differs from that of the corona or in which the number of flowers, the size, floriferousness, etc., vary. The medium-sized, piriform bulb is not very proliferous. There are two to four glaucous-green, linear, arcuate or erect, fairly thick leaves about 9–12 in. (23–30 cm.) long. The solitary flowers (*N. poeticus*), or those borne in umbels of two to ten (*N. tazetta*), are carried at the apex of an upright, often slightly pendulous, scape. Their perigonium has six open, stellate lobes and a small cup-shaped corona that varies in color and, slightly, in shape.

Height of plant 5½–16 in. (14–40 cm.).

Size of flower 1⅛–2 in. (3–5 cm.).

Place of origin Hybrids derived from parents originating from Southern Europe and the Mediterranean region.

Flowering time Spring.

Cultivation A sunny or slightly shady position. Temperate climate. Can withstand the cold well. Suited to any type of fertile, rich, moist ground. The bulbs need be planted only to a depth of about 6 in. (15 cm.) and then do not like to be moved. The clumps of bulbs may need to be split up, however, every three or four years. Watering is unnecessary. The surface soil should be lightly dug over during the resting period, after the leaves have died down. Trouble-free.

Propagation By bulblets, removed from parent bulbs during the resting stage and left to grow in a well-prepared nursery bed. It will be at least three years before they come into flower. Alternatively, by seed, although this method is seldom used because it is so slow; nor is it always possible, since the seeds cannot be relied on to ripen on the plants.

Qualities Hardy. Easy to grow.

Opposite: above, Narcissus tazetta x poeticus *cv.; below,* Narcissus tazetta x poeticus *cv. "Geranium."*

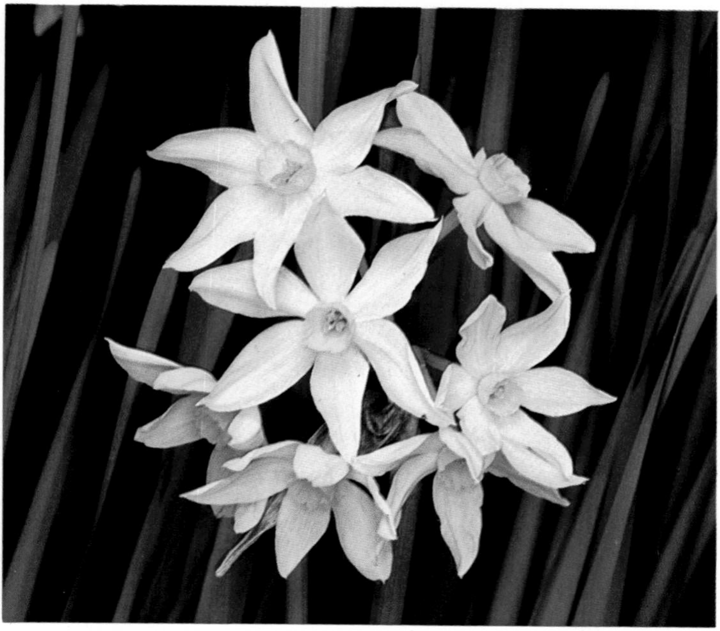

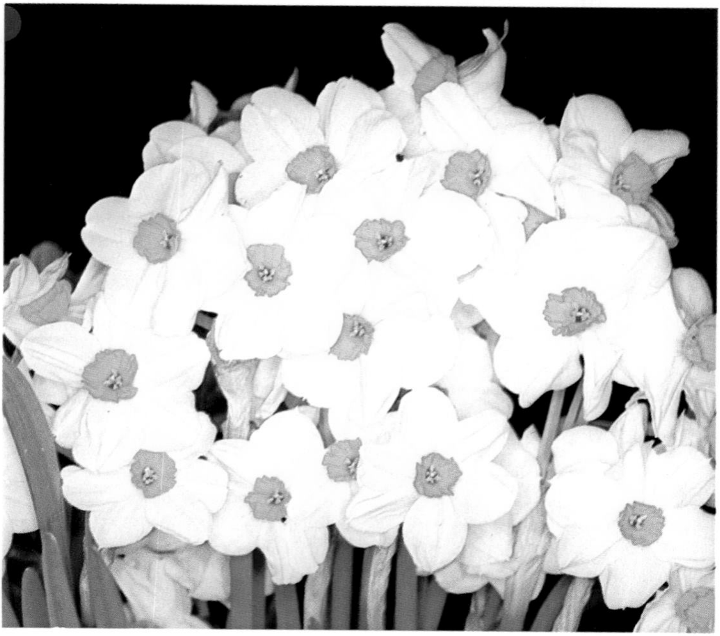

236 NELUMBO NUCIFERA Joseph Gaertner
Syn.: *N. speciosum*. Common names: Indian or Chinese lotus

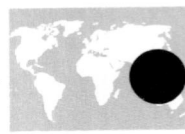

Family Nymphaeaceae.
Description Aquatic plant with whitish rhizome irregularly enlarged into cylindrical, vesiculose parts with root crowns. Peltate leaves almost rotund with slightly raised limb, upper surface impermeable and velutinate-cereous, prominent venation on lower; float just above water on long, fibrous, sturdy petioles. Large flowers borne singly on a long, erect peduncle, in various shades of red and pink.
Height of plant 4–5 ft. (1.20–1.50 m.).
Size of flower 10–12 in. (25–30 cm.).
Place of origin Southern Asia, Australia.
Flowering time Summer.
Cultivation Full sun in ponds, pools or water gardens. Warm-temperate climate. Still, tepid water not below 60° F. (15.5° C.) and between 1½ and 5 ft. (0.50–1.50 m.) deep. Deep mud in the bottom with plenty of fertile sediment. Frost-tender. Winter is resting period; cut down withered stems and leaves.
Propagation By rhizome division in spring. Occasionally by seed, sown as soon as it has been collected or stored in damp sphagnum moss, since conservation time extremely limited.
Qualities Hardy in its own environment. Easy to grow.

237 NERINE SARNIENSIS (Carolus Linnaeus) William Herbert
Syn.: *Amaryllis sarniensis* Linnaeus. Common name: Guernsey lily

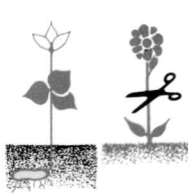

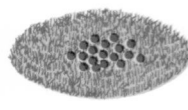

Family Amaryllidaceae.
Description This plant has a medium-sized, rotundate-oblong bulb covered in chestnut-brown scales. The sparse leaves are linear, obtusely acute and carnosect. The numerous flowers (eight to ten) are borne in globose terminal umbels on strong, upright scapes. The perigonium has a short tube with abruptly reflexed linear lobes; its erect stamens are very protrusive. This charming plant is grown for garden ornament and for cutting. It has several rose-pink and red-flowered cultivars.
Height of plant 12–18 in. (30–45 cm.).
Size of flower 3⅛–4 in. (8–10 cm.).
Place of origin South Africa.
Flowering time Summer.
Cultivation Full sun to slight shade. Temperate climate. Fairly resistant to cold, especially if grown in a sheltered position. Suitable for any light, fertile, moist, well-drained soil. Requires plenty of water while in flower but considerably less during germination and none at all during the resting period of the bulb. It likes to be left undisturbed. Pests and diseases: insects during flowering; various rots in cold, damp places.
Propagation By removal of bulblets after flowering.
Qualities Half-hardy to tender. Suitable for terraces, etc. Easy to grow.

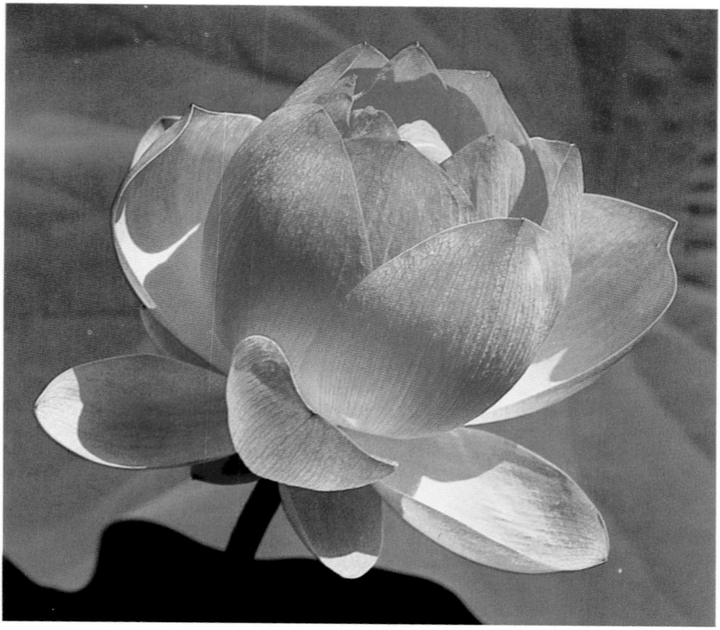

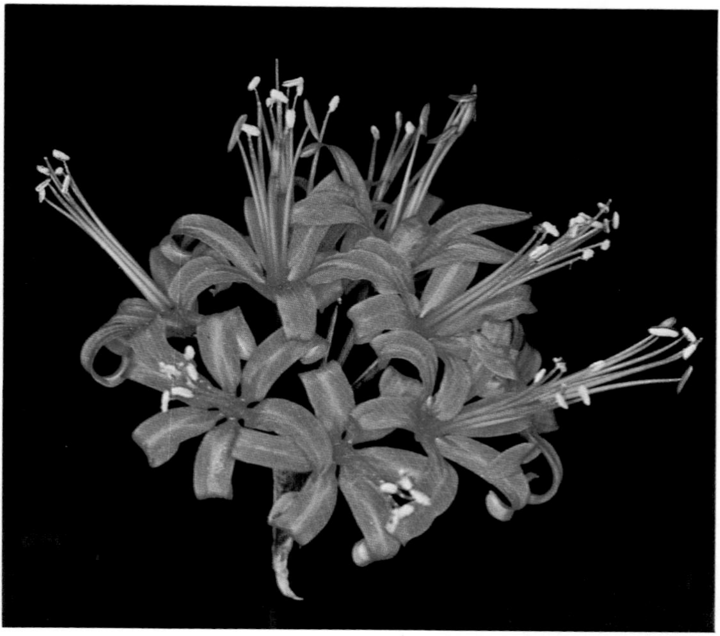

238 NERIUM OLEANDER Carolus Linnaeus
Common names: Oleander, rose bay

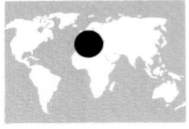

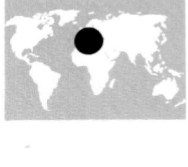

Family Apocynaceae.
Description An evergreen shrub or small tree, well branched, spreading and diffuse. The bark of the branches as well as the leaves and seeds are very poisonous due to the presence of alkaloids (nerin and oleandrin). The narrow dark-green leaves are lanceolate, coriaceous and verticillate in groups of three. The abundant flowers, which have a distinctive fragrance, are carried in corymbous and terminal cymes. The corolla is usually pink but may also be found in purplish-red, white, various yellowish shades and striate. Flowers are long-lasting and showy; they may be single, semidouble or double.
Height of plant 5–20 ft. (1.50–6 m.).
Size of flower 1¼–2 in. (3.3–5 cm.).
Place of origin Mediterranean regions and Middle East.
Flowering time Summer.
Cultivation Full sun. Temperate climate. Even if damage is sustained to the crown, the plant will survive and throw up new growth from the base. Grows in almost any type of soil, even if poor. Its flowering period is lengthened if a periodic application of a general organic/mineral fertilizer is given. Although it likes a lot of moisture in the summer, it can withstand dry conditions. Light autumn pruning; but it can be encouraged to make new growth by cutting back hard to the base.
Propagation By air layering in spring–summer. By cuttings taken in summer and rooted in a propagating frame.
Qualities Hardy in its own environment. Easy to grow.

239 NICOTIANA ALATA Heinrich Friedrich Link and Friedrich Otto
Syn.: *N. affinis* Thomas Moore. Common name: Flowering tobacco

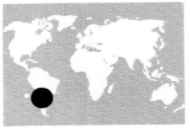

Family Solanaceae.
Description Perennial usually grown as an annual. Its erect stem is well branched and the whole plant is pilose-glandulous. Its purplish-red leaves are sessile, ovate-lanceolate and arranged in a rosette at the base. This is a plant that deserves to be more widely grown for its long and abundant floriferousness and delicate fragrance.
Height of plant 2½–5 ft. (0.80–1.50 m.).
Size of flower 2⅜–3⅛ in. (6–8 cm.).
Place of origin South America.
Flowering time Summer.
Cultivation A bright, sheltered position. Flowering is held up or growth arrested if the temperature falls below 50° F. (10° C.). It grows in any type of soil that is light, fertile, moist and kept in good condition with manure and phospho-potassic fertilizers. Frequent and plentiful watering. After flowering, plants can be pulled up. Pests and diseases: insects; chlorosis, viruses and various fungus diseases.
Propagation By spring sowing in pans under glass. In warm areas the seeds can be sown directly in the garden.
Qualities Half-hardy. Very easy to grow.

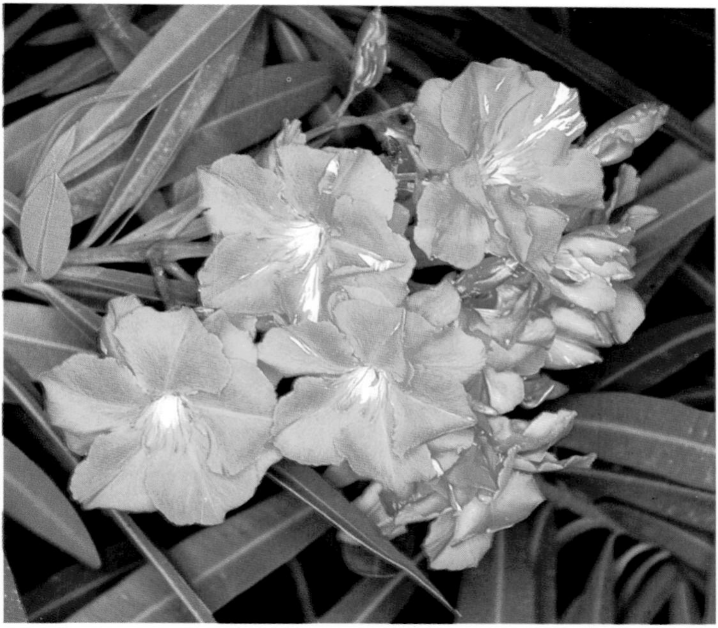

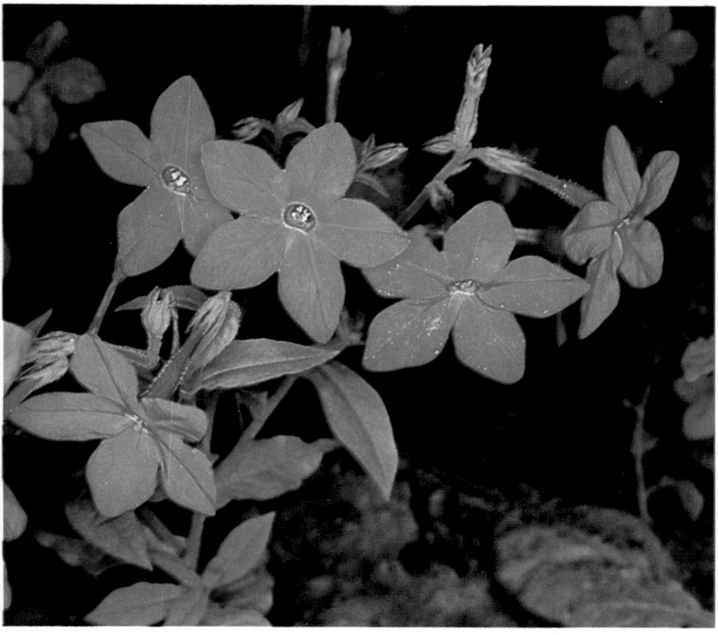

240 NYMPHAEA RUBRA William Roxburg
Common name: Red water lily

Family Nymphaeaceae.
Description Water lilies are herbaceous perennials with fairly robust rhizomes furnished with long roots. Their leaves are borne on long petioles; the reddish-green, floating blades are rotund-cordate, somewhat dentate, macular or striate, and sometimes with a crinkled margin. The flowers are large and numerous, with rayed or erect petals in various colors. Found in all latitudes and climates. Can be grown in ponds, tanks, ornamental pools, etc.

The leaves of *N. rubra* are orbicular-cordate and carnosect with a dentate margin. Its flowers are borne singly on a peduncle that carries them just above the surface of the water. A deep purplish-red, the erect petals open at night and in the early morning.

Water depth 12–40 in. (0.30–1 m.).
Size of flower 6–10 in. (15–25 cm.) diameter (water lilies in general 4–10 in. [10–25 cm.]).
Place of origin India.
Flowering time Summer.
Cultivation The depth of water varies from a few inches to about 3½ feet. They prefer soft mud rich in sedimentary organic material. Hardy water lilies do not require any particular attention. Half-hardy water lilies should almost always be over-wintered in a greenhouse or the rhizomes stored under cover in damp sand. Tropical water lilies can be grown in tanks in large greenhouses at moderate temperature or outdoors in ponds or tanks during the summer with the water at least 65°–68° F. (18°–20° C.).

Another system of classification is based on size: the miniature requiring water depth of 6–8 in. (15–20 cm.).

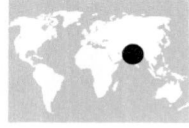

Water lilies can be planted directly into the mud at the bottom of natural ponds or lakes or in suitable containers that can easily be immersed, affording ease of feeding and cleaning the plants as well as for propagation and winter storage. The soil should be a mixture of 1 part argillaceous garden soil, 1 part humus, 1 part well-seasoned farmyard manure and 1 part wet river sand.

Propagation By rhizome division, cutting the tubers into pieces and putting them into 5-in. (12-cm.) pots with plain loam; then immerse in warm water. In 30 days repot and immerse in their flowering position. Seeds can be used.
Qualities Hardy. Easy to grow.

---

241 NYMPHAEA ODORATA William Aiton
Common name: Water lily

Family Nymphaeaceae.
Description The leaves of *N. odorata* are entire and subrotund-cordate, each with a very long petiole. The white flowers, which appear to rest lightly on the water, are short-lived.
Size of flower 3⅛–6 in. (8–15 cm.) in diameter.
Place of origin Eastern United States.
Flowering time Summer.
Cultivation and **Propagation** See *Nymphaea rubra*.
Qualities Hardy.

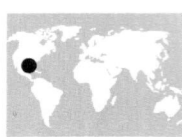

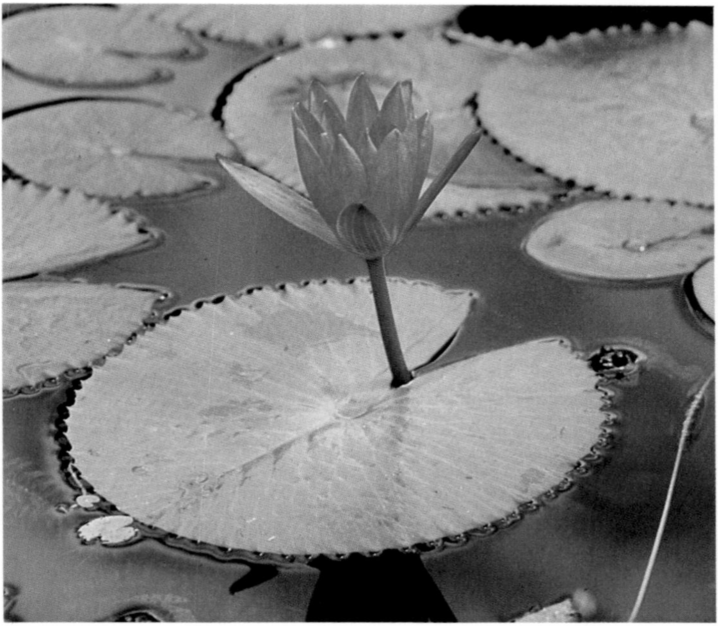

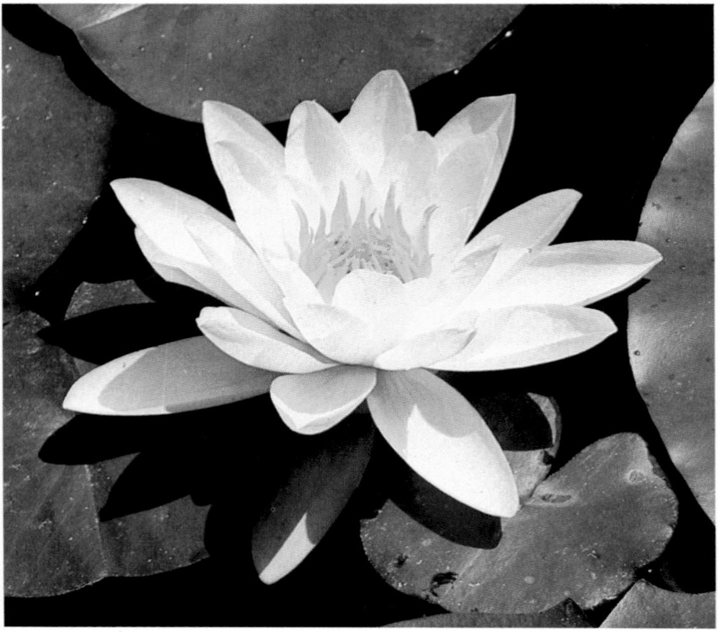

242 **NYMPHAEA x MARLIACEA** Henry Shoe-maker Conrad cv. ''Chromatella''
Common name: Water lily

Family Nymphaeaceae.
Description Glossy, subrotund-cordate leaves. Large flowers, appearing to rest on the surface of the water, with pale-yellow petals and bright-yellow stamens.
Size of flower 6–8 in. (15–20 cm.).
Place of origin A horticultural hybrid derived from crossing *Nymphaea alba* or *Nymphaea tuberosa* with *Nymphaea mexicana*.
Cultivation and **Propagation** See *Nymphaea rubra*.
Qualities Very Hardy.

---

243 **NYMPHAEA x LAYDEKERI** Hortorum
Common name: Water lily

Family Nymphaeaceae.
Description Reddish- or brownish-green, subrotund-cordate leaves. Medium-sized, bright-red flowers tinged with pink appear to rest on the surface of the water.
Size of flower 6–8 in. (15–20 cm.).
Place of origin A horticultural hybrid probably derived from the crossing of *Nymphaea alba* var. *rubra* with *Nymphaea tetragona*.
Flowering time Summer.
Cultivation and **Propagation** See *Nymphaea rubra*.
Qualities Hardy. Easy to grow.

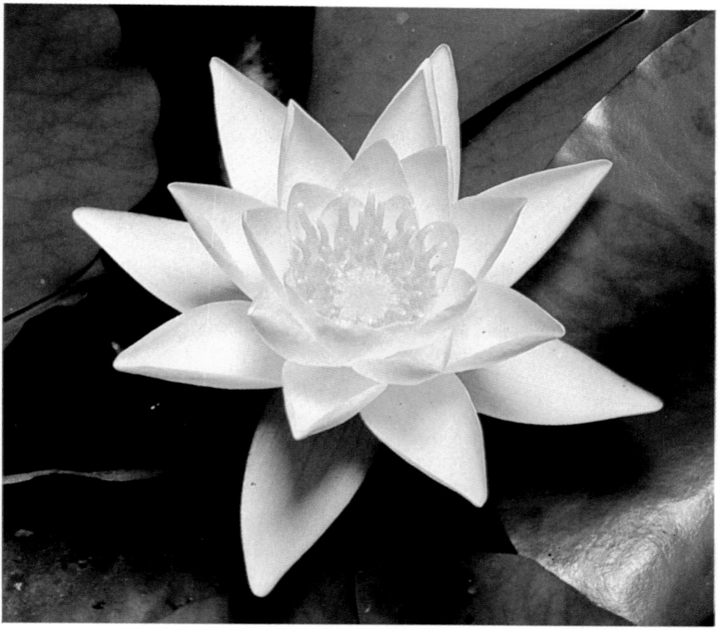

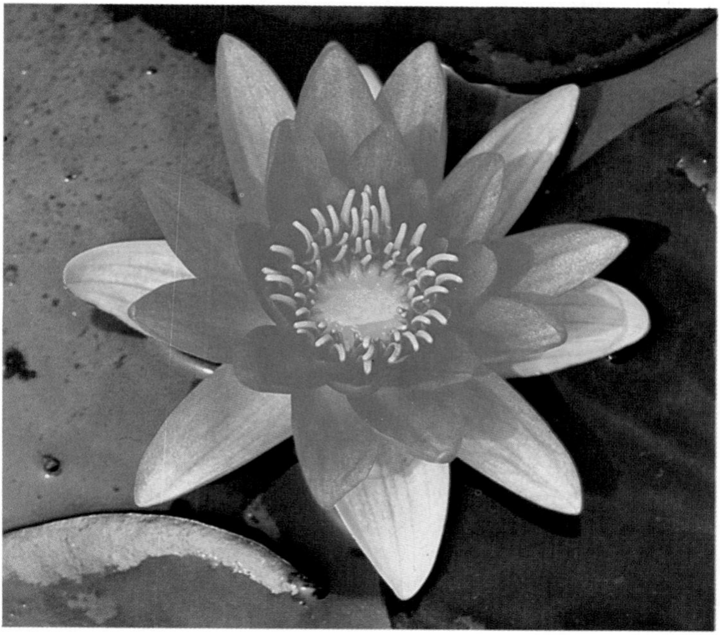

244 OTHONNA CARNOSA C. F. Lessing

Family Compositae.
Description A distinctive plant because of its pale-green, porcelainlike leaves and suffruticose habit, it lends itself particularly to gardens near the sea due to its resistance to a salty atmosphere. Its prostrate-diffuse stems are ligneous at the bottom, becoming carnose toward the top. Its rather thick, alternate leaves, which grow close together, are linear, spatulate and rotundate or obtuse. The solitary, bright-yellow flowers are in capitula and grow from the foliar axils.
Height of plant 1–4 ft. (0.30–1.20 m.).
Size of flower ¾–2 in. (2–5 cm.).
Place of origin South Africa.
Flowering time Spring–summer.
Cultivation A very sunny position or in full sun. Temperate climate. Can withstand a certain amount of cold. Prefers moist, rich, permeable, argillaceous-sandy soil. Appreciates periodic applications of organic manure. Although it can survive well in dry conditions, it responds to a little regular watering. Dead flowers should be removed and the plants given a light trim at the end of the season.
Propagation By cuttings taken in the spring–summer and rooted in a box under glass. By division.
Qualities Suitable for terraces, balconies. Hardy. Easy to grow.

245 OXALIS FLORIBUNDA Johann George Christian Lehmann

Family Oxalidaceae.
Description An acauline plant with a long, small, very proliferous bulb, this forms broad, dense clumps quite close to the ground. Its leaves consist of three to five obcordate, pilosect segments with a long, slender petiole. Flowers are borne in groups of ten to twelve in alternate umbels and are an attractive bright pink.
Height of plant 8–10 in. (20–25 cm.).
Size of flower ½–¾ in. (1.5–2 cm.).
Place of origin Chile.
Flowering time Spring–summer.
Cultivation A sunny position. Temperate climate. Cannot withstand very cold weather. Suitable for any warm, dry, well-aerated, acid or calcareous soil. It requires almost no watering at all and no particular attention. It often becomes invasive. It dislikes frosts and excessive dampness.
Propagation By bulbs in spring or autumn.
Qualities Suitable for balconies and terraces. Easy to grow.

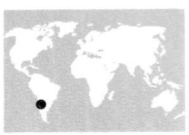

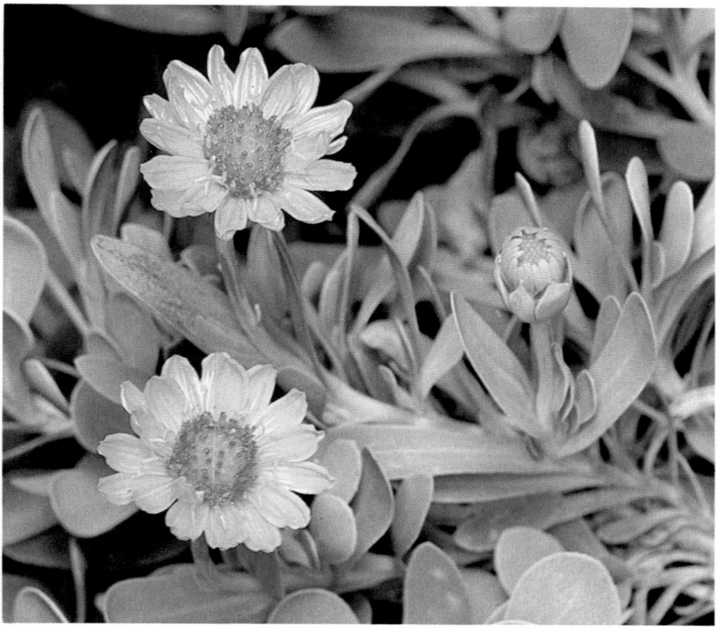

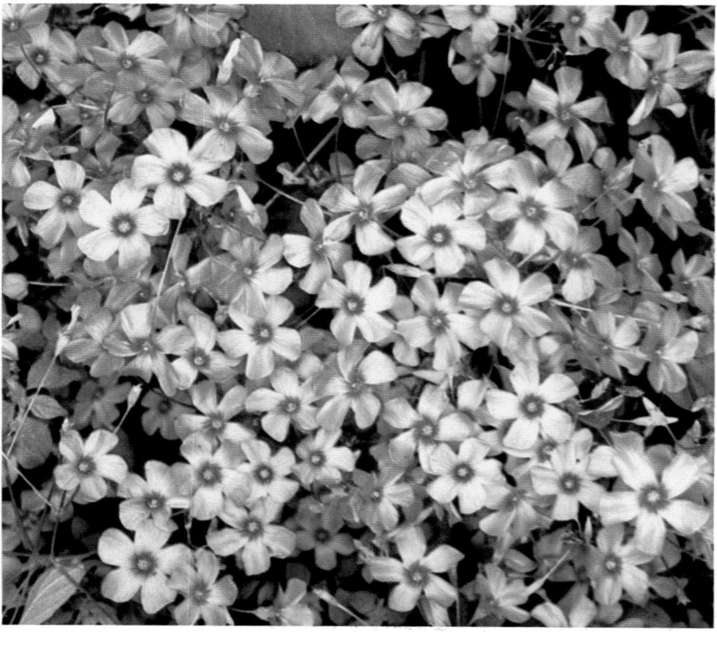

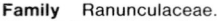

246 PAEONIA LACTIFLORA Peter Simon Pallas
cv. "Flore Pleno"
Syn.: *P. albiflora* Pallas cv. Common name: Peony

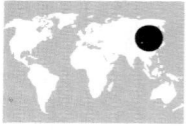

Family Ranunculaceae.
Description A cespitose herbaceous plant, particularly notable for very lovely flowers, with single or ramose herbaceous
stems. Its alternate leaves are ternate or biternate with oval-
lanceolate leaflets, often fused at the base. The large, fragrant
flowers are borne on long, upright peduncles with three to five
blooms to a stem. There are a great many attractive cultivars in
white and various shades of pink with double and semidouble
flowers.
Height of plant 2–2¾ ft. (60–85 cm.).
Size of flower 4–6 in. (10–15 cm.).
Place of origin China, Siberia, Mongolia.
Flowering time Late spring–early summer.
Cultivation A light to partially shady position. Temperate climate. Can withstand the cold well. Suitable to any ground that
is not too light or alkaline. Does not like to be transplanted.
Benefits from periodic seasonal surface dressings of or-
ganic/mineral fertilizers and from regular watering. All foliage
should be cut down to ground level in autumn, and in very cold
areas the crowns should be well mulched. Trouble-free.
Propagation By clump division in autumn. By root cuttings in
late winter or spring in a greenhouse.
Qualities Hardy. Easy to grow.

247 PAEONIA SUFFRUTICOSA Henry C. Andrews
cv. flore semipleno
Syns.: *P. arborea* James Donn, *P. moutan* John
Sims. Common name: Tree peony

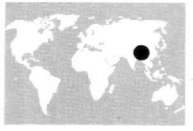

Family Ranunculaceae.
Description A cespitose, shrubby plant with few branches.
Its large, bipinnate leaves consist of three to five lobed leaflets;
they are reddish when young, becoming glaucous and pruin-
ose as the summer passes. The fragrant terminally borne flowers are very decorative, double, semidouble and single, according to the various cultivars. Wide range of colors and color
combinations. Free-flowering.
Height of plant 2½–5 ft. (0.80–1.50 m.).
Size of flower 4–10 in. (10–25 cm.).
Place of origin China and Tibet.
Flowering time Spring.
Cultivation A sunny or slightly shady position. Temperate
climate. Frost-resistant. Suited to any type of rich, moist soil,
even if fairly compact; if necessary, soil can be amended with
peat. A seasonal application of a general organic/mineral fer-
tilizer is beneficial, as is regular watering. Very slow-growing.
Does not usually require pruning. Trouble-free.
Propagation Graft onto pieces of root of *P. erbacea* and root
in a greenhouse at summer's end. By seed, but this is slow. By
division of rooted basal suckers in late winter.
Qualities Hardy. Easy to grow.

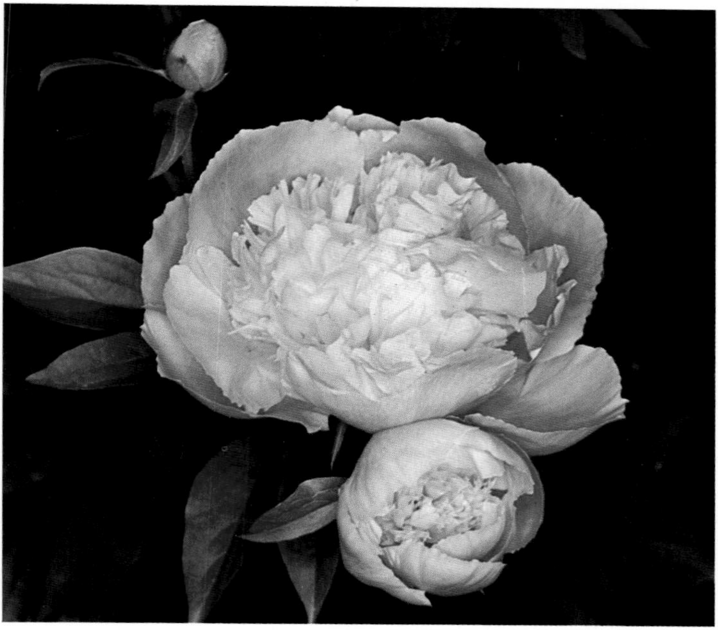

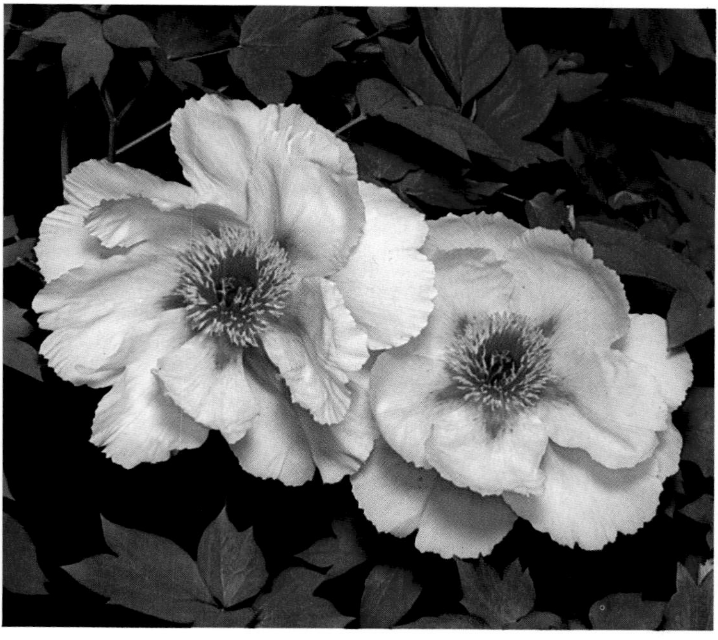

248 PAPAVER NUDICAULE Carolus Linnaeus
Common name: Iceland poppy

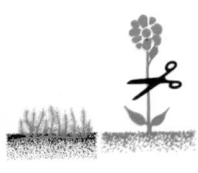

Family Papaveraceae.
Description A cespitose, herbaceous perennial that is often treated as an annual. Its erect, slender, pilose scapes rise in close formation from a basal rosette of pinnate-partite, glaucous-green leaves. Its large flowers, borne singly on long stems, have a corolla that may be golden-yellow, sulfur yellow, pink, scarlet, white or orange. Its flowering period is quite long.
Height of plant 12–16 in. (30–40 cm.).
Size of flower 1⅛–3⅛ in. (3–8 cm.).
Place of origin Subarctic regions of North America, Europe and Asia.
Flowering time Summer.

Cultivation A very bright position or in full sun. Cool-temperate climate. Grows in any kind of soil that is rich in lime and organic material, but not in soil that is argillaceous-siliceous. Likes regular watering and an occasional application of liquid fertilizer. Prone to root rot and distortion (rickets) due to unsuitable soil.

Propagation By spring sowing in flowering site. Does not like to be transplanted.
Qualities Very hardy. Easy to grow.

---

249 PAPAVER RHOEAS Carolus Linnaeus cv. "Flores Rhoeados"
Common Names: Shirley poppy, corn poppy

Family Papaveraceae.
Description A herbaceous annual plant. Its upright, ramified stem is pilose with a lactiferous line. Its leaves are pilose, with a basal rosette; the upper leaves are alternate, oblong and deeply pinnate with irregularly incised-lobate segments. Numerous singly borne, simple flowers with two green pilose concave sepals and four delicately textured scarlet petals with black markings at the base. Also semidouble and double varieties. The ovary consists of a capsule surrounded by numerous stamens with black anthers. Young plants make an excellent vegetable and their essence is used medicinally as a sedative and to induce sleep.

Height of plant 1¼–3 ft. (40–90 cm.).
Size of flower 2–3 inches (5–9 cm.).
Place of origin Temperate Europe.
Flowering time Spring–summer.

Cultivation A very sunny position. Temperate climate. Fairly frost-resistant. Likes open, cool soil with a little organic manure. Moderate watering. Pick faded flowers to prolong bloom. Remove plants immediately after flowering.
Pests and diseases Greenfly and blackfly; oidium if ground is too wet.

Propagation By autumn sowing, directly in flowering site, in mild climates; early spring sowing elsewhere.
Qualities Hardy. Very easy to grow.

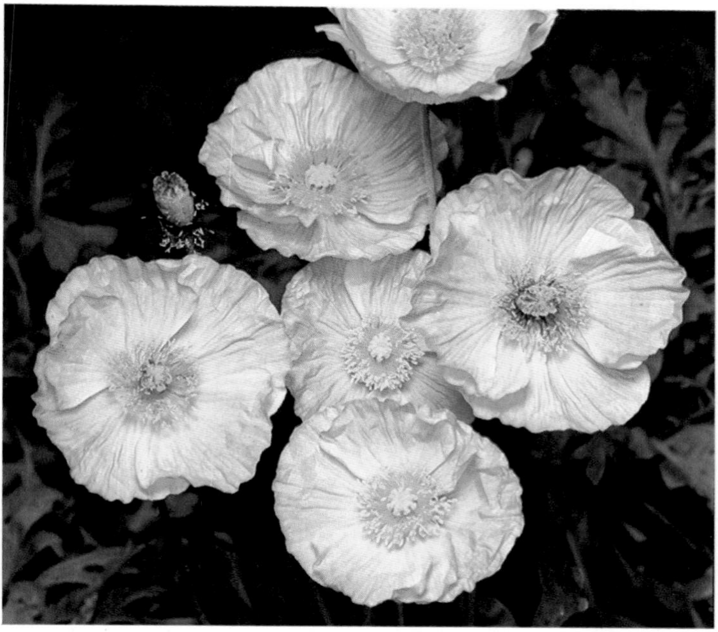

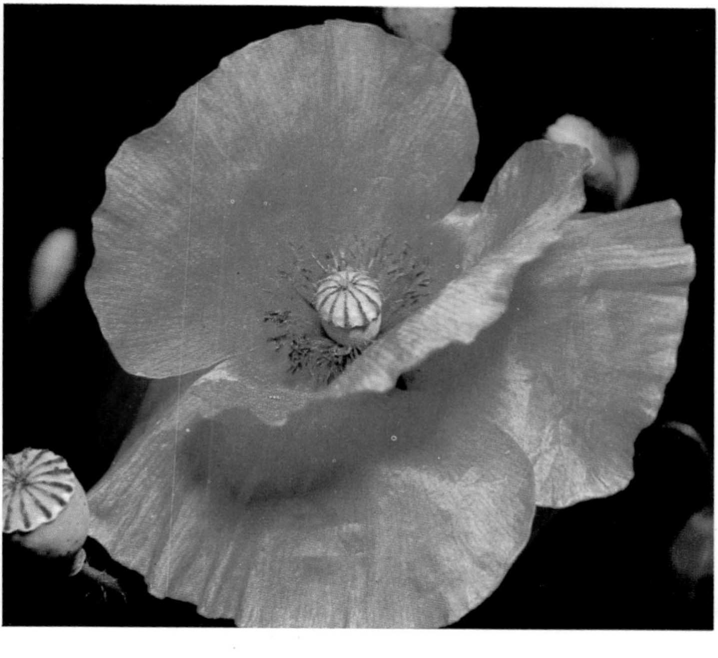

250 PASSIFLORA COERULEA Carolus Linnaeus
Common name: Passion flower

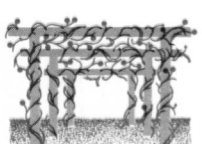

Family   Passifloraceae.
Description   A climbing, evergreen perennial. Its numerous slender branches are furnished with long tendrils with which it clings to any support provided. Its leaves are palmatisect with five to seven oblong lobes. The axillary flowers are borne on long peduncles and have a very distinctive form: the rayed petals have a corona formed of numerous filiform appendages in the shape of a star and shaded from deep purplish-blue to white. The fruits are like small orange eggs.
Height of plant   13–20 in. (4–6 m.).
Size of flower   3⅛–4 in. (8–10 cm.).
Place of origin   Brazil, Peru, Argentina.
Flowering time   Summer–autumn.
Cultivation   Full sun. Temperate climate. Survives some frost but top growth usually dies back and new growth emerges from the base in the spring. Suited to almost any type of garden soil, preferably of only average fertility and moderately manured, since in ground that is overrich the plant produces too many leaves in relation to the flowers. The long growth can be shortened by about one-third, but the short shoots should not be pruned because they produce the flowers. Regular watering.
Propagation   By spring sowing in a coldframe. By layering and by cuttings taken in the spring–summer.
Qualities   Suitable for balconies. Hardy. Easy to grow.

---

251 PASSIFLORA QUADRANGULARIS Carolus Linnaeus
Common names: Passion flower, apple ball

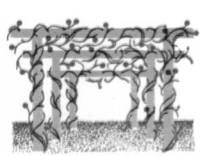

Family   Passifloraceae.
Description   A perennial that is evergreen in temperate zones. Its quadrangular, sarmentose stems are furnished with cirri that cling to any available support. Its alternate leaves are ovate-oblong with a short petiole. The solitary fragrant flowers, which are showy both in form and color, grow from the foliar axils. The elongated calyx opens into a quinquelobate cup, a double or triple corona and five petals. Fruits are ovoidal with a thick skin; there are many seeds in the edible pulp.
Height of plant   23–26 ft. (7–8 m.).
Size of flower   3⅛–4 in. (8–10 cm.).
Place of origin   Unknown but probably tropical America.
Flowering time   Summer.
Cultivation   A sunny to partially shaded sheltered position, perhaps against a wall. Warm-temperate climate. Suited to any kind of rich, open, well-manured soil. Plentiful watering during the summer. Light pruning after fruiting.
Propagation   By autumn or spring sowing in pots in a temperate greenhouse. By cuttings taken in autumn or spring–summer and rooted in a greenhouse.
Qualities   Half-hardy. Relatively easy to grow.

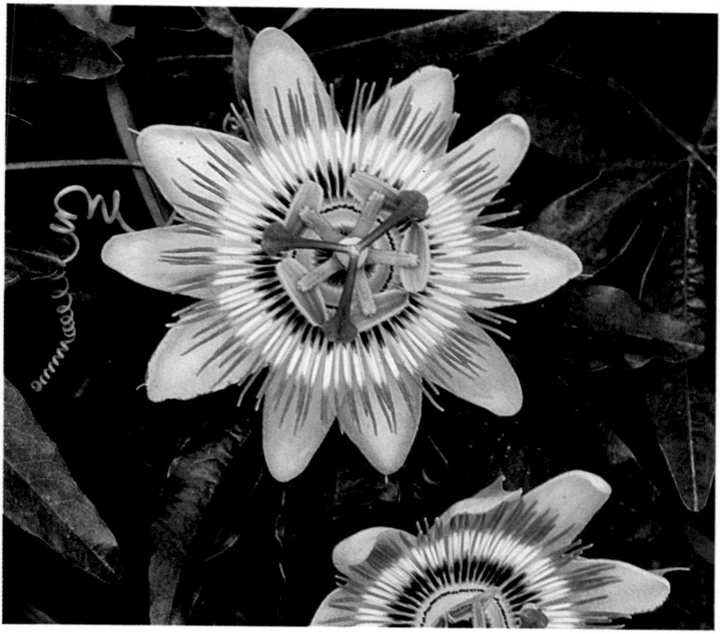

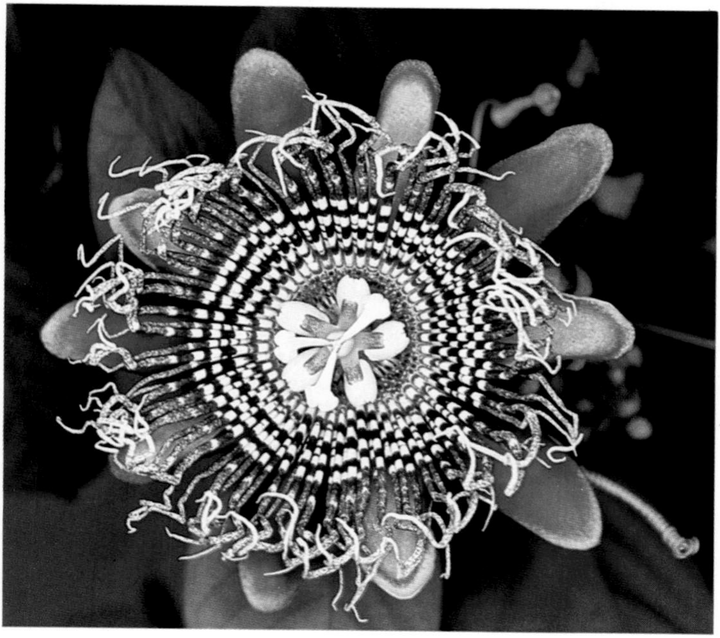

252 PAULOWNIA TOMENTOSA (Carl Peter Thunberg) Ernst Gottlieb Steudel

Syn.: *P. imperialis* Philipp Franz von Siebold and Joseph Gerhard Zuccarini. Common name: Empress tree

Family Bignoniaceae.
Description A deciduous tree of upright, spreading habit and a globose head. The bark on trunk and branches is a blackish hue. Its large, alternate leaves are cordate, acute, entire or slightly lobate, with long petioles. Its sizable flowers are borne in erect racemes that open in early spring before the leaves unfurl. The tubulous corolla is asymmetrical, like that of the catalpa.

Height of plant 16–45 ft. (5–13.7 m.).
Size of flower 1½–2⅜ in. (4–6 cm.).
Place of origin China.
Flowering time Early spring.
Cultivation Full sun. Temperate climate. Frost-resistant. Suited to any type of moist, open soil, even if only moderately fertile. No particular care is usually necessary and it is inadvisable to prune the tree as the branches are very sappy inside and do not heal easily.

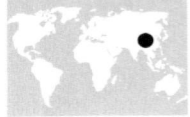

Propagation By spring sowing in a sheltered seedbed outdoors. By root cuttings in a propagating frame in a warm greenhouse or in pans in a coldframe.
Qualities Hardy. Easy to grow.

253 PELARGONIUM ZONALE C. L. L'Héritier de Brutelle

Common name: Zonal geranium

Family Geraniaceae.
Description A perennial generally grown as an annual. The original species is now hard to find since it has been supplanted by many hybrid forms. Through innumerable crossings, it is now known as *P. x hortorum*. It has a shrubby stem with carnosect ramifications. Its alternate leaves are orbicular-reniform, crenulate and velutinate with a blackish-green or bronze medial zone. Its single, varicolored flowers are borne in dense, semi-globose umbels. Aromatically scented.

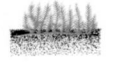

Height of plant 1½–5 ft. (0.50–1.50 m.).
Size of flower 1⅛ in. (3 cm.).
Place of origin South Africa.
Flowering time Spring, summer, autumn.

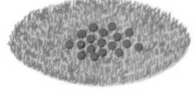

Cultivation In full sun or a very bright position. Warm-temperate climate. Frost-tender. In other than warm zones, it must be kept under cover, in a frost-free place, during the winter. Suited to any type of soil, it prefers good, well-aerated ground that is fertile, rich and moist. Regular watering in the summer but less frequent in the autumn and winter. Renew every two or three years. Remove dead growth in spring, shorten long branches. Diseases: rust, leaf spot, fungus diseases.

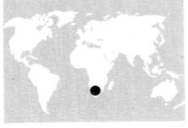

Propagation By cuttings or late winter sowing of seeds under glass. Pot on twice before planting outdoors.
Qualities Suitable for terraces, balconies. Hardy in a warm climate, otherwise tender. Easy to grow.

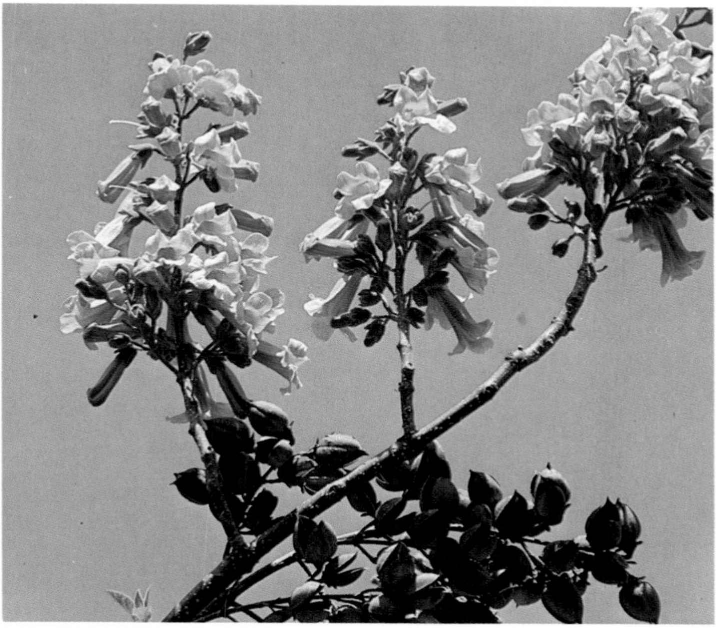

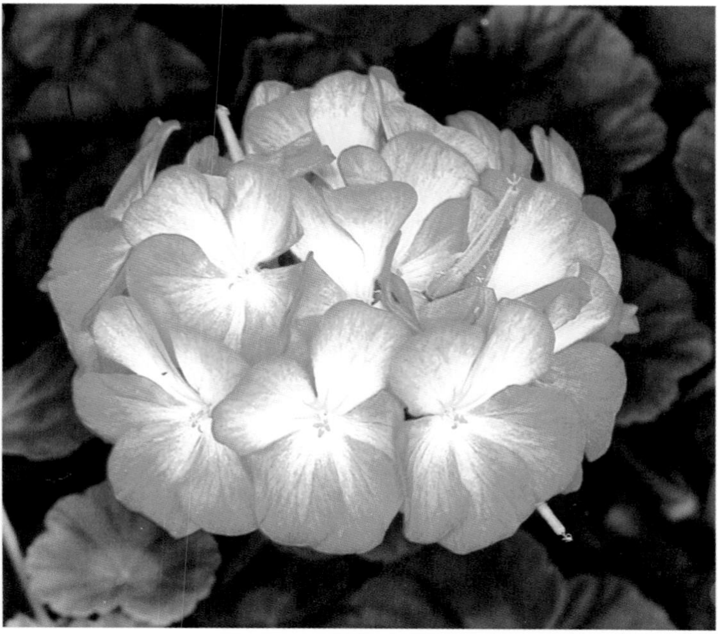

254 PELARGONIUM x DOMESTICUM Hortorum

Syns.: *P. macranthum* Hortorum, *P. x grandiflorum* Hortorum. Common names: Regal geranium, Lady Washington geranium, Martha Washington geranium

Family   Geraniaceae.

Description   A suffruticose evergreen usually grown as a pot plant. Its upright stems are woody and lightly ramified; rather loose habit. Its dark-green, alternate leaves are peltate-reniform, dentate and consistent, usually trilobed and with a long petiole. The flowers are borne in spreading umbels. Cultivar colors are white, purple and shades of pink.

Height of plant   3 ft. (0.9 m.).

Size of flower   1½–2⅜ in. (4–6 cm.).

Place of origin   Hybrids of horticultural origin, derived from crossings of *P. cucullatum, P. angulosum* and *P. grandiflorum.*

Flowering time   Spring–summer.

Cultivation   Treat as an annual in full sun or very bright position. Temperate climate. Cannot withstand the cold. Requires overwintering in a temperate greenhouse. It likes argillaceous soil mixed with good woodland mold, well-rotted manure and a little sand. Regular watering alternated with liquid feeding. Growing tip and laterals can be pinched out in the early stages of development to encourage a more compact formation. Subject to rust and various fungus diseases.

Propagation   By cuttings taken in the summer or early spring and rooted in a sheltered place in a coldframe or greenhouse.

Qualities   Suitable for balconies, terraces. Hardy in a warm region, otherwise tender. Easy to grow.

Opposite: two cultivated varieties of Pelargonium x domesticum. *Above,* Pelargonium macranthum *or five-spotted geranium; this is a sturdy, suffruticose evergreen with erect, rather sparse, ramifications. Its alternate, peltate-reniform leaves are tougher and rougher-textured than in other varieties. The flowers are large and characterized by five dark blotches; it blooms abundantly but does not bloom twice in one season. Below,* Pelargonium x grandiflorum, *butterfly pelargonium—a favorite with commercial growers. It is a suffruticose plant with a rather ligneous, sub-articulate, nodose stem; its alternate leaves are roughly peltate-reniform, dentate, lobate and pubescent; its numerous large flowers resemble butterflies and are borne in axillary cymes. This type of geranium blooms only once during the season.*

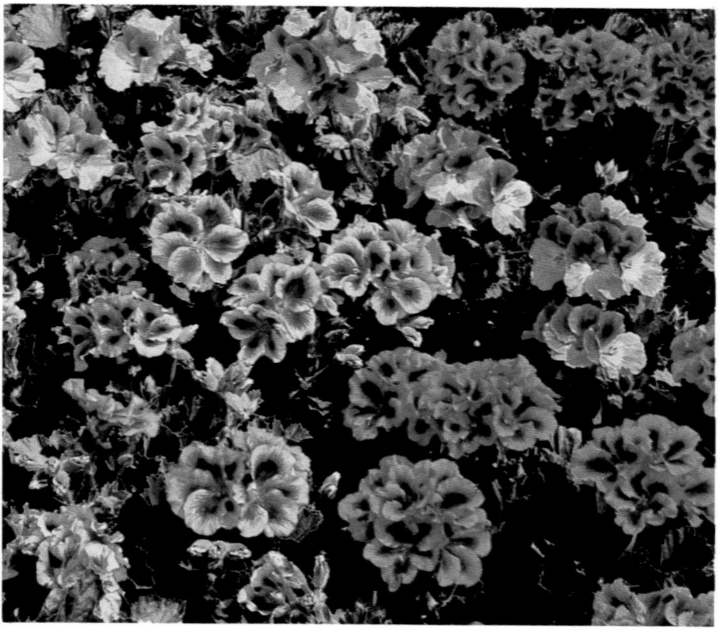

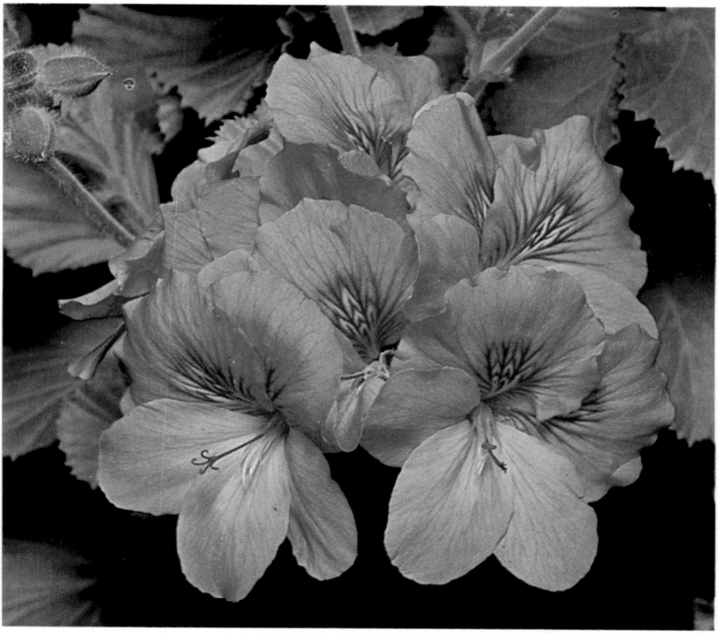

255 PELARGONIUM x HORTORUM L. H. Bailey

Syn.: *Pelargonium zonale* hybrid. Common names: Zonal geranium, garden geranium

Family Geraniaceae.

Description Innumerable species derived from crossings of *P. zonale* x *P. inquinans* are included in this category. Further divisions: according to leaf color—silver, tricolor, gold, bronze, etc.; height—tall, medium, dwarf, miniature; flower—single, semidouble, double. Generally treated as annuals and can be grown from seed as annuals; the cv. "Carefree," for instance, is in flower within five months of sowing. Flower colors include white, salmon pink, scarlet, rose-pink.

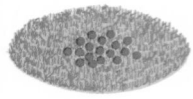

Height of plant 12–32 in. (30–80 cm.).

Size of flower ¾–1½ in. (2–4 cm.).

Place of origin A horticultural hybrid.

Flowering time Spring, summer, autumn.

Cultivation A very bright position or in full sun. Warm-temperate climate. In fairly cold regions, overwinter in a frost-free place. Suited to any type of ground but prefers good, rich garden soil with a general organic/mineral fertilizer. Regular watering in the summer but reduced during the autumn and winter. Can be lightly cut back in spring. Renew in second or third year. Subject to fungus diseases.

Propagation By cuttings taken in the winter for summer bloom and in the summer for winter bloom. By scarified seed sown in late winter under glass.

Qualities Suitable for terraces, balconies. Easy to grow.

---

256 PELARGONIUM PELTATUM William Aiton cv. "Rouletta"

Syn.: *P. hederaefolium* Hortorum. Common name: Ivy geranium

Family Geraniaceae.

Description Widely grown for its floriferousness, ivy geranium has a prostrate-ascendent stem with spreading, articulate, nodose, fragile ramifications. Its alternate leaves are peltate-reniform, angular, quinquelobate and carnosect. Its numerous flowers are grouped in umbels of varying compactness, according to the various species, on very long peduncles. There are many cultivars in colors including white, pink, red, purple, striate, with single, semidouble or double flowers.

Height of plant 3 ft. (0.9 m.).

Size of flower 1⅛–2 in. (3–5 cm.).

Place of origin South Africa.

Flowering time Spring–summer. Sporadically otherwise.

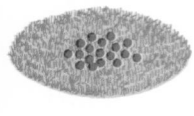

Cultivation Treat as an annual in full sun or a very bright position. Temperate climate. Limited resistance to cold; Overwinter under cover in frost-prone areas. Prefers rich, moist garden soil or a mixture of argillaceous woodland mold enriched with well-rotted manure and a little sand. Liquid fertilizer during the early growing period. Trim lightly after flowering. Subject to fungus diseases.

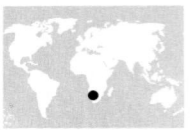

Propagation By cuttings taken in spring–summer and rooted under glass in a frame.

Qualities Suitable for terraces, balconies. Easy to grow.

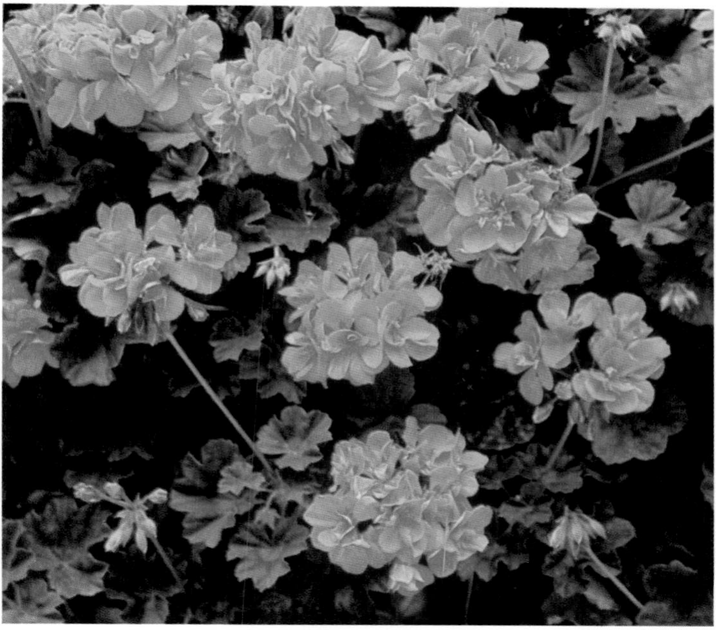

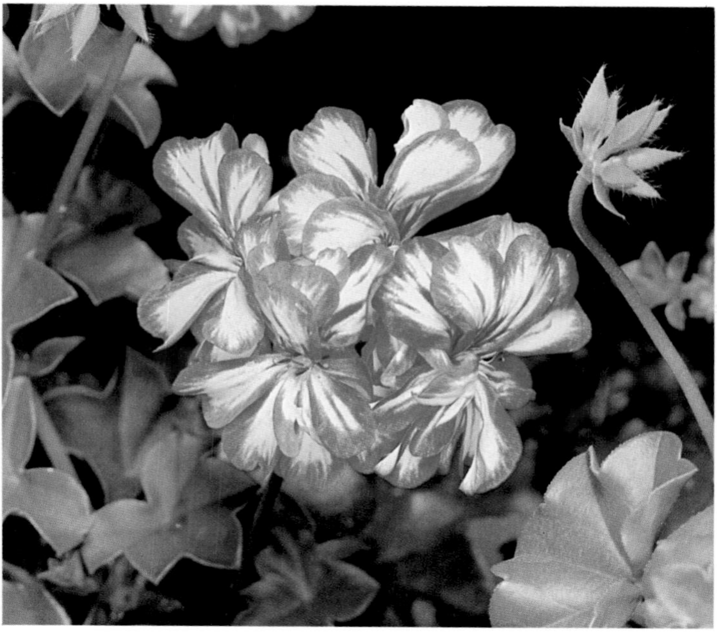

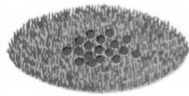

257 **PETUNIA x HYBRIDA** Hortorum
Common name: Petunia

Family Solanaceae.
Description A herbaceous perennial grown as an annual. Upright, herbaceous, ramified, glandular stems. Alternate, oval or oblong, obtuse, rather thick leaves with an unpleasant smell. Its numerous fragrant flowers are axillary with a flaring-infundibuliform corolla. This hybrid originates from crossings derived from the species *P. axillaris*, *P. inflata* and *P. violacea*. There are numerous horticultural varieties with flowers of various colors and different habits. These consist of four main groups—"multiflora," which includes those with a bicolor corolla like a pink-and-white star; "grandiflora," in which the flowers are larger (3–4 inches/7.5–10 cm. in diameter) and sometimes double with ruffled petals; "nana compacta" covers the dwarf (6 in./15 cm. high) varieties; and "pendula" includes the long and trailing varieties.
Height of plant 1–2 ft. (30–60 cm.).
Size of flower 2⅜–6 in. (6–15 cm.).
Place of origin A hybrid of horticultural origin.
Flowering time Summer–autumn.
Cultivation A sunny position. Temperate climate. Does not like the cold and prefers an open, sheltered site. Suited to any type of light, moist, rich, sandy garden soil. Plenty of organic material should be worked into the ground before planting and applications of liquid fertilizer given during the growing period. It is sometimes necessary to pinch out the tops to encourage side growth. Supports are often required. Plentiful watering. Plants can be pulled up after flowering. Remove the dead flowers to ensure continued bloom. Pests: frequently attacked by red spider mites and aphids.
Propagation By late winter–early spring sowing in pans under glass. When ready, seedlings can be pricked off into seed boxes and put in a coldframe for planting out when the plantlets have hardened off and are sufficiently bushy.
Qualities Suitable for balconies, terraces. Half-hardy. Very easy to grow.

Opposite: two cultivars of Petunia x hybrida. Above, small-flowered petunia, dwarf multiflora cv. "Satellite"; below, medium large-flowered petunia cv. "Grandiflora."

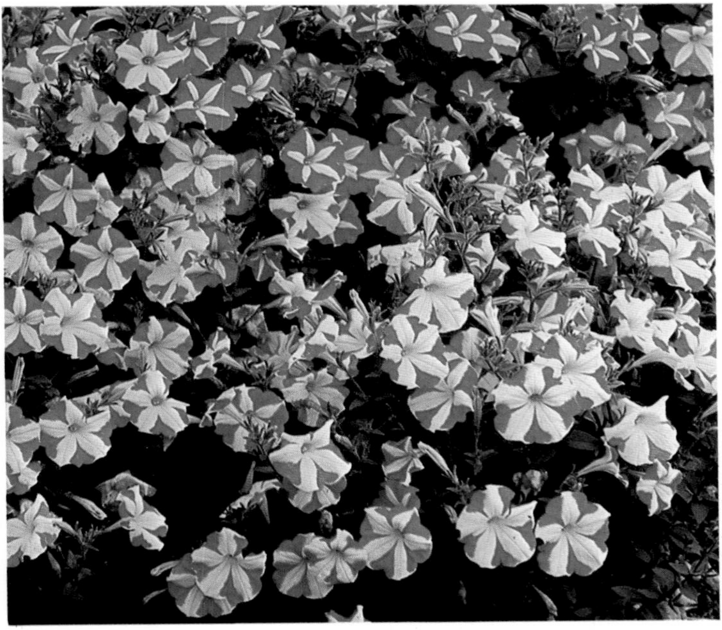

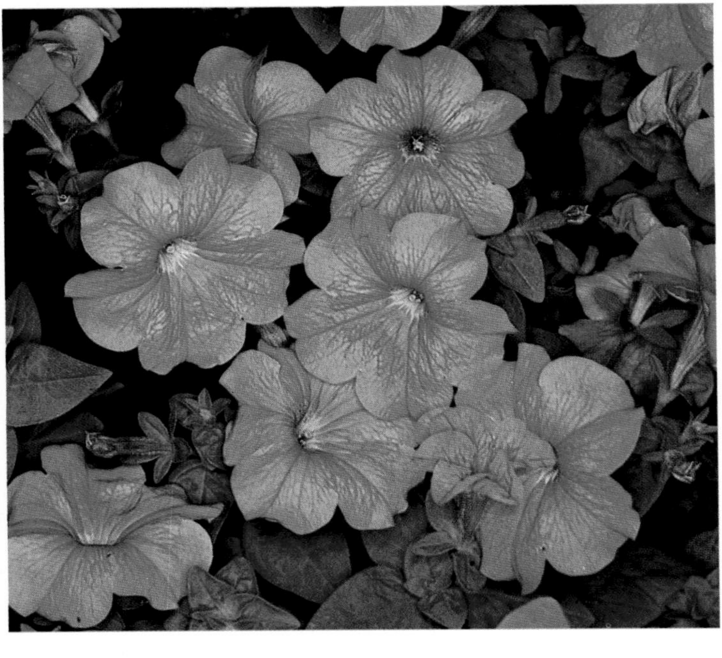

258 PEN(T)STEMON x GLOXINOIDES Hortorum

Syn.: *P. hartwegii* George Bentham cv. Common name: Beard-tongue

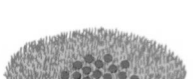

Family Scrophulariaceae.

Description A short-lived, herbaceous perennial with a bushy appearance. It has an upright stem with bright-green, lanceolate or ovate, opposite leaves, sometimes retroflexed. Its numerous flowers are borne in large, elongated panicles on erect peduncles that lean slightly downward. The tubulous corolla is digitate bilabiate, rather like a gloxinia, in a range of colors including red, pink, purple, white, pale blue, etc.

Height of plant 2–3 ft. (60–90 cm.).

Size of flower 1½–2 in. (4–5 cm.).

Place of origin A horticultural hybrid derived from *P. hartwegii* or from crossings between *P. hartwegii* and *P. cobaea*. (*P. hartwegii* is a rare species originating from Mexico.)

Flowering time Summer.

Cultivation A sunny, sheltered position. Temperate climate. Frost-tender. Likes a fertile, organically enriched soil. Requires watering during dry spells. Advisable to renew the plants every two years. Cut flowered branches back as soon as the blooms fade. Plants should be cut down to ground level in the autumn and given a good protective mulch.

Propagation By division of the crown in spring or autumn. Also by seed sowing in a nursery bed in spring or autumn.

Qualities Very hardy in a warm-temperate climate. Easy to grow.

259 PHILADELPHUS GRANDIFLORUS Karl Ludwig Willdenow

Syn.: *Ph. inodorus* Carolus Linnaeus var. *grandiflorus* (Willdenow) Asa Gray. Common name: Mock orange

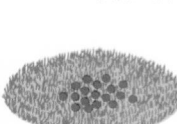

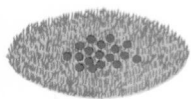

Family Saxifragaceae.

Description A deciduous shrub with numerous fragile chestnut-colored branches springing from the base; they lose their bark in their second year. Its leaves are ovate-elliptical, acuminate, dentate, rounded at the base and pubescent along the central rib. The flowers are larger than in the other species, growing singly or in groups of two or three at the ends of short lateral branches. This is undoubtedly one of the best of the mock oranges being grown as a garden plant, although it has no perfume.

Height of plant 5–6½ ft. (1.50–2 m.).

Size of flower 1¾–2 in. (4.5–5 cm.).

Place of origin Southeastern United States.

Flowering time Early summer.

Cultivation A sunny to partially shaded position. Temperate climate. Frost-resistant. Suited to any type of soil that is fairly heavy, argillaceous, rich and moist. Regular watering. Periodic applications of organic/mineral fertilizer. Remove old, weak or distorted wood in late autumn. Usually trouble-free.

Propagation By herbaceous and semi-hardwood cuttings taken in the spring–summer and rooted in a coldframe.

Qualities Hardy. Easy to grow.

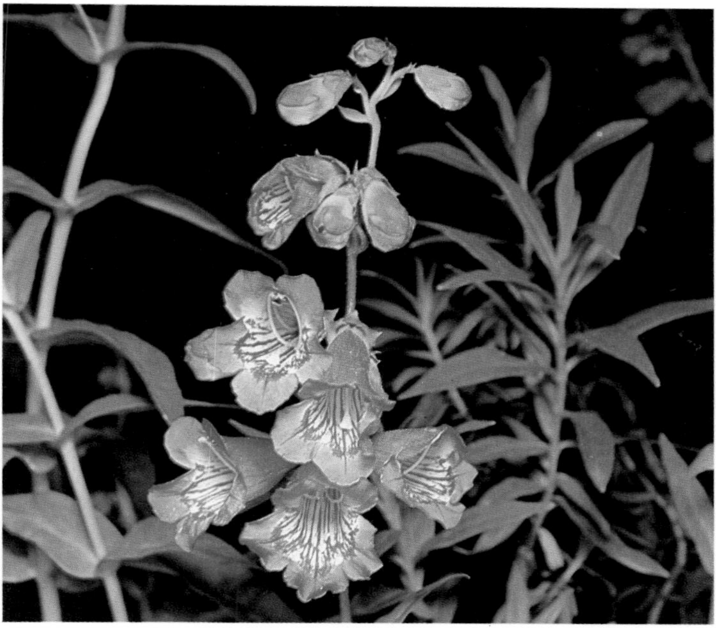

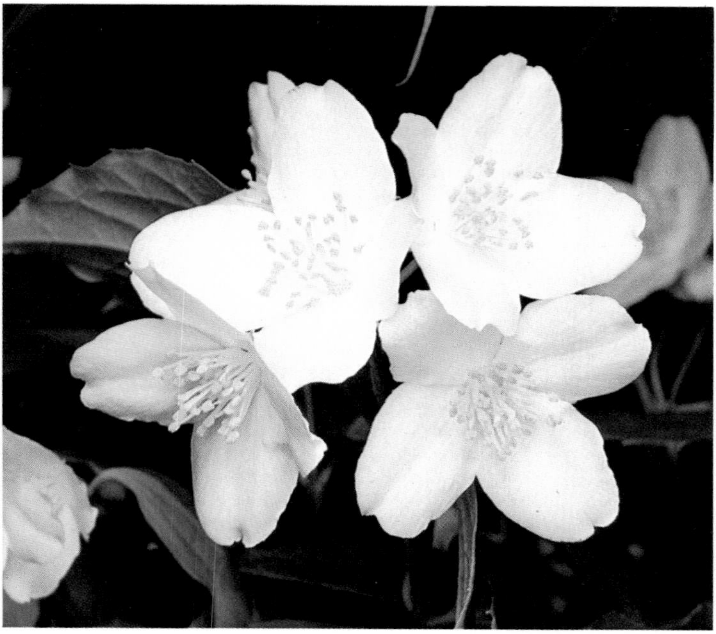

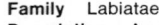

260 PHLOMIS FRUTICOSA Carolus Linnaeus
Common name: Jerusalem sage

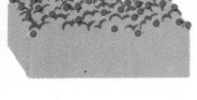

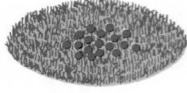

Family Labiatae.
Description A very hardy shrub, it is undemanding and most adaptable. Its numerous ramifications form dense bushes. Its silvery-whitish-green, opposite leaves are ovate-elliptical, subcordate and pubescent. Without its flowers, it could easily be mistaken for *Salvia officinalis*. Its numerous large flowers are bilabiate and grouped in spaced-out whorls. It makes a fine display and has a long flowering period.
Height of plant 3 ft. 4 in.–5 ft. (1–1.50 m.).
Size of flower 1 ⅛–1 ½ in. (3–4 cm.).
Place of origin Mediterranean region.
Flowering time Summer.
Cultivation A sunny or slightly shady position. Temperate climate. Fairly frost-resistant. Suited to any kind of soil, even if stony and dry or near the sea. Requires no particular attention but appreciates being watered during very dry spells. Flowered branches should be shortened in the winter. Trouble-free.
Propagation By semi-herbaceous cuttings taken in summer–autumn. By spring sowing in a coldframe.
Qualities Hardy. Easy to grow.

261 PHLOX DRUMMONDII Joseph Dalton Hooker
Common name: Annual phlox

Family Polemoniaceae.
Description A herbaceous annual with dichotomous ramifications and upright stems. Its leaves are sessile, the lower ones opposite and the upper ones alternate, oblong-lanceolate. Its numerous fragrant flowers are borne in lax capitaliform cymes. The corolla is tubulous at first, expanding into a flat, rotate form consisting of five broad, ovate lobes of red, purple, crimson or white.
Height of plant 10–20 in. (25–50 cm.).
Size of flower ¾–1 ⅛ in. (2–3 cm.).
Place of origin Texas.
Flowering time Summer–autumn.
Cultivation A sunny, sheltered position. Temperate climate. Cannot withstand heavy frosts. Likes a light, rich soil with a low clay content, enriched with plenty of organic material; if compact, the soil should be amended with heath mold and sand when preparing the ground. Plentiful watering. Pests and diseases: slugs on young plants and eelworms (stem and bulb types); chlorosis in unsuitable soil, and various rots.
Propagation By spring sowing in pans under glass or directly in the garden.
Qualities Suitable for balconies, terraces. Half-hardy. Rather demanding to grow.

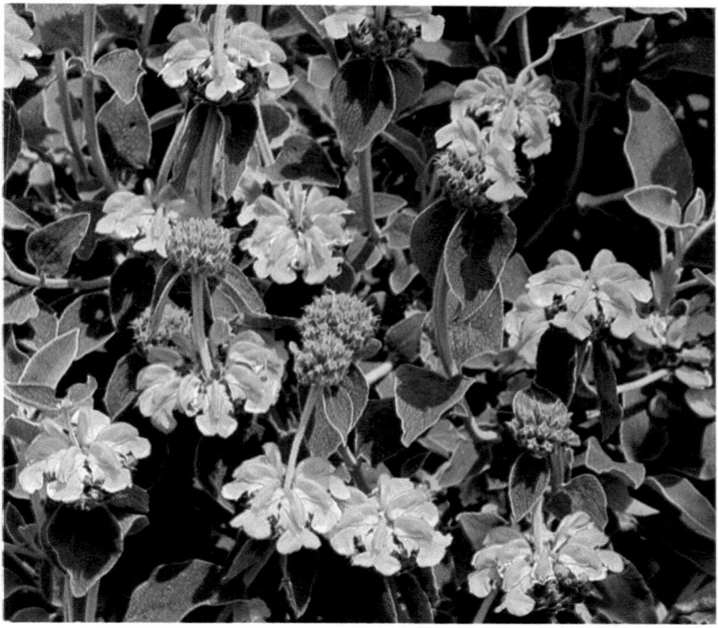

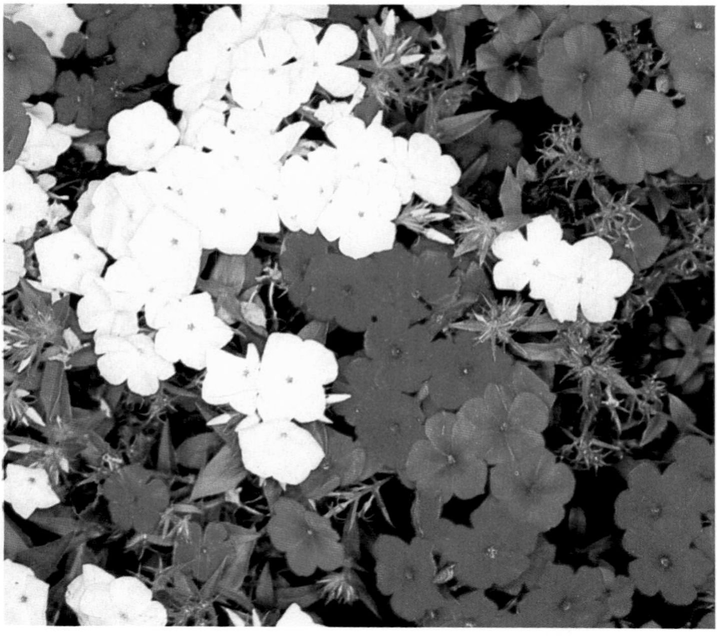

262 PHLOX PANICULATA Carolus Linnaeus
Syns.: *P. decussata* (Lyons) Frederick T. Pursh, *P. scabra* Robert Sweet. Common name: Perennial phlox

Family Polemoniaceae.
Description A herbaceous perennial with upright, slender, solitary stems. Its leaves are about 3⅛–4 in. (8–10 cm.) long, ternate or opposite and oblong-lanceolate. The fragrant flowers are grouped in dense terminal panicles. Each tubulous corolla has five expanded lobes. Color range includes pink, violet-purple, white and salmon-orange.
Height of plant 10–14 in. (25–35 cm.).
Size of flower ¾–1⅛ in. (2–3 cm.).
Place of origin Eastern United States.
Flowering time Summer–autumn.

Cultivation A sunny position. Temperate climate. Rich soil with low clay content mixed with peat and sand. Plenty of organic material should be worked into the ground prior to planting and liquid fertilizer applied during growing period. Plentiful watering. Cut down to ground level in the winter and protect with mulch. Pests and diseases: young plants vulnerable to slugs, stem and bulb eelworms; chlorosis, stem and leaf distortion (rickets).

Propagation By late-spring sowing in a nursery bed and planting out in the spring. But propagation by spring division of clumps is preferable. Also by cuttings taken in the spring, but this method is seldom used.
Qualities Half-hardy to hardy. Very easy to grow.

263 PHLOX SUBULATA Carolus Linnaeus
Syns.: *P. setacea* Linnaeus, *P. frondosa* Hortorum. Common name: Moss pink

Family Polemoniaceae.
Description A small, dense, subshrubby perennial with ascending or descending ramifications. Its evergreen leaves are ciliate and linear-acuminate or subulate. Its numerous flowers have a tubulous corolla with five open, rotate lobes. Colors include purple, pink, lavender-blue and white, according to the variety.

Height of plant 2–4¾ in. (5–12 cm.).
Size of flower 1–1⅛ in. (2.5–3 cm.).
Place of origin Eastern United States.
Flowering time Spring.

Cultivation A very sunny position. Temperate climate. Frost-tender. Suited to any type of good garden soil that is naturally humus-rich or amended with heath mold and peat, enriched with well-rotted manure. Regular watering. After flowering, the cymes that carried the blooms should be lightly trimmed.
Propagation By cuttings or clump division in spring.
Qualities Very hardy. Fairly easy to grow.

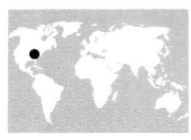

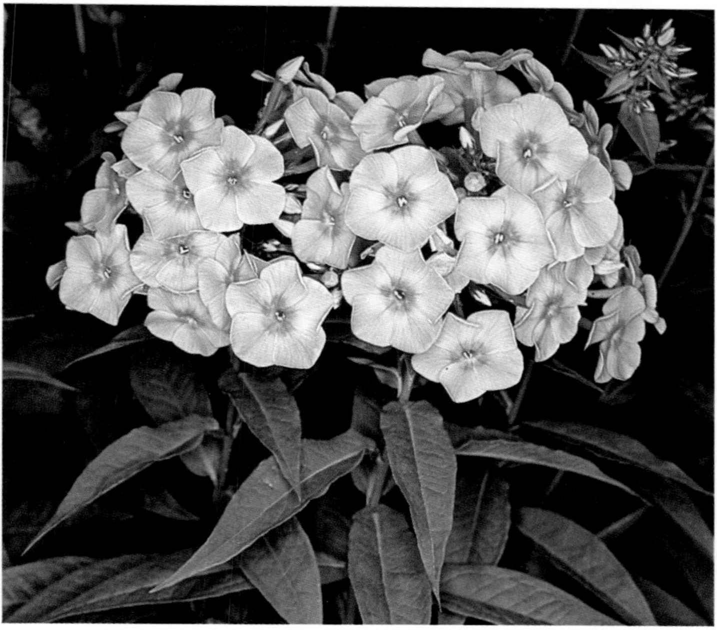

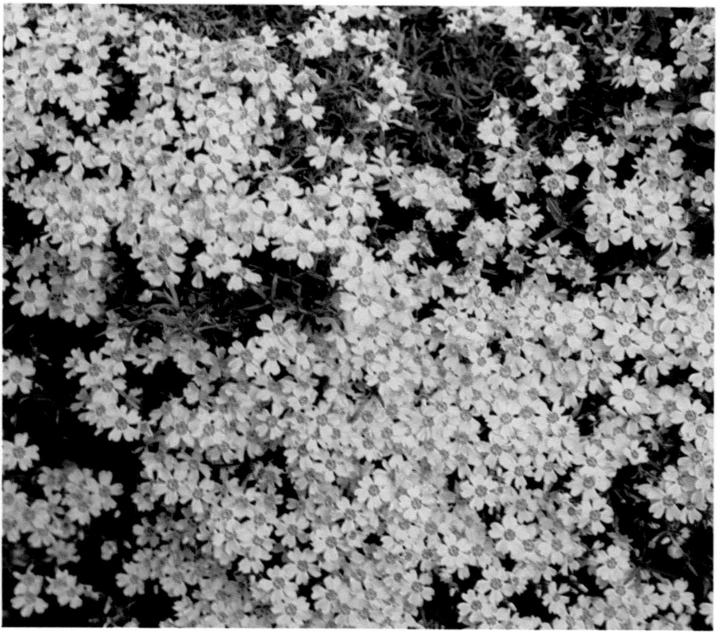

264 PHOTINIA SERRULATA John Lindley
Syn.: *Crataegus glabra* Conrad Loddiges

Family Rosaceae.
Description An arborescent shrub with strong, spreading branches. Its alternate, evergreen leaves are oblong-lanceolate, serrulate and coriaceous; when young they are a glowing red tinged with bronze, and dark green during the intermediate periods. The numerous white, rather unpleasant-smelling flowers are borne in large corymbs. Bright-red berries in the autumn.
Height of plant 10–30 ft. (3–9.1 m.).
Size of flower ¼–⅜ in. (0.6–0.8 cm.).
Place of origin Japan and China.
Flowering time Spring.
Cultivation A bright position, even in full sun. Temperate climate. Frost-resistant. Likes deep, heavy soil, even argillaceous, provided it is moist. Periodic applications of general organic/mineral fertilizers. Does not usually require watering apart from a little in a dry summer. After an initial shaping, it is better to leave this plant to grow naturally. Diseases: sometimes subject to oidium and other fungus diseases.
Propagation By spring sowing, but this is a very slow method. Cuttings and grafting are more advisable.
Qualities Hardy in a mild zone. Easy to grow.

265 PHYLICA ERICOIDES Carolus Linnaeus

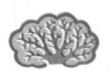

Family Rhamnaceae.
Description A bushy shrub, rather like the *Erica* with which it has much in common culturally. It has numerous slender, whitish stems and a great many small, alternate, sessile, linear-acuminate leaves with a glossy upper surface and a whitish lower one. Its numerous fragrant flowers are borne in dense terminal capitula, each having a lanate calyx. It is a useful plant, since it comes into bloom during the autumn–winter period when most flowers have finished.
Height of plant 20–40 in. (0.50–1 m.).
Size of flower ¾–1⅛ in. (2–3 cm.) each capitulum.
Place of origin South Africa.
Flowering time Autumn–winter.
Cultivation A semi-shaded position. Warm-temperate climate. Frost-tender. Prefers rich, moist, argillaceous-sandy soil that has been well manured. Regular watering. This plant can be shaped if it is trimmed regularly after flowering. Very suitable as a pot plant. Pests and diseases: fungus diseases in damp sites.
Propagation By cuttings or layering in spring–summer. Cuttings can also be taken in autumn and rooted in a warm greenhouse.
Qualities Tender. Very easy to grow.

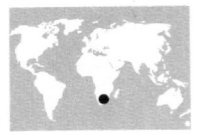

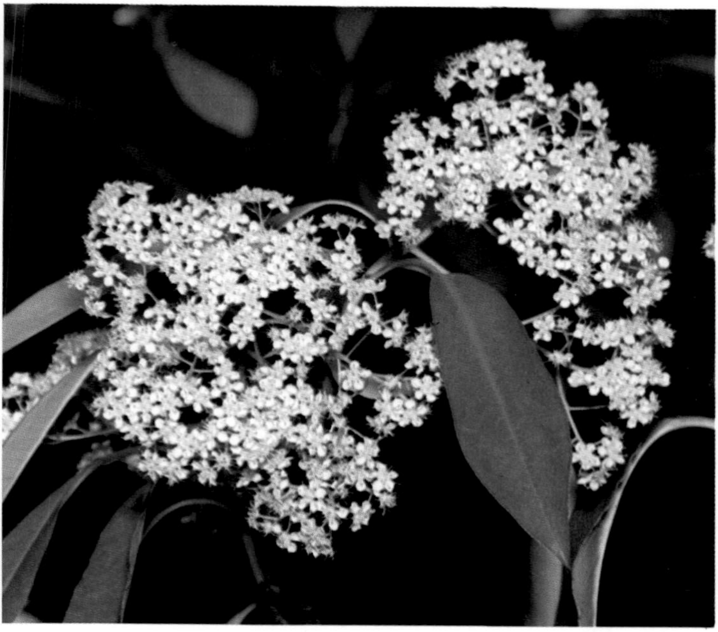

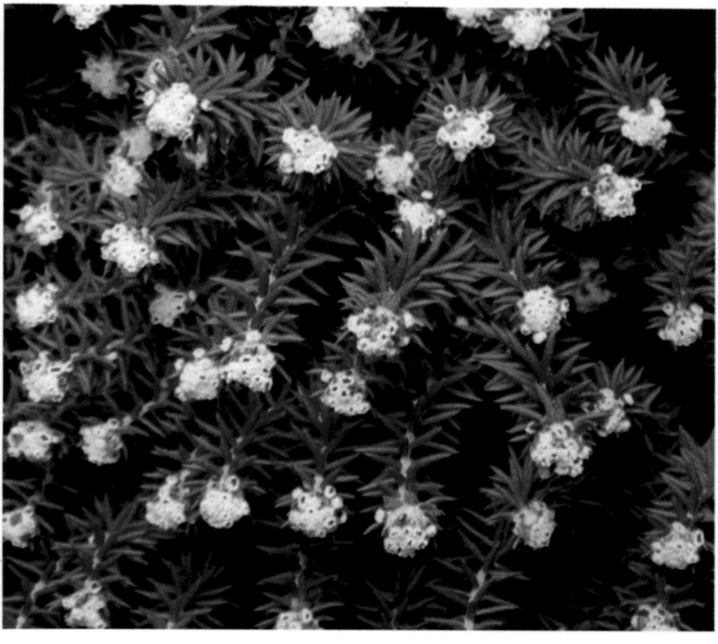

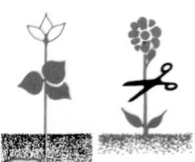

266 PHYSALIS ALKEKENGI Carolus Linnaeus
Common names: Chinese lantern, bladder cherry, cape gooseberry

Family Solanaceae.
Description A herbaceous perennial often grown as an annual. It is often allowed to naturalize. Its stems are prostrate-ascendent with sub-cordate or broadly ovate, ondulate, velutinate leaves. Its solitary flowers are axillary and insignificant although the plant becomes more attractive when its rather strange fruits develop on each pedicel. These consist of coral-red berries, each one enclosed in an inflated-vesiculose, ovoid-acuminate, orange or reddish calyx in the form of a lantern. They are dried for use as a colorful winter decoration.
Height of plant 12–24 in. (30–60 cm.).
Size of flower ½–¾ in. (1.5–2 cm.), diameter of inflated calyx.
Place of origin Europe to central Asia.
Flowering time Early summer.
Cultivation A shady to partially shady position. Temperate climate. Withstands the cold quite well. Suited to any type of moist, rich garden soil. Regular watering. The stems should be cut to ground level in the autumn. Requires no special attention. Rests during the winter.
Propagation In spring, by division of its rhizomatose roots or by seed sown in a coldframe.
Qualities Hardy. Easy to grow.

267 PITTOSPORUM TOBIRA William Aiton
Syn.: *P. chinense* David Don. Common name: Japanese pittosporum

Family Pittosporaceae.
Description A strong, bushy evergreen shrub with numerous compact ramifications. Its leaves, alternate or in whorls, are oblong-spatulate, obtusely acute and coriaceous; bright, dark green on the upper surface, pale on the lower. Its numerous ivory-white, orange-scented flowers are borne in umbelliferous cymes.
Height of plant 8–20 ft. (2.50–6 m.).
Size of flower 1 in. (2.5 cm.).
Place of origin China and Japan.

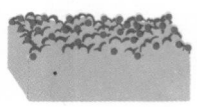

Cultivation Full sun or partial shade. Frost-tender. Can withstand a salty atmosphere particularly well. Prefers a rich, moist, argillaceous-sandy soil. Can survive well during very dry periods. In poor soil a periodic application of a general organic/mineral fertilizer keeps this plant in good condition. Does not usually require watering except perhaps in exceptionally dry weather. Can be pruned to shape in autumn or late winter. Pests: sometimes attacked by scale insects.

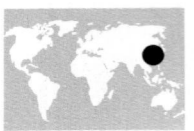

Propagation Usually by spring sowing outdoors in a nursery bed. It is also possible to take semi-hardwood cuttings in the spring–summer or to layer some of the branches during the same period.
Qualities Suitable for terraces if kept small. Tender t ~ hardy in a warm-temperate region. Easy to grow.

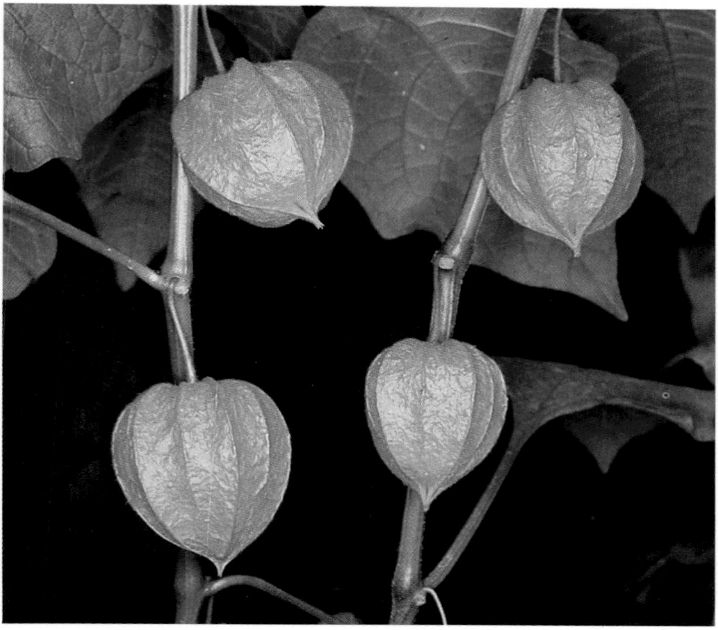

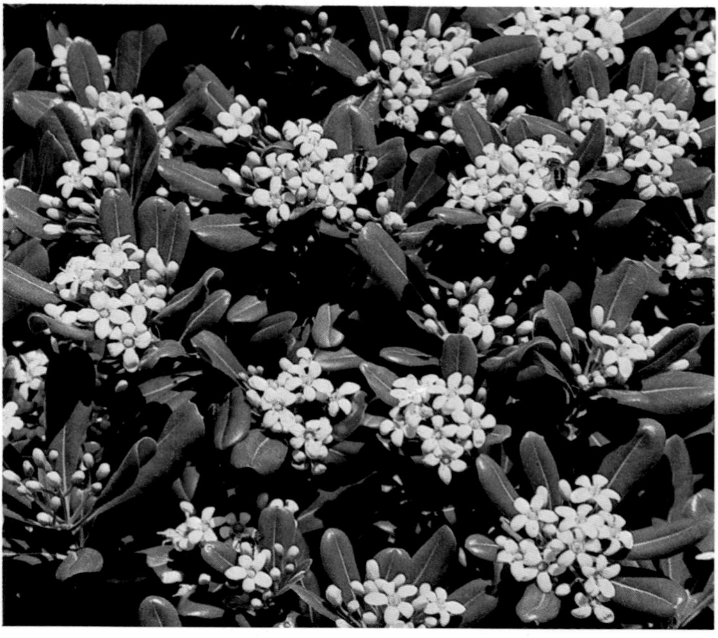

268 PLATYCODON GRANDIFLORUM (Nicolaus Joseph Jacquin) Augustin Pyramus De Candolle

Syn.: *Campanula grandiflora* Jacquin. Common name: Balloonflower

Family Campanulaceae.

Description A deciduous cespitose perennial with numerous upright stems, ramified toward the top. Its lustrous green, alternate leaves are consistent, serrate and oblong or ovate-lanceolate. Its numerous flaring-campanulate flowers are borne in lax, foliose racemes. Its cultivars are particularly appreciated for the length of their flowering period as well as for their colors, which include white, lilac-mauve and dark blue, and for their semidouble and double varieties.

Height of plant 15–24 in. (40–60 cm.).

Size of flower 2–2¾ in. (5–7 cm.).

Place of origin China, Siberia, Korea and Japan.

Flowering time Summer.

Cultivation A slightly shady position. Temperate climate. Fairly frost-resistant, especially if well mulched or provided with protective screens. Suited to almost any kind of soil, even if compact, provided it is rich. Requires regular watering during its flowering period, after which it rests. All flowered stems should be cut off; the plant then disappears completely, so its location must be marked. A top dressing of organic/mineral fertilizer should be worked lightly on the surface from time to time. Pests: aphids and red spider mites.

Propagation By spring sowing in pans or pots and germinated under glass. Alternatively, by clump division in spring.

Qualities Good for balconies, etc. Hardy. Easy to grow.

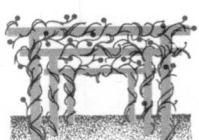

269 PLUMBAGO CAPENSIS Carl Peter Thunberg

Syns.: *P. auriculata,* Jean Baptiste Lamarck, *P. grandiflora* Michele Tenore. Common name: Leadwort

Family Plumbaginaceae.

Description A perennial widely grown as a creeper or climber for its wealth of flowers. Its stem is sarmentose-climbing or bushy-decumbent. Its alternate leaves are oblong-obtuse at the apex and often fasciculate and almost persistent in a warm–temperate climate. The blue flowers are borne in short, terminal sub-umbelliferous spikes rather like jasmine. Also white-flowered and scarlet varieties.

Height of plant 10–16 ft. (3–5 m.).

Size of flower 1–1⅜ in. (2.5–3.5 cm.).

Place of origin South Africa.

Flowering time Spring–autumn.

Cultivation A bright position, even in full sun. Cannot withstand the cold although it may survive a few light frosts with damage only to the top growth. Prefers a sheltered position, ideally against a wall. Suited to any type of soil provided it is fertile, moist, rich in organic material and well drained. Benefits from a periodic application of a general fertilizer. Regular watering. Requires hard pruning in autumn or, better still, in spring; all secondary growth should be shortened and weak or straggly branches removed.

Propagation Semi-hardwood cuttings in spring–summer.

Qualities Suitable for terraces and balconies. Tender but hardy in a warm-temperate climate. Easy to grow.

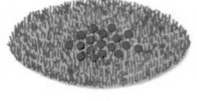

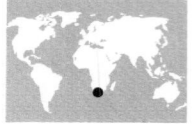

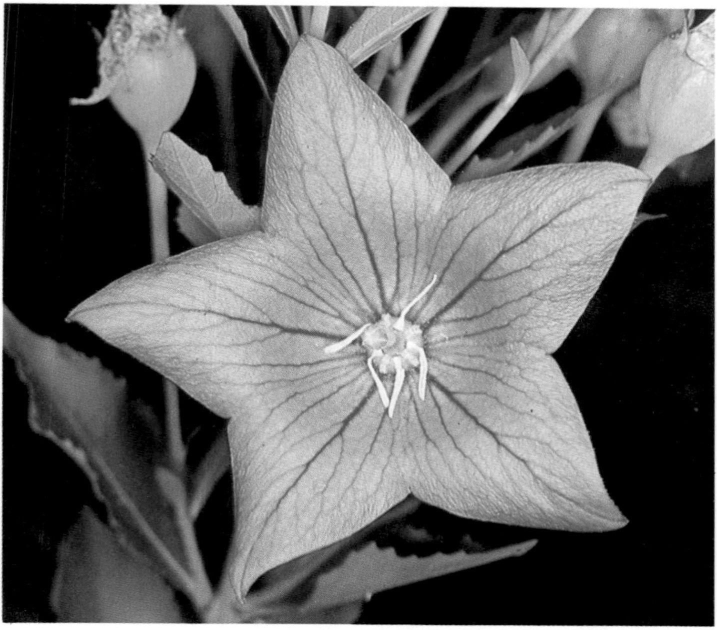

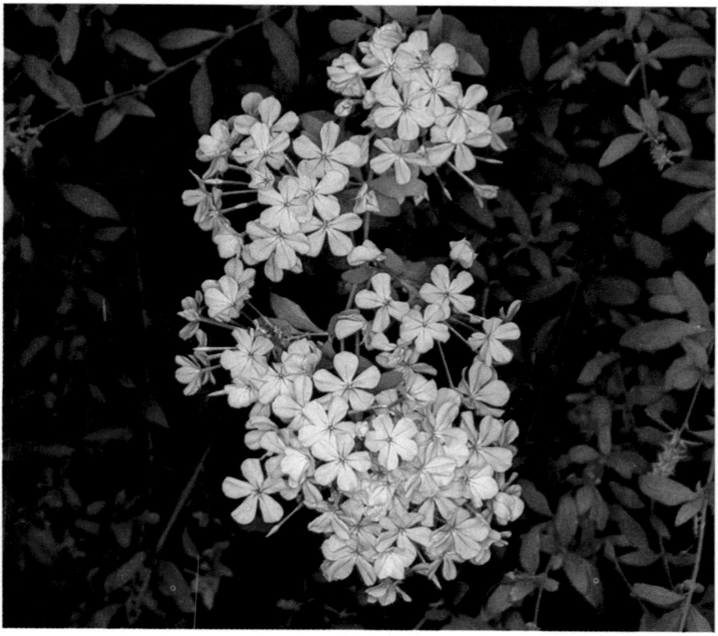

270 PONCIRUS TRIFOLIATA (Carolus Linnaeus) Constantino Samuel Rafinesque-Schmaitz

Syns.: *Pseudaegle sepiaria* Linnaeus, *Citrus trifoliata* Linnaeus, *Limonia trifoliata*. Common name: Hardy orange

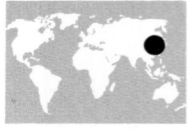

Family Rutaceae.

Description A slow-growing shrubby arborescent with glossy green ramifications. Decorative, with abundant flowers, it is also a protective hedge, with its formidable spines. Its alternate, trifoliate leaves, which are sparse, consist of obovate or elliptical leaflets. It has numerous white axillary flowers. Its spherical fruits are deep yellow and have a velutinate skin, like small mandarins. It can be used as a rootstock for citrus plants.

Height of plant 6½–15 ft. (2–4.50 m.).

Size of flower 1⅜–2 in. (3.5–5 cm.).

Place of origin China, Korea, Japan.

Flowering time Spring.

Cultivation Full sun to partial shade. Warm–temperate climate. It can survive the cold down to a few degrees below freezing point. Suitable for almost any type of soil that is argillaceous-humic, rich and moist. An undemanding plant, it does not usually require watering. Responds well to pruning and can even be cut to shape, although it is very lovely if left to grow naturally. Generally trouble-free.

Propagation By seed, using fresh seed or seed that has been stratified in sand; sowing should be done in a sheltered seedbed and the seedlings transplanted into a nursery bed in the spring. Also by cuttings in late summer.

Qualities Only half-hardy outside its own environment.

---

271 PORTULACA GRANDIFLORA William Jackson Hooker

Common name: Rose moss

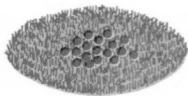
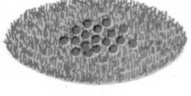

Family Portulacaceae.

Description A prostrate-diffuse perennial grown as an annual. Its ramifications are either creeping or erect (semiprostrate). Its alternate leaves are cylindrical-acuminate, succulent and slightly pilose. It bears numerous roselike flowers with four to six petals—more in the double varieties—in colors that include yellow, orange, red, pink, white. The flowers, which are produced from the foliar axils, bloom in succession.

Height of plant 4–8 in. (10–20 cm.).

Size of flower 1½–2 in. (4–5 cm.).

Place of origin South America.

Flowering time Summer.

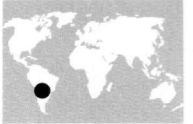

Cultivation Full sun. Warm-temperate climate. Thrives in dry, even poor, soil or gravelly screes. Suitable for any type of soil provided it is sandy, moderately fertile and rather dry. Very limited watering. Requires no particular care. The plants can be pulled up after flowering but they will often already have self-seeded and will germinate naturally the following year.

Propagation By spring sowing in the flowering site.

Qualities Suitable for balconies, terraces. Easy to grow.

272 POTENTILLA ATROSANGUINEA Conrad Loddiges
Common name: Cinquefoil

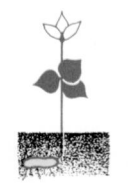

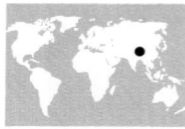

Family Rosaceae.
Description A bushy, herbaceous perennial with trifoliate leaves consisting of elliptical-ovate, dentate leaflets. Its flowers are borne in terminal panicles and may be single or double, according to the species. There are several varieties in different shades of red.
Height of plant 21–26 in. (55–65 cm.).
Size of flower ¾–1 in. (2–2.5 cm.).
Place of origin Himalayas.
Flowering time Spring–summer.
Cultivation A light or slightly shady position. Temperate climate. It can withstand the cold well, especially if given a protective mulch. It thrives equally well in calcareous or acid soil provided it is deep, fairly damp and well dug. Regular watering. Appreciates light seasonal dressings of organic material. The flowered cymes should be cut down. Trouble-free.
Propagation By clump division in spring or autumn.
Qualities Suitable for balconies, terraces. Hardy. Easy to grow.

273 PRIMULA MALACOIDES A. Franchet
Common name: Fairy primrose

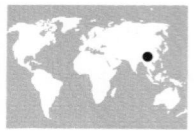

Family Primulaceae.
Description A herbaceous, bushy, pubescent perennial grown as an annual. Its pale-green leaves grow in rosettes and are oblong, lobate-cordate at the base and rotundate at the top. Its numerous delicately fragrant flowers are borne in multiple verticels on whitish, pulverulent scapes.
Height of plant 10–14 in. (25–35 cm.).
Size of flower ⅜–½ in. (1–1.5 cm.).
Place of origin China.
Flowering time Winter–spring.
Cultivation A delicate plant, this requires a bright, sheltered position. Can be grown outdoors only in warm-temperate regions. It is often grown in a greenhouse and transferred to the flowering site just before the buds open. It likes a light, rich, humic, moist soil. Frequent watering. Pests and diseases: aphids; various rots and fungus diseases.
Propagation By spring sowing; the pans should be kept under glass and subsequently pricked off into boxes before transferring the young plants into pots or garden in the fall.
Qualities Tender—usually regarded as a pot or greenhouse plant. Rather demanding to grow.

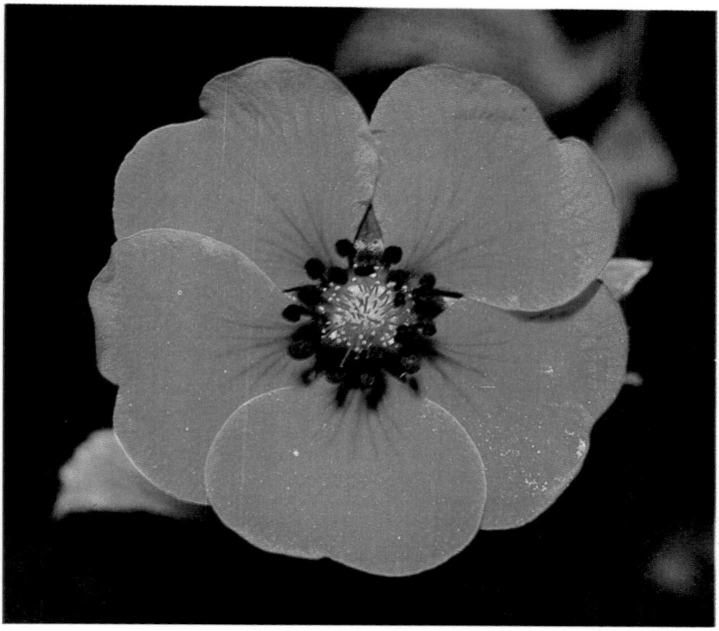

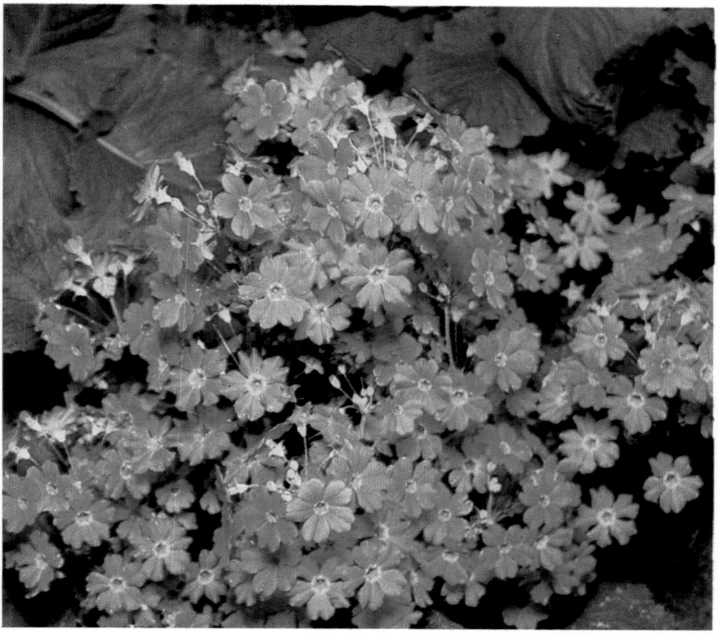

274 **PRIMULA OBCONICA** Hance

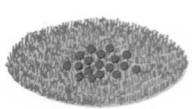

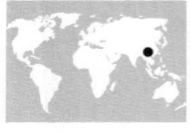

Family Primulaceae.
Description A cespitose perennial usually grown as an annual, it has a wealth of obovate-oblong leaves with an undulate margin, cordate at the base and pilose. The rather sweetly scented flowers are borne on a long, rigid scape and are grouped in a globose umbel, each one carried on a pedicel an inch or so in length. Colors include pink, violet, red, white with yellow.
Height of plant 6–12 in. (15–30 cm.).
Size of flower 1–1½ in. (2.5–4 cm.).
Place of origin China.
Flowering time Spring.
Cultivation A bright, sheltered position, not in direct sunlight, since this fades the color of the flowers. Warm-temperate climate. Frost-tender. Usually taken from the greenhouse and placed outdoors just as flowering is about to start in the spring, when danger of frost has passed. It likes a light, rich, moist, woodland-type soil, organically enriched. Frequent and plentiful watering. Pests and diseases: often subject to aphids and red spider mites; oidium.
Propagation By autumn or spring sowing in pans in a light, sandy compost in a temperate greenhouse. The seedlings require pricking out and subsequent potting up or planting out, if the temperature is sufficiently high.
Qualities Suitable for balconies, terraces and indoors. Tender to half-hardy, depending upon the climate. Fairly demanding to grow.

275 **PRIMULA PALINURI** Petagna
Common name: Palinuro cowslip

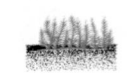

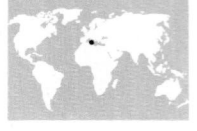

Family Primulaceae.
Description A bushy herbaceous perennial. Its glaucous-green leaves are evergreen, carnose, obovate-spatulate and about 2¾–6 in. (7–15 cm.) long by 1–1½ in. (2.5–4 cm.) wide. Its numerous flowers are erect or semipendulous and borne in a dense umbel at the top of a strong scape, with a white-farinose calyx and sulfur-yellow corolla. It is one of the hardiest of the primulas.
Height of plant 4¾–8 in. (12–20 cm.).
Size of flower ¾–1 in. (2–2.5 cm.).
Place of origin Capo Palinuro in the province of Salerno, Italy.
Flowering time Spring.
Cultivation A bright, even sunny position. Temperate climate. Can withstand a few light frosts. It likes a fairly heavy, calcareous soil, amended with woodland mold mixed with a little sand. Animal manures should be avoided. These plants should be watered only if the weather is very dry, since they prefer the moisture from evaporation rather than a waterlogged condition. After flowering, stalks should be removed. Subject to root rot.
Propagation By spring sowing in pans of light, fibrous soil, germinated under glass in a frame or greenhouse and subsequently pricked out. When the plantlets are sufficiently large, pot up into 2-in. (5 cm.) pots before planting out.
Qualities Relatively easy to grow.

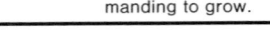

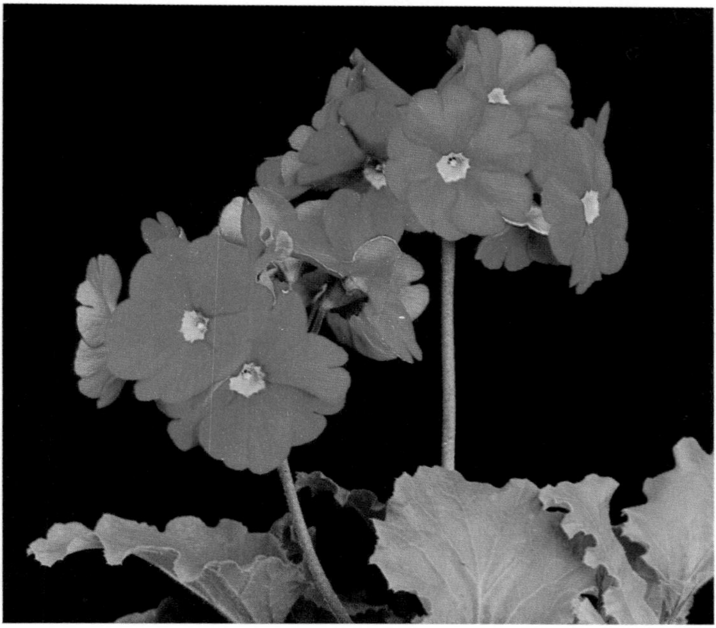

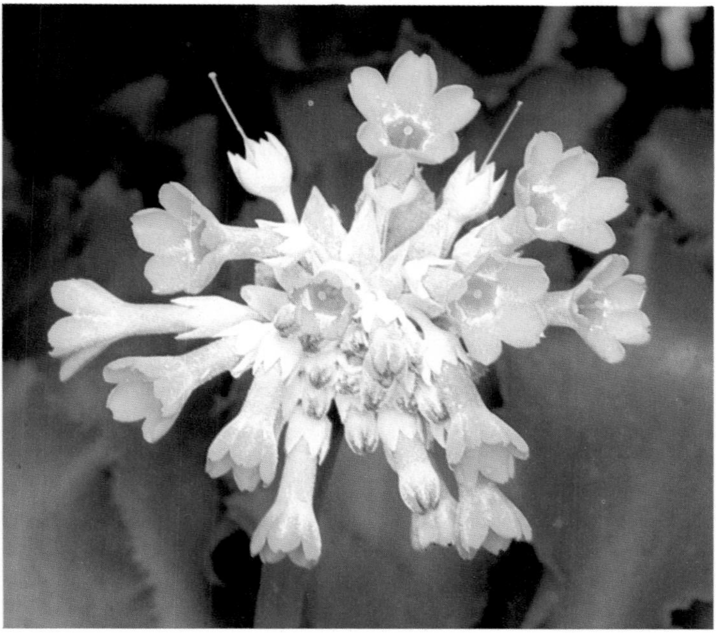

276 PRIMULA x POLYANTHA Hortorum
Common name: Polyanthus primrose

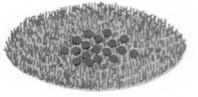

Family Primulaceae.
Description A sturdy, herbaceous biennial often grown as an annual. It has abundant, broad, obovate or spatulate light-green leaves that form a tight basal clump. Its flowers are borne in dense globose groups at the top of upright scapes. The color range includes white, pink, yellow and various shades of blue, cream and violet.
Height of plant 10–14 in. (25–35 cm.).
Size of flower 1⅛–1¾ in. (3–4.5 cm.).
Place of origin A horticultural hybrid obtained from crossings between *P. elatior*, *P. veris* and *P. vulgaris*.
Flowering time Spring.

Cultivation Partial shade. Temperate climate. Neutral or moderately acid soil, consisting of equal parts of woodland or heath mold, peat and sand, enriched with well-rotted organic compost; animal manure should be avoided, since it may prove harmful. Liquid fertilizer during early stages of growth. Frequent watering. Pests and diseases: aphids, caterpillars, slugs, snails, cutworms and vine weevils; various rots and fungus diseases.
Propagation By division in spring or early summer. By spring sowing in pans; seedlings subsequently pricked off.
Qualities Suitable for balconies, terraces. Half- to very hardy, depending on the strain. Moderately easy to grow.

277 PRUNUS AVIUM Carolus Linnaeus
Common name: Sweet cherry

Family Rosaceae.
Description A tree with upright branches and dark-brown, glossy bark that desquamates easily. Its leaves are ovate-acuminate or oblong-lanceolate with a serrate margin and pubescent lower surface. The numerous flowers open as the leaves unfurl. They are borne in clusters of four to eight with scarious leaf-bud scales at the base of the floral peduncles. The fruits (drupes) have a bitter-sweet, juicy pulp.
Height of plant 26–40 ft. (8–12 m.).
Size of flower ¾–1⅛ in. (2–3 cm.).
Place of origin Europe.
Flowering time Spring.

Cultivation Full sun. Cool-temperate climate. Frost-resistant. Suited to any type of deep, moist, rich soil that is not too calcareous. Benefits from periodic applications of organic/mineral fertilizers. Plentiful watering during very dry weather. Does not like to be pruned. Pests and diseases: caterpillars and scale insects; leaf curl.

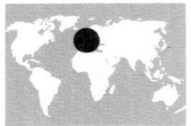

Propagation By seed, but the new plants may not be true to type. By grafting in spring–summer onto the wild cherry to obtain cultivated varieties.
Qualities Hardy. Easy to grow.

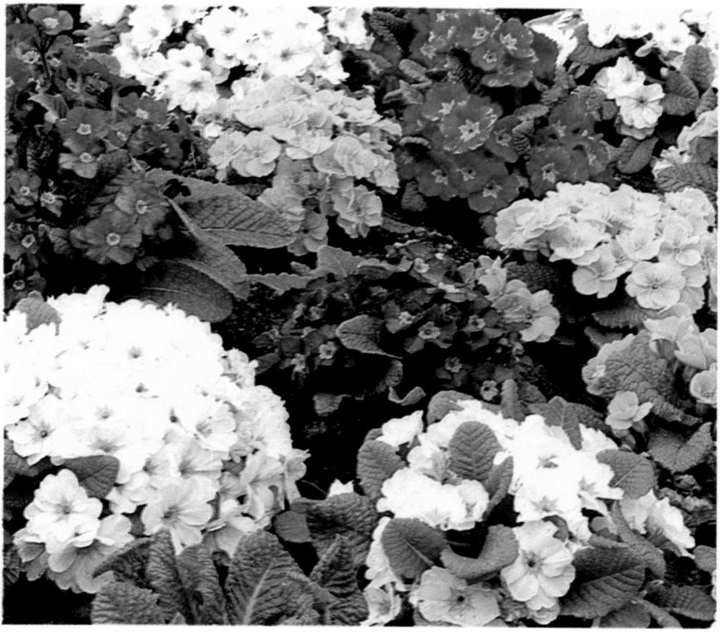

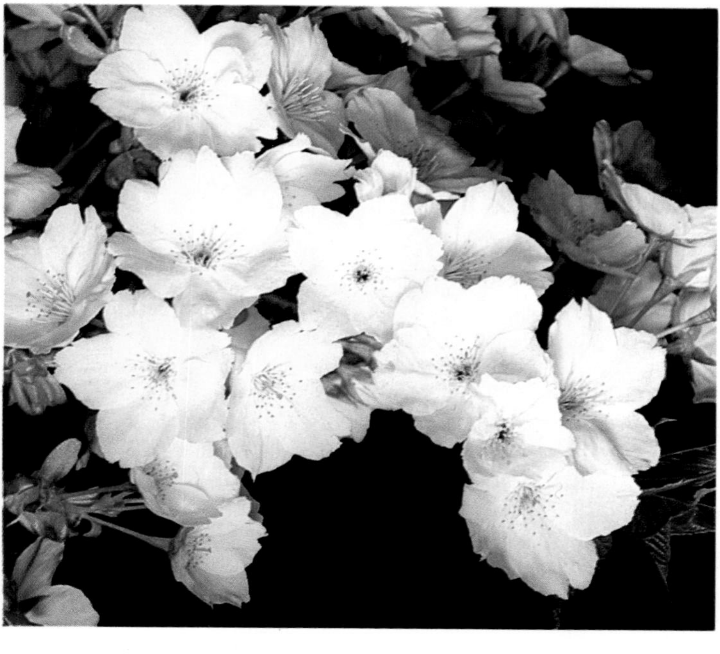

278 PRUNUS CERASIFERA Friedrich Ehrhart var. "Pissardii" L. H. Bailey
Common names: Cherry plum, Myrobalan plum

Family Rosaceae.
Description This little tree is very decorative because of the constant dark plum-red color of its foliage. It has an arborescent stem with numerous ramifications and a compact, symmetrical head. Its alternate leaves, carried on a short petiole, are ovate-acute and serrate. Its abundant pink flowers, which open before the leaves unfurl, grow either singly or in groups and are positioned alternately along the branches. There are several cultivated single- or double-flowered varieties in various tones of pink. It bears cherry-shaped, edible plums.
Height of plant 16–23 ft. (5–7 m.).
Size of flower ½–¾ in. (1.5–2 cm.).
Place of origin Balkans, Asia Minor, Iran.
Flowering time Early spring.
Cultivation Full sun. Temperate climate. Withstands the cold very well. Suited to almost all types of soil but prefers it moderately argillaceous, rich and moist. Likes a periodic application of a general organic/mineral fertilizer. Requires watering during very dry spells. Does not react adversely to pruning. Usually trouble-free.
Propagation The double and semidouble varieties can be grafted onto Myrobalan. The other types can be propagated from seed in an outdoor, sheltered seedbed in autumn or spring.
Qualities Hardy. Easy to grow.

279 PRUNUS GLANDULOSA Carl Peter Thunberg cv. "Albiplena"
Syns.: *P. japonica* Thunberg, *P. chinensis* Karl Ludwig Blume. Common name: Dwarf flowering almond

Family Rosaceae.
Description This delightful shrub, which may be better known to the amateur gardener as *P. chinensis,* is widely grown, since it makes attractive cut flowers and can be forced to bloom early. The stem is cut down to a few inches from the ground, thus inducing the plant to throw up numerous slender branches that are literally covered with flowers and are always in great demand by florists. Its leaves are lanceolate and denticulate-serrate.
Height of plant 40–47 in. (1–1.20 m.).
Size of flower ¾–1 in. (2–2.5 cm.).
Place of origin China and Japan.
Flowering time Late winter–spring.
Cultivation In full sun or a bright position. Temperate climate. Fairly frost-resistant. Suited to argillaceous-calcareous soil, generously enriched with well-matured manure and mineral fertilizers. Liquid fertilizer should also be applied during the initial stage of growth. Plentiful watering. Each branch should be pruned back to two or three buds from the base immediately after flowering. Diseases: sometimes prone to fungus diseases.
Propagation By semi-hardwood cuttings taken in spring or summer or by grafting during the same period.
Qualities Hardy. Easy to grow.

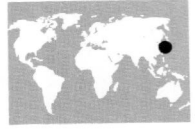

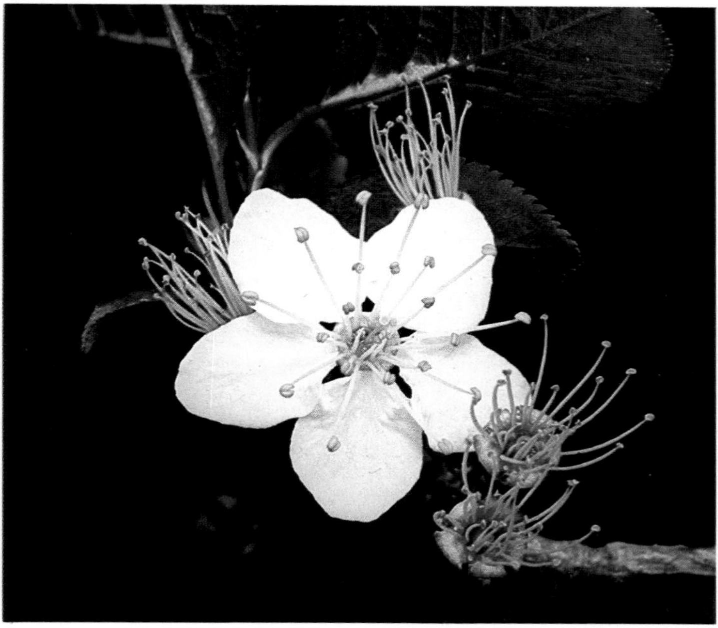

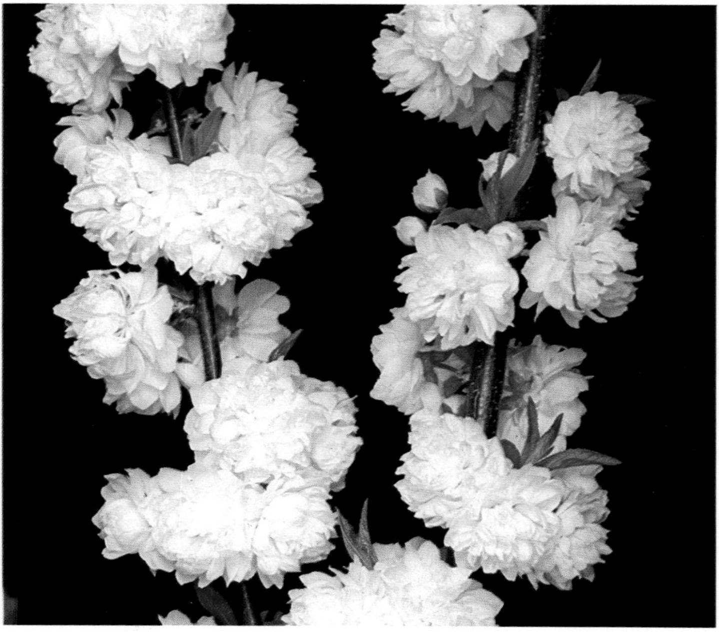

280 PRUNUS GLANDULOSA Carl Peter Thunberg
cv. "Rosea Plena"
Syns.: *P. japonica* Thunberg, *P. chinensis* Karl Ludwig Blume. Common name: Dwarf flowering almond

Family Rosaceae.
Description   This variety is often grown for its qualities as a cut flower, although it is less in demand than "Albiplena" because it is inclined to throw up fewer flowering branches. With its magnificent floriferousness, however, it makes a delightful ornamental plant. There are several cultivars in various shades of pink. It is a small, bushy shrub with upright branches. It blooms profusely before the leaves unfurl.
Height of plant   40–47 in. (1–1.20 m.).
Size of flower   ¾–1 in. (2–2.5 cm.).
Place of origin   China and Japan.
Flowering time   Late winter–spring.

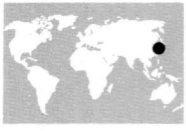

Cultivation   Full sun or partial shade. Temperate climate. Frost-resistant. It lends itself well to being forced in a greenhouse to advance the flowering period. Suited to any type of soil provided it is fertile, moist and has plenty of organic material. Diseases: Leaf spot, and is sometimes attacked by the parasitic fungus exoascales (*Exoascus*).
Propagation   By cuttings and grafting in spring–summer.
Qualities   Hardy. Easy to grow.

---

281 PRUNUS LAUROCERASUS Carolus Linnaeus
Syn.: *Laurocerasus officinalis,* Johann Jacob Roemer. Common name: Cherry laurel

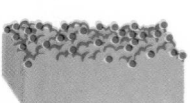

Family   Rosaceae.
Description   A well-known shrub extensively used as a garden hedge or in shrubberies. Its arborescent stems are ramified from the base with upright branches. Its alternate leaves are coriaceous, oblong, obtuse, acuminate and serrate, with a slightly recurved margin. Its fairly ornamental flowers are borne in dense axillary racemes. Its fruits are rather like small cherries in appearance; the pulp is edible but the kernel contains a poisonous almond. A special liqueur is made from these fruits. There are various cultivated forms.
Height of plant   10–20 ft. (3–6 m.).
Size of flower   ⅜ in. (1 cm.).
Place of origin   Balkans, Asia Minor, Caucasus.
Flowering time   Spring.

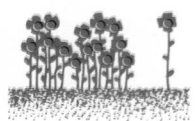

Cultivation   A sunny or even shady position. Cool-temperate climate. Fairly frost-resistant. Suited to almost any kind of well-aerated, rich, moist soil. Watering is usually unnecessary except during very dry spells. Can be cut to shape. Pests: often attacked by various species of scale insect.
Propagation   By semi-hardwood cuttings taken in spring or late summer and rooted in a sheltered position in a nursery bed. Sometimes grown from seed, but this is rare.
Qualities   Hardy. Easy to grow.

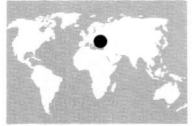

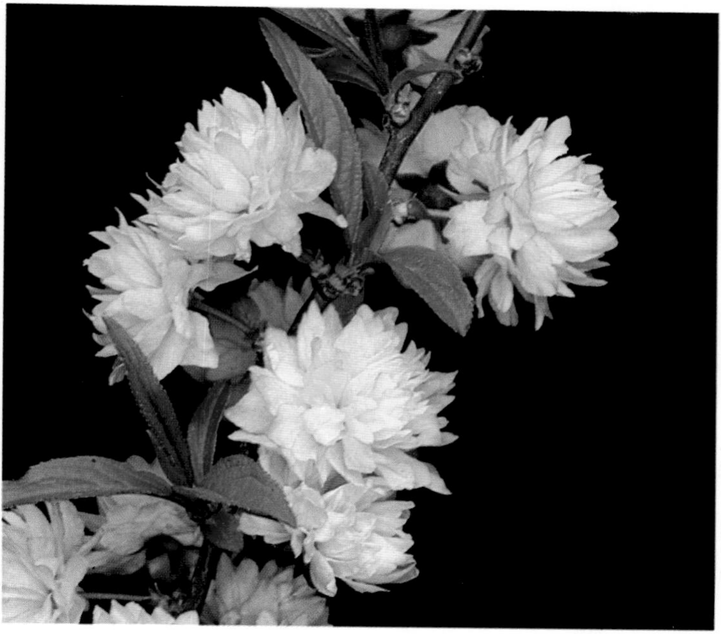

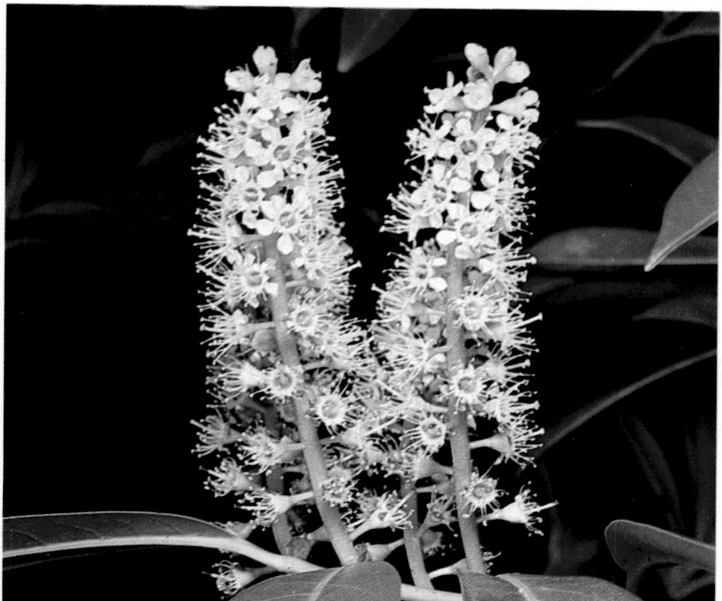

282 PRUNUS PERSICA Philipp Franz von Siebold and Joseph Gerhard Zuccarini cv. flore pleno Hortorum
Syn.: *Amygdalus persica* Carolus Linnaeus. Common name: Peach

Family Rosaceae.
Description A shrub or small tree, extremely ornamental. It is rather short-lived, however. It has arborescent stems, which are often contorted, with divaricate ramifications. Its alternate leaves are lanceolate and biserrate. Numerous axillary flowers borne singly or in groups of two to four. Ornamental varieties generally produce little fruit, but those raised for their delicious fruit have plenty of less ornamental flowers.
Height of plant 6½–13 ft. (2–4 m.).
Size of flower ¾–1½ in. (2–4 cm.).
Place of origin Wild species indigenous to China.
Flowering time Spring.
Cultivation In full sun or a very bright position. Temperate climate. Frost-resistant. Suited to almost any type of permeable, well-aerated, rich soil. Periodic applications of a general organic/mineral fertilizer. Plentiful watering in the summer. Should be pruned rather hard after blooming to force the new growth on which next year's flowers will appear. Pests and diseases: aphids; exoascales, leaf spot and chlorosis.
Propagation By budding in summer onto a seed-raised peach or an almond, plum or apricot, with dormant bud.
Qualities Hardy. Easy to grow.

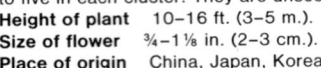

283 PRUNUS SERRULATA John Lindley cv.
Common name: Japanese cherry

Family Rosaceae.
Description A medium-sized tree with erect branches and dark-brown, glossy bark. All the cultivated hybrids of *Prunus serrulata* belong to this group of *Prunus (Cerasus)*. The leaves of *P. serrulata* are shiny, ovate or oblong, acuminate lengthwise, dentate and 2–6 in. (5–15 cm.) long. The flowers appear at the same time as the leaves or a little earlier; there are three to five in each cluster. They are unscented.
Height of plant 10–16 ft. (3–5 m.).
Size of flower ¾–1⅛ in. (2–3 cm.).
Place of origin China, Japan, Korea.
Flowering time Spring.
Cultivation Full sun or partial shade. Cool-temperate climate. Frost-resistant. Suited to any type of soil, whether acid or calcareous, provided it is rich, moist and well drained. A general organic/mineral fertilizer worked into the surrounding surface soil periodically. Plentiful watering during dry spells. Pruning should be restricted to a minimum.
Propagation By grafting onto wild-cherry rootstock in the spring–summer.
Qualities Hardy. Easy to grow.

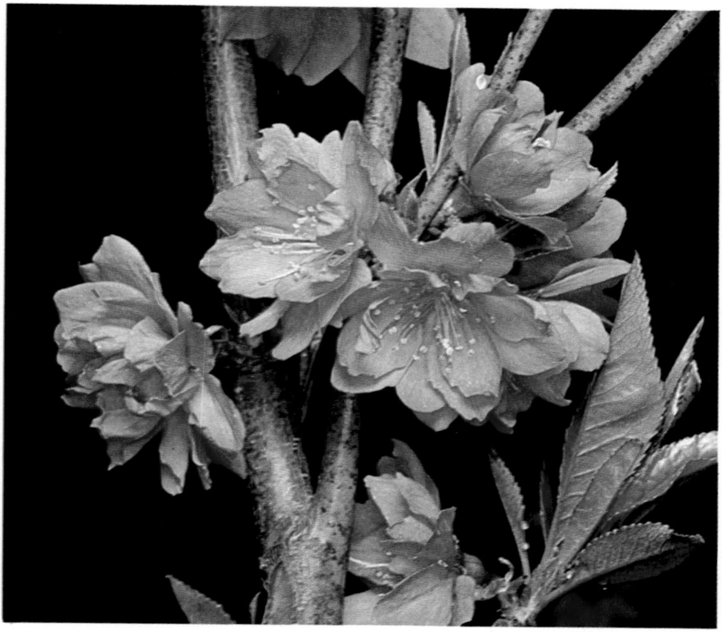

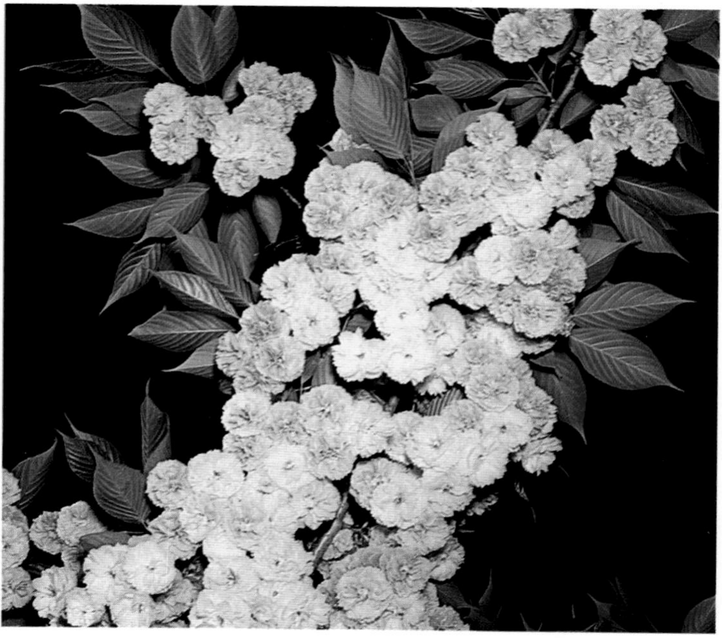

284 PRUNUS SUBHIRTELLA Friedrich Anton Wilhelm Miquel
Common name: Higan cherry

Family Rosaceae.
Description This is one of the best of the small-flowered ornamental cherries. The tree is medium size, very ramified, with slender secondary branches. Its leaves are ovate-acuminate, doubly serrate, slightly pubescent and with well-marked venation. Its numerous flowers are borne in clusters of two or three. Fruits are reddish drupes. Among its various cultivars, two are particularly attractive: the cv. ''Pendula,'' with pink flowers covering the drooping branches in the spring, and cv. ''Autumnalis,'' with semidouble flowers in autumn and spring.
Height of plant up to 33 ft. (10 m.).
Size of flower ¾ in. (2 cm.).
Place of origin Japan.
Flowering time Spring.

Cultivation A sunny to partially shaded position. Temperate climate. Fairly frost-resistant. Grows in calcareous as well as acid soil but prefers moderately calcareous, moist, fertile ground. Benefits from periodic applications of a general organic/mineral fertilizer. Should be well watered in when planted and afterward during very dry spells. Like all cherry trees, it does not like to be pruned. It is subject to chlorosis in unsuitable ground; treat with iron chelate if necessary.
Propagation By budding or splice grafting, in the spring, onto wild cherry or a cherry tree raised from seed.
Qualities Hardy. Easy to grow.

285 PTILOTRICHUM SPINOSUM (Carolus Linnaeus) Edmond Boissier
Syn.: *Alyssum spinosum* Linnaeus

Family Cruciferae.
Description A delightful herbaceous perennial often grown in rock-garden borders. Semishrubby, its stems tend to turn upward. Its silvery-greenish leaves are obovate-lanceolate and pilose on the lower surface. The white flowers are borne in racemes. There are some horticultural cultivars.
Height of plant 10–16 in. (25–40 cm.).

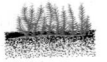

Size of flower $^1/_{10}$–$^3/_{20}$ in. (0.3–0.4 cm.).
Place of origin Southwestern Alps. Naturalized in southern Europe, including Italy.
Flowering time Spring.

Cultivation Full sun. Temperate climate. Can withstand a few light frosts. Grows in any soil, even if poor and dry, calcareous and stony. Watering restricted to very dry spells. The dead flowers should be lightly trimmed. Pests and diseases: insects; various rots and rust in damp sites.
Propagation By spring sowing in pans in a coldframe; also directly into the flowering position.
Qualities Hardy. Easy to grow.

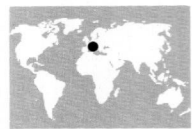

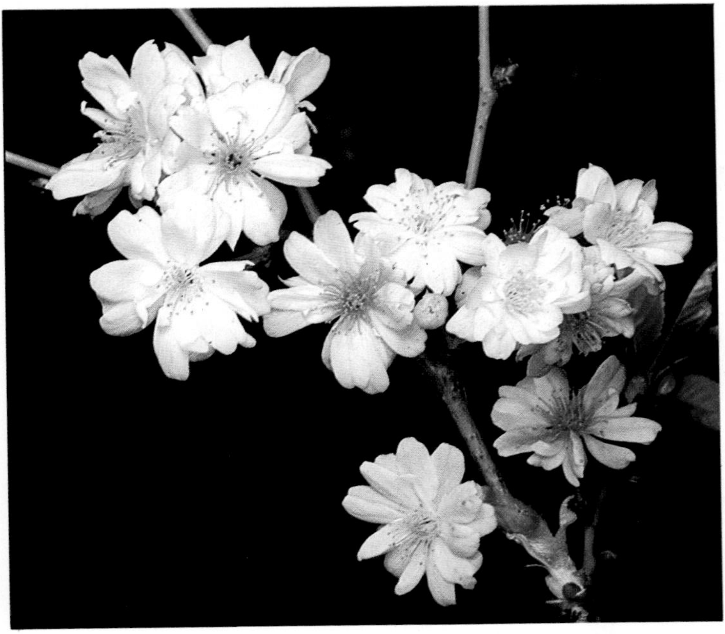

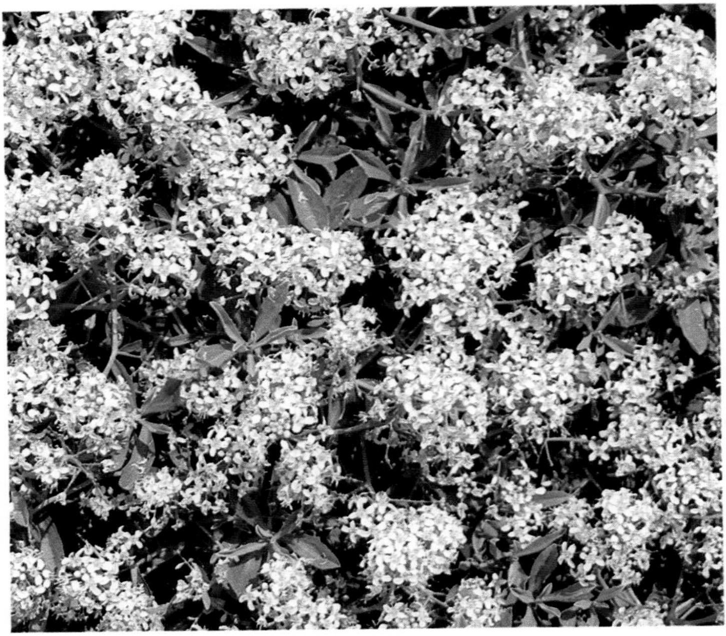

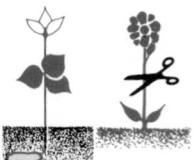

286 PULSATILLA VULGARIS Phillip Miller
Syn.: *Anemone pulsatilla* Carolus Linnaeus. Common name: Pasqueflower

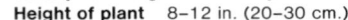

Family Ranunculaceae.
Description A charming deciduous, herbaceous perennial with a taproot. It only has a few leaves, which are radical, tripinnatosect and villose with linear-acute laciniae. Its floral stem is erect and villose with a collarette of bipartite linear bracts set just under the flower. An attractive little rock-garden plant. Its solitary flowers grow terminally.
Height of plant 8–12 in. (20–30 cm.).
Size of flower 2 in. (5 cm.).
Place of origin Central Europe; from cool, moist sites in the hilly and mountainous areas.
Flowering time Late spring–early summer.
Cultivation A moist, shady position. Cool-temperate climate. Frost-resistant. Prefers ground that is moderately compact, rich and moist—the woodland-mold type. Undemanding, it lends itself to being allowed to run wild. Requires watering during very dry spells. It rests through the summer.
Propagation By spring sowing in pans or, even better, in pots and germinated in a coldframe. Sometimes, too, by division.
Qualities Hardy in the hills and mountains of its natural environment. Very easy to grow.

287 PUNICA GRANATUM Carolus Linnaeus cv. flore pleno
Common name: Pomegranate

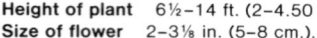

Family Punicaceae.
Description A plant with a shrubby, arborescent habit, its ramifications are slender and dense, slow-growing and sometimes spiny. Grown for the decorativeness of its flowers and foliage. Its leaves are opposite or alternate, oblong-lanceolate and ondulate. Its large flowers are either solitary or in clusters of two to five at the end of the branches. Double-flowered varieties are sterile but some single ones produce sour fruits and others sweet fruits.
Height of plant 6½–14 ft. (2–4.50 m.).
Size of flower 2–3⅛ in. (5–8 cm.).
Place of origin Southeastern Europe, Middle East, Iran.
Flowering time Late spring–summer.
Cultivation A position in full or almost full sun. Warm-temperate climate. Cannot withstand much frost. Grows in any deep, moist, fertile soil. Benefits from a periodic application of a general organic/mineral fertilizer. Requires watering during very dry spells. All flowered, dead or weak growth should be cut back in the autumn. A very beautiful plant when left in its natural shape.
Propagation The horticultural varieties can be propagated by cuttings, air layering or splice grafting in the spring. Also by seed, but may not be true to type.
Qualities Suitable for balconies, etc. Hardy. Easy to grow.

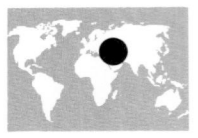

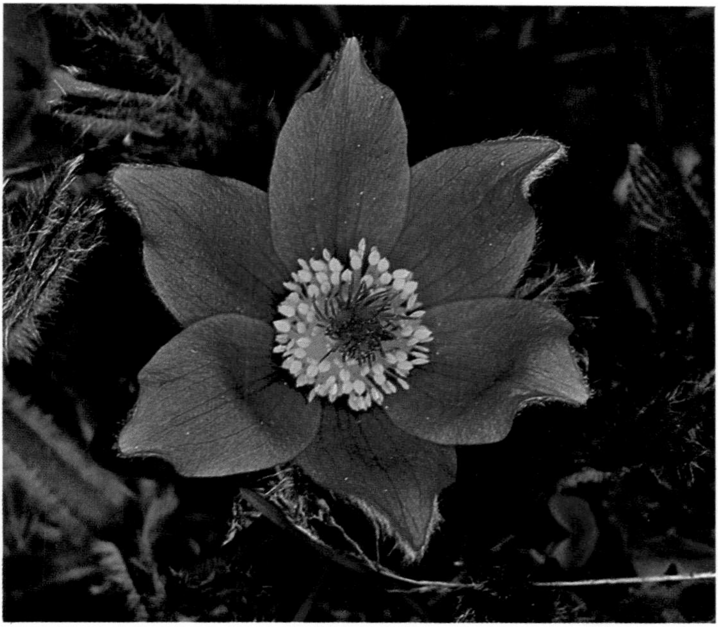

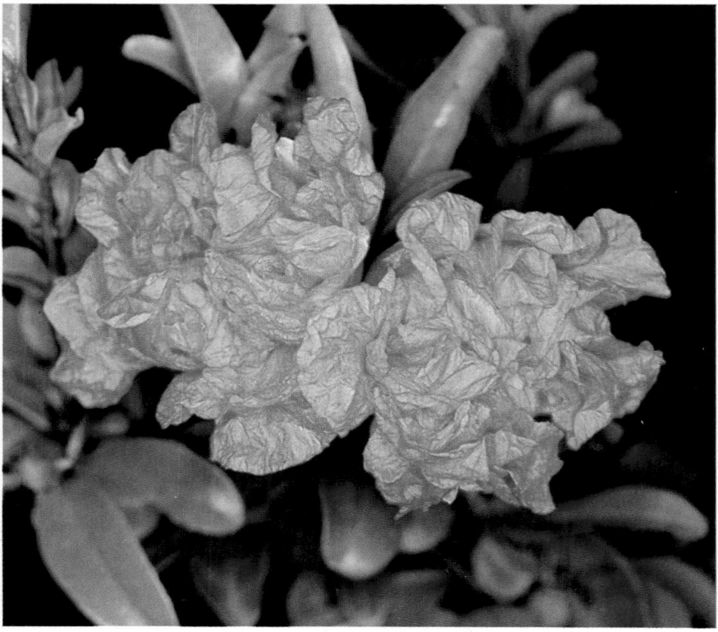

288 PUNICA GRANATUM Carolus Linnaeus var. "Nana" (Linnaeus) Christian Hendrick Persoon cv. "Flore Simple." Common name: Dwarf pomegranate

Family Punicaceae.

Description A small shrub with slender ramifications with bright-green, opposite leaves. Its flowers are a brilliant red and the edible fruit variegated and decorative. It is a form of *Punica granatum* with fruit very like that of the wild species; in fact, it retains all the features of the original plant but in miniature. This single-flowered fertile species produces very ornamental little fruits, about the size of a walnut or an egg. There are some very floriferous cultivars: "Rosea," "Rubra Plena" and "Nana Racemosa."

Height of plant 20–60 in. (0.50–1.50 m.).
Size of flower 1⅛–1½ in. (3–4 cm.).
Place of origin Southeastern Europe, Middle East.
Flowering time Late spring–summer.

Cultivation In full sun or a very sunny position. Temperate climate. Can withstand only a few light frosts. Suited to any type of well-aerated, fertile, moist soil. Appreciates an occasional application of a general organic/mineral fertilizer. Regular watering. It is very beautiful when left to grow naturally.

Propagation By spring or autumn sowing in pots or pans and germinated in a propagating frame or warm greenhouse. Will begin to flower after two years.

Qualities Suitable for balconies, terraces. Easy to grow.

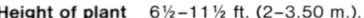

289 PYRACANTHA COCCINEA Johann Jacob Roemes cv. "Lalandei" Common name: Scarlet firethorn

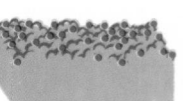

Family Rosaceae.

Description An evergreen or semi-evergreen shrub with dense, strong, blackish branches and sharp spines. Its alternate leaves are fasciculate, oblong or oval, crenulate-denticulate and coriaceous. Its numerous small white flowers are borne in corymbs on long pedicels; they have a rather unattractive scent. The whole plant seems to turn to coral-red in the autumn when its ornamental and abundant berries ripen.

Height of plant 6½–11½ ft. (2–3.50 m.).
Size of flower ⅛ in. (0.5 cm.).
Place of origin Southeastern Europe, Asia Minor.
Flowering time Spring.

Cultivation A sunny or partially shaded position. Temperate climate. Frost-resistant. Suited to almost all types of soil, with a preference for moist, siliceous-argillaceous, humus-rich ground. Plentiful watering in the summer. Lends itself well to being trimmed to shape for hedges, espaliers, etc. Plenty of well-rotted manure should be dug into the ground when it is planted and periodic applications of a mineral-based fertilizer given if the plant shows signs of being unhealthy. Pests: often attacked by woolly aphids (*Eriosoma lanigerum*).

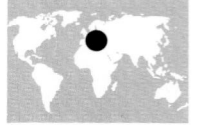

Propagation By semi-hardwood cuttings in late summer; these should be treated with a hormone root stimulant before planting. By spring sowing in a nursery bed or coldframe.

Qualities Hardy. Easy to grow.

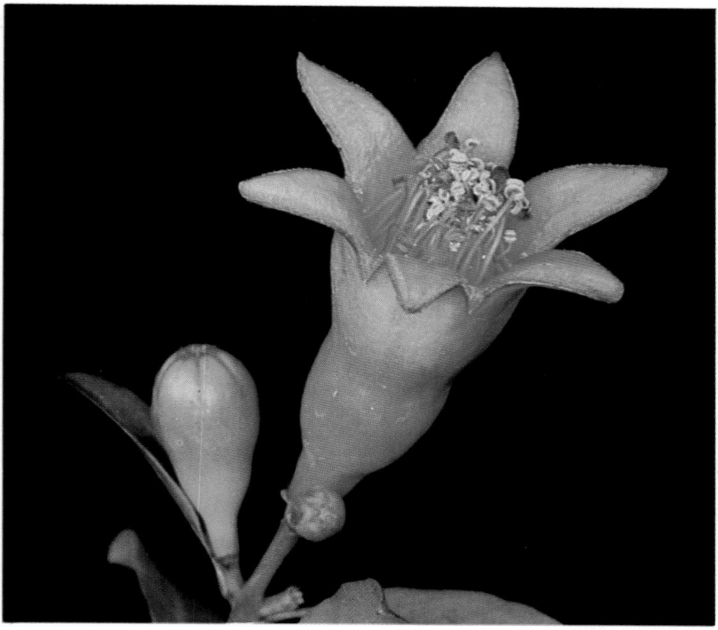

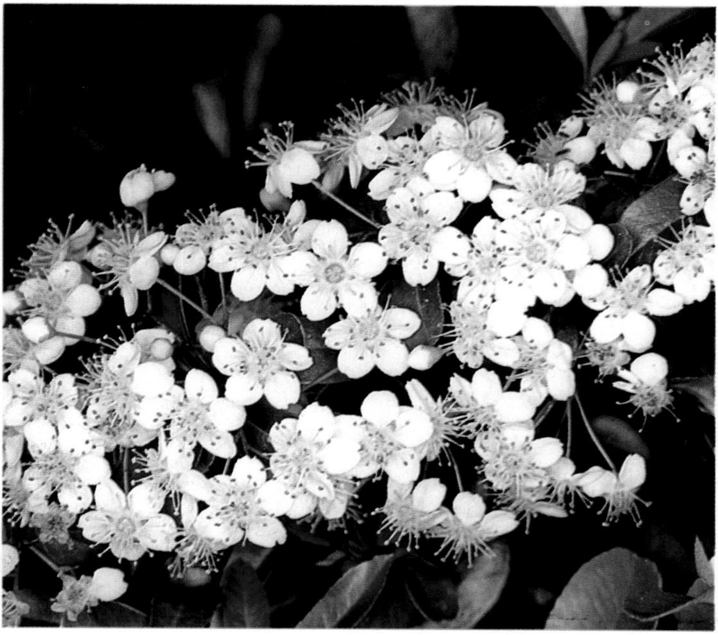

290 PYRACANTHA CRENULATA (David Don) Johann Jacob Roemer var. "Rogersiana" Jacks
Common name: Firethorn

Family Rosaceae.
Description A medium-size, very spiny evergreen shrub with compact, sturdy, dense ramifications. Its small, alternate leaves are oblong or oval and coriaceous. Numerous white hawthornlike flowers are borne in corymbs; they have a rather unattractive scent. The plant is again covered in color in the autumn when the yellow fruits ripen. Other cultivars with very decorative yellow fruits are "Flava," "Flava Nova," "Aurantiaca," "Superba" and "Sungold."
Height of plant 10–13 ft. (3–4 m.).
Size of flower ⅛ in. (0.5 cm.).
Place of origin China.
Flowering time Spring.
Cultivation In full sun or slight shade. Temperate climate. Frost-resistant. Suited to any soil, even if argillaceous-calcareous. Plentiful watering during dry spells. Benefits from a spring application of organic manure. Pruning: This plant can be shaped or grown as a hedge; it can also be left to grow as a bush or small tree, in which case only distorted and dead branches need to be removed. Pests: aphids are sometimes a problem.
Propagation By sowing in autumn or, even better, in spring in a sheltered nursery bed or in boxes in a coldframe.
Qualities Hardy. Easy to grow.

291 RAPHIOLEPIS INDICA (Carolus Linnaeus) John Lindley
Syn.: *Crataegus indica* Linnaeus. Common name: India hawthorn

Family Rosaceae.
Description A compact, ramified evergreen shrub. Its alternate leaves are serrate and ovate-acuminate or lanceolate. Its numerous flowers are borne in lax terminal racemes 2⅜–4 in. (6–10 cm.) long with tomentose peduncles and calyces, and subulate bracts. The corolla is shaded from white to pink.
Height of plant 40–60 in. (1–1.50 m.).
Size of flower ½–¾ in. (1.5–2 cm.).
Place of origin Southern China.
Flowering time Spring–summer.
Cultivation A sunny or slightly shady position. Warm-temperate climate. Does not like the cold and is treated as a greenhouse plant in cold zones. Prefers open, rich, well-manured soil. Overall watering, reduced in winter. Pruning limited to opening up of branches and removal of dead or weak growth in the autumn–spring. Usually trouble-free. If growth is sluggish, apply a foliar feed.
Propagation By spring sowing in pans in a warm greenhouse or propagating frame. By well-ripened shoots taken in late summer and rooted in a greenhouse. May also be grafted on to the *Crataegus* species.
Qualities Half-hardy. Very easy to grow.

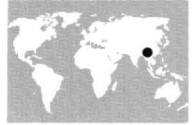

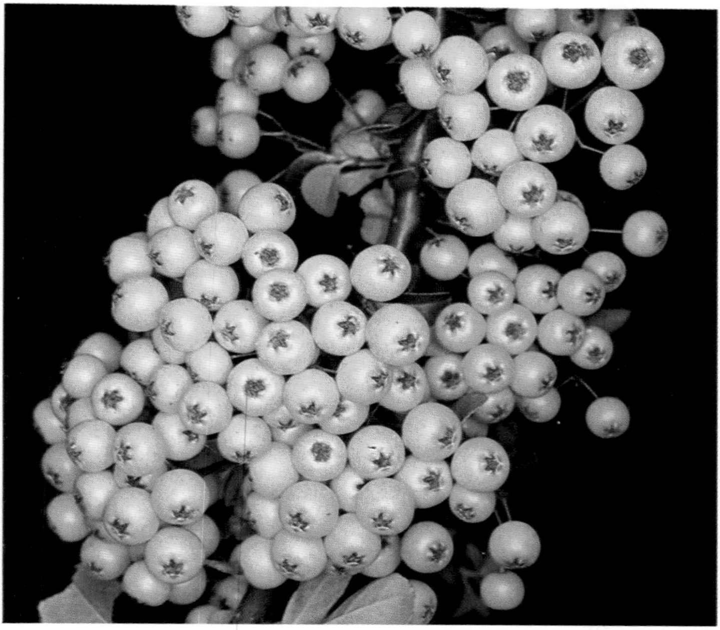

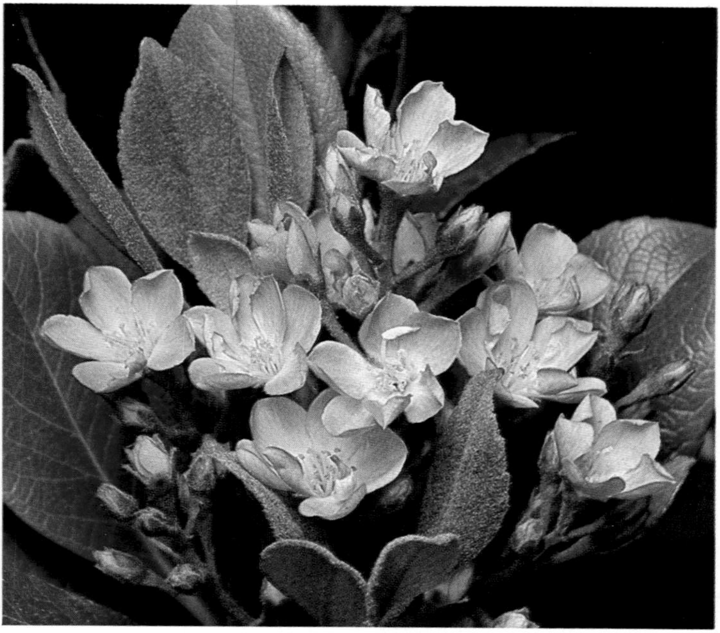

292 RHODODENDRON FERRUGINEUM Carolus Linnaeus
Common name: Alpenrose

Family Ericaceae.
Description A beautiful shrub but very difficult to grow outside its natural alpine surroundings. Its stem is treelike and well branched. Its alternate leaves grow close together and are oblong-lanceolate, coriaceous, glabrous and green on the upper surface but rust-colored on the lower. Its numerous flowers, borne in terminal corymbs, vary in color from pale pink to purple and scarlet.
Height of plant 12–32 in. (30–80 cm.).
Size of flower ½–¾ in. (1.5–2 cm.).
Place of origin The mountains of central Europe.
Flowering time Summer.
Cultivation In full sun or a bright position. Cool-temperate climate. Frost-resistant and prefers a mountainous site with an acid soil, rich in natural organic material. Very regular watering with rainwater. Does not like to be pruned or disturbed.
Propagation By spring–summer sowing in peat pots that are plunged into the ground in a cool, sheltered place. As soon as the plantlets are sufficiently large, they can be planted in their flowering site.
Qualities Hardy. Very demanding to grow.

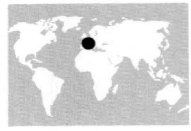

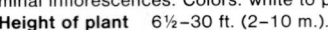

293 RHODODENDRON ARBOREUM Smith cv.
Common name: Rhododendron

Family Ericaceae.
Description Shrub or small ornamental tree. It has woody branches, springing from the base, and its persistent, oblong, coriaceous leaves are 6 in. (15 cm.) long and 2 in. (5 cm.) wide with dark-green upper sides and often rust-colored undersides. Its numerous campanulate flowers are clustered in terminal inflorescences. Colors: white to pink, purple and red.
Height of plant 6½–30 ft. (2–10 m.).
Size of flower 1½–2⅜ in. (4–6 cm.).
Place of origin Himalayas.
Flowering time Spring.
Cultivation A semishaded position in a cool-temperate climate. Stands cold quite well. Likes a constantly moist acid soil. Ideal potting compost mixes heath or fibrous woodland mold with leaf mold and composted beech leaves. Requires periodic feeding with an organic-mineral fertilizer. Plentiful overall watering and spraying. Prune by removing dead and weak growth and straggly shoots. Pests and diseases: scale and gnawing insects; fungus diseases and chlorosis.
Propagation By cuttings taken in the summer from the branch ends of the current year's growth; by layering; by grafting; or by seed.
Qualities Suitable for growing either in groups or singly in special conditions on a terrace, in pots or containers. Half-hardy. A demanding plant.

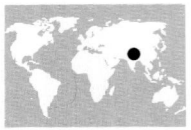

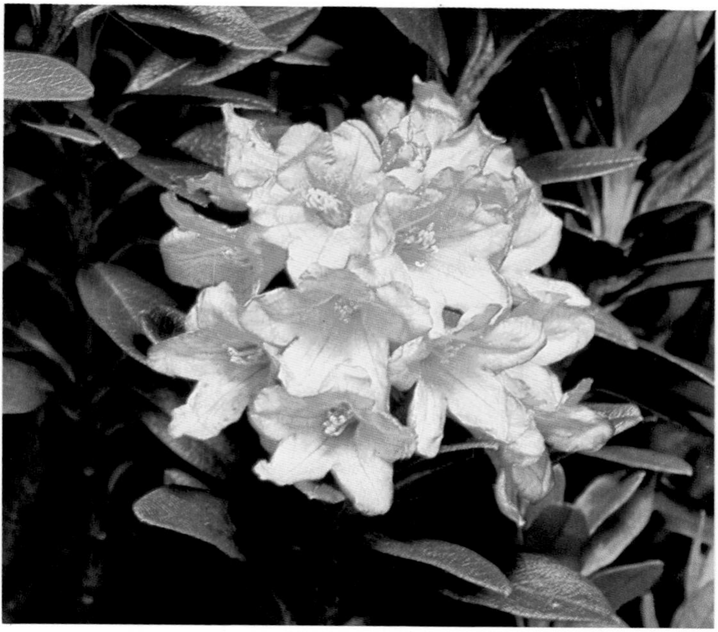

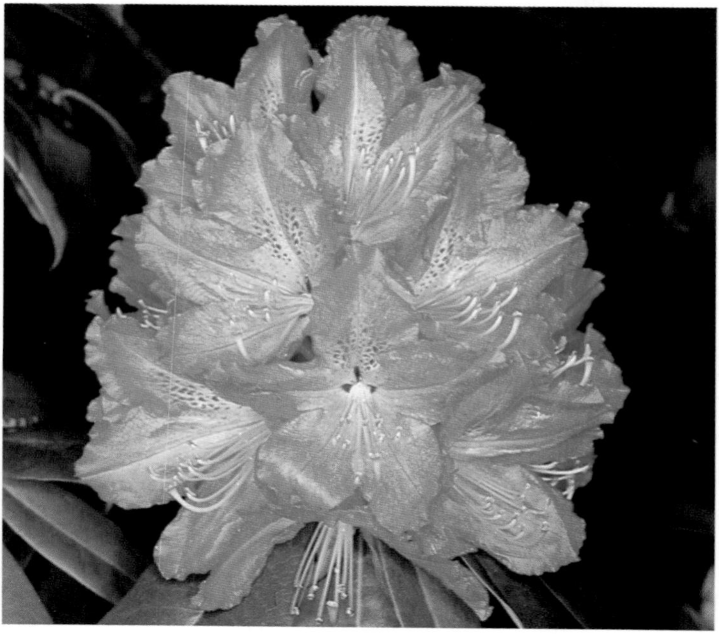

294 RHODODENDRON KIUSIANUM Tomitaro
Makino cv. "Apricot"
Syns.: *R. obtusum* (John Lindley) Jules Emile Planchon *japonicum* form (Karl Johann Maximowicz) Ernest H. Wilson, *Azalea obtusa* Hortorum. Common name: Hiryu azalea

Family Ericaceae.
Description A diffuse, well-branched, evergreen shrub. Its rather small leaves are lanceolate, acuminate-rotundate, tomentose and coriaceous. Its infundibuliform, terminally borne flowers are carried singly or in clusters. There are a great many cultivars of various sizes and flower colors.
Height of plant 20–40 in. (0.50–1 m.).
Size of flower ¾–1⅛ in. (2–3 cm.).
Place of origin Japan.
Flowering time Late spring.
Cultivation A very bright position. Cool-temperate climate. Suffers from the cold as much as from excessive heat. It likes an acid, light, fibrous, moist soil. If pot-grown, a compost consisting of heath mold, fibrous peat, leaf mold and silicate sand with a base of natural organic material such as ground lupine seeds, hoof-and-horn, etc. Lime-free water should be used plentifully. Pruning limited to light trimming and shortening of straggly branches. Pests and diseases: scale insects and red spider mites; fungus diseases.
Propagation By cuttings taken in early summer and rooted under glass.
Qualities Half-hardy. A demanding plant to grow.

295 RHODODENDRON LUTEUM Robert Sweet
Syns.: *R. flavum* George Don, *Azalea pontica* Carolus Linnaeus. Common name: Pontic azalea

Family Ericaceae.
Description A vigorous deciduous shrub. The young, pubescent branches have an open, erect habit with viscid buds. This species has given rise to many cultivated hybrids and is often used as a rootstock because of its vigor. Its alternate leaves are oblong-lanceolate and ciliate with a serrulate margin. Its numerous flowers are borne in terminal corymbs of seven to twelve. It flowers before its leaves unfurl.
Height of plant 5–8 ft. (1.5–2.5 m.).
Size of flower 1½–2 in. (4–5 cm.).
Place of origin Asia Minor and the Caucasus.
Flowering time Spring.
Cultivation An open, bright but shady position. Cool-temperate climate. Can withstand the cold well. Prefers slightly argillaceous-sandy soil, rich in organic material or amended with a generous introduction of peat, heath mold and leaf mold with some slow-releasing organic fertilizer. Plentiful watering with lime-free water. Pruning is not usually necessary but any straggly, weak or dead growth should be removed. Scale insects are often troublesome.
Propagation By half-ripened cuttings taken in the spring–summer and rooted under glass. By seed in pans in a temperate greenhouse. By layering in the spring.
Qualities Hardy. A demanding plant to grow.

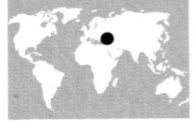

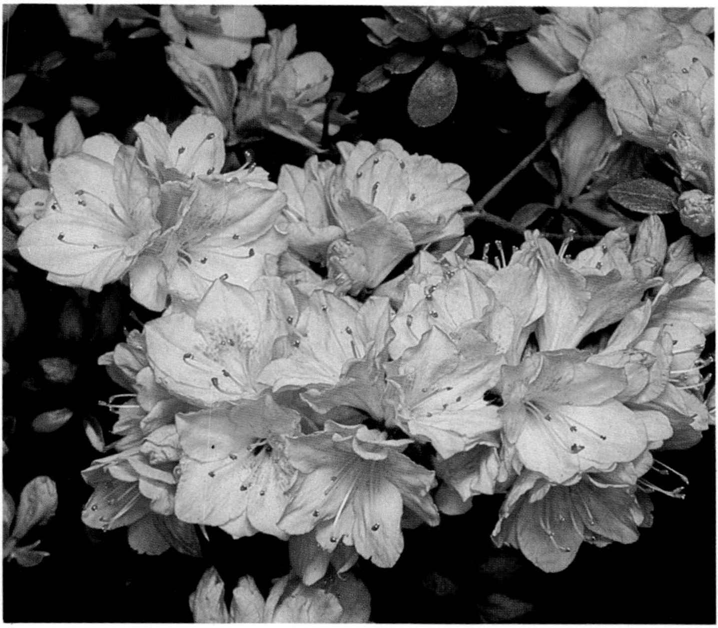

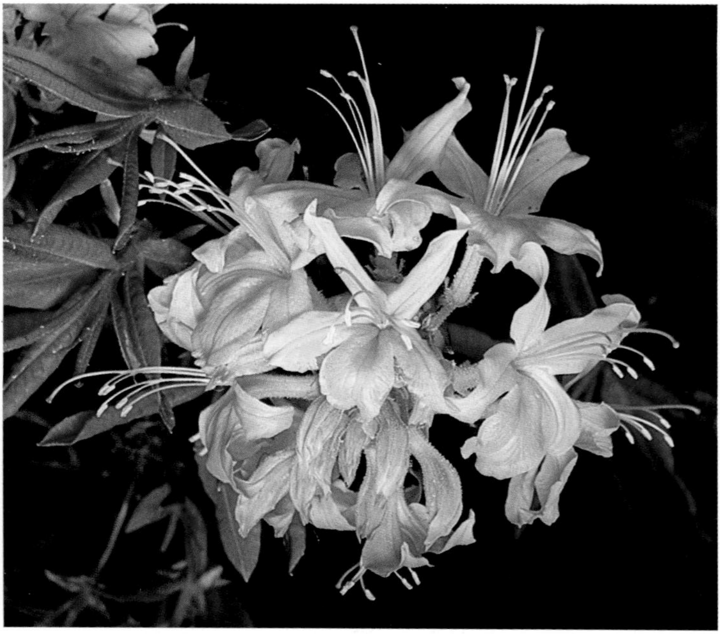

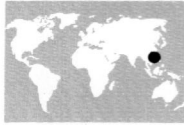

296 RHODODENDRON MOLLE (Karl Ludwig Blume) George Don

Syns.: *Azalea mollis* Blume, *A. sinensis* Conrad Loddiges. Common name: Mollis azalea

Family Ericaceae.

Description As a result of frequent crossings with *R. japonicum*, this species—of Chinese origin—has become the parent of a series of horticultural hybrids. Most of these are cultivated in the flower-growing industry as pot plants, especially in Holland, under the collective name of Mollis azaleas. They lend themselves particularly well to forcing under glass. The plants are usually sturdy, ligneous and of bushy habit with open ramifications. The pale-green, alternate leaves are sub-lanceolate, ciliate and often slightly revolute, with a short petiole. The flowers are numerous and showy, clustered together in globose terminal racemes of ten to twelve in various colors including pink, yellow and orange.

Height of plant 5–6½ ft. (1.5–2 m.).

Size of flower 2–3⅛ in. (5–8 cm.).

Place of origin China.

Flowering time Spring.

Cultivation A sunny, slightly shady position. Cool-temperate climate. Cannot withstand heavy frosts. This plant grows in argillaceous-sandy, moist, humus-rich soil, or where the ground has been enriched with fibrous peat, heath mold and leaf mold. Benefits from applications of liquid fertilizer during the growing period. Frequent and plentiful watering. Pruning limited to removing weak or straggly branches and dead growth. Pests: scale insects and red spider mites.

Propagation By cuttings or layering in the spring–summer. Sometimes by grafting. Also by seed in the spring but this is a slow process.

Qualities Fairly hardy. A demanding plant to grow.

Opposite: two cultivated varieties of Rhododendron molle. *Above,* Rhododendron molle *cv. "Hotspur Red"; below,* Rhododendron molle *cv. "Spek's Brilliant."*

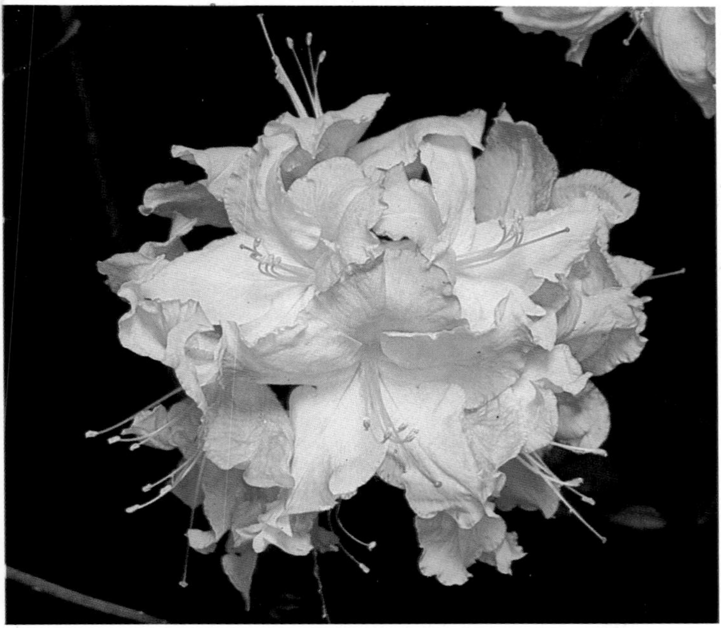

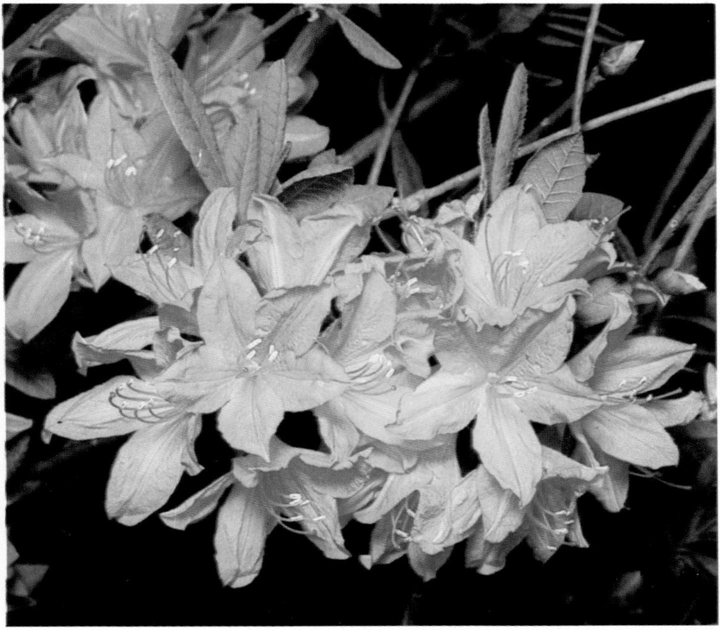

297 RHODODENDRON OBTUSUM (John Lindley)

Jules Emile Planchon
Syns.: *Azalea amoena* Lindley, *A. obtusa* Lindley.
Common name: Hiryu azalea

Family   Ericaceae.

Description   An evergreen shrub so densely ramified with slender branches as to form a compact, umbel-like head. Its small, numerous leaves are persistent, tomentose, oblong-elliptical and sub-lanceolate. Its abundant wine-red flowers are campanulate and single or fasciculate.

Height of plant   2–8 ft. (0.60–2.50 m.).

Size of flower   ¾–1 in. (2–2.5 cm.).

Place of origin   Japan.

Flowering time   Spring.

Cultivation   A bright, even sunny, position. Temperate climate. Ideal temperature between 41°–77° F. (5°–25° C.). Can withstand a few light frosts. Likes an acid soil (pH 4–5) or soil that has been amended with fibrous peat and leaf mold or heath mold with a little sand. Benefits from periodic applications of liquid fertilizer. Plentiful watering and, in the summer months, regular spraying. Pruning is limited to a little light trimming and removal of straggly or dead growth. Pests: scale insects and red spider mites.

Propagation   By half-ripened cuttings under glass in spring–summer.

Qualities   Half-hardy. A demanding plant to grow.

Opposite: two varieties of Rhododendron obtusum.
Above, Rhododendron obtusum *cv. "Amoenum," below,*
Rhododendron obtusum *cv. "Toreador Red."*

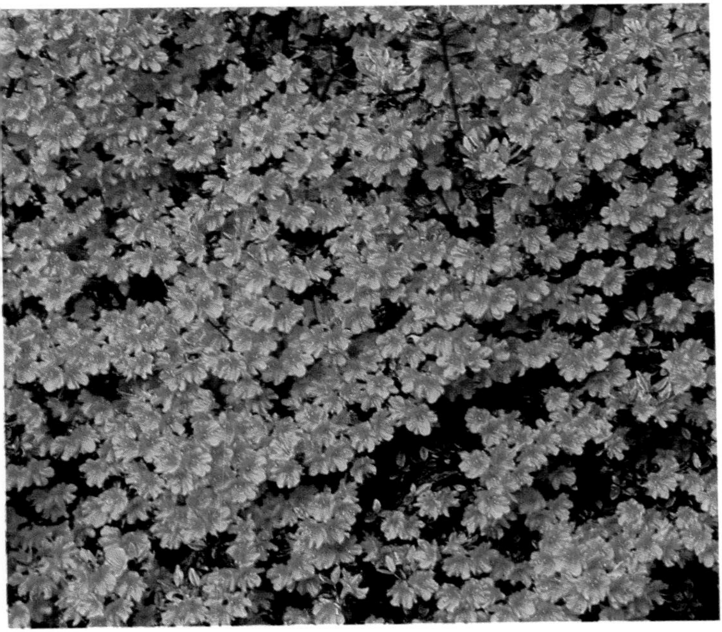

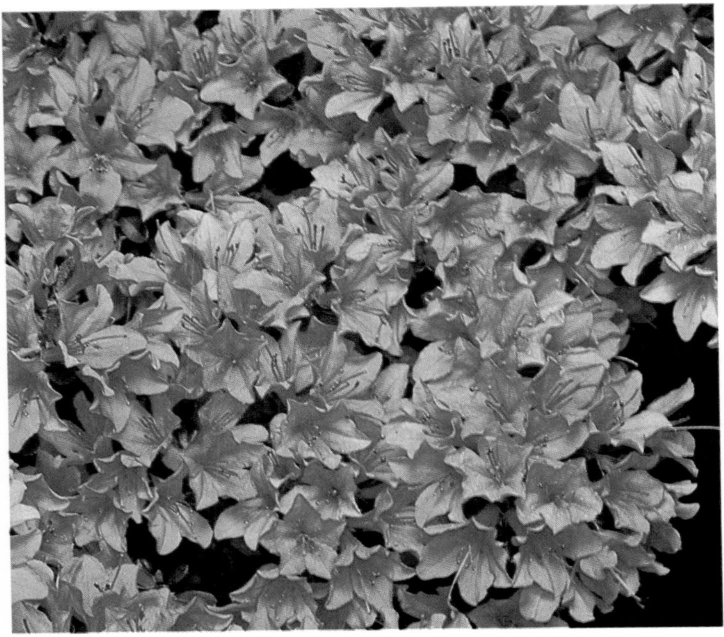

298 RHODODENDRON species cv.

Syns.: *Azalea indica* Hortorum, *R. indicum* Hortorum.
Common name: Azalea

Family Ericaceae.
Description The majority of azaleas available commercially as pot plants belong to this type. It is a bushy, compact plant with slender, fragile, ligneous branches. Its leaves are oblong-lanceolate and either alternate or arranged in terminal rosettes on the branches. Its numerous flowers, borne at the end of the branches, are white, pink, purple, variegated or flecked.
Height of plant 40–60 in. (1–1.50 m.).
Size of flower 1½–3 in. (4–8 cm.).
Place of origin Derived from *R. indicum,* in Japan.
Flowering time Spring.
Cultivation A shady but bright position. Cool-temperate climate. Prefers a light, humus-rich, lime-free soil with an acid reaction; if pot-grown, the compost should consist of woodland mold mixed with heath mold, peat and leaf mold. Periodic applications of an organic/mineral fertilizer. Regular and plentiful watering. Pests and diseases: scale insects and red spider mites; chlorosis, in unsuitable soil.
Propagation By half-ripened cuttings taken in the spring–summer and rooted under glass. By layering and/or air layering in the summer.
Qualities Very hardy. A demanding plant to grow.

---

299 RIBES SANGUINEUM Frederick T. Pursh
Common name: Flowering currant

Family Saxifragaceae.
Description A small deciduous shrub with bushy habit. Its deep-green alternate leaves are palmate-lobate. Its abundant blooms are carried gracefully in racemes, which spring from the foliar axils, of pendulous clusters of florets. The deep-pink flowers, which are unscented, are followed by black berries gleaming with pruina. There are several cultivars whose flowers vary in depth of color.
Height of plant 5–6½ ft. (1.50–2 m.).
Size of flower $^{3}/_{16}$–$^{5}/_{16}$ in. (0.5–0.8 cm.).
Place of origin Northwestern United States.
Flowering time Spring.

Cultivation A moderately sunny position. Temperate climate. Can withstand the cold well. Suited to almost any soil, even if slightly calcareous, provided it is rich and moist. Benefits from a top dressing of manure and mineral fertilizer in late winter. Plentiful watering in summer. Flowered branches should be cut back in autumn and the oldest removed altogether. Pests and diseases: various insects; fungus may sometimes attack.
Propagation By hardwood cuttings, about 8–12 in. (20–30 cm.) long, taken in late autumn and rooted in a sheltered nursery bed or propagating frame. By clump division in autumn or spring. Sometimes by grafting.
Qualities Hardy. Easy to grow.

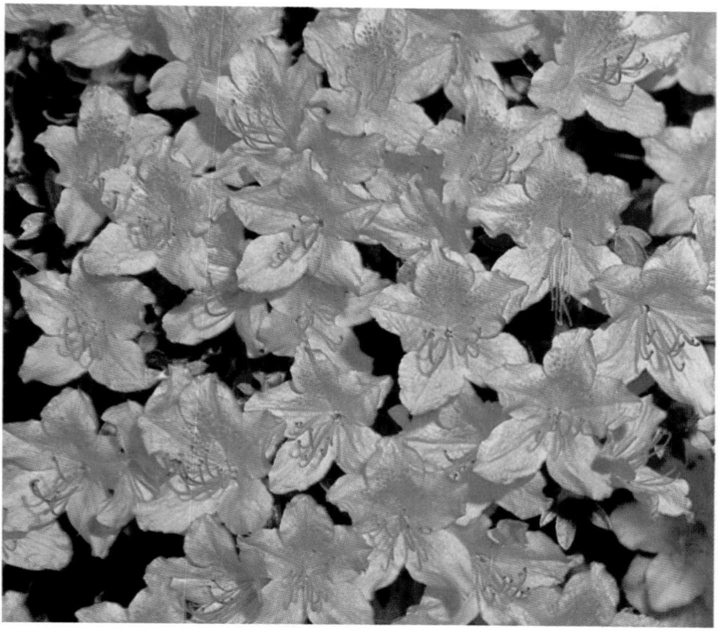

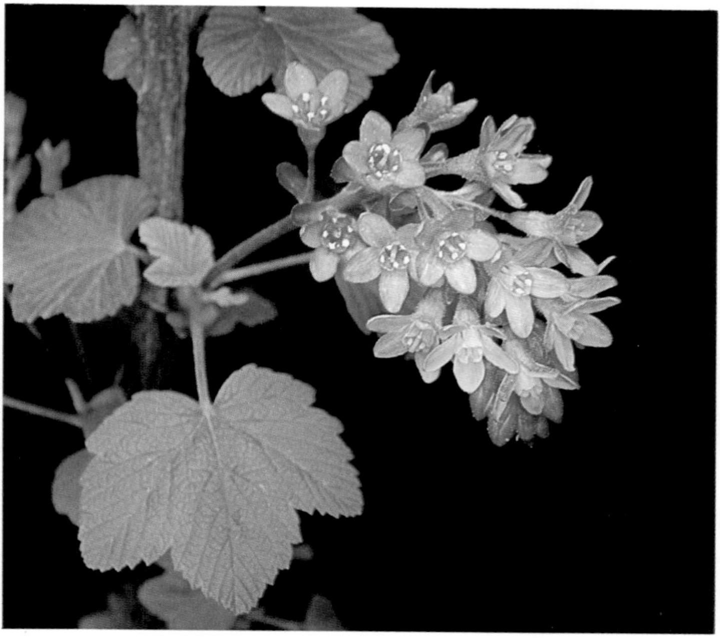

300 ROBINIA HISPIDA Carolus Linnaeus
Syn.: *R. rosea* Humphrey Marshall. Common name: Rose acacia

Family Papilionaceae.
Description A deciduous shrub, this is one of the most graceful and ornamental of the genus because of its foliage and delicately pink flowers. It has long, fragile, sometimes slightly pendulous ramifications which, with their covering of reddish hairs, are hybrid. Its alternate, imparipinnate leaves are composed of seven to thirteen ovate elliptical leaflets. The numerous flowers are borne in pendulous axillary racemes and have a long flowering period. The small tree forms are often obtained by grafting onto *R. pseudoacacia*.
Height of plant 5–8 ft. (1.50–2.50 m.).
Size of flower 1–1 ⅛ in. (2.5–3 cm.).
Place of origin Florida and Virginia.
Flowering time Spring and sporadically in summer.

Cultivation A well-exposed, sunny position. Temperate climate. Well able to withstand the cold. No special soil requirements but prefers siliceous-argillaceous, rich, moist ground. Does not need any particular care. Slow growth can be overcome by a spring application of manure and minerals. To achieve a nicely balanced plant, prune to shape in late winter.
Propagation Generally by grafting on to *R. pseudoacacia*.
Qualities Hardy. Easy to grow.

---

301 ROBINIA PSEUDOACACIA Carolus Linnaeus
Common name: Black locust

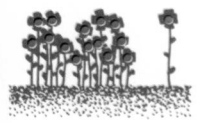

Family Papilionaceae.
Description A tree with open ramifications. A very hardy plant that naturalizes easily and is often invasive. Because of its strong roots and strong, decay-resistant wood, it is very useful for reinforcing sloping sites where soil erosion is a threat. Its numerous melliferous flowers are quite ornamental; they are scented and borne in pendulous racemes. Its alternate leaves are imparipinnate with oblong or elliptical leaflets. There are several cultivars.
Height of plant 16–80 ft. (5–24.4 m.).
Size of flower 1–1 ⅛ in. (2.5–3 cm.).
Place of origin Eastern United States.
Flowering time Spring.
Cultivation Full sun. Temperate climate. Well able to withstand the cold. Suited to any soil. Does not require particular attention. Can be pruned hard without ill effects; pollarding and basal cutting encourage a tremendous number of radical shoots to develop. Trouble-free as long as it is kept away from areas where not wanted.

Propagation It often reproduces itself freely by seed or by radical shoots.
Qualities Hardy. Very easy to grow.

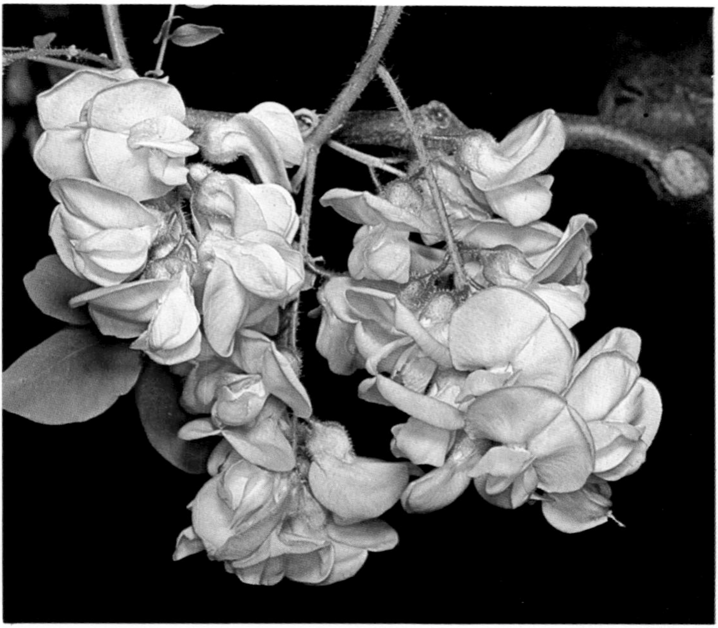

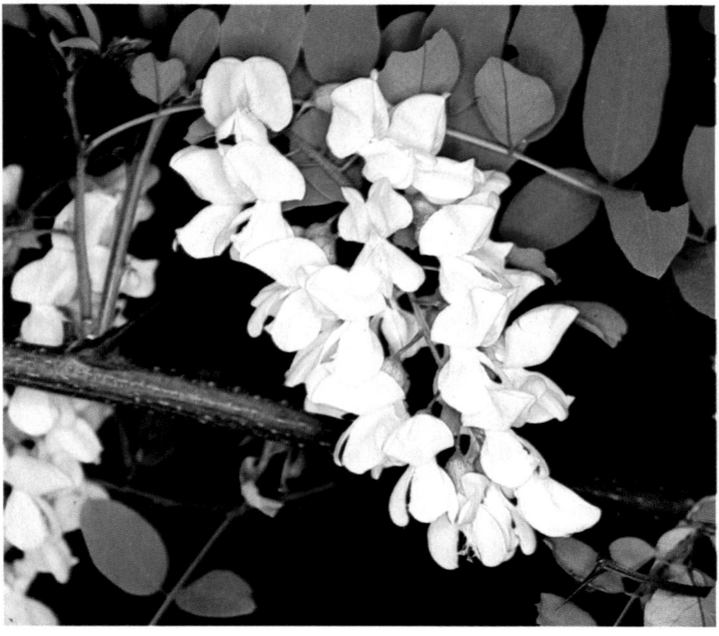

302 ROSA
Common name: Rose

The rose is an ancient plant, its origins lost in prehistory. Fossils bear witness to its presence in Europe, Asia and America many millions of years ago. Even then, there were numerous species that in the course of their evolutive pattern have given rise to more than 200 species now in existence in the temperate and subtropical regions of the boreal hemisphere.

Roses were introduced at least 5,000 years ago, established by references in the history of the Sumerian civilization during the fourth and third millennia B.C. as well as in that of Babylonia and Persia. At about the same time the Chinese were extracting the oil to use in the making of perfumes. The rose has been extensively used in the representation of floral motifs since antiquity in pictorial art, architecture, etc. Found frequently in heraldic devices, it has always been a symbol of elegance, nobility and decorum. A rose without thorns is still the symbolic flower of England.

Wild roses, used frequently in cultivation, are recognized easily by five-petaled single flowers. In floriculture they are referred to as "botanical roses" and include the hybrids subsequently obtained from crossings of different wild species.

Some of the best known botanical roses include: *R. gallica, R. damascena*, and *R. sempervirens*. All other roses are the result of multiple successive crossings, and it is therefore difficult to establish the parentage of these hybrid forms. Only those hybrids produced by the few world-renowned growers have a reliable genealogy, which gives great distinction to such crosses. Classification is very complex and has undergone several variations through the years. The main groups are:

Old roses
These are the oldest hybrids, which include such classic forms as *gallica* (species), "Bourbon," "Portland," "Peychnal," "Tea Rose," *x alba* (species), *centifolia* (species).

Hybrid tea roses
A very numerous group identifiable by the rather large blooms. Several varieties produce flowers 4–6 in. (10–15 cm.) in diameter, with a strong fragrance. Flowering continues for most of the summer, from June to October. A few examples are "Alexander," "Bonsoir," "Chicago Peace," "Fragrant Cloud," "Piccadilly."

Floribundas
These roses are usually smaller than the hybrid teas. The flowers, borne in clusters, may be single, semidouble or double, and several of the varieties are scented. They bloom from June to October. Also included in this group are the so-called *R. polyantha* and it is difficult to distinguish between the two. Examples are "Allgold," "Anna Wheatcroft," "Elizabeth of Glamis," "Iceberg."

Modern shrub roses
Typified by a number of large-flowered, nonclimbing roses that sometimes bloom from June to September. May reach a height of about 6–7 ft. (2 m.) and form thick bushes. Examples: "Angelina," "Kathleen Ferrier," "Will Scarlet."

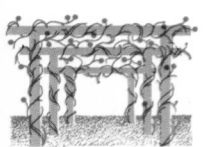

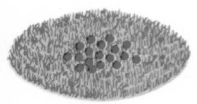

Opposite: above, "Mermaid" rose (1918), a climber/rambler; below, "Clair Matin" rose (Sélection Meilland, 1962), a modern shrub.

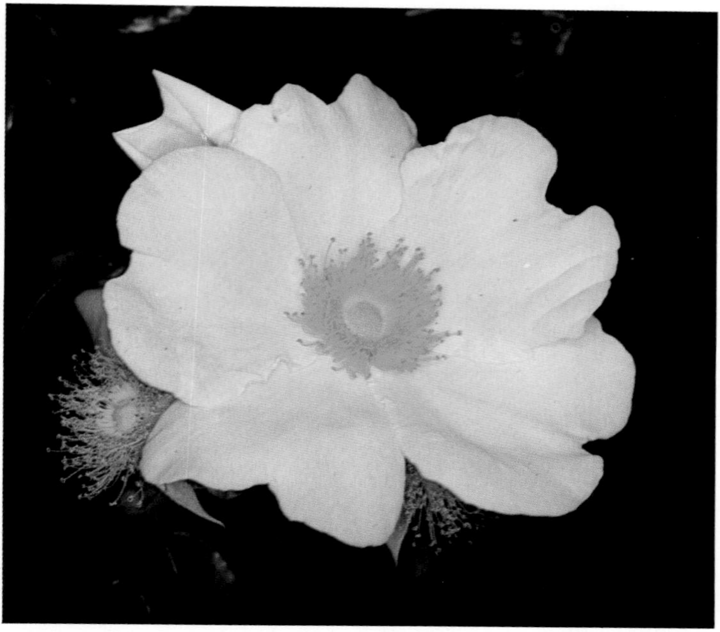

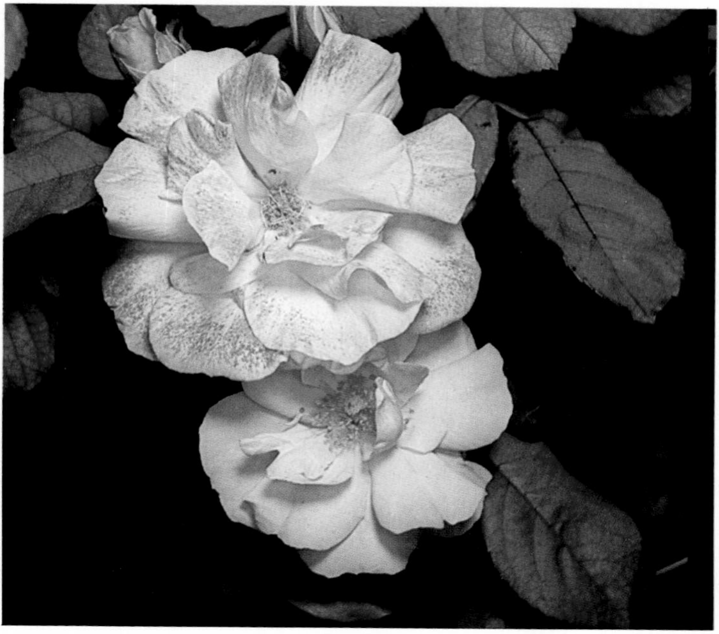

Climbers and Ramblers

Climbing roses have a vigorous habit. Some varieties bloom almost continuously and some have two distinct flowering periods. They may grow as high as 50 ft. (15 m.) and therefore need to be supported, either with poles, pergolas, etc., or against a wall. Examples are "Mermaid" (climber), "Dorothy Perkins" (rambler—double), "Excelsa" (rambler—double), "Sander's White" (rambler—double).

Miniature

These grow as tiny bushes with semidouble or double flowers about ¾–1⅛ in. (2–3 cm.) in diameter. Plants vary in height from 6–15 in. (15–40 cm.). This group does not have a great range of varieties but some of the better known are "Baby Masquerade," "Perla de Alcanada," "Cinderella."

Roses are versatile plants and adapt to almost any kind of soil and almost any site. The ideal conditions, however, for a rose garden are an open position in full or almost full sun; deep, rich soil, moderately compact to well aerated, sandy, moist and with a slightly acid reaction. Amend soil that is either too light or too heavy. Soil that is very open and sandy requires a great deal of organic material worked into it. Before laying out a rose garden

Opposite: above, "Princesse Grace de Monaco" rose (Sél. Meilland, 1956), a hybrid tea; opposite, below, "Princess Stephanie" rose (Sél. Meilland), a modern shrub. Below: "Catherine Deneuve" rose (Sél. Meilland, 1981), hybrid tea by floribunda.

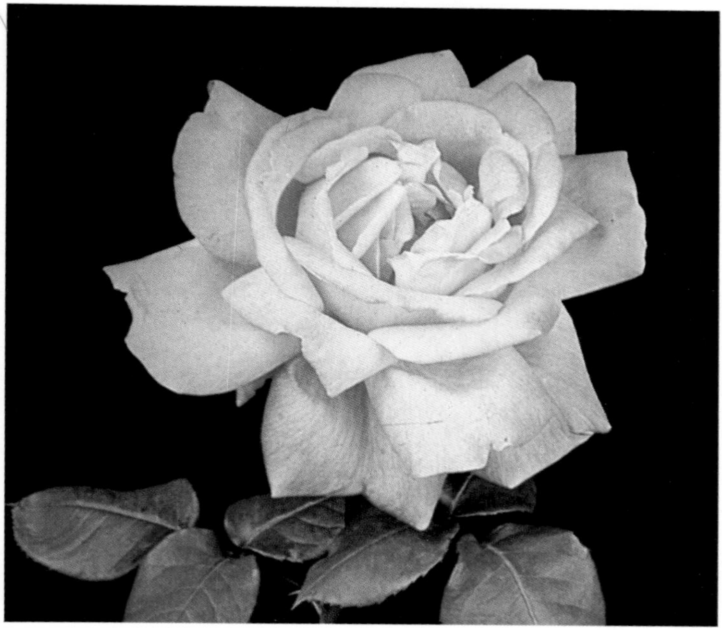

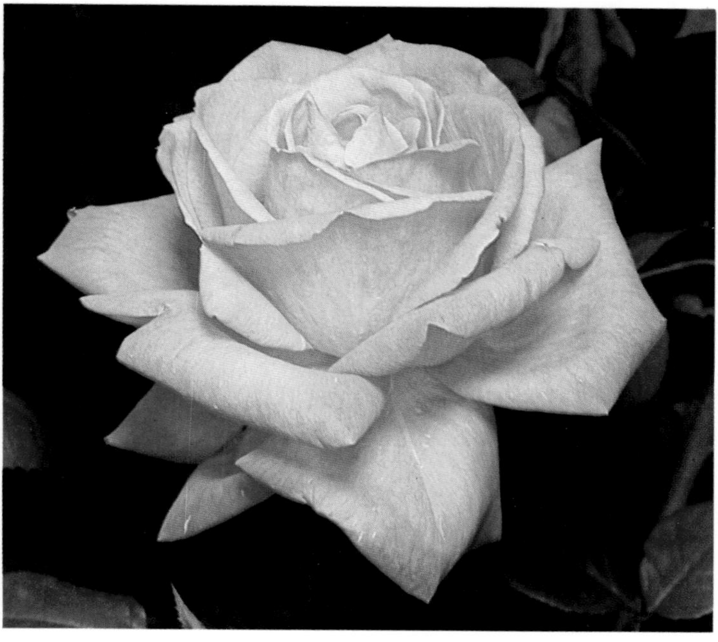

or planting a specimen rose tree or bush, the ground should be well dug to a depth of at least 12–14 in. (30–35 cm.) at least a month before planting. At the same time incorporate plenty of well-rotted manure with an organic base—about 12–20 pounds (6–10 k.) per square yard (meter)—and finish off with an application of about ¾–1 ounce (25–30 g.) per square yard (meter) of a slow-acting complete mineral fertilizer.

The best time of year for planting is the spring. Shrub roses, if not container grown, are often supplied with their roots bare and need to be prepared for planting in the following way:

1. Cut away any damaged, very old or distorted roots and reduce the others by a quarter or a third.

2. Check the branches, making sure that they have been pruned to 8–10 in. length (20–25 cm.) and cutting away any that are weak, damaged or overcrowded. Branches that are too long should be cut back to two or three buds.

3. If the roots are dry, immerse them for 4 to 12 hours in a solution of water and argillaceous soil mixed with cow manure. Planting can then be carried out, ensuring that the roots are well plastered with this compound.

4. Make sure each individual hole is the right size and shape to take the root system of the particular plant.

5. Put a layer of good, rich compost at the bottom of the hole,

Opposite: above, "Fragrant Cloud" rose, 1964, hybrid tea; opposite, below, "Super Star" rose (= "Tropicana"), 1960, hybrid tea. Below: "Mme. Edouard Herriot" rose, hybrid tea.

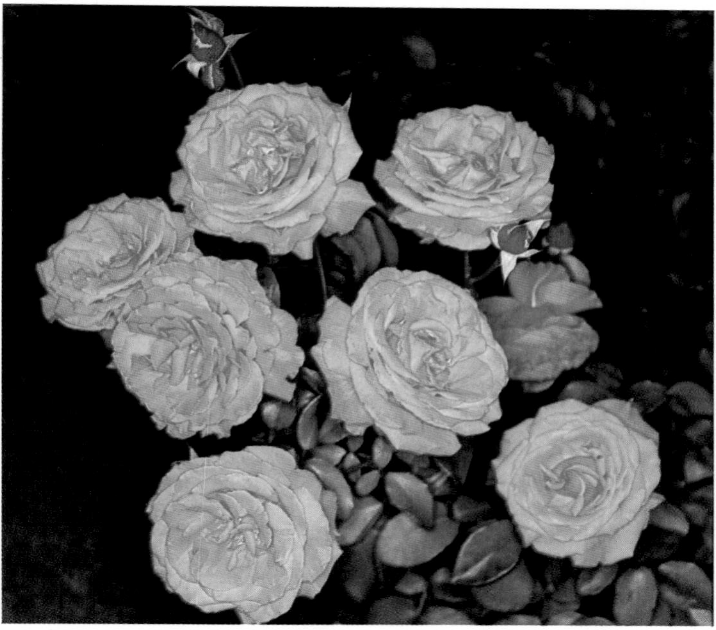

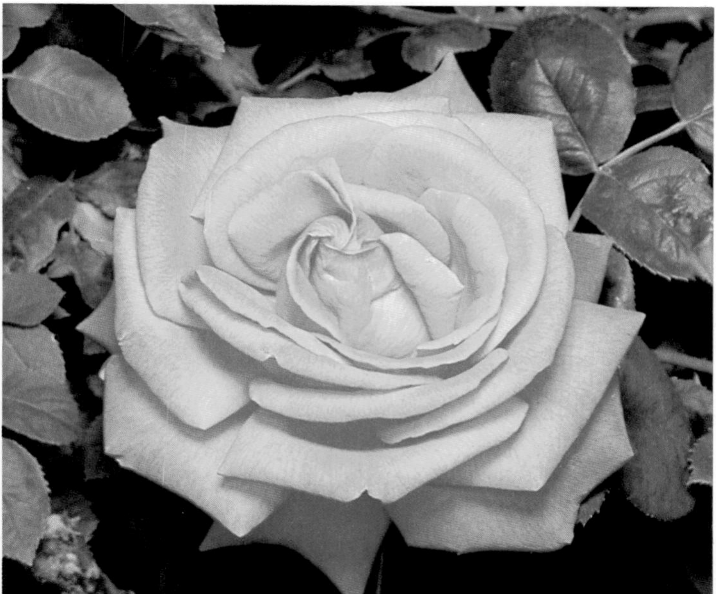

spread the roots out over it and cover them with more, but finer, planting compost. Press this well down all around the stem but make sure that the union of stock and scion (the crown) remains at soil level.

6. If planting in dry weather, follow with a thorough watering.

7. Standard and climbing roses should be staked or tied to an appropriate support.

Periodic feeding

A top dressing about 2 in. (5 cm.) deep of well-rotted manure or organic compost should be spread around the plants toward the end of winter or in early spring and lightly dug into the topsoil. If no manure is available, leaf mold, peat, grass clippings, etc., can be used. During the spring, a further dressing of a complete mineral fertilizer should be given—about 1 ounce (30 g.) per square yard (meter). At about midsummer, the mineral feeding can be completed with a dressing of about 1 ounce (30 g.) per square yard (meter) of sulfate of potash to encourage lignification of the branches.

Watering

Roses can usually survive a certain amount of dryness quite well. In very open, sandy, light or calcareous soils, and during very dry spells, however, they require plenty of water, preferably provided through irrigation and directly applied at the foot

Opposite: above, "Jelcanodir" rose (Sél. Meilland), hybrid tea by floribunda; opposite, below, "Mascotte" rose, (Sél. Meilland), hybrid tea. Below: red "H. T." rose, hybrid tea.

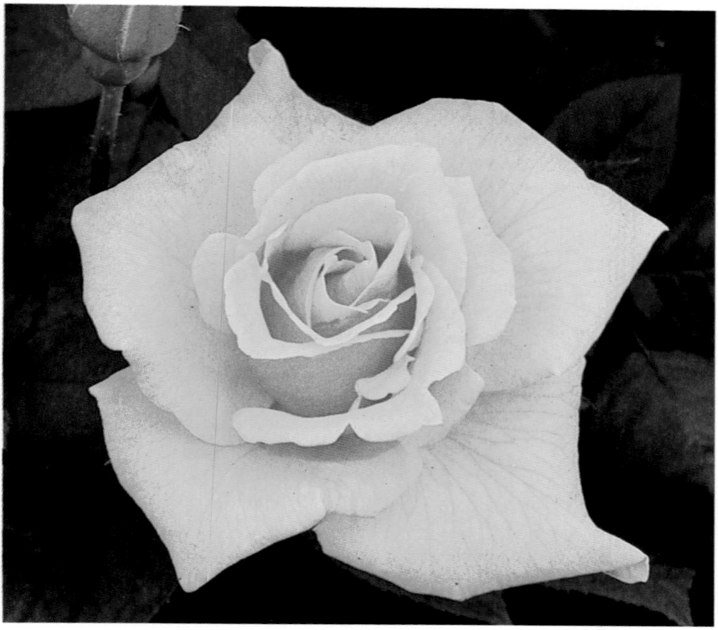

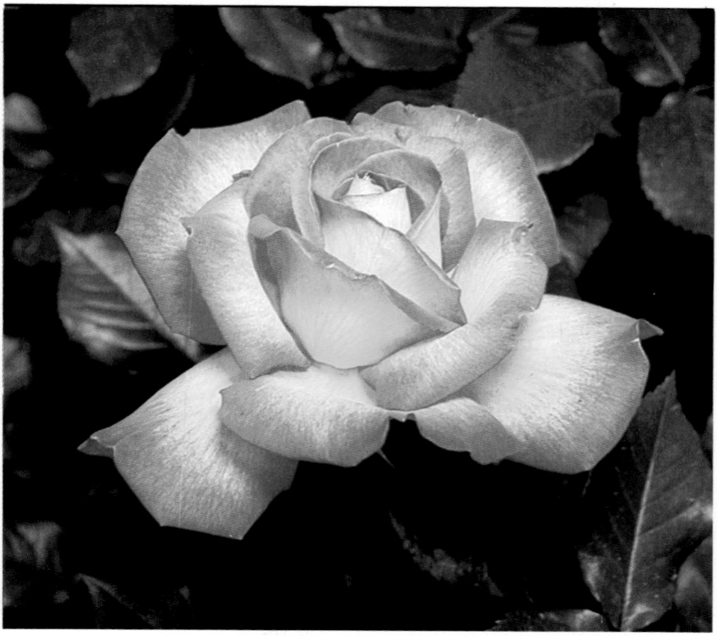

of each plant. Do not get water on the foliage or flowers since these may be damaged and diseases encouraged.

Pruning

Green pruning. All suckers springing from the roots, below the crown, must be removed. Also any that emerge from the stem of a standard rose must be removed close to the stem. To obtain large blooms, remove all buds that grow laterally to the main flower buds.

In the case of hybrid tea roses, shorten all flowering stems to one bud on the main ramification. In the case of *R. floribunda,* remove the flowering stem by cutting above the first bud.

Pruning individual shrub roses. To obtain large, strong blooms prune to two or three buds. For normal-size and more numerous blooms, prune to three to five buds. Remove weak growth or branches that cross or overlap, to open up the plant into a shape rather like a flowerpot.

Pruning bush roses or a rose hedge. Remove any dead or exhausted branches and shorten the longest by one-third. The lateral branches growing on the main branches should be shortened, too, by pruning back to one or two buds from the point of insertion. New shoots should be encouraged by cutting the old ones back to the point from which the new ones spring.

Pruning climbing roses. Prune in autumn or winter, cutting out dead, thin or weak branches. Leave the long new shoots to

Opposite: above, "Cocktail" rose (Sél. Meilland, 1957), modern shrub; opposite, below, garden rose "Paso Doble" (Sél. Meilland), floribunda. Below: "Charleston" rose (Sél. Meilland), floribunda.

replace the old weak ones. Shorten the old main branches by one-third and their lateral ramifications to one or two buds. If no new shoots have been formed, cut back the main ramifications to half their length.

Pruning rambling roses. The long growths produced by ramblers from their base are the flowering branches for the following year. Pruning, therefore, entails removing as much of the old growth as is necessary to equalize the amount of old growth and new shoots in order to balance the alternation of new branches and flowering growth (i.e., half will be in bloom each summer and half will be preparing to bloom the following year). New shoots will often be produced on old wood, rather than from the foot, probably 15–24 in. (40–60 cm.) from the base. If these are quite strong, it is a good idea to cut the old branch back to the point at which the new growth is springing.

Pruning standard rose trees. The same method can be applied as for shrub roses because a rose tree is really a shrub rose grafted on to a taller stem.

Pests and diseases Prone to infestation by aphids, leafhoppers, caterpillars and red spider mites; and to various fungus diseases such as oidium, rust, black spot, powdery mildew, honey fungus; and diseases of the root system.

Propagation By budding, cuttings and layering. Seed is a long process used by hybridizers to obtain new varieties.

Below: "Iskra" rose (Sél. Meilland), climber by floribunda. Opposite: above, "Chorus Mémoire" rose (Sél. Meilland), floribunda; opposite, below, "Imperator" (Sél. Meilland), floribunda.

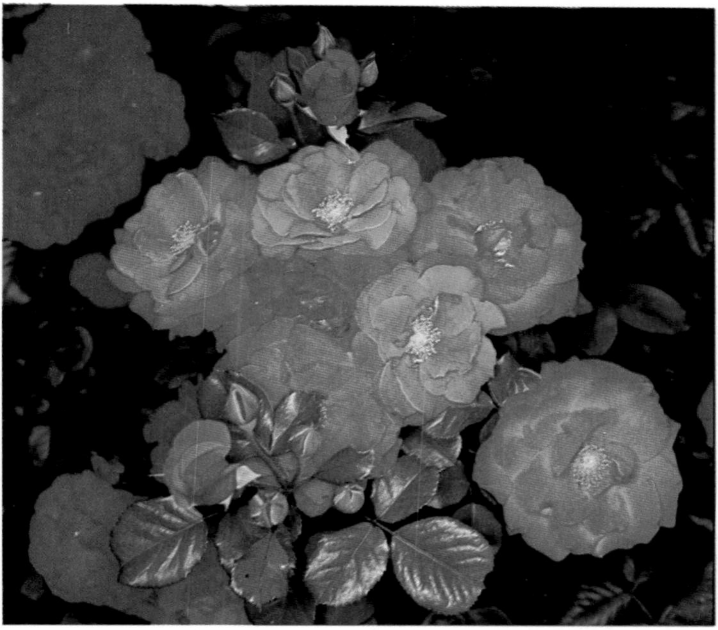

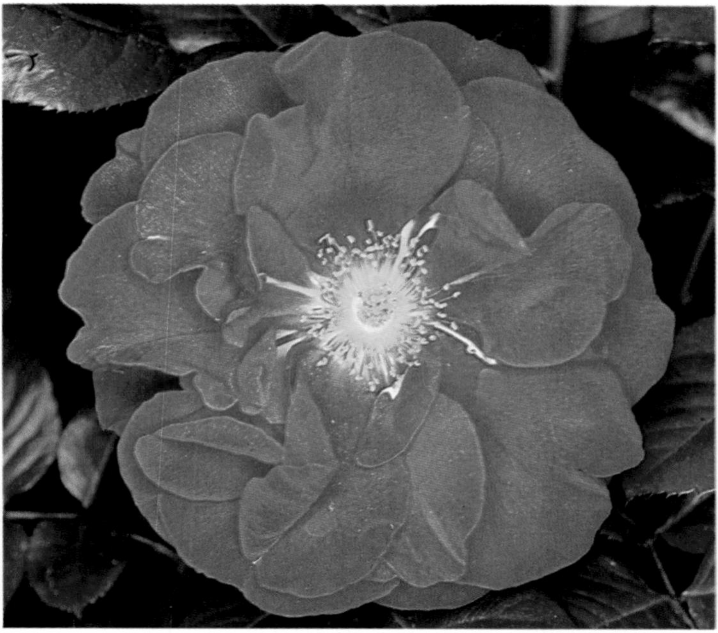

303 ROSA BANKSIAE William Townsend Aiton
Common name: Banks' rose

Family Rosaceae.
Description A vigorous climbing rose, partially deciduous, it is thornless, with long, slender ramifications. Its alternate leaves are composed of three to five leaflets, ⅞–2 in. (2.2–5 cm.) long and ⅜–1⅛ in. (1–3 cm.) wide, oblong-lanceolate, dentate and glabrous. The numerous sweetly scented white or yellow flowers are single in the wild form although under cultivation they may be single, double or semidouble. This rose comes within the category of climbing roses.
Height of plant 23–26 ft. (7–8 m.).
Size of flower ¾–1⅜ in. (2–3.5 cm.).
Place of origin China.
Flowering time Spring.
Cultivation Full sun. Sheltered position. Temperate climate. Fairly frost-resistant. Good garden soil, even if calcareous, provided it is fertile and moist. Periodic dressings of organic/mineral fertilizers. Autumn pruning to remove the old branches and to prepare the new ones by shortening the season's growth to two or three buds. Diseases: oidium and various fungus diseases.
Propagation By layering in spring–summer. By hardwood cuttings taken in autumn and rooted in a sheltered nursery bed.
Qualities Hardy. Easy to grow.

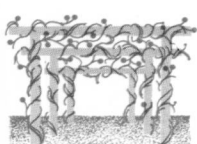

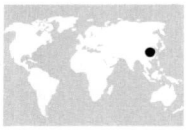

304 ROSA LAEVIGATA André Michaux
Syn.: *Rosa sinica* William Aiton. Common name: Cherokee rose

Family Rosaceae.
Description One of the typical old roses introduced from China, it is sarmentose and evergreen. It has a vigorous stem and bright-green trifoliate leaves with oval, dentate, coriaceous leaflets. Its very numerous single white flowers are sweetly scented and very similar to the "Mermaid" rose. It bears red hips in autumn and winter. This rose comes within the category of climbing roses.
Height of plant 16–23 ft. (5–7 m.).
Size of flower 3–4 in. (8–10 cm.).
Place of origin China.
Flowering time Summer.
Cultivation Full sun or very sunny. Temperate climate. In a cool-temperate climate it is inclined to be tender. Dislikes the cold and thrives in warm coastal regions. It likes a moderately heavy, rich, moist soil. Periodic dressings of organic and mineral fertilizers. Requires watering during the summer. It should be pruned to two or three buds if grown as an espalier. When growing freely, this plant can be rejuvenated by allowing the new growth to replace the old, flowered wood. Pests and diseases: aphids; oidium.
Propagation By semi-ripened cuttings; by layering; by budding and by seed.
Qualities Half-hardy. Easy to grow.

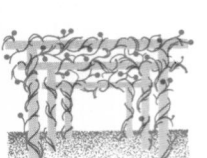

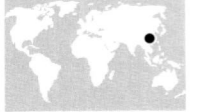

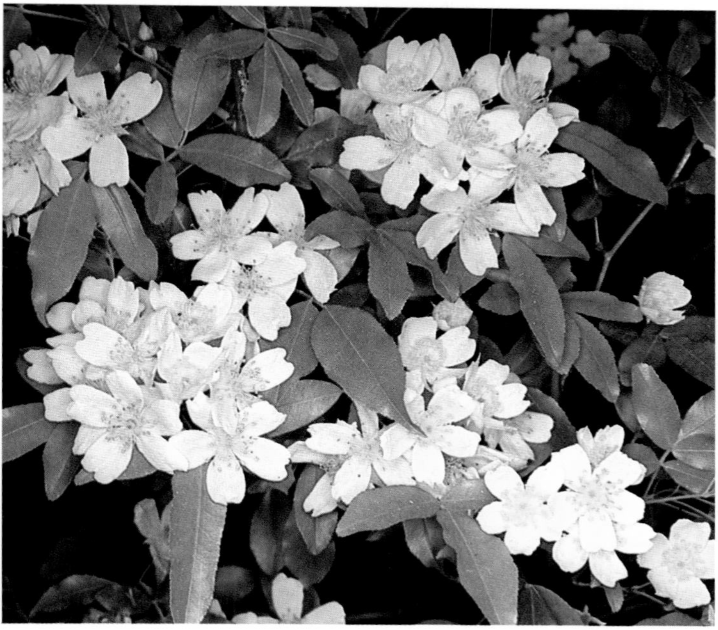

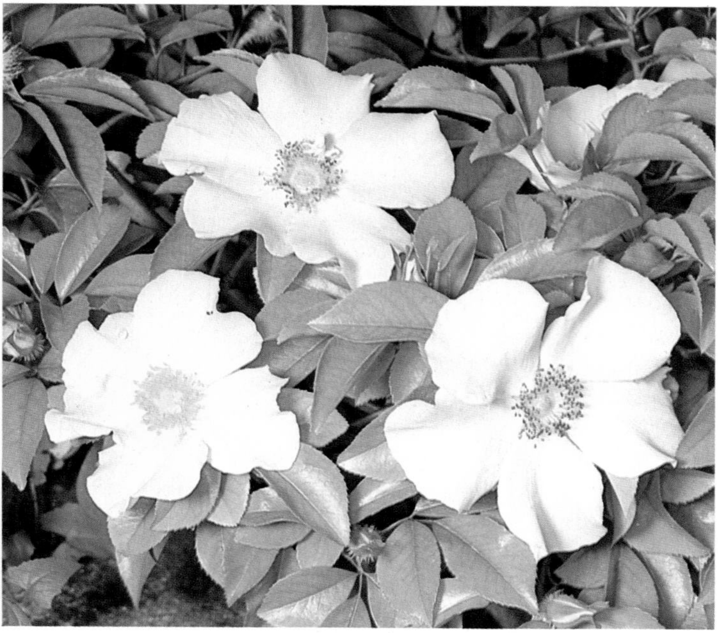

305 ROSMARINUS OFFICINALIS Carolus Linnaeus
Common name: Rosemary

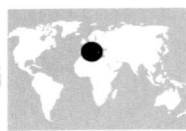

Family Labiatae.
Description A bushy evergreen shrub with numerous upright ramifications. Its small persistent leaves are opposite or grouped in clusters; they are linear and coriaceous, green on the upper surface and a silvery-whitish color on the lower. The numerous flowers are borne in foliaceous racemes toward the top of the branches. The whole plant exudes a pleasant aromatic scent and is well known for its medicinal qualities and as a culinary herb. It is very attractive to bees, which produce excellent honey from it.
Height of plant 20–60 in. (0.50–1.50 m.).
Size of flower ⅜–½ in. (1–1.5 cm.).
Place of origin Mediterranean coast.
Flowering time Spring.
Cultivation An exposed, sunny position. Temperate climate. Is able to withstand temperatures down to a few degrees below freezing point with only slight damage. Prefers argillaceous-sandy, rich, moist soil but can adapt very well to a dry site. Does not require watering. Can be made into a hedge. Pests: red spider mites are sometimes troublesome when this plant is growing in shade.
Propagation By division of basal shoots. By hardwood cuttings in autumn and spring. Sometimes by seed.
Qualities Also suitable for balconies, terraces. Hardy. Easy to grow.

306 RUDBECKIA HIRTA Carolus Linnaeus var. *bicolor* Thomas Nuttall
Syns.: *R. bicolor* Nuttall, *R. hirta* Linnaeus var. *pulcherrima*. Common name: Black-eyed Susan, gloriosa daisy

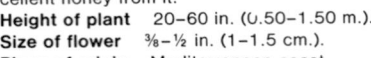

Family Compositae.
Description A herbaceous, bushy plant, it is a biennial grown as an annual. Its leaves are sessile, the lower ones lanceolate, and often ovate-acute. The flowers are borne in capitula on single or slightly ramified stems. The ray florets are deep yellow with red or reddish-brown shading at the base and a chestnut-brown disc. Foliage and stems are hispid.
Height of plant 2–3 ft. (60–90 cm.).
Size of flower 2⅜–4 in. (6–10 cm.).
Place of origin Northeastern United States.
Flowering time Summer.
Cultivation Grows well in a sunny to partially shaded position. Frost-tender. Likes moist, fertile, fairly heavy soil, even if argillaceous, but not siliceous. A top dressing of manure should be given when the ground is dug over. Plentiful watering in the summer. Usually trouble-free.
Propagation By spring sowing in boxes under glass.
Qualities Hardy. Easy to grow.

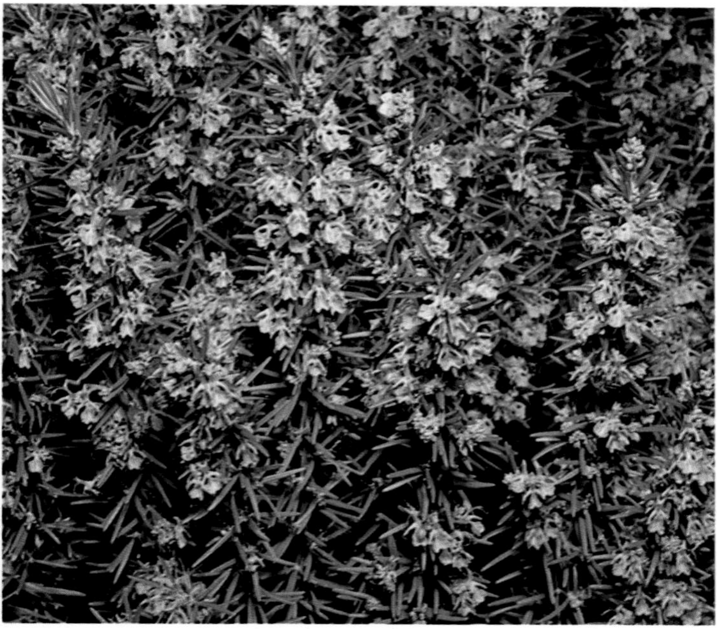

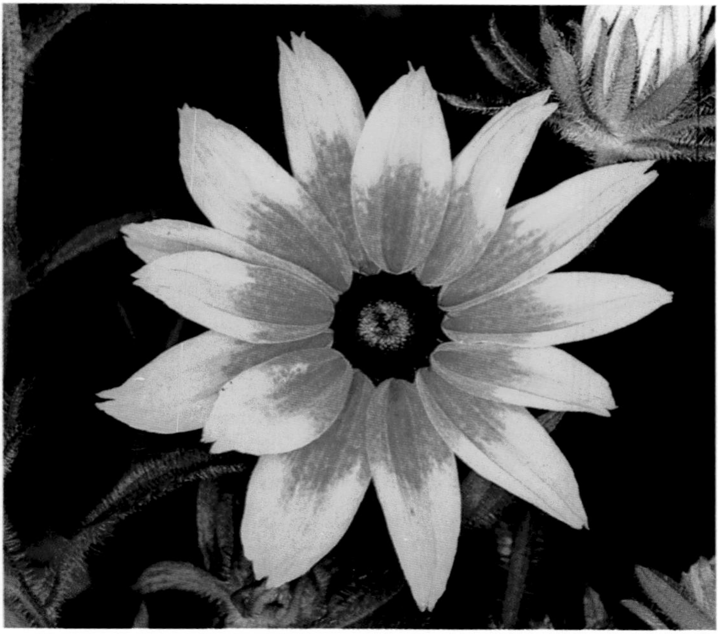

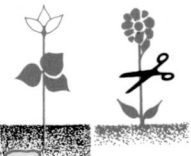

307 RUDBECKIA FULGIDA William Aiton

Syns.: *R. speciosa, R. newmanii, R. deamii.* Common name: Coneflower

Family Compositae.
Description A bushy herbaceous perennial. Its leaves are difform, sometimes cordate, linear, lanceolate and equipped with long petioles, although the top ones are almost sessile. The flowers are borne in isolated or small groups of capitula, originating from the axils of the leaves on the upper part of the stem. The ray carries about 20 yellow ligulate florets and the disc is a dark chestnut-brown.
Height of plant 16–22 in. (40–55 cm.).
Size of flower ¾–1¾ in. (2–4.5 cm.).
Place of origin Eastern United States.
Flowering time Summer–autumn.
Cultivation A sunny to partially shaded position. Temperate climate. It likes moist, humus-rich soil that tends to be heavy, even if calcareous. Can withstand a few frosts, especially if well mulched. Plentiful watering in the summer. Dry and yellowed foliage should be removed in the autumn. Usually trouble-free.
Propagation Mainly by clump division in spring. Also by spring sowing in boxes in a coldframe or cool greenhouse.
Qualities Hardy. Easy to grow.

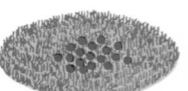

308 RUSSELIA EQUISETIFORMIS Diedrich Franz Leonhard von Schlectendahl and Adalbert von Chamisso

Syn.: *Russelia juncea* Joseph Gerhard Zuccarini. Common name: Coral plant

Family Scrophulariaceae.
Description A cespitose, shrubby plant, its main branches are decumbent while its secondary ones are slender, verticillate and filiform. Its few small leaves are opposite, ovate-lanceolate, denticulate and often reduced to linear scales. Its numerous pendulous flowers have a tubulous corolla and, when in full bloom, the plant appears to be raining red flowers. It makes a fine pot plant and is suitable for hanging baskets.
Height of plant 4–5 ft. (1.20–1.50 m.).
Size of flower 1⅛ in. (3 cm.).
Place of origin Mexico.
Flowering time Summer.
Cultivation An exposed, sunny position. Can live outdoors in a warm-temperate climate. Frost-tender. It is regarded as a temperate greenhouse plant in the colder regions. Prefers good, rich garden soil with occasional dressings of organic manure. If grown in a pot it should be repotted at least every two years. Pruning: exhausted branches should be cut out and any that are too long should be shortened.
Propagation By clump division. By basal shoot cuttings in the spring, rooted in a light compost in a propagating frame or greenhouse, then transferred to small individual pots.
Qualities Half-hardy to tender. Very easy to grow.

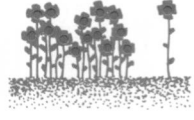

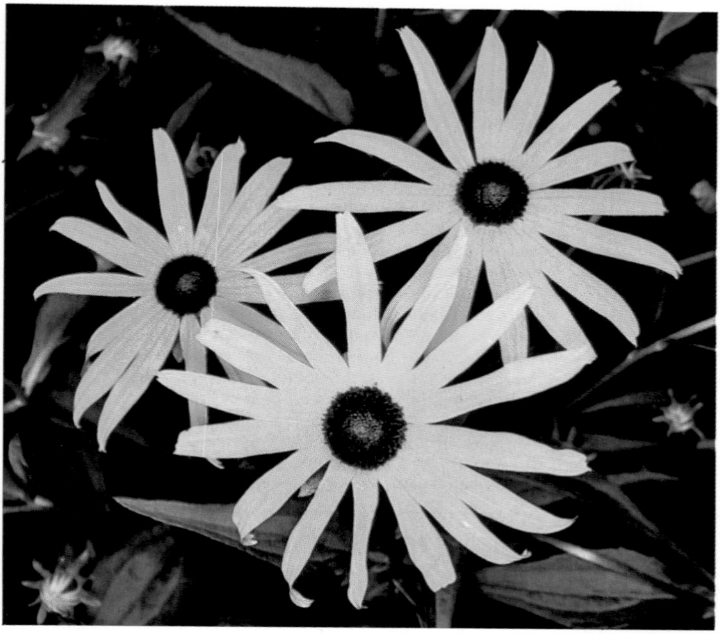

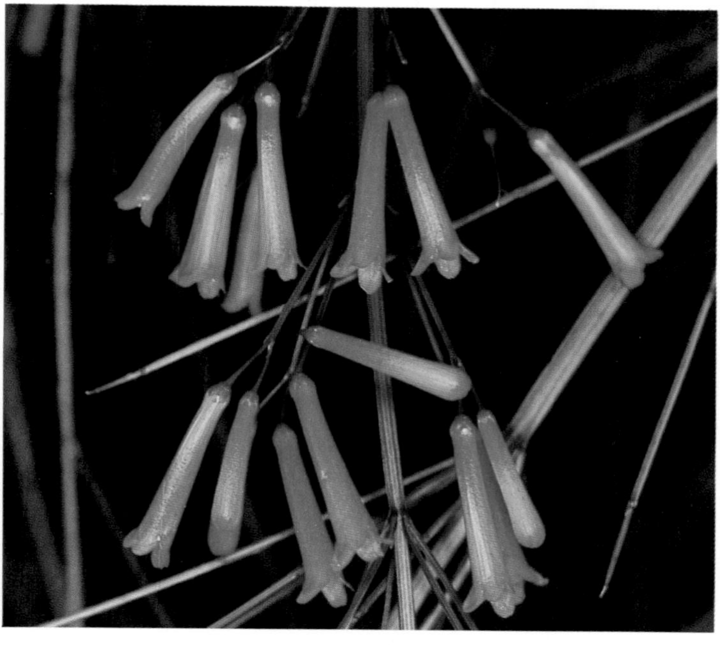

309 SALVIA SPLENDENS John Bellenden Ker
Common name: Scarlet sage

Family Labiatae.
Description Popular bedding plant—a perennial grown as an annual. Its frutescent, quadrangular stems are ramified from the base. Its leaves are opposite, ovate-acuminate and sub-cordate. Abundant flowers in terminal racemes that have a long life; most striking features are their brightly colored calyx and bracts, the same shade as the corolla. Several cultivated varieties are produced commercially in several brilliant colors.
Height of plant 8–28 in. (20–70 cm.).
Size of flower 1⅜–2 in. (3.5–5 cm.).
Place of origin Brazil.
Flowering time Summer–early autumn.
Cultivation Full sun to partial shade. Temperate climate. Grows in any garden soil, well worked and generously enriched with thoroughly rotted organic manure. If the ground is too compact, open up with peat or leaf mold. Frequent watering. Pests and diseases: red spider mites and leafhoppers; various types of rot and fungus diseases.
Propagation By late winter sowing in pans under glass.
Qualities Half-hardy. Easy to grow.

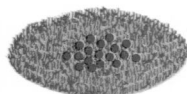

310 SALVIA INVOLUCRATA Antonio Jose Cavanilles

Family Labiatae.
Description Frutescent, cespitose subshrub with ovate-acuminate leaves. Numerous flowers in dense, difform, terminal racemes; the last flowers frequently do not fully blossom. Broad rose-pink bracts and a purplish-pink corolla.
Height of plant 5 ft. (1.50 m.).
Size of flower 1⅛–1½ in. (3–4 cm.).
Place of origin Mexico.
Flowering time Autumn.
Cultivation A bright position. Temperate climate. Frost-tender. Likes well-aerated, rich, sandy soil and periodic dressings of organic manure. Regular watering. Cut back flowered branches to an inch or two (a few centimeters), leaving the new basal growths untouched.
Propagation By clump division in the autumn. By half-ripened cuttings taken in spring–summer.
Qualities Suitable for balconies, terraces. Hardy only in its own environment. Very easy to grow.

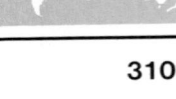

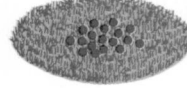

311 SALVIA LEUCANTHA Antonio Jose Cavanilles
Common name: Mexican bush sage

Family Labiatae.
Description Cespitose perennial; upright stems are tomentose and nodose, with lanceolate, pubescent leaves. Numerous flowers in verticillasters and strange bluish-white inflorescences.
Height of plant 40–50 in. (1–1.30 m.).
Size of flower ¾ in. (2 cm.).
Place of origin Mexico.
Flowering time Summer–autumn.
Cultivation, Propagation and **Qualities** As for *S. involucrata*.

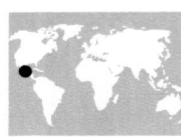
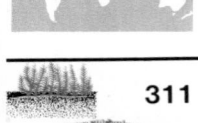
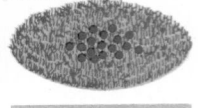

312 SANTOLINA CHAMAECYPARISSUS
Carolus Linnaeus
Syn.: *S. incana* Jean Baptiste Lamarck. Common name: Lavender-cotton

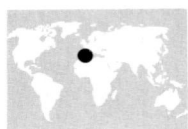

Family Compositae.
Description An evergreen low-growing bushy shrub with foliage that is rather more ornamental than its flowers. It grows in an attractive, compact cushion form and exudes a penetrating aromatic odor. Its tiny silvery-gray leaves are almost cylindrical, with obovate segments, and arranged in cupressus-like branchlets. The yellow flowers are borne in isolated, subglobose-hemispheric, terminal capitula.
Height of plant 12–27 in. (50–70 cm.).
Size of flower ⅜–¾ in. (1–2 cm.).
Place of origin Mediterranean regions.
Flowering time Summer.
Cultivation Full sun or partial shade. Temperate climate. Can withstand a few light frosts quite well. Grows in any type of soil, even if poor and dry. Very limited watering. Can be shaped as a hedge by trimming the plants lightly. Trouble-free.
Propagation By cuttings taken in spring or late summer.
Qualities Suitable for balconies and terraces. Hardy. Easy to grow.

313 SAPONARIA OCYMOIDES Carolus Linnaeus
Common name: Rock soapwort

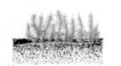

Family Caryophyllaceae.
Description A herbaceous perennial with prostrate-articulate, nodose stems. Its opposite leaves are about 1⅛ in. (3 cm.) long and elliptical or oval. Its carmine-pink or pale-pink flowers, which are similar to those of the Silene, are borne in corymbiform cymes; the calyx is tubulous with a stellate corolla.
Height of plant 8–18 in. (20–45 cm.).
Size of flower ¾–1 in. (2–2.5 cm.).
Place of origin Southwestern Europe.
Flowering time Spring–summer.
Cultivation Full sun. Warm-temperate climate. Arid, rocky or gravelly soil, tending to be calcareous. Requires no particular attention. Limited watering during the driest spells. All stems after flowering should be cut back lightly. Is able to grow in altitudes of up to 6,500 ft. (2,000 m.) above sea level. Cannot withstand heavy frosts.
Propagation By spring sowing in pots or directly in the flowering site.
Qualities Hardy. Easy to grow.

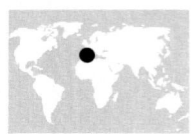

314 **SAXIFRAGA MOSCHATA** F. X. von Wulfen
Syn.: *S. muscoides* von Wulfen. Common name:
Saxifrage

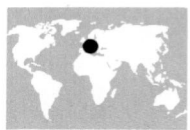

Family Saxifragaceae.
Description A herbaceous perennial with a creeping habit, forming a compact hummock. This plant is very ornamental when in bloom, the flowers so densely borne as to create a purplish-pink cushion. Its minute leaves are opposite or alternate, oblong, linear or spatulate. The flowers, either solitary or in small groups, are carried on a short peduncle. The elliptical-oblong petals vary in color according to the variety or hybrid. A suitable plant for a hilly or mountain-sited garden.
Height of plant 1⅛–3⅛ in. (3–8 cm.).
Size of flower ⅜ in. (1 cm.).
Place of origin Central Europe.
Flowering time Spring.
Cultivation A very sunny position. Cool-temperate climate. Withstands the cold well. Prefers gravelly, porous, moist, humus-rich soil. Plentiful watering in the summer. Does not require any particular care. Subject to various kinds of rot or blight in unsuitable surroundings or at too low an altitude.
Propagation By spring sowing in pans under glass or by separating the runners from the clump.
Qualities Hardy. Very easy to grow.

315 **SCHIZANTHUS PINNATUS** Hipolito Ruiz
Lopez and Jose Pavon
Common name: Butterfly flower

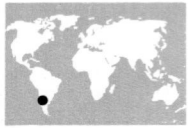

Family Scrophulariaceae.
Description A bushy annual with numerous erect, slender ramifications springing from the base. Its alternate leaves are pinnatifid and decreasing, divided into entire, oblong, dentate segments. It is extremely free-flowering and attractive with rather unusual flowers borne in compact, spicate, ramose racemes. The corolla is lobate in various colors including pink, red and white.
Height of plant 10–20 in. (25–50 cm.).
Size of flower ¾–1⅛ in. (2–3 cm.).
Place of origin Chile.
Flowering time Spring–summer.
Cultivation A bright or slightly shady position. Warm-temperate climate. Cannot withstand the cold and likes to be sheltered but open to the sun. Likes a fairly light, permeable, rich, sandy soil. Frequent but even watering, as this plant is susceptible to various kinds of rot. Requires frequent spraying with pesticides to ward off invasions of insects, especially aphids. Violent rain can damage the plants severely.
Propagation By sowing seeds under glass in late winter.
Qualities Half-hardy. A demanding plant to grow.

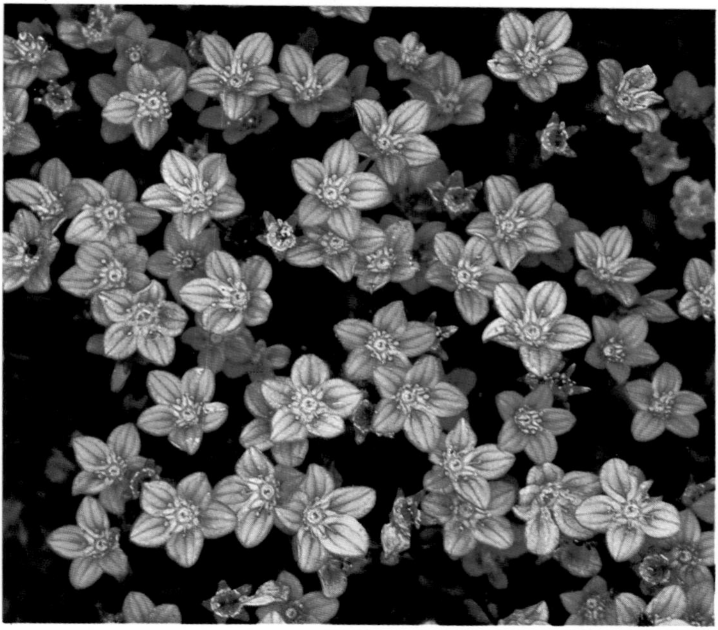

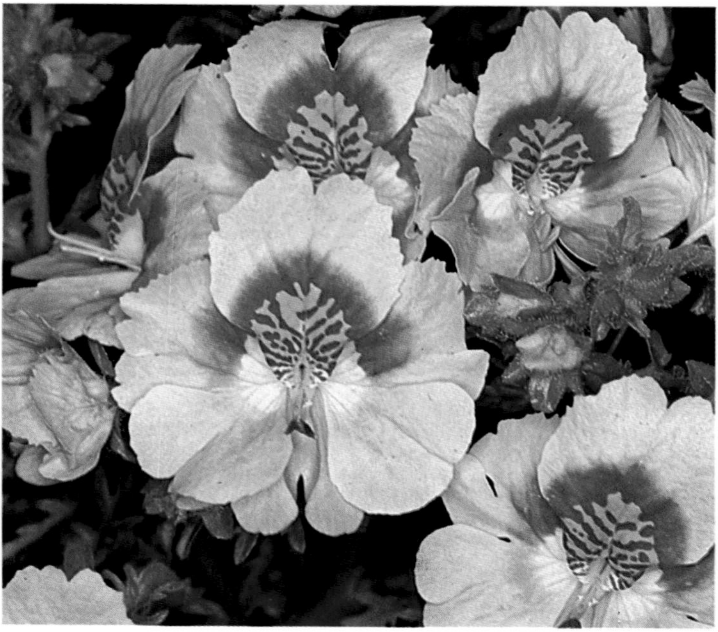

316 SCILLA PERUVIANA Carolus Linnaeus
Syn.: *S. clusii* F. Parlatore. Common name: Cuban lily

Family Liliaceae.
Description A plant with a large piriform bulb, its leaves are about 12–16 in. (30–40 cm.) long, carnose, linear-acute and arranged in a rosette. Its numerous flowers are borne in dense, conical, umbelliferous racemes with slender peduncles accompanied by two bracts of which one is long and the other short. The open, campanulate perigonium ranges from azure to dark blue.
Height of plant 6–10 in. (15–25 cm.).
Size of flower ¾–1⅛ in. (2–3 cm.).
Place of origin Western Mediterranean region.
Flowering time Spring.
Cultivation A moderately sunny position. Temperate climate. Can withstand light frosts. Likes rich, moist garden soil. This plant should be watered until it blooms, after which it rests. Does not require any particular attention. Very long-lived. Not prone to diseases.
Propagation By bulblets. By seed, but it will be two to three years before the first flowering.
Qualities Hardy. Easy to grow.

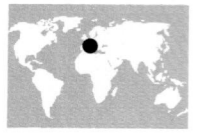

317 SEMPERVIVUM ARACHNOIDEUM Carolus Linnaeus
Common name: Cobweb houseleek

Family Crassulaceae.
Description A very proliferous herbaceous perennial. It forms compact groups of persistent, globose, acauline rosettes with acute, oblong, succulent, glandular, hispid, imbricate leaves covered at the top with fine white threads like a cobweb. Its numerous small, stellate, pink or reddish flowers are borne at the apex of foliose scapes.
Height of plant 4–6 in. (10–16 cm.).
Size of flower ½–¾ in. (1.5–2 cm.).
Place of origin Mountainous regions of southern Europe.
Flowering time Spring.
Cultivation Full sun in very shallow soil. Temperate climate. Can withstand a few light frosts. Likes porous soil even if calcareous and arid. Very resistant to dry conditions. Watering should be kept to a minimum. Feeding limited to a little powdered organic fertilizer. Exhausted rosettes should be removed after flowering period.
Propagation By detaching some of the numerous offsets. By spring sowing in boxes of light, very sandy compost, to germinate in a greenhouse or coldframe.
Qualities Hardy. Easy to grow.

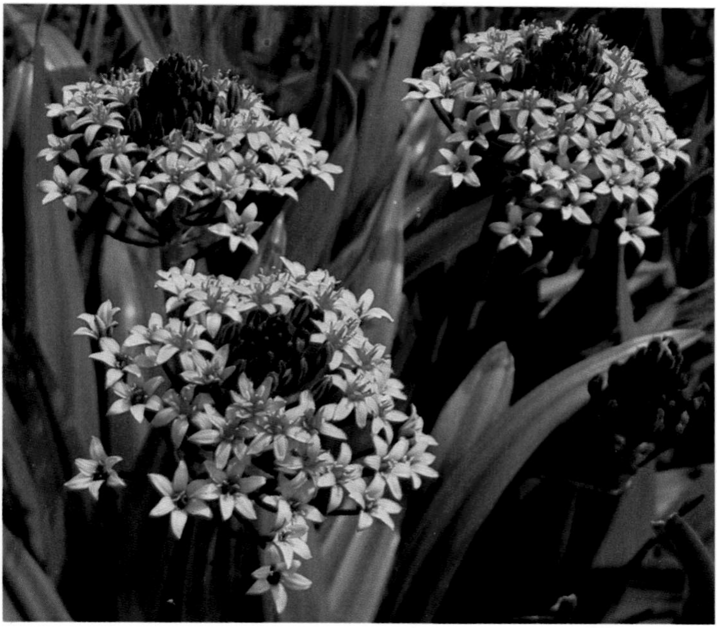

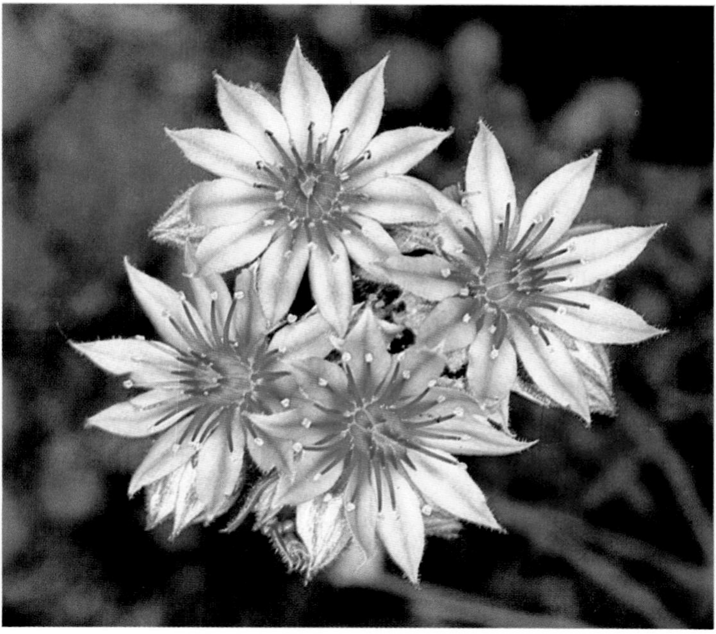

318 **SENECIO CINERARIA** Augustin Pyramus De Candolle
Syns.: *Cineraria maritima* Carolus Linnaeus, *S. maritimus* (Linnaeus) Heinrich Gottlieb Ludwig Reichenbach, *S. bicolor, C. bicolor.* Common name: Dusty miller

Family Compositae.
Description A bushy, suffruticose plant with weak, untidy ramifications. Its persistent leaves are oblong-pinnatosect and incised. Its leaves and stems are covered in a silvery sericerous down that gives them a decorative appearance. The flowers, less decorative than the leaves, consist of yellow daisylike capitula, borne in corymbs at the end of the branches.
Height of plant 2–3 ft. (60–95 cm.).
Size of flower ½–¾ in. (1.5–2 cm.).
Place of origin Western Mediterranean region.
Flowering time Spring–summer.

Cultivation A sunny position, even near the sea. Temperate climate. Cannot withstand much frost. Grows in almost any well-aerated soil that is sufficiently fertile and moist. Can survive dry conditions very well. Watering limited to particularly dry spells in the summer. Dead, weak and exhausted growth should be removed after flowering and any straggly branches trimmed. Trouble-free.
Propagation By cuttings taken in spring–summer and rooted in a sandy compost in boxes in a propagating frame. By clump division in autumn or spring. Also by seed.
Qualities Hardy. Easy to grow.

---

319 **SENECIO CRUENTUS** (Masson) Augustin Pyramus De Candolle
Syns.: *Cineraria cruenta* Masson, *C. multiflora.* Common name: Cineraria

Family Compositae.
Description Herbaceous perennial with lobate leaves of various sizes, and marginally dentate. Its flowers are in capitula borne in large corymbs. Colors include white, pink, light blue, dark blue, red, etc. Numerous hybrids divided into three groups: "Hybrida Grandiflora," 12–16 in. (30–40 cm.), with single capitula and large, broad-petaled flowers; "Multiflora Nana," with single capitula and broad ray petals; "Stellata," with double capitula and narrow ray petals.
Height of plant 8–16 in. (20–40 cm.).
Size of flower 1⅛–3⅛ in. (3–8 cm.).
Place of origin Canary Islands.
Flowering time Spring.

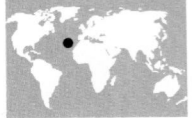

Cultivation Partial shade. Warm-temperate climate. Frost-tender. Likes porous-fibrous compost of leaf mold, peat and some sand with some well-rotted organic manure and a pinch of dried blood. Plentiful watering and liquid fertilizer every 15–20 days. Attacked by aphids and fungus diseases.
Propagation By summer sowing in pots or pans to germinate in a coldframe at 55° F. (13° C.); seedlings will require pricking off into boxes, followed by potting up and then potting on at least once more. Flowering takes seven or eight months.
Qualities Half-hardy. A demanding plant to grow.

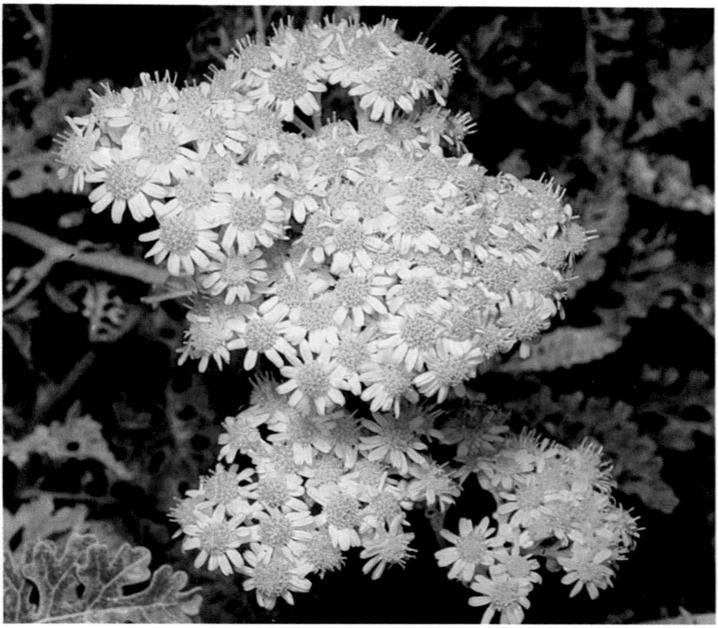

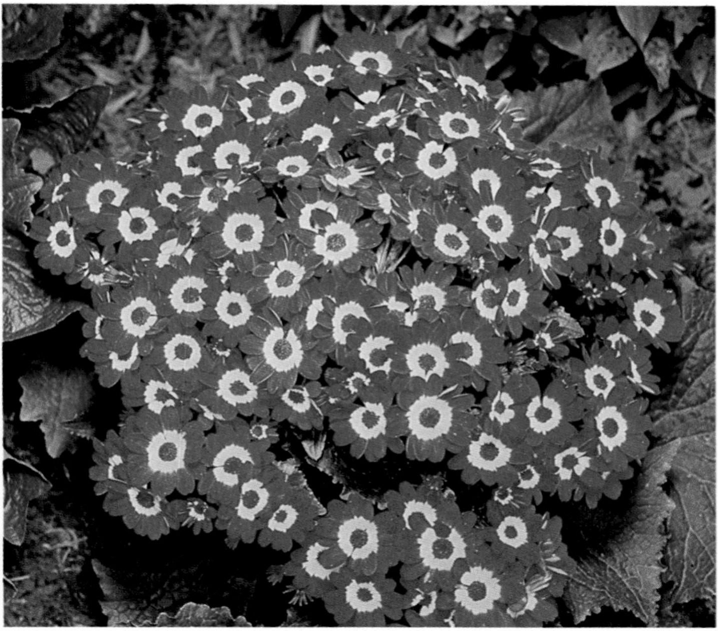

320 SENECIO PETASITIS (John Sims) Augustin Pyramus De Candolle
Syn.: *Cineraria platanifolia* Schrad

Family   Compositae.
Description   A dense, bushy shrub with rather thick, pubescent ramifications. Its large, alternate leaves are rotundate and lobate, the angular lobes having irregular, cottony venation on the lower surface. The flowers are borne in small capitula in large terminal, corymbiform, ramose cymes. It is seen to best effect when growing by itself in a lawn or on a grassy bank. It needs space.
Height of plant   40–60 in. (1–1.50 m.).
Size of flower   ¾ in. (2 cm.).
Place of origin   Mexico.
Flowering time   Late winter–spring.
Cultivation   A shady position. Temperate climate. Can withstand a little cold. Prefers a damp, woodland-type soil, rich in organic material, even if calcareous. Frequent and plentiful watering. Heads should be removed after flowering, and old, exhausted branches cut back to the base. Usually trouble-free.
Propagation   By division in autumn (an easy method) or by cuttings taken in the spring.
Qualities   Hardy. Easy to grow.

---

321 SILENE PENDULA Carolus Linnaeus
Common names: Campion, catchfly

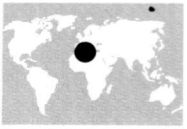

Family   Caryophyllaceae.
Description   A small herbaceous plant with a bushy habit. It has numerous rather sticky, nodose, dichotomous ramifications. Its lower leaves are oblong-spatulate and arranged in a rosette while the upper are lanceolate and alternate. Its numerous flowers are borne in ramified dichasia. The calyx is globose-piriform with dark-red venation and a rose-pink, stellate corolla with bifid petals. It is widely grown as an edging or bedding plant. There is a double-flowered cultivar.
Height of plant   8–12 in. (20–30 cm.).
Size of flower   1–1⅛ in. (2.5–3 cm.).
Place of origin   Mediterranean regions.
Flowering time   Spring.
Cultivation   Full sun or partial shade. Temperate climate. Prefers well-worked, humus-rich or generously manured garden soil, even if calcareous. Some feeding with liquid fertilizer after planting. Frequent watering. Plants should be removed after flowering.
Propagation   By summer sowing in a sheltered seedbed or in pans in a coldframe. Seedlings should be pricked off into a nursery bed for planting out in late winter or early spring.
Qualities   Hardy. Easy to grow.

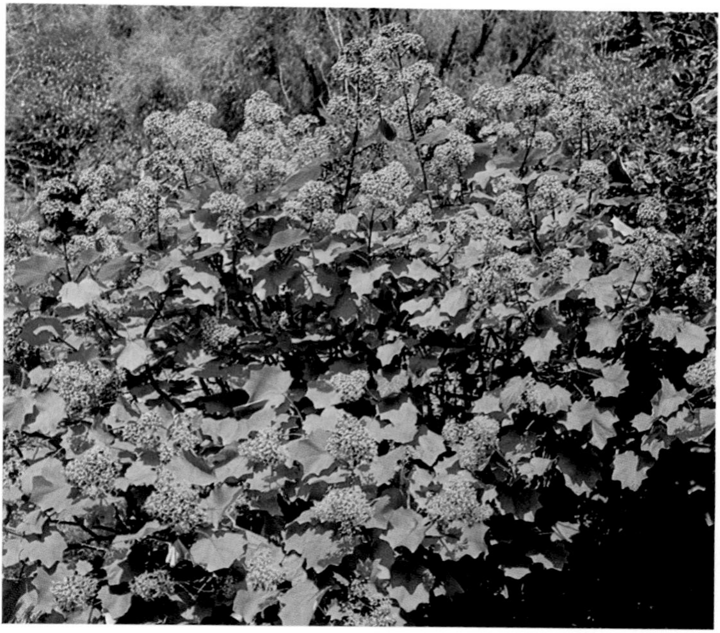

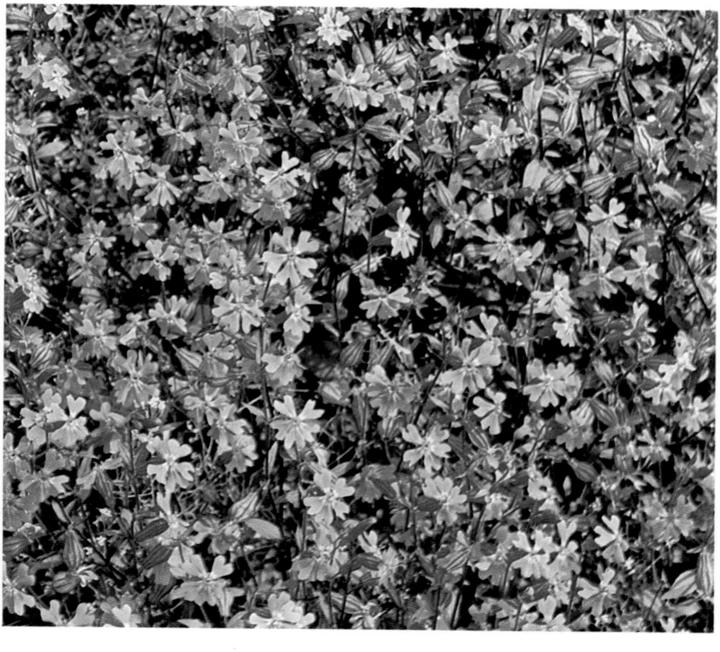

322 **SOLANUM CAPSICASTRUM** Heinrich Friedrich Link
Syn.: *S. pseudo-capsicum* Hortorum. Common name: Jerusalem cherry

Family Solanaceae.
Description A small, woody evergreen subshrub. Its persistent, alternate leaves are oblong-lanceolate or acute. Its flowers are small and insignificant but these give way to large berries ranging from yellow to coral-red, which are very decorative. The foliage of the cultivar ''Variegatum'' is variegated in white and cream.
Height of plant 24–31 in. (60–80 cm.).
Size of flower, berry flowers ⅛–⅜ in. (0.5–0.8 cm.); berries about ⅜–½ in. in diameter.
Place of origin Brazil.
Flowering time Late summer. The berries appear almost all the time.
Cultivation Partial shade. This plant likes a warm, relatively humid atmosphere. Frost-tender. Grows in almost any type of well-aerated, rich, moist garden soil. Requires dressings of organic manure. Frequent watering. Prune by removing dead growth and shortening straggly branches. Trouble-free.
Propagation By spring sowing in small pots or pans to germinate in a greenhouse or propagating frame (64° F./18° C.). Seedlings should be potted up and then potted on at least once before planting out.
Qualities Not hardy except in its natural environment. Easy to grow.

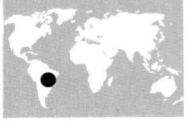

---

323 **SOLANUM RANTONNETII** Elie Abel Carrière
Syn.: *S. japonicum* Hortorum

Family Solanaceae.
Description A deciduous, occasionally evergreen shrub with dark-colored angular branches. Its dark-green leaves are ovate-lanceolate, undulate and often gibbous, with a short petiole. Its numerous flowers are borne in purplish-blue terminal corymbiform cymes, each one having a white star in the center and yellow stamens. The berries are like yellow cherries.
Height of plant 5–8 ft. (1.50–2.50 m.).
Size of flower ¾–1⅛ in. (2–3 cm.).
Place of origin Argentina, Paraguay.
Flowering time Summer.
Cultivation Full sun. Warm-temperate climate. A sheltered position. Cannot withstand the cold. Grows in any soil, preferably deep, well-aerated, humus-rich and moist. Can also be grown in a pot provided it can be overwintered under cover. It is subject to attack by fungus diseases if grown under too damp conditions.
Propagation By spring sowing in a cool greenhouse. By half-ripened cuttings taken in the late spring–summer.
Qualities Half-hardy. Very easy to grow.

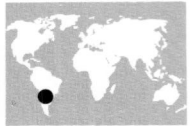

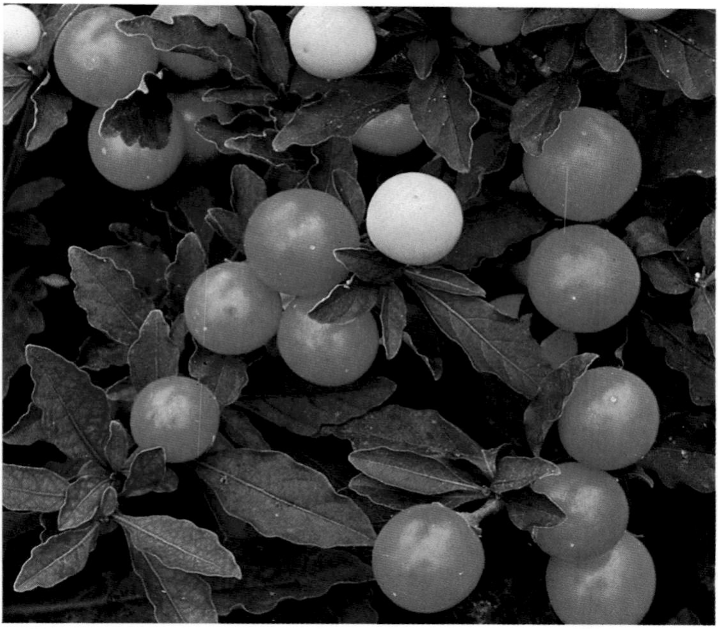

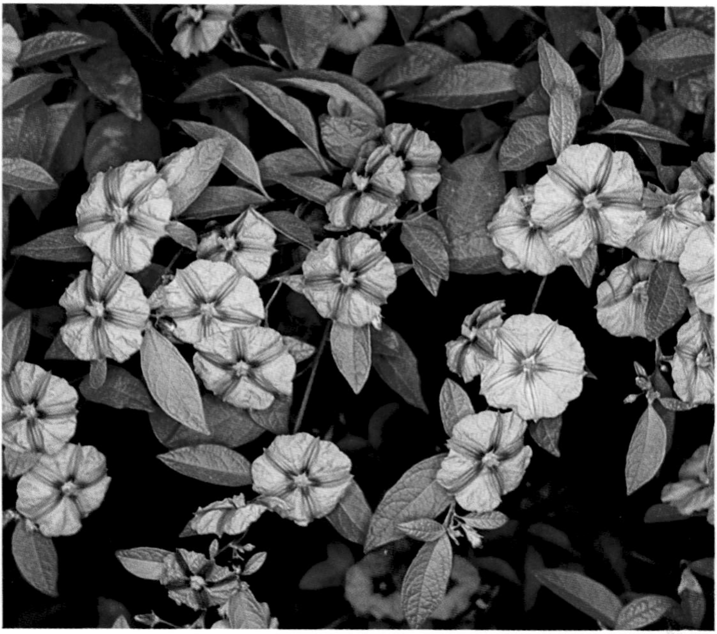

324 **SOLANUM WENDLANDII** Joseph Dalton Hooker
Common name: Costa Rican nightshade

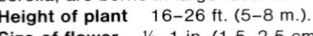

Family Solanaceae.
Description A climbing semi-evergreen shrub. Its abundant branches, which have a few thorns, are sarmentose and need to be supported. Its dark-green leaves are somewhat polymorphic, alternate and obovate-lanceolate or pinnate-parted. Its abundant lilac-blue flowers, each with a rotate-pentagonal corolla, are borne in large racemes.
Height of plant 16–26 ft. (5–8 m.).
Size of flower ½–1 in. (1.5–2.5 cm.).
Place of origin Costa Rica.
Flowering time Summer–autumn.
Cultivation A light, slightly shady, sheltered position. Cannot withstand the cold. Prefers any soil that is humus-rich and moist, even if moderately calcareous. Regular watering. Requires pruning in the autumn to remove dead or weak growth and to shorten the branches. Benefits from a periodic application of organic/mineral fertilizers.
Propagation By layering. By unripened shoots taken as cuttings in the spring–summer and rooted in a greenhouse or frame. By spring sowing in small pots in a propagating frame or greenhouse.
Qualities Hardy only in its natural environment. Easy to grow.

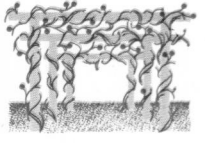

---

325 **SPARMANNIA AFRICANA** Carl von Linne
Common name: African linden

Family Tiliaceae.
Description Although not well known, this evergreen shrub is hardy and easily adapts to temperate regions. Its abundant flowers are very attractive and long-lasting. It has a shrubby habit with hispid ramifications springing from the base. Its large leaves, also hispid, are alternate, cordate-ovate, rugose and slightly palmate-lobate. Its umbelliferous axillary inflorescences bear as many as 30 to 40 white flowers, each with numerous red stamens that are yellow at their base. There are single, semidouble and double varieties.
Height of plant 6½–10 ft. (2–3 m.).
Size of flower 1⅛–1½ in. (3–4 cm.).
Place of origin South Africa.
Flowering time Winter–spring.
Cultivation Full sun or partial shade. Warm-temperate climate. Frost-tender. Suitable for warm coastal districts. Grows in any well-manured garden soil. Lends itself well to being grown as a greenhouse plant. Regular watering. A periodic application of organic/mineral fertilizers. Cutting back is limited to removal of dead and flowered growths as well as of any weak branches.
Propagation By clump division in the spring. A better method, however, is by semi-ripened or hardwood cuttings taken in spring–summer and rooted in a greenhouse (61° F./16° C.).
Qualities Half-hardy. Very easy to grow.

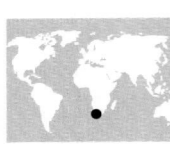

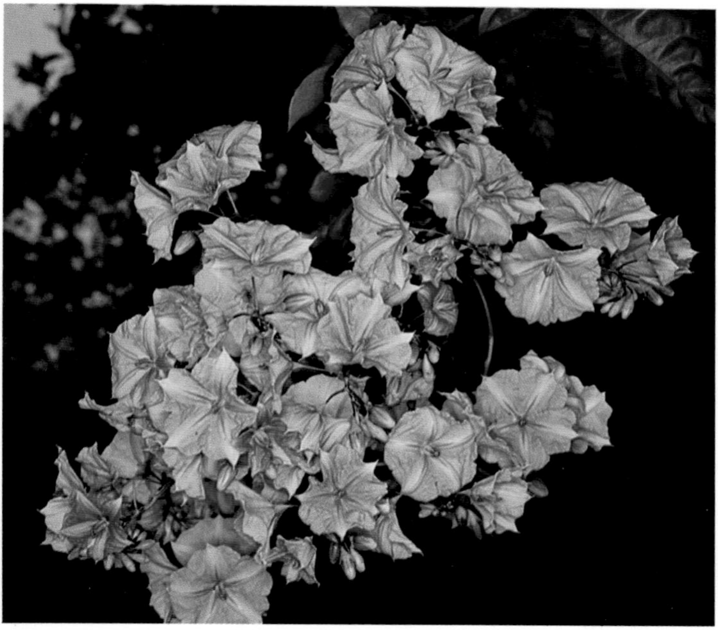

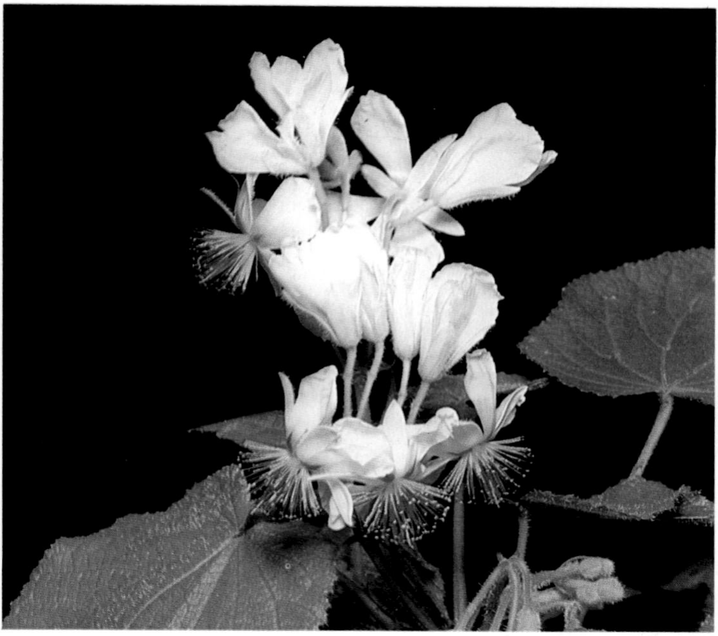

326 SPARTIUM JUNCEUM Carolus Linnaeus

Syn.: *Genista juncea* Jean Baptiste Lamarck. Common name: Spanish broom

Family Papilionaceae.

Description A diffuse bushy shrub with numerous slender, upright, cylindrical, tapering ramifications. Its small, deciduous leaves are oblong-lanceolate and well spaced. Its numerous yellow, strongly scented flowers are borne in terminal racemes; the rather showy, papilionaceous corolla has a broad standard (vexillum). It adapts extremely well to sterile soil where it provides a decorative splash of color.

Height of plant 5–11½ ft. (1.50–3.50 m.).

Size of flower 1 in. (2.5 cm.).

Place of origin Mediterranean regions.

Flowering time Spring–summer.

Cultivation Full sun. Temperate climate. Damaged by heavy frost. Grows in poor, arid soil, even if sandy. Does not require watering or feeding. Pruning is limited to removal of dead growth and the cutting back of straggly branches. Lovely when left to grow naturally. Young plants are vulnerable to attack by caterpillars, snails and slugs; otherwise generally trouble-free.

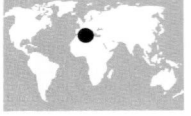

Propagation By seed sown in the flowering site in spring.

Qualities Hardy. Easy to grow.

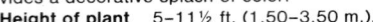

327 SPIRAEA CANTONIENSIS Juan Loureiro

Syn.: *S. reevesiana* John Lindley

Family Rosaceae.

Description A bushy, perennial, deciduous shrub. Its dense, slender upright ramifications are slightly recurved at the end. Its alternate leaves are lanceolate and irregularly incise-dentate. Extremely free-flowering, with the flowers borne in short corymbs of 15 to 25 or more and carried at the end of very short peduncles over the whole length of the main branch. Slightly scented.

Height of plant 40–60 in. (1–1.50 m.).

Size of flower ⅛–⅜ in. (0.5–1 cm.).

Place of origin China.

Flowering time Spring.

Cultivation A moderately sunny or partially shaded position. Temperate climate. Withstands the cold well. Flowering can be affected by late frosts. Grows in almost any soil. Requires watering only in exceptionally dry spells. Does not usually require any particular attention except to be thinned out periodically. Generally trouble-free.

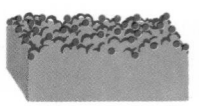

Propagation By hardwood cuttings taken in autumn or spring and rooted in a sheltered nursery bed. Also by layering.

Qualities Hardy. Easy to grow.

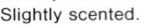

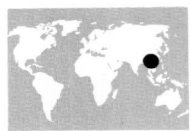

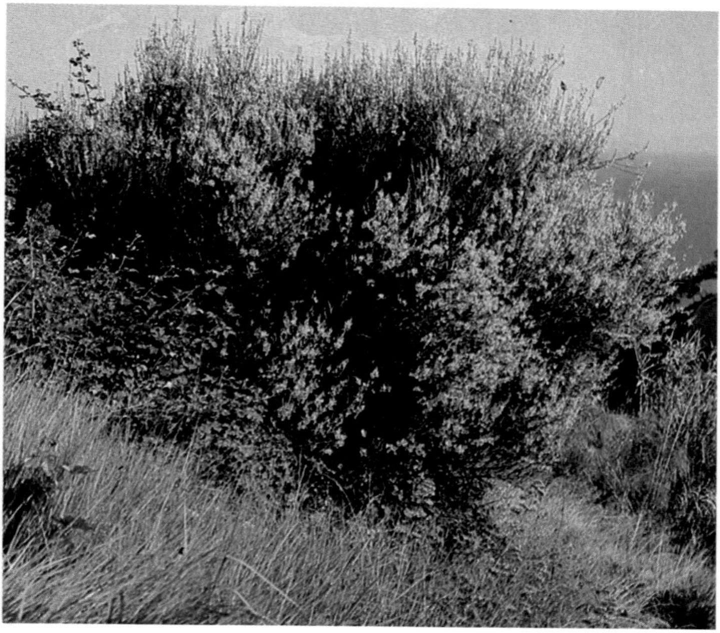

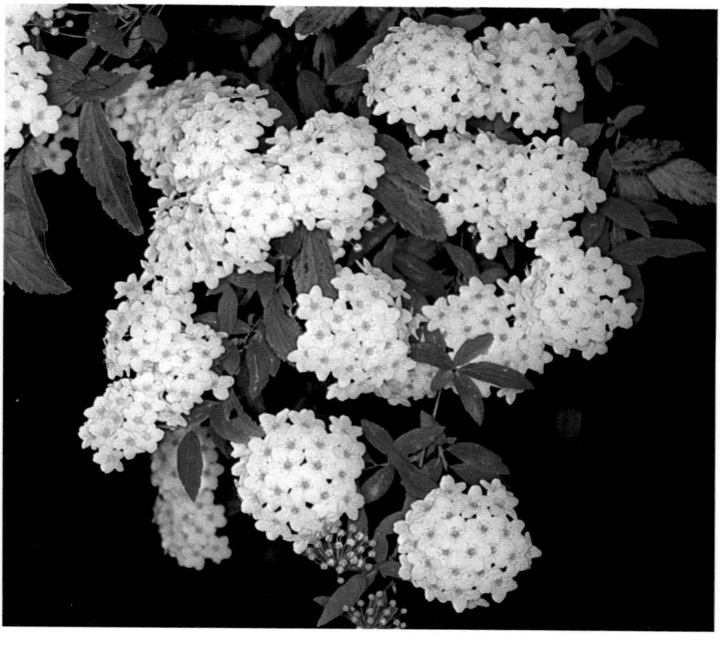

328 SPIRAEA JAPONICA Carolus Linnaeus
Syns.: *S. callosa* Carl Peter Thunberg, *S. fortunei* Jules Emile Planchon

Family Rosaceae.
Description One of the prettiest varieties of spiraea, widely grown because of its attractive appearance and the length of time it remains in flower. It has a suffrutescent, shrubby habit, bushing out with slender, erect, ligneous ramifications. Its deciduous alternate leaves are ovate-lanceolate, rugose and venose with a serrate margin. The numerous small flowers are borne in large terminal, compound corymbs in varying shades of pink.

Height of plant 40–60 in. (1–1.50 m.).
Size of flower ⅛ in. (0.5 cm.).
Place of origin Japan.
Flowering time Spring, summer, autumn.
Cultivation Full sun or partial shade. Temperate climate. Frost-resistant. Grows in almost any type of garden soil, with a preference for ground that is well aerated, humus-rich and moist. A little light top dressing with organic material ensures strong, vigorous plants. Limited watering during very dry spells. The oldest branches should be removed and any dead growth cut out. Generally trouble-free.

Propagation By division of basal shoots, which always grow freely around adult plants. By green or semi-ripened shoots in the spring–summer.
Qualities Hardy. Suitable for terraces, etc. Easy to grow.

329 SPREKELIA FORMOSISSIMA (Carolus Linnaeus) William Herbert
Syn.: *Amaryllis formosissima* Linnaeus. Common name: Jacobean lily

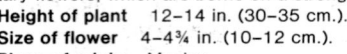

Family Amaryllidaceae.
Description This deciduous bulbous plant, which is very easy to grow, deserves to be better known because of its unusual shape and the beauty of its scarlet-crimson flower. From the tunicate bulb spring acute, linear, distichous, carnose, slightly recurved leaves that unfold at the same time as the solitary flowers, which are borne on a strong, carnose scape.

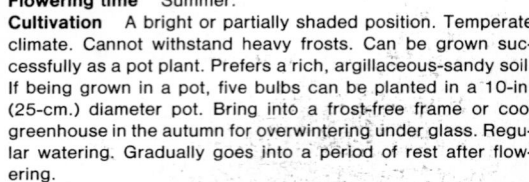

Height of plant 12–14 in. (30–35 cm.).
Size of flower 4–4¾ in. (10–12 cm.).
Place of origin Mexico.
Flowering time Summer.
Cultivation A bright or partially shaded position. Temperate climate. Cannot withstand heavy frosts. Can be grown successfully as a pot plant. Prefers a rich, argillaceous-sandy soil. If being grown in a pot, five bulbs can be planted in a 10-in. (25-cm.) diameter pot. Bring into a frost-free frame or cool greenhouse in the autumn for overwintering under glass. Regular watering. Gradually goes into a period of rest after flowering.

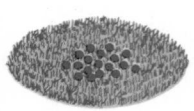

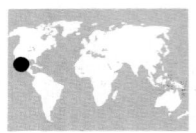

Propagation By removal of bulblets during the resting stage.
Qualities Not hardy except in its natural environment. Easy to grow.

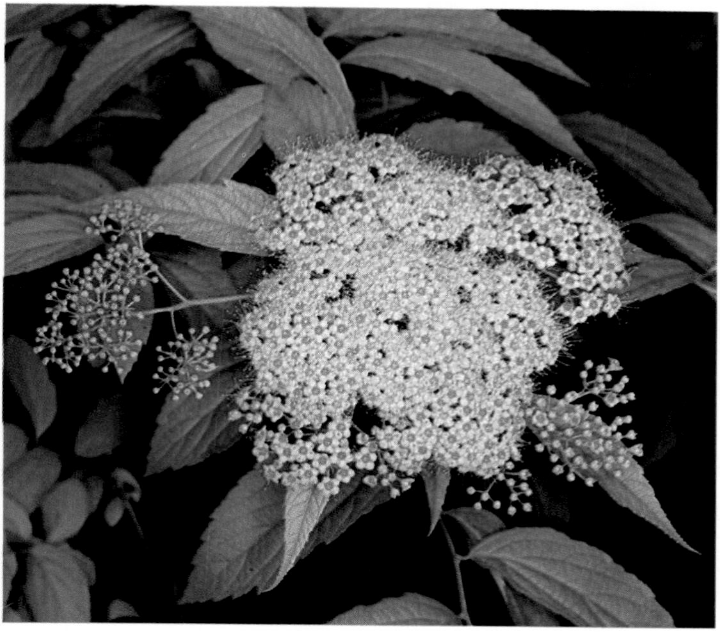

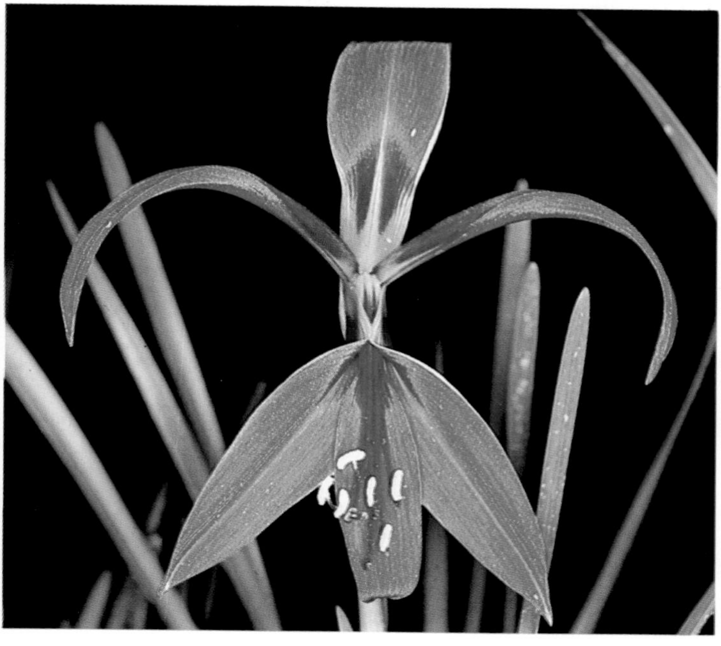

330 STAPHYLEA TRIFOLIA Carolus Linnaeus
Common name: Bladdernut

Family Staphyleaceae.
Description An attractive deciduous shrub whose flowers resemble white lilac. Its arborescent stem has strong, erect ramifications. The leaflets of its trifoliate leaves are ovate-elliptical, serrate, slightly pubescent underneath and 2⅜–3⅛ in. (6–8 cm.) long. Its numerous, scented flowers are borne in dense, pendulous panicles. The fruits are bi- or trilobed vesiculose capsules containing two or three seeds.
Height of plant 6½–13 ft. (2–4 m.).
Size of flower ⅜–¾ in. (1–2 cm.).
Place of origin Northwestern United States.
Flowering time Spring.
Cultivation A bright, slightly shady position. Temperate climate. Withstands the cold quite well. Undemanding, it grows in almost any type of well-aerated, moderately fertile, moist soil. Plentiful watering in the summer. Pruning limited to removal of flowered and dead growth as well as some shortening of overgrown branches. Generally trouble-free.

Propagation By seeds, cuttings or layers in the spring–summer.
Qualities Hardy. Easy to grow.

331 STRELITZIA ALBA (Carl von Linne) H. C. Skeels
Syn.: *S. augusta* Carl Peter Thunberg

Family Musaceae.
Description An arborescent plant that is grown for the imposing beauty of its foliage. Its ringed cylindrical stem may grow to a diameter of over 8 in. (20 cm.). Its persistent leaves can be 40–80 in. (1.2–2.4 m.) long; they are fasciculate, subcordate at the base and rounded at the apex with a long, sheathing petiole at the base. Its unusually shaped irregular, pinkish-white flowers spring from the foliar axils. They consist of three divergent, external, colored tepals and three internal ones, two of which form an arrowhead shape.
Height of plant 6½–33 ft. (2–10 m.).
Size of flower 8–12 in. (20–30 cm.).
Place of origin South Africa.
Flowering time Summer.

Cultivation In full sun or a very bright position. A warm-temperate climate. Cannot withstand the cold. Requires a rich soil. It can be grown as a pot plant using a small amount of very good garden soil mixed with woodland mold, peat, a little sand and plenty of well-rotted manure. Periodic feeding with organic/mineral fertilizers and repotting every two or three years. Regular and plentiful watering. Cut back old leaves.

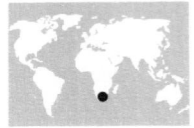

Propagation By division of young suckers and basal roots, rooted in pots in a warm greenhouse.
Qualities Not hardy except in its natural environment. Easy to grow.

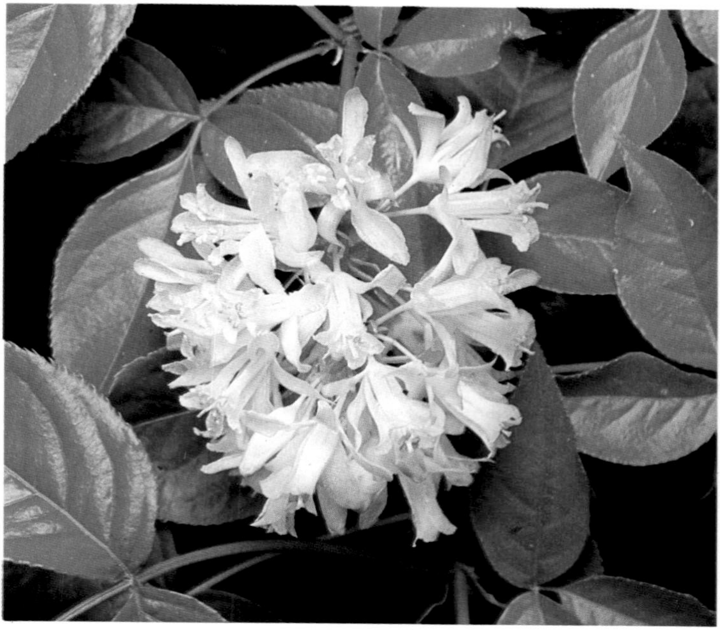

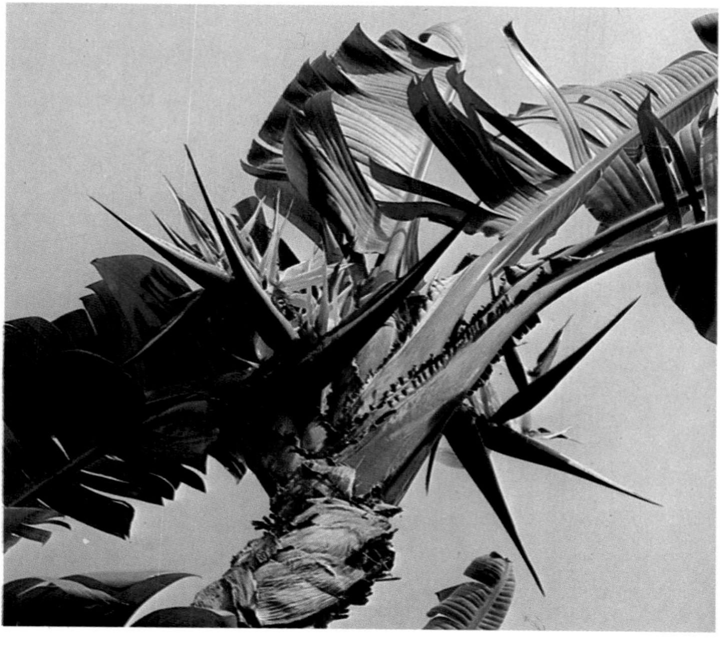

332 STRELITZIA REGINAE William Aiton
Common name: Bird of paradise flower

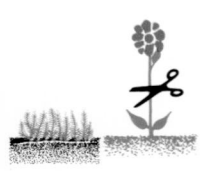

Family Musaceae.
Description An acauline, herbaceous, evergreen perennial, slightly cespitose, with large, carnose roots. Its large, erect, rigid leaves are oval-oblong and coriaceous with a raised margin, while the very decorative petiole is long, sturdy and sheathed at the base. Its elegant flowers are borne on strong scapes with two or three joined together to form a strange apical inflorescence that gives the impression of the head of a heron with a gracefully curved and slender neck. It is usually grown in warm coastal areas as a greenhouse plant or as a pot plant on sunny verandas.

Height of plant 2–4 ft. (0.60–1.20 m.).
Size of flower 4–6 in. (10–15 cm.).
Place of origin South Africa.
Flowering time At various times of the year, according to position; usually in the autumn.
Cultivation A moderately sunny but bright position. Warm-temperate climate. Frost-tender. Likes a deep, fertile soil, even if a little calcareous, amended with peat, woodland mold and well-rotted farmyard manure. Regular watering. Does not like to be disturbed by being transplanted frequently. Is subject to root rot.

Propagation By seed in a temperate greenhouse but this is a very slow process. By division in the spring of basal shoots from strong plants for rooting in a temperate greenhouse.
Qualities Half-hardy to tender. A demanding plant to grow.

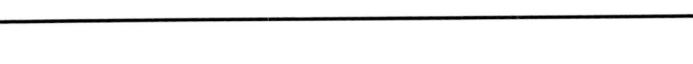

333 STREPTOSOLEN JAMESONII (George Bentham) Miers

Family Solanaceae.
Description A bushy, ramified, evergreen shrub, the ends of whose branches are pubescent. Often grown in warm coastal areas for its floriferousness and long flowering period. Its large, alternate leaves are entire, oval and slightly velutinate. Its tubulous flowers open out into four or five widely expanded lobes borne in terminal inflorescences.

Height of plant 2½–6½ ft. (0.80–2 m.).
Size of flower ½–¾ in. (1.5–2 cm.).
Place of origin Colombia, Ecuador.
Flowering time Summer–autumn.
Cultivation A sunny, sheltered position. Temperate climate. Cannot withstand the cold. Needs to be protected from autumn to late spring. Can be grown as a greenhouse pot plant in a compost of equal parts of good garden soil mixed with woodland mold, peat and well-rotted farmyard manure. Regular watering. Requires repotting every two years. Benefits from light pruning after flowering.

Propagation By half-ripened cuttings taken in the summer. By layering.
Qualities Half-hardy to tender. Very easy to grow.

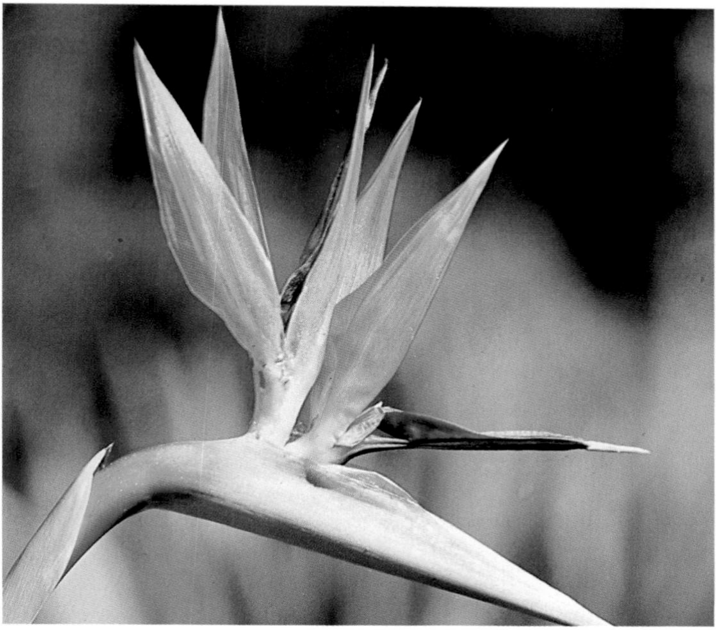

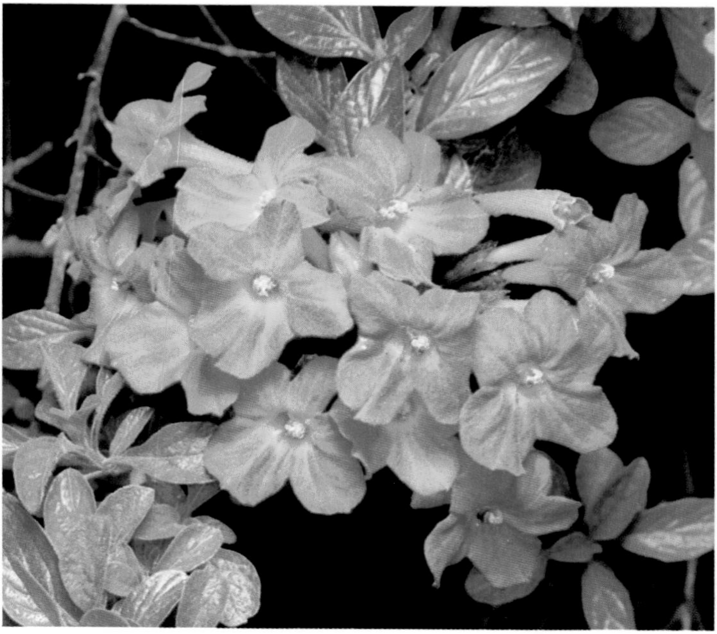

334 SYRINGA LACINIATA Phillip Miller

Syn.: *Syringa x persica* Carolus Linnaeus, var. *Laciniata* Miller. Common name: Lilac

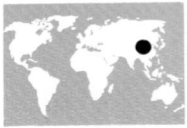

Family   Oleaceae.
Description   A bushy deciduous shrub with spreading, slender, rather weak, light ramifications. Its opposite leaves are pinnatosect, lanceolate and delicately laciniate. It flowers abundantly on the wood of the previous year. Its sweetly scented flowers are small and infundibuliform with a corolla that opens out into four oval lobes. The flowers are borne in long ramified panicles with an open, light appearance; they are delicate and decorative.
Height of plant   6½–10 ft. (2–3 m.).
Size of flower   ⅜ in. (1 cm.).
Place of origin   China.
Flowering time   Spring.
Cultivation   A sunny to partially shaded position. Temperate climate. Frost-resistant. Grows in almost any garden soil, even if only moderately fertile. Appreciates a periodic application of a complete organic/mineral fertilizer. Watering may be necessary during the summer. No pruning required since this removes the flower buds for the following year.
Propagation   By semi-hardwood cuttings taken in the spring–summer and rooted in a frame or greenhouse. By root suckers.
Qualities   Hardy. Easy to grow.

335 SYRINGA VULGARIS Carolus Linnaeus

Common name: Common lilac

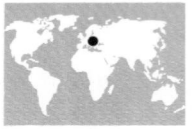

Family   Oleaceae.
Description   A deciduous, well-branched shrub or small tree. It is floriferous and has a long flowering period. Its opposite leaves are cordate-acuminate. Its numerous sweetly scented flowers are borne in dense terminal panicles; they may be mauve, violet, white or in various shades of these colors. There are single, semidouble and double-flowered forms according to the different horticultural varieties, of which there are about 80.
Height of plant   16–23 ft. (5–7 m.).
Size of flower   ⅜ in. (1 cm.).
Place of origin   Southeastern Europe.
Flowering time   Spring.
Cultivation   A sunny to partially shaded position. Temperate climate. Frost-resistant. Grows in any soil, preferably moderately argillaceous, well aerated, rich and moist. Regular watering during dry spells. Weak plants should be given a liquid feed. Branches can be shortened, if necessary. Prone to attack by the lilac leaf miner.
Propagation   By suckers and semi-hardwood cuttings. In the case of many cultivars, grafting is the only method of reproduction.
Qualities   Hardy. Easy to grow.

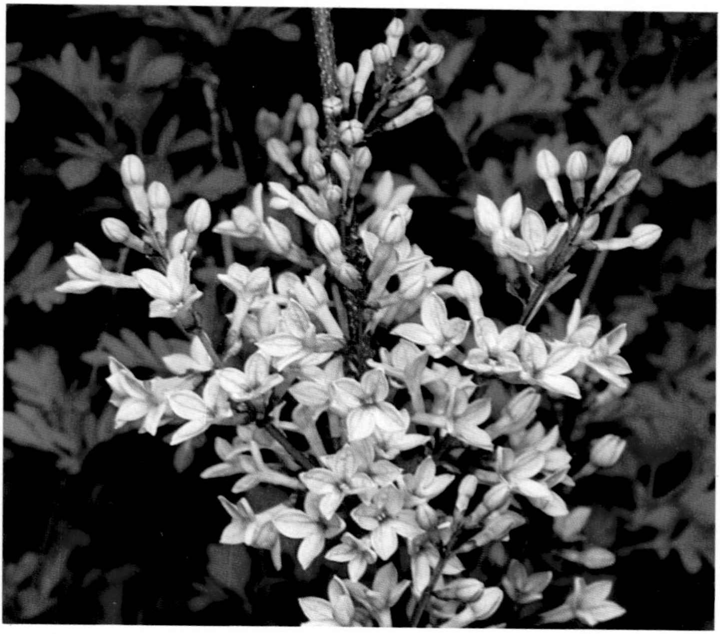

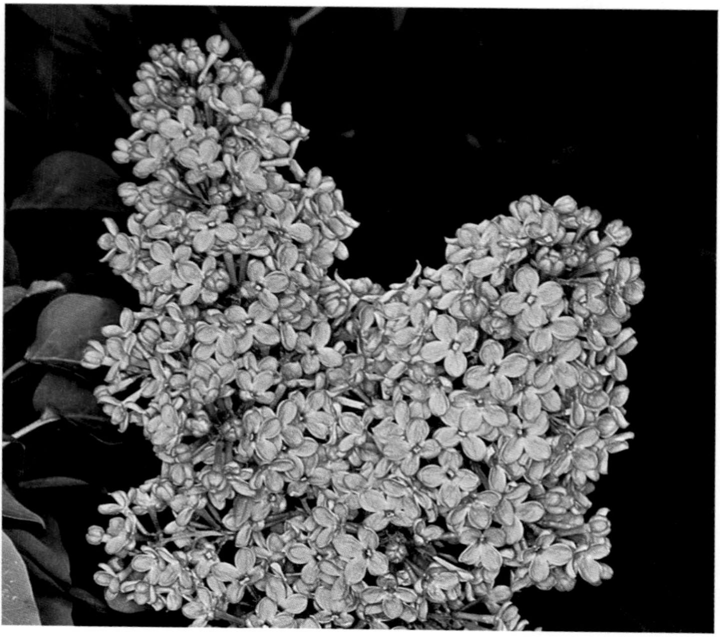

336 TACSONIA VAN-VOLXEMII William Jackson Hooker

Syns.: *Passiflora van-volxemii* Hooker, *P. antioquiensis* Hermann G.K.W. Karsten. Common name: Passion flower

Family Passifloraceae.

Description A climbing plant with numerous slender branches equipped with tendrils. Its palmate—almost trifoliate—leaves are acute and slightly dentate. Its large, isolated flowers are borne on long peduncles that spring from the foliar axils. The crimson corolla has an elongated central column consisting of the style and stamens. There is no corona made up of filaments.

Height of plant   20–33 ft. (6–10 m.).
Size of flower   4–5 in. (10–12 cm.).
Place of origin   Colombia.
Flowering time   Autumn.

Cultivation A sunny position. Warm-temperate climate. Grows well in sheltered sites in warm coastal areas. Cannot withstand the cold. Likes open, rich, moist but well-drained ground. Requires an occasional top dressing of well-rotted manure and a complete mineral fertilizer in generous quantities. Limited watering during the summer and any particularly dry spells. Pruning can be carried out in the winter to shorten overlong branches and remove flowered and dead wood.

Propagation By cuttings and layering during spring–summer. By spring sowing in a temperate greenhouse.

Qualities Not hardy except in its natural environment. Easy to grow.

337 TAGETES ERECTA Carolus Linnaeus

Common name: African marigold

Family   Compositae.

Description A herbaceous annual with strong, ramified stems. Its opposite leaves are imparipinnate with dentate, oblong-lanceolate leaflets. It exudes a rather unpleasant smell. Its numerous double, sulfur-yellow flowers are produced in large, crispate, pompon capitula, rather like carnations.

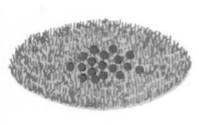

Height of plant   20–40 in. (0.50–1 m.).
Size of flower   2–4 in. (5–10 cm.).
Place of origin   Mexico.
Flowering time   Summer–autumn.

Cultivation A sunny position. Temperate climate. Not very demanding, it grows in any garden soil, even if only moderately fertile, if enriched with plenty of organic material. It appreciates feeding with a liquid fertilizer during the early stages of growth and plenty of watering. Usually trouble-free.

Propagation By spring sowing in pans under glass.

Qualities Suitable for balconies, terraces. Hardy. Easy to grow.

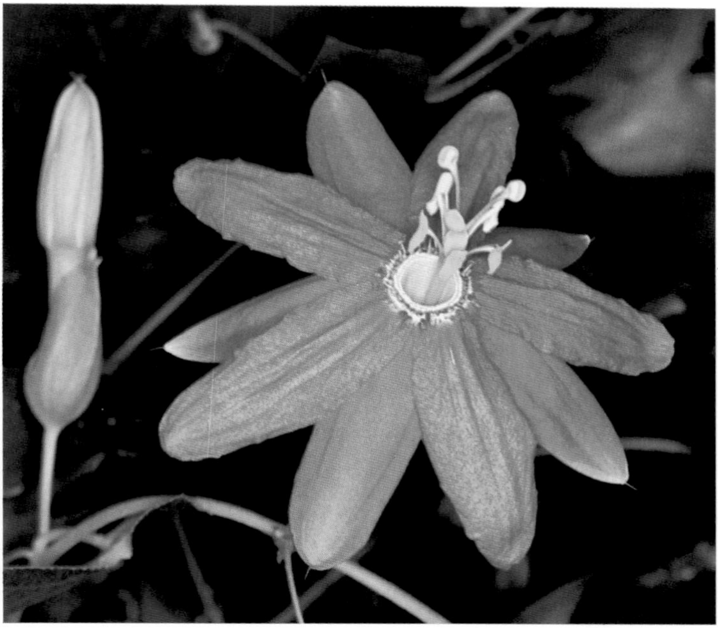

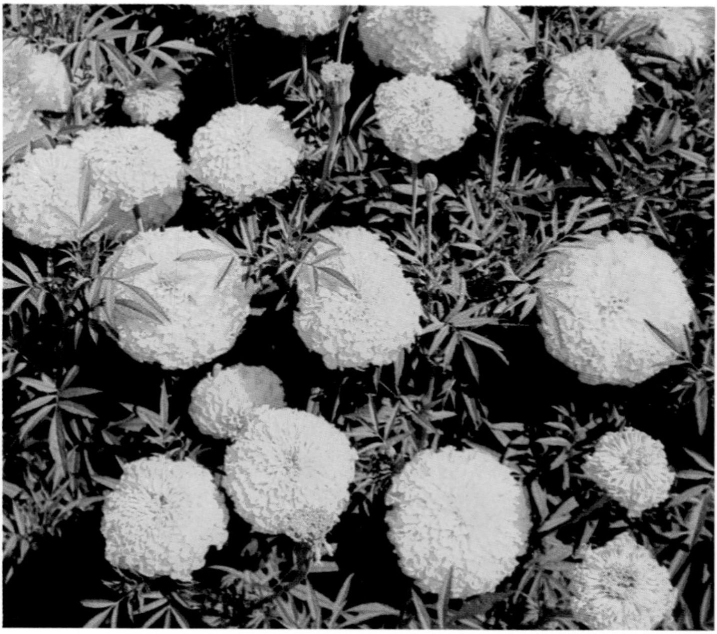

338 TAGETES PATULA Carolus Linnaeus
Common name: French marigold

Family Compositae.
Description An erect, bushy herbaceous annual that gives off a rather unpleasant penetrating smell. Its leaves are alternate or opposite and imparipinnate with sessile, lanceolate, dentate leaflets. The flowers are borne in capitula and may be single or double, according to the variety, and carried on a long peduncle. The color ranges from golden-yellow with striations to a velvety reddish-brown.
Height of plant 6–20 in. (15–50 cm.).
Size of flower 1⅜–2 in. (3.5–5 cm.)
Place of origin Mexico.
Flowering time Summer–autumn.

Cultivation A sunny position. Temperate climate. Grows in any type of well-worked garden soil that has been enriched with plenty of organic material. Requires generous watering interspersed with a few applications of liquid fertilizer after planting out. The plants should be removed after flowering. Usually trouble-free.
Propagation By spring sowing in pans under glass.
Qualities Suitable for balconies, terraces. Hardy. Easy to grow.

339 TAMARIX PARVIFLORA Augustin Pyramus DeCandolle
Syn.: *T. tetrandra* Hortorum. Common name: Tamarisk

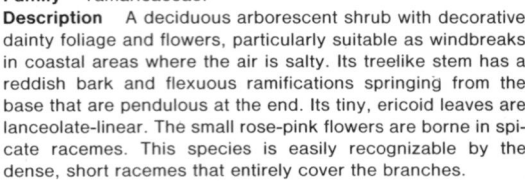

Family Tamaricaceae.
Description A deciduous arborescent shrub with decorative dainty foliage and flowers, particularly suitable as windbreaks in coastal areas where the air is salty. Its treelike stem has a reddish bark and flexuous ramifications springing from the base that are pendulous at the end. Its tiny, ericoid leaves are lanceolate-linear. The small rose-pink flowers are borne in spicate racemes. This species is easily recognizable by the dense, short racemes that entirely cover the branches.
Height of plant 10–16 ft. (3–5 m.).
Size of flower ⅛ in. (0.5 cm.).
Place of origin Eastern Mediterranean region.
Flowering time Spring.

Cultivation In full sun or a very sunny position. Temperate climate. Can withstand a few frosts but the young branches may be damaged. It prefers damp, siliceous-sandy ground but also grows in ordinary garden soil provided it is well aerated and moist. Plentiful watering. An occasional application of organic/mineral fertilizer assists growth, which is very slow. Pruning limited to removal of dead or straggly wood.
Propagation By hardwood cuttings taken in autumn or spring and rooted in a sheltered nursery bed.
Qualities Hardy. Easy to grow.

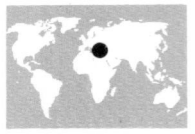

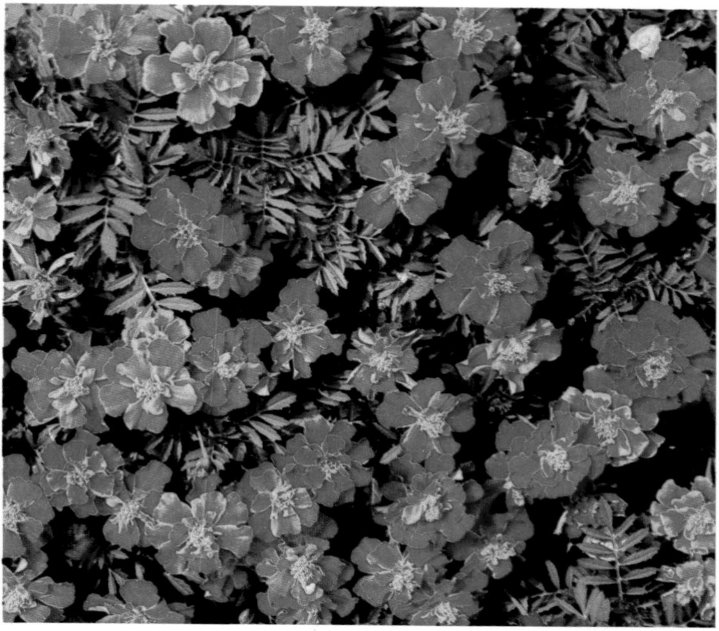

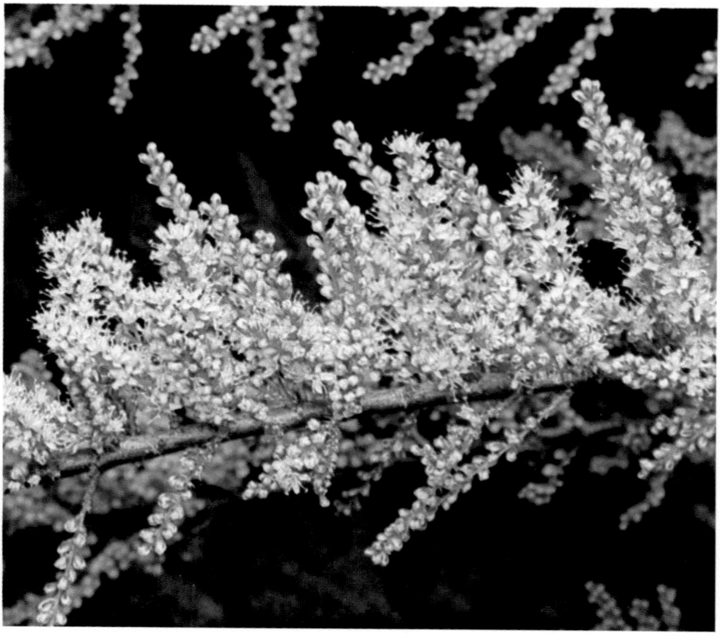

340 TELEKIA SPECIOSA (J.C.D. von Schreber) J.C.G. Baumgarten
Syn.: *Buphthalmum speciosum* von Schreber

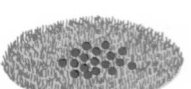
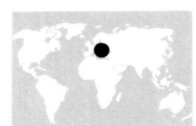

Family Compositae.
Description A shrubby perennial with numerous ramified stems. Its alternate leaves are sessile, ovate-lanceolate or cordate-triangular, dentate and rough-textured. Its golden-yellow flowers are borne in numerous capitula, like large single daisies, with a prominent disc. This is a little-known plant but well worth growing for its hardiness and showy flowers.
Height of plant 24–32 in. (60–80 cm.).
Size of flower 2⅜–3⅛ in. (6–8 cm.).
Place of origin Eastern Europe.
Flowering time Summer.
Cultivation A bright, sunny or partially shaded position. Temperate climate. Can withstand the cold well. Grows in any type of soil, preferably calcareous, moist and humus-rich. Even thrives in a rocky site. Regular watering. Responds well to an occasional top dressing of organic material. Generally trouble-free.
Propagation By clump division in the spring. By spring sowing in a frame.
Qualities Hardy. Easy to grow.

---

341 TEUCRIUM FRUTICANS Carolus Linnaeus
Syn.: *T. tomentosum* Konrad Moench. Common name: Germander

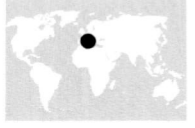

Family Labiatae.
Description An evergreen shrub, well ramified from the base, with whitish, quadrangular stems. Its opposite leaves are oblong-lanceolate, pubescent, rugose and silvery underneath. Its lavender-violet flowers are borne either singly or in bilabiate racemose cymes with a conspicuous trilobate lower lip.
Height of plant 40–80 in. (1–2 m.).
Size of flower 1–1⅛ in. (2.5–3 cm.).
Place of origin Western Mediterranean region.
Flowering time Summer.
Cultivation Full sun or partial shade. Warm-temperate climate; requires a sheltered position. Grows quickly in any garden soil, even if calcareous. Requires regular watering during the driest spells. Benefits from light periodic applications of organic/mineral fertilizers. Makes a fine hedge and, once the shape has been achieved, requires only trimming and occasional cutting out of dead or straggly material. Generally trouble-free.
Propagation By half-ripened or hardwood cuttings taken in the spring. By layering. Sometimes, too, by seed in pans germinated in a propagating frame.
Qualities Half-hardy to tender; hardy in its own environment. Easy to grow.

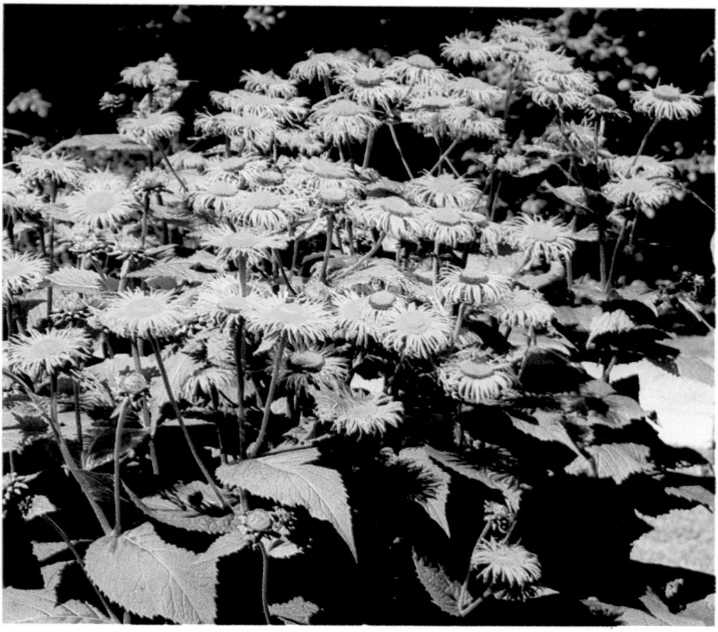

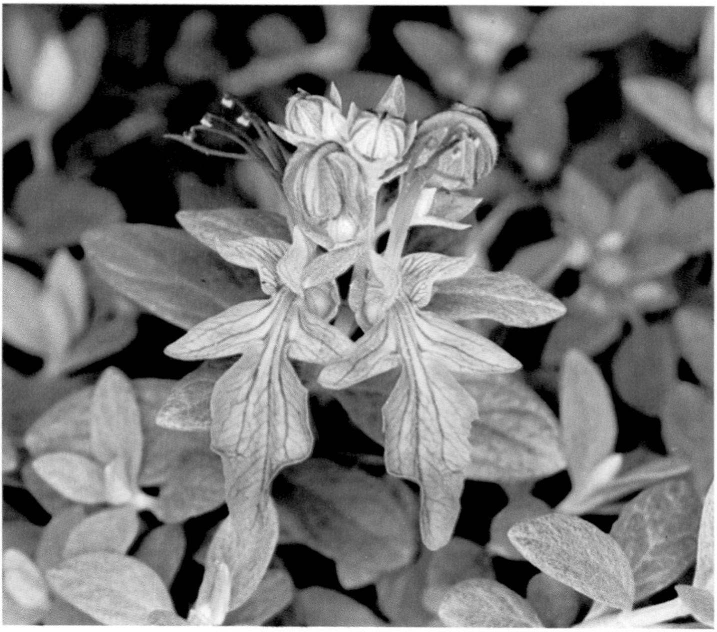

342 THUNBERGIA GRANDIFLORA William Roxburg
Common name: Sky vine

Family Acanthaceae.

Description A perennial evergreen climber with an articulate, nodose stem. Its brownish-green leaves are opposite, ovate-cordate and lobate-truncate at the base, with a long petiole. Its axillary flowers are borne singly and have a tubulous corolla with a limb opening out into five sub-rotund pale-azure lobes with purple markings and a yellow throat.

Height of plant 6½–10 ft. (2–3 m.).

Size of flower 2–3⅛ in. (5–8 cm.).

Place of origin India.

Flowering time Summer–autumn.

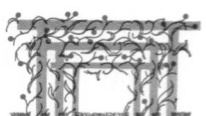

Cultivation A bright, sunny position. Warm-temperate climate. Sheltered site; more frequently grown in a cool greenhouse. Soil should be well aerated and mixed with heath mold, leaf mold and a little sand, enriched with some well-rotted organic material. It requires supporting as its stems are delicate at the nodes. Regular watering. At the first hint of cold weather the leafy branches die back, but the stock will survive and should be transferred to a cool greenhouse.

Propagation Mainly by cuttings of stem sections taken in the spring and rooted in a greenhouse.

Qualities Tender. A demanding plant to grow.

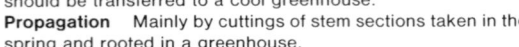

343 THYMUS SERPYLLUM Carolus Linnaeus
Common names: Creeping thyme, mother of thyme

Family Labiatae.

Description A suffruticose plant with slender-prostrate, downward-growing, ramose stems forming dense cushionlike tufts. The whole plant exudes a pleasant aromatic perfume. Its tiny flowers with pink-purple corollas are grouped in dense racemes or whorls (verticels) and are so prolific that they cover most of the plant when in full bloom. It is used in the making of aromatic essences and as a culinary herb.

Height of plant 1⅛–2 in. (3–5 cm.).

Size of flower ⅛ in. (0.5 cm.).

Place of origin Europe.

Flowering time Spring, summer, autumn.

Cultivation In full sun or a very bright position. Temperate climate. Frost-resistant. Likes hilly or mountainous terrain in a natural setting, even if stony, with humus-rich soil. Does not usually require watering or any particular attention. The flowered cymes should be cut off to retain shape and vigor of the plant.

Propagation By clump division in spring. By cuttings of lateral shoots after flowering. Sometimes, too, by spring sowing.

Qualities Hardy. Easy to grow.

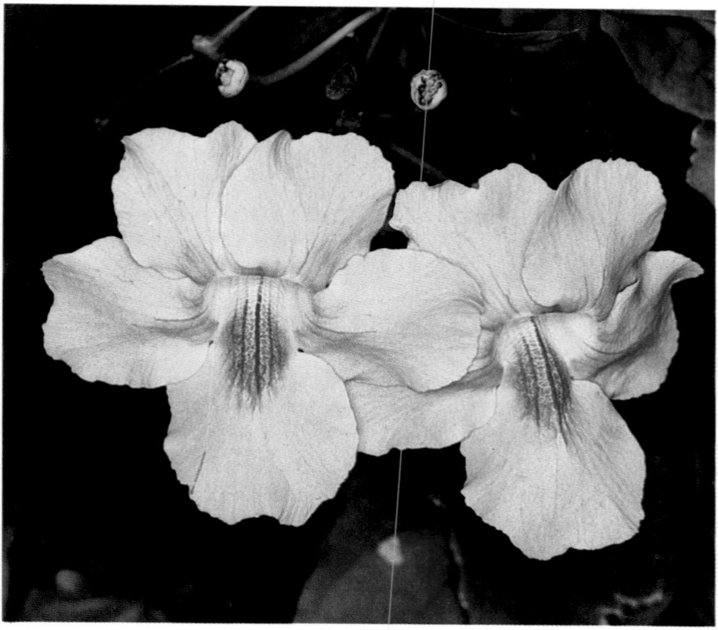

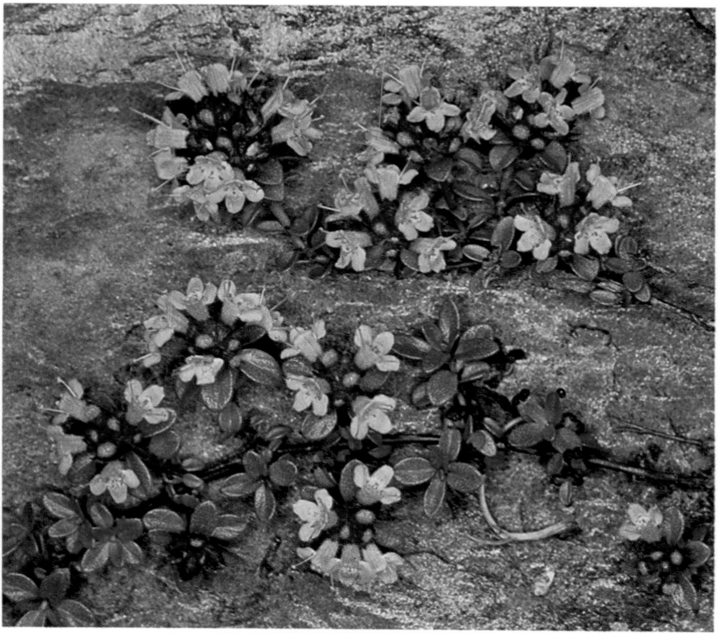

344 THYMUS VULGARIS Carolus Linnaeus
Common name: Common thyme

Family Labiatae.
Description A delightful suffruticose, dwarf shrub that combines decorative and useful qualities. In addition to its use as a culinary herb, it is used pharmaceutically in the production of the essence known as thymol. Its numerous dense, slender ramifications are partially ligneous. Its evergreen, opposite leaves are oblong-lanceolate, with revolute margins and somewhat tomentose on the lower surface. The numerous flowers are borne in dense racemes arranged in whorls (verticels) at the end of the branches.

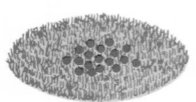

Height of plant 8–16 in. (20–40 cm.).
Size of flower ⅛ -⅜ in. (0.5–0.8 cm.).
Place of origin Western Mediterranean region.
Flowering time Spring–early summer.
Cultivation Full sun. Temperate climate. Fairly frost-resistant. Prefers stony, even rocky, ground with a low fertility level. Does not usually require watering or feeding. After flowering, the dry floriferous cymes can be trimmed to retain the cushiony shape of the plants. Generally trouble-free.

Propagation By cuttings of lateral shoots taken in spring and rooted in a coldframe. By spring sowing in pans in a coldframe.
Qualities Suitable for terraces and balconies. Hardy. Easy to grow.

---

345 TRACHELOSPERMUM JASMINOIDES
(John Lindley) Charles Lemaire cv. ''Variegatum''
Syn.: *Rhynchospermum jasminoides* Lindley. Common names: Confederate jasmine, star jasmine

Family Apocynaceae.
Description A climbing evergreen that is widely grown in temperate regions and is often mistaken for jasmine. It is a vigorous but slow-growing plant with voluble stems and milky sap. Its persistent, opposite leaves are lanceolate-acuminate and coriaceous. It is very floriferous, the whole plant becoming enveloped in a cloud of sweetly scented flowers like little white stars. This variegated cultivar is less floriferous than the green-leaved variety. Its flowers have a rotate corolla with asymmetrical linear lobes.

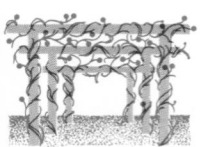

Height of plant 10–23 ft. (3–7 m.).
Size of flower ¾–1 in. (2–2.5 cm.).
Place of origin China.
Flowering time Summer.
Cultivation A bright position, even in full sun. Temperate climate. Can be irreparably damaged by frost. Grows in almost any kind of well-aerated, fertile, moist garden soil. Appreciates periodic dressings of manure and a complete mineral fertilizer. Regular watering in the summer. Should be lightly pruned to remove dead or exhausted growth and to shorten straggly branches. Pests: sometimes attacked by various scale insects.

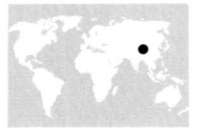

Propagation By layering or by lateral shoot cuttings rooted in a warm greenhouse.
Qualities Half-hardy to hardy, depending on temperature. Suitable for terraces, balconies. Easy to grow.

346 TRADESCANTIA x ANDERSONIANA W. W. Ludwig and Roweder
Syn.: *T. virginiana* Hortorum. Common name: Spiderwort

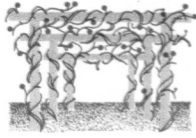

Family   Commelinaceae.

Description   A perennial, but not long-lived. Grows in thick clumps in a temperate climate. Its herbaceous, erect stems are carnose and nodose. Its leaves are tender, linear-lanceolate and sheathed. Its numerous, brightly colored flowers last only a short time but open in succession; they consist of three deep blue-purple or rose-pink sub-rotund tepals.

Height of plant   20–28 in. (50–70 cm.).

Size of flower   1⅛ in. (3 cm.).

Place of origin   A cultivated hybrid derived from crossings between *T. chiensis*, *T. subaspera* and *T. virginiana*, all originally from the east-central United States.

Flowering time   Summer.

Cultivation   A bright, partially shaded, position. Warm-temperate climate. The foliage and stems are frost-tender. Prefers a sheltered site but grows in almost any type of soil that is open and humus-rich, provided it is moist to damp. Requires plentiful watering and some organic dressing. Cutting back limited to thinning out and removal of flowered or straggly growth. Generally trouble-free. Also suitable as a pot plant.

Propagation   By clump division in the spring. By spring sowing in pans to germinate in a coldframe.

Qualities   Half-hardy to hardy; top growth will die back at first frosts, but crowns will invariably survive. Easy to grow.

347 TROPAEOLUM MAJUS Carolus Linnaeus
Common name: Nasturtium

Family   Tropaeolaceae.

Description   A creeping and climbing annual. It has a rather thick, smooth, very ramified stem. Its alternate leaves, medium-green on the upper surface and pale on the lower, are peltate-rotundate, slightly angular and carnose. Its abundant axillary flowers are very showy. Their tubulous-flaring corollas are bright yellow or deep orange and have reddish-brown blotches and a long spur at the back. Each one is carried on a long peduncle. Height and color vary according to the different cultivars.

Height of plant   1–8 ft. (0.30–2.50 m.).

Size of flower   1½–3 in. (4–8 cm.).

Place of origin   Peru, Ecuador, Colombia.

Flowering time   Summer–autumn.

Cultivation   In full sun or a very sunny position. Temperate climate. Cannot withstand the cold. Grows in any well-aerated, rich, moist soil. Before planting, the ground should be enriched with organic material. Plentiful watering. Appreciates a few applications of liquid fertilizer in the early stages of growth. The plants are usually removed after flowering. Subject to aphids and several virus diseases.

Propagation   By spring sowing in the flowering site.

Qualities   Suitable for terraces, balconies. Easy to grow.

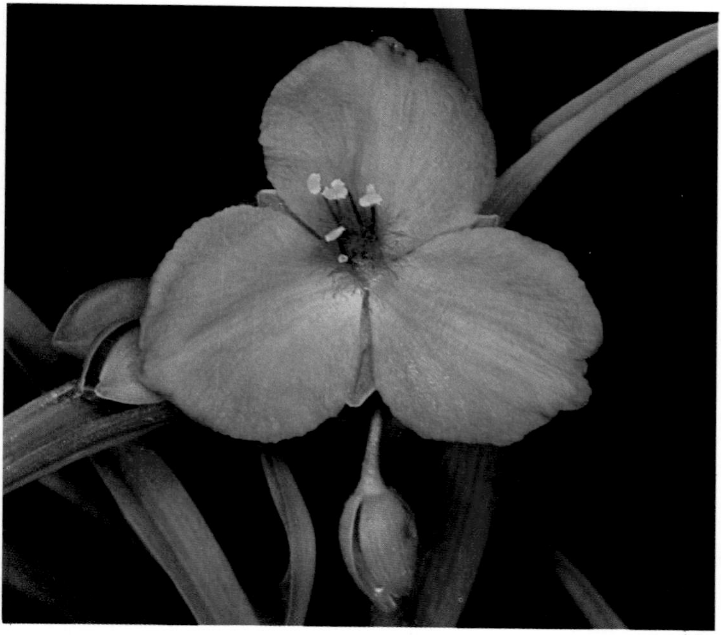

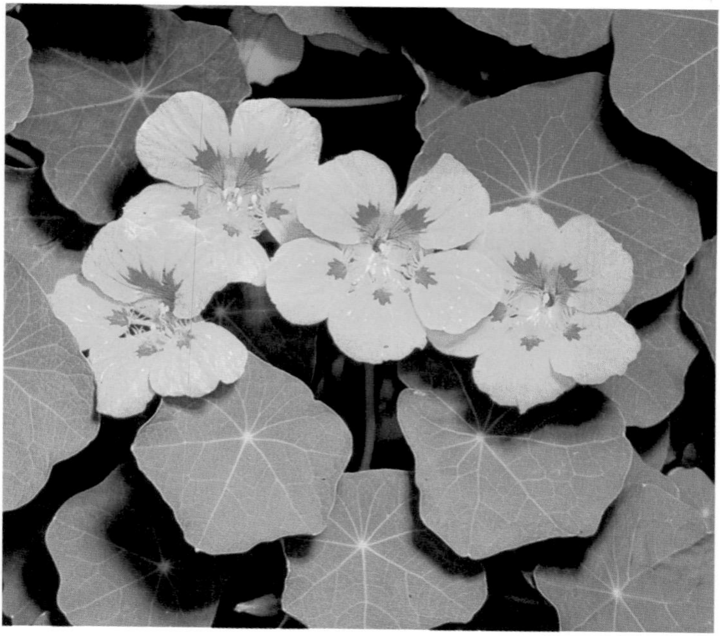

348 TROPAEOLUM PENTAPHYLLUM Jean Baptiste Lamarck

Family Tropaeolaceae.
Description A little-known but attractive tuberous-rooted plant. Its unusual flowers make it very decorative. It has dark-reddish, slender, voluble, cylindrical stems. Its compound leaves are digitate-quinate with a long spiral petiole; the leaflets are entire and ovate-acute. The axillary, solitary, pendulous flowers are red with greenish lobes and a cylindrical tubulous corolla.

Height of plant 40–60 in. (1–1.50 m.).
Size of flower 1⅜–2 in. (3.5–5 cm.).
Place of origin Argentina, Chile.
Flowering time Summer–autumn.
Cultivation In full sun or a very sunny position. Temperate climate. Frost-tender. Grows in any well-aerated, moist garden soil with good humus content. Can be grown as a pot plant, supported by canes. Overall watering, especially in the summer. A few applications of liquid fertilizer during early growth greatly strengthens the plant. Subject to infestation by aphids.
Propagation By spring sowing. By basal shoots or division of the tubers in autumn or spring.
Qualities Half-hardy. Very easy to grow.

349 TULIPA x GESNERIANA Hortorum cv. "Darwin"
Common name: Darwin tulip

Family Liliaceae.
Description A perennial plant with a piriform bulb covered with a chestnut-brown tunic (epicarp). Its basal and caulinary leaves are mainly lanceolate, ondulate, glabrous, glaucescent and rather thick. Its decorative, solitary flowers are borne terminally on a cylindrical, upright, carnose floral scape. Colors include white, yellow, pink, bright red, purplish-red, according to the numerous cultivars. These plants are subject to rapid exhaustion.

Height of plant 20–28 in. (50–70 cm.).
Size of flower 2–3⅛ in. (5–8 cm.).
Place of origin A cultivated hybrid of horticultural origin.
Flowering time Spring.
Cultivation A sunny or partially shaded position. Temperate climate. Can withstand the cold well. Likes rich, well-aerated garden soil with a good humus content or amended with peat or leaf mold and sand. Animal manures should be avoided. Regular watering before flowering. The scapes should be cut down when the leaves turn yellow. Diseases: various types of rot, rust and leaf spot (a virus disease).
Propagation By bulblets removed during the resting period. Selected Dutch bulbs are usually bought each year, however, and planted directly to a depth of 2–4 in. (5–10 cm.) in the flowering site in the autumn.
Qualities Suitable for balconies. Hardy. Easy to grow.

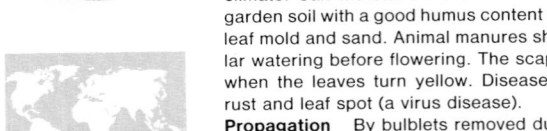

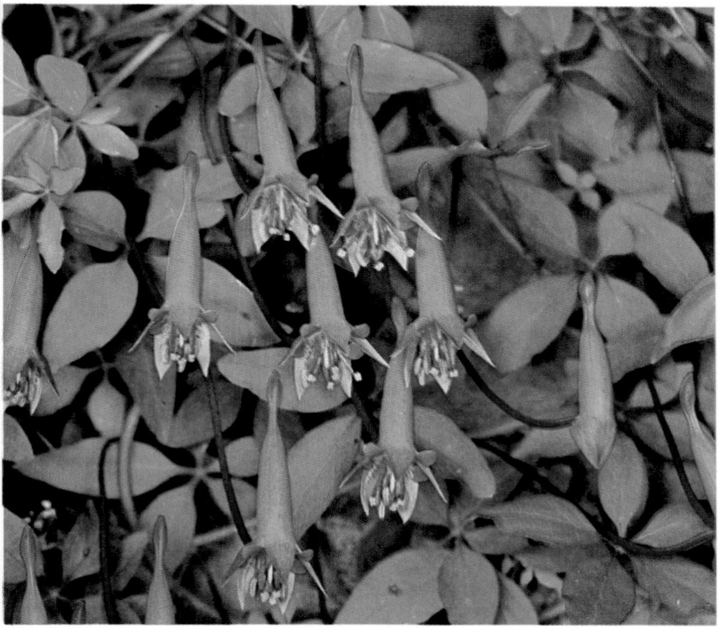

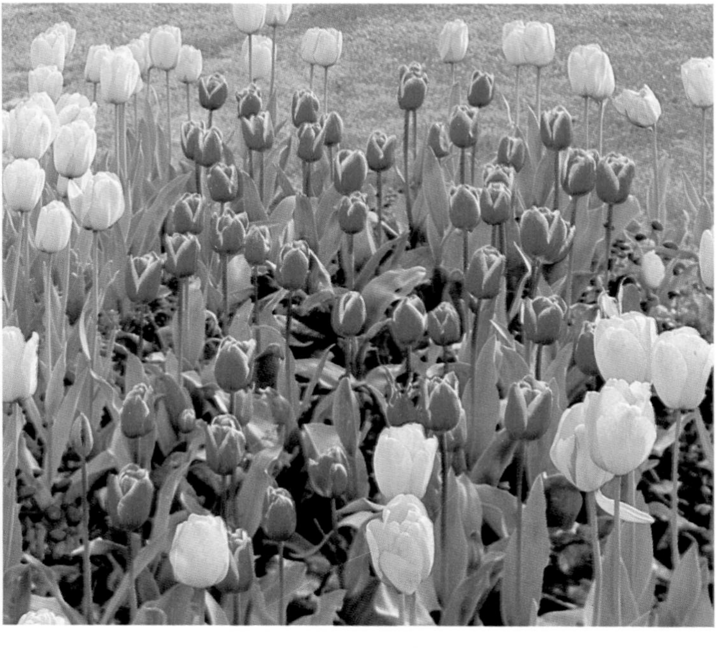

350 TULIPA x GESNERIANA Hortorum cv. "Dracontia"
Common name: Parrot tulip

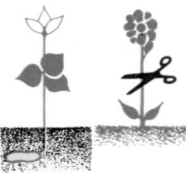

Family Liliaceae.
Description A bulbous perennial with a piriform tunicate bulb. Its basal and caulinary leaves are mainly lanceolate, ondulate, glabrous, glaucescent and rather thick. It produces a bizarre flower with deeply cleft and laciniately dentate petals. Although usually single, some of the many cultivars are double-flowered. The parrot tulip has more curiosity value than beauty. Its range of colors includes salmon-pink, white, rose-pink, scarlet and variegated.
Height of plant 12–16 in. (30–40 cm.).
Size of flower 3⅛–4 in. (8–10 cm.).
Place of origin A cultivated hybrid of horticultural origin.
Flowering time Spring.
Cultivation A sunny or partially shaded position. Temperate climate. Can withstand the cold well. Likes rich, well-aerated garden soil with a good humus content or amended with peat or leaf mold and sand. Avoid animal manures. Moderate watering. When the leaves start to become dry after flowering, remove them. The bulbs then can be dug up and kept in a cool, dry place, but are usually left in the ground. Subject to various types of rot as well as to fungus and virus diseases.
Propagation By bulblets removed during the resting period. Selected Dutch bulbs are usually bought each year.
Qualities Suitable for balconies. Hardy. Easy to grow.

351 VERBENA CANADENSIS (Carolus Linnaeus) Nathaniel Lord Britton
Syn.: *V. aubletia* Nicolaus Joseph Jacquin

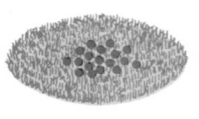

Family Verbenaceae.
Description A perennial that is often grown as an annual in cool-temperate regions, it is widely used as a ground cover because of its large number of fast-growing, prostrate-ascendent, creeping stems and its abundant and prolonged flowering period. It is also easily cultivated. Its opposite leaves are oblong-lanceolate and incise-dentate. Its flowers are borne in compact terminal spikes. There are cultivars whose colors include deep and pale pink, mauve, etc.
Height of plant 12–16 in. (30–40 cm.).
Size of flower ⅜–½ in. (0.8–1.2 cm.).
Place of origin Southwestern United States and Mexico.
Flowering time Spring–autumn.
Cultivation In full sun or a very sunny, sheltered position. Temperate climate. Frost-tender. Grows in any well-aerated, rich soil, preferably a mixture of woodland mold, peat and sand incorporated with organic material. Plentiful watering. A few applications of liquid fertilizer after planting encourage growth. Eelworms tend to attack its roots.
Propagation By early-spring seed sowing under glass.
Qualities Suitable for balconies, terraces, hanging containers. Hardy. Easy to grow.

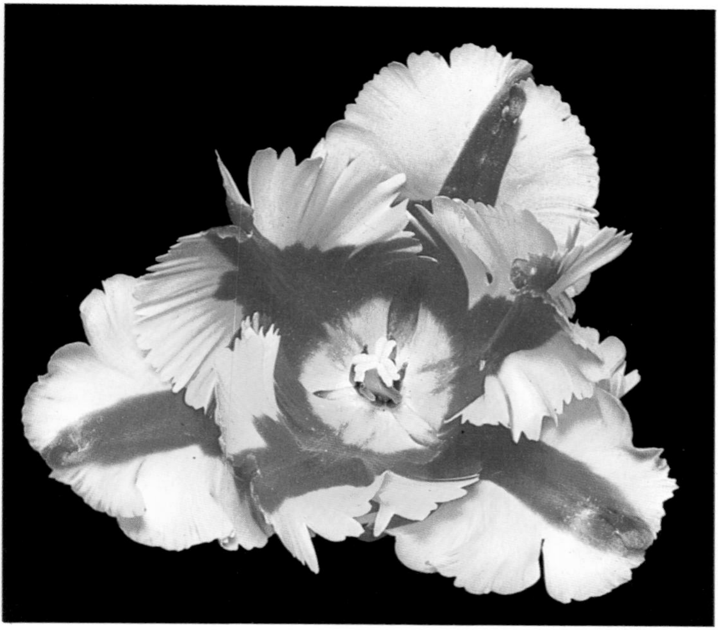

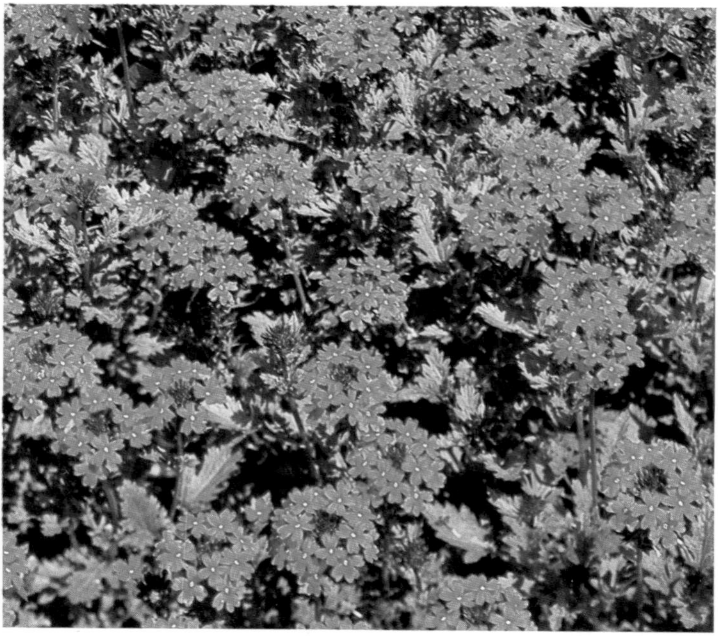

352 VERBENA x HYBRIDA A. Voss
Syn.: *V. hortensis* Hortorum

Family Verbenaceae.

Description A cespitose perennial grown as an annual with prostrate-ascendent, quadrangular stems and diffuse ramifications, often radicant. Its opposite leaves are oblong-lanceolate and irregularly incise-dentate. Its numerous flowers are borne in flattened umbels. The name *V. hortensis* covers a great many varieties of hybrids that differ widely. They include dwarf, medium, tall and creeping plants, in single or mixed colors. They are extremely decorative.

Height of plant 6–12 in. (15–30 cm.).

Size of flower ⅛ in. (0.5 cm.).

Place of origin A horticultural hybrid achieved by crossings of *V. peruviana* with a great many other species such as *V. incana, V. platensis,* etc.

Flowering time Summer.

Cultivation In full sun or a very sunny position. Temperate climate. Does not like the cold. Prefers a light soil or one that has been amended with equal parts woodland or leaf mold, peat and sand mixed with well-rotted manure. Regular watering, especially plentiful in the summer. A few applications of liquid fertilizer before flowering. Bushy growth is encouraged by pinching out the leading shoot after planting out. Keep dead flowers picked off. Often prone to oidium and various fungus diseases in the autumn.

Propagation By late winter or spring sowing under glass.

Qualities Suitable for balconies, etc. Easy to grow.

---

353 VIBURNUM BITCHIUENSE Tomitaro Makino

Family Caprifoliaceae.

Description An ornamental deciduous shrub similar to *V. carlesii,* but smaller and less floriferous, with a very compact habit. Its ramifications are erect and stiff. Its opposite leaves are ovate-rotundate, dentate and acuminate. Its small, numerous, fragrant flowers are borne in dense umbelliferous cymes. Black berries in the autumn.

Height of plant 8–10 ft. (2.50–3 m.).

Size of flower corolla: ¼–⅝ in. (0.6–0.7 cm.).; inflorescence: 1⅛–2 in. (3–5 cm.).

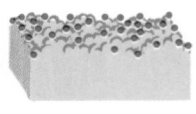

Place of origin Japan.

Flowering time Spring.

Cultivation Partial shade. Temperate climate. Can withstand the cold well. Arid soil and dry climates should be avoided. Prefers ground that is deep, fertile and moist, tending to be wet. Benefits from a periodic top dressing of organic/mineral fertilizers. Generous watering in the summer. Branches should be shortened in the autumn and any dead, weak or exhausted growth removed. This plant tends to become easily exhausted if not fed regularly and pruned adequately.

Propagation By spring sowing in pans under glass. By cuttings taken in spring or autumn; these should be treated with a rooting hormone powder before putting in a frost-free cold-frame.

Qualities Hardy. Easy to grow.

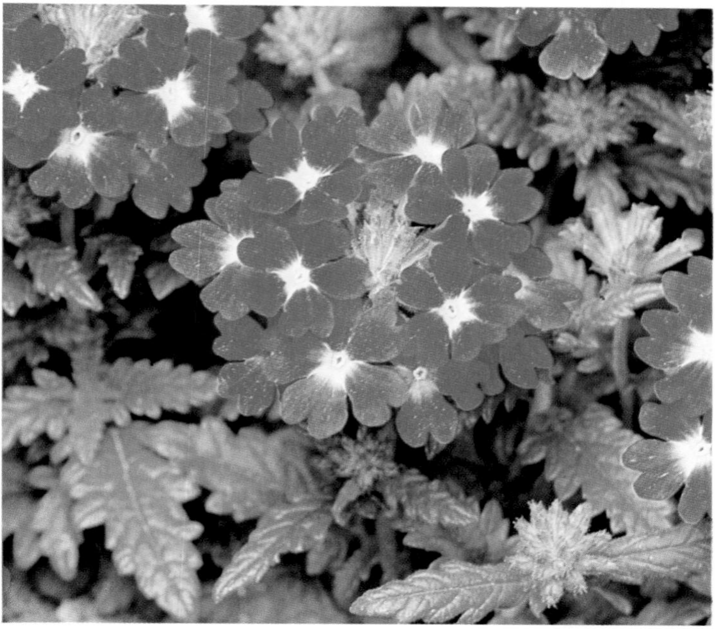

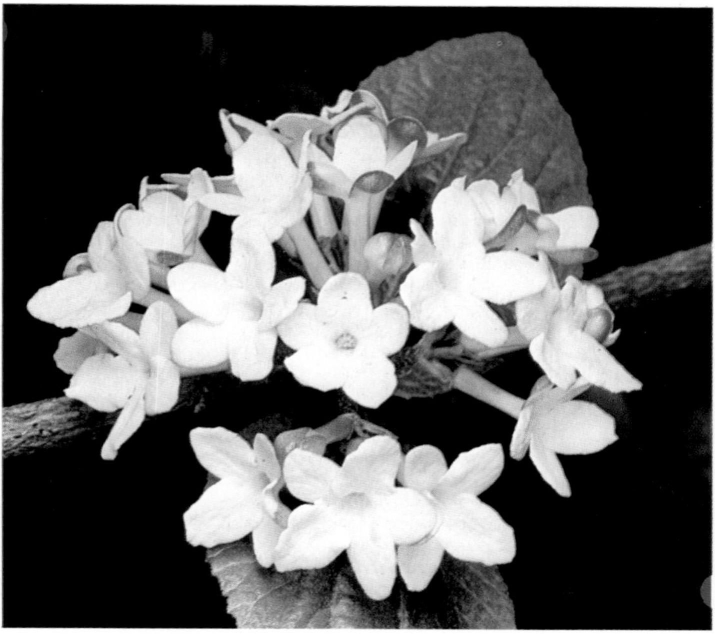

354 **VIBURNUM OPULUS** Carolus Linnaeus cv. ''Sterile''
Common name: European cranberry bush

Family Caprifoliaceae.
Description A well-known, widely grown deciduous flowering shrub with a cespitose habit and numerous upright branches. Its opposite leaves are palmate-lobate, rotundate at the base, with three to five acute, dentate lobes. Its numerous sterile white flowers are borne in rather pendulous, spherical, umbelliferous cymes that are very effective. Other cultivars quite frequently grown are: ''Compactum,'' ''Nanum,'' ''Variegatum'' and ''Xanthocarpum.''
Height of plant 8½–10 ft. (2–3 m.).
Size of flower ½–¾ in. (1.5–2 cm.).
Place of origin A horticultural form; the original species grows wild throughout Europe.
Flowering time Spring.
Cultivation A moderately sunny site. Temperate climate. Can withstand the cold well. Likes a cool, sheltered, even hilly, position. Grows in almost any type of fertile, moist soil. Watering limited to summer. Benefits from a light organic/mineral top dressing from time to time. In autumn, when the leaves have fallen, the plant should be pruned to remove dead, weak or straggly growth and to thin out if overgrown.
Propagation By removal in the spring of the many suckers that rise from the roots. By softwood cuttings taken in the spring.
Qualities Hardy. Easy to grow.

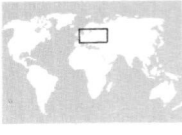

355 **VIBURNUM RHYTIDOPHYLLUM** W. Botting Hemsley
Common name: Leatherleaf viburnum

Family Caprifoliaceae.
Description A bushy, slow-growing evergreen shrub with abundant ramifications springing from the base and tomentose toward the top. Its large dark-green leaves are opposite, oblong-lanceolate, rugose and consistent; they are glossy on the upper surface and pulverulent underneath. Its numerous yellowish-white flowers are borne in broad umbelliferous corymbs. Its autumn fruits consist of red berries that gradually turn black.
Height of plant 10–13 ft. (3–4 m.).
Size of flower ⅛ in. (0.5 cm.).; the whole inflorescence, 6–8 in. (15–20 cm.).
Place of origin China.
Flowering time Spring.
Cultivation A shady position. Temperate climate. Frost-resistant. Likes moderately compact, rich, moist soil with a humus content. Plentiful watering in the summer. A light pruning to remove dead growth after flowering. Hard pruning should be avoided as this plant is so lovely in its natural form. Usually trouble-free.
Propagation By cuttings taken in the spring. By seed sown as soon as it is ripe (early autumn) in a coldframe, but this is a very slow process.
Qualities Hardy. Easy to grow.

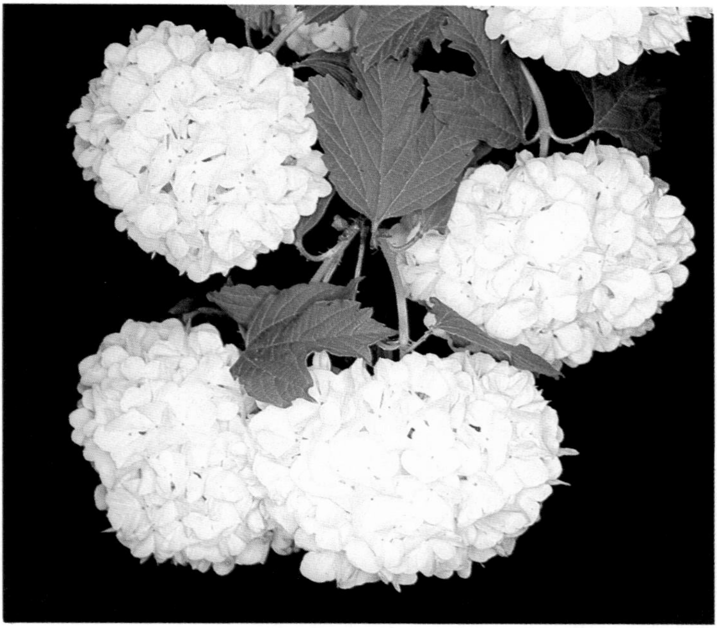

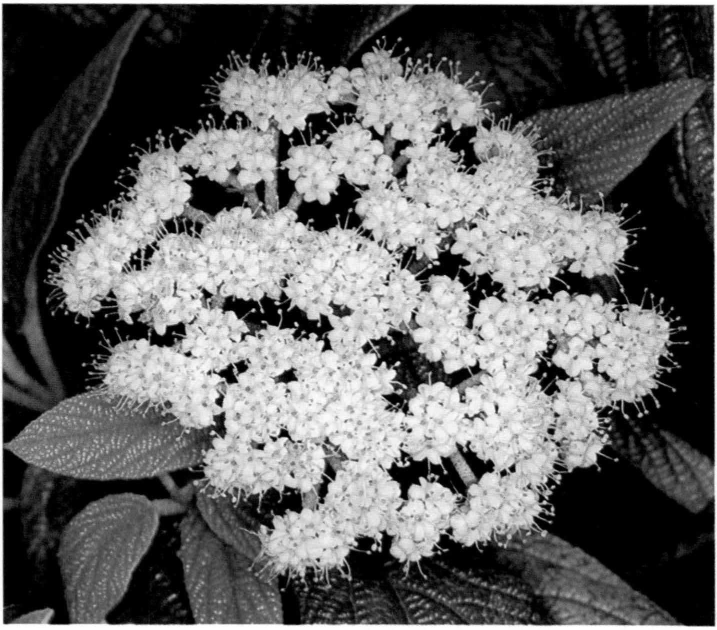

356 VIBURNUM TINUS Carolus Linnaeus
Common name: Laurestinus

Family Caprifoliaceae.
Description A compact, well-ramified, evergreen shrub. Its opposite leaves are ovate-elliptical, glossy on the upper surface, pale and tomentose on the lower. Its numerous flowers, rose-pink at first but gradually becoming white when in full bloom, are borne in dense umbelliferous cymes. Its glossy dark-blue berries are very decorative.
Height of plant 8–11½ ft. (2.50–3.50 m.).
Size of flower ⅛–⅜ in. (0.5–0.8 cm.).
Place of origin Mediterranean regions.
Flowering time Spring and sporadically in autumn.
Cultivation A very bright position but also adapts to a shady site. Grows in almost any type of soil providing it is humus rich and moist. Can withstand the cold and dry spells very well. Requires watering only in exceptionally dry weather. Dead and flowered wood should be removed and plants thinned out if overgrown. These shrubs can be shaped into a hedge but at the expense of the flowers. Pests: often attacked by lacebugs and red spider mites.

Propagation By autumn or spring sowing outdoors in a sheltered nursery bed. By clump division or by cuttings in the spring.
Qualities Hardy. Easy to grow.

---

357 VIBURNUM TOMENTOSUM Carl Peter Thunberg cv. "Mariesii"
Syn.: *V. plicatum* Friedrich Anton Wilhelm Miquel cv. "Mariesii." Common name: Doublefile viburnum

Family Caprifoliaceae.
Description This deciduous shrub has all the good qualities required of any plant: an elegant habit; lovely leaves (oval, acuminate-dentate), bright green turning to multicolored in the autumn; showy flowers. These are in flat corymbs, those on the outside being sterile like those of *Hydrangea petiolaris*. They give way to coral-red berries as the leaves fall in the autumn.
Height of plant 6½–10 ft. (2–3 m.).
Size of flower ¾–1⅜ in. (2–3.5 cm.).
Place of origin A horticultural form, the wild form native to China and Japan.
Flowering time Spring–early summer.

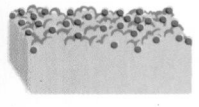

Cultivation A partially shaded position. Cool-temperate climate. Can withstand the cold well. Prefers a woodland-type soil that is moist and rich in humus or organic material. Generous watering in the summer. Requires seasonal feeding with organic/mineral fertilizers. Pruning limited to shortening the branches to retain a balanced shape and to ensure that it does not outgrow its strength. Susceptible to attack by lacebugs and red spider mites.

Propagation By softwood cuttings in spring–summer. Sometimes by grafting. By spring sowing in individual pots in a propagating frame with bottom heat (61° F./16° C.).
Qualities Hardy. Easy to grow.

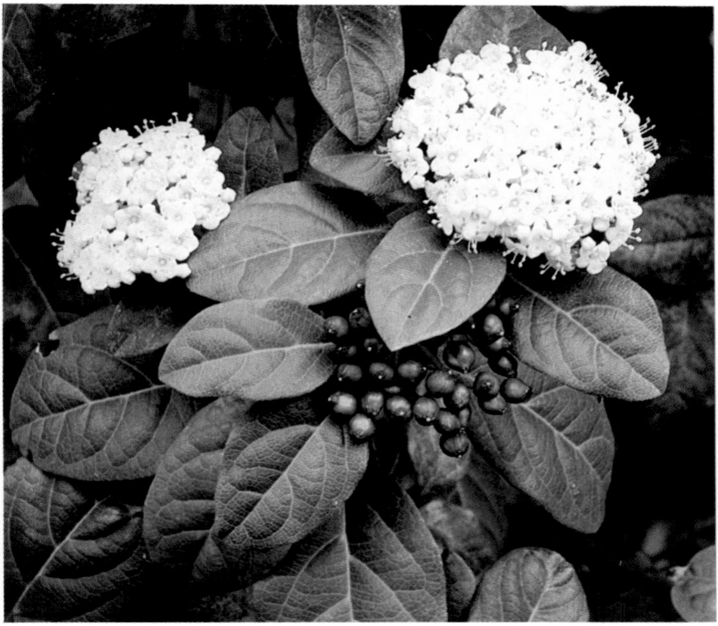

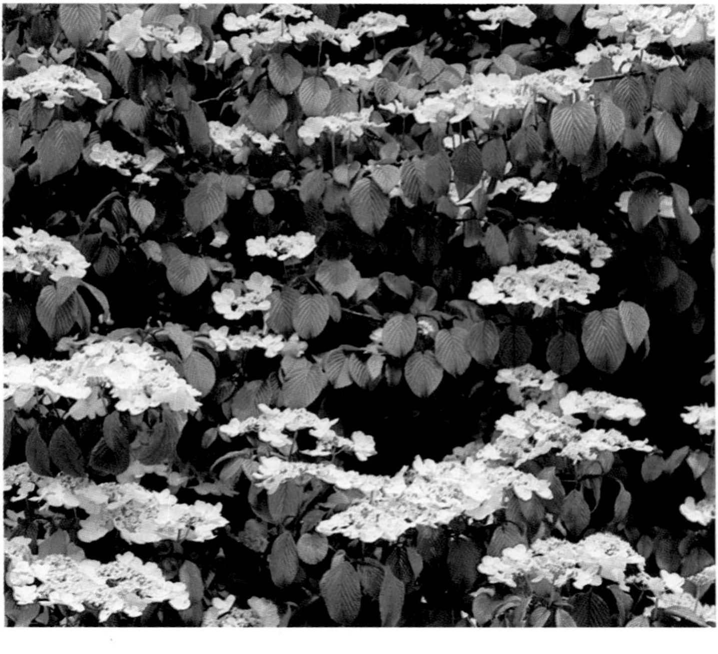

358 VINCA MAJOR Carolus Linnaeus cv. "Variegata"
Common name: Greater periwinkle

Family Apocynaceae.
Description An evergreen, suffruticose, herbaceous subshrub. Its long, creeping, trailing stems frequently put roots down at their tips. Its floriferous shoots are erect. Its opposite leaves are oblong-ovate, glabrous, carnose and variegated with white or pale yellow. Its axillary flowers are sky-blue to mauve. It is a delightful and decorative plant both for its flowers and for its foliage. Very undemanding, it grows well in shady sites.

Height of plant 1–2¼ ft. (30–70 cm.).
Size of flower 1⅛–1½ in. (3–4 cm.).
Place of origin A cultivated form derived from the wild form originating from the Mediterranean regions.
Flowering time Spring.
Cultivation A shady position. Temperate climate. Can withstand the cold very well. Does not require any particular care. Watering limited to very dry spells. Pruning limited to removal of dead, weak or straggly growth and the elimination of the oldest stems. Usually trouble-free.
Propagation By clump division and by layering in the spring or autumn.
Qualities Hardy. Easy to grow.

359 VINCA MINOR Carolus Linnaeus
Common names: Dwarf periwinkle, myrtle

Family Apocynaceae.
Description A herbaceous, evergreen subshrub. It has numerous slender stems that are partly creeping and rooting and partly erect. Its dark-green, opposite leaves are elliptical-lanceolate, coriaceous and glabrous, with a short petiole. Its numerous axillary flowers are of a deep mauve-blue that varies according to the soil type. This plant is a very useful ground cover in a shrubbery or under trees. There are several cultivars in various colors, some with variegated leaves.

Height of plant 6–10 in. (15–25 cm.).
Size of flower ¾–1⅛ in. (2–3 cm.).
Place of origin Europe.
Flowering time Spring and sometimes in autumn.
Cultivation A light to deep shady site. Temperate climate. Frost-resistant. Prefers an open, rich, moist, woodland type of soil with a humus content. Watering limited to very dry spells. Does not usually require any particular care. If the plants become too old or straggly, a light trim with shears rejuvenates them.
Propagation By clump division or by the natural layering of the trailing stems of adult plants, 6 in. (15 cm.) lengths of which can be cut off and rooted by planting on the diagonal in the flowering site.
Qualities Hardy. Easy to grow.

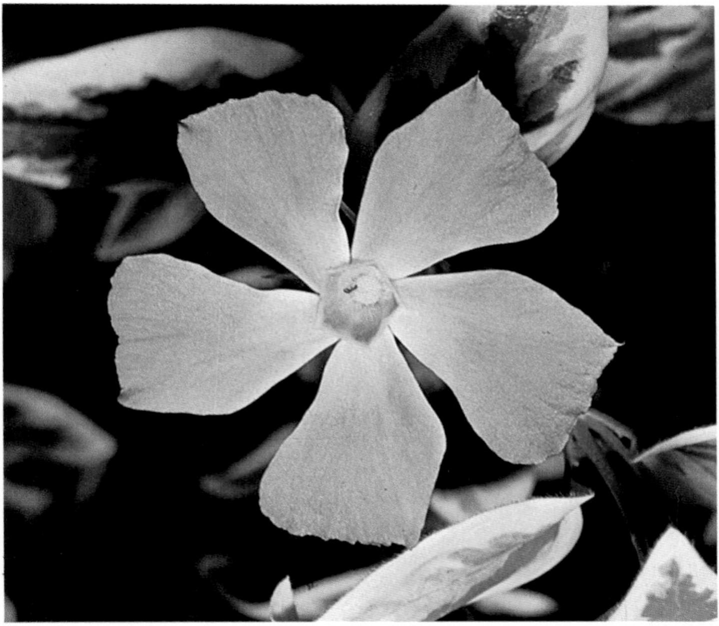

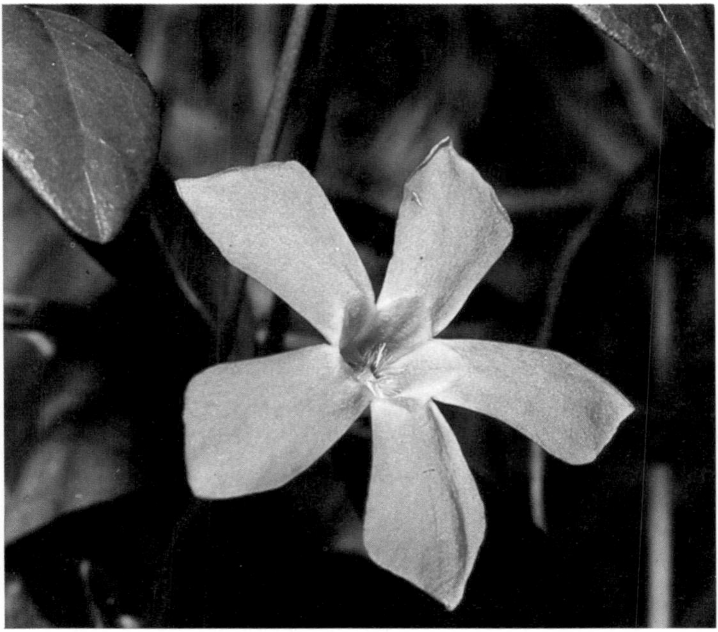

360 VIOLA ODORATA Carolus Linnaeus
Common name: Sweet violet

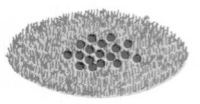

Family Violaceae.
Description A herbaceous perennial. The cultivated varieties of *Viola odorata* often differ from the species although all are recognizable by the delicacy of their flowers and delightful fragrance. The plant is stoloniferous and spreads by means of runners. Its leaves, which are produced in tufts, are rotundate-cordate with ovate-acuminate stipules. Its singly borne flowers open out into five petals. There are many horticultural varieties, one of the best known being *V. pallida plena* "Nicholson," usually called the Parma violet.
Height of plant 2–4 in. (5–10 cm.).
Size of flower ¾–1⅛ in. (2–3 cm.).
Place of origin Woodlands of Europe.
Flowering time Winter–spring.

Cultivation A shady position and under shrubs, trees, etc. Cool-temperate climate. Can withstand the cold well. Prefers a rich, fibrous, moist-damp woodland soil. Requires frequent watering if being grown in dry conditions. Does not usually need any particular attention. Pests: aphids and other insects often cause the leaves to dry out and become papery.
Propagation By clump division in the autumn or spring, and after flowering. It is possible to reproduce the fertile varieties by seed, sowing them in pans in light, sandy compost in a cool, partially shaded position.
Qualities Hardy. Easy to grow.

361 VIOLA TRICOLOR Carolus Linnaeus cv.
Syn.: *V. tricolor* var. *Hortensis* Augustin Pyramus De Candolle. Common names: Pansy, Johnny-jump-up

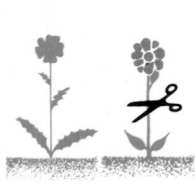

Family Violaceae.
Description Delightful little biennial or short-lived perennial. Erect hollow stem with alternate, oblong, acute, crenate-serrate leaves. The flowers are hybrid forms very different from the original plants used in the numerous crossings that achieved the *V. wittrockiana*. The *V. tricolor* produces numerous singly borne, axillary flowers, very pretty, abundant, and long blooming. They are slightly scented. Many horticultural varieties in a selection of colors.
Height of plant 6–8 in. (15–20 cm.).
Size of flower 1⅛–2 in. (3–5 cm.).
Place of origin The species originated in Europe.
Flowering time Spring–summer.

Cultivation A bright or slightly shady position. Cool-temperate climate; too much warmth prevents flowering. Fairly frost-resistant. Prefers a fertile, moist, humus-rich woodland type of soil. Regular watering. Compact ground can be amended with peat, heath mold and sand. A few applications of liquid fertilizer shortly after planting accelerate growth. Plants should be removed after flowering. Pests and diseases: young plants are attractive to snails and slugs; root rot.
Propagation By summer sowing, pricking off into a seedling bed and planting in flowering positions in autumn or spring.
Qualities Hardy. Suitable for terraces. Easy to grow.

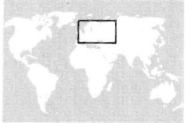

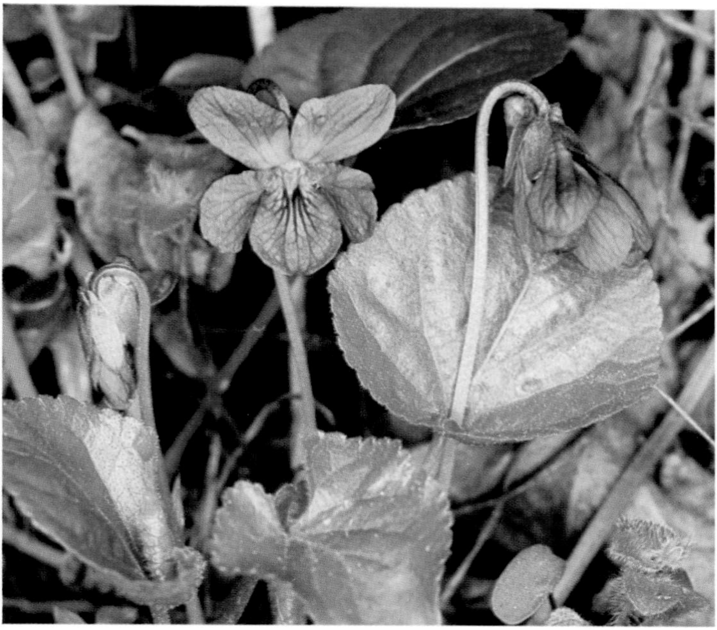

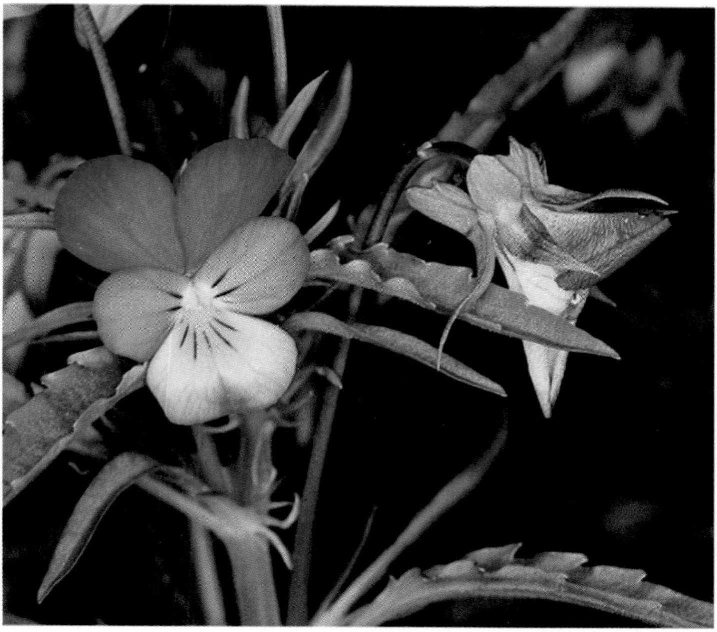

362 VIOLA x WITTROCKIANA Gams
Common name: Pansy

Family   Violaceae.
Description   A herbaceous biennial. It has an erect, hollow, ascendent stem with numerous angular, hollow ramifications. Its alternate leaves are oblong, crenate and carnose with pinnatifid stipules. Its large, numerous, axillary flowers are borne singly. There are many varieties, selected for their shape, color or size of the flower.
Height of plant   6–12 in. (15–30 cm.).
Size of flower   2–4 in. (5–10 cm.).
Place of origin   A hybrid of horticultural origin obtained by crossings and recrossings of *V. tricolor* with other species, especially *V. lutea* and *V. altaica*.
Flowering time   Spring–summer.
Cultivation   Full sun to partial shade. Temperate climate. Can withstand a few frosts. Likes a well-aerated, rich garden soil, even if calcareous. Organic feeding and regular watering. A few applications of liquid fertilizer after planting encourage luxuriant growth. The plants should be removed after flowering. Pests: sometimes attacked by eelworms and aphids.
Propagation   By summer sowing under glass or in a sheltered position; seedlings should be pricked off into a seedling bed for planting out in the late autumn or spring.
Qualities   Suitable for balconies, terraces. Hardy. Easy to grow.

---

363 WEIGELA FLORIDA (Alexander von Bunge) Augustin Pyramus De Candolle
Syns.: *W. rosea* John Lindley, *Diervilla florida* Philipp Franz von Siebold and Joseph Gerhard Zuccarini, *D. amabilis*

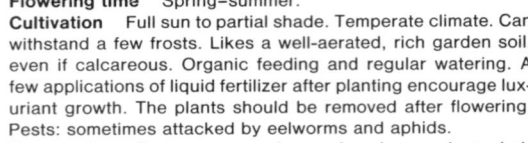

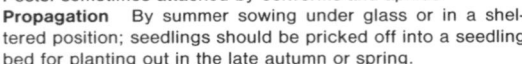

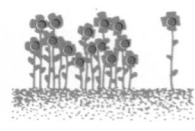

Family   Caprifoliaceae.
Description   One of the best spring-flowering garden shrubs. Deciduous. It has an erect, bushy habit with abundant ramifications. Its opposite leaves are irregularly ovate-acuminate and crenulate-dentate. Its flowers are borne in axillary and terminal dense umbels or whorls (verticels). The corolla, usually pink, is infundibuliform. The species is relatively rare and the cultivated plants are nearly all hybrid forms of *W. florida* x *W. japonica* or of *W. florida* x *W. floribunda* or *W. coreaensis*.
Height of plant   5–6 ft. (1.50–3 m.).
Size of flower   1⅛ in. (3 cm.).
Place of origin   China, Korea.
Flowering time   Spring.
Cultivation   A moderately sunny position. Temperate climate. Frost-resistant. Grows in any soil, preferably moderately compact, rich and moist. Benefits from an occasional top dressing of a complete organic/mineral fertilizer. Plentiful watering; dry conditions harm the plant. Prune immediately after flowering. Usually trouble-free.
Propagation   By hardwood cuttings taken at the end of winter and rooted in sand in a temperate greenhouse. By half-ripened cuttings taken in summer and rooted similarly.
Qualities   Hardy. Easy to grow.

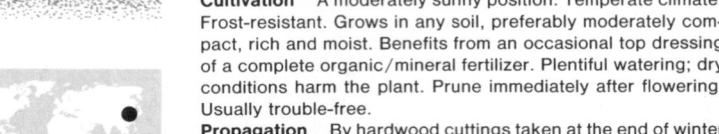

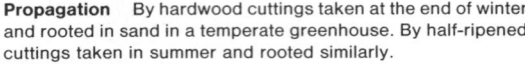

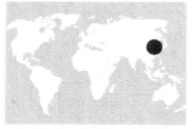

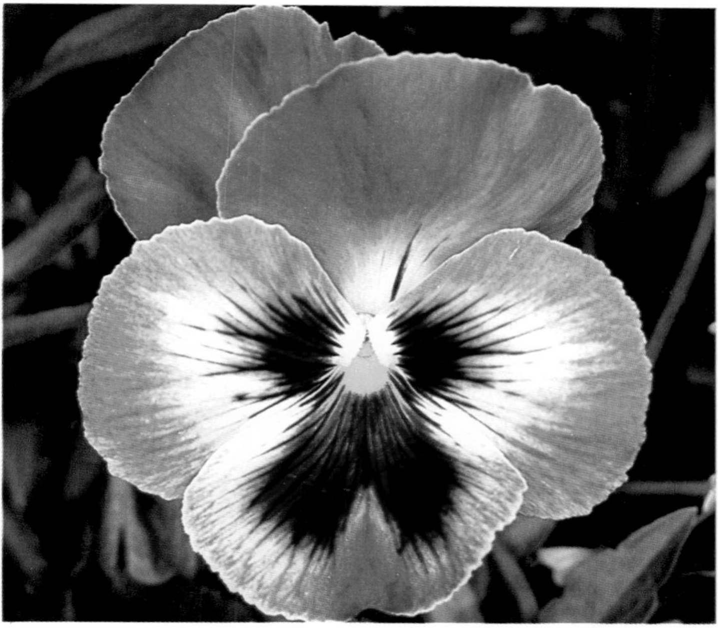

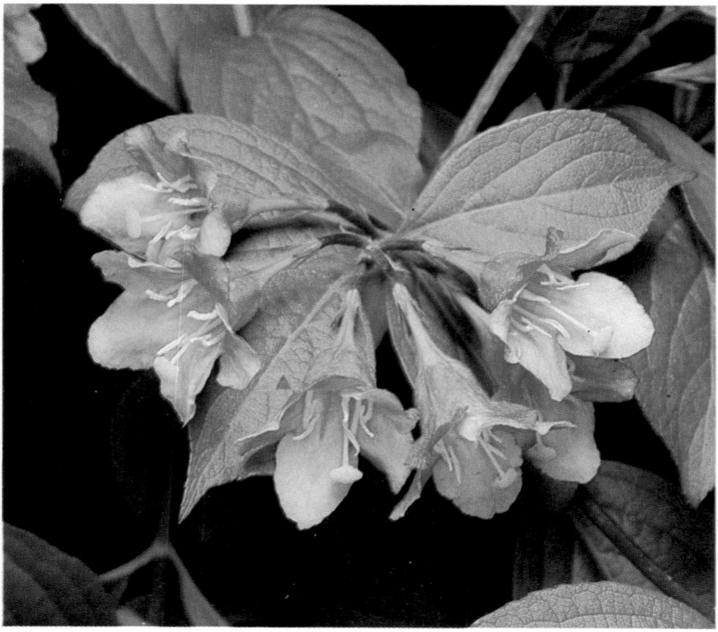

364 WIGANDIA CARACASANA Friedrich Alexander von Humboldt and Karl Sigismund Kunth

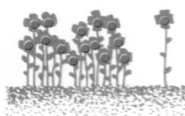

Family Hydrophyllaceae.
Description A climbing shrub, sometimes with an arborescent habit. Its branches are pubescent and sericerous. Its alternate, ovate leaves are dentate, cordate at the base with a long petiole and covered with slightly irritating hairs. Its flowers are in terminal, scorpioid cymes borne in dense panicles. The corolla is campanulate with a white tube and a violet-colored five-lobed limb.
Height of plant 1½–8 ft. (1–2.50 m.).
Size of flower ⅜–1 in. (1–2.5 cm.).
Place of origin Mexico, Venezuela.
Flowering time Spring.

Cultivation A sheltered, very bright or very slightly shaded position. Temperate climate. Frost-tender. Thrives outdoors in a warm coastal region. Grows in any type of rich, moist garden soil. Benefits from a seasonal top dressing of a complete organic/mineral fertilizer. Requires plentiful watering during the summer. Flowered heads should be removed. Pruning limited to cutting back of the old wood. Pests and diseases: aphids and caterpillars; chlorosis in unsuitable soil or soil that is too wet.
Propagation By division of the shrub. By basal shoots and root cuttings in spring–summer. By seed, although seeds do not always ripen despite a fairly high temperature; if mature seed is available, it can be germinated in pans in a greenhouse.
Qualities Half-hardy. Very easy to grow.

---

365 WISTERIA FLORIBUNDA (Karl Ludwig Willdenow) Augustin Pyramus De Candolle
Syn.: *W. multijuga*. Common name: Japanese wisteria

Family Papilionaceae.
Description Climbing deciduous plant with a voluble stem and many ramifications. Its deciduous, alternate leaves are imparipinnate with 13 to 19 ovate elliptical leaflets. Numerous slightly scented flowers borne in very decorative pale-pink, simple racemes about 8–14 in. (20–35 cm.) long and up to 20–24 in. (50–60 cm.) in the cultivar "Macrobotrys." It blooms later than *W. sinensis*, and loses its leaves earlier in autumn.
Height of plant 16–26 ft. (5–8 m.).
Size of flower ½–1 in. (1.5–2.5 cm.).
Place of origin Japan.
Flowering time Spring.

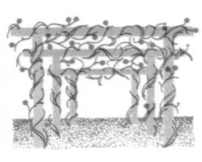

Cultivation In full sun or partial shade. Temperate climate. Frost-resistant. Needs to be supported. Grows in any type of moist, rich soil. Water well only when planted. Cut back flowered growth as soon as blooms have died, then prune hard to two or three buds from the base of previous year's wood, in autumn or early winter. If growth is sparse, apply organic/mineral fertilizer.

Propagation By layering during spring–summer. By root and hardwood cuttings rooted in a propagating frame or greenhouse in spring–summer.
Qualities Hardy. Easy to grow.

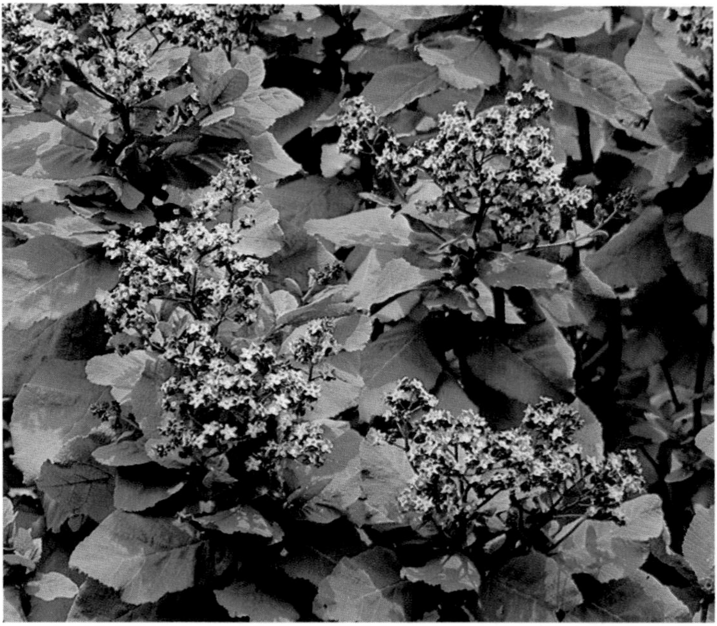

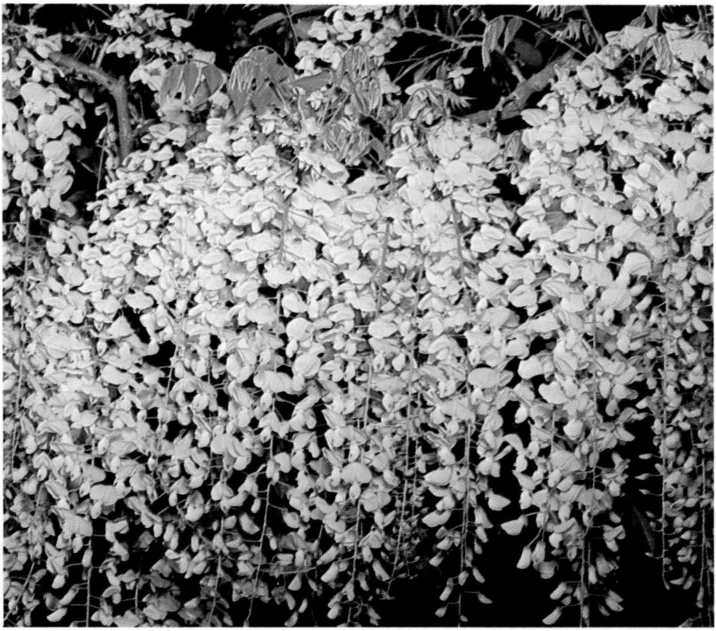

366 **WISTERIA SINENSIS** (John Sims) Robert Sweet
Syn.: *W. chinensis* Augustin Pyramus De Candolle.
Common name: Chinese wisteria

Family Papilionaceae.
Description A climbing deciduous plant with a strong, ligneous, voluble, ramified stem. Its imparipinnate leaves are composed of nine to thirteen ovate-lanceolate, acuminate leaflets. Its numerous violet-blue, scented flowers are borne in drooping racemes, growing close together or fairly far apart, about 6–12 in. (15–30 cm.) long. The abundant blooms appear on its bare branches before the leaves have unfurled.
Height of plant 15–50 ft. (5–15 m.).
Size of flower ¾–1 in. (2–2.5 cm.).
Place of origin China.
Flowering time Spring.
Cultivation In full sun or partial shade. Temperate climate. Frost-resistant. Needs to be supported or grown against a wall. Grows in any type of soil, preferably one that is moderately argillaceous, rich and moist. Does not like to be transplanted. When first planted, watering helps it to become established. It should be pruned twice: a light pruning in August to remove flowered growth and hard pruning in autumn or at the end of winter.
Propagation By layering in summer–autumn. By root and hardwood cuttings taken in spring–summer and rooted under glass.
Qualities Hardy. Easy to grow.

---

367 **YUCCA GLORIOSA** Carolus Linnaeus
Common name: Spanish dagger

Family Agavaceae.
Description A ligneous-fibrous plant with a short, upright trunk with few ramifications. Its alternate linear leaves are 2–2½ ft. (60–80 cm.) long, clustered spirally on the trunk and equipped with a terminal acuminate point. Its large flowers are pale pink or whitish and borne in long, erect, terminal panicles. The perigonium is cup-shaped, formed of six more or less separate, pendant lobes.
Height of plant 5–8 ft. (1.50–2.50 m.).
Size of flower 2¾–4 in. (7–10 cm.).
Place of origin Southeastern United States
Flowering time Spring–summer.
Cultivation In full sun and a dry position. It suffers in cold weather but can withstand some freezing weather. Grows in any soil, even if not very fertile, but preferably sandy or well aerated. It thrives even in rocky terrain near the sea. Does not require watering or any particular care. The dry leaves should be removed periodically. If it becomes too tall for the site, with a tendency to topple over, cut back to its base; it will nearly always throw up suckers. Usually trouble-free.
Propagation By seed sown in pans in a frame or greenhouse but it takes at least two or three years before the young plants are ready to be planted out. By basal suckers or root cuttings brought on in a warm greenhouse.
Qualities Hardy. Suitable for terraces. Easy to grow.

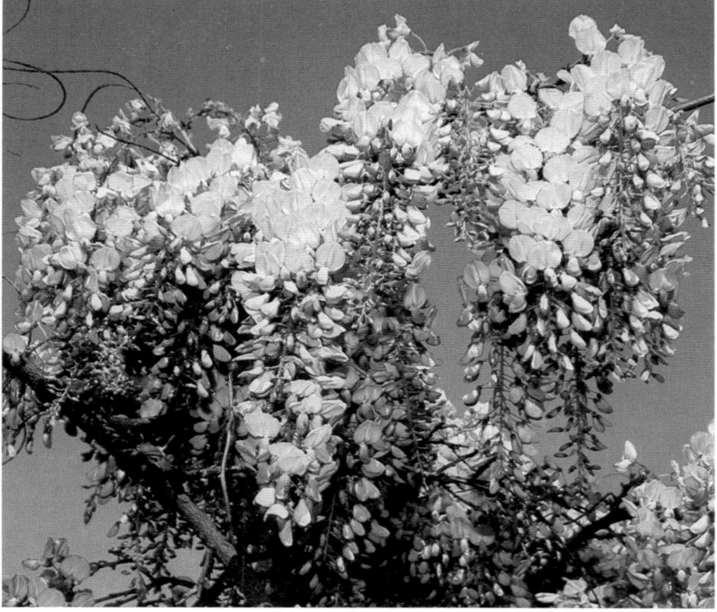

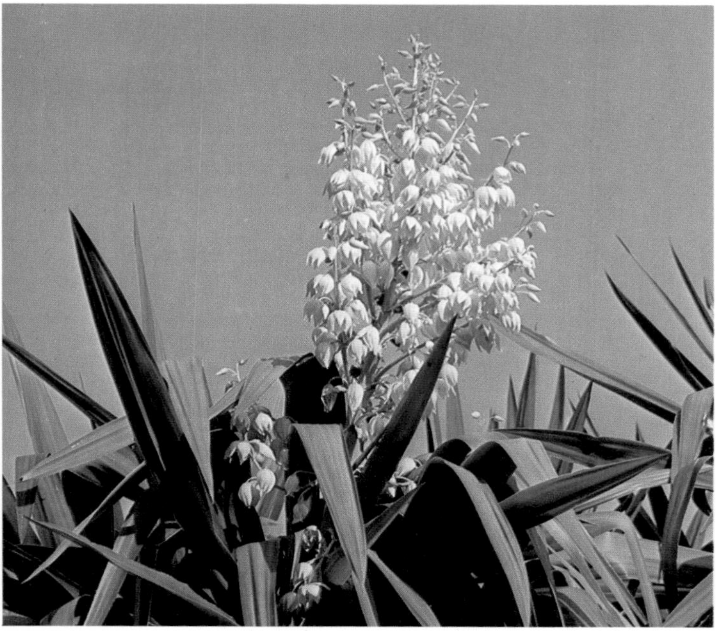

368 ZANTEDESCHIA AETHIOPICA (Carolus Linnaeus) Kurt Sprengel

Syn.: *Richardia africana* Karl Sigismund Kunth, *Calla aethiopica* Carolus Linnaeus. Common names: Common calla lily, lily of the Nile

Family Araceae.
Description Large, proliferous, oblong tubers truncated at the base. Basal leaves have a large, long, carnose petiole, sheathed at the base; leaf blade is large, sagittate or cordate and undulate. The whole plant contains a caustic-vesicant. Yellow flowers borne singly on a spadix surrounded by a large creamy-white bract (spathe) on a long, carnose, erect, sturdy peduncle.
Height of plant 24–40 in. (0.60–1 m.).
Size of flower 4–6⅜ in. (10–16 cm.).
Place of origin South Africa.
Flowering time Spring–summer.

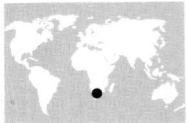

Cultivation Full sun or very bright position. Warm-temperate climate. Cannot withstand cold. Likes moist, well-manured soil and grows well in slightly warm, still, shallow water. Feed with a complete liquid fertilizer; water generously. In cooler climates lift rhizomes and store in a cool but frost-free place during their resting period; elsewhere leave in the ground. Diseases: corm rot and fungus diseases.
Propagation By offsets removed from the parent rhizomes during their resting stage. Flowers in about two years.
Qualities Hardy in its natural environment, otherwise half-hardy. Very easy to grow.

369 ZINNIA ELEGANS Nicolaus Joseph Jacquin

Syn.: *Z. violacea* Antonio Jose Cavanilles

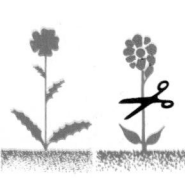

Family Compositae.
Description An erect, bushy annual, ramified from the base with fragile, expansive branches. Its medium-green, opposite leaves are sessile, ovate or sub-cordate and rough-textured. Its flowers are borne singly on strong peduncles; their colors include white, pink, red, purple, yellow. They remain in bloom for a considerable time and make a fine display. Many of the distinct horticultural varieties, such as *Z. hybrida*, derive from this species.
Height of plant 20–28 in. (50–70 cm.).
Size of flower 2⅜–4¾ in. (6–12 cm.).
Place of origin Mexico.
Flowering time Summer–autumn.

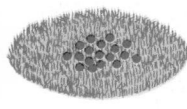

Cultivation In full sun or a very bright position. Temperate climate. Prefers calcareous soil but grows in any soil provided it is well worked and manured with organic material and a good supply of lime and phosphorus. The growing tips should be pinched out shortly after the young plants have been planted out in order to encourage them to branch. Frequent and plentiful watering. Subject to various types of rot and fungus diseases, especially oidium.

Propagation By spring sowing directly in the garden or under glass.
Qualities Hardy. Easy to grow.

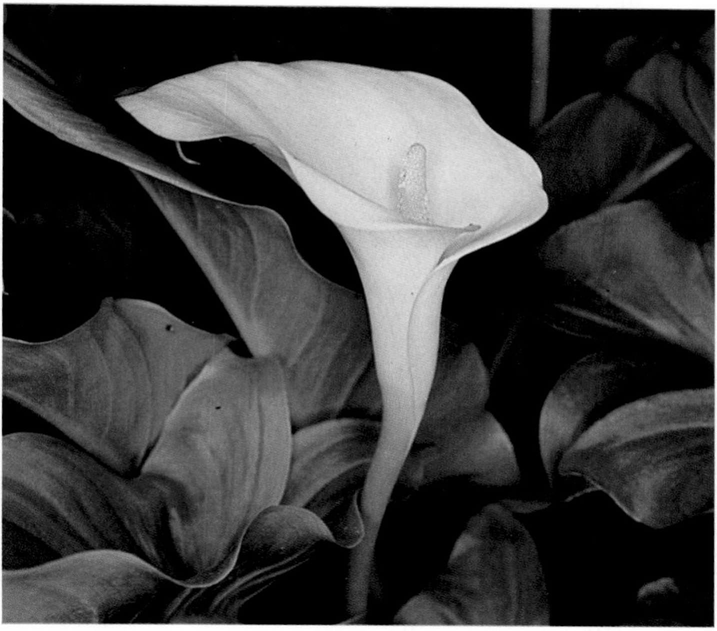

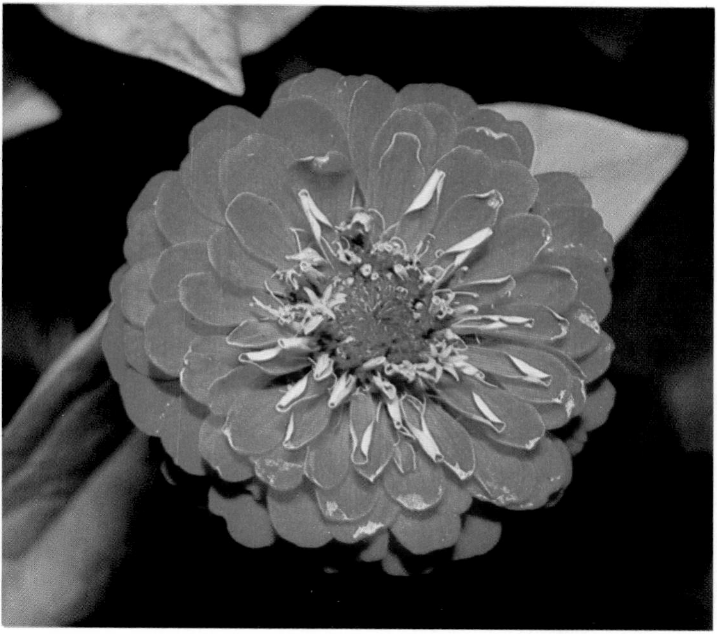

GLOSSARY

Acauline/Acaulose/Acaulescent   having no stem or almost none.
Achene   type of indehiscent dry fruit containing only one seed.
Actinomorphic   roughly speaking, symmetrical. Divisible vertically into similar halves.
Acuminate   graduating to a point.
Acute   ending in a point.
Acyclic structure   spiral arrangement of the parts of a flower.
Adventitious   appearing in abnormal places; for example, roots growing from a branch.
Air layering/Aerial layering   type of vegetative propagation carried out by means of a specially treated area of a branch, which is enclosed in a sleeve until rooting takes place. Then the new plant can be detached and planted.
Alate   winged: said of a leafstalk when it is closely flanked by two small, leaflike membranes (stipules).
Albinism   condition of a plant that turns white as a result of deficiencies in the function of chlorophyll in photosynthesis.
Alluvial soil   the fine soil formed from sediment brought by running water and deposited on low-lying ground.
Alternate leaves   leaves arranged at different heights on the stem. Compare "Opposite leaves."
Amplexicaul   a sessile leaf whose base envelops the stem horizontally.
Androecium   the male organs of the flower formed by the stamens.
Anther   the fertile part of a stamen, consisting of two pollen sacs.
Arborescent   treelike in growth or general appearance.
Arcuate   bent in a bowlike curve.
Argentate   having a silvery appearance.
Articulate   jointed, usually referring to a stem or fruit in which there is natural separation.
Ascendent/Ascending   said of a stem or branch growing more or less horizontally at first, then turning upward gradually to an erect position.
Averse   turned back on itself.
Axillary flowers   flowers that grow from the axil of a leaf, i.e., between leaf and stem.
Bacciform   berry-shaped.
Basal leaves   leaves at the base of a plant.
Berry   a fleshy fruit with high water content and hard-coated seeds.
Bifid   forked; almost divided into two parts by a deep cleft.
Bilabiate corolla   formed into two lips, an upper and lower.
Binate   composed of two equal parts; growing in pairs.
Bipinnate leaf   doubly compound-pinnate or pinnatisect leaf; i.e., divided in turn into compound-pinnate or pinnatisect parts.
Bract   a sort of modified leaf at the base of a flower or inflorescence.
Bud terminal or axillary   embryonic shoot capable of forming a new branch with leaves; it grows at the tip of a stem or from a leaf axil.
Budding   see Grafting and Budding.

Bulb ovoid underground stem made up of a compressed stem surrounded by several overlapping modified leaves (tunics) and leaf bases, papery on the outside and fleshy on the inside. Some bulbs (for example, lilies) consist of individual scale leaves.

Bulbil a small bud in the shape of an aerial bulb situated on the branches at the leaf axil.

Bulblet a small underground bulb produced as an offset of the main (parent) bulb.

Caducous deciduous; said of leaves that remain on the plant for only one growing season and then fall off.

Calcifuge/Calciphobe/Calcifobous lime-hating; having a preference for an acid soil.

Calyx external involucre of a flower made up of sterile floral components that are usually green (sepals).

Campanulate corolla bell-shaped corolla.

Canaliculate see Channeled.

Capitulum inflorescence consisting of numerous sessile florets all on the same level and borne on the apex of the peduncle on the receptacle.

Capsule a dry seedcase that opens on ripening by a parting of its valves.

Carina a ridge-shaped structure or keel consisting of two fused lower petals enclosing stamens and stigma.

Carinate keel-like.

Carnose/Carnous of a fleshy consistency.

Carpels modified fertile floral leaves that collectively form the gynoecium.

Cartilagenous hardened and tough but still pliable.

Cauline relating to the stem; especially, growing from the stem rather than from the base of the plant.

Cavity (of the anther) the part of the anther formed by the pollen sacs.

Cavity (of the ovary) a sector of a polycarpic ovary.

Cereous waxy.

Cespitose growing in tufts; said of a plant that sends up a number of stems, growing fairly close together, from its base.

Channeled describing a leaf so shaped as to form a channel.

Chlorosis yellowing of leaves due mainly to mineral deficiencies or waterlogging.

Ciliate having margins fringed with hairs.

Cirrus/Cirrhus a tendril.

Cladode flattened, green stem or branch resembling a leaf.

Claviform club-shaped.

Clay a very compact type of soil made up of minute particles.

Climber a plant that is unable to support itself unless it clings to a support by means of special appendages such as tendrils, prickles, adventitious roots, twining stems, etc.

Clump division reproduction of plants by dividing a crown or clump in two or more parts.

Collar/Collet the junction of root and shoot.

Coldframe low, boxlike construction with a glass or plastic sash or removable lights for the protection of plants and for hardening them off.

Compost highly nutritious soil produced through the natural fermentation of layers of soil and various organic substances.

Compound leaf a leaf that branches from a central midrib and is divided into several units called leaflets or segments, each one having the form of a leaf.

Compressed flattened.

Connate having similar parts joined by growth.

Contorted entwined.

Coriaceous of a practically rigid consistency, almost leathery.

Corolla the involucre of a flower consisting of sterile, colored floral parts (petals).

Corymb an indeterminate inflorescence in which the pedunculate flowers spring from different points of the main stalk, yet all reach the same height.

Crenate with a notched or scalloped margin (crenature).

Crenulate with very small crenatures along the margins.

Crispate a fluted, crisped or curled margin.

Cristate crested.

Crop rotation the alternation of crops or plants so they don't grow in the same places year after year. It helps to keep soil in good tilth and discourages insects and buildup of disease.

Cruciate or Cruciform corolla four petals growing in the form of a cross.

Culm the stem of the gramineae (grasses), usually unbranched, which features very prominent nodes, elongated internodes and, frequently, cavities.

Cultivar a variety of plant that has been achieved by cultivation through selection and hybridization.

Cuneate/Cuneal/Cuneiform wedge-shaped and attached by the point.

Cutting a section of softwood, semi-hardwood, hardwood, leaf, root, etc., cut from a living plant and put in contact with a rooting medium to form a new plant.

Cutting back reduction in length of the main and secondary branches of a plant.

Cyclic structure the parts of a flower arranged in whorls or cycles.

Cyme a determinate inflorescence in which the terminal flower of the primary axis opens first.

Dead-heading cutting off the heads of flowers to encourage new blooms.

Deciduous losing leaves for part of the year.

Decumbent lying on the ground but with the tip growing upward.

Decussate when each pair of opposite leaves is at right angles to the pair below.

Determinate growing no further than the flowers at the ends of the stems.

Dentate a margin with sharp toothlike notches.

Depressed flattened from the end.

Desquamate having a loose, scaly surface.

Dialypetalous corolla, Choripetalous corolla with separate petals.

Dialysepalous calyx with separate calyxes.

Dialytepalous perigonium with separate tepals.

Dichasium a cymose inflorescence in which two secondary stems grow from the same point on each side of the main stem (simple and compound dichasium).

Dichotomous branching a primitive form of branching in which forked branches form two branches of equal size.

Difform/Difformed unusual or irregular in shape.

Diffuse stem a free- and loosely branching prostrate stem that spreads extensively.

Digitate leaf a leaf consisting of five leaflets springing from the same point.

Dioecious plant bearing male flowers on one plant and female flowers on another.

493

Disc florets or Disc flowers   the tiny flowers in the center of a capitulum type of inflorescence.

Dissemination or Dispersal   the dispersion of seeds—or of the fruit contained in them—for the propagation of the species.

Distant   spaced apart.

Distichous leaves   leaves arranged alternately in two vertical rows on opposite sides of the stem.

Divaricate branch   a wide-spreading, forked branch.

Drainage   correct working of the ground to ensure that it is permeable and to enable excess water to drain away.

Drip watering or Trickle watering   method of watering by which water drips or trickles slowly into the soil.

Drupe   a fruit with a fleshy pericarp and a single hard seed (kernel), the whole being enclosed in a very tough involucre.

Elliptic   ellipse-shaped.

Ensiform   sword-shaped.

Epiphyte   a plant that grows on the stems or branches of trees and other plants without harm to the host, since it has special means of storing water such as aerial roots.

Equitant leaves   leaves springing from the base in rosette form; they overlap each other to store water.

Ericoid   having heatherlike leaves.

Evergreen   a plant with persistent leaves. Old leaves are shed throughout the year and replaced with new; thus the plant always seems covered with foliage.

Eye   bud containing the primordia of a new branch or flower.

Falciform   sickle-shaped.

Farinose/Farinosus/Farinaceous   covered with very short, whitish hairs that disintegrate easily into a white, waxy powder.

Fasciculate roots   see Fibrous roots.

Fibrous roots   a mass of thin spreading roots, fairly uniform in size, that spring from the collar of a plant.

Filament   part of a stamen, this is the thin stalk that supports the anther.

Fimbriate   with a fringed margin.

Fistulose/Fistular   cylindrical and hollow, like a pipe.

Flexuous/Fluxuose   term used to describe a stem which changes direction at its nodes to form a semi-zigzag line.

Floral appendages, Parts or Components   the modified leaves of which a flower is composed.

Floral terminal bud   the tip of a flowering branch that bears the flower bud.

Foliaceous/Foliose   flat and leaflike.

Foliar feeding   the application of specially prepared nutritive substances by spraying the exposed parts of the plant for absorption by the leaves.

Gamete   one of the sex cells of a plant—either male or female.

Gamopetalous, Monopetalous or Sympetalous corolla   petals partly or entirely fused to each other.

Gamosepalous or Monosepalous calyx   sepals partly or entirely fused to each other.

Gamotepalous perigonium   tepals partly or entirely fused to each other.

Gibbous/Gibbose   swollen, particularly on one side or near the base.

Glabrous   free of hair.

Glandulous   covered with hairs that emit a viscous fluid when touched.

Glaucescent/Glaucous   covered with a whitish bloom.

Grafting and Budding   methods used in horticulture to form a union between plants of different species by means of skillful notching and the insertion of shoots or scions.

494

Gramineous   grass-like; relating to grasses.

Guano   organic manure made from the excrement of sea birds; in its original, meaning from the Pacific islands off South America.

Gynoecium   the female organ of a flower consisting of carpels.

Harden off   to move a plant into a colder location so it will adjust to life in the garden.

Habit   the growth pattern of a plant.

Helicoid   coiled spirally.

Hermaphrodite   a flower that has an androecium and a gynoecium.

Hirsute or Hispid   covered with stiff, bristly hairs (or with shaggy hairs, as in some cacti).

Hoof and horn   an organic fertilizer made from ground and pulverized animal horns and hooves; it is often roasted.

Humus   natural organic constituent of the soil created by decomposed plant and animal matter.

Hydroponics   soilless culture in water impregnated with nutritive solutions.

Imparipinnate or Odd-pinnate   a pinnate compound leaf with a single leaflet at the apex.

Indehiscent   not opening at maturity; a seedpod, for example.

Indeterminate   growing on from the apex, especially the apex of the main stem.

Inflorescence   the grouping of flowers on the same axis.

Infundibuliform   funnel-shaped.

Inorganic or Mineral fertilizer   made up of various soluble mineral substances.

Involucre   a whorl of small leaves or bracts close under a flower or flower cluster.

Laciniate   divided into deep, narrow, irregular lobes.

Lamina   the broad, expanded part of a leaf or petal; the blade

Lanate   woolly.

Lanceolate   lance-shaped, tapering at each end.

Lax   arranged loosely.

Layer   the part of a branch that has been in contact with the ground and has struck root, either spontaneously or with help.

Leaf-bud scale   each of the small modified leaves wrapped around the buds for their protection.

Leaflet   one division of a compound leaf.

Leaf mold   soil of various types, usually from the forest floor or a leaf pile, produced by the breaking down and decomposition of leaves and other organic substances.

Leaf rosette   a close grouping of leaves at the base of a stem.

Liana/Liane   a climbing and twining plant.

Ligneous/Lignose   woody.

Lignification   the deposition of a complex carbohydrate, lignin, in the cellulose material of the cell walls of woody tissue.

Liguliform/Ligulate   strap-shaped. Describes a very short-tubed corolla that is prolonged above into a flattened group of united petals; or a capitulum in which every flower has a ligulate corolla.

Limb   the blade of a leaf. The broad, upper part of a petal. The upper, often spreading, part of a sympetalous corolla.

Linear   long and narrow.

Lobed   with an irregular margin formed by numerous rounded or curved projections.

Macular   blotched or spotted with a contrasting color.

Medial   in the middle; central.

Median plane   the plane passing through the center of an organ.

Medulla/Medullate   the central part of an organ, i.e., the pith of a stem.
Melliferous   yielding or producing honey.
Monochasium (simple and compound)   a cymose inflorescence in which only one secondary stalk grows on the main stem.
Monoecious plant   a plant bearing both male and female flowers.
Mulch   a thick layer of compost, straw, dried leaves, peat, etc., spread around the base of plants as a protection against frost and to conserve water; also cuts down on weeds and weeding.
Nanism   subnormal growth producing a dwarf plant.
Nervature   the arrangement of veins, as in a leaf.
Nodes   points at which leaves and buds are positioned on the stem or branch.
Obcordate leaf   heart-shaped leaf, attached at its apex.
Oblong leaf   elongated leaf with margins almost parallel.
Obovate leaf   reversed egg-shaped leaf, with the point at the base.
Obtuse leaf   leaf with a rounded top.
Offset   a young plant developing near the base of the parent plant. A bulblet.
Opposite leaves   a pair of leaves at each node, one on each side, at the same height on the stem. Compare Alternate leaves
Orbiculate   rounded.
Organic fertilizer   made up of substances of an organic nature.
Ovary   fertile part of the gynoecium containing the ovules.
Ovate/Oval leaf   egg-shaped leaf.
Ovule   internal organ of the ovary that produces the female spores and, after fertilization, the embryo.
Palmate   a leaf shape in which the veins are arranged like fingers.
Palmatisect   having the leaf blade cut almost to the base to form several diverging lobes.
Panicle   a type of raceme composed of multiple branching flower stalks.
Papilionaceous corolla   butterfly-like, it consists of five petals—an external one (vexillum), two equal laterals (wings) and two internal ones fused together (carina).
Pappus   calyx modified into a downy or scaly material, typical of the fruit of the composite family.
Parent plant   a plant selected for the production of seeds for reproduction.
Paripinnate leaf   a compound pinnate leaf with an even number of leaflets.
Peat   decomposed organic vegetable matter that has undergone comparatively recent fossilization.
Pedate leaf   a compound leaf, palmately divided into three main divisions, the outer ones being divided several times like toes or the claws of a bird.
Pedicel   stem of a single flower in a cluster.
Peduncle   main stalk bearing a flower or an inflorescence.
Pedunculate   having a peduncle or growing on a peduncle.
Peltate   shield-shaped or umbrella-like leaf with the leaf-stalk attached near the center.
Perianth   floral envelope consisting of the sterile parts of a flower (sepals and petals).
Pericarp   the external part of a fruit surrounding the seeds.
Perigonium   a type of perianth consisting of the sterile floral components (tepals), all equal and usually colored.
Persistent leaf   a leaf that stays on the plant for more than one growing season and falls only after a few years.

Personate refers to a bilabiate corolla that somewhat resembles a mask or face of an animal.

Pesticides substances designed to prevent the spread of various pests and to control or destroy them. Insecticides are used to combat insects; fungicides, to combat diseases.

Petals floral leaves that constitute the corolla.

Petiole leaf-stalk extending from the stem joint to the base of the leaf blade.

pH symbol used to describe the acidity or alkalinity of soil. Soil with a pH of about 7 is neutral. Below 7 it is acid; above, alkaline.

Phyllode a petiole so flattened as to resemble a leaf blade.

Phytophagous feeding on vegetal material (plants).

Phytohormone chemical or natural substances that control the growth and/or development of plants.

Pilose/Pilous covered with hair.

Pinching out removing buds or the ends of stems to encourage plant to bush out or to put out fewer but larger flowers.

Pinna the primary division of a pinnate leaf.

Pinnate describing a leaf or bract in which the leaflets are positioned like the barbs of a feather.

Pinnatifid leaf pinnate leaf whose margin is cut into lobes for about two-thirds its width.

Pinnatisect leaf pinnate leaf whose margin is cut deeply into lobes, down to the main rib.

Piriform/Pyriform pear-shaped.

Pistil a part of the gynoecium made up of one or more carpels.

Plantule seedling.

Plicate folded like a fan.

Pollarding drastic pruning operation on the main branches of the crown——or even on the stem——of a plant.

Pollen collection of tiny grains that form in the pollen sacs of the anther.

Pollen grain or granule male reproductive cell (microspore) whose purpose is to land on the stigma of a flower and form male gametes.

Pollen sac that part of the cavity in the anther that produces pollen.

Pollination the process of transporting pollen from the anther to the stigma.

Pollinator an insect or other medium that carries pollen from the stamens of one flower to the pistil of another.

Polycarpic having a gynoecium with two or more ovaries.

Potting bench a raised bench on which sowing, transplanting, etc. can be done in the greenhouse.

Potting on transferring a plant from one flower pot to a slightly larger one.

Pricking out/Pricking off transplanting tiny seedlings.

Primordia first stages in the development of an organ.

Procumbent see Prostrate.

Propagation any operation whereby plants are reproduced.

Propagator/Propagating frame special container or small box——such as a dish with a cover——for germinating seeds.

Proliferous bulb producing one or more offsets.

Prostrate growing along the ground.

Pruina a powdery bloom or secretion on the surface of a plant, especially on the fruit.

Pruning the cutting away of dead or living parts of a plant.

Pubescent covered with very short, soft hairs.

Pulverulent appearing to be covered with dust or powder.

Quinate leaf a leaf with five leaflets.

Quinquelobate five-lobed.

Raceme an indeterminate inflorescence of pedunculate flowers, borne on one long stem, in which the terminal flower is the last to open.

Radicant rooting from the stem.

Ramification a branch.

Ramified branched.

Ramose much branched.

Ray florets or flowers peripheral flowers in a capitulum-type inflorescence.

Receptacle the base of a flower on which the floral components are carried.

Recurved bent or curved backward.

Regular see Actinomorphic.

Reniform kidney-shaped.

Reticulate with veins or nerves arranged in netlike fashion.

Retrocurved/Retroflexed turned backward.

Revolute rolled backward, generally downward.

Rhizome an elongated, horizontal underground stem with a bud at one end. It grows into an aerial stalk with leaves and flowers.

Root ball see Soil ball

Rosaceous corolla a corolla consisting of five rayed petals.

Rotate corolla wheel-shaped or rayed corolla.

Rotund approximately circular.

Rotundate see Orbiculate.

Rugose wrinkled.

Sagittate leaf a leaf shaped like an arrowhead.

Saprophyte a plant that lives on organic materials derived from dead organisms.

Sarmentose/Sarmentous having runners.

Scaly bulb a bulb whose swollen leaf bases do not form a complete circle in cross section.

Scape the long stalk of a herbaceous plant coming directly from the root with leaves only at the base and flowers at the top.

Scarious/Scariose thin and dry with a generally dried-up appearance, especially at the tips and edges.

Scorpioid describes an inflorescence that curls up at the end like the tail of a scorpion and uncurls as flowers develop.

Seedbed a piece of ground specially prepared for sowing or for the transplanting of seedlings.

Seed box small container used for rooting cuttings, potting on, etc.

Seedling young plantlet produced by the germination of a seed.

Seed pan a small box or tray in which seeds are sown.

Segment leaflet.

Sepals floral leaves that form the calyx.

Sericeous covered with soft down; silky.

Serrated tooth-edged, like a saw.

Serrulate/Serratulate serrate, but with very small teeth.

Sessile describing a flower or leaf attached directly by its base, without pedicel or peduncle; stalkless

Setaceous/Setiform bristle-shaped.

Sheath basal part of some leaves that wraps around the stem or branch. A more or less tubular structure surrounding a part of a plant.

Shoot new growth of varying degrees of vigor.

Shrub woody plant, branching out from its base, bushy or treelike in habit.

Siliqua/Silique the long, narrow seed vessel of cruciferous plants.

Sinuate with a wavy edge, as a leaf.

Soil ball the lump of soil retained by the root system of some plants when they are transplanted.

Spadix a spike of flowers with a fleshy axis and enclosed in a spathe.

Spathe a large bract, which may be colored or membranous, enclosing a spadix.

Spatulate/Spathulate spatula-shaped; narrow at the base and broadening at the end.

Spicate spike-shaped.

Spike an indeterminate inflorescence with sessile flowers arranged along a long stem, the terminal flower being the last to open.

Spindly or leggy growth long, weak growth caused by lack of light.

Spinose/Spinous spiny.

Sporophylls the reproductive parts of a flower (stamens and carpels); modified leaves.

Spurred corolla corolla with a straight or curved cylindrical appendage (spur) at its base.

Spur-pruning a type of short pruning to one, two or three short fruit-bearing branches (spurs).

Squamous/Squamate/Squamose scaly.

Stamen male reproductive part of a flower consisting of a filament and an anther.

Standard the large petal standing up at the back of a papilionaceous flower.

Stellate starlike.

Stellulate like a small star.

Stem or Stalk central support of a plant that bears the leaves, to which it conducts water and minerals.

Stigma the tips of the gynoecium that receive the pollen grains.

Stipules small leaflike appendages arranged in pairs at the base of some leaves.

Stolon a long, creeping branch that puts out roots and leaves from its nodes.

Stopping see Pinching out

Style the stalk linking the ovary to the stigma.

Subsoil the layer of soil immediately beneath the topsoil.

Succulent having thick, fleshy leaves and stems that retain a water supply. A type of plant with such structure.

Sucker/Side-shoot a fairly vigorous adventitious shoot that usually springs from the stem or root of a plant just below ground level.

Suffrutescent/Suffruticose a woody plant, with softwood branches springing from its base. It is usually less than about 20 in. (50 cm.) in height.

Symmetrical see Actinomorphic

Taproot a thick, cylindrical or tapering root growing straight down into the ground.

Tendrils threadlike organs that can twine themselves around a support. Some are modified leaves and others are modified stems.

Tepals floral leaves (petals and sepals) that form the perigonium.

Terminal flowers flowers growing at the end of a branch or stem.

Ternate growing in threes, as a compound leaf with three leaflets.

Tetragonous having four angles and four convex faces.

Thalamus see Receptacle

Thinning out removing seedlings to give space to others. Removing weak and invasive growth.

Thyrsiform having a racemose primary axis and a cymose secondary one.

Tomentose   densely covered with matted woolly hairs.
Topping   removal of shoots and main buds, especially the top growing point, to encourage growth.
Trifoliate leaf   a leaf divided into three leaflets.
Trigonal   triangular in cross section.
Triquetrous   said of a stem or branch that is triangular in cross section.
Truncate   ending abruptly as if cut off at the tip.
Tuber   an underground stem of irregular shape that acts as a reservoir of nutrients. Its growth buds are dispersed irregularly over its surface.
Tubulous corolla   a corolla that is cylinder-shaped, like a tube.
Tunicate bulb   a bulb enveloped in several imbricate, papery scales.
Twining plant   a plant that twists its stem spirally around a support.
Umbel   an inflorescence in which the flowers are borne on short stalks (peduncles) that spring from a common stem, all reaching the same height.
Unisexual   having only an androecium (male reproductive parts) or a gynoecium (female reproductive parts).
Under glass   a shortcut phrase used when seeds or cuttings are propagated in a coldframe, greenhouse or indoors in your own house.
Urceolate corolla   a pitcher-shaped corolla, with a narrow mouth.
Vagina   see Sheath.
Vaginate or Sheathed   equipped with a sheath.
Velutinate/Velutinous   with a velvety surface.
Venation   see Nervature
Venose   with veins.
Vernalization   exposing seeds, bulbs or plants to low temperatures to induce flowering ahead of the plant's normal schedule.
Verticil   an arrangement of leaves grouped round each node.
Verticillaster   an inflorescence consisting of numerous flowers arranged in whorls at each node.
Verticillate   arranged in verticels (whorls).
Vesiculose   swollen like a bladder. Appearing to be made up of small bladders. Made up from, or full of, vesicles.
Vexillum   see Standard.
Villous/Villose   wtih long, soft, weak hairs; shaggy.
Viscid   covered with a sticky substance.
Whorl   see Verticil
Zygomorphic   divisible in half by only one longitudinal plane.

BIBLIOGRAPHY

Bailey, L.H., *The Standard Cyclopedia of Horticulture,* Macmillan Publishing Company, New York and London, 1963.

Bailey, L.H. and Bailey E.Z., *Hortus Third. A Concise Dictionary of Plants Cultivated in the United States and Canada.* Macmillan Publishing Company, New York and London, 1976.

Brosse, J., *Atlas des Arbustes, Arbrisseaux et Lianes de France et d'Europe Occidentale,* Bordas, Barcelona, 1979.

Gibson, M., *The Book of the Rose,* MacDonald and Jane's, London and Sydney, 1980.

Princess Grace of Monaco and Robins, G., *My Book of Flowers,* Sidgwick and Jackson Ltd., London, 1980.

Graf, A.B., *Exotica 3,* Roehrs Co., Rutherford, New Jersey, 1963.

Hay, R. and Synge P., *Fiori e Piante,* Sansoni Editore, Florence, 1970.

Huxley, A., *An Illustrated History of Gardening,* Paddington Press Ltd., New York and London, 1978.

Pizzetti, I., and Cocker, H., *Il Libro dei Fiori,* Vol. 1–3, Garzanti, Milan, 1968.

The New York Botanical Garden Illustrated Encyclopedia of Horticulture, Garland Publishers, Inc., New York, 1979.

Traverso, O., *Botanica Orticola,* Pavia, 1926.

INDEX OF ENTRIES

(*The numbers refer to the entry number.*)

506

ACKNOWLEDGMENTS

The Publisher gratefully acknowledges the cooperation of: Piergiorgio Compodonico, Hanbury Botanical Garden at Ventimiglia; Le Conservatoire et Jardin Botaniques de la Ville de Genève; le Vicomte de Noailles, Grasse; the Garden Club of Monaco; Jean Giovannini and Gilbert Viethel, Division Jardins de Monaco; l'Istituto Sperimentale per la Floricoltura, San Remo; le Jardin Botanique Exotique, Menton-Garavan; Marcel Kroenlein, Jardin Exotique de Monaco; Gabriel Olliver, Keeper of the Rose Garden and National Museum of Monaco; Sélection Meilland, Cap d'Antibes; la Société des Bains de Mer, Monaco.

Edited by Fabrizio Tolu
Symbols by Giorgio Seppi and Raffaele Curiel
Makeup and maps by Raffaello Segattini
Editorial secretary: Adalisa De Gobbi
Translator: Sylvia Mulcahy
Illustrator: Raffaella Giacometti Piva
Photographer: Giuseppe Mazza
Photocomposition by the Composition Center OGAM, Verona

Picture Credits

Photographs: Giuseppe Mazza, Monte Carlo
Drawings: Raffaella Giacometti Piva, Verona
(New York Public Library, Astor, Lenox and Tilden Foundations: 13.
British Museum, London: 14. Curtis' Botanical Magazine: 17.
Arnoldo Mondadori Editore, Verona: 18. L. Giugnolini, Florence: 20. Uffizi, Florence: 52. Louvre, Paris: 53.)